STALIN'S WARS

Also by Geoffrey Roberts

The Unholy Alliance: Stalin's Pact with Hitler
The Soviet Union and the Origins of the Second World War
The Soviet Union in World Politics, 1945–1991
Ireland and the Second World War (co-edited with Brian Girvin)
The History and Narrative Reader (editor)
Victory at Stalingrad: The Battle That Changed History
Stalin – His Times and Ours (editor)

STALIN'S WARS

FROM WORLD WAR TO COLD WAR, 1939–1953

GEOFFREY ROBERTS

YALE UNIVERSITY PRESS
OCM 70673207
NEW HAVEN AND LONDON

For information about this and other Yale University Press publications, please contact:

U.S. Office: sales.press@yale.edu   www.yalebooks.com
Europe Office: sales@yaleup.co.uk www.yaleup.co.uk

Set in Minion by J&L Composition, Filey, North Yorkshire
Printed in Great Britain by St Edmundsbury Press Ltd, Bury St Edmunds

Library of Congress Cataloging-in-Publication Data

Roberts, Geoffrey, 1952–
    Stalin's wars: from World War to Cold War: 1939–1953/Geoffrey Roberts.
        p. cm.
    Includes bibliographical references and index.
    ISBN 0–300–11204–1 (alk. paper)
    1. Stalin, Joseph, 1879–1953—Influence. 2. Stalin, Joseph, 1879–1953—Military leadership. 3. World War, 1939–1945—Diplomatic history. 4. Soviet Union—History, Military. 5. World politics—1945– I. Title.
    DK268.S8R574 2006
    947.084'2092—dc22
    [B]
                                                                                        2006023395

A catalogue record for this book is available from the British Library.

10 9 8 7 6 5 4 3 2 1

In Memory of Dennis Ogden (1927–2004)

Contents

List of Illustrations   *viii*

List of Maps and Figure   *x*

Preface and Acknowledgements   *xi*

Chronology of Major Events   *xvi*

1 Introduction: Stalin at War   1

2 Unholy Alliance: Stalin's Pact with Hitler   30

3 Grand Illusions: Stalin and 22 June 1941   61

4 War of Annihilation: Stalin versus Hitler   82

5 Victory at Stalingrad and Kursk: Stalin and his Generals   118

6 The Politics of War: Stalin, Churchill and Roosevelt   165

7 Triumph and Tragedy: Stalin's Year of Victories   192

8 Liberation, Conquest, Revolution: Stalin's Aims in Germany
and Eastern Europe   228

9 Last Battles: Stalin, Truman and the End of the Second World War   254

10 The Lost Peace: Stalin and the Origins of the Cold War   296

11 Generalissimo at Home: The Domestic Context of Stalin's
Postwar Foreign Policy   321

12 Cold War Confrontations: Stalin Embattled   347

13 Conclusion: Stalin in the Court of History   372

Notes   *375*

Select Bibliography   *430*

Index   *447*

Illustrations

Ribbentrop, the German Foreign Minister, signing the Nazi–Soviet pact on 23 August 1939. Stalin and Molotov stand in the background. Interfoto.

Stalin and members of the Politburo on their way to a parade in Red Square. AKG Images.

Hitler and his generals. AKG Images.

Text of Stalin's radio broadcast of 3 July 1941, published in *Pravda*. David King Collection.

Stalin giving his speech to the troops in Red Square, 7 November 1941. David King Collection.

Molotov and Eden in Moscow. David King Collection.

Churchill, Averell Harriman, Stalin and Molotov at the Kremlin during Churchill's visit in August 1942. Corbis.

Victorious Soviet soldiers marching through the ruins of Stalingrad. Interfoto.

Ruins of the factory district in besieged Stalingrad. Interfoto.

President Franklin Delano Roosevelt and American Secretary of State, Cordell Hull. Getty Images.

Insurgents of the Warsaw uprising surrender to the Germans. David King Collection.

Notes from the Churchill–Stalin percentages agreement. David King Collection.

Soviet soldiers with former prisoners of Auschwitz after the camp's liberation, January 1945. AKG Images.

Churchill, Roosevelt and Stalin at the Yalta conference, February 1945. AKG Images.

Red Army soldiers hoisting the Soviet flag on top of the Reichstag building in Berlin, May 1945. AKG Images.

Soviet troops display captured Nazi banners at the victory parade in Red Square, 24 June 1945. AKG Images.

Stalin and President Harry Truman at the Potsdam conference, July 1945. AKG Images.

Atomic bomb damage in Hiroshima, Japan, following the explosion on 6 August 1945. Corbis.

Berlin children greet the arrival of a 'Raisin Bomber' during the Berlin blockade. AKG Images.

Lavrentii Beria. David King Collection.

Marshal I.S. Konev. AKG Images.

Marshal Zhukov with officials of the Red Army. AKG Images.

Georgi Dimitrov with Stalin on his left and Voroshilov, Kaganovich and Molotov on his right. AKG Images.

Floral tributes to Stalin piled up against the Kremlin wall at the time of his funeral. AKG Images.

Stalin's funeral in March 1953. Beria, Malenkov, Molotov and Bulganin carry Stalin's coffin as it leaves the union building. AKG Images.

Maps and Figure

Maps

1 The Nazi–Soviet Pact, August–September 1939   40
2 The Soviet–Finnish War, 1939–1940   49
3 Soviet Plans for Offensive War Against Germany, 1941   75
4 Operation Barbarossa, June–December 1941   83
5 German Encirclement of Soviet Troops, 1941   86
6 The Soviet Counter-Offensive at Moscow, December 1941   113
7 The Plan for Operation Blau, April 1942   120
8 The German Advance in the South, Summer 1942   127
9 The Battle for Stalingrad, September–November 1942   146
10 Operation Uranus, November 1942   150
11 'Mars', 'Jupiter', 'Saturn' and 'Uranus'   152
12 The Battle of Kursk, July 1943   158
13 Soviet Military Operations, 1944   193–4
14 Operation Bagration   201
15 The Soviet Advance on Warsaw, Summer 1944   205
16 The Vistula–Oder Operation, January–February 1945   255
17 The Berlin Operation, April 1945   262
18 The Manchurian Campaign, August 1945   286
19 The Postwar Division of Germany   351
20 The Korean War, 1950–1953   365

Figure

The structure of Soviet military and political decision-making during
the Great Patriotic War   96

Preface and Acknowledgements

This study of Stalin as warlord and peacemaker began life as an investigation of the Soviet role in the Grand Alliance of the Second World War. The aim was to explore how the Grand Alliance emerged and developed, the way Stalin, Churchill, Roosevelt and Truman fought their diplomatic and political battles, and why the coalition collapsed after the Second World War. That aim remains a central strand of this book but in 2001–2002 I conducted a study of the battle of Stalingrad that made me grapple more extensively with the military dimensions of Stalin's war leadership.[1] I also became more interested in Soviet domestic politics and in the social history of the Stalin regime in the 1940s. The result is the present book – a detailed and sustained study of Stalin's military and political leadership in the final and most important phase of his life and career.

Baldly stated, my conclusions are threefold. First, that Stalin was a very effective and highly successful war leader. He made many mistakes and pursued brutal policies that resulted in the deaths of millions of people but without his leadership the war against Nazi Germany would probably have been lost. Churchill, Hitler, Mussolini, Roosevelt – they were all replaceable as warlords, but not Stalin. In the context of the horrific war on the Eastern Front, Stalin was indispensable to the Soviet victory over Nazi Germany. Second, that Stalin worked hard to make the Grand Alliance a success and wanted to see it continue after the war. While his policies and actions undoubtedly contributed to the outbreak of the cold war, his intentions were otherwise, and he strove in the late 1940s and early 1950s to revive *détente* with the west. Third, that Stalin's postwar domestic regime was very different to the Soviet system of the prewar years. It was less repressive, more nationalistic, and not so dependent on Stalin's will and whimsy for its everyday functioning. It was a system in transition to the relatively more relaxed social and political order of post-Stalin times. The process of 'destalinisation' began while Stalin was still alive, although the cult of his personality reigned supreme in the Soviet Union until the day he died.

This portrait of Stalin as the greatest of war leaders, as a man who preferred peace to cold war, and as a politician who presided over a process of postwar domestic reform will not be to everyone's taste. There are some for whom the only acceptable image is Stalin the evil dictator who brought nothing but woe to the world. This is the mirror-image of the Stalin cult – the dictator as devil not deity. It is a picture of Stalin that pays perverse homage to his abilities as a political leader. Certainly, Stalin was a skilled politician, an intelligent ideologue and a superb administrator. He was also a quietly charismatic figure who personally dominated everyone who came into close contact with him. But Stalin was not superhuman. He miscalculated, misperceived, and allowed himself to be misled by his own dogma. He was not always clear about what he wanted or how he wanted events to develop. He was as capricious as he was calculating and frequently took decisions that worked against his own best interests. The other thing this book does is to cut Stalin down to human size. This is not to deny the tumultuous times in which he lived nor to underrate the momentous or awful nature of many of his actions. But I do suggest that Stalin was more ordinary, and therefore all the more extraordinary in his impact, than either his devotees or his denouncers imagine. This normalisation of Stalin carries with it the danger of making his many crimes seem commonplace. That is not my intention and I have tried to provide as many details as I can of the murderous activities of Stalin and his regime. But this book is not a catalogue of Stalin's crimes. Its goal is greater understanding of Stalin. As my colleague Mark Harrison has argued, we can undertake that task without fear of moral hazard and having achieved greater understanding we can condemn Stalin even more if we want to.[2] To me, however, the lesson of Stalin's rule is not a simple morality tale about a paranoid, vengeful and bloodthirsty dictator. It is a story of a powerful politics and ideology that strove for both utopian and totalitarian ends. Stalin was an idealist prepared to use whatever violence it took to impose his will and achieve his goals. In the titanic struggle with Hitler his methods were unpalatable but effective, and perhaps unavoidable if victory was to be secured. Equally, Stalin's ambitions were limited; he was a realist and a pragmatist as well as an ideologue, a leader prepared to compromise, adapt and change, as long as it did not threaten the Soviet system or his own power.

As Robert H. McNeal, one of Stalin's greatest biographers, said: there is no point 'in trying to rehabilitate Stalin. The established impression that he slaughtered, tortured, imprisoned and oppressed on a grand scale is not in error. On the other hand, it is impossible to understand this immensely gifted politician by attributing solely to him all the crimes and suffering of his era, or to conceive him simply as a monster and a mental case.'[3] The aim of this book is not to rehabilitate Stalin but to re-vision him. In these pages you will find many Stalins: despot and diplomat, soldier and statesman, rational bureaucrat and paranoid politician. They add up to a complex and contradictory picture of a highly talented dictator who created and controlled a system that was strong enough to survive the ultimate test of total war. The failure in the long run of the Stalinist system should not blind us to its virtues, not least its vital role in winning the war against Hitler. Rather than trumpet the west's victory in the cold war we should remember the Soviet Union's role in preserving the long postwar peace.

A book such as this would not have been possible without the enormous accretion of knowledge that has resulted from the opening up of the Soviet archives in the last 15 years – directly in terms of archival access or through the publication of thousands of new documents from the archives. Lytton Strachey complained that 'the history of the Victorian Age will never be written: we know too much about it'.[4] Faced with the mountain of new evidence on Stalin and his era, I now know how he felt. Strachey's solution to his dilemma was to compose a series of debunking portraits of eminent Victorians. I have adopted a similar strategy except that I want to demystify Stalin rather than debunk him. This is not a conventional biography but it does present an intimate portrait of Stalin as a political leader. I have also tried to allow Stalin to speak with his own voice so that readers can form their own impressions and judgements of him. Even so, the research task was enormous. But, thankfully, there was help at hand from the galaxy of distinguished scholars who have tackled many aspects of Stalin and his times. I include among their number people like McNeal who wrote in the pre-archival era and relied mainly on public sources such as Stalin's speeches, newspaper articles and the bare record of events. One thing that my research in the Russian archives has taught me is the importance of using the public as well as the confidential Soviet sources. Most of what Stalin was thinking and doing you can read all about in the Soviet newspapers. The challenge facing historians is to integrate and combine such traditional sources with the new ones from the Russian archives. That means, too, the resuscitation of the vast body of scholarship from the days when the Soviet Union still existed and archival access was blocked. The works of McNeal, Isaac Deutscher, John Erickson, William McCagg, Paulo Spriano, Alexander Werth and others are an invaluable resource that we cannot afford to ignore. The old scholarship is venerable but not outdated.

My own research in the Russian archives concentrated on my specialist field of foreign policy and international relations. My research in Moscow was supported and facilitated by Professor Alexander Chubar'yan's Institute of General History in the Russian Academy of Sciences, in particular by my dear friends in the War and Geopolitics section, headed by Professor Oleg Rzheshevskii and Dr Mikhail Myagkov. I owe very special thanks to Dr Sergey Listikov who has helped me in innumerable ways during the past 10 years.

Among the many friends and colleagues working in the same field with whom I have swapped ideas and materials are: Lev Bezymenskii, Michael Carley, Aleksei Filitov, Martin Folly, David Glantz, Kathleen Harriman, David Holloway, Caroline Kennedy-Pipe, Jochen Laufer, Mel Leffler, Eduard Mark, Evan Mawdsley, Vladimir Nevezhin, Alexander Orlov, Vladimir Pechatnov, Silvio Pons, Alexander Pozdeev, Vladimir Poznyakov, Robert Service, Teddy Uldricks, Geoffrey Warner and the late Derek Watson. I am immensely grateful to them all. Albert Resis read virtually the whole manuscript and tried to save me from as many mistakes as he could. I hope I have not betrayed his magnificent labour on my behalf. I benefited greatly, too, from the comments of the Yale University Press reviewers. A big thanks to my friend and teacher, Svetlana Frolova, for checking my transliterations and for advising on some translations.

In institutional terms I have, above all, to thank my employers University College Cork for granting me the privilege of several terms of sabbatical leave so that I could conduct research in Britain, the United States and Russia. The Arts Faculty at UCC has been an indispensable source of funding for my research trips, including the award in 2000 of the faculty's coveted research achievement prize. In September 2001 I made my first trip to the United States, courtesy of a short-term grant from the Kennan Institute for Advanced Russian Studies. This enabled me to do extensive research on the invaluable Harriman Papers in the Library of Congress in Washington, DC. In 2004–2005 I was awarded a Senior Research Fellowship by the Irish Research Council for Humanities and Social Sciences. During this sabbatical the Fulbright Commission granted me an award that allowed me to spend three months at Harvard University. At Harvard I was the guest of Mark Kramer and the Cold War Studies Program of the Davis Center for Russian Studies. Mark's prodigious researches in Russia's archives have been an inspiration to us all and his program has accumulated thousands of reels of microfilm of Soviet archives, many of which I was able to work on during my time at Harvard.

I have presented a number of conference and seminar papers on my research, and special mention must be made of the annual meetings of the British International History Group, occasions that have allowed me to share my thinking with fellow International History specialists. The Moscow conference circuit was opened up to me by Professor Gabriel Gorodetsky in 1995 and the benefit in terms of ideas and contacts has been immeasurable. His own book on Stalin and 22 June 1941 is a classic study that illuminated my path.[5] In Moscow the two main archives I worked in were those of the Foreign Ministry and the Russian State Archive of Social-Political History, where the communist party archives for the Stalin era are housed. I also spent a lot of time reading Soviet newspapers in the Moscow State Public Historical Library. I would like to thank the archivists and librarians for their patience and persistence in dealing with me over the years. My mainstays in London were, as always, the libraries of the London School of Economics and the School of Slavonic and East European Studies.

The book is dedicated to the late Dennis Ogden. Dennis was of the generation of British communists who had to come to terms with the debunking of the Stalin cult by Khrushchev in 1956. He was in Moscow at the time, working as a translator, and attended a party meeting at his publishing house where the 'secret speech' was read out. He often recalled the dismay, disbelief, shock and silence of those attending the meeting. When I met him in the 1970s he was in the vanguard of the critical study of the Soviet experiment in socialism and prominent in the public criticism of Soviet authoritarianism and repression of dissidents. His independent, critical spirit has inspired me ever since.

This is the fourth book I have worked on with my publisher, Heather McCallum. I continue to be impressed by her outstanding professionalism and by her dedication to the publishing of history books that are both scholarly and popular.

This is the eighth book I have worked on with my partner, Celia Weston. Her input was intellectual as well as editorial, emotional as well as material. No one has contributed to this book more than Celia. I really don't know what I would do without her.

This is a narrative history. It tells the story of Stalin's thinking, decisions and actions during the Second World War and in the cold war more or less chronologically. But the book begins by setting the scene with an overall picture and assessment of Stalin at war.

Chronology of Major Events

1939

23 August	Nazi–Soviet Pact
1 September	German invasion of Poland
3 September	Britain and France declare war on Germany
17 September	Red Army invades eastern Poland
	Soviet Union declares its neutrality in the European war
28 September	Soviet–German Boundary and Friendship Treaty
	Soviet–Estonian Treaty of Mutual Assistance
5 October	Soviet–Latvian Treaty of Mutual Assistance
10 October	Soviet–Lithuanian Treaty of Mutual Assistance
30 November	Soviet attack on Finland

1940

5 March	Politburo resolution authorising the execution of 20,000 Polish POWs
12 March	Soviet–Finnish peace treaty signed
9 April	Germany invades Demark and Norway
10 June	Italy enters the European war
22 June	France surrenders to Germany
25 June	USSR proposes spheres of influence agreement in the Balkans
28 June	Bessarabia and Northern Bukovina annexed by the USSR
21 July	Baltic States agree to incorporation in the USSR
27 September	Germany, Italy and Japan conclude tripartite pact
12–14 November	Molotov–Hitler–Ribbentrop talks in Berlin
25 November	Soviet proposal for a four-power pact with Germany, Italy and Japan
18 December	Hitler directive on Operation Barbarossa

1941

25 March	Soviet–Turkish statement on neutrality
5 April	Soviet–Yugoslav Treaty of Friendship and Non-Aggression
6 April	German invasion of Yugoslavia and Greece
13 April	Soviet–Japanese neutrality pact
4 May	Stalin appointed Chairman of the Council of People's Commissars
5 May	Stalin speech to the graduates of the Red Army staff academies
14 June	Tass statement on Soviet–German relations
22 June	Operation Barbarossa
	Molotov radio broadcast on the German invasion
23 June	Establishment of Stavka
28 June	Fall of Minsk
30 June	Establishment of the GKO (State Defence Committee)
3 July	Stalin radio broadcast on the German invasion
10 July	Stalin becomes Supreme Commander
12 July	Soviet–British Agreement on joint action against Germany
16 July	German capture of Smolensk
19 July	Stalin appointed People's Commissar for Defence
14 August	Atlantic Charter
6 September	Leningrad surrounded
19 September	Germans capture Kiev
1 October	Anglo-American–Soviet supplies agreement
2 October	Germans launch Operation Typhoon to capture Moscow
16 October	Fall of Odessa
6–7 November	Stalin speeches in Moscow
5 December	Moscow counter-offensive by Red Army
7 December	Japanese attack at Pearl Harbor
11 December	Hitler declares war on the US
15–22 December	Eden trip to Moscow

1942

1 January	Declaration of the United Nations
5 April	Hitler directive on Operation Blau
19–28 May	Battle of Kharkov
22 May–11 June	Molotov trip to London and Washington
26 May	British–Soviet Treaty of Alliance
11 June	Soviet–American agreement on mutual aid

12 June	Anglo-Soviet–American communiqués on the opening of a second front in 1942
26 June	Vasilevskii appointed Chief of the General Staff
28 June	Beginning of German summer offensive in the south
4 July	Sebastopol falls to the Germans
12 July	Formation of the Stalingrad Front
23 July	Rostov captured by the Germans
	Hitler orders capture of Stalingrad and Baku
28 July	Stalin Order 227 ('Not a Step Back'!)
12–15 August	Churchill–Stalin conference in Moscow
25 August	State of siege declared at Stalingrad
26 August	Zhukov made Deputy Supreme Commander
10 September	Germans reach the Volga
8 November	Operation Torch begins in North Africa
19 November	Operation Uranus (Stalingrad counter-offensive by the Red Army)
23 November	German 6th Army surrounded in Stalingrad

1943

10 January	Launch of Operation Ring at Stalingrad
18 January	Leningrad blockade broken
24 January	Casablanca declaration on unconditional surrender
31 January	German 6th Army surrenders at Stalingrad
14 February	Rostov recaptured by the Red Army
6 March	Stalin appointed Marshal of the Soviet Union
13 April	Germans announce discovery of mass graves at Katyn
26 April	USSR breaks off diplomatic relations with the Polish government in exile in London
22 May	Publication of resolution proposing the dissolution of the Comintern
5–13 July	Battle of Kursk
26 July	Mussolini falls from power
3 September	Allied invasion of Italy
25 September	Smolensk recaptured by the Red Army
13 October	Italy declares war on Germany
19–30 October	Moscow Conference of Foreign Ministers
6 November	Kiev recaptured by the Red Army
28 November– 1 December	Tehran Conference
12 December	Soviet–Czechoslovak Treaty of Friendship, Mutual Aid and Postwar Co-operation

1944

27 January	Leningrad blockade completely lifted
10 April	Odessa recaptured by the Red Army
10 May	Sebastopol recaptured by the Red Army
6 June	D-Day landings in Normandy
23 June	Beginning of Operation Bagration to liberate Belorussia
3 July	Minsk recaptured by the Red Army
20 July	Attempt on Hitler's life
1 August	Beginning of Warsaw Uprising
21 August– 28 September	Dumbarton Oaks conference
5 September	Soviet–Finnish ceasefire USSR declares war on Bulgaria
9 September	Soviet–Bulgarian ceasefire
12 September	Romania surrenders
19 September	Finland surrenders
2 October	End of the Warsaw Uprising
9–18 October	Churchill–Stalin conference in Moscow
20 October	Red Army enters Belgrade
28 October	Bulgaria surrenders
2–10 December	De Gaulle visit to Moscow
10 December	Franco-Soviet Treaty of Alliance
16–24 December	German Ardennes offensive

1945

4 January	USSR recognises the Polish Committee of National Liberation as the Provisional Government of Poland
12 January	Vistula–Oder operation begins
17 January	Warsaw captured by the Red Army
27 January	Auschwitz captured by the Red Army
4–11 February	Yalta conference
13 February	Budapest falls to the Red Army
5 April	USSR renounces its pact of neutrality with Japan
11 April	Soviet–Yugoslav Treaty of Friendship, Mutual Aid and Postwar Co-operation
12 April	Roosevelt dies; Truman becomes President
13 April	Vienna falls to the Red Army
16 April	Red Army's Berlin Operation begins
25 April– 26 June	San Francisco conference on the foundation of the UN

30 April	Hitler commits suicide
2 May	Berlin surrenders to the Red Army
7–8 May	Germany surrenders unconditionally
9 May	Red Army captures Prague
24 May	Stalin's toast to the Russian people
24 June	Victory parade in Red Square
28 June	Stalin proclaimed Generalissimo
17 July– 2 August	Potsdam conference
17 July	US tests atom bomb
24 July	Truman informs Stalin about the atom bomb
6 August	Atom bomb dropped on Hiroshima
8/9 August	USSR declares war on Japan
9 August	Atom bomb dropped on Nagasaki
14 August	Japan agrees to surrender Sino-Soviet Treaty of Friendship and Alliance
2 September	Japan signs treaty of capitulation
11 September– 2 October	First meeting of the Council of Foreign Ministers (CFM) in London
16–26 December	Moscow conference of American, British and Soviet foreign ministers

1946

10 January– 14 February	First session of the UN General Assembly
9 February	Stalin's election speech
10 February	Elections to Supreme Soviet
5 March	Churchill's 'Iron Curtain' speech in Fulton, Missouri
25 April– 16 May	CFM meeting in Paris
15 June– 12 July	CFM meeting in Paris
29 July– 15 October	Paris Peace Conference
7 August	USSR demands joint control of the Black Sea Straits with Turkey
16 August	*Zhdanovshchina* begins
4 November– 12 December	CFM meeting in New York

1947

10 February	Signing of peace treaties with Bulgaria, Finland, Hungary, Italy and Romania
10 March– 24 April	CFM meeting in Moscow
12 March	Truman speech to US Congress
5 June	Marshall Plan speech
27 June– 2 July	Paris conference on the Marshall Plan
22–28 September	Founding conference of the Cominform
25 November– 15 December	CFM meeting in London

1948

25 February	Communist coup in Czechoslovakia
24 June	Beginning of Berlin blockade
28 June	Yugoslavia expelled from the Cominform

1949

4 March	Vyshinskii replaces Molotov as Foreign Minister
4 April	Signing of NATO treaty
8 May	Establishment of West German state
12 May	Lifting of Berlin blockade
23 May– 20 June	CFM meeting in Paris
29 August	Soviet atom bomb test
1 October	Chinese People's Republic proclaimed in Peking
7 October	Establishment of East German state

1950

14 February	Sino-Soviet Treaty of Friendship, Alliance and Mutual Aid
25 June	North Korea invades South Korea
19 October	Chinese forces cross the Yalu into North Korea

1951

5 March– 21 June	Paris conference of the deputy foreign ministers of the USSR, France, the UK and the USA
8 July	Peace talks begin in Korea

1952

10 March	'Stalin note' on the terms for a peace treaty with Germany
9 April	Second 'Stalin note' on the German question
5–14 October	19th Congress of the Soviet communist party
21 December	Stalin's last public statement welcomes the idea of negotiations with the new Eisenhower administration

1953

5 March	Death of Stalin

Introduction
Stalin at War

In the pantheon of twentieth-century dictators Joseph Stalin's reputation for brutality and criminality is rivalled only by Adolf Hitler's. Yet when he died in March 1953 his passing was widely mourned. In Moscow weeping crowds thronged the streets and there were displays of mass public grief throughout the Soviet Union.[1] At Stalin's state funeral, party leaders queued up to eulogise their dead boss in reverential tones that suggested the passing of a saint, not a mass murderer. 'The deathless name of Stalin will always live in our hearts, in the hearts of the Soviet people and of all progressive humanity,' claimed Vyacheslav Molotov, the Soviet foreign minister. 'The fame of his great deeds in the service and happiness of our people and the workers of the whole world will live forever!'[2] None of this was particularly surprising. During the last 20 years of his life the cult of Stalin's personality had ruled supreme in Soviet Russia. According to cult mythology Stalin was not just the great helmsman of the Soviet state, the political genius who had led his country to victory in war and to superpower status in peace, but the 'father of the peoples'.[3] He was, the slogan went, the 'Lenin of today', and, fittingly, Stalin's body was laid alongside that of the founder of the Soviet state in his mausoleum on Red Square.

But Stalin's reputation soon began to take a battering in the Soviet Union. Only three years later, in February 1956, Nikita Khrushchev, the new Soviet leader, denounced the cult of personality as a perversion of communist principles and depicted Stalin as a despot who had executed his comrades, decimated his military commanders, and led the country to one disaster after another during the Second World War.[4]

Khrushchev's speech was delivered to a secret session of the 20th congress of the Soviet communist party but within a few months a resolution of the party's central committee 'On Overcoming the Cult of Personality and its Consequences' gave many of the critical themes a public airing.[5] At the 22nd party congress in 1961 Khrushchev returned to the attack on Stalin, this time in public, and he was joined by a number of other speakers. The congress voted to remove Stalin's body from Lenin's mausoleum, one delegate in the debate on this resolution claiming that she had 'sought Ilich's advice, and it was as if he stood before me alive and said: It is unpleasant for me to be beside Stalin, who has brought so much harm to the Party'.[6] Stalin's body was duly taken from Lenin's side and buried in a modest grave beside the Kremlin wall.

After Khrushchev's fall from power in 1964 the new Soviet leadership found it expedient to partly rehabilitate Stalin. The problem with the Khrushchevite critique was that it raised dangerous questions about the failure of the party to control Stalin's dictatorship and about the culpability of other members of the Soviet military and political elite in his wrongdoings. Stalin continued to be criticised in the post-Khrushchev era, but negative assessments were balanced by a positive appraisal of his achievements, particularly his role in the socialist industrialisation of the USSR.[7]

In the late 1980s a new phase of condemnation and criticism of Stalin began in the Soviet Union. But this time the critique of Stalin became linked to a more general rejection of the Soviet communist system. The original sponsor of this anti-Stalin campaign was the reform communist leader Mikhail Gorbachev, who encouraged critical discussion of the Soviet past as a weapon in his struggle against opponents of political change.[8] Gorbachev failed to reinvigorate Soviet communism but his reform programme destabilised the political system sufficiently to precipitate its collapse in 1991. By the end of that year the multinational Soviet state had fallen apart, Gorbachev had resigned as President of the now defunct Union of Soviet Socialist Republics, and Boris Yeltsin was the leader of a post-Soviet Russia. In the Yeltsin era discussion of the Stalin question knew no bounds and was fuelled by the opening of party and state archives which revealed for the first time the details of the means and mechanisms of his dictatorial rule.

It might have been expected that the 1990s would see Stalin's reputation in Russia reduced to the same level as Hitler's in Germany: he would continue to be worshipped by a neo-Stalinist cult but the general verdict would be that his impact on Russia and the world was mostly negative. But that did not happen. For many Russians the material deprivations of the forced transition from authoritarian communism to unbridled capitalism during the Yeltsin years made Stalin and his era seem more attractive, not less.[9] Among historians there was condemnation and criticism of Stalin aplenty, but his regime had defenders as well as detractors, particularly among those who argued that he had played an indispensable role in defeating the Nazis' attempt to impose their racist empire on Russia and Europe.

By the early twenty-first century, with the former KGB officer Vladimir Putin in power, Stalin was more alive in Russia than at any time since his death. The Moscow bookshops were full of tomes debating his life and legacy.

Posthumously published memoirs of Stalin's cronies, or the recollections of their children, were among the best-selling works.[10] Russian television showed endless documentaries about Stalin and his inner circle. Post offices sold postcards reproducing classic paintings and graphics of the Stalin cult, while stalls and kiosks on Red Square offered sweatshirts and other memorabilia emblazoned with his image.

On the 50th anniversary of his death Russian public opinion was much less enamoured of Stalin than it had been in the cult era, but his reputation was still riding high. An opinion poll of 1,600 adults in the Russian Federation, conducted in February–March 2003, revealed that 53 per cent approved of Stalin overall, while only 33 per cent disapproved. Twenty percent of those polled thought that Stalin was a wise leader, while a similar number agreed that only a 'tough leader' could have ruled the country in the circumstances of the time. Just 27 per cent of respondents agreed that Stalin was 'a cruel, inhuman tyrant responsible for the deaths of millions', while a similar percentage thought that the full truth about him was not yet known.[11]

In the west the political and historical treatment of Stalin followed a similar trajectory. When he died in 1953 the cold war was at its height but newspaper coverage of Stalin's death was respectful and the obituaries mostly balanced. At this time Stalin was still seen as a relatively benign dictator, as a statesman even,[12] and in popular consciousness an affectionate memory lingered of 'Uncle Joe', the great war leader who had led his people to victory over Hitler and helped save Europe from Nazi barbarism.

Equally, it was no secret that Stalin had been responsible for the deaths of millions of his own citizens: peasants deported or starved to death during the forced collectivisation of Soviet agriculture; party and state officials purged during hunts for 'enemies of the people'; ethnic minorities condemned as wartime collaborators of the Nazis; and returning Soviet POWs suspected of cowardice, treason and betrayal. Yet still the commentators found much to commend in Stalin's life and career. One of his first serious biographers, Isaac Deutscher, argued that Stalin had used barbarous methods to drive backward-ness and barbarism out of Russia. 'The core of Stalin's genuine historic achieve-ment,' wrote Deutscher in 1953 just after the dictator's death, 'lies in the fact that he found Russia working with the wooden plough and left her equipped with atomic piles.'[13] Deutscher, it should be noted, was a former adherent of Stalin's great rival, Trotsky (murdered by a Soviet security agent in Mexico in 1940), and was not personally sympathetic to the communist dictator.

While Khrushchev's 'secret speech' to the 20th party congress remained unpublished in the Soviet Union until the Gorbachev era, a copy was leaked to the west[14] and soon became one of the key texts of western historiography of the Stalin era. But many western historians were sceptical about

Khrushchev's efforts to lay all the blame for past communist crimes on Stalin and the cult of his personality. Khrushchev himself was a member of Stalin's inner circle and a participant in many of the policies and events that he now found it expedient to condemn. It became apparent, too, that one set of myths was being replaced by another when there developed a minor cult of Khrushchev's personality.[15]

While western historians did not go along with the 1960s rehabilitation of Stalin, the rebalancing of the Soviet discussion about his regime offered new evidence and perspectives. Particularly valuable was the contribution of Soviet military memoirs.[16] After 1956 these memoirs had been mainly devoted to embellishing and elaborating Khrushchev's critique of Stalin's wartime record. After Khrushchev's fall in 1964 the memoirists were free to provide a more positive account of Stalin's role and to correct the simplistic and often incredible assertions of the secret speech; for example, that Stalin had planned military operations using a globe of the earth![17]

Both in Russia and the west much of the discussion of Stalin's life and legacy has centred on his role during the Second World War. Stalin's biography encompasses several very different phases – years of illegal political activity in Tsarist Russia, participation in the Bolshevik seizure of power in 1917 and in the ensuing civil war, the inner-party leadership struggles of the 1920s, the industrialisation and collectivisation drives of the 1930s, and the cold war conflict with the west in the 1940s and 1950s. But the central episode in his life was what the Soviets called the Great Patriotic War.[18] The war tested to the limit both Stalin's leadership and the system he had done so much to create and shape. 'For our country this war was the most cruel and difficult of all the wars experienced by our motherland . . . The war was a sort of test of our Soviet system, our state, our government, our communist party,' said Stalin in a speech of February 1946.[19]

The Red Army's recovery from the devastating blow of the German invasion of June 1941 and its victorious march to Berlin by May 1945 was the greatest feat of arms the world had ever seen. The Soviet victory in the war led to the spread of communism to Eastern Europe and to other parts of the globe and provided new sources of legitimacy for the communist system and for Stalin's leadership. For the next 40 years the Soviet system was seen as a viable alternative to western liberal democratic capitalism, a state that competed effectively with the west, economically, politically and ideologically during the cold war. Indeed, at the peak of the Soviet challenge in the 1950s and 1960s it seemed to many that Stalin's vision of the global triumph of the communist system would eventually be realised.[20]

While the Second World War had fateful political consequences for the communist system it was a catastrophe for the Soviet people. During the war

70,000 Soviet cities, towns and villages were laid waste. Destroyed were 6 million houses, 98,000 farms, 32,000 factories, 82,000 schools, 43,000 libraries, 6,000 hospitals and thousands of miles of roads and railway track.[21] In terms of casualties, during Stalin's lifetime the official Soviet figure was 7 million fatalities. Later this figure was raised to 'over 20 million'. In post-Soviet times numbers as high as 35 million war-related deaths were quoted, but the generally accepted figure is about 25 million, two-thirds of them civilians.[22]

To what extent was Stalin responsible for the disastrous impact of the war on the Soviet Union? Khrushchev's critique of Stalin's war record focused, in particular, on his responsibility for the disaster of 22 June 1941 when the Germans were able to launch a successful surprise attack on Russia that took their armies to the gates of Moscow and Leningrad. This theme was taken up by many western historians, who broadened it to include a more wide-ranging critique of the controversial Nazi–Soviet non-aggression pact of 1939–1941.

The Nazi–Soviet Pact

When Hitler invaded Poland in September 1939 he did so secure in the knowledge that while he might face war with Britain and France in the west, his eastern flank was safeguarded by Soviet neutrality in the form of a non-aggression pact agreed with Stalin on 23 August 1939. Stalin concluded this pact in return for a secret agreement guaranteeing a Soviet sphere of influence in Eastern Europe. Stalin's decision to do this deal with Hitler on the very eve of a new European war was a dramatic, last-minute improvisation. Only a few days before this radical turn in Soviet policy Stalin had been negotiating the terms of military alliance with Britain and France, but he feared London and Paris were manoeuvring to provoke a Soviet–German war that would allow them the luxury of standing aside while the Nazis and the communists slugged it out on the Eastern Front. Stalin's pact with Hitler was designed to turn the tables on the western powers and to give him freedom of manoeuvre in the coming war. [23]

After the outbreak of war Stalin moved to occupy eastern Poland, allocated by the pact to the Soviet sphere of influence. The Baltic States of Estonia, Latvia and Lithuania were next on Stalin's list, as was Finland. While the Baltic States acceded to Soviet demands to site military bases on their territory and signed mutual assistance pacts with the USSR, the Finns refused. So at the end of November 1939 the Red Army invaded Finland. Contrary to Stalin's expectations of a quick and easy victory, the war with Finland dragged on and proved to be very costly, diplomatically as well as militarily. The greatest danger to Stalin came when Britain and France began assembling an expeditionary force to Finland with the aim of using the 'Winter War' as an excuse to occupy the iron ore fields of northern Sweden. In those circumstances the Germans would have intervened to protect raw materials vital to their war economy and the Soviet Union would have been dragged into the greater European war. The Finns were also fearful of an escalation of the war and sued for peace. Under the terms of the peace treaty signed in March 1940 Finland conceded the Soviet territorial demands but retained its independence as a state.

The only state to back the Soviet Union diplomatically during the war with Finland was Germany, an action that constituted one aspect of extensive Soviet–German political, economic and military co-operation in 1939–1940. In summer 1940, however, the Stalin–Hitler alliance began to crack under the impact of mutual suspicion of the other's intentions and war re-emerged as the most likely scenario in Soviet–German relations. But Stalin continued to believe that war could and would be delayed until 1942. It was this miscalculation that led him to restrain Soviet military mobilisation until the very last minute. Only when Hitler's armies were flooding across Soviet borders did Stalin finally accept that war had definitely come.

The controversy about Stalin's pact with Hitler is fundamentally an argument about the costs and benefits of that unholy alliance. On one side are those who contend that Stalin turned his back on an anti-German alliance with Britain and France in August 1939 and thereby facilitated the Nazi takeover of most of continental Europe. The price of this miscalculation was the devastating blow of 22 June 1941 and the near success of the German invasion of the Soviet Union. On the other side are those who argue that the USSR was not ready for war with Germany in 1939 and that Stalin as well as Hitler made a number of strategic gains from the pact which, crucially, bought the Soviets time to prepare their defences.

In the 1990s the debate about the Stalin–Hitler pact took a new turn when a number of Russian historians began to argue that the root cause of the disaster of June 1941 was not Stalin's efforts to maintain peace with Hitler but his preparations to launch a pre-emptive strike against Germany.[24] According to this view the main reason for the initial Soviet defeats was that the Red Army was deployed for attack, not defence. The Soviet military were not so much caught napping as caught in the middle of preparations for their own attack on Germany. The novelty of this interpretation was its utilisation of new evidence from Russian archives, including the Soviet war plans of 1940–1941, which indicated that the Red Army did indeed intend to wage an offensive war against Germany. But the proffered analysis of why Stalin might want to launch an attack on Germany was of a much older vintage. Throughout the 1920s and 1930s anti-communist commentators had highlighted the so-called 'war–revolution nexus':[25] the idea that Stalin was plotting to precipitate a new world war that – like the First World War – would open the way to revolutionary upheavals throughout Europe. Taking up this theme, Nazi propagandists claimed the German invasion of Russia was a pre-emptive strike against an imminent Soviet attack and depicted the war as a crusade in defence of civilised Christian Europe from the Asiatic Bolshevik hordes.

In truth, far from plotting war and revolution, there was nothing that Stalin feared more than a major military conflict. War offered opportunities – and Stalin certainly took them when they came along – but also posed great dangers. While the First World War had led to the Russian Revolution of 1917, it was followed by a civil war in which the communists' enemies almost succeeded in strangling Bolshevism at birth. Included among the Bolsheviks' opponents in the civil war were the great capitalist powers – Britain, France and the United States – who aided anti-communist forces in Russia and imposed an economic and political blockade – a cordon sanitaire – to contain the contagion of Bolshevism. The Bolsheviks were able to survive the Russian civil war and in the 1920s to break out of international isolation, but for the next two decades they feared the revival of a grand capitalist coalition dedicated to crushing the Soviet socialist system. By the early 1940s Soviet Russia was much stronger and Stalin was confident about the Red Army's ability to defend the socialist motherland, but the nightmare scenario of involvement in a war against a united front of hostile capitalist states still persisted. Even as radical a realignment of states as an Anglo-German alliance against Russia was not ruled out by Stalin in 1940 and 1941. For this reason, while some of Stalin's military commanders were urging the preparation of a pre-emptive strike against Germany, the Soviet dictator himself calculated that such an action could provoke a premature war and he decided to gamble everything on the possibility of maintaining peace with Hitler.

Stalin as Warlord

Alongside debate on the Nazi–Soviet pact the other sustained focus of historical discussion has been Stalin's military and political leadership during the Great Patriotic War. During the war Stalin was Supreme Commander of the Soviet armed forces, head of the State Defence Council and People's Commissar for Defence, as well as the head of government and the leader of the communist party. He signed all the major directives and orders to the armed forces. His speeches and statements were major milestones in the declaration of Soviet military strategy and political aims and played an important role in boosting popular morale. Stalin represented the country at summit meetings with the Soviet Union's wartime allies, Great Britain and the United States,[26] and corresponded on a regular basis with the British Prime Minister, Winston Churchill, and the American President, Franklin Delano Roosevelt.[27] Before 1939 Stalin had received few foreigners, apart from fellow communists, but during the Second World War he became a familiar figure to a stream of visiting dignitaries, diplomats, politicians and military men. In Soviet wartime propaganda Stalin was depicted as the central, steadfast symbol of the country's unity in the struggle against the Germans. Paeans for Stalin's military genius filled the pages of the Soviet press during the latter stages of the war and when at the end of the war Stalin was crowned 'Generalissimus' – the superlative General – it seemed only appropriate.[28]

To outside observers Stalin appeared as both the key figure and the linchpin of the Soviet war effort. This contemporary perception was summed up in Deutscher's 1948 biography of Stalin:

> Many allied visitors who called at the Kremlin during the war were astonished to see on how many issues, great and small, military, political or diplomatic, Stalin took the final decision. He was in effect his own commander-in-chief, his own minister of defence, his own quartermaster, his own minister of supply, his own foreign minister, and even his own chef de protocole . . .Thus he went on, day after day, throughout four years of hostilities – a prodigy of patience, tenacity, and vigilance, almost omnipresent, almost omniscient.[29]

Sixty years later Deutscher's appraisal has been amply borne out by new evidence from Russian sources which now provides a detailed picture of Stalin's policies, decisions and activities during the war. In Stalin's appointments diary we can see who visited him in his Kremlin office and how long they stayed.[30] We have access to thousands of military, political and diplomatic reports and briefings that flowed into Stalin's office. We have a nearly complete record of Stalin's political and diplomatic conversations during the war, including those with foreign communist leaders, with whom he was generally the most frank. We have the transcripts of many of Stalin's telephone and telegraphic conversations with his military commanders on the front line. We have the memoirs and diaries of some of his closest associates. This new body of evidence is far from complete; there is still limited evidence of Stalin's most private thoughts and calculations.[31] But we now know a considerable amount about Stalin's detailed conduct of the Soviet war effort and about the context in which he formulated and took his military and political decisions.

Averell Harriman, the American ambassador in Moscow from 1943 to 1945, probably had more direct dealings with Stalin than any other foreigner during the war. In an interview given in 1981 he made this assessment of Stalin's war leadership:

> Stalin the War Leader . . . was popular, and there can be no doubt that he was the one who held the Soviet Union together . . . I do not think anyone else could have done it, and nothing that has happened since Stalin's death induces me to change that opinion . . . I'd like to emphasize my great admiration for Stalin the national leader in an emergency – one of those historical occasions when one man made such a difference. This in no sense minimizes my revulsion against his cruelties; but I have to give you the constructive side as well as the other.[32]

In the same interview Harriman presented a fascinating sketch of the qualities that, in his eyes, made Stalin such an effective war leader. In Harriman's view Stalin was a man of keen intelligence, by no means an intellectual, but a smart operator, a practical man who knew how to use the levers of power to good effect. As a personality Stalin was very approachable, albeit blunt and prepared to use shock tactics as well as flattery to get his way in negotiations. On social occasions Stalin showed concern for everybody and drank toasts with everyone, but – unlike some of his associates – never got drunk or lost his self-control. Harriman was at particular pains to deny that Stalin was paranoid (as opposed to just 'very suspicious') or that he was a 'mere bureaucrat':

> He had an enormous ability to absorb detail and to act on detail. He was very much alert to the needs of the whole war machine . . . In our negotiations with him we usually found him extremely well informed. He had a masterly knowledge of the sort of equipment that was important for him. He knew the caliber of the guns he wanted, the weight of the tanks his roads and bridges would take, and the details of the type of metal he needed to build aircraft. These were not characteristics of a bureaucrat, but rather those of an extremely able and vigorous war leader.[33]

Stalin the social charmer, Stalin the master of his brief, Stalin the effective negotiator; above all, Stalin the determined but practical man of action – these themes of Harriman's recur time and again in the reports of those who worked with the Soviet dictator during the war.

Among historians the retrospective verdict on Stalin is more mixed but even his most severe critics accept that the war was an exceptionally positive period in his life and career. A common view is that while Stalin's rule was generally horrific, the vices of his dictatorship became the virtues of his war leadership. Richard Overy, for example, offered this assessment of Stalin in his classic text, *Why the Allies Won*:

> Stalin brought a powerful will to bear on the Soviet war effort that motivated those around him and directed their energies. In the process he expected and got exceptional sacrifices from his besieged people. The personality cult developed around him in the 1930s made this appeal possible in wartime. It is difficult to imagine that any other Soviet leader at that time could have wrung such efforts from the population. There is a sense in which the Stalin cult was necessary to the Soviet war effort . . . revelations of the brutality of the wartime regime should not blind us to the fact that Stalin's grip on the Soviet Union may have helped more than it hindered the pursuit of victory.[34]

Apart from his closest political associates,[35] the group that had the most intense and frequent contacts with Stalin during the war were the members of his High Command. Accounts by Stalin's generals provide an intimate portrait of the Soviet dictator's daily routine during wartime.[36] Stalin – a man in his sixties – was a hard taskmaster who worked 12–15 hours a day throughout the war and demanded the same of his subordinates. He was briefed on the strategic situation three times a day by his General Staff officers. He expected accurate, unblemished reporting and was quick to spot inconsistency and error. He had a phenomenal memory for facts, names and faces. He was prepared to listen to arguments but expected proponents to stick to the point and kept his own contributions short and decisive.

However, the main focus of Soviet military memoirs is not these personal abilities but Stalin's performance as Supreme Commander, as a military leader. As Seweryn Bialer pointed out, what impressed westerners was Stalin's grasp of grand strategy and his control of the technical and tactical details of the Soviet war effort.[37] But what mattered to his generals was Stalin's operational art – his ability to direct big battles and control large-scale military operations. In this respect Soviet military memoirs report many mistakes by Stalin: ill-conceived, costly offensives; refusal to order strategic retreats in the face of enemy encirclement; and the mishandling of major battles. Other complaints concern Stalin's excessive meddling in frontline operations, his loss of composure during critical situations, and the scapegoating of others for his own mistakes. Above all there is the criticism that Stalin was profligate with men and materiel and that the Soviet victory over Germany was achieved at too high a cost.

During the course of the Eastern Front war the Soviets destroyed more than 600 enemy divisions (Italian, Hungarian, Romanian, Finnish, Croat, Slovak and Spanish as well as German). The Germans alone incurred 10 million casualties on the Eastern front (75 per cent of their total wartime losses), including 3 million dead, with Hitler's Axis allies losing another million. The Red Army destroyed 48,000 enemy tanks, 167,000 guns and 77,000 aircraft.[38] However, Soviet losses were two to three times greater than those of the Germans. Soviet military casualties, for example, totalled about 16 million, including 8 million killed.[39]

Marshal Georgii Zhukov, Stalin's Deputy Supreme Commander during the war, fiercely contested the idea that the Soviet High Command was profligate with men and materiel, arguing that while it is easy to claim in retrospect that fewer forces could have been used and fewer casualties suffered, on the field of battle conditions are immeasurably more complex and unpredictable.[40] Arguably, the major proportion of the Red Army's casualties was the result of two factors. First, the massive losses incurred during the catastrophic first few months of the war, which included the encirclement and capture of millions of Soviet troops by the Germans, most of whom then died in Nazi captivity. Then, during the second half of the war, there were the high costs of large-scale offensive action against an enemy that conducted a ferocious and highly skilled retreat all the way back to Germany. As late as April 1945, during the battle of Berlin, the Wehrmacht was still capable of inflicting 80,000 fatalities on the Red Army.

While there is no evidence that Stalin suffered even the slightest remorse about sending millions of his citizens to death in battle, he was not without emotion. He wore the mask of command very well and was ruthless in pursuit of victory but his hatred of the Germans was plain and he was genuinely shocked by Hitler's war of annihilation on the Eastern Front, a war whose aim was the complete destruction of the communist system, the razing of the USSR's cities, and the mass murder or enslavement of millions of Soviet citizens. 'If the Germans want to have a war of extermination, they will get it,' warned Stalin in November 1941.[41] Throughout the war Stalin favoured the imposition of a punitive peace on Germany, one that would provide a guarantee against the rise of another Hitler. Although Stalin consistently distinguished between Nazi war guilt and that of the German people as a whole, he displayed no pity for the enemy and only ever restrained the revenge of his armies when it suited his political or economic purposes. In public he never betrayed any emotion about the death of his son, Yakov – who died in German captivity during the war – but the loss united him in bereavement with millions of his fellow citizens who lost loved ones.

One of Stalin's most emotive and revealing outbursts about Germany and the Germans was contained in a statement to a visiting Czechoslovak delegation in March 1945:

Now we are beating the Germans and many think the Germans will never be able to threaten us again. This is not so. I hate the Germans. But that must not cloud one's judgement of the Germans. The Germans are a great people. Very good technicians and organisers. Good, naturally brave soldiers. It is impossible to get rid of the Germans, they will remain. We are fighting the Germans and will do so until the end. But we must bear in mind that our allies will try to save the Germans and come to an arrangement with them. We will be merciless towards the Germans but our allies will treat them with kid gloves. Thus we Slavs must be prepared for the Germans to rise again against us. [42]

One of the sternest critics of Stalin's war leadership was his 'glasnost' biographer, General Dmitrii Volkogonov. Joining the Red Army in 1945, Volkogonov worked in the armed forces propaganda department for 20 years and then became head of the Soviet Institute of Military History. Because of his background and position, Volkogonov was able, particularly during the Gorbachev years, to gain access to a wide range of Soviet military, political and intelligence archives.[43] His 1989 biography of Stalin was widely regarded as the first serious and genuinely critical treatment of the Soviet dictator published in the USSR. Volkogonov's verdict on Stalin as a warlord was that he 'was not the military leader of genius depicted in countless books, films, poems, monographs and stories' and that 'he had no professional military skills' and 'came to strategic wisdom only through blood-spattered trial and error'. At the same time, Volkogonov was not blind to the positive aspects of Stalin's warlordship, in particular the Soviet leader's ability to see 'the profound dependence of the armed struggle on an entire spectrum of other, non-military factors: economic, social, technical, political, diplomatic, ideological and national'.[44]

Since the publication of Volkogonov's book, opinion among Russian military historians has swung back in Stalin's favour, although many authors continue to argue that it was Stalin's generals who won the war and that without his leadership victory could have been secured at a much lower cost. [45]

The detailed reconstruction and interpretation of Stalin's war record is the main subject of this book, as is the validity of this continuing critique and counter-critique, but some general points are in order here.

Stalin was no general but he did have experience of high command in the field and of serving in the combat zone, although not on the front line. During the Russian civil war he served as a political commissar, a representative of the communist party's central committee responsible for securing and maintaining supplies for the Red Army, a job that involved him in high-level military decision-making. Stalin's most famous action during the civil war was his role in the successful defence of Tsaritsyn in 1918 – a city renamed Stalingrad in his honour in 1924. Located in the southern USSR at a crucial point on the River Volga, Tsaritsyn guarded the route to Moscow's food and fuel supplies from the Caucasus. In the 1920s and 1930s Stalin maintained an interest in military affairs and became a persistent critic of what he called the civil war mentality, insisting that the Red Army had to constantly modernise its doctrines and arms and resist the temptation to bask in former glory.

Especially salient to his role as a warlord during the Second World War was Stalin's experience of defeat and near catastrophe in 1919–1920. At the height of the civil war the Bolsheviks were besieged by counter-revolutionary White Armies attacking from every direction and were barely able to hang on to the territory they controlled in the central part of the country. Stalin also witnessed General Pilsudski's blocking of the Red Army's march on Warsaw in 1920 and the successful Polish counter-offensive that resulted in the Soviet loss to the newly created Polish state of Western Belorussia and Western Ukraine.[46] These experiences of severe setback should be borne in mind when considering Stalin's extraordinary faith in victory during the Second World War, which never wavered even when the Germans occupied half his country and besieged Leningrad, Moscow and Stalingrad.

During the Great Patriotic War Stalin assumed the role of general but he showed no inclination (unlike Churchill) to witness the military struggle at first hand or (unlike Hitler) to direct operations close to the front line. He made only one brief visit to a combat zone. He preferred to exercise supreme command in his imagination, within the confines of his Kremlin office or at his dacha (country house) just outside Moscow.

Any criticism of Stalin's operational errors has to be balanced by a recognition that he got things right too, often contrary to the advice of his professional military advisers. That was especially true when operational issues overlapped with matters of morale, politics and psychology. As Volkogonov noted, Stalin's 'thinking was more global, and it was this that placed him above the others in the military leadership'.[47]

It should not be assumed that all the criticisms levelled against Stalin are either accurate or true. In many instances Stalin was acting on the advice of his military commanders and the responsibility for mistakes must be shared. Nor is it wise to assume that because mistakes can be identified in retrospect they were rectifiable at the time. Quite often the knowledge and foresight required to avoid costly errors simply was not available to anyone at the time. Like armchair generals all over the world, Soviet military memoirists have not been immune to the temptation to re-fight battles after the event, when the winning is so much easier, and cost-free.

Finally, although it would be easy to accumulate and quote critical comments on Stalin from the pages of Soviet military memoirs, to do so would distort the main impression they convey – that of a leader who learned from his mistakes and got better at his job as the war progressed. This was certainly the view of his two closest military associates during the war, Marshals Alexander Vasilevskii and Georgii Zhukov.

Vasilevskii, chief of the Soviet General Staff for most of the Eastern Front war, was involved in the planning and direction of all the Red Army's major operations. He was in daily contact with Stalin, either in person or on the telephone, and was frequently dispatched to the front line as the Supreme Commander's personal representative. In his memoirs, published in 1974, Vasilevskii distinguished between two periods of Stalin's war leadership: the first few months of the war when his 'inadequate operational and strategic training was apparent' and the period from September 1942 when – with the battle of Stalingrad at its height – he began to listen to and accept professional advice and tutoring and as a result gained a 'good grasp of all questions relating to the preparation for and execution of operations'. In sum, it was Vasilevskii's

> profound conviction that Stalin, especially in the latter part of the war, was the strongest and most remarkable figure of the strategic command. He successfully supervised the fronts and all the war efforts of the country ... I think that Stalin displayed all the basic qualities of a Soviet general during the strategic offensive of the Soviet Armed Forces ... As Supreme High Commander, Stalin was in most cases extremely demanding but just. His directives and commands showed front commanders their mistakes and shortcomings, taught them how to deal with all manner of military operations skillfully.[48]

While Vasilevskii is generally seen as one of the brains behind the Red Army's war effort, Zhukov is usually regarded as its greatest frontline general. He directed the successful defence of Moscow in autumn 1941 – the first great turning point of the Eastern Front war – and played a key role in the battles of Stalingrad (1942), Kursk (1943) and Berlin (1945). From August 1942 he served as Stalin's Deputy Supreme Commander and in June 1945 led the victory parade in Red Square. His reputation is as a determined, wilful and ruthless commander, one of the few Soviet generals willing to challenge directly Stalin's judgements on military matters and to stand his ground in the ensuing rows. After the war Zhukov fell from Stalin's favour, was demoted, and posted to a regional military command. After Stalin's death Zhukov returned from the wilderness and served as Minister of Defence but then fell out with Khrushchev and was forced to retire in 1957. After Khrushchev's fall from power Zhukov was again rehabilitated and in the mid-1960s published a series of seminal studies of the major battles of the Great Patriotic War.[49]

Zhukov's memoirs, published in 1969, presented a flattering portrayal of Stalin's abilities as Supreme Commander:

Is it true that Stalin really was an outstanding military thinker, a major contributor to the development of the Armed Forces and an expert in tactical and strategic principles? . . . Stalin mastered the technique of the organisation of front operations and operations by groups of fronts and guided them with skill, thoroughly understanding complicated strategic questions . . . He had a knack of grasping the main link in the strategic situation so as to organise opposition to the enemy and conduct a major offensive operation. He was certainly a worthy Supreme Commander. Of course Stalin had no knowledge of all the details with which troops and all command echelons had to deal meticulously in order to prepare for an operation properly by a front or group of fronts. For that matter, this was something he didn't need to know . . . Stalin's merit lies in the fact that he correctly appraised the advice offered by the military experts and then in summarised form – in instructions, directives and regulations – immediately circulated them among the troops for practical guidance.[50]

These two laudatory portraits of Stalin as a very able Supreme Commander are hardly surprising given the closeness of the two marshals to Stalin. They were appointed and promoted by him. They were loyal servants of the Soviet state. They were true believers in communism, subscribers to the Stalin cult and they had shared in the glory of the Soviet victory in the Great Patriotic War. Above all they had survived Stalin's bloody purge of the Soviet military in 1937–1938.

Stalin's Terror

Stalin's prewar purge of the Soviet armed forces began in dramatic fashion. In May 1937 the deputy People's Commissar for Defence, Marshal M.N. Tukhachevskii was arrested and accused of treason and involvement in a conspiracy with Nazi Germany to overthrow the Soviet government. Promoted to Marshal by Stalin in 1935, Tukhachevskii was the Red Army's most innovative and eloquent strategic theorist and a vigorous proponent and organiser of the Red Army's modernisation and re-equipment.[51] Arrested at the same time as Tukhachevskii were seven other high ranking generals and in June all the accused were tried in secret, found guilty and shot. The verdict and the sentence were announced in the Soviet press and within ten days of the trial another 980 officers had been arrested.[52] By the time the purge had run its course more than 34,000 officers had been dismissed from the armed forces. While some 11,500 of these officers were eventually reinstated, the great majority were executed or died in prison.[53] Among those who perished were 3 marshals, 16 generals, 15 admirals, 264 colonels, 107 majors and 71 lieutenants. The category of officer that suffered most losses was that of political commissar, thousands of whom perished in the purges.[54]

After Stalin's death the purge was repudiated by the Soviet military and political leadership and its victims exonerated and rehabilitated.[55] Subsequently a debate developed about the impact of the purge on the military performance of the Red Army, especially during the early stages of the war with Germany. Among those purged were some of the most experienced and talented members of the Soviet officer corps. It was argued that the purge stymied military innovation, initiative and independence and that it resulted, said some, in the complete subordination of the Red Army and its High Command to Stalin's will – with the price being paid in the blood of millions of Soviet citizens who died because of the Soviet dictator's unrestrained military errors and miscalculations.

If Stalin's aim was to cow his High Command, then he certainly succeeded: even in the face of complete disaster in 1941, there was no challenge to Stalin's authority from his generals, nor any dissent when he blamed military failures on incompetent commanders and had them shot.[56] But it would be misleading to say that Stalin dominated a High Command consisting of a cohort that had stepped trembling into the bloodstained shoes of their purged predecessors. When they had gained battle experience and learned from their mistakes Stalin's wartime commanders performed outstandingly and developed a positive, collaborative relationship with the Soviet dictator in which they displayed initiative, flair and a good deal of independence. Whether or not their purged colleagues would have done any better in the circumstances remains a matter of speculation. What is certain is that the purged officers were innocent and that the purge meant an important loss of command expertise precisely at a time when the Soviet armed forces were undergoing a massive expansion in preparation for war. From a 10 per cent share of the national budget in 1932–1933 defence spending increased to 25 per cent in 1939 and army numbers grew from under a million to more than four million.[57] By 1941 the Red Army was the largest and most extensively equipped force in the world and that process of re-equipment, retraining and reorganisation of the armed forces continued until the outbreak of war with Germany later that year.

Stalin's purge of the armed forces was not an isolated phenomenon. After the assassination of Sergei Kirov, the head of the Leningrad Communist Party, in December 1934, thousands of party members were arrested, suspected of involvement in a plot to kill Soviet leaders.[58] In the mid-1930s there was a series of public political show trials of former leading members of the Bolshevik party who were accused of being spies, saboteurs and plotters against Stalin.[59] Then came the so-called *Yezhovshchina* – named after Stalin's security chief, Nikolai Yezhov – a frenzied hunt for the alleged 'enemy within' that resulted in mass arrests and executions of party and state officials. These events are known collectively as the 'Great Terror', an intense period of political repression and violence in which millions were arrested and hundreds of thousands shot, mostly in 1937–1938.[60]

Neither the extent nor the full ramifications of the Great Terror became known until much later but there was no secret about this hunt for 'enemies of the people'. The terror was a public spectacle, a mass participation event in which everyone was encouraged to denounce and inform on anyone suspected of political heresy, economic sabotage, or involvement in the machinations of foreign governments. Widespread belief in the guilt of the victims of repression fuelled popular enthusiasm for the process and was reinforced by the multiplication and intensification of international threats and tensions, particularly after Hitler came to power in January 1933. Soviet society really did seem to be under siege from its external and internal enemies.[61]

But what did Stalin believe? What were his motives for the Great Terror and the decapitation of his High Command? This is a question that goes to the heart of the debate about Stalin and the nature of his regime.

Broadly, there are two schools of thought among historians. First, that Stalin used the Terror to consolidate his dictatorship and system of power. This view tends to be associated with explanations of Stalin's actions based on one or other of his personality traits: that he was paranoid, vengeful, sadistic, bloodthirsty, driven by a will to power. The second view is that Stalin saw the terror as necessary for the defence of the Soviet system against a potentially lethal combination of internal subversion and external threat. This latter interpretation tends to be associated with a view of Stalin which stresses that he was an ideologue – a true believer in communism and convinced by his own propaganda about the class enemy.

These two analyses of Stalin are not wholly incompatible. In order to conduct the terror Stalin needed the character to authorise the execution of hundreds of thousands of his citizens and imprison many millions more. But that does not mean the process was driven by his psychological traits or by purely personal ambitions. Equally, while Stalin was a true believer in the virtues of communism he came to identify the interests of the Soviet system as synonymous with the strengthening of his own personal power position and used the Great Terror to that end.

However, perhaps the most important key to Stalin's motivations lies in the realm of ideology. The leitmotif of Soviet communist ideology in the 1920s and 1930s was class struggle – the inbuilt antagonism between mutually incompatible economic interest groups. This conflict between contending class forces was seen as a struggle waged between states as well as within states. Stalin's particular contribution to this class-conflict ideology was his emphasis on the intensification of the class struggle that takes place between capitalist and socialist states in an international epoch of imperialist wars and revolutionary upheavals. The Soviet Union, according to Stalin, was the target of imperialist intrigue because it was a threatening, alternative social system to capitalism that had to be subverted by espionage, sabotage and murderous conspiracies directed against its communist leadership.

Stalin's apocalyptic vision of the communist–capitalist class struggle at the state level reached its apotheosis in February–March 1937 at a plenum of the party's central committee:

> The wrecking and diversionary-spying work of agents of foreign states has touched to one degree or another all or almost all of our organisations, administrative and party as well as economic . . . agents of foreign states, including Trotskyists, have penetrated not only into the lower organisation, but even into certain responsible posts . . . Is it not clear that as long as capitalist encirclement exists we will have wreckers, spies, diversionists and murderers sent to the interior by agents of foreign states?
>
> We must smash and throw out the rotten theory that with each forward movement we make the class struggle will die down more and more, that in proportion to our successes the class enemy will become more and more domesticated . . . On the contrary, the more we move forward, the more success we have, then the more wrathful become the remnants of the beaten exploiter classes, the more quickly they turn to sharper forms of struggle, the more mischief they do the Soviet state, the more they grasp at the most desperate means of struggle . . .[62]

Stalin's frequent repetition of this theme, both publicly and privately, suggests that he really did believe he was waging an authentic struggle against the capitalist subversion of the Soviet system. According to the recollections of Molotov, Stalin's closest political associate, the object of the Great Terror was to get rid of a potential fifth column in advance of the inevitable war between the Soviet Union and the capitalist states.[63]

While it strains credibility to suggest that Stalin genuinely believed the absurd treason charges levelled against Tukhachevskii and the other generals, the potential for such a military conspiracy against his leadership was not so far-fetched. Tukhachevskii was a very strong personality with ideas about rearmament, strategic doctrine and civil–military relations that did not always chime with those of Stalin. Tukhachevskii clashed personally with his immediate chief, People's Commissar for Defence and long-time Stalin crony, Kliment Voroshilov, and there was a background of tension between the Red Army and the communist party which placed a question mark over the military's political loyalty in times of severe crisis.[64]

Apparently unreliable elements in the military and the communist party were not the only groups targeted by Stalin as part of his preparations for war. Living in the borderlands of the Soviet Union were a number of ethnic groups considered potentially disloyal in the event of war. Along the western border were Ukrainians, Poles, Latvians, Germans, Estonians, Finns, Bulgarians, Romanians and Greeks. In the Near East there were Turks, Kurds and Iranians and in the Far East there were Chinese and Koreans. Integral to the Great Terror was a process of ethnic cleansing involving the arrest, deportation and execution of hundreds of thousands of people living in border areas. According to one estimate, up to a fifth of those arrested and a third of those executed during the *Yezhovshchina* were members of such ethnic minorities.[65] According to another estimate 800,000 non-Russians were deported to Soviet Central Asia between 1936 and 1938. While the mass repression of party members, state officials and military officers came to an end in 1939, Stalin continued his ethno-political cleansing of borderland populations. After the Soviet invasion of eastern Poland in 1939, 400,000 ethnic Poles were arrested, deported and/or executed; among those shot were 20,000 Polish POWs – victims of the infamous 'Katyn massacre' of April–May 1940.[66] The Red Army's occupation of the Baltic States in summer 1940 led to the deportation of several hundred thousand Estonians, Latvians and Lithuanians. After the outbreak of the Soviet–German war in June 1941 Stalin's ethnic cleansing reached new heights of frenzy in the face of feared collaboration with the enemy. During the course of the Great Patriotic War 2 million members of ethnic minorities – Volga Germans, Crimean Tartars, Chechens and other Transcaucasian populations – were deported to the Soviet interior.[67]

Soviet Patriotism

Stalin's war against his borderland populations represented not so much personal as political paranoia – a fear of the threat that nationalist secessionism could pose to the survival of the Soviet state in time of war. But repression was not his only weapon against perceived separatist or disloyal tendencies among the ethnically mixed Soviet population. His other tactic was to reposition the Soviet state as the patriotic defender of Russia against foreign exploitation and occupation. This did not entail abandoning communist ideology or revolutionary internationalism or the socialist goals of the Soviet state. Rather it meant the adoption by Stalin and the Soviet system of a patriotic as well as a communist identity. One label for this repositioning is 'national bolshevism',[68] another is 'revolutionary patriotism'.[69] Stalin's own term was simply 'Soviet patriotism', which referred to the dual loyalty of citizens to the Soviet socialist system and to a Soviet state that represented and protected the various national traditions and cultures of the USSR. The multinational USSR was 'proletarian in content, national in form', declared Stalin: it was a class-based state that fostered national cultures and traditions as well as those of the proletariat. The agency integrating and organising this dual loyalty and identity was the communist party led by Stalin.

Stalin was ideally suited to personify the multiple identities and loyalties expected of Soviet citizens. He was a Georgian who ostentatiously valued his native traditions but also embraced Russian culture, language and identity. His humble origins as the son of a cobbler denoted a plebeian class identity but like millions of others he had benefited from the Bolshevik Revolution and the social mobility resulting from the socialist reconstruction of Russia. Stalin was a man of the borderlands who stood for a strong, centralised Soviet state that would defend all the peoples of the USSR. In short, Stalin was a Georgian, a worker, a communist and a Soviet patriot.[70]

An early sign of this patriotic repositioning of the communist party and of his own persona came in a much-quoted speech by Stalin in February 1931 on the urgency of the need to industrialise and modernise, a speech which illustrates his deft handling and melding of class-political and patriotic themes:

The history of old Russia consisted, among other things, in her being ceaselessly beaten for her backwardness. She was beaten by the Mongol khans. She was beaten by the Turkish beys. She was beaten by the Swedish feudal rulers. She was beaten by the Polish-Lithuanian lords. She was beaten by the Anglo-French capitalists. She was beaten by the Japanese barons. Everyone gave her a beating for her backwardness. For military backwardness, for cultural backwardness, for state backwardness, for industrial backwardness, for agricultural backwardness. They beat her because it was profitable and could be done with impunity. You remember the words of the pre-revolutionary poet: 'You are wretched, you are abundant, you are mighty, you are powerless, Mother Russia' ... Such is the law of the exploiters: beat the backward, you are weak – so you are in the wrong and therefore you can be beaten and enslaved ... We have fallen behind the advanced countries by fifty to a hundred years. We must close that gap in ten years. Either we do this or we'll be crushed. This is what our obligations before the workers and peasants of the USSR dictate to us.[71]

Together with Lenin, Stalin had been the architect of the Soviet nationalities policy.[72] Before 1917 Stalin had authored the main Bolshevik theoretical analysis of the so-called national question[73] and after the revolution served as People's Commissar for the Nationalities.[74] As revolutionary internationalists Lenin and Stalin believed in working-class unity across and superseding national boundaries and opposed nationalist separatism as a matter of principle. However, they recognised both the continuing appeal of national sentiment and the possibility of utilising native cultures and traditions in the political struggle against Tsarism and in the construction of a socialist state. Bolshevik ideology was adapted to take on board the project of fostering cultural and linguistic nationalism among the nationalities and ethnic groups of the USSR while at the same time struggling for the class-based political unity of all Soviet peoples. The USSR's first constitution, adopted in 1922, was highly centralist but also theoretically federalist and ostensibly based on a voluntary union of national republics.

In the 1920s the Bolsheviks' nationalities policy had two main practical prongs: 'nativisation' – the appointment of members of ethnic minorities to official positions in their localities; and fostering cultural and linguistic nationalism among the peoples of the USSR, including some who had no discernible national identity before the Soviet era. But one section of the population remained exempt from the nativisation policy and cultural nationalism: the Russians. The Russian population was larger than all the other Soviet nationalities put together. Lenin and Stalin feared that, because of their size and cultural sophistication, the Russians would dominate the other nationalities and that encouraging Russian national consciousness would unleash chauvinist tendencies. In the 1930s, however, Stalin's attitude towards the Russians underwent a radical change. A specifically Russian patriotism was rehabilitated and Russian patriotic heroes from the pre-revolutionary past were admitted into the Bolshevik heroic pantheon. The Russians were now depicted as the core group of the historic gathering of the peoples that constituted the Soviet multinational state. In cultural terms Russians were deemed first among equals of the Soviet nations – the cement of the USSR's 'friendship of the peoples'. Politically, the Russians were seen as the group most committed to the communist cause and the most loyal to the Soviet state.

Before the revolution the Bolsheviks had campaigned against Tsarist russification policies. By the end of the 1930s Russian had been returned to its status as the dominant language of education, the armed forces and the state, while Russian music, literature and folklore formed the backbone of a newly invented Soviet cultural tradition.[75] Among the many reasons for this 'Russian turn' in Stalin's nationalities policy was that with war coming a degree of russification was now seen as necessary to bind together the hundred or so nationalities that made up the USSR. Appeals to patriotism were also seen as a useful means of popular political mobilisation for the construction of the socialist state, and most of that modernisation and industrialisation was taking place in Russia. Above all, Stalin saw the powerful political appeal of a populist historical narrative that linked Russia's endeavours in the past with the struggles of the Soviet present. As Stalin put it in a toast at a private party at Voroshilov's dacha in November 1937:

> The Russian tsars did much that was bad. They robbed and enslaved the people. They led wars and seized territory in the interests of the landowners. But they did one good thing – they put together an enormous Great Power. . .We inherited this Great Power. We Bolsheviks were the first to put together and strengthen this Great Power, not in the interests of the landowners and capitalists, but for the toilers and for all the great peoples who make up this Great Power.[76]

Stalin's vision of the Soviet state as the inheritor of Russia's struggle to attain the power that could protect its peoples had an obvious utility in a feverish atmosphere of foreign threat, international crisis and approaching war. When war came in 1941 Stalin was able to mobilise the Soviet Union, particularly its Russian population, in a patriotic war of national defence against the latest in a long line of foreign invaders. As Stalin told Harriman in September 1941, 'we know that the people won't fight for world revolution and they won't fight for Soviet power, but perhaps they will fight for Russia'.[77] In a war as closely fought as the Soviet–German one, Stalin's ability to draw upon national senti-ment and patriotic loyalties as well as political commitment to the Soviet system was of critical importance. At the same time strenuous efforts were made to propagate the idea of a distinct Soviet patriotism that bound together all the nations and peoples of the USSR. Russian nationalism and Soviet patri-otism were supplemented by concepts of a broader Slavic solidarity and iden-tity and by Stalin's search for an alliance of Slavic states to combat any future German menace.[78]

The new patriotic identity of Stalin's Russia had an important bearing on what happened after the war. Having won a great victory Stalin expected his just rewards in the form of an expansion of Soviet power and influence, including the attainment of such traditional objectives of Tsarist foreign policy as control of the Black Sea Straits and warm water ports for an ocean-going navy. But Stalin's ambitions were frustrated by Britain and the United States – his partners in the Grand Alliance that defeated Hitler – who saw Soviet expansionism in the Black Sea, the Mediterranean and the Pacific as a threat to their own national strategic and political interests. In December 1945 Stalin complained to Ernest Bevin, the British Foreign Secretary, that 'as he saw the situation, the United Kingdom had India and her possessions in the Indian Ocean in her sphere of interest; the United States had China and Japan, but the Soviet Union had nothing'.[79]

However, Stalin's main strategic interest lay in Soviet expansion into Central and Eastern Europe so he backed away from confrontation with the western powers in peripheral areas. He refused to support the communist insurgency in Greece after the war, drew back from the demand for control of the Black Sea Straits, and acquiesced in the British and American refusal to give him a share of defeated Italy's North African colonies. But the damage to Soviet patriotic pride and prestige inflicted by his erstwhile allies remained and contributed to a pronounced xenophobic turn in Stalin's foreign and domestic policy after the war.

Publicly the first major manifestation of this new trend in Stalin's postwar policy was a speech by his ideology chief A.A. Zhdanov in August 1946 criticising Soviet journals and writers for their obsequiousness in the face of western literature and culture. This speech launched what became know as the *Zhdanovshchina* – an ideological campaign against western influence that extolled the unique virtues of Soviet science and culture. Zhdanov's speech was heavily edited by Stalin and the campaign itself conducted at his behest.[80] Privately, Stalin had already berated his inner circle for their 'liberalism' and 'servility' towards the west and urged his Foreign Minister, V.M. Molotov, to concede nothing in diplomatic negotiations with the United States and Great Britain.[81] In 1947 Stalin talked to Sergei Eisenstein about his new film, *Ivan the Terrible*, and advised him that

> Tsar Ivan was a great and wise ruler . . . Ivan the Terrible's wisdom rested on the fact that he stood for the national point of view and did not allow foreigners into his country, shielding the country from foreign influence . . . Peter the First was also a great ruler, but he related to foreigners too liberally, opened the gate too wide to foreign influence and allowed the Germanification of the country. Catherine allowed even more. After that – was Alexander I's court really a Russian court? Was the court of Nicholas I really a Russian court? No, they were German courts.[82]

The Cold War

The emergence and development of the *Zhdanovshchina* was intimately linked to the emerging cold war struggle with the west. Although the cold war did not get under way until 1947 the rift between Stalin and his Grand Alliance partners began to develop almost as soon as the war ended. While there were a number of diplomatic disputes with the west – about Poland, the occupation regime in Japan, the control of atomic energy – most worrying for Stalin were developments on the ideological front. During the war the Soviet Union, the Red Army and Stalin's leadership had received exemplary and laudatory coverage in the western press. Indeed, the Stalin cult in the USSR had branches in Britain, the United States and the other countries of the allied camp. When the war ended, however, Stalin's propaganda chiefs complained about the inauguration of a wide-ranging anti-Soviet campaign in the western media. The Soviets believed this campaign was linked to the postwar re-emergence of anti-communist political trends in Britain, the United States and Western Europe that augured an anti-Soviet turn in western foreign policy.[83] An early manifestation of this sinister development was Winston Churchill's 'Iron Curtain' speech in Fulton, Missouri in March 1946. While Churchill spoke of the need for continued co-operation with the Soviet Union his main theme was a clarion call to an anti-communist crusade. Although Churchill was no longer British Prime Minister, Stalin felt it necessary to issue a lengthy public reply printed on the front page of *Pravda*, denouncing him as an inveterate anti-communist and warmonger.[84] In general, however, Stalin exercised restraint in his public pronouncements on relations with the west, emphasising the possibility of continued coexistence and co-operation. The reason for Stalin's public moderation and reticence was, quite simply, that he did not want a cold war with the west and hoped for continued negotiations with Britain and the United States about the postwar peace settlement. As he told the visiting Republican Senator Harold Stassen in April 1947:

> The economic systems of Germany and the USA are the same but nevertheless there was war between them. The economic systems of the USA and the USSR are different but they fought side by side and collaborated during the war. If two different systems can collaborate in war, why can't they collaborate in peacetime?[85]

As Albert Resis has argued, 'although Stalin's crimes were numberless, one crime was falsely charged to him; that he bears sole responsibility for starting what came to be called the "Cold War". In fact he neither planned nor desired it.'[86] But Stalin's own actions and ambitions did contribute to the outbreak of the cold war. At the end of the Second World War the Red Army occupied half of Europe and Stalin was determined to establish a Soviet sphere of influence in the states that bordered European Russia. There was also a great political swing to the communist parties across the continent and Stalin had visions of a people's democratic Europe – a Europe of left-wing regimes under Soviet and communist influence. Stalin did not see this ideological project as incompatible with prolonged postwar collaboration with his partners in the Grand Alliance, including an equitable division of interests across the globe.[87] He did muse on the possibility of a future war with the western powers but saw such a conflict as remote. 'I am completely certain that there will be no war, it is rubbish. They [the British and Americans] are not capable of waging war against us,' Stalin said to the Polish communist leader Wladyslaw Gomulka in November 1945. 'Whether in thirty years or so they want to have another war is another issue.'[88]

Apart from establishing a Soviet sphere of influence in Eastern Europe, Stalin's priorities after the war were economic reconstruction, postwar security arrangements – above all the future containment of German power – and the establishment of a mutually beneficial long-term *détente* with Britain and the United States. The cold war disrupted all his plans. It came about because the west saw Stalin's political and ideological ambitions as presaging unlimited Soviet and communist expansionism. Hence Britain and the United States resisted what they saw as Stalin's attempt to establish Soviet hegemony in Europe, making him in turn fear that his former allies were trying to roll back his wartime gains.

While western leaders spoke of Soviet expansionism, Stalin complained of Anglo-American globalism. Stalin could not understand why the west felt so threatened by Soviet actions in Europe when he considered them to be natural, defensive and limited. He was also blinded by his ideological conviction that the postwar swing to the left in Europe was an aspect of an inevitable and irreversible historical process leading towards socialism. But Stalin was also realistic and pragmatic enough to see that in an open political and ideological contest with the west he was likely to be the loser. As the Grand Alliance fell apart and the cold war approached he increasingly chose to close off the USSR and the Soviet sphere in Eastern Europe from western influence. Domestically, Stalin again played the patriotic card, this time with an even more pronounced xenophobic emphasis than in the 1930s. In the international arena Stalin's ideological banner became the defence of the national independence of European states from British and American domination.

The cold war itself broke out in 1947 with Truman's announcement in March of a worldwide struggle against communist aggression and expansionism and then, in June, the unveiling of the Marshall Plan for the political and economic reconstruction of postwar Europe. Stalin responded by imposing complete communist and Soviet control of Eastern Europe and by announcing through a speech of Zhdanov's in September 1947 that two conflicting trends in postwar international politics had solidified into a split into two camps – a camp of imperialism, reaction and war, and a camp of socialism, democracy and progress.[89]

But even after this mutual declaration of cold war Stalin still hoped to avert a complete split with the west and to keep the door open to negotiation and compromise. He was particularly concerned about the revival of the German threat. At the end of the war Germany had been divided into Soviet and American, British and French occupation zones. Stalin's fears that the western zones of Germany would become the mainstay of an anti-Soviet bloc prompted him to provoke the first great crisis of the cold war – the Berlin airlift of 1948–1949. Berlin had been divided in 1945, too, but it lay deep in the Soviet zone of occupation in eastern Germany. In order to force further negotiations about the future of Germany, Stalin cut off land supply routes to the western sectors of Berlin. But he was thwarted by the airlift of supplies to West Berlin and had to back down. If anything, the Berlin crisis accelerated the process leading to the establishment of an independent West German state in May 1949 and the signing a month earlier of the NATO treaty – an American-led military and political alliance pledged to defend Western Europe from Soviet attack or intimidation.

The Soviet failure in relation to Germany was one of Stalin's many miscalculations during the cold war. The most costly and dangerous was the Korean War. Urged on by the North Korean leader Kim-Il Sung, Stalin authorised an attack on South Korea in June 1950. At first all went well and within weeks North Korean forces occupied most of the country. However, an American-led military intervention under the auspices of the United Nations rapidly reversed the tide of war. Kim-Il Sung's army was pushed back north and it was only the reluctant intervention of communist China that saved his regime from complete collapse. This development led to a souring of relations between Stalin and the Chinese leader Mao Tse-tung and the war itself proved to be very costly militarily, politically and economically.

These foreign setbacks were counterbalanced by some positive developments. Stalin was able to consolidate his grip on Eastern Europe, although his power was challenged by Tito and this led to a split in 1948 with communist Yugoslavia – hitherto the most loyal of Soviet allies. In August 1949 the Soviet Union tested its first atomic bomb, and in October Mao's communists came to power in China. Most important, despite the tense international atmosphere, a direct military clash with the west was avoided and in the late 1940s and early 1950s Stalin strove to regain the political initiative by launching an international peace campaign.

No amount of foreign difficulties could threaten Stalin's position at home. His victory in the war made his leadership unquestionable and unchallengeable, while popular adulation reached new heights of absurdity.

Stalin's domestic policy after the war is often characterised as a return to communist 'orthodoxy' and 'normalcy' and there is some truth in this. During the war Stalin had adapted his mode of rule to the needs of the situation. He accepted the need for more flexibility in military, cultural and economic affairs and was prepared to permit a greater diversity of voices to express themselves in the Soviet press. In the context of the Grand Alliance he opened up the country to external influences. However, neither Stalin nor the communist party – his main instrument of power – was well suited to the continuation of this style of leadership in peacetime and the deteriorating international situation also encouraged a return to orthodoxy in both ideology and political methods. But the war had changed everything and the system Stalin presided over was not the same as before. The communist system now had a new source of legitimacy – the Great Patriotic War – but it also had to deal with a new set of popular expectations about the future. Millions of returning war veterans had to be integrated into party and state structures. Nor could the nationalist genie easily be put back into the bottle. The mobilisation of Russian national sentiment helped to win the war but it also provoked counter-nationalisms among other ethnic groups in the USSR that had to be combated, both by political means and by repression.[90]

Stalin's most impressive feat during the war was the way he changed both the style of his leadership and the functioning of the system he presided over. Stalin's power and popularity at the end of the war meant that he had a number of choices open to him, but the complex and challenging situation he faced at home and abroad made reversion to a strong form of communist authoritarianism a likely outcome. The tragedy of the cold war was that it provided Stalin with an incentive to consolidate his personal dictatorship rather than continue to explore the possibilities of a more pluralistic regime glimpsed during the war. It may be that Stalin was personally incapable of making any other choice, but the flexibility and creativity that he displayed in wartime suggested otherwise. Moreover, there was no return to the mass terror of the 1930s. Instead, there was a significant reduction in the overall level of political repression. Stalin's postwar regime was a system in transition and its destination was the more relaxed Soviet political order that emerged after his death in 1953.

Age and the strains of war caught up with Stalin in 1945 and he took to spending several months each year on vacation at one of his dachas on the Black Sea.[91] He gave up trying to run and interfere with everything, concentrating mainly on foreign affairs and on calculated interventions to keep his entourage on their toes. One description of Stalin's system of postwar rule is that it was *neopatrimonial*. Like his Tsarist predecessors, or any other powerful autocrat, Stalin through his patrimony controlled and, in a sense, owned the state. Before and during the war he had exercised his 'ownership' by involving himself in making a myriad of decisions and in detailed supervision of the day-to-day activities of the government. In the postwar years he became more restrained, allowing much government business to be conducted by committees and commissions headed by his Politburo colleagues. This resulted in a much more orderly conduct of government and party affairs, albeit heavily bureaucratised and highly conservative as no one wanted to upset the 'boss'. Still, notwithstanding his unlimited power and increasing caprice, Stalin's postwar leadership was much more modern and rational than previously.[92]

At the 19th party congress in October 1952 – the first such gathering since 1938 – Stalin did not even bother to deliver the main political report, entrusting this task to Politburo member G.M. Malenkov.[93] Stalin's own intervention at the congress was restricted to a few brief, concluding remarks aimed at visiting fraternal delegates. Significantly, he harped again on the patriotic theme:

> Previously the bourgeoisie was considered the head of the nation, the defender of the rights and independence of the nation . . . Now there is no sign of the 'national principle'. Now the bourgeoisie will sell the rights and independence of the nation for dollars. The banner of national independence and national sovereignty has been thrown overboard. Without doubt, this banner must be raised by you, the representatives of the communist and democratic parties, and carried forward, if you want to be the patriots of your country, if you want to become the leading force of the nation.[94]

'Victors are not judged' goes the old Russian saying, often attributed to Catherine the Great. Stalin knew better than his Tsarist predecessor, and said so in his February 1946 speech:

> They say that victors are not judged, that they should not be criticized or controlled. This is wrong. Victors may and must be judged, they may and must be criticized and checked up on. That is useful not only for the work but for the victors themselves; there will be less presumption, there will be more modesty.[95]

The need to learn from one's mistakes was a recurrent theme of Stalin's public and private discourse, but he knew that the only judgement that would really matter while he lived would be his own. Even outside the Soviet Union the judgement of most people in the immediate aftermath of the war – those on the winning side, at any rate – was that Stalin's victory, despite its high cost, had been worth it. A barbaric threat to European civilisation had been thwarted, and that was good enough for most people. The cold war had yet to begin in earnest and many hoped that Stalin's dictatorship would evolve into a more benign regime, one worthy of the sacrifices of the Soviet people and of the great victory over Nazi Germany. These hopes were dashed by the outbreak of the cold war and by Stalin's abandonment of wartime liberalisation in favour of the consolidation of communist authoritarianism.

But Stalin continued to occupy an uneasy, contradictory place in Soviet and western discourse about the war. For some, Stalin was the reason for victory; for others the cause of catastrophe. He was deemed the greatest of war leaders and the most disastrous. His path to victory was terrible but perhaps unavoidable. He had created a repressive and terroristic system that massacred millions, but maybe it was the only system that could have won the titanic struggle against Hitler.

2

Unholy Alliance
Stalin's Pact with Hitler

The Nazi–Soviet pact of August 1939 was not Stalin's first foray into the field of foreign affairs but it was by far his most significant and dramatic since coming to power in the 1920s. On the very eve of the Second World War the enmity that had bedevilled relations between Soviet Russia and Nazi Germany since Hitler came to power in 1933 was declared dissolved as the two states signed a treaty pledging non-aggression, neutrality, consultation and the friendly resolution of disputes.

The first public inkling of this extraordinary turn of events was the announcement on 21 August 1939 that Joachim von Ribbentrop, the Nazi Foreign Minister, was to fly to Moscow for negotiations about a German–Soviet non-aggression treaty. Ribbentrop arrived in the Soviet capital on 23 August and the deal was struck later that day. On 24 August *Pravda* and *Izvestiya* carried news of the pact, complete with the now infamous front-page picture of Soviet foreign commissar, Vyacheslav Molotov, signing the treaty with a smiling Stalin looking on.

'The sinister news broke upon the world like an explosion,' wrote Winston Churchill. 'There is no doubt that the Germans have struck a master blow,' the Italian Foreign Minister, Count Ciano, recorded in his diary; 'the European situation is upset.' The Berlin-based American journalist William L. Shirer spoke for millions when he recalled that he 'could scarcely believe it' and 'had the feeling that war was now inevitable'.[1]

The reason for the shock and surprise was that for the previous six months Stalin had been negotiating an *anti-Hitler* alliance with the British and French. These negotiations had begun after the Nazi occupation of Czechoslovakia in March 1939 and were prompted by the German threat to Poland, Romania and other East European states. In April the Soviets proposed a full-blown triple alliance between Britain, France and the USSR – a military coalition that would guarantee European security against further German expansion and, if necessary, go to war with Hitler. By the end of July agreement had been reached on the political terms of the alliance and the negotiations moved into their final phase with the opening of military talks in Moscow.

The triple alliance negotiations were conducted in private, but there was little of their content that did not leak to the press. When the Anglo-French military delegation arrived in Moscow on 10 August it was greeted with suitable public fanfare and the talks were conducted in the sumptuous splendour of the Tsarist Spiridonovka Palace. Hopes were high that a triple alliance would be formed and that Hitler would be deterred from turning the dispute with Poland over Danzig and the 'Polish Corridor' into a new European war. But after a few days the military negotiations broke down and on 21 August were adjourned indefinitely, destined never to be resumed.[2]

The ostensible reason for the breakdown was the Soviet demand that the British and French guarantee that Poland and Romania would allow the Red Army passage through their territory upon the outbreak of war with Germany. The problem was that Poland and Romania – two authoritarian, anti-communist states, both with territorial disputes with the USSR – dreaded Soviet intervention almost as much as they feared German invasion and were unwilling to concede the Red Army an automatic right of passage in the event of war. The Soviets insisted, however, that their military plans depended on advancing through Poland and Romania to repulse a German attack and that they had to know now where they stood. For the Soviets a triple alliance with Britain and France meant, above all, a co-ordinated military plan to fight a common war against Germany. Without such a military agreement there was no point to a political front against Hitler, who would not be deterred from war by any diplomatic agreement, or so the Soviets believed.

Beyond the issue of Soviet right of military passage across Romania and Poland, there was a deeper reason for Moscow's decision to halt the triple alliance negotiations: Stalin did not believe that the British and French were serious about fighting Hitler; he feared, indeed, that they were manoeuvring to get him to do their fighting for them. As Stalin later told Churchill, he 'had the impression that the talks were insincere and only for the purpose of intimidating Hitler, with whom the Western Powers would later come to terms'.[3] On another occasion Stalin complained that Neville Chamberlain, the British Prime Minister, 'fundamentally disliked and distrusted the Russians' and stressed that 'if [I] could not get an alliance with England, then [I] must not be left alone – isolated – only to be the victim of the victors when the war was over'.[4]

When Stalin ended the triple alliance negotiations he was not certain what would happen next, notwithstanding the pact with Hitler he concluded a few days later. For months the Germans had been hinting that they could offer better terms than the British and French. In early August these overtures reached a crescendo when Ribbentrop told the Soviet diplomatic representative in Berlin, Georgii Astakhov, that 'there was no problem from the Baltic to the Black Sea that could not be solved between the two of us'.[5] Until now Stalin had not given Ribbentrop any encouragement and Astakhov remained uninstructed about how to respond to the increasingly extravagant promises made by his German contacts. The Germans were obviously trying to disrupt the triple alliance negotiations and while Stalin did not trust the British and French, he trusted Hitler even less. As an ideologue himself Stalin took Hitler's fervent anti-communism seriously and did not doubt the Nazi dictator intended, if he could, to implement the programme of German expansion into Russia he had advocated in *Mein Kampf.* Stalin feared, too, that the vacuum left by a failed triple alliance would be filled by an Anglo-German understanding directed against the Soviet Union. By the end of July, however, the triple alliance negotiations had dragged on for months and the dilatory approach of the British and French to the forthcoming military talks indicated that London and Paris intended to spin them out even longer, in the hope that Hitler would be deterred from attacking Poland by just the possibility of an Anglo-Soviet–French alliance. So, instead of flying to Moscow the Anglo-French military delegation sailed to Leningrad on a slow steamer and arrived with no detailed strategic plans for a joint war against Germany.

While the British and French thought Hitler could be deterred by talks, Stalin had no such confidence and believed instead his intelligence reports that Hitler would soon attack Poland. In these circumstances – the disintegration of the triple alliance project and the coming Polish war – the German offer of negotiations demanded more serious consideration and Astakhov was authorised to sound out exactly what was being proposed. The turning point in these soundings came when the Germans agreed to sign a special protocol delineating Soviet and German foreign policy interests. In an urgent, personal message to Stalin on 20 August Hitler pressed for Ribbentrop to be allowed to go to Moscow to negotiate the protocol, pointing out that 'the tension between Germany and Poland has become intolerable' and that there was no time to lose. Stalin replied the next day, agreeing to Ribbentrop's visit:

I hope that the German–Soviet non-aggression pact will mark a decided turn for the better in political relations between our countries. The people of our countries need peaceful relations with each other. The assent of the German Government to the conclusion of a non-aggression pact provides the foundation for eliminating the political tension and for the establishment of peace and collaboration between our countries.[6]

Stalin personally received Ribbentrop in the Kremlin and displayed all the acumen, charm and intelligence for which he was to become famous in diplomatic circles. To Ribbentrop's offer to mediate problems in Soviet–Japanese relations, Stalin responded that he was not afraid of the Japanese and that they could have war if they liked, although peace would be so much better! He probed Ribbentrop about Mussolini's attitude to the German–Soviet pact and wanted to know what the Turks were up to. Stalin opined that while Britain was weak militarily it would wage war craftily and that the French army was still worthy of consideration. He proposed a toast to Hitler's health, telling Ribbentrop that he knew 'how much the German nation loves its Führer'. As Ribbentrop was leaving Stalin told him that 'the Soviet Government takes the new Pact very seriously. He could guarantee on his word of honor that the Soviet Union would not betray its partner.'[7]

But what had Stalin agreed with Ribbentrop and what was the nature of the new Soviet–German partnership? The published text of the non-aggression treaty was the same as the many other non-aggression pacts the Soviet Union had concluded in the 1920s and 1930s, apart from the notable absence of a provision for the denunciation of the agreement in the event of aggression by Germany or the USSR against a third party. As this omission indicated, the pact was fundamentally a pledge of Soviet neutrality during the coming German–Polish war. In return, Stalin received Hitler's promises of friendship and non-aggression and, more importantly, the provisions of a 'secret additional protocol' attached to the published pact. The first clause of this secret protocol specified that the Baltic States of Finland, Estonia and Latvia fell within the Soviet sphere of influence. The second clause divided Poland into Soviet and German spheres of influence along the line of the rivers Narew, Vistula and San and stated that 'the question of whether the interests of both parties make desirable the maintenance of an independent Polish state and how such a state should be bounded can only be definitely determined in the course of further political developments'. The third and final clause of this short protocol drew attention to the Soviet interest in Bessarabia, a piece of Romanian territory, which Moscow claimed had been 'stolen' from Russia in 1918, while the German side disclaimed any interest in this dispute.[8]

In relation to the Baltic States, the Germans had conceded what the Soviets had demanded of the British and French during the triple alliance negotiations – a free hand in the Baltic to secure their strategic position in an area considered vital to the security of Leningrad. In the context of the triple alliance negotiations a 'free hand' meant Moscow's right to take pre-emptive action to avert Nazi subversion of the Baltic States and the flexibility to counter a German invasion of the Baltic States as it saw fit, irrespective of what the Balts themselves might want. But it was not so clear how Stalin would choose to exercise his freedom of manoeuvre in the Baltic sphere of influence he had just acquired from the Germans. Would he occupy the Baltic States or seek some other means of securing Soviet interests in the area? A similar uncertainty hung over Stalin's policy in relation to Poland. The Germans had agreed to stay out of a Soviet sphere of influence in the east of the country, but what would be the meaning and consequences of that promise in practice? The answer to that question depended on a great unknown: the course of the German–Polish war and the response of Britain and France to Hitler's attack on Poland. In August 1939 it was not obvious that Poland would succumb as easily as it did to German invasion. Britain and France were pledged to defend Poland but a new 'Munich' – an appeasement deal betraying the Poles to Hitler – was not ruled out, at least not by Stalin. What, then, would be the fate of the Soviet sphere of influence in eastern Poland? Until the situation became clearer Stalin decided to tread carefully, maintaining Soviet neutrality in the developing international crisis over Poland and refraining from the active pursuit of Soviet interests in relation to Poland and the Baltic States, even keeping the door open to a revival of negotiations with Britain and France.

Stalin's prevaricating position was articulated by his foreign commissar, Molotov, who in a speech to the Supreme Soviet on 31 August 1939 proposed formal ratification of the German–Soviet pact. The most significant point of Molotov's speech was that while he announced the dealignment of the Soviet Union in European politics – the USSR would not now participate in an alliance against Hitler – there was no realignment alongside Germany. Indeed, Molotov was at particular pains to argue that the German–Soviet non-aggression treaty was the *consequence* not the cause of the failure of the triple alliance negotiations, implying that the deal with Hitler was a second-best alternative to coalition with Britain and France. He defended the non-aggression pact on grounds that it had narrowed the zone of possible hostilities in Europe and thwarted the designs of those who wanted to set the Soviet Union and Germany against each other in order to provoke 'a grand new slaughter, a new holocaust of nations'.[9] Here Molotov was echoing Stalin's critique of British and French foreign policy at the 18th Congress of the Soviet Communist Party in March 1939. According to Stalin,

the policy of non-intervention means conniving at aggression, giving free rein to war . . . The policy of non-intervention reveals an eagerness, a desire, not to hinder the aggressors in their nefarious work: not to hinder Japan, say, from embroiling herself in a war with China, or, better still, the Soviet Union; not to hinder Germany, say, from . . . embroiling herself in a war with the Soviet Union; to encourage them surreptitiously in this; to allow them to weaken and exhaust one another; and then, when they have become weak enough, to appear on the scene with fresh strength, to appear, of course, 'in the interests of peace', and to dictate conditions to the enfeebled belligerents.[10]

Did Stalin take a leaf out of the western appeasers' handbook when he concluded the Nazi–Soviet pact? Was Stalin an adherent of the 'war–revolution' nexus – the idea that provoking a new world war would precipitate the kind of revolutionary upheavals that had engulfed Europe at the end of the First World War? Many anti-communist commentators thought so at the time and it is a view of Stalin's aims echoed by those historians seeking to establish that the main cause of the Second World War was not Hitler's designs, but Stalin's. One of the key texts in this *oeuvre* is a speech Stalin supposedly made to the Politburo on 19 August 1939 in which he reviewed the prospects for the 'soviet-isation' of Europe as a result of a war that he intended to provoke and then prolong by signing the Nazi–Soviet pact.[11] The problem is that the 'speech' is a forgery. Not only was there no such speech, but it is doubtful that the Politburo even met on that day (it rarely met at all by the late 1930s). It is, as the Russian historian Sergei Sluch has termed it, 'the speech of Stalin's that never was'.[12]

Stalin's so-called speech made its first appearance at the end of November 1939 in the French press. Its publication was plainly a piece of black propaganda designed to discredit Stalin and to sow discord in Soviet–German relations. The text's content marked it out as obviously false. Stalin was reported as saying, for example, that already – on 19 August – he had an agreement with Hitler giving him a Soviet sphere of influence in Romania, Bulgaria and Hungary. It was not taken very seriously outside France, although Stalin himself was moved to issue a statement denouncing the reported speech as a lie.[13]

Far from plotting war in 1939, Stalin feared that he and his regime would become the chief victims of a major military conflict. Ultimately, that is why he gambled on a pact with Hitler; it was no guarantee of peace and security, but it did offer the best chance of keeping the Soviet Union out of the coming war. No doubt like everyone else Stalin expected that if Britain and France did declare war on Germany there would be a prolonged conflict, a war of attrition – one which would provide some time and space for the Soviet Union to strengthen its defences. But he was far too cautious to gamble everything on a simple repeat of the First World War.

The Partition of Poland

From Stalin's point of view the most important question after the signing of the Nazi–Soviet pact was: what would happen to Poland? That question was answered by the stunning success of the German blitzkrieg invasion of Poland. As early as 3 September Ribbentrop was telling the Soviets that the Polish army would be beaten in a few weeks and urging them to send their forces into the Russian sphere of influence in eastern Poland.[14] That same day, however, Britain and France declared war on Germany. On 5 September Molotov replied evasively to Ribbentrop's request, agreeing that Soviet action was necessary but saying that premature intervention 'might injure our cause and promote unity among our opponents'.[15] It was not until 9 September that Molotov informed the Germans that Soviet forces would move into Poland in the next few days.

Stalin's own thinking on the war and on the Polish question was revealed at a meeting with Georgi Dimitrov, the leader of the Communist International, on 7 September 1939:

A war is on between two groups of capitalist countries . . . for the redivision of the world, for the domination of the world! We see nothing wrong in their having a good hard fight and weakening each other. It would be fine if at the hands of Germany the position of the richest capitalist countries (especially England) were shaken. Hitler, without understanding it or desiring it, is shaking and undermining the capitalist system . . . We can maneuver, pit one side against the other to set them fighting with each other as fiercely as possible. The non-aggression pact is to a certain degree helping Germany. Next time we'll urge on the other side . . . Formerly . . . the Polish state was a national state. Therefore, revolutionaries defended it against partition and enslavement. Now [Poland] is a fascist state, oppressing the Ukrainians, Belorussians and so forth. The annihilation of that state under current conditions would mean one fewer bourgeois fascist state to contend with! What would be the harm if as a result of the rout of Poland we were to extend the socialist system onto new territories and populations?[16]

These statements derive from Dimitrov's diary – the most important source on Stalin's private thinking during the war years – and require some comment since they can be interpreted as evidence for the 'war–revolution' nexus hypothesis. The occasion for the meeting was the announcement by Stalin of a change in the Comintern's political line, which since its 7th World Congress in 1935 had been based on an anti-fascist popular front, including support for an alliance between the Soviet Union and the western bourgeois democracies.

After the Nazi–Soviet pact the Comintern and its member parties continued with the popular front policy, supporting Moscow's diplomatic manoeuvre in signing the non-aggression treaty with Germany but continuing to advocate a war of national defence against fascist aggression. Stalin did not retrospectively repudiate the popular front policy, indeed Dimitrov also records him saying that 'we preferred agreements with the so-called democratic countries and therefore conducted negotiations. But the English and the French wanted us for farmhands and at no cost!' Circumstances had changed, however, and the war that had actually broken out was an inter-imperialist conflict and the 'division of capitalist states into fascist and democratic no longer makes sense'. Stalin spoke, too, of the 'prospect of the annihilation of slavery' during the war but he did not advocate, as Lenin had done during the First World War, turning the imperialist war into a revolutionary civil war. Stalin's immediate purpose was to present an ideological rationale for the Red Army's forthcoming invasion of Poland – the first such act of military expansion in the history of the Soviet state – and his main message to Dimitrov was that communists had to oppose war, not wage one.

The Red Army crossed into Poland on 17 September 1939. In announcing the action Molotov declared on the radio that the German–Polish war had demonstrated the bankruptcy of the Polish state. In these circumstances, said Molotov, the Soviet armed forces were entering the country to aid and protect Ukrainians and Belorussians living on Polish territory. This patriotic rationale was reinforced by Soviet newspaper reports of Polish repression of Ukrainians and Belorussians and of the cheering welcome given to their Red Army 'liberators' from the east.[17]

The Polish territories occupied by the Red Army – broadly those allocated to Stalin under the Nazi–Soviet pact – were, in fact, the western regions of the Ukraine and Belorussia. They lay east of the so-called 'Curzon Line' – the ethnographical frontier between Russia and Poland drawn up by a commission of the Paris Peace Conference in 1919 and named after the British Foreign Secretary who chaired it. The commission's aim was to provide a basis for a ceasefire in the Russo-Polish war that had just broken out. The final border, however, was determined by Polish military successes in the war and the Soviet Union ceded Western Ukraine and Western Belorussia to Poland in the Treaty of Riga signed in March 1921. But the Soviets never reconciled themselves to the loss of those territories, which contained only a minority of Poles. Diplomatically the territorial dispute between the two states remained dormant but it hovered in the background, particularly in the 1930s when Stalin's Russia began to adopt a more patriotic identity. There was also constant concern in Moscow that non-Soviet Ukrainians and Belorussians living in Poland could be used as a base for the subversion of their compatriots within the USSR. Indeed, in 1938, Nazi propagandists and Ukrainian nationalists had waged a press and propaganda campaign for a reunified and independent Ukraine. The Soviet invasion of eastern Poland embodied, therefore, a peculiar 'nationalist' logic as well as the obvious geo-strategic rationale that the Red Army's move into the country had secured a shift of the Soviet defence line westwards and established a definite limit on German eastward expansion.

One person who welcomed the Soviet move into Poland was Churchill – the British politician had just returned from a long spell in the wilderness and was back in the cabinet as First Lord of the Admiralty. In a famous radio broadcast on 1 October 1939 he argued:

> Russia had pursued a cold policy of self-interest. We could have wished that the Russian armies should be standing on their present line as the friends and allies of Poland instead of as invaders. But that the Russian armies should stand on this line was clearly necessary for the safety of Russia against the Nazi menace.

Churchill offered a further comfort to his listeners:

> I cannot forecast to you the action of Russia. It is a riddle wrapped in a mystery inside an enigma; but perhaps there is a key. That key is Russian national interest. It cannot be in accordance with the interest or the safety of Russia that Germany should plant itself upon the shores of the Black Sea, or that it should overrun the Balkan States and subjugate the Slavonic peoples of south-eastern Europe. That would be contrary to the historic life-interests of Russia.[18]

Churchill was right. Russian national interest was one key to Stalin's foreign policy; the other was communist ideology. Although Stalin's statement to Dimitrov on 7 September contained a good deal of rhetoric designed to ratio-nalise the Comintern's abandonment of its anti-Nazi policy it also embodied much authentic belief. Underlying Stalin's calculations about the Nazi–Soviet pact was a fundamentalist vision of the inevitability of capitalist crises and imperialist wars. Throughout the 1920s and 1930s Stalin had warned that if the imperialists attempted to resolve their internal difficulties by waging war on the Soviet Union it would be their own downfall as they would be faced with working-class revolt and revolution in their own countries. But Stalin was too much of a realist to base Soviet security on the hope of revolution abroad; experience had taught him that the revolutionary movement in the advanced capitalist states was very weak and not to be relied upon. Hence

Stalin's political directives to Dimitrov after the outbreak of war were cautious and conservative. At a meeting with Dimitrov on 25 October 1939 Stalin observed that 'during the first imperialist war the Bolsheviks overestimated the situation. We all got ahead of ourselves and made mistakes . . . there must be no copying now of the positions the Bolsheviks held then . . . It should also be remembered that the current situation is different: at that time there were no Communists in power. Now there is the Soviet Union!' On 7 November Stalin told Dimitrov: 'I believe that the slogan of turning the imperialist war into a civil war (during the first imperialist war) was appropriate only for Russia . . . For the European countries that slogan was inappropriate . . .'[19]

Stalin's point that a major difference between the First and Second World Wars was the existence of the Soviet Union would have required no emphasis for Dimitrov, who like all communists of his era was schooled in the belief that his first duty was action in defence of the USSR, not least in time of war when the very existence of the socialist state could come under threat. What Stalin required of his communist supporters in 1939 was not the waging of a revolutionary war but a political campaign in favour of peace, including support for Hitler's pleas to the British and French to end the conflict over Poland.

The Soviet–German 'peace offensive' had begun after a second round of meetings between Stalin and Ribbentrop on 27–28 September. Ribbentrop had flown to Moscow to discuss Soviet proposals for changes to the Soviet–German boundary in occupied Poland. Stalin told Ribbentrop that the Soviet–German division of Poland should as far as possible be along ethnographic lines. That would entail the transfer of Polish territory from the Soviet to the German sphere of influence; in exchange Lithuania would be transferred to the Soviet sphere of influence in the Baltic. In presenting this deal to Ribbentrop, Stalin emphasised that a demarcation line that separated ethnic Poland from the predominantly non-Polish ethnic areas bordering the USSR would pre-empt possible future nationalist agitation for a united Poland.[20] The upshot of these discussions was a new Nazi–Soviet pact in the form of the 'German–Soviet Boundary and Friendship Treaty' of 28 September 1939 that specified the new boundary in Poland and (in a secret protocol) transferred Lithuania to the Soviet sphere of influence (*see Map 1 on p. 40*).[21] That same day the Soviet Union and Germany issued a joint statement calling for an end to the European war now that the Polish state had been liquidated.[22] This was followed by calls from Hitler for a negotiated peace, a demand echoed by Molotov in his speech to the Supreme Soviet at the end of October 1939 in which he blamed the British and French for the continuation of the war, arguing that the motive was the defence of their colonial possessions and the ongoing inter-imperialist struggle for world supremacy.[23]

The Nazi–Soviet Pact, August–September 1939

The 'New Rapallo'

But did Stalin really want the European war to come to an end? Probably not, but he had no idea how long it would last or what course it might take, and there was no guarantee that any outcome would be favourable to the Soviet Union. Britain and France had declared war on Germany in support of Poland but had taken little action in support of the Poles and seemed content for the moment to fight a war with Germany from behind the 'Maginot Line' of defensive fortifications along the Franco-German border. The German conquest of Poland had changed fundamentally the balance of power in Europe, but it was difficult to predict what the precise consequences of that would be. In such circumstances Stalin had no option but to strengthen the Soviet strategic position in whatever ways he could while avoiding involvement in the European war. For the moment that meant close co-operation with the Germans, including support for Hitler's 'peace proposals'. At the same time Stalin did not want to burn his bridges with Britain and France and he attempted to balance his commitments to Hitler by keeping open the door to a reconstruction of Soviet relations with the western powers.[24]

How long the new relationship with Hitler would last was difficult to say but Stalin did not, at this stage, rule out a long-term partnership. Indeed, there was an important precedent for prolonged Soviet–German co-operation. In 1922 the Soviet Union and Germany had signed the Treaty of Rapallo, an agreement that re-established diplomatic relations between the two states (they had been severed in 1918) and led to a decade of intensive economic, political and military co-operation. The 'Rapallo relationship', as it was called, only broke down when Hitler came to power in 1933. Even so, throughout the 1930s there were intermittent efforts by both sides to restore a degree of co-operation, particularly in trade relations.[25] In his discussions with Ribbentrop on 27 September Stalin emphasised the Rapallo precedent:

Soviet foreign policy has always been based on belief in the possibility of co-operation between Germany and the Soviet Union. When the Bolsheviks came to power they were accused of being paid German agents. It was the Bolsheviks who concluded the Rapallo agreement. It provided the basis for the expansion and deepening of mutual relations. When the National-Socialists came to power in Germany, relations worsened as the German government deemed it necessary to give priority to internal political considerations. After a while this issue exhausted itself and the German government displayed the will to improve relations with the Soviet Union . .. Historically the Soviet Government never excluded the possibility of good relations with Germany. Hence it is with a clear conscience that the

Soviet Government begins the revival of collaboration with Germany. This collaboration represents a power that all other combinations must give way to.[26]

Of course, Nazi Germany was not the Weimar Republic and Hitler was no ordinary German politician, but Stalin tended to view democratic and fascist states as co-existing on a common capitalist continuum rather than as qualitatively different phenomena.[27] In the 1930s Nazi Germany had posed a dire threat to the Soviet Union and Stalin sought common cause with the western democracies. Circumstances had changed and now Hitler represented not a threat but an opportunity. The 'opportunity' might become a threat in the future but for the time being Stalin was content to make as many gains as possible from the 'new Rapallo' with Germany.

During the 1920s the Soviet Union and Germany had been very important trading partners, a relationship that collapsed when Hitler came to power. But with the Nazi–Soviet pact there was a significant revival of economic relations between the two states. Under the aegis of economic agreements signed in August 1939, February 1940 and January 1941 Soviet–German exports and imports increased tenfold, reaching levels they had not attained since the early 1930s.[28] The pattern of trade was the same as in that earlier period: the Germans provided the Russians with credits to buy machinery and manufactured goods; in return the Soviets exported raw materials to Germany. Between January 1940 and June 1941 the following raw materials were supplied by the Soviet Union to Germany:

1.5 million tons of grain
100,000 tons of cotton
2 million tons of petroleum products
1.5 million tons of timber
140,000 tons of manganese
26,000 tons of chromium[29]

Particularly important were grain, petroleum, manganese and chromium – vital ingredients of the German war economy that now faced a British naval blockade. The Soviets also signed a secret protocol with the Germans to act on their behalf as a third-party buyer and ship goods to Germany via the USSR. For their side of the deal the Soviets received an equivalent amount of machine tools, finished metals, chemical products and military and other equipment.[30] In value terms the imports and exports balanced out at around 500 million marks each way, but the strategic gain to Hitler was far greater than that to Stalin. As Edward E. Ericson commented:

without Soviet deliveries ... Germany could barely have attacked the Soviet Union, let alone come close to victory. Germany's stockpiles of oil, manganese, and grain would have been completely exhausted by the late summer of 1941. And Germany's rubber supply would have run out half a year earlier ... In other words, Hitler had been almost completely dependent on Stalin to provide him the resources he needed to attack the Soviet Union. It was no wonder that Hitler repeatedly insisted Germany fulfill the terms of the economic treaties. He could not conquer any Soviet territory until he first received enough Soviet raw materials.[31]

Stalin's co-operation with Hitler in the military sphere was more circumscribed but still valuable to the Germans. When German bombers attacked Poland in September 1939 they were aided by directional signals from a Soviet radio station. This was followed by co-ordination of the Soviet and German armed forces after the Red Army invaded Poland on 17 September 1939. The Soviets opened their ports in the Arctic Sea to German ships requiring refuge and allowed the Germans to establish a secret U-boat base on Soviet territory near Murmansk – a base that remained operational until it became redundant after the German invasion of Norway in April 1940.[32]

On the ideological front the Soviet press stopped its attacks on fascism and Nazism, while in the cultural sphere a number of steps were taken to re-establish and develop links between Germany and the USSR. But by far the most important dimension of Stalin's partnership with Hitler was geopolitical. While the war continued, and while Hitler needed friendship with Stalin to protect his eastern flank, the Germans did not compete with the Soviets in their designated sphere of influence in the Baltic.

Spheres of Influence

Even before the final settlement of the Polish question Stalin had begun to make his move in the Baltic. On 24 September 1939 the Estonian Foreign Minister, in Moscow to sign a trade agreement, was confronted with a demand from Molotov for a mutual assistance pact that would provide for Soviet air and naval bases in Estonia. On 27 September Stalin became involved in the negotiations and reassured the Estonians about the proposed Soviet military bases:

Do not be afraid of these garrisons. We have assured you that the Soviet Union does not want in any way to affect Estonian sovereignty, her government, or her economic system, nor her internal life or foreign policy ... the

Soviet troops will refrain from everything that is not in harmony with these promises.[33]

Formally speaking, Stalin was as good as his word and the text of the Soviet–Estonian Pact of Mutual Assistance signed on 28 September 1939 contained clauses forbidding Soviet interference in Estonia's internal affairs.[34]

It was the Latvians' turn next. Like all the Baltic governments they hoped for German intercession on their behalf, but Stalin quickly dispelled that illusion. 'I tell you frankly a division into spheres of influence has taken place,' he informed the Latvian Foreign Minister on 2 October. 'As far as the Germans are concerned we could occupy you. But we want no abuse.'[35] At a further meeting the next day Stalin was even more explicit: 'The Germans might attack. For six years German fascists and the communists cursed each other. Now in spite of history there has been an unexpected turn, but one cannot rely upon it. We must be prepared in time. Others, who were not prepared, paid for it.'[36]

The Latvians signed their mutual assistance treaty with the Soviet Union on 5 October, as did the Lithuanians on 10 October. As in the Estonian treaty, there were provisions for Soviet military bases and promises of non-interference. Stalin told the Lithuanians that the military bases were 'the most precious element in the service of Lithuanian security'[37] and quipped that 'our troops will help you put down a communist insurrection should one occur in Lithuania'.[38]

Actually, Stalin was only half joking. In line with its stated policy Moscow issued strict instructions to its diplomatic representatives and military units in the Baltic States to refrain from interference in local politics and not to do anything that could fuel rumours of a future 'sovietisation' of the area.[39] As Stalin explained to Dimitrov on 25 October:

We believe that in our pacts of mutual assistance [with the Baltic States] we have found the right form to allow us to bring a number of countries into the Soviet Union's sphere of influence. But for that we have to maintain a consistent posture, strictly observing their internal regimes and independence. We are not going to seek their sovietisation. The time will come when they will do that themselves![40]

Stalin's restraint in relation to the Baltic States was in sharp contrast to Soviet policy in Western Belorussia and Western Ukraine. After the Red Army's occupation of these territories in September 1939 the Politburo ordered an election campaign under the slogans of the establishment of Soviet power and the reunification of the eastern and western regions of Belorussia and the

Ukraine. Instructions were also issued on the nationalisation of big business, the takeover of the banking system and the collectivisation of agriculture.[41] Needless to say, the elections were rigged and in November these 'people's assemblies' voted unanimously for incorporation into the USSR. In pursuit of total political control the Soviet authorities were ruthless in their use of terror and in the encouragement of inter-ethnic communal violence and class war.[42] A particularly repressive policy was pursued in relation to the Polish minority in Western Belorussia and Western Ukraine, who were seen as the most likely source of opposition to the new Soviet regime. Some 400,000 Poles (out of a total population of 12 million) were imprisoned, deported or, in many cases, executed. Among the victims were 20,000 Polish officer POWs and political prisoners, shot in March–April 1940, most infamously in the Katyn forest near Smolensk.[43]

Did Stalin intend to visit the same fate on the Baltic States? That is certainly the conclusion that some have drawn from the fact that in summer 1940 the Baltic States were occupied by the Red Army, incorporated into the USSR and, like Western Belorussia and Western Ukraine, subjected to forced sovietisation. However, both Soviet behaviour and Stalin's statements in autumn 1939 were consistent with a commitment to a more restrained policy, at least at that time. Moreover, the more radical policy pursued in eastern Poland had very specific roots. As noted earlier, the Soviets had never reconciled themselves to the loss of Western Belorussia and Western Ukraine to the Poles and Stalin intended from the outset of the Red Army invasion to incorporate these territories into the USSR. Sovietisation of eastern Poland did not create a precedent for the Baltic States but it did provide a model of how it could be done, including the deportation from Estonia, Latvia and Lithuania in June–July 1940 of some 25,000 'undesirables'.[44]

The other area that greatly interested Stalin was the Balkans. Unlike Poland and the Baltic States there was no agreement with the Germans on spheres of influence in this region but that did not deter Stalin from pursuing one. At the centre of Stalin's design were two countries – Bulgaria and Turkey – both of which were offered mutual assistance pacts with the Soviet Union. The Bulgarians politely declined, pointing out that it was not clear what aid the Soviets could offer them in the event of war and that such an agreement would arouse suspicion in the already tense atmosphere in the Balkans in autumn 1939.[45] The Turkish position was more complex. They were prepared to sign a mutual assistance pact with the Soviets but were intent as well on concluding mutual assistance agreements with Britain and France. This was unacceptable to Stalin, as he graphically explained to the Turkish Foreign Minister on 1 October 1939:

Events have their own logic: we say one thing, but events go another way. With Germany we divided Poland. England and France did not declare war on us, but they might. We don't have a pact of mutual assistance with Germany but if the English and French declare war on us, we will have to fight them. How would the [Anglo-French–Turkish] agreement look then? . . . [You] might reply that you have made provision for such an outcome, that the Turks will decide their own action or that Turkey will be neutral. But we will have to make the provision that if Turkey does enter the war our pact loses its force. We will never come out against Germany . . . Do we want to conclude a pact with the Turks? We do. Do we want friendship with Turkey? Yes. But in the circumstances I have spoken about the pact [between the Soviet Union and Turkey] would be transformed into a piece of paper. Who is to be blamed for the fact that things have turned out unfavourably for the conclusion of such a pact with Turkey? Nobody. It is circumstances, the development of events. The action in Poland played its role. The English and French, especially the English, did not want an agreement with us, considering that they could manage without us. If we are guilty of anything it is of not having foreseen all this.[46]

Despite Stalin's plea the Turks went ahead and signed a mutual assistance agreement with Britain and France on 19 October 1939. The treaty precluded Turkey's involvement in a war with the Soviet Union, but this was small compensation for the failure of Stalin's grand vision of a Soviet-led neutral Balkan bloc of Turkey, Bulgaria and the USSR.

Stalin was obviously trying to scare the Turks with his talk of unforeseen circumstances and unintended consequences and he made plain his primary commitment to the partnership with Germany. But his statement also expressed Stalin's sense that these early weeks of the European war were a fluid, fast-moving scene and that it was difficult to anticipate the final alignment of states in the conflict. Stalin was being more prescient than he might have imagined. Within a few weeks events in the Baltic had taken a turn that brought the Soviet Union to the brink of war with Britain and France.

The Winter War

The Soviet–Finnish war of 1939–1940 was Stalin's first real test as a military leader since the Russian civil war. During the Spanish civil war Stalin had supervised Moscow's aid to the Republican side of the conflict, including the dispatch of some 2,000 Soviet 'volunteers' to fight Franco's fascist forces. Throughout the 1930s there had been intermittent military clashes with Japan along the Sino-Soviet border, sometimes of divisional strength. But neither case bore any comparison with the full-scale invasion of a neighbouring sovereign state. Poland was a more relevant example of Soviet military action but by the time of the Red Army invasion the Polish armed forces had been well and truly smashed by the Germans.

The 'Winter War' with Finland was not of Stalin's choosing. He would have preferred a negotiated solution to the border and security issues that sparked the conflict. But when political negotiations with Finland broke down he had no hesitation in authorising military action.

The road to war began on 5 October 1939 when the Soviet Union invited Finland to send a delegation to Moscow to discuss a Soviet–Finnish mutual assistance pact. In Moscow the Finnish delegation was presented not only with demands for a pact but with demands for the concession or leasing of a number of islands in the Gulf of Finland for the construction of Soviet naval fortifications. Most importantly, Stalin wanted to shift north-westwards the Soviet–Finnish border, which was only 20 miles from Leningrad. In return the Finns were offered territorial compensation in Soviet Karelia in the far north.

In preparation for the negotiations the Soviet Foreign Ministry formulated a series of maximum and minimum demands. Among the maximum Soviet demands were military bases in Finland, ceding of the nickel-mining area of Petsamo in northern Finland, and veto rights over Finnish military fortifications in the Baltic.[47] The Finnish delegation, however, was prepared to make few, if any, concessions and the Soviets retreated to their minimum territorial demands, even dropping the proposed Soviet–Finnish mutual assistance pact. Negotiations dragged on throughout October but achieved no positive result.[48] Indeed, in mid-October the Finns mobilised their army and, anticipating a war, arrested a number of Finnish communists.[49]

It seems that Stalin decided quite early on that war with Finland might be necessary. On 29 October the Leningrad military district presented the defence commissar Kliment Voroshilov with a 'plan of operation for the destruction of the land and naval forces of the Finnish army'.[50] In mid-November 1939 Stalin reportedly told his Military Council that 'we shall have to fight Finland'.[51] Around the same time Voroshilov ordered that the concentration of Soviet forces in the Leningrad area be completed by 20 November and local commanders prepared for action by 21 November.[52] A *casus belli* was found in border clashes between Soviet and Finnish forces and on 28 November Molotov renounced the 1932 non-aggression pact between the USSR and Finland. The following day the Soviet Union severed diplomatic relations with Finland.[53] That night Stalin began an eight-hour meeting in his Kremlin office with his closest associates, including Voroshilov.[54] The Red Army attacked Finland the next day.

According to Khrushchev the Soviet leadership did not expect a drawn-out conflict with Finland and believed the Finns would back down in the face of the threat of military action or, at worst, would surrender when the first shots were fired.[55] Moscow's belief in an easy war and a quick victory was evident in its political preparations for the conflict. On 30 November Molotov told the German ambassador that 'the formation of another government in Finland was not excluded – one friendly to the Soviet Union and to Germany. This government would not be Soviet but a democratic republic. Nobody will set up soviets there, but we hope that it will be a government that we can reach agreement with on safeguarding the security of Leningrad.'[56] What Molotov meant was revealed the next day when the Soviets set up their own puppet government – the 'People's Government of Finland' headed by the Finnish communist Otto Kuusinen. On 2 December the Kuusinen government solemnly concluded a mutual assistance pact with the USSR that conceded Stalin's main territorial and security demands in exchange for 70,000 square kilometres of Soviet Karelia.[57]

To an extent the creation of the Kuusinen government was merely an ideological fig leaf for the Soviet attack on Finland. But setting up that government also expressed the Soviets' genuine belief – or hope – that the Red Army's invasion would be hailed by a popular uprising against the bourgeois Helsinki government.[58] Stalin's spin on the ideological dimension of the Finnish conflict was expressed in a remark to Dimitrov in January 1940 in which he linked the Soviet war with Finland to the worldwide political struggle for socialism: 'World revolution as a single act is nonsense. It transpires at different times in different countries. The Red Army's activities are also a matter of world revolution.'[59] However, Stalin was blinkered by his ideology, not blinded by it. As soon as it became clear that Finnish political developments were not moving according to the ideological blueprint the Kuusinen government disappeared from view. Indeed, in the same conversation with Dimitrov Stalin had indicated a retreat to a much more limited ambition for Finland: 'we have no desire for Finland's territory. But Finland should be a state that is friendly to the Soviet Union.'[60]

On the military front the Soviet–Finnish war had two main phases (see Map 2 on p. 49). In December 1939 the Red Army launched a broad-front attack on Finnish defences, employing five separate armies with about 1.2 million men between them, supported by 1,500 tanks and 3,000 aircraft. The main attack was against the 'Mannerheim Line' on the Karelian isthmus. Named after the Commander-in-Chief of the Finnish armed forces this was a belt of defences, natural and constructed, that ran the width of the isthmus. The main assault on the Mannerheim Line was by the 7th Army under the leadership of K.A. Meretskov, who commanded the Leningrad military district. The Soviet aim

The Soviet–Finnish War, 1939–1940

was to breach the Mannerheim Line, occupy the town of Viipuri and then turn west towards the Finnish capital, Helsinki. The initial Soviet attacks failed. Defences were formidable, the Finns fought well, the weather was bad and the Soviet offensives were clumsy and badly co-ordinated. In January 1940 the Soviets regrouped, reinforced their armies and Stalin appointed S.K. Timoshenko to overall command of the Soviet assault on Finland. In mid-February Timoshenko launched a well-prepared offensive, again concentrated against the Mannerheim Line. This time the Soviets succeeded in breaching Finnish defences and in driving back Mannerheim's men along a broad front.[61]

By March 1940 the Red Army was in a position to collapse the remnants of the Finnish defence, advance on Helsinki and then overrun and occupy the whole country. Stalin chose, however, to respond to Finnish peace feelers and to negotiate and conclude a treaty ending the war. Under the terms of the treaty, signed on 12 March 1940,[62] the Finns conceded all the main Soviet territorial demands but retained their independence and sovereignty and, unlike the other Baltic States, were spared a mutual assistance pact and Soviet military bases on their mainland territory. Stalin's relative moderation towards Finland was a response to the wider ramifications of the conflict which, by spring 1940, threatened to drag the Soviet Union into full-scale involvement in the European war.

The international response to the Soviet attack on Finland had been extremely hostile. As Ivan Maiskii, the Soviet ambassador in London noted in his memoirs, he 'had lived through quite a number of anti-Soviet storms, but that which followed 30 November 1939 broke all records'.[63] In France the atmosphere was even more tense and Ya. Z. Suritz, the Soviet ambassador in Paris, reported to Moscow on 23 December that 'our embassy has become a plague zone and is surrounded by a swarm of plainclothes cops'.[64] In Italy the virulence of popular demonstrations against the USSR led Moscow to withdraw its ambassador from Rome in protest. In the United States a 'moral embargo' on the export of war-related goods to the Soviet Union was announced by the government. On 14 December the League of Nations expelled the USSR from its ranks – the first and last time in its history the organisation took such action against an aggressor state (Germany, Italy and Japan had all left of their own accord). By this time the League had little authority and respect left, but the Soviet Union had been the great champion of collective security against aggression in the 1930s, and the expulsion rankled in Moscow.

Stalin articulated his own irritation at this turn of events in a conversation with the head of the Estonian armed forces in December 1939:

In the world press there is unfolding an orchestrated campaign of attack against the USSR, which is accused of carrying out an imperialist expansion policy, especially in connection with the Finnish–Soviet conflict. Widespread rumours allege that the Soviet Union in its negotiations with Britain and France required for itself the right to seize Finland, Estonia and Latvia . . . It is typical that the English and French, who are spreading and fabricating rumours about us, have decided not to publish confirmation of these rumours in official documents. The reason is very simple . . . steno-graphic records show that the French and English had no serious desire to achieve a fair and honest agreement with us, which could have averted war. All the time they only dodged.[65]

The political fallout from the Winter War was bad enough, but far more worrying were reports reaching Moscow of British and French preparations to send an allied expeditionary force to aid the Finns. There were even reports in early 1940 of allied plans to bomb the Baku oilfields to cut off Soviet oil supplies to Germany.[66]

The Anglo-French aim in relation to Finland was to transport 'volunteers' to the war zone via Norway and Sweden. During the course of this operation the Anglo-French force would seize control of Narvik in Norway and also occupy the iron ore fields of northern Sweden – a vital resource of the German war economy. Churchill, who was interested in any action that expanded the war against Germany, was an enthusiastic supporter of the expedition and while he minimised the danger of a Soviet–Western war over Finland, he was evidently prepared to risk one.[67] Churchill's judgement is a difficult one to justify in retrospect. The allied expedition would have entailed significant violations of Norwegian and Swedish neutrality. The Germans would have taken action to protect their iron ore supplies from Sweden, while the Swedes told the Finns that they would defend their neutrality and resist an allied expedition by force. Stalin did not want a conflict with Britain and France but, faced with allied forces on his doorstep and the outbreak of a major war in Scandinavia, he might well have felt he had no choice but to line up militarily alongside Hitler.

In his *English History, 1914–1945* A.J.P. Taylor concluded of the planned expedition to Finland that 'the British and French governments had taken leave of their senses',[68] a sentiment that Stalin might well have shared, except that he had another theory: Anglo-French manoeuvres in relation to Finland fed his favourite fear that Britain and France were trying to turn the European war against the Soviet Union. One possible scenario was sketched by Maiskii in a dispatch to Moscow on 23 December 1939. In British ruling circles there were two views of Anglo-Soviet relations, said Maiskii. One view supported the maintenance of Soviet neutrality in the war, in the hope that this neutrality could become friendlier and might even develop into an alliance against Germany. The other view was that Soviet neutrality was not working to the British and French advantage and that the Finnish events presented an opportunity to precipitate the entry of the USSR into the war on Germany's side. Soviet participation in the war would exhaust the USSR and there was the possibility of the United States siding with the western allies in such circumstances. Moreover, in the context of a war-exhausted Soviet Union it might be possible to form an international capitalist coalition, including even Germany, to fight Bolshevik Russia.[69]

These fears and suspicions were given a public airing by Molotov on 29 March 1940, in a speech to the Supreme Soviet devoted to a blistering attack on Britain and France. 'When war began in Finland,' said Molotov, 'the British and French imperialists were prepared to make it the starting point of war against the USSR in which not only Finland itself but also the Scandinavian countries – Sweden and Norway – were to be used.' London and Paris, Molotov argued, viewed Finland as a *place d'armes* for a possible attack on the Soviet Union. Pointing to the aid Finland had received from foreign states, Molotov stated 'that what was going on in Finland was not merely our collision with Finnish troops. It was a collision with the combined forces of a number of imperialist states.' Molotov also presented an overview of the Winter War from the Soviet point of view. As might be expected, he lauded the Red Army for breaching the Mannerheim Line and extolled the virtues of the peace treaty – which had thwarted imperialist designs, safeguarded Soviet security, and maintained Finland as an independent state. Soviet casualties in the war were stated by Molotov to be 48,745 dead and 158,863 wounded, while Finnish fatalities were 60,000 and another 250,000 wounded.[70]

Notwithstanding Molotov's triumphalist gloss on the war, behind closed doors the Soviets were undertaking a thorough and searching examination of the results and lessons of the conflict. This process began with a lively discussion of a critical report by Voroshilov on the conduct of the war held at a plenum of the central committee of the communist party on 28 March.[71] This was followed on 14–17 April by a special conference of the High Command on 'the experience of military operations against Finland'. Stalin was present throughout the proceedings, intervened frequently in the discussion, and closed the conference with his own summation on the lessons of the war.

Stalin began his concluding remarks by defending the decision to go to war, pointing out that the security of Leningrad was vital: it was the country's second city and the centre for 30–35 per cent of the state's defence industry. On the timing of the war Stalin argued that rather than wait a few months until preparations for invasion were more complete it had been better to take advantage of the propitious circumstances of the European war. To wait a couple of months might have meant a delay of 20 years before Leningrad's position could be secured, if Britain, France and Germany suddenly made it up with each other. On the duration of the war Stalin revealed that the Soviet leadership thought it might have lasted until August or September 1940 and pointed to a number of past Russian campaigns in Finland that went on for years. However, the Soviet military had not taken the war with Finland seriously enough, expecting it to be a walkover like the invasion of eastern Poland. Furthermore, the cult of the Russian civil war was still prevalent in the armed forces, said Stalin, but 'the civil war was not a contemporary war because it was a war without artillery, planes, tanks and rockets'. Stalin criticised the Finnish army for its defensive orientation, arguing that a passive army was not a real, contemporary army, which had to be an army of attack. Stalin ended by pointing out that the Soviet Union had defeated not only the Finns but their 'European teachers': 'We beat not only the Finns – that was not such a big task. The main thing about our victory was that we beat the techniques, tactics and strategies of the leading states of Europe. This was the main thing about our victory.'[72]

After the conference a commission was established to further distil the experience of the Finnish war.[73] The work of this commission and its subsidiary bodies contributed to a series of reforms of the Soviet armed forces over the next few months. These reforms were presided over by Timoshenko, who had replaced Voroshilov as defence commissar in May. That same month a government decree restored the titles of general and admiral at the higher levels of command and in June announced the promotion to these ranks of hundreds of experienced, combat-blooded officers. Among those promoted were Timoshenko, who became a marshal, and Meretskov, who was made a general of the army. Around the same time Stalin agreed to recall thousands of purged and disgraced officers to the armed forces. Among the returnees was Colonel K.K. Rokossovskii, promoted to general in June 1940 and destined to become a famed marshal of the Soviet Union during the Great Patriotic War. On 16 May 1940 the regulations governing the training of Soviet troops were revised to provide for more realistic preparation for combat. In July the armed forces' disciplinary code was beefed up and in August unitary command was restored at the tactical level. This meant that field officers no longer had to agree their command decisions with a political commissar. At the same time steps were taken to improve propaganda work in the armed forces and to recruit more officers and men into the communist party.[74]

The Winter War is often depicted as a great failure of Stalin's leadership: it was a costly campaign that greatly embarrassed the Red Army and encouraged

Hitler to think that an invasion of Russia would be relatively easy; it isolated the Soviet Union diplomatically and brought it to the brink of war with Britain and France; it made an enemy of the Finns, who joined in the German attack on the USSR in June 1941. But that was not how the war and its outcome were seen by Stalin. The war had been won, after all, and it only took three months, despite difficult terrain and weather conditions. The Soviet Union had achieved its territorial goals and the timely conclusion of the war had thwarted Anglo-French imperialist intrigues. The war had exposed some flaws in the armed forces' training, equipment, structure and doctrine but that was a good thing, as long as steps were taken to correct them. If anything, the Finnish war gave Stalin confidence that the Soviet Union was strong enough to deal with the unpredictable ramifications of the wider European war.

The Finnish war was highly revealing of Stalin's style of supreme command. His decision to abandon the ideological project of a 'people's democratic Finland' and his willingness to bring the war to a rapid conclusion demonstrated his ability to step away from dogmatic positions when reality demanded. Similarly, Stalin's removal of his long-time crony Voroshilov as defence commissar, the rehabilitation of the purged officers, and the promotion to high rank of young, talented military commanders displayed his flexibility in crucial matters of personnel. The internal post-mortem on the war showed that the assumption of Stalin's infallibility – a pervasive feature of all Soviet decision-making – did not preclude full and frank discussion of a range of issues or the correction of mistakes and the implementation of radical reforms. However, Stalin's interventionist style and the deference paid to his opinions during the various discussions meant that the Soviet command structure was highly dependent on Stalin making the right decisions at the strategic level. Fortunately, Stalin's Bolshevik futuristic belief in the virtues of modernity and technology happened to serve him well in many military matters. His oft-expressed belief in the virtues of modern military technology meant that he grasped quickly the significance of the German armoured blitzkrieg conquest of France in May–June 1940. In July 1940 Stalin reversed an earlier decision to abolish the Red Army's tank corps and authorised the formation of a number of large and heavily armoured mechanised corps.[75] Around the same time decisions were taken on the procurement and production of the models of many of the tanks, guns and planes that were to be the mainstay of the Soviet armed forces during the Great Patriotic War.[76] In a meeting with his senior commanders in January 1941 Stalin defended mechanisation against critics who thought that horses were more reliable than tanks and that the latter were, anyway, highly vulnerable to artillery. Stalin insisted that 'modern warfare will be a war of engines. Engines on land, engines in the air, engines on water and under water. Under these conditions, the winning side will be the one with the greater number and the more powerful engines.'[77]

The Fall of France and the End of the Nazi–Soviet Pact

Until the fall of France in June 1940 the Nazi–Soviet pact served Stalin well. The deal with Hitler had kept the USSR out of the war, averted the nightmare of a Soviet–German clash on the Eastern Front while Britain and France stood on the sidelines, and provided more time to prepare the country's defences. Political and territorial gains had been made in Poland and the Baltic States. The revival of the Rapallo relationship with Germany offered many economic benefits and Hitler's neutrality during the Winter War had been very welcome. It was by no means a one-sided balance sheet; Hitler made many gains, too, notably the freedom to attack Poland without fear of having to fight a major war on two fronts. The stunning success of the German blitzkrieg in Western Europe upset that balance. When France surrendered on 22 June 1940 Hitler dominated continental Europe. Britain under the new Churchill leadership seemed determined to fight on but its capacity to resist either Hitler or the siren voices of appeasement calling for a peace deal seemed doubtful. Stalin now faced the prospect of an end to the European war and a peace settlement whose terms would be dictated by the victorious Germans.

Stalin's response to this new situation was a series of initiatives to optimise his strategic gains while the war continued. In mid-June 1940 Stalin moved to strengthen his control of the Baltic States. Fearing Baltic nationalist intrigues and German penetration of the region, Stalin demanded the establishment of pro-Soviet governments in Estonia, Latvia and Lithuania and Red Army occupation of all three countries. He made renewed efforts to build a Soviet sphere of influence in the Balkans. Responding to reports of Italy's imminent entry into the war, Molotov made overtures to Rome about a 'spheres of influence' deal in the Balkans with Italy and Germany. On 10 June Italy did enter the war and Soviet soundings increased in intensity, culminating in a proposal on 25 June that Italy recognise the USSR's predominance in the Black Sea area in return for Soviet recognition of Italian hegemony in the Mediterranean.[78] On 26 June Molotov presented the Romanian ambassador with an ultimatum demanding the return of Bessarabia (now part of modern-day Moldova). He also demanded that the Romanians cede North Bukovina, a territory with a Ukrainian population but which the Soviet Union had never claimed before. Two days later, the Romanians caved in to the Soviet demands. The reacquisition of Bessarabia added depth to the defence of the Soviet navy's Black Sea bases in Odessa and Sebastopol, while the occupation of North Bukovina secured land links between Bessarabia and the Ukraine. The Soviet border with Romania now ran along the north-eastern bank of the mouth of the Danube and gave Moscow a claim to participate in the regime controlling traffic on the river.[79] Like Western Belorussia and Western Ukraine, Bessarabia and North Bukovina were rapidly incorporated as territories of the USSR. A similar process of incorporation began in the Baltic States in July 1940. While opposed by the majority of the population, an urban-based, activist left-wing minority welcomed the Red Army occupation and demanded Soviet power and incorporation into the USSR. This radical mood among sections of the population prompted Moscow to rethink its opposition to 'sovietisation' and by mid-August rigged elections had been held to new people's assemblies in the three Baltic States, which then duly voted for the incorporation into the USSR.[80]

Stalin saw these moves as defensive and as preliminaries to a peace conference at which the next phase of the Soviet–German alliance would be negotiated. To Hitler, however, Stalin's actions appeared provocative and threatening. Stalin's takeover of the Baltic States was interpreted as part of a Soviet military build-up along Germany's eastern borders. Moscow's attempt to use Italy to broker a spheres of influence deal in the Balkans was seen as expansionist. The Red Army's move into Bessarabia and Bukovina imperilled German oil supplies from Romania's Ploesti fields.

Hitler's suspicions were further aroused by the appointment of a new British ambassador to the Soviet Union. Stafford Cripps arrived in Moscow in mid-June and brought with him a personal message from Churchill to Stalin. Churchill warned Stalin of the threat represented by German hegemony in Europe and suggested discussions about the problems it posed to Soviet and British interests. Stalin met Cripps on 1 July and rebuffed the British overture. To Cripps's point that Britain was fighting to maintain the balance of power in Europe, Stalin replied that he 'wanted to change the old equilibrium in Europe, which worked against the USSR. As negotiations showed, the British and French did not want to meet us halfway on this question. This served to bring about a rapprochement between Germany and the USSR . . . If the issue is the restoration of equilibrium, including the establishment of a balance in relation to the USSR, then we have to say that we cannot agree with this.' He further told Cripps that it was 'premature to speak of German domination of Europe. The defeat of France did not signify such domination. Such domination over Europe by Germany would require German domination of the seas, and that was hardly possible . . . In all his meetings with German representatives he had noted no desire for German domination of the world . . . he did not deny that among the nationalsocialists there were those who spoke of German domination of the world.

But ... in Germany there are intelligent people who understand that Germany does not have the power to dominate the world.'[81] Two weeks after this meeting Molotov provided Count Friedrich von der Schulenburg, the German ambassador, with a sanitised but not inaccurate report of the exchanges between Stalin and Cripps.[82] Stalin's message to Hitler was clear: he wanted to continue the Nazi–Soviet pact. That message was reinforced by Molotov in his speech to the Supreme Soviet on 1 August 1940 when he derided press speculation that the Soviet Union found Germany's new power position in Europe disagreeable and intimidating. On the contrary, said Molotov, the Nazi–Soviet pact was now more important than ever and was based not on 'fortuitous considerations of a transient nature, but on the fundamental political interests of both countries'.[83]

Hitler believed, however, that something was brewing in Anglo-Soviet relations and that Britain was taking heart from the USSR's newfound role as a counterbalance to German power in Europe. On 31 July Hitler told his High Command:

England's hope lies in Russia and America ... Russia – this is the factor which England is relying on most. Something must have happened in London ... But if Russia suffered defeat the last hope of England would be gone. Domination of Europe and the Balkans would then be Germany's. Decision: in this conflict Russia must be finished off. Spring 1941. The sooner Russia is destroyed the better. The operation will only have meaning if we destroy this state in one blow.[84]

As the quotation shows, Hitler's preoccupation at this time was with Britain, not Russia, and he could not understand why the British had rejected yet another offer of peace negotiations. While German military planners began mapping out an invasion of Russia, Hitler gave the go-ahead to Ribbentrop to try to involve the Soviet Union in a 'continental bloc' of Germany, Italy, Japan and the USSR that would range itself against the United States as well as Britain.[85] It is difficult to judge how seriously Hitler took this pet project of the anti-British Ribbentrop, but he seems to have been prepared to give it a chance. Certainly, it was only after the collapse of the proposed continental bloc that Hitler issued a formal directive to prepare for an invasion of Russia.

Ribbentrop's continental bloc required Russia to join the three-power pact signed by Germany, Italy and Japan on 27 September 1940. Under the terms of this tripartite pact the signatories pledged to assist one another should they be attacked by a power then not involved in the war. In addition, Ribbentrop envisaged the signing of a secret protocol in which each state would specify the direction of their future expansion.[86]

On 13 October Ribbentrop wrote to Stalin, inviting Molotov to Berlin for negotiations:

> I should like to state that in the opinion of the Führer . . . it appears to be the historic mission of the four powers – the Soviet Union, Italy, Japan and Germany – to adopt a long-range policy and to direct the future development of their peoples into the right channels by delimitation of their interests on a world-wide scale.[87]

Stalin replied positively on 22 October: 'I agree with you that a further improvement in the relations between our two countries is entirely possible on the permanent basis of a long-range delimitation of mutual interests.'[88]

But behind the friendly tones the tension in Soviet–German relations was rising. On 31 August Germany and Italy had arbitrated a long-standing Hungarian–Romanian territorial dispute, awarding Transylvania to Hungary but guaranteeing the territorial integrity of what was left of Romania pending the settlement of some Bulgarian claims. Moscow was furious that it was not consulted about this decision, which meant that Romania was now under German domination, and in September a German military mission arrived in the country. Later that month German military units appeared on Finnish soil as well. Signs were also accumulating that Italy intended to attack Greece (which it did on 28 October), thus spreading the European war to the Balkans.

In a directive to Molotov on 9 November 1940 Stalin set out his aims for the negotiations with Ribbentrop and Hitler. Molotov was instructed to probe German intentions and find out how the Soviet Union figured in Hitler's plans. Soviet interests in relation to a whole series of international questions were to be asserted, above all in relation to the incorporation of Bulgaria into the USSR's sphere of interest, which Stalin designated 'the most important question of the negotiations'. [89]

Stalin's instructions to Molotov indicate that he was prepared to negotiate a wide-ranging deal with the Germans and still thought a partnership with Hitler was possible. Molotov arrived in Berlin on 12 November and attempted to fulfil Stalin's brief. But he found himself faced not with negotiations about a new spheres of influence deal but with the offer of a junior partnership in a German-led global alliance, in which Soviet expansion was to be directed towards India and a clash with Britain. Stalin had no interest in such an arrangement and an impasse was quickly reached. Molotov persisted in trying to tie the Germans down to specific agreements on immediate issues but to no avail. The log jam in the negotiations was summed up by this sharp exchange between Molotov and Ribbentrop at their last meeting on 14 November:

The questions which interested the Soviet Union in the Near East, concerned not only Turkey, but Bulgaria ... the fate of Rumania and Hungary was also of interest to the Soviet Union and could not be immaterial to her under any circumstances. It would further interest the Soviet Government to learn what the Axis contemplated with regard to Yugoslavia ... Greece ... and Poland ... (Molotov)

He could only repeat again and again that the decisive question was whether the Soviet Union was prepared and in a position to co-operate with us in the great liquidation of the British Empire. On all other questions we would easily reach an understanding if we could succeed in extending our relations and in defining the spheres of influence. Where the spheres of influence lay had been repeatedly stated. (Ribbentrop)[90]

According to Yakov Chadaev, a senior administrator in the Council of People's Commissars, when Molotov gave his report to the Politburo on the discussions in Berlin, Stalin was convinced that Hitler was intent on war.[91] However, the formal Soviet response to the Berlin negotiations suggests that Stalin had not given up completely on a deal with Hitler. On 25 November Molotov presented Schulenburg with a memorandum setting out the conditions of Soviet adherence to the tripartite pact: (1) the withdrawal of German troops from Finland; (2) a Soviet–Bulgarian mutual assistance pact, including the establishment of Soviet military bases; (3) recognition of Soviet aspirations in the direction of the Persian Gulf; (4) an agreement with Turkey providing for Soviet military bases on the Black Sea Straits; and (5) Japanese renunciation of rights to coal and oil concessions in North Sakhalin.[92] As John Erickson commented: 'Stalin's response ... was in every sense a test of Hitler's intentions: the Soviet terms for joining a four power pact amounted to giving Hitler full freedom in the west only at the price of foreclosing his option to wage a successful war against the Soviet Union.'[93] At the same meeting Molotov informed Schulenburg that the new Soviet ambassador to Germany, Vladimir G. Dekanozov, was leaving for Berlin the next day. Dekanozov met Hitler on 19 December. The German dictator told him that the negotiations that had begun with Molotov would be continued in an official fashion, but refused to be drawn any further.[94] In reality, Hitler had already decided on war. The previous day, 18 December 1940, Hitler had issued his directive on Operation Barbarossa – the code name for the German invasion of Russia.[95]

In December 1939 Stalin had replied to Ribbentrop's congratulatory telegram on his 60th birthday with a dramatic public affirmation of the durability of the Soviet–German alliance: 'the friendship between the peoples of the Soviet Union and Germany, cemented by blood, has every reason to be solid and lasting'.[96] A year later, however, the two states had begun the countdown to war.

3

Grand Illusions
Stalin and 22 June 1941

After Molotov's failed negotiations in Berlin the signs pointing to a Soviet–German war grew ever more ominous. As Stalin told Dimitrov on 25 November, 'our relations with Germany are polite on the surface, but there is serious friction between us'.[1] Dimitrov was ordered to begin a Comintern campaign in Bulgaria in support of Moscow's proposal to Sofia that the two countries sign a mutual assistance pact, an offer reactivated after Molotov's return to Moscow from Berlin.[2] Once again the Bulgarians politely declined the Soviet offer, and signalled their intention to align with the Axis by signing the tripartite pact.[3] Faced with this prospect the Soviets protested to Berlin that they considered Bulgaria within their security zone in the Balkans. To no avail: Bulgaria signed the tripartite pact in March 1941, adding its signature to those of Hungary, Romania and Slovakia which had all joined the Axis alliance in November 1940. Adding to Moscow's concerns was the position in Greece, invaded by Italy in October 1940, which now had 100,000 British troops fighting on its soil. This threatened an extension of the European war to the rest of the Balkans.

By spring 1941 the only independent state left in Eastern Europe, apart from embattled Greece, was Yugoslavia. Moscow took steps to enrol Yugoslavia in an anti-German front in the Balkans as early as October 1940 and then took heart from a popular coup in Belgrade at the end of March 1941 that overthrew the pro-German government. From Belgrade the Soviet embassy reported on mass demonstrations demanding 'Alliance with Russia!', while the Yugoslav communist party began a campaign for a mutual assistance pact with the USSR.[4] On 30 March the new Yugoslav government approached the Soviet embassy with proposals for a military and political alliance between Yugoslavia and the USSR, stressing, in particular, the need for arms to defend the country's neutrality. The next day Molotov invited Belgrade to send a delegation to Moscow for urgent negotiations.[5] Talks took place in Moscow on 3–4 April, with negotiations being conducted on the Soviet side by Deputy

Foreign Commissar Andrei Vyshinskii. The Yugoslavs wanted a military alliance but what was on offer from Stalin was a 'pact of non-aggression and friendship'. Vyshinskii was quite frank about the reason for this: 'We have an agreement with Germany and we do not want to give the impression that we are violating this agreement. Above all, we do not want to disturb this agreement.'[6] In accordance with this priority Molotov called in Schulenburg on the evening of 4 April to tell him that the Soviet Union was going to sign a non-aggression treaty with Yugoslavia. Schulenburg protested that relations between Yugoslavia and Germany were tense at the moment since the question of Yugoslavia's membership of the tripartite pact was uncertain. Molotov replied that there was no contradiction between Yugoslavia's adherence to the Axis and the proposed pact and that issues in German–Yugoslav relations were a matter for settlement by Berlin and Belgrade. For its part, said Molotov, the Soviet Union saw its non-aggression and friendship pact with Yugoslavia as a contribution to peace and the lessening of tensions in the Balkans.[7]

The Soviet–Yugoslav pact of non-aggression, although dated 5 April, was actually signed in the early hours of 6 April 1941.[8] After the signing ceremony a banquet was held in the Kremlin. Among the participants was the Soviet diplomat Nikolai Novikov, who recalled in his memoirs this exchange between Stalin and Savich, the head of the Yugoslav delegation:

Savich: If they [the Germans] attack us we will fight to the last man and you Russians will also have to fight, whether you like it or not. Hitler will never stop himself. He has to be stopped.

Stalin: Yes, you are right, Hitler will not stop by himself. He has far to go with his plans. The Germans are trying to intimidate us but we are not afraid of them.

Savich: You know, of course, about the rumours that Germany intends to attack the Soviet Union in May?

Stalin: Let it try. We have strong nerves. We do not want war. Hence we concluded a pact of non-aggression with Hitler. But how does he implement it? Do you know how many troops the Germans have moved to our borders?[9]

But Stalin's verbal bravado was not matched by his actions. Later that day the Germans, concerned about the Italians' faltering Greek campaign as well as about the hostility of the new government in Belgrade, launched an invasion of Yugoslavia and Greece. Within a fortnight Belgrade was suing for peace. British forces fighting in Greece held out a little longer, but by early May they had been expelled from the Greek mainland and that country was under German occupation, too. The Yugoslavs received neither supplies nor much sympathy from the Soviets. It is possible that if the Yugoslavs had held out for longer then some Soviet aid would have been forthcoming,[10] but faced with yet another easy German blitzkrieg victory, Stalin chose to avoid conflict with Hitler over Yugoslavia. Indeed, with the fall of Yugoslavia Stalin seems to have decided that henceforth the best way to deal with Hitler was by appeasement.

Appeasement Soviet-Style

Before the Second World War, Stalin had often criticised the Anglo-French policy of appeasement on the grounds that making concessions to Hitler only whetted his appetite for more territorial gains. That consideration was put aside in the three months before 22 June 1941 as Stalin sought to deflect Hitler from war by a series of extravagant gestures of friendship designed to demonstrate his peaceful intentions towards Germany.

The first of these gestures was the signing on 13 April 1941 of a neutrality pact with Japan. Since Japan was one of Germany's partners in the tripartite pact the signature of the Soviet–Japanese treaty was a clear message to Hitler that Stalin was still interested in negotiations and deals with the Axis. Indeed, the neutrality pact was depicted in the Soviet press as the logical outcome of previous proposals that the USSR should join the three-power pact.[11] Of course, the pact with Japan also protected the Soviet Union's Far Eastern flank in the event of war with Germany. But Stalin did not have much faith in Japan's commitment to neutrality in such circumstances. It was the political symbolism that mattered more than the strategic significance of the pact. Stalin himself reinforced the message to Berlin by a public demonstration of affection for Germany on the occasion of the departure of Matsuoka, the Japanese Foreign Minister, from Moscow by train on 13 April. After bidding goodbye to Matsuoka at the station Stalin sought out and publicly embraced Schulenburg, saying to him, 'we must remain friends and you must do everything to that end'. Later he turned to the German military attaché Colonel Krebs and told him, 'We will remain friends with you – in any event.'[12]

On 7 May it was announced in the Soviet press that Stalin had been appointed Chairman of the Council of People's Commissars, i.e. had become head of the government as well as retaining his post of General Secretary of the Soviet communist party. Molotov, who had held the post of Soviet premier since 1930 and had continued in a dual role when he was appointed People's Commissar for Foreign Affairs in May 1939, was made Stalin's deputy. According to the Politburo resolution of 4 May that recorded this decision, the reason for Stalin's appointment was the need to improve the co-ordination of party and state organs in a tense international situation that demanded significant strengthening of the country's defences.[13]

Moscow had long cultivated Stalin's image as a peacemaker and conciliator and, sure enough, Schulenburg cabled Berlin that he was 'convinced that Stalin will use his new position in order to take part personally in the maintenance and development of good relations between the Soviets and Germany'.[14] Stalin's appointment as premier was followed by a series of further appeasement signals. On 8 May the Soviet news agency, Tass, issued a denial of rumours of troop concentrations along the Soviet border. The next day the Soviets withdrew diplomatic recognition of the governments-in-exile of German-occupied Belgium, Norway and Yugoslavia. On 12 May the Soviet Union recognised an anti-British regime in Iraq. On 24 May Schulenburg reported home that Stalin's policy was 'above all, directed at the avoidance of conflict with Germany' as shown 'by the attitude of the Soviet government during the last few weeks, the tone of the Soviet press . . . and the observance of the trade agreements concluded with Germany'.[15] In early June the fall of Crete to the Germans was followed by a rapid withdrawal of Soviet recognition of Greek sovereignty. Stalin's appeasement campaign reached a climax on 13 June 1941 with the publication by Tass of a statement denying rumours of conflict and impending war between the Soviet Union and Germany. The USSR, said Tass, was adhering to the Soviet–German non-aggression pact, as was Germany, and contrary reports were all lies and provocations. The statement denied that Germany had made any new demands on the USSR but hinted that there could be negotiations were that to be the case.[16] In the remaining days of peace the Soviets dropped a number of further hints to the Germans that they were open to talks.

Misleading Signals

Did Stalin, the great realist and cynic, really believe that such gestures could make any difference to Hitler's course of action? Stalin's innermost thoughts and calculations in the days and weeks before the German attack on the Soviet Union remain shrouded, but it seems he really did believe that Hitler was not set on war in summer 1941 and that diplomacy could preserve peace, for a while longer at least.

For a start the signals emanating from the Soviet–Japanese neutrality pact were, from Stalin's point of view, a two-way affair. Moscow and Tokyo had been talking for 18 months about signing a Soviet–Japanese version of the Nazi–Soviet pact that would resolve their disputes about borders, fishing rights, and Japan's oil and mining concessions in North Sakhalin. The final negotiations took place during the course of a European tour by Matsuoka in March–April 1941. Matsuoka visited Moscow in March and again in April, having just been to Berlin to talk to Hitler. Matsuoka did not know that Hitler intended to make war on Russia and in his conversation with Stalin on 12 April he gave no hint that he thought any trouble was brewing in Soviet–German relations.[17] If Hitler was bent on war, Stalin must have reasoned, he would surely have steered his Japanese ally away from a pact with the Soviet Union. Japan's willingness to sign a neutrality pact was a positive signal from Berlin as well as Tokyo. In the tense aftermath of the Yugoslav events Stalin sensed an opportunity to send a message to Hitler about his peaceful intentions and he dropped long-standing Soviet demands that the Japanese give up their economic rights in North Sakhalin and agreed to sign a straightforward neutrality pact.

Then there was the role of Schulenburg, a committed Rapallite, a true believer in the eastern orientation of German foreign policy and in the alliance with Russia, whose reports to Berlin often put a positive gloss on Soviet–German relations. In mid-April 1941 he returned home for consultations. When he met Hitler on 28 April the Führer complained bitterly about Soviet actions during the Yugoslav crisis. Schulenburg defended Soviet behaviour and tried to persuade Hitler 'that Stalin was prepared to make even further concessions'.[18] But the meeting concluded on an indeterminate note and Schulenburg returned to Moscow in early May with deep forebodings about the future of German–Soviet relations. In a series of meetings with Dekanozov, the Soviet ambassador to Germany, who was on leave from Berlin, Schulenburg tried to prod the Soviets into a major diplomatic initiative to ease the tensions in Soviet–German relations. At the first meeting, on 5 May, Schulenburg gave Dekanozov a fairly accurate report of his discussion with Hitler, highlighting the Führer's concerns about the Soviet–Yugoslav treaty episode. Schulenburg was more concerned, however, about reports of a coming war between Russia and Germany and said that something had to be done to blunt these rumours. Dekanozov asked what could be done but Schulenburg would only say that they should both think about it and meet again for further discussion. At the second meeting, on 9 May, Schulenburg proposed that Stalin send a letter to Hitler and the other Axis leaders professing the Soviet Union's peaceful intentions. For his part, Dekanozov suggested a joint Soviet–German communiqué and Schulenburg thought this a good idea, too, but action had to be taken quickly. At their third and final meeting, on 12 May, Dekanozov reported that Stalin had agreed to a joint communiqué and to an exchange of letters with Hitler about the rumours of war but that Schulenburg should negotiate the texts with Molotov. At that point Schulenburg drew back from his personal initiative, saying that he had no authority to conduct such negotiations.[19] That evening Dekanozov met Stalin for nearly an hour, presumably to report on his conversation with Schulenburg.[20]

Schulenburg's initiative was purely personal but he was the German ambassador and he had just returned to Moscow having met and talked to Hitler in Berlin. Stalin could be forgiven for interpreting his approach to Dekanozov as an informal but official sounding-out. This interpretation also fitted in with the growing perception in Moscow that there was a split in German ruling circles between the advocates of war with the Soviet Union and those who favoured further co-operation with the USSR. In this light Schulenburg's sounding could be read as evidence of the activities of a 'peace' party in Berlin. The 'split theory', as Gabriel Gorodetsky has called it, had circulated in Moscow in one form or another since Hitler came to power. This belief reflected the reality of the strong Rapollite tradition in Germany but was underpinned by Marxist dogma about the division in German capitalism between economic groups that favoured eastern territorial expansion and those that preferred to trade with the Soviet Union. Moscow's predisposition to believe in the existence of 'hawks' and 'doves' in Berlin was reinforced by many Soviet intelligence reports, including those submitted by a Gestapo double agent who had infiltrated one of Moscow's spy rings in Germany.[21]

Another event that seemed to underline the split theory was the dramatic flight of Hitler's Deputy, Rudolf Hess, to Britain on 10 May 1941. Hess flew to Britain on a personal mission to broker a peace deal between Britain and Germany. In Moscow one spin put on the affair was that Hess's aim was a peace that would pave the way for an Anglo-German alliance against Bolshevik Russia. A more optimistic reading was that Hess's defection was further evidence of the split between those who wanted war with Russia and those who still saw Britain as the prime enemy. Hess's defection coloured Stalin's view of the many intelligence reports on the coming German attack that were now crossing his desk. Were the reports accurate or were they rumours circulated by those who wanted to precipitate a Soviet–German war? Stalin's suspicions in this regard were not far wrong. The British did use the Hess affair to sow discord in Soviet–German relations by circulating rumours that he was on an official mission to form an Anglo-German alliance against Russia.[22] The dreadful irony was that when the British became convinced that the Germans were indeed about to invade Russia and attempted to warn Stalin of the danger, they were not believed. At meetings with Maiskii on 2, 10, 13 and 16 June British officials gave him chapter and verse on German troop movements along the Soviet frontier.[23] Maiskii duly reported this information to Moscow but it had little impact.

In this uncertain situation Stalin relied on his own reasoning to assess Hitler's likely intentions: it did not make sense for Germany to turn against Russia before Britain was finished off. Why fight a two-front war when the Soviet Union self-evidently posed no immediate danger to Germany? In May 1941 Stalin told the graduating cadets of the Red Army academies that Germany defeated France in 1870 because it fought on only one front but had lost the First World War because it had to fight on two fronts. This rationalisation was reinforced by the assessment in some of the intelligence reports presented to him. For example, on 20 March 1941 General Filip Golikov, the chief of Soviet military intelligence, presented a summary of reports on the timing of German military action against the USSR. Golikov concluded, however, that 'the most likely date for the beginning of military action against the USSR is after victory over England or after the conclusion of an honourable peace with Germany. Rumours and documentation that war against the USSR is inevitable in the spring of this year must be considered as disinformation emanating from English or even, perhaps, German intelligence.'[24] Golikov's subsequent reports to Stalin, however, presented the information on the concentration of German (and Romanian) forces along the Soviet border in a much more balanced manner.[25] On 5 May, for example, Golikov reported that the number of German divisions concentrated on the Soviet border had in the past two months increased from 70 to 107, including an increase in tank divisions from six to 12. Golikov further pointed out that Romania and Hungary had between them about 130 divisions and that German forces along the Soviet border were likely to increase further following the end of the war with Yugoslavia.[26]

Another source of persistent warnings about German preparations for war with the USSR were two highly placed Soviet spies in Germany. 'Starshina', who worked in the headquarters of the Luftwaffe and 'Korsikanets', in the German economics ministry. Between them they sent dozens of reports to Moscow containing evidence of the coming German attack.[27] On a report based on information from these two dated 17 June 1941 Stalin wrote to his intelligence chief, V.N. Merkulov: 'perhaps you can send your "source" from the staff of the German air force to go fuck his mother. This is not a "source" but a disinformer.'[28] However, Stalin did not comment on the information from Korsikanets, which was equally suggestive of an imminent German invasion. As Gabriel Gorodetsky argued, Stalin's outburst was a sign that he was getting rattled by these reports that a German attack was coming soon and had begun to fear they could be true.[29]

Another stream of warnings came from the Far East. Richard Sorge was a Soviet spy in Tokyo working under cover as a German journalist. His main sources of information were the German ambassador and the German military attaché in Tokyo. Sorge's reports were based on the expressed opinions of these two sources and they did not prove to be wholly accurate. Early reports from Sorge suggested Germany would invade the USSR only after finishing off Britain. His first predicted date for the German attack was May 1941. As late as 17 June 1941 Sorge was reporting that the military attaché was not sure whether there would be war or not. On 20 June, however, Sorge reported that the ambassador thought that war was now inevitable.[30]

Closer to home there were the reports submitted by Dekanozov from Berlin. Again, there was an element of equivocation in them. On 4 June he reported on widespread rumours of an imminent Soviet–German war, but also on stories that there would be a *rapprochement* between the two countries on the basis of Soviet concessions to Germany, a new spheres of influence deal and a promise from Moscow not to interfere in European affairs.[31] On 15 June Dekanozov cabled Moscow that the Danish and Swedish military attachés believed that the concentration of German forces on the Soviet border was no longer a demonstration designed to extract concessions from Moscow but part of the 'immediate preparation for war with the Soviet Union'.[32] He did not, however, make it clear that he shared these views.

Adding to the uncertainty was the extensive disinformation campaign waged by the Germans, which was designed to explain away the massive concentration of their forces along the Soviet border. The Germans began by asserting that the military build-up was a defensive measure. Then they put it about that their build-up in the east was a ruse to lull the British into a false sense of security. Another story was that the German divisions were there not to invade but to intimidate the Soviets into economic and territorial concessions. One of the most prevalent rumours was that even if Hitler did attack he would first present an ultimatum to Stalin – an idea designed to cover up the surprise attack that the Germans were actually planning.[33]

After the event it was easy to identify which reports were true and which were false and to see through the equivocations of many of Stalin's sources. At the time, however, there was room for doubt, particularly about the timing of a German attack. Stalin's calculation was that Hitler would not attack yet and that evidence suggesting otherwise could be explained by the split theory or by the machinations of British intelligence. At the same time Stalin could not afford to discount the possibility of war in the short term. Stalin was never foolhardy and while he might disparage foreign intelligence as false reporting by stupid spies or *agents provocateurs*, the evidence of the German military build-up from Soviet border reconnaissance was just too weighty to ignore. As Field Marshal Alan Brooke, Chief of the Imperial General Staff during the war, noted later of Stalin:

Stalin is a realist . . . facts only count . . . plans, hypotheses, future possibilities mean nothing to him, but he is ready to face facts, even when unpleasant.[34]

While Stalin could hope, even believe, that Hitler would not attack, the evidence was clear that the German dictator *might* be planning to attack soon. Stalin responded to this possibility by the continuation and, indeed, acceleration of his preparations for war, including a massive build-up of Soviet frontline forces:

— In May–June 800,000 reservists were called up.
— In mid-May 28 divisions were ordered to the western districts of the USSR.
— On 27 May these districts were ordered to build field command posts.
— In June 38,500 men were sent to the fortified areas of the border districts.
— On 12–15 June the districts were ordered to move forces to the frontier.
— On 19 June, district HQs were ordered to move to new command posts. Orders were also issued to districts to camouflage targets and disperse aircraft.[35]

By June 1941 the Red Army had more than 300 divisions, comprising some 5.5 million personnel, of whom 2.7 million were stationed in the western border districts.[36] On the night of 21–22 June this vast force was put on alert and warned to expect a surprise attack by the Germans.[37]

But still the question remains: why didn't Stalin order full-scale mobilisation of Soviet forces well in advance of a possible attack, if only as a precautionary measure? Part of the answer is that Stalin did not want to provoke Hitler into a premature attack. 'Mobilisation means war' was a commonplace of Soviet strategic thinking. It derived from Russia's experience during the crisis that led to the outbreak of the First World War. Tsar Nicholas II's decision to mobilise the Russian army as a precautionary measure in July 1914 had provoked, it was believed, a German counter-mobilisation and hence the escalation of the 'July Crisis' into a European war. Stalin was determined not to repeat that mistake. Besides, he did not think it mattered much if Hitler was able to spring a surprise attack because according to Soviet military doctrine the outbreak of hostilities with Germany would be followed by a period of 2–4 weeks during which both sides would mobilise and concentrate their main forces for battle. In the meantime, there would be tactical battles along the frontier and limited penetrations and incursions by mobile forces probing for weaknesses and preparing the way for major outflanking movements. In any event, the decisive battles would be fought a few weeks after the outbreak of war. Again, the model was the First World War, but Stalin's generals were not stupid, they were not – as the cliché goes – simply preparing to fight the last war again. They had observed the German blitzkrieg victories over Poland and France and noted the effectiveness of concentrated tank offensives and massive encirclement manoeuvres by the Wehrmacht's highly mobile forces. But they did not think the Red Army would share the fate of their French and Polish counterparts. They saw Poland as weak militarily and the French, with their 'Maginot mentality', as having no stomach for a fight. They were confident Soviet defences would hold and provide cover while the Red Army mobilised its main forces for battle. As Evan Mawdsley has argued, 'Stalin and the Soviet High Command believed that they were dealing with Hitler from a *position of strength*, not from one of weakness.'[38]

In the context of this analysis of the future war Stalin was not frightened of a surprise attack by Hitler. At most it would cost the loss of a few tactical frontier battles. On that calculation Stalin's gamble on the preservation of peace makes a lot more sense. The payoff could be a delay of war until 1942, by which time Soviet defences would be much stronger and the country's preparations for war complete. Paradoxically, then, the German surprise attack on 22 June 1941 surprised no one, not even Stalin. The nasty surprise was the nature of the attack – a *strategic* attack in which the Wehrmacht committed its main forces to battle from day one of the war, slamming through and shattering Red Army defences and penetrating deep into Russia with strong armoured columns that surrounded the disorganised and immobile Soviet armies.

The failure of Stalin and his generals to imagine a strategic surprise attack was only partly a consequence of misconceived military doctrine. It was also a matter of focus. What preoccupied the Soviet High Command on the eve of war was not how they were going to defend against a German invasion but when and where they were going to *attack*. They were planning and preparing to wage an offensive war against Germany, not a defensive one.

Soviet Plans for Offensive War

To say that the Soviet Union was preparing to take offensive action against Germany is not to endorse the idea that Stalin was preparing a preventative war against Hitler and intended to launch a pre-emptive strike.[39] Stalin's political and diplomatic manoeuvres show that he was desperate for peace in summer 1941. Had Stalin succeeded in delaying war until 1942 it is possible that he might have decided to take the initiative and strike first, but his inclination was always to postpone war for as long as possible. He was confident of the Red Army's military prowess but he feared the consequences of Soviet involvement in a major war, which carried with it the danger that the USSR's capitalist foes might unite against a common, communist enemy. At the same time Stalin's gamble on maintaining peace with Hitler in summer 1941 required the covering contingency of adequate defence being in place if his calculations proved to be wrong. His generals, however, were focused not on defence but on their own plans for attack and counterattack. There was, in practical terms, a mismatch between Stalin's diplomatic strategy and his generals' military strategy. Arguably, this dangerous disconnection between political strategy and operational doctrine, plans and preparations was the most important factor in the calamity that befell the Red Army on 22 June 1941.

The source of this disconnection was the offensive-oriented military doctrines of the Red Army dating back to the 1920s. The Soviet High Command intended to fight the next war by taking the battle to the enemy, by launching attacks and counterattacks and by the deep penetration and invasion of the opponent's territory. This policy commitment to offensive action was reinforced by interwar developments in military technology – by the increase in the power, mobility and reliability of tanks, planes and artillery – which made feasible highly mobile attacks and rapid flanking movements and the breaching of even the best-prepared defences. In Red Army doctrine, defence was definitely second best to attack, a mere phase in the preparation of offensive action. This doctrinal order of priorities was reinforced by observations of the German victories in Poland and France and by the Soviets' own experience of breaching the strong defences of the Mannerheim Line in Finland in 1940.

In his concluding speech to a conference of the High Command held at the end of December 1940 Defence Commissar Timoshenko summed up state of the art Soviet strategic thinking, devoting most of his remarks to problems of the offensive. Timoshenko did not ignore the question of defence. Indeed, his speech contained a whole section on defence in which he argued strongly that there was no 'crisis of contemporary defence' and against the idea that the rapid defeat of Poland and France showed that defenders could not defend effectively against modern firepower and mobile attackers. Effective defence was possible in modern conditions, said Timoshenko, but it had to be defence in depth and there had to be a number of zones and echelons of defence. But Timoshenko was clear, even in this section of his report, that 'defence is not the decisive means of defeating the enemy: only attack can achieve that in the end. Defence should only be resorted to when there is insufficient force for attack, or when it helps in the establishment of conditions necessary for the preparation of an attack.'[40]

The other main speaker at the conference was General Georgii Zhukov, a former cavalry officer and an advocate of armoured mobile warfare, who had made his name as a frontline commander by waging a successful offensive against the Japanese at Khalkin Gol in August 1939 following border clashes on the Sino-Mongolian border. He delivered a report on 'the character of contemporary offensive operations'. His theme was that the Red Army needed to learn from the recent experience of the European war and to update its preparations for offensive action.[41] After the conference, in January 1941, two sets of war games were played by members of the High Command. Both games were based on offensive actions and manoeuvres on the Soviet Union's western borders. The victor in each case was Zhukov, who was then made Chief of the General Staff. As Evan Mawdsley says, 'it is difficult to see Zhukov's appointment as anything other than Stalin's endorsement of the offensive orientation of the Red Army'.[42]

Stalin was steeped in the doctrine of offensive action. As well as sharing the military rationale for the strategy he had a long-standing commitment to the aggressive defence of the sacred Soviet soil. 'We do not want a single foot of foreign territory,' he told the 16th party congress in 1930, 'but of our territory we shall not surrender a single inch to anyone.'[43] Offensive concepts and themes – dating back to the civil war – were also pervasive in Stalinist political culture where the solution to social and economic problems was typically seen in terms of squads of vanguard workers using shock tactics to root out and destroy entrenched enemies holding back the implementation of party policy. The Red Army's concept of fighting the future war on the territory of the enemy dovetailed, too, with the messianic tendencies of Soviet ideology. Stalin did not believe in exporting revolution by force of arms.[44] But he did see the Red Army as a liberating force whose incursion into foreign territory could have a positive political impact from a communist point of view. As Stalin later famously said, 'whoever occupies a territory also imposes on it his own social system. Everyone imposes his own system as far as his army can reach. It cannot be otherwise.'[45] What Stalin had in mind at the time was the Red Army's role in supporting the establishment of communist-dominated popular front governments in Eastern Europe in 1944–1945. In 1939–1940, however, the model was the role played by the Red Army in the 'revolutions' that took place in Western Belorussia, Western Ukraine, Bessarabia, Bukovina and the Baltic States. Set against this was the cautionary example of the failure of the Red Army's 'liberation mission' in Finland during the Winter War. But the Red Army's commitment to offensive action and the counter-invasion of enemy territory was primarily driven by strategic not ideological considerations. Quite simply, attack was seen as the best defence and the potential political benefits of the Red Army's forward movement were no more than a bonus. Nevertheless, an integral part of the Red Army's preparation for war was to imbue its soldiers with the idea that military action was an aspect of a wider political struggle between the Soviet Union and the capitalist world. In 1940–1941 this ideological propaganda was stepped up as the Soviet authorities sought to shore up the myth of the invincible Red Army after the battering it had taken during the war with Finland.[46]

Strategically, the Red Army's offensive orientation was embodied in its war plans. These 'plans' consisted of documents that identified potential enemies, assessed the scale and possible disposition of opponents' forces and predicted likely avenues of enemy attack. The plans also outlined the Red Army's grand strategy – how in general terms the Soviet Union planned to counter enemy invasion. Seven such plans were drawn up between 1928 and 1941. The last to be drafted before the outbreak of the Second World War was prepared in March 1938 under the supervision of the then Chief of the General Staff, Marshal Boris Shaposhnikov.[47] Shaposhnikov's document identified the main enemies as Germany and its allies in Europe, and Japan in the Far East. Although the Soviet armed forces had to be prepared to fight a war on two fronts, Germany was identified as the primary threat and the west as the main theatre of operations. The Germans, said the document, would attempt an invasion of the Soviet Union either north of the Pripiat marshes in the direction of Minsk, Leningrad and Moscow or south of the marshes, with the aim of advancing on Kiev and conquering the Ukraine. Which route was taken would depend on the political situation in Europe and the precise line-up against the Soviet Union of Germany and its allies in Eastern Europe. The document then detailed two variants of Soviet operational plans to counter a German-led invasion. If the Germans attacked in the north the Red Army would counterattack in that sector and remain on the defensive in the south. If the Germans attacked in the south the Red Army would counterattack there and remain on the defensive in the north. In both variants the aim was to engage and destroy the main concentrations of the enemy's armed forces.

The next version of the plan was prepared in the very different circumstances of summer 1940,[48] following Timoshenko's replacement of Voroshilov as defence commissar. In outline it was very similar to the 1938 document. However, the 1940 version predicted the Germans would attack in the north with a thrust from East Prussia (now, after the conquest of Poland, reattached to the main body of Germany) into Lithuania, Latvia and Western Belorussia (all now part of the Soviet Union). Therefore the bulk of the Red Army's forces should be concentrated in the north, said the plan. Again, the object of the exercise was to engage and destroy the enemy's main forces, wherever they might be.

This later version of the war plan was also prepared by Shaposhnikov's staff officers. However, in summer 1940 he stepped down as Chief of Staff due to bad health and was replaced by General Meretskov. Further work was done on the plan and a new draft dated 18 September was prepared.[49] The September plan repeated the idea that the Germans were most likely to attack in the north but did not exclude the possibility that they might concentrate their main forces in the south, thus reasserting the need for a plan with two variants of the Soviet strategic response. If the Germans concentrated in the south the Red Army would also concentrate there and launch a counterattack that would head for Lublin and Krakow in German-occupied Poland and then on to Breslau in southern Germany, with the aim of cutting off Hitler from his Balkan allies and from the crucial economic resources of that region. If the Germans made their move in the north, the Red Army would invade East Prussia. Again, the aim was to find and fight the main German forces.

The September plan was submitted to Stalin and the Soviet leadership for discussion. Out of this consultation there came, in early October, a crucial amendment: the Red Army's main attack forces were to be concentrated in the south and tasked with an advance on Lublin, Krakow and Breslau. Although the reason for this change was not specified in the memorandum that Timoshenko and Meretskov sent to Stalin,[50] the most likely explanation is the expectation that when war broke out the main concentration of German forces would be found in the south. Certainly in the next version of the war plan, prepared in March 1941, the south was identified as the most likely site for the concentration of German forces, although concentration in the north and an attack from East Prussia were not ruled out.[51] From spring 1941 onwards Soviet intelligence reports emphasised that if the Germans did attack it would mainly be in the south. These misleading assessments reflected the effectiveness of the German disinformation campaign which aimed to cover up their real intention: to concentrate their attack in the north along the Minsk–Smolensk–Moscow axis (*see Map 3 on p. 75*).

The decision to plump for a southern concentration of the Red Army was a fateful one, which Zhukov and others were keen to explain away in their memoirs. In their version of events the decision was made by Stalin who believed that Hitler wanted to seize the economic and mineral resources of the Ukraine and southern Russia, including the oil of the Caucasus. While it is true Stalin thought that the struggle for raw materials would be crucial in the coming war, there is no direct evidence that the decision to concentrate forces in the south was specifically his, although he must have gone along with it. Another possibility, suggested by Gabriel Gorodetsky, is that when the 1940 war plan was being drawn up the Soviet leadership was obsessed with what was going on in the Balkans and wholly focused on isolating Hitler from his Balkan allies.[52] From this perspective the decision to concentrate in the south was perhaps driven more by political than military considerations. Then there is the suggestion made by Marshal Matvei Zakharov in his study of the Soviet General Staff: that personal preferences and bureaucratic factors may have played a critical role in the decision.[53] The main beneficiary in terms of

Soviet Plans for Offensive War Against Germany, 1941

resources was the Kiev military district. Both Meretskov and Timoshenko were former commanders of the Kiev military district and Zhukov was in that post when he was appointed Chief of the General Staff in January 1941. A number of the junior General Staff officers involved in drafting the war plans had also served on the south-western front. Certainly, the Kiev military district became a very active proponent of the idea that the Germans were concentrating in the south-west and lobbied heavily for more forces to counter this development.[54] Finally, there is the more radical and controversial argument that the reason Stalin and his generals chose to concentrate in the south was that the Red Army was planning a pre-emptive strike against Germany, and the plains of southern Poland offered an easier invasion route than the rivers, lakes, bogs and forests of East Prussia.[55]

The key piece of evidence for the proponents of the pre-emptive strike hypothesis is a new version of the war plan prepared in mid-May 1941.[56] The status of this particular document – which has been the subject of extensive controversy in Russia[57] – is uncertain. It was a handwritten document prepared by General Vasilevskii, at that time Deputy Chief of Operations, in the name of Zhukov and Timoshenko but not signed by either of them. It is not certain that Stalin saw the document or was even told about it.[58]

This May 1941 document was a less elaborate and less formally structured version of the earlier war plans. It has the air of being, as Cynthia A. Roberts has suggested, 'less a plan than a working document for one'.[59] According to this document, Germany and its allies (Finland, Hungary and Romania) would be able to deploy 240 divisions against the USSR and the main German force of about a 100 divisions would in all probability be deployed in the south for an attack in the direction of Kovel', Rovno and Kiev. The document further noted that the German army was in a state of mobilisation and that 'it had the possibility to pre-empt us in deployment and to deliver a sudden blow'. The document continued:

> In order to prevent this (and to destroy the German army), I consider it necessary not to give the initiative to the German command under any circumstances, to forestall the enemy in deployment and to attack the German army at that moment when it is still at the deployment stage and has not yet managed to organise a front or co-ordinated the different branches of the army. The primary strategic goal of the Red Army will be to destroy the main force of the German army deploying south of Demblin. . .The main blow of the forces of the South-Western Front to be inflicted in the direction of Krakow and Katowitze, cutting off Germany from its southern allies. [There will be] a supporting blow by the left flank of the Western Front in the direction of Sedletz and Demblin with the aim

of containing the Warsaw formations and helping the South-Western Front to destroy the Lublin formations of the enemy. An active defence to be conducted against Finland, East Prussia, Hungary and Romania and preparations made for the delivery of a strike against Romania under favourable conditions.

The document concluded with some requests to Stalin for action, including acceptance of the proposed plan of deployment in the event of war with Germany and, crucially, the secret mobilisation of all the High Command's reserve armies.

Read as part of the sequence of successive war plans there was nothing surprising in the May document. It was a logical development of the idea that in the coming war the Red Army would attack the German main force that was being deployed in the southern sector. The document's proposal to pre-empt the final stage of German mobilisation and deployment reflected, no doubt, the anxiety provoked by accumulating intelligence reports of massive Wehrmacht concentrations along the Soviet frontier in spring 1941 and the growing realisation that war was coming sooner rather than later. The proposal to counterattack in the form of an invasion of southern Poland was the same as before and the proposed secret movement of the reserve armies was an extension of existing and ongoing measures of covert mobilisation.

The problem with the document was twofold. First, it was deeply ambiguous about the timing of a Soviet pre-emptive strike. If the aim was to destroy the German armies, the best moment to do that would be when they were not quite fully mobilised, deployed, concentrated and co-ordinated. But who could judge accurately when that would be? Second, there was no possibility that Stalin would accept the new plan while he believed there was still a chance of peace, unless he could be persuaded that Soviet defences would crumble if the Germans were able to attack first – and there is no evidence that such a view was articulated within the Soviet military. It was only after the event, after the disaster of 22 June 1941, after the war, and after Stalin's death, that senior Soviet commanders began to say that more attention should have been paid to defence and to parrying a potentially devastating sudden German blow.

It has been suggested that the appearance of the May plan was linked to Stalin's speech to the 2,000 graduates of the Red Army staff academies on 5 May 1941. By this time it was normal for every public or semi-public remark of Stalin's to be widely disseminated in the Soviet Union. On this occasion, however, there was no published text, only a short report in *Pravda* the next day under the headline 'We must be prepared to deal with any surprises':

In his speech, Comrade Stalin noted the profound changes that had taken place in the Red Army in the last few years, and emphasised that, on the strength of the experience of modern war, its organisation had undergone important changes, and it has been substantially re-equipped. Comrade Stalin welcomed the officers who had graduated from the military academies and wished them all success in their work.[60]

Not surprisingly, rumours began to circulate about what else Stalin might have said to his graduating cadets. According to one report Stalin warned that war with Germany was definitely coming; according to another he advocated an offensive war to expand the socialist system. The version the Soviets leaked to the Germans was that Stalin talked about a new compromise with Hitler. The truth, as is usually the case, was more prosaic than any of the rumours. According to the text of Stalin's speech, which came to light in 1995, his main theme was as *Pravda* reported – the reform, reorganisation and re-equipment of the Red Army. However, the speech contained a number of details about the reforms and about the Red Army's strength – not the kind of information to make public on the eve of war. Stalin also spoke critically of the German army, denying that it was as invincible as it seemed and arguing that it would not be as successful in the future as it had been in the past if it fought under the banner of aggression and conquest. Again, remarks that it would not have been politic to publish when Stalin was trying to persuade Hitler of his peaceful intentions.

After the graduation ceremony there was a reception in the Kremlin at which Stalin, as usual, proposed several toasts. Some of his pre-toast remarks have been preserved for posterity. According to Dimitrov, for example, Stalin 'was in an exceptionally good mood' and said 'our policy of peace and security is at the same time a policy of preparation for war. There is no defence without offence. The army must be trained in a spirit of offensive action. We must prepare for war.' Another observer recorded Stalin saying 'good defence means attack. The offensive is the best defence.' According to the official record Stalin also said:

The policy of peace is a good thing. We have up to now . . . carried out a line [based on] defence. . . And now, when our army has been reconstructed, has been amply supplied with equipment for modern battle, when we have become stronger, now it is necessary to go from defence to offence. Defending our country we must act offensively. From defence to go to a military doctrine of offensive actions. We must transform our training, our propaganda, our agitation, our press in an offensive spirit. The Red Army is a modern army, and a modern army is an offensive army.

Was this statement a call to arms, a rallying of the troops for a pre-emptive strike, a signal to the General Staff to draw up the necessary plans? It is not credible that Stalin would have signalled any such intentions in such a public setting. Besides, the statement's pro-offence content was not that different from Stalin's private remarks a year earlier to the command conference on the experience of the Finnish war. More credible is that Stalin wanted to impress upon his young officers the need for an attacking spirit and probably saw his casual remarks as a boost to morale, a confidence-building fillip in face of the impending war with Germany. But that is a long way from planning and preparing to provoke such a war.

After Stalin's speech the pace of Soviet war preparations picked up but they were not of the scale and character necessary to make a pre-emptive strike in summer 1941.[61] In this connection some scholars have made much of the fact that on 24 May 1941 Stalin held a three-hour conference in his Kremlin office with virtually all his top military commanders. The suggestion is that this was the meeting that decided on a pre-emptive strike against Germany, a suspicion magnified by the absence of any subsequent information about what was discussed. However, according to his appointments diary, Stalin did not meet again with Timoshenko, his defence commissar, with Zhukov, his Chief of Staff, or with any of his generals for 10 days.[62] This was hardly behaviour consistent with implementing a momentous decision to launch an attack on Germany. It is more likely the conference on 24 May was simply part of the ongoing defensive preparations for war.

In retrospect the most common criticism of Stalin's behaviour during the last weeks of the Soviet–German peace has not been that he was preparing to attack but that he refused to bring the Red Army to a full state of alert in advance of the German invasion. Vasilevskii in his memoirs supported Stalin's policy of maintaining peace for as long as possible but argued that 'the whole problem . . . boiled down to the length of time we had to continue that policy. After all Nazi Germany actually had made war preparations on Soviet borders quite openly, especially in the last month; that was exactly the time when we should have carried out a speedy mobilization and transferred border districts to a full war footing, building up strong and deep-lying defences.'[63] In a posthumously published interview Vasilevskii defined the problem as one in which Stalin arrived at the Rubicon of war in June 1941 but failed to take the hard next step forward.[64] Zhukov, however, was of a different view: 'Vasilevskii's opinion does not fully correspond with reality. I believe that the Soviet Union would have been beaten early on if we had deployed all our forces on the borders on the eve of war, and the German troops would have been able to accomplish their plan, encircle and destroy them at the border . . . Then Hitler's troops could have stepped up the campaign and Moscow and

Leningrad would have fallen in 1941.'[65] In his memoirs Marshal Rokossovskii took this argument further when he said that the main force of the Red Army should not have been deployed on the border at all, but much deeper in Soviet territory. That way it would have avoided annihilation by the initial German attack and been in a position to conduct concentrated mobile counterattacks against the advancing Wehrmacht.[66]

The idea that the best way to deal with Operation Barbarossa would have been some kind of mobile strategic defence posture has also been canvassed by a number of western analysts, such as Cynthia A. Roberts. Whether the Red Army was capable of implementing such a strategy, or whether it would have worked out any better for the Soviets, is a matter of speculation. But whatever its alleged intrinsic merits, the concept of strategic defence had no place in the doctrinal universe of the Soviet High Command at the time. As Zhukov admitted in his memoirs, 'at that time our military-theoretical science generally did not consider the profound problems of strategic defence, mistakenly considering it not so important'.[67] When the Germans attacked on 22 June 1941 Timoshenko and Zhukov responded by issuing orders for the implementation of long-standing plans for offensive action. Even as the Germans drove deep into Soviet territory and arrived at the gates of Moscow and Leningrad, the Red Army's preferred counter-measure was to attack when and where they could. Eventually the Red Army learned the virtues of defence but only because it had to, and the doctrine of offensive action persisted throughout the war. In strategic terms the Red Army conducted a wholly offensive campaign on the Eastern Front. Only during the battle of Kursk in summer 1943 did the Red Army temporarily adopt a strategic defence posture, absorbing the great German tank offensive before launching a massive counterattack.

After the war the Red Army's retreats and defeats in 1941–1942 were sanitised and mythologised as all part of the great Stalin's plan to draw the German army deep into Russia in order to destroy it, much as the Tsar's generals had done to the French army during the Napoleonic war. After Stalin's death a more realistic and critical picture of the disaster of 22 June 1941 began to emerge. But the new myth was that it was Stalin's predilection for offensive action that was responsible for the disastrous attacking tactics of the Red Army during the early months of the war. In fact the cult of attack and counterattack represented a consensus in the Soviet High Command and responsibility for the doctrine and its consequences was shared by all.

The extent of the tragedy of 22 June 1941 from the Soviet point of view was summed up by the fate of the massive army Stalin had assembled to counter the German invasion. By the end of that year the Red Army had lost 200 divisions in battle and suffered over 4 million casualties. Among the losses were

142,000 officers (out of 440,000), including 40 generals killed and 44 captured.[68] Many contemporary observers expected the battle-hardened German army that had so easily conquered Poland and France to achieve similar results in Russia. Others thought the Soviets might have made a better fight of it. What surprised everyone, though, was that the Red Army could survive the enormous damage inflicted by the Germans and then begin to push back what had been the greatest invasion in military history.

War of Annihilation
Stalin versus Hitler

The German invasion of the Soviet Union began a little before dawn on Sunday 22 June 1941. Leading the assault across a 1,000-mile front were 152 German divisions, supported by 14 Finnish divisions in the north and 14 Romanian divisions in the south.[1] Later, the 3.5-million-strong invasion force was joined by armies from Hungary and Italy, by the Spanish 'Blue Division', by contingents from Croatia and Slovakia, and by volunteer units recruited from every country in Nazi-occupied Europe.

The invasion force was organised in three massed army groups: Army Group North attacked from East Prussia and fought its way along the Baltic coastal lands towards Leningrad; Army Group Centre advanced towards Minsk, Smolensk and Moscow; while Army Group South headed for the Ukraine and its capital, Kiev (*see Map 4 on p. 83*).

The strategic goals of the invasion had been set out by Hitler in his directive of 18 December 1940:

> The German Wehrmacht must be prepared to defeat Soviet Russia in one rapid campaign . . . The mass of the [Red] army stationed in Western Russia is to be destroyed in bold operations involving deep and rapid penetrations by panzer spearheads, and the withdrawal of combat-capable elements into the vast Russian interior is to be prevented . . . The Operation's final objective is the establishment of a defensive barrier against Russia running along the general line of the Volga to Arkhangel.[2]

The code name for the invasion was Operation Barbarossa, in honour of Frederick I ('Red Beard'), the Holy Roman Emperor who led a twelfth-century crusade to liberate Christianity's holy places from Muslim control. On 22 June Hitler declared he had attacked the USSR to pre-empt a Soviet strike against the Reich.[3] Thereafter Nazi propagandists presented the German

Operation Barbarossa, June–December 1941

Under German rule or influence by June 1941

General direction of the German advance

Occupied by German forces between June and December 1941

Cities besieged by Germans 1941

NORWAY

SWEDEN

FINLAND

Murmansk

Kandalaksha

Arkhangel

Lake Ladoga

Helsinki

Leningrad

Tikhvin

Vologda

Novgorod

Pskov

Gorkii

Riga

Dvina

Moscow

Smolensk

Riaizin

Baltic Sea

Danzig

Tula

Bialystok

Minsk

Orel

Warsaw

Pripiat Marshes

Dnepr

U S S R

Lublin

Kursk

Voronezh

Kiev

Belgorod

HUNGARY

Lvov

Kharkov

Stalingrad

Rostov

ROMANIA

Odessa

YUGOSLAVIA

Sebastopol

BULGARIA

Black Sea

GREECE

campaign in Russia as a defensive crusade against an unholy Bolshevik empire that threatened European civilisation.

The Nazi ideological framing of Operation Barbarossa signalled the kind of war the Germans planned to fight in Russia – a war of destruction and exter-mination, a *Vernichtungskrieg*.[4] Not only the Red Army, but the entire Soviet communist regime was to be destroyed. Driving this determination was the Nazi view of the USSR as a Judaeo-Bolshevik state – a communist regime under Jewish control, whose destruction necessitated the extermination of the Jewish cadres who ran the Soviet state. Nazi racist ideology also defined the Slavic peoples of the Soviet Union as an inferior race of *Untermenschen* or sub-humans, but the German attitude to the Slavs was more exploitative than specifically genocidal. As Hitler said later of the Slavs, 'our guiding prin-ciple is that the existence of these people is justified only by their economic exploitation for our benefit'.

The ideological and racist war that Hitler wanted to wage against Russia was incorporated into the military preparations for Operation Barbarossa. As Hitler told his generals on 30 March 1941, 'the war against Russia will be such that it cannot be conducted in a knightly fashion; the struggle is one of ideolo-gies and racial differences and will have to be conducted with unprecedented, unmerciful and unrelenting harshness.'[5]

In March 1941 agreement was reached between the Wehrmacht and the SS on the role of the *Einsatzgruppen* – the special 'action teams' that were to follow the German armies into Russia to eliminate 'Judaeo-Bolshevik' offi-cials, activists and intellectuals. On 13 May 1941 Hitler issued a decree which effectively exempted German soldiers from punishment for any atrocities they might commit in Russia. A few days later the Wehrmacht issued 'Guidelines for the behaviour of the fighting forces in Russia':

1. Bolshevism is the mortal enemy of the National Socialist German people. Germany's struggle is aimed at that disruptive ideology and its exponents.
2. That struggle demands ruthless and energetic action against Bolshevik agitators, guerrillas, saboteurs, Jews and the complete liquidation of any active or passive resistance.
3. Extreme reserve and the most alert vigilance are called for towards all the members of the Red Army – even prisoners – as treacherous methods of fighting are to be expected. The Asiatic soldiers of the Red Army in particular are inscrutable, unpredictable, insidious and unfeeling.

On 6 June the Wehrmacht issued 'Guidelines on the treatment of commissars'. This was the infamous 'Commissar Order', which dealt with the fate of commissars – the political officers of the Red Army – who 'if captured in battle, or while resisting, are as a matter of principle to be finished off with weapons at once'.

This ideological framing of the coming war with Russia helps to explain why the Germans imagined they could destroy the Red Army in the course of a single, lightning campaign. German military planners thought the Red Army had been significantly weakened by the prewar purges and had not been impressed by its performance during the Finnish war, but as important was their ideologically distorted perception of the political weakness of Stalin's regime. 'You only have to kick in the door and the whole rotten structure will come crashing down,' said Hitler.[6] Far from expecting serious resistance in Russia, the Germans envisaged they would be welcomed as liberators by large sections of the Soviet population

In the early days of Operation Barbarossa it seemed that Hitler's prediction of a quick and easy victory would be fulfilled. On day one the Luftwaffe struck 66 enemy airfields and destroyed 900 Soviet aircraft on the ground and another 300 in the air.[7] Within days the Germans had complete air superiority across the entire breadth of the battle zone. On 3 July General Franz Halder, Chief of the German Army General Staff, noted in his diary: 'on my part it would not be too bold to assert that the campaign against Russia has been won in the space of two weeks'.[8] Within three weeks the Soviets suffered three-quarters of a million casualties and lost 10,000 tanks and 4,000 aircraft. Within three months the Germans had captured Kiev, encircled Leningrad and reached the gates of Moscow.[9]

The Germans employed much the same tactics as they had in Poland and France. Concentrated columns of powerful armoured divisions punched their way through enemy defences and encircled Soviet forces from the rear. The German panzers were followed by infantry divisions tasked to destroy encir-cled enemy forces and to hold captured territory. In the June encirclement of Minsk the Germans bagged 400,000 Soviet prisoners. In July it was the turn of Smolensk (300,000 prisoners) and in September Kiev (500,000 prisoners) to fall to German encirclement. In October the Briansk and Viazma encir-clements near Moscow netted another half-million or more Soviet soldiers (*see Map 5 on p. 86*). By the end of 1941 the Germans had captured 3 million Soviet prisoners. By February 1942, 2 million of those POWs were dead, mainly from starvation, disease and maltreatment. In addition, the Germans simply executed those prisoners they suspected were communists. By the end of the Eastern Front war 160,000 captured 'commissars' had been killed by the Germans.

German Encirclement of Soviet Troops, 1941

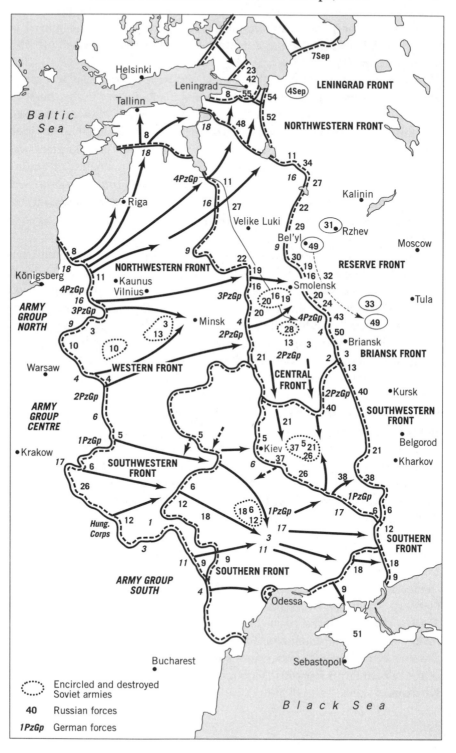

Helsinki

7Sep

23
42

Leningrad

8
55
54

LENINGRAD FRONT

(4Sep)

Tallinn

Baltic
Sea

18
8

18
48
52

NORTHWESTERN FRONT

Riga

4PzGp
11
11
16

11
34
27

Kalinin

16
27

16
22

Velike Luki

29

(31) Rzhev

Moscow

Königsberg
11
Kaunus
Vilnius

NORTHWESTERN FRONT

9
22
19

Bel'yl
30

19
16

(49)

RESERVE FRONT

19
32

16
20
24

(33)
Tula

(49)

**ARMY
GROUP
NORTH**
4PzGp
16
3PzGp

3PzGp
16
20

20
16
19

Smolensk

9
3
10
(10)
(13)
(3)
Minsk
4
2PzGp

4PzGp
28
13
3
4

(28)

43
50

Briansk

Warsaw
4
4

WESTERN FRONT

21
2PzGp

2
13

BRIANSK FRONT

3

**ARMY
GROUP
CENTRE**
2PzGp
6

**CENTRAL
FRONT**

2PzGp
40

Kursk

40

**SOUTHWESTERN
FRONT**

1PzGp
5
Krakow
17
5

**SOUTHWESTERN
FRONT**

6
6

5
Kiev
37
37

(37) 5 21
26

21

Belgorod

Kharkov

26
26
5
18 6
12
38
38

1PzGp

Hung.
Corps
12
1

12
18
(18 6
12)
1PzGp
17

17

6
6

3
1
9

**SOUTHERN
FRONT**

17
11

12

**SOUTHERN
FRONT**

11
9

SOUTHERN FRONT

18
18
9

**ARMY GROUP
SOUTH**

4
Odessa
9

Bucharest

51

Sebastopol

⬭ Encircled and destroyed
Soviet armies

40   Russian forces

1PzGp   German forces

Black Sea

The fate of the Soviet POWs was shared by many other Soviet citizens, above all those of Jewish origin. About a million Soviet Jews were massacred by the Germans, mostly during 1941–1942.[10] The main instrument of this mass murder were the SS *Einsatzgruppen*. Initially, the *Einsatzgruppen* were tasked with killing able-bodied Jewish men. However, in August 1941, Himmler, the SS Chief, gave the order for the wholesale slaughter of entire Jewish communities to commence – men and women, parents and children, old and young, the sick and the healthy. Illustrative of the change of policy was the shooting of 30,000 Jews at Babi Yar, a ravine outside Kiev, at the end of September 1941.

The reason for this transition from the selective killing of Jewish males to the mass murder of all Jews has been the subject of extensive discussion among historians of the Holocaust.[11] It seems to have been connected to the escalation of the Germans' anti-partisan tactics. Soviet partisan actions in the rear of the invading German armies began within days of the outbreak of the war, often initiated, inspired and aided by retreating Red Army units fighting their way out of encirclement. The German response – as in Greece, Yugoslavia and Poland – was to burn villages and execute those suspected of aiding the partisans. In September 1941 the Wehrmacht issued orders that between 50 and 100 'communists' should be killed for every German who fell victim to a partisan attack.

There was an intimate connection between the Wehrmacht's anti-partisan tactics and the anti-Jewish campaign of the SS. All Jews were stigmatised as communists and partisans, and all partisans branded Jews. 'The Jew is a partisan. The Partisan is a Jew.' 'A Jew is a Bolshevik is a partisan.' These were the German slogans that served the dual purpose of rationalising the mass murder of Soviet Jews and legitimising the harsh and indiscriminate anti-partisan measures.[12] The Babi Yar massacre, for example, was ostensibly in retaliation for the killing of a number of German officers, blown up by delayed-action time bombs left by the retreating Red Army in the centre of Kiev.

Notwithstanding their spectacular successes, the tide of war did not flow entirely in the Germans' direction. Not all Soviet defences crumbled. Some positions held and fought on for weeks, months even. In the Brest fortress on the border with German-occupied Poland 3,000 Soviet soldiers fought almost to the last man, holding out for a week against an assault by 20,000 Germans. Odessa, the Soviet Navy's main port on the Black Sea, held out against an attack by the 4th Romanian army for nearly 10 weeks between August and October 1941. Its sister port of Sebastopol faced an even greater onslaught but did not fall until summer 1942. While millions of Soviet soldiers were taken prisoner, tens of thousands of others – individuals, small groups, platoons, battalions, brigades and whole divisions – fought their way out of encirclement to rejoin the main body of the Red Army.[13] The Soviets launched numerous counterattacks, forcing the Germans to retreat and regroup on many occasions. The Soviet defence of Kiev held up the German advance on Eastern Ukraine for nearly a month, while the battles in the Smolensk region in July–August 1941 held up the German advance on Moscow for two months. Fierce counterattacks in the Leningrad area thwarted Hitler's aim to capture and raze to the ground the Soviet Union's second city.

The ferocity of the fighting shook the Germans out of their initial complacency about an easy war. By 11 August General Halder was beginning to have his doubts: 'At the beginning of the war we calculated that there would be about 200 enemy divisions against us. But already we have counted 360. These divisions are not armed and equipped according to our understanding of these words and their tactical leadership is not very satisfactory. But they exist. If we destroy a dozen the Russians present us with another dozen.'[14]

The price the Red Army exacted for German victories was very high. In the first three weeks of war the Germans suffered 100,000 casualties, and lost 1,700 tanks and assault weapons and 950 planes. By July they were suffering 7,000 casualties a day. By August total casualties were nearly 180,000.[15] These were nothing compared to the astronomical Soviet losses but were nevertheless far higher than the Germans were used to. During the course of the entire West European campaign of 1940, total German losses were only 156,000, including 30,000 dead.[16] Crucially, despite its spectacular advance into Russia, the Wehrmacht failed to achieve its strategic objectives. Leningrad was besieged but it did not fall. The German advance in the south reached Rostov-on-Don – the gateway to the Caucasus and oilfields of Baku – but ran out of steam and by the end of November the city had been recaptured by the Russians.

Hitler's last chance to win the war in the course of a single campaign was to capture Moscow. The Germans launched their assault on the Soviet capital in October 1941, utilising more than 70 divisions – a million men, with 1,700 tanks, 14,000 artillery pieces and almost 1,000 aeroplanes. The attack brought Army Group Centre to within 20 miles of the Kremlin, but no further. On 5 December the Red Army launched a counter-offensive in front of Moscow, which pushed the Germans 40–50 miles back from the city. It was the Wehrmacht's first significant defeat of the Second World War. It signalled that Operation Barbarossa had failed and that Hitler now faced a long war of attrition on the Eastern Front. As two wartime observers of events concluded, 'the Russian campaign of 1941 was a serious *strategic* defeat for the Germans'.[17]

By December 1941 the European war had been transformed into a global war. Following the Japanese attack on Pearl Harbor on 7 December the United States was locked in combat with Germany's ally in the Far East, and Hitler's declaration of war on America on 11 December brought the US into the European theatre. This set the seal on the American–British–Soviet coalition that had been forming since summer 1941. In these new circumstances Hitler began to consider what resources he would need to sustain a global war against the allied coalition. His gaze fell increasingly on the oil, industry and raw materials of the Ukraine, southern Russia and the Caucasus.

Stalin's Response to the German Attack

An oft-told tale about Stalin's response to Operation Barbarossa is that he was shocked and surprised by the German attack, refused to believe that it was happening and then descended into a depression which he did not snap out of until urged to do so by his Politburo colleagues. As with so many stories about Stalin, the origin of this one is Khrushchev's secret speech to the 20th party congress in 1956:

> It would be incorrect to forget that after the first severe disaster and defeats at the front, Stalin thought this was the end. In one of his speeches in those days he said: 'All that which Lenin created we have lost forever'. After this Stalin for a long time actually did not direct the military operations and ceased to do anything whatever. He returned to active service only when some members of the Political Bureau visited him and told him that it was necessary to take certain steps immediately in order to improve the situation at the front.[18]

Khrushchev – who was in Kiev when the war began – elaborated on the story in his memoirs, reporting that Beria told him that Stalin had at one point resigned the leadership and retreated to his dacha in despair.[19]

Another version of this particular incident was put forward in the memoirs of Anastas Mikoyan, Stalin's Trade Minister. According to Mikoyan the Politburo members went to Stalin's dacha and told their skulking leader that they had decided to create a State Defence Committee which they wanted him to head up. The instigators of this action were Beria and Molotov, said Mikoyan.[20] However, as Roy and Zhores Medvedev have argued, this is a most unlikely story. Molotov and Beria were among the most submissive of Stalin's inner circle and would not have dared to be so forthright.[21] Then there is the testimony of Yakov Chadaev, which broadly backs up Mikoyan's story that the Politburo members went to see Stalin at his dacha and, led by Molotov, asked him to come back to work. However, Chadaev's account of this incident is not that of an eyewitness but based on hearsay. Chadaev's direct reportage of his memory of Stalin's state of mind during the first few days of war gives the impression that the Soviet dictator's behaviour was highly contradictory: on the one hand, strong and decisive; on the other, reticent and faltering.[22] Furthermore, in an interview in 1982 Chadaev stated the following in response to a question about Stalin's behaviour during the first months of the war: 'During the days of crisis, of critical situations on the front, Stalin controlled himself very well on the whole, displaying confidence and calmness and demonstrating great industriousness.'[23] Other memoir evidence includes Molotov's response when asked about the episode at the dacha: 'Stalin was in a very agitated state. He didn't curse, but he wasn't quite himself. I wouldn't say that he lost his head. He suffered, but didn't show any signs of this. Undoubtedly he had his rough moments. It's nonsense to say he didn't suffer. But he is not portrayed as he really was . . . As usual he worked day and night and never lost his head or his gift of speech. How did he comport himself? As Stalin was supposed to, firmly.'[24] According to Zhukov, 'Stalin himself was strong-willed and no coward. It was only once I saw him somewhat depressed. That was the dawn of June 22, 1941, when his belief that the war could be avoided was shattered. After June 22, 1941, and throughout the war Stalin firmly governed the country . . .'[25] When Lazar Kaganovich, another Politburo member, was asked if Stalin had lost his nerve when the war broke out, he replied 'it's a lie!'[26] Molotov and Kaganovich were diehard Stalin loyalists, whereas Khrushchev and Mikoyan were apostates who led the anti-Stalinist struggles of the 1950s. Zhukov was purged by Stalin after the war, but fell out with Khrushchev in 1957 and then found himself on the receiving end of Khrushchevite accusations about *his* conduct of the war.

Perhaps a better guide to Stalin's personal response to the German attack is the contemporary evidence of his actions during the first days of the war. According to his appointments diary, when war broke out Stalin held numerous meetings with members of the Soviet military and political leadership.[27] The early days of the war required many decisions by Stalin. On the day war broke out he authorised 20 different decrees and orders.[28] On 23 June he established a Stavka (Headquarters) of the Main Command, a mixed political and military body – chaired by Defence Commissar Timoshenko – to oversee the strategic direction of the war. On 24 June it was resolved to establish a Council of Evacuation to organise the evacuation of people and materials from the war zone and to create a Soviet Information Buro (Sovinform) to co-ordinate and direct the propaganda war.[29] On 29 June Stalin issued an urgent directive to party and state organisations in frontline areas, ordering them to fight to the last drop of blood in defence of every inch of Soviet soil. The supplies and rear areas of the Red Army were to be fully protected and all cowards and panic-mongers immediately arraigned before military tribunals. Partisan detachments were to be formed in enemy-occupied areas and in the event of forced retreat a scorched earth policy was to be followed and the enemy was to be left no roads, railways, factories or food supplies that they could make use of. These instructions formed the basis of the text of a radio broadcast by Stalin to the Soviet people a few days later.[30]

On 22 June the day began in Stalin's office at 5.45 a.m. when Molotov returned from a meeting with Schulenburg bearing news of the German declaration of war.[31] One of the first decisions was that Molotov rather than Stalin should give a radio address to the nation at midday. According to Molotov, Stalin decided to wait until the situation clarified itself before making his own speech to the country.[32] Molotov's draft of his speech was heavily edited by Stalin on the spot. He expanded its content in a number of ways. First, Molotov was to state at the outset that he was speaking on Stalin's behalf and then to call in his conclusion for the country to rally round Stalin's leadership. Second, Molotov was to make clear that the Soviet Union had not infringed the non-aggression pact with Germany in any way. Third, Molotov was to stress that the war had been forced on the Soviet Union not by the German workers, peasants or intelligentsia but by the German fascists who had also enslaved France, Poland, Yugoslavia, Norway, Belgium, Denmark, the Netherlands, Greece and other countries. Fourth, Molotov was to compare Hitler's invasion of Russia with that of Napoleon and to call for a patriotic war in defence of the motherland. Whilst Stalin's emendations were extensive, the most memorable lines of the speech – its concluding peroration which became one of the main propaganda slogans of the Soviet war effort – appear to have been Molotov's own: 'Our cause is just. The enemy will be defeated. Victory will be ours.'[33]

Another early visitor to Stalin's office that day was Comintern leader Georgi Dimitrov, who recorded in his diary:

At 7.00 a.m. I was urgently summoned to the Kremlin . . . Striking calmness, resoluteness, confidence of Stalin and all the others . . . For now the Comintern is not to take any overt action. The parties in the localities are mounting a movement in defence of the USSR. The issue of socialist revolution is not to be raised. The Soviet people are waging a patriotic war against fascist Germany. It is a matter of routing fascism, which has enslaved a number of peoples and is bent on enslaving still more.[34]

In and out of Stalin's office that day was Deputy Foreign Commissar, Andrei Vyshinskii, who reported on diplomatic developments. He had some good news. From London Maiskii had telegraphed Foreign Secretary Anthony Eden's reassurance that Britain would fight on and that there was no question of London concluding a separate peace with Germany, regardless of the rumours arising out of the Hess mission. Eden also informed Maiskii that

Churchill would speak that evening on the radio about the German attack and about Anglo-Soviet relations.[35] Churchill's broadcast must have come as a considerable relief to Stalin:

> No one has been a more consistent opponent of Communism than I have for the last 25 years. I will unsay no word that I have spoken about it. But all this fades away with the spectacle that is now unfolding. The past with its crimes, its follies and its tragedies flashes away . . . We have but one aim and one single, irrevocable purpose. We are resolved to destroy Hitler and every vestige of the Nazi regime. From this nothing will turn us, nothing . . . . It follows, therefore that we shall give whatever help we can to Russia and the Russian people . . . if Hitler imagines that his attack on Soviet Russia will cause the slightest division of aims or slackening of effort in the great Democracies who are resolved upon his doom, he is woefully mistaken . . . His invasion of Russia is no more than a prelude to an attempted invasion of the British Isles . . . The Russian danger is therefore our danger and the danger of the United States, just as the cause of any Russian fighting for his hearth and home is the cause of free men and free peoples in every quarter of the globe.[36]

The United States was ostensibly neutral but had been supplying substantial aid to Britain for nearly a year and, at a White House press conference on 24 June, Roosevelt announced that this policy would be extended to the Soviet Union.[37] On 12 July Britain and the Soviet Union signed an agreement on joint action in the war against Germany and pledged that neither side would conduct separate negotiations with Hitler about an armistice or a peace treaty.[38] At the end of July Roosevelt sent his personal representative, Harry Hopkins, to Moscow to discuss with Stalin the supply of American aid for the Soviet war effort.[39] In early August the two states exchanged notes which formalised the US pledge to supply the USSR with war materials.[40] At the end of September Lord Beaverbrook, the British Supplies Minister, travelled to Moscow with Averell Harriman, Roosevelt's lend-lease administrator in London, to sign a formal agreement on Anglo-American supplies to Russia.[41]

But the most important developments and decisions were being made on the military front. In the early hours of 22 June Timoshenko and Zhukov had issued a directive warning of a surprise German attack. Border districts of the Red Army were ordered to bring their forces to a state of full combat readiness and to disperse and camouflage aircraft before dawn on 22 June. At the same time commanders were ordered to avoid any 'provocative actions'. Following a meeting with Stalin in the Kremlin, a second directive was issued by Timoshenko and Zhukov at 7.15 a.m. Reporting on German air and artillery attacks, troops were ordered to attack the Germans where they had crossed the Soviet border but not to cross the frontier themselves without special authorisation. At 9.15 p.m. Timoshenko and Zhukov issued a third directive, ordering the North-Western and Western Fronts of the Red Army to attack, encircle and destroy Army Group North and the South-Western Front to attack and encircle Army Group South. The Red Army's Northern and Southern Fronts (respectively bordering Finland and Romania) were ordered to remain on the defensive. The Western Front was instructed to contain Army Group Centre's advance along the Warsaw–Minsk axis while assisting the offensive action of the North-Western Front.[42] This directive was broadly in line with prewar plans for Red Army counter-offensive action in the event of war. It indicates that Stalin and the High Command fully expected the Red Army would be able to cope with the German attack and to carry out its own strategic missions, including mounting an effective counter-invasion of German territory. Indeed, according to the third directive, the Red Army was expected to achieve its initial objectives in East Prussia and southern Poland within two days. In line with these expectations Zhukov was immediately dispatched to Kiev to oversee the offensive operations on the South-Western Front, where the bulk of Soviet forces had been concentrated in anticipation of a main force German advance on the Ukraine. Shaposhnikov, the former Chief of the General Staff, and Kulik, Chief of Soviet artillery, were sent to help out on the Western Front.[43] The calm and confidence underlying these initial moves were noted by General Shtemenko in his memoirs: 'From the outset the atmosphere at the General Staff, though tense, was businesslike. None of us doubted that Hitler's surprise tactics could give him only a temporary advantage. Both chiefs and their subordinates acted with their usual confidence.'[44] Confidence in victory was shared by the general Soviet population. In Moscow many people were amazed that the Germans had dared to attack, while thousands more flocked to join the armed forces and people's militias.[45]

When the Soviet counter-offensives of 23–25 June failed to make any significant progress and the Wehrmacht continued to advance on all fronts, it became apparent that the General Staff had grossly underestimated the weight of the initial German attack. As Zhukov noted in his memoirs:

We did not foresee the large-scale surprise offensive launched at once by all available forces which had been deployed in advance in all major strategic directions. In short, we did not envisage the nature of the blow in its entirety. Neither the People's Commissar, nor myself or my predecessors – B.M. Shaposhnikov, K.A. Meretskov nor the General Staff top officers – expected the enemy to concentrate such huge numbers of armoured and motorised troops and, on the first day, to commit them to action in powerful compact groupings in all strategic directions with the aim of striking powerful wedging blows.[46]

For Stalin the awful realisation that not all was going to plan came with reports that Minsk, the capital of Belorussia, had fallen to the Germans. According to Zhukov (back in Moscow after the failure of the South-Western Front's counter-offensive) Stalin visited the People's Commissariat of Defence twice on 29 June to express his concern about the situation that had developed on the Western Front.[47] By 30 June not only had Minsk fallen but the best part of four Soviet armies had been encircled west of the Belorussian capital and 'the [Soviet] Western Front virtually ceased to exist as an organised force'.[48] That same day Stalin issued a decree establishing a State Defence Committee (GKO – *Gosudarstvennyi Komitet Oborony*) that he would chair himself.[49]

The formation of the GKO was announced by Stalin in his radio broadcast of 3 July. According to some reports Stalin's delivery was hesitant and halting (he never was a great public speaker) but as a text – which was published in all Soviet newspapers that day – it was a bravura performance. Stalin began his speech with the salutation 'Comrades! Citizens! Brothers and Sisters! Fighters of our army and navy! It is to you that I am appealing, my friends!' Stalin emphasised the immense danger facing the country, revealing that the enemy had already captured large tracts of Soviet territory. How had this situation come about? asked Stalin. 'The fact of the matter is that the troops of Germany, a country at war, were already fully mobilised and the 170 divisions brought to the Soviet frontiers and hurled against the USSR were in a state of complete readiness . . . whereas the Soviet troops had still to effect mobilisation and move up to the frontiers.' Was the Nazi–Soviet pact a mistake? No, said Stalin, it had gained the country time and space to prepare for war and while the Germans had made short-term military gains from their surprise attack, politically they had exposed themselves yet again as bloodthirsty aggressors. Stalin emphasised that it was a patriotic war, in defence not only of the Soviet system but of the national culture and national existence of 'the Russians, the Ukrainians, Byelorussians, Lithuanians, Latvians, Estonians, Uzbeks, Tartars, Moldavians, Georgians, Armenians, Azerbaijanians and the other free peoples' of the USSR. Equally pronounced was Stalin's emphasis on the anti-fascist theme and his insistence that the war was a struggle for the liberation of Europe from German domination, one that would be waged in conjunction with Britain and the United States. Although Stalin's tone was urgent it was also confident. He denied that the Germans were invincible, pointing out that only in the Soviet Union had they encountered serious resistance. 'Comrades, our forces are numberless. The overweening enemy will soon learn this to his cost.'[50] The popular reaction to Stalin's speech was mixed but on the whole positive, at least in Moscow, where party and police reports noted its role in lifting morale and inspiring patriotic enthusiasm.[51]

Behind the brave words, however, the military situation was going from bad to worse. By mid-July the Red Army had lost 28 divisions, while another 70 had lost half their men and equipment and the Germans had penetrated 300–600 kilometres into Russia across a broad front.[52]

Coping with Catastrophe

During his political career Stalin had faced many emergencies: the 1917 Revolution, the civil war, the collectivisation of Soviet agriculture, the industrialisation drive, the 1930s hunt for the enemy within, the prewar crisis and, now, the disintegration of Soviet defence plans. His response to this latest emergency was typical: reorganisation, purges, personnel changes and the concentration of more and more direct decision-making power in his own hands.

The State Defence Committee, or GKO, stood at the pinnacle of Stalin's decision-making system during the war (*see Figure on p. 96*). As a sort of war cabinet chaired by Stalin, it was a political body charged with directing and controlling all aspects of the Soviet war effort. Initial members were Foreign Commissar Molotov, security chief Lavrentii Beria, Politburo member Georgii Malenkov and Marshal Voroshilov, Stalin's long-time military crony. Although the party's Politburo continued to exist and function in a formal sense during the war, it rarely met as a body and the GKO in effect took its place as the highest collective body of the Soviet leadership. Subordinate to the GKO was the Council of People's Commissars and the various government ministries and state planning bodies.

On 10 July the Stavka, or headquarters, of the Main Command was reorganised as the Stavka of the High Command with Stalin in the chair. On 8 August it was renamed Stavka of the Supreme Command (*Stavka Verkhovnogo Glavnokommandovaniya*) and Stalin became Supreme Commander of the Armed Forces.[53] Supported by the General Staff, Stavka was responsible for military strategy and for the planning, preparation and conduct of big operations.

The top level of Soviet war organisation was completed by the People's Commissariat of Defence (NKO: *Narodnyi Kommissariat Oborony*). Stalin was appointed People's Commissar for Defence on 19 July 1941.[54] The NKO consisted of a number of directorates – Artillery, Armour, Airborne, Air Defence, Communications, Reserve Forces, Rear Area Service, Education, Military Intelligence and Counterintelligence, and Propaganda – which served as organs of the GKO.[55]

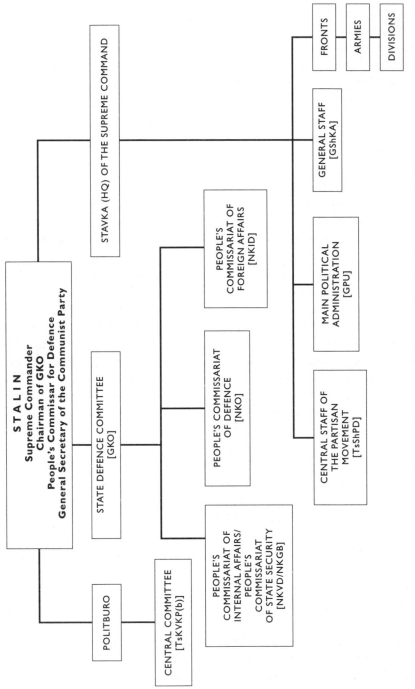

Figure: *The structure of Soviet military and political decision-making during the Great Patriotic War*

The effect of this reorganisation was formally to unify in the person of Stalin the control and direction of the entire Soviet war effort. Stalin's personal control over his country's war effort was more extensive and more complete than that of any of the other warlords of the Second World War. In practice, however, Stalin concentrated on military decision-making. He supervised and took many decisions in relation to other areas of state activity, but he tended to devolve initiative and responsibility to trusted subordinates such as Beria (internal security), Nikolai Voznesenskii (the economy), Mikoyan (supplies), and Lazar' Kaganovich (transport). Only in foreign policy was Stalin's decision-making as continuous and detailed as in the military domain and Molotov remained Stalin's closest associate, spending more time than anyone else with the Soviet dictator during the war.

The reorganisation of the armed forces was equally drastic. On 10 July the five 'Fronts' of the Red Army (Northern, North-Western, Western, South-Western and Southern) were reduced to three multi-front strategic 'Directions' (*Napravlenii*). Marshal Voroshilov was sent to command the North-Western Direction, Marshal Timoshenko to the Western Direction, and Marshal Budennyi to the South-Western Direction.[56] On 15 July Stavka issued a directive abolishing the large mechanised corps formed only a year earlier and reallocated the reduced-in-size tank divisions to an infantry support role. The Directions were ordered to abolish large, unwieldy armies and replace them with smaller and more flexible field armies of no more than five or six divisions. The directive also envisaged the establishment of a number of highly mobile cavalry units to strike at the rear of the enemy, disorganising the Germans' command and control systems and attacking supply lines.[57]

On 16 July the political propaganda directorate of the NKO was reorganised as the Main Political Administration of the Red Army (GPU: *Glavnoe Politicheskoe Upravlenie RKKA*). Simultaneously, the Institution of Military Commissars was reintroduced into the armed forces.[58] This meant that political officers would once again have the power to veto command decisions and would act as deputy commanders at every level of the armed forces. On 20 July Stalin and the new head of the GPU, General Lev Mekhlis, issued a directive to all political commissars on the gravity of the situation, stressing the commissars' special responsibility for maintaining discipline in the armed forces and for dealing harshly with cowards, deserters and panic-mongers. There could be no retreats without authorisation and it was the commissars' personal responsibility to ensure this policy was carried out.[59] This directive was one of a series issued by Stalin that reflected his belief that the Red Army's initial defeats and retreats were caused partly by indiscipline, particularly among those in command positions. On 17 July a GKO resolution established a special department (*Osobyi Otdel'*) of the NKVD (*Narodnyi Kommissariat*

Innostrannyk Del – People's Commissariat of Internal Affairs) charged with the struggle against spies and traitors in the Red Army and armed with the authority to execute deserters on the spot.[60] On 16 August Stalin issued Order 270 – a directive to all members of the armed forces instructing them that cowards and deserters were to be eliminated and that any commander displaying 'shyness' in the face of battle was to be immediately replaced. Units finding themselves encircled were instructed to fight to the last man. Most harshly, Stalin announced that henceforth the families of cowards, deserters and traitors would be liable to arrest.[61] On 12 September Stalin directed front-line commanders to form 'blocking detachments' (*zagraditel'nye otriady*) to stop Red Army soldiers from fleeing to the rear and to liquidate the instigators of panic and desertion. Interestingly, Stalin also stipulated that the role of these detachments was to support those soldiers who refused to succumb to panic and the fear of encirclement.[62]

Stalin's determination to impose a harsh disciplinary regime on his armed forces was demonstrated by his purge of the senior commanders of the ill-fated Western Front that suffered such catastrophic defeat at Minsk. Heading the list of those arrested was General Dmitrii Pavlov, the Commander-in-Chief of the Western Front. In a GKO resolution of 16 July announcing the arrests Stalin made it clear that he was delivering an object lesson for any senior officer who broke discipline.[63] When he was arrested in early July Pavlov was accused of involvement in an anti-Soviet conspiracy – much as Tukhachevskii had been in 1937 – but when the military tribunal sentenced him to death on 22 July it was for cowardice, panic-mongering, criminal negligence and unauthorised retreats.[64] The other group of senior commanders to fall victim to Stalin's wrath was a number of high-ranking officers of the Red Air Force, arrested and blamed for the devastating attacks of the Luftwaffe on Soviet airfields on 22 June 1941. Among those arrested were Generals Proskurov, Ptukhin, Rychagov and Smushkevich, all shot without trial in October 1941.[65] Almost a victim of Stalin's purge, the former Chief of the General Staff, Meretskov, was arrested when Pavlov was tortured into naming him as a co-conspirator in an anti-Soviet plot. However, although Meretskov was subjected to a severe interrogation by the NKVD he was released without charge and, in September, sent back to his old stamping ground of Leningrad, where he served as a Stavka representative until his transfer to the Far Eastern theatre in 1945.[66]

Pavlov's replacement as commander of the Western Front was General A.I. Yeremenko. When the fronts were reorganised into Directions in mid-July Yeremenko retained his command but Timoshenko was made overall commander of the Western Direction (i.e. the Minsk–Smolensk–Moscow axis) and Shaposhnikov was appointed his Chief of Staff.[67] At the end of July,

Shaposhnikov was recalled to Moscow to replace Zhukov as Chief of the General Staff. Zhukov's new appointment was the command of two reserve armies forming up behind the Western Direction in the central sector in front of Moscow.[68] Zhukov's new command was an important assignment – to take part in a major counter-offensive against Army Group Centre in the Smolensk region, in his case an operation centred on the city of Yel'nya. As Zhukov noted in his memoirs, 'the Yel'nya operation was my first independent operation, the first test of my operational-strategic ability in the great war with Hitlerite Germany'.[69] The operation began in mid-August and by early September Zhukov's forces had recaptured the city and regained a sizeable chunk of territory from the Germans.[70] In the Soviet press the success at Yel'nya was hailed as a great victory and arrangements were made for foreign correspondents to visit the battlefield.[71]

The Yel'nya offensive was one of a complex series of Red Army operations in the Smolensk region in summer 1941. The city itself fell to the Germans in mid-July but fierce battles continued to rage in the area. At stake for Soviet troops was blocking the Germans' path to Moscow – less than 200 miles from Smolensk. However, Stavka did not fight a defensive battle at Smolensk; its strategy was offensive and took the form of numerous counter-strokes, counterattacks, and counter-offensives like the one at Yel'nya. Often criticised, in retrospect, the strategy had its successes. The Germans were held up at Smolensk for two months and the difficulties experienced by the Wehrmacht persuaded Hitler to delay his march on Moscow and to divert forces to the seemingly softer targets of Leningrad in the north and Kiev in the south. The psychological boost to the Red Army of halting and in some places throwing back the advance of Army Group Centre was also significant. But the cost of these achievements was very high. Zhukov's 100,000-strong army, for example, suffered one third casualties in the Yel'nya operation and when the Germans resumed their thrust to Moscow at the end of September the Red Army was unable to hold the ground it had recaptured at such great cost just a few weeks earlier.[72] The Red Army's total losses in the two-month struggle with the Germans in the Smolensk region approached half a million dead or missing, with another quarter of a million wounded.[73]

This pattern of costly Soviet offensives that achieved little except to delay the German advance was repeated across the Eastern Front throughout summer 1941. It is a strategy that has been criticised severely, the main suggestion being that a defensive orientation would have been more effective and less costly and that timely withdrawal would have been wiser than standing ground and fighting to the last man. Particular fire has been directed against Stalin, who is accused of being the moving spirit behind the Red Army's offensive orientation in summer 1941. However, the doctrine of offensive action was not Stalin's personal creation or responsibility but part of the Red Army's strategic tradition and military culture. Stalin embraced it, not least because it was a strategy and style that chimed with his politics and ideology. Stalin was above all a voluntarist – a believer in the transformative power of human will and determination. The military goals he set for the Red Army were as demanding and ambitious as the economic and political targets he expected his industrial managers and party cadres to achieve. 'There are no fortresses that Bolsheviks cannot storm' was a party slogan close to Stalin's heart, and he constantly invoked the maxim that once the correct policy had been decided (usually by himself) organisation and cadres 'determine all'. Unfortunately, Stalin's military commanders were no more capable of meeting his triumphalist expectations than were his economic or political cadres of meeting their tragets. As David Glantz has argued, 'Stavka thoroughly misunderstood the capabilities of its own forces and those of the Wehrmacht . . . it congenitally overestimated the former and underestimated the latter. Consequently, the Stavka assigned its forces unrealistic missions; the results were predictably disastrous . . . Stavka's misconceptions about what its forces could accomplish produced ever more spectacular defeats.'[74]

Stalin fully shared these misconceptions and, as Supreme Commander, bore ultimate responsibility for their disastrous practical consequences. As A.J.P. Taylor noted, Stalin's dedication to the doctrine of the offensive 'brought upon the Soviet armies greater catastrophes than any other armies have ever known'.[75] There were many occasions, too, when it was Stalin's personal insistence on the policy of no retreat and of counterattack at all costs that resulted in heavy Soviet losses. The best-known example of this is the disaster at Kiev in September 1941.

Because it had been allocated the major share of the Red Army's frontline divisions, including much of its armour, Stavka's South-Western Front was more successful in slowing the German advance after 22 June 1941 than its counterparts in central and northern Russia. Nevertheless, by early August Army Group South was approaching Kiev and Stalin's military advisers began warning him that a withdrawal from the Ukrainian capital might become necessary.[76] On 18 August, however, Stalin and Stavka issued a directive that Kiev must not be taken by the enemy.[77] By the end of August the Red Army had been forced back to a line of defence along the River Dnepr and Kiev now lay exposed at the end of a long and vulnerable salient. At this point General Heinz Guderian – the famed German tank commander – and his 2nd Panzer Army was detached by Hitler from Army Group Centre and ordered south to attack the South-Western Front from the rear and threaten the encirclement of Soviet forces in and around Kiev. Stavka observed this move but Stalin was confident that a newly formed Briansk Front under Yeremenko's command would be able to deal with the threat. On 24 August there was a telegraph exchange with Yeremenko in which Stalin asked him if the allocation of additional forces to his front would enable him to destroy the 'scoundrel' Guderian. Yeremenko replied: 'As regards this scoundrel Guderian, have no doubt that we will endeavour to fulfil the task you have given us of destroying him.'[78] By 2 September, however, Stalin was beginning to have his doubts and sent Yeremenko the following message: 'Stavka is still not happy with your work ... Guderian and his whole group must be smashed to smithereens. Until this is done all your assurances of success are worthless. We await your reports of the destruction of the Guderian group.'[79] According to Vasilevskii, on 7 September the Military Council of the South-Western Front requested permission to withdraw some forces to the Desna River to protect their right flank from Guderian's advance. Vasilevskii and Shaposhnikov went to Stalin with this proposal, intent on convincing him that the abandonment of Kiev and a withdrawal east of the Dnepr were long overdue. 'The conversation was tough and uncompromising,' recalled Vasilevskii. 'Stalin reproached us saying that like [Marshal Budennyi], we took the line of least resistance – retreating instead of beating the enemy.'[80] On 9 September Stalin did authorise a partial withdrawal but 'the mere mention of the urgent need to abandon Kiev', says Vasilevskii, 'threw Stalin into a rage and he momentarily lost his self-control. We evidently did not have sufficient will-power to withstand these outbursts of uncontrollable rage or a proper appreciation of our responsibility for the impending catastrophe.'[81] In a telephone conversation with Shaposhnikov on 10 September Budennyi, the overall commander of the South-Western Direction, pointed up the failure of Yeremenko's forces to achieve their tasks and said that without reinforcements he would be forced to order withdrawals.[82] Budennyi asked Shaposhnikov to convey his views to the Supreme Commander but the next day he sent a telegram to Stalin direct: 'The Military Council of the South-Western Front considers that in the situation that has arisen it is necessary to allow a general withdrawal of the Front to the rear ... Delaying the withdrawal of the South-Western Front could result in the loss of troops and a great deal of material. As a last resort, if the question of withdrawal cannot be considered I ask for permission to withdraw forces and equipment from the Kiev area that could undoubtedly help the South-Western Front to counteract encirclement.'[83] Later that day Stalin spoke to General Kirponos, the commander of the South-Western Front and told him: 'your proposal to withdraw forces ... we consider dangerous ... Stop looking for lines of retreat and start looking for lines of resistance and only resistance.'[84] Stalin also decided that day to remove Budennyi from command of the South-Western Direction and to appoint Timoshenko in his place.[85] On 13 September Kirponos's Chief of Staff submitted a report to Shaposhnikov saying that catastrophe was only a couple of days away. Infuriated, Stalin dictated the reply himself: 'Major-General Tupikov sent a panic-ridden dispatch . . . to the General Staff. The situation, on the contrary, requires that commanders at all levels maintain an exceptionally clear head and restraint. No one must give way to panic . . . All troops of the front must understand the need to put up a stubborn fight without looking back. Everyone must unswervingly carry out the instructions of Comrade Stalin.'[86] Despite Stalin's exhortations, the end came quickly. On 17 September Stavka finally autho- rised a withdrawal from Kiev to the eastern bank of the Dnepr.[87] It was too little, too late; the pincers of the German encirclement east of Kiev had already closed. Four Soviet armies, 43 divisions in all, were encircled. The South- Western Front suffered three-quarters of a million casualties, including more than 600,000 killed, captured or missing during the battle of Kiev.[88] Among the dead were Kirponos and Tupikov.

One survivor of the Kiev disaster was General Ivan Bagramyan, Kirponos's Chief of Operations, who managed to fight his way out of encirclement. In his memoirs Bagramyan speculated that the reason Stalin was so insistent on defending Kiev was that he had told Roosevelt's emissary, Harry Hopkins, that the Red Army would be able to hold a line of defence from Kiev to Moscow to Leningrad.[89] In this conversation with Hopkins at the end of July Stalin exuded confidence, saying that the Germans were tired and no longer had an attacking spirit. Stalin told Hopkins that because of heavy rains the Germans would not be able to conduct significant operations after 1 September and, in any event, the front would be stabilised by 1 October.[90] But a month was a very long time on the Eastern Front and by early September Stalin was reporting to Churchill that the front had been destabilised by the arrival of fresh enemy forces. He urged Churchill to open a second front, either in the Balkans or France, that would divert 30–40 enemy divisions from the Eastern Front. This was not the first time that Stalin had called on Britain to open a second front but the appeal had much greater urgency than before. When Churchill informed him that it would not be possible to open a second front in 1941 Stalin suggested that 25–30 British divisions be shipped to the USSR to fight on Soviet soil.[91]

While the prestige factor undoubtedly played a part – Kiev was the historic birthplace of the Russian state as well as the capital of the Ukraine – the main reason for the débâcle, as Vasilevskii suggested in his memoirs, was that Stalin underestimated the threat of German encirclement and overestimated the capacity of his own forces to deal with that threat.[92]

Evan Mawdsley has commented that the German encirclement of Kiev was 'their greatest triumph of the war in the East and the Red Army's greatest single military disaster'.[93] But the battle of Kiev was not a complete disaster for

Stalin. It cost Hitler dear, too (100,000 casualties and 10 divisions, according to Vasilevskii).[94] And while Guderian was busy in the south, Army Group Centre was unable to resume its advance on Moscow. Following their victory at Kiev the Germans advanced into Eastern Ukraine, into the Crimea and towards Rostov-on-Don, the gateway to the Caucasus. The Germans captured Rostov in November 1941 but they were unable to hold the city, and in the Crimea embattled Sebastopol fought on until July 1942.

From the point of view of Stalin's Supreme Command the Kiev episode demonstrated that the Soviet warlord's optimism of the will was not tempered by sufficient pessimism of the intellect. It showed as well the ease with which Stalin could impose his wishes on his generals and the difficulties they had in getting him to accept their advice once his mind was made up. If Stalin did not learn to make better decisions, or to accept better advice, the Red Army's prospects for survival would be bleak indeed.

The Battle for Leningrad

The final outcome of Operation Barbarossa was settled by the battle of Moscow in October–November 1941, but when the Germans first invaded Russia their main goal was to capture Leningrad.[95] Only after Army Group North had seized Leningrad were German forces to be concentrated against Moscow. Initially, everything went according to plan. Soviet defences on the Lithuanian border were easily penetrated and Stavka's attempted counter-offensive on 23–24 June against Army Group North failed. Within three weeks the Germans had advanced 450 kilometres across a wide front and occupied much of the Baltic region. Thereafter the German rate of advance began to decrease, from 5 kilometres a day in July to 2.2 kilometres in August and 1.4 kilometres in September. In mid-August the Soviets attempted another counter-offensive, this time in the area of Staraya Russa near Novgorod. It too, failed, but forced the Germans to transfer forces from Army Group Centre to support Army Group North and added to their mounting losses. Stalin's response to the plans of his front commanders for this counter-offensive showed that he was learning some caution:

The operational plan . . . is unrealistic at this time. It is necessary to take into account those forces you have at your disposal and, therefore, you must assign [a] limited mission . . . Your notion of an operational tempo of 15 km per day is clearly beyond your capability to fulfill. Experience indicates that, during our offensive, the enemy will deliberately withdraw in front of our shock group. Then, while creating the appearance of a rapid and easy offensive, he will simultaneously regroup his forces to the flanks of our shock group with the mission of subsequently encircling it and cutting it off from the main front lines. Therefore, I order you not to go too far forward during the offensive . . . Prepare the operation with the utmost secrecy . . . so that the enemy, as so often happens, does not discover our plan at the beginning of the operation and does not disrupt our offensive.[96]

After the failure of the Soviet counter-offensive at Staraya Russa the German advance resumed, and by early September Army Group North had reached the outskirts of Leningrad. At this point, however, Hitler switched to Moscow as his main target and decided that, rather than take Leningrad by storm, the city would be encircled and starved into submission. Supported by a continuing Finnish attack north of Leningrad, the Germans were confident the city would fall sooner rather than later. On 22 September Hitler issued a directive on Leningrad: 'The Führer has decided to erase the city of Petersburg from the face of the earth. I have no interest in the further existence of this large population point after the defeat of Soviet Russia . . . We propose to closely blockade the city and erase it from the earth by means of artillery fire of all calibre and continuous bombardment from the air.'[97]

To Stalin the threat to Leningrad was even more dangerous than the collapse of the Soviet position in the Ukraine. If Leningrad fell the road would be open for the Germans to make a flanking attack on Moscow; the Soviet Union would have been deprived of an important centre of defence production; and the psychological impact of losing the cradle of the Bolshevik Revolution to the Nazis would be devastating. Stalin's anxieties about the Leningrad situation were reflected in his prickly relations with the local leadership. The Leningrad party boss was Politburo member A.A. Zhdanov, unquestionably a Stalin loyalist, but one with talent, energy and initiative.[98] The day after the GKO was established he set up his own local version of the defence committee in Leningrad. Later, on 20 August 1941, Zhdanov established a Military Council for the Defence of Leningrad, whose designated task was to prepare for a street-by-street, house-by-house defence of the city. Stalin had not been consulted, however, and he was not pleased. In a telegraph exchange with Zhdanov on 22 August he stated:

1.   You have formed a Military Council for the defence of Leningrad. You must understand that a Military Council can only be formed by the government or by its representative, Stavka . . .
2.   Neither Voroshilov [the commander of the North-Western Direction] nor Zhdanov are on this Military Council . . . This is incorrect and even harmful politically. The workers are given to understand that Zhdanov

and Voroshilov don't believe in the defence of Leningrad, have washed their hands of it and assigned the defence to others . . .

3. In your decree on the formation of the Military Council . . . you propose the election of battalion commanders [of workers' detachments]. This is incorrect organizationally and harmful politically . . .

4. According to your decree . . . the defence of Leningrad will be restricted to workers' battalions . . . We think that the defence of Leningrad must above all be an artillery defence.

Zhdanov wired back that the council had limited powers and functions and that he and Voroshilov remained in overall charge of Leningrad's defence but Stalin reiterated that they had no right to establish such a body and feared that they might again take it into their heads to contravene normal procedures. Zhdanov admitted that the proposal to elect commanders might have been mistaken but experience had shown that the workers' detachments replaced commanders who had run away with those of their own choice. Stalin insisted, however, that if such a practice spread to the whole army it would mean anarchy.[99] On 24 August the GKO passed its own resolution on the establishment of a Military Defence Council in Leningrad, one that included Zhdanov and Voroshilov among its membership. On 26 August the GKO decided to send a high-powered commission to Leningrad to examine issues relating to the defence of the city and the possible evacuation of its industry and population. The commission, headed by Molotov, arrived in Leningrad on 27 August. Two days later it recommended the evacuation of 250,000 women and children from the city and another 66,000 people from nearby frontline areas. It also urged the deportation of 96,000 people of German and Finnish origin from the region.[100]

Stalin remained unhappy with the performance of the Leningrad Front commander General M.M. Popov, as well as with those of Zhdanov and Voroshilov. On 29 August he telegraphed Molotov in Leningrad:

I fear that Leningrad will be lost by foolish madness. What are Popov and Voroshilov doing? They don't even tell us of the measures they are taking against the danger. They are busy looking for lines of retreat. As far as I can see this is their only purpose . . . This is pure peasant fatalism. What people! I can't understand anything. Don't you think someone's opening the road to the Germans in this important direction? On purpose? Who is this man Popov? What is Voroshilov doing? How is he helping Leningrad? I write this because I'm disturbed by the lack of activity of Leningrad's commander . . . Return to Moscow. Don't be late.[101]

That same day the North-Western Direction was abolished and the commands of the North-Western and Leningrad Fronts merged. On 5 September Voroshilov was named as commander of the new Leningrad Front and Popov became his Chief of Staff. However, Voroshilov was soon relieved of his command and on 11 September Stavka appointed Zhukov in his place.[102]

Zhukov's chosen method for defending Leningrad was to order counter-attacks and impose draconian discipline. On 17 September he issued an order concerning the defence of Leningrad's southern sector: 'all commanders, political workers and soldiers who abandon the indicated line without a written order from the front or army military council will be shot immediately'. Stalin wholeheartedly endorsed both the spirit and the letter of Zhukov's threat. On 20 September he wrote to Zhukov and Zhdanov ordering them to pass on this message to local commanders:

> It is said that, while advancing to Leningrad, the German scoundrels have sent forward among our forces . . . old men, old women, wives and children . . . with requests to the Bolsheviks to give up Leningrad and restore peace.
>
> It is said that people can be found among Leningrad's Bolsheviks who do not consider it possible to use weapons and such against these individuals. I believe that if we have such people among the Bolsheviks, we must destroy them . . . because they are afraid of the German fascists.
>
> My answer is, do not be sentimental, but instead smash the enemy and his accomplices, the sick or the healthy, in the teeth. The war is inexorable, and it will lead to the defeat . . . of those who demonstrate weakness and permit wavering . . .
>
> Beat the Germans and their creatures, whoever they are, in every way and abuse the enemy; it makes no difference whether they are willing or unwilling enemies.[103]

By the end of September 1941 the front around Leningrad had stabilised. The city was almost completely encircled and besieged by German and Finnish forces (and later by the Spanish 'Blue Division') but resupply by air and across Lake Ladoga was still possible. The great drama of Leningrad had begun. More than a million Soviet soldiers lost their lives fighting in the Leningrad region. In nearly three years of siege 640,000 civilians died of starvation while another 400,000 perished or disappeared during the course of evacuations. As Evan Mawdsley has pointed out, the siege of Leningrad was an ordeal experienced mainly by women. Most of the male population were in the Red Army or conscripted in the People's Militia.[104] The Germans tried on many occasions to breach the city's defences and break the defenders' will to resist but never came as close to success as they had in 1941. The siege was a major test for Zhdanov and the communist party. By a combination of sustained ruth-lessness and popular mobilisation the civilian population of the city was held together and the legend of heroic Leningrad created.[105]

In strategic terms the siege pinned down large numbers of enemy forces (a third of the Wehrmacht in 1941) and helped to safeguard Moscow. Of particular importance was the successful Tikhvin counter-offensive of November–December 1941, which secured Moscow against a German encir-clement manoeuvre from the north-west. But friction between Stalin and the Leningrad comrades continued to surface from time to time. For example, in a telegraph exchange with Zhdanov on 1 December 1941 Stalin began by sarcastically observing that 'it is extremely strange that Comrade Zhdanov does not feel it necessary to come to the apparatus to demand from us the mutual exchange of information in such difficult times for Leningrad. If the Muscovites did not call you to the apparatus, it is likely that Comrade Zhdanov would forget all about Moscow and the Muscovites . . . One might conclude that Comrade Zhdanov's Leningrad is not located in the USSR but in the Pacific Ocean.' As this quote illustrates, there was undoubtedly an element of Moscow–Leningrad rivalry in Stalin's relations with Zhdanov but more important was Stalin's obsession with the defence of Moscow. As he said to Zhdanov later in the same communication: 'Don't waste any time. It is not only every day that is precious but every hour. The enemy is gathering all his forces in front of Moscow. All the other fronts now have a good opportunity to attack the enemy, including your front.'[106]

Stalin Saves Moscow

The battle of Moscow began with two disasters for Stalin. In early October the Germans trapped seven Soviet armies in massive encirclements at Viazma and Briansk. The encirclements were a devastating blow to the Briansk, Western and Reserve Fronts defending the approaches to Moscow. Between them they lost 64 rifle divisions, 11 tank brigades and 50 artillery regiments.[107] Personnel losses numbered a million, including nearly 700,000 captured by the Germans. As David Glantz says, 'the disasters . . . the Red Army suffered in October exceeded those of June, August and September in nearly every respect'.[108] The débâcle was partly the result of the Germans' superior numbers. Army Group Centre's attacking force of a million men, 1,700 tanks and assault guns, 14,000 artillery guns and mortars and 950 planes outnum-bered the defending forces of the three Soviet fronts consisting of 800,000 men, 6,808 guns and mortars, 782 tanks and 545 planes.[109] Soviet forces had also been weakened by offensive exertions in August and September and had since then not had time to dig in properly and create a multi-echelon defence.

As always, there were operational mistakes but the simple truth may be that the Germans fought and manoeuvred better and it was this, together with their superiority in men and materiel, that brought them victory. In any event, the German success meant the Soviet capital was now directly and immediately under threat.[110]

Stalin responded to the deteriorating military situation by recalling Zhukov from Leningrad to Moscow on 5 October and on 10 October placing him in command of a new Western Front.[111] On 5 October Stavka ordered the formation of 10 reserve armies east of Moscow.[112] During the course of the Moscow battle nearly 100 divisions were transferred to the central sector of the front, including nine from the Far East, as Stalin had decided that the Japanese were unlikely to join in the German attack at this stage.[113]

Despite this concentration of forces, plans were drawn up for the part evacuation of the Soviet capital, which began to be implemented on 15 October. Among the first to be evacuated to Kuibyshev, located 500 miles south-east of Moscow on the Volga, were foreign diplomats and journalists, the People's Commissariat of Foreign Affairs and the People's Commissariat of Defence. Most of the General Staff were sent to Arzamas halfway between Moscow and Kuibyshev. Beria was ordered to plant explosives to blow up a major part of the city, should that become necessary.[114] These were precautionary measures and not necessarily in anticipation that Moscow was going to fall to the Germans, but they sparked off wild rumours and a general panic among sections of the population, who began to flee the capital of their own accord. Nerves were steadied by a radio broadcast on 17 October by A.A. Shcherbakov, the Moscow party boss, which assured citizens that Stalin was staying in the capital. The situation was stabilised further by a GKO resolution on 19 October that declared a state of siege, imposed a curfew and placed the city's security in the hands of Beria's NKVD.[115] Despite all that has been written about the so-called 'big skedaddle' (*bolshoi drap*),[116] the great majority of ordinary Muscovites remained unwavering in the face of the imminent German threat to the capital.[117] Among the defenders of the Soviet capital in October–November 1941 were five divisions of volunteers, who, barely trained and poorly equipped, suffered extremely high casualty rates in frontline fighting with the Germans. Another half a million civilians in the Moscow region helped construct defensive fortifications in front of the city.

When Zhukov took charge of the capital's defence of the city the plan was to defend a line that ran through Mozhaisk, about 75 miles west of Moscow. But Zhukov also made plans to pull back to defensive positions closer to the city.[118] By the end of October the Germans had either breached or circumvented the Mozhaisk line and were converging on Moscow from the north-west and south-west as well as advancing in the centre. By early November the

Wehrmacht was within 50 miles of the Soviet capital but had failed to make a decisive breakthrough. This was the moment when Stalin made his own, possibly decisive, contribution to saving Moscow from the Germans. The occasion was the annual celebration of the anniversary of the Bolshevik Revolution, traditionally marked by a speech from a party leader and a military parade in Red Square. According to Zhukov, on 1 November Stalin asked him if the situation at the front would allow the festivities to proceed as normal. Zhukov replied that the Germans were in no condition to start a major offensive in the next few days.[119] However, because of the danger of German bombing the traditional eve of anniversary meeting was held underground, in the Mayakovsky metro station.

Stalin rose to the occasion and produced a masterly performance. With the enemy at the gates of Moscow he could hardly deny the seriousness of the danger. Indeed, he frankly admitted the full extent of the territorial losses to the Germans. But Stalin pointed out that the Wehrmacht's blitzkrieg strategy had failed and asked why the 'lightning war' had succeeded in Western Europe but not in the Soviet Union. There were, said Stalin, three reasons. First, Hitler's failure to enlist Great Britain and the United States into an anti-Bolshevik coalition. Second, the Germans had counted on the instability and unreliability of the Soviet home front – on class and ethnic differences leading to the rapid disintegration of the USSR. Third, the Germans had under-estimated the strength of the Red Army and its capacity to maintain morale and wage an effective defence of its native land. Regarding what he characterised as the 'temporary reverses' of the Red Army, Stalin highlighted two factors: the absence of a second front in Europe and shortages of tanks. He then addressed the politics and ideology of the 'Hitlerite invaders'. They were not, as they claimed, nationalists or socialists but imperialists, said Stalin. In fact, 'the Hitler regime is a copy of the reactionary regime which existed in Russia under Tsardom. It is well-known that the Hitlerites suppress the rights of the workers, the rights of the intellectuals and the rights of nations as readily as the tsarist regime suppressed them, and that they organise medieval Jewish pogroms as readily as the tsarist regime organised them. The Hitlerite party is a party of enemies of democratic liberties, a party of medieval reaction and [anti-semitic] Black-Hundred pogroms.' Stalin stressed that 'the German invaders want a war of extermination with the peoples of the USSR' and highlighted, in particular, the exterminationist threat to 'the great Russian nation' and its culture. Stalin refuted Nazi claims of any parallel between Hitler and Napoleon, mindful perhaps that the French emperor had actually captured Moscow before being forced to retreat from Russia. According to Stalin, 'Napoleon fought against the forces of reaction and relied on progressive forces, whereas Hitler . . . relies on the forces of reaction and is fighting the progressive forces'. This assertion was part of Stalin's argument that the German rear was unstable and subject to resistance from progressive forces in Germany as well as in Nazi-occupied Europe. But what spelled real doom for Hitler, argued Stalin, was the American–British–Soviet coalition, a mighty economic alliance that would win the decisive 'war of engines': 'The war will be won by the side that has an overwhelming preponderance in engine production.' Stalin concluded by defining the struggle with Hitler as a just war, a struggle for the liberation of the 'enslaved peoples of Europe' as well as the Soviet Union.[120]

The next day, 7 November 1941, Stalin addressed the troops parading through Red Square. The situation was grave, Stalin told them, but the Soviet regime had faced even greater difficulties in the past:

> Remember the year 1918, when we celebrated the first anniversary of the October Revolution. Three-quarters of our country was . . . in the hands of foreign interventionists. The Ukraine, the Caucasus, Central Asia, the Urals, Siberia and the Far East were temporarily lost to us. We had no allies, we had no Red Army . . . there was a shortage of food, of armaments . . . Fourteen states were pressing against our country. But we did not become despondent, we did not lose heart. In the fire of war we forged the Red Army and converted our country into a military camp. The spirit of the great Lenin animated us . . . And what happened? We routed the interventionists, recovered our lost territory, and achieved victory.

In conclusion Stalin returned to the patriotic theme, invoking past Russian struggles against foreign invaders:

> A great liberation mission has fallen to your lot. Be worthy of this mission . . . Let the manly images of our great ancestors – Alexander Nevsky [who defeated the Swedes], Dimitry Donskoy [who beat the Tartars], Kurma Minin and Dimitry Pozharsky [who drove the Poles out of Moscow], Alexander Suvorov and Mikhail Kutuzov [the Russian hero generals of the Napoleonic Wars] – inspire you in this war. May the victorious banner of the great Lenin be your lodestar.[121]

In later years there was much comment on the specifically Russian patriotic content of these speeches. Alexander Werth, for example, wrote of 'Stalin's Holy Russia Speech'. However, as Werth also noted, Stalin's patriotic persona was nothing new. He had long positioned himself as a nationalist, as a state builder and a state protector. And while the Russian patriotic theme was particularly marked it was balanced by references to the Soviet system and to the USSR and the friendship of its peoples. What was really striking about these speeches was the complete absence of any reference to the Soviet communist party. Although Lenin was mentioned, it was in his role as a member of the Russian heroic pantheon, not as the founder of the Bolshevik party. Stalin had not discarded the communist party; far from it, the party remained the key instrument for the country-wide mobilisation for war. But the silence about the party in Stalin's speech carried the message that he was seeking a patriotic unity that extended far beyond the ranks of committed communists.

Stalin's speeches were reprinted in the Soviet press and distributed in leaflet form throughout the armed forces. The speeches were translated and millions more leaflets were printed in German, Italian, Finnish, Hungarian, Romanian and Spanish for use in the propaganda war on the front line.[122] In the days following the speeches Soviet military censors examined millions of citizens' letters to and from the front and reported a significant upswing in the popular mood.[123] From Leningrad the NKVD reported that 'the speech of Comrade Stalin and his Red Square statement of 7 November are being widely discussed by the working people . . . Workers, officials and intellectuals are saying that Comrade Stalin's speech inspired confidence and clarified for everyone the immediate perspective on the war. The inexhaustible reserves and forces of the Soviet Union guarantee the complete destruction of German Fascism. The aid from America and England that Stalin spoke about will hasten the defeat of the German-Fascist invaders.'[124] While it is impossible to assess with any degree of accuracy the contribution Stalin's intervention made to Soviet success in the battle of Moscow, it may well have made the difference between victory and defeat.

In mid-November the Germans resumed their attack on the capital and in a number of places advanced to within sight of the city centre. Soviet defences buckled but held at critical points, such as the city of Tula south-west of Moscow. It was touch and go until Stavka reserves became available to plug defensive gaps and halt the German advance. These reserves, originally intended to spearhead a major counter-offensive, had to be deployed prematurely in a defensive role. By early December the German attack on Moscow had petered out. The exhaustion of German troops, the Wehrmacht's logistical difficulties in maintaining long supply chains, and the inclement winter weather had all played their role but the decisive factor was Stavka's manpower reserves. These reserves were sufficent not only to defend the capital but to attack, and Zhukov was now ready to make his counter-move.

On the Offensive

Zhukov submitted his plan for a counter-offensive in front of Moscow to Stalin on 30 November and the operation began five days later (*see Map 6 on p. 113*). Zhukov's plan was to attack the enemy forces flanking Moscow north and south and to drive them away from the Soviet capital. Stalin was in ebullient mood on the eve of the counter-offensive. 'The Russians have been in Berlin twice already, and they will be there a third time,' he told Wladyslaw Sikorski, the leader of the Polish government in exile, on 3 December 1941.[125]

By mid-December the Germans had been forced back 100–200 miles from Moscow across a broad front. On 16 December the commander of Army Group Centre, Field Marshal Fedor von Bock, asked Hitler for permission to make a defensive withdrawal. Hitler refused and issued a 'stand fast' order on 18 December, forbidding retreat and insisting on fanatical resistance to the Soviet advance[126] – an action that may well have saved the Wehrmacht from a general rout. As a result the Soviet counter-offensive was halted and contained, most crucially along the Moscow–Smolensk axis.

While the Germans were digging into their defensive positions Stavka was hatching a yet more ambitious project: the launch of a general offensive right across the Eastern Front. The strategic aims of this operation were to encircle Army Group Centre and recapture Smolensk; to annihilate Army Group North and lift the blockade of Leningrad; and to force Army Group South back in the Ukraine, relieve Sebastopol and reoccupy the Crimea. The aim was to incapacitate the Wehrmacht and deliver a war-winning blow in the course of a single strategic operation – in effect, Operation Barbarossa in reverse. The chronology of the emergence and preparation of this grand design is complex,[127] but it seems that Soviet plans began to be drawn up and preliminary orders issued in mid-December. At the same time elements of the incipient general counter-offensive began to be implemented, although the main effort did not take place until January 1942.

It is common to ascribe this grand schema to Stalin. John Erickson, for example, called it 'Stalin's First Strategic Offensive'. Given Stalin's predilection for gigantic projects and the triumphalism in the Soviet press that accompanied the successful Moscow counter-offensive – the Germans' first major defeat in the war – it is not difficult to imagine Stalin formulating and driving forward such a plan. However, there is no evidence – *post hoc* memoir claims apart[128] – that Stalin's generals dissented from the idea of a strategic counter-offensive. It was an operation that fitted perfectly the Red Army's offensive doctrine, it would provide an opportunity to nullify the failure of previous efforts to win back the strategic initiative and, if successful, would collapse the German invasion.

The Soviet Counter-Offensive at Moscow, December 1941

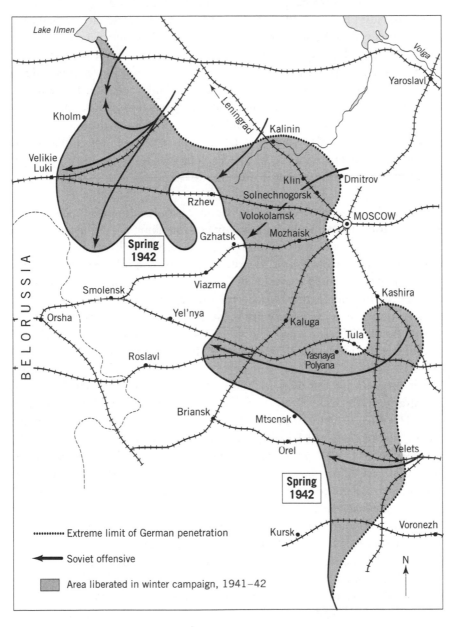

Lake Ilmen

Volga

Yaroslavl

Kholm

Leningrad

Kalinin

Velikie
Luki

Klin

Dmitrov

Solnechnogorsk

Rzhev

Volokolamsk

MOSCOW

Gzhatsk

Mozhaisk

**Spring
1942**

BELORUSSIA

Viazma

Kashira

Smolensk

Yel'nya

Kaluga

Tula

Orsha

Roslavl

Yasnaya
Polyana

Briansk

Mtsensk

Orel

Yelets

**Spring
1942**

Voronezh

•••••••• Extreme limit of German penetration

Kursk

◀━━━ Soviet offensive

N

Area liberated in winter campaign, 1941–42

Stalin's confidence in the coming operation was evident in a conversation with Anthony Eden, the British Foreign Secretary on 16 December:

> We are at the turning point now. The German army is tired out. Its commanders had hoped to end the war before winter and did not make the necessary preparations for the winter campaign. The German army today is poorly dressed, poorly fed, and losing morale. They are beginning to feel the strain. Meanwhile the USSR has prepared large reinforcements and put them into action in recent weeks. This has brought about a fundamental change on the front ... Our counterattacks have gradually developed into counter-offensives. We intend to follow a similar policy during the whole winter ... It is hard to guess how far we shall advance in the course of our drive but, in any case, such will be our line until spring ... We are advancing and will continue to advance on all fronts.[129]

Eden was in Moscow to discuss the terms of an Anglo-Soviet alliance and postwar co-operation. Stalin had already begun talking about the need for an agreement on the postwar world as well as a postwar alliance in his discussions with Beaverbrook and Harriman at the end of September 1941. Subsequently, he raised these issues in his correspondence with Churchill, who agreed to send Eden to Moscow for a wide-ranging exchange of views. In Moscow, Eden was presented with a much more radical proposal than the British had anticipated. There should be two Anglo-Soviet agreements, said Stalin, one on mutual military aid during the war and another on the settlement of postwar problems. To the second agreement would be attached a secret protocol on the reorganisation of European borders after the war. According to the Soviet draft of the proposed protocol, the USSR's borders would be those extant in June 1941 (i.e. inclusive of the Baltic States, Western Belorussia and Western Ukraine, Bessarabia and North Bukovina, and the territory ceded by Finland in March 1940). Poland would be compensated for its loss of eastern provinces by expansion into German territory in the west. Finland would concede the Petsamo area to the USSR. Czechoslovakia, Greece, Albania, Yugoslavia and Austria would be restored as independent states. As a reward for maintaining its neutrality, Turkey would get the Dodecanese islands, some Bulgarian territory and, perhaps, some Syrian territory. Germany would be weakened by disarmament and by dismemberment – its break-up into a number of smaller political units. Britain would have an alliance with Belgium and Holland and military bases in Western Europe, while the USSR would have military bases in Finland and Romania. Finally, there would be a postwar military alliance in Europe to safeguard the peace.[130]

Compared to the sphere of influence in Eastern Europe that Stalin actually achieved in 1945, these were quite modest proposals; essentially, the restoration of the European status quo, punishment of enemy states (above all, Germany), and the enhancement of British and Soviet security. In conversation with Eden, however, Stalin made it clear that his main and immediate priority was British recognition of the territorial gains the USSR had made under the Nazi–Soviet pact. As he told Eden: 'It is very important for us to know whether we shall have to fight with Britain over our western frontiers at a peace conference.'[131]

From Stalin's point of view the war looked as if it could be over in only a few months. How the war would come to an end was difficult to foresee. Confident of short-term military success, Stalin was attempting to maximise his political position in advance of the war's end. But Eden resisted Stalin's demands, saying that he needed to consult Churchill and the Cabinet and that the Americans also had an interest in what was being proposed. Eden left Moscow on 22 December 1941 but it was not until April 1942 that the British responded formally to Stalin's proposals, offering a series of anodyne generalities about wartime and postwar co-operation which committed them to nothing and conceded none of the essential Soviet demands. On 22 April Stalin wrote to Churchill that he proposed to send Molotov to London to discuss the differences between the Soviet and British positions.[132] Arriving in London on 20 May, Molotov, as instructed, doggedly restated the Soviet position. Then a curious thing happened. Molotov suddenly agreed to accept the British offer of a wartime treaty of alliance that contained no more than vague commitments to postwar co-operation. Molotov's initial response to the British offer, which he cabled to Moscow, had been that it was an 'empty declaration' and should be rejected. On 24 May, however, Stalin ordered a change of line:

We have received the draft treaty Eden handed you. We do not consider it an empty declaration but regard it as an important document. It lacks the question of the security of frontiers, but this is not bad, perhaps, for it gives us a free hand. The question of frontiers, or to be more exact, of guarantees for the security of our frontiers at one or another section of our country, will be decided by force.[133]

Prompting Stalin's change of policy was the deteriorating military situation at home. In December he had been musing on the shape of the postwar world; now his priority was to shore up the Anglo-Soviet alliance and to obtain a commitment from the British and Americans to open a second front in Europe in 1942 that would relieve pressure on the Eastern Front.

Stalin had entered 1942 confident of victory. In early January Stavka regrouped its forces and prepared to launch a counter-offensive to collapse the German position all along the Eastern Front. On 10 January Stalin issued the following directive to his commanders:

> After the Red Army had succeeded in wearing down the German fascist troops sufficiently, it went over to the counter-offensive and pursued the German invaders to the west. So as to hold up our advance, the Germans went on the defensive . . . The Germans intend thereby to delay our advance till the spring so that then, having assembled their forces, they can once again take the offensive against the Red Army . . .
>
> Our task is not to give the Germans a breathing space, to drive them westwards without a halt, force them to exhaust their reserves before springtime when we shall have fresh big reserves, while the Germans will have no more reserves; this will ensure the complete defeat of the Nazi forces in 1942.[134]

The Soviet offensive secured some local gains but failed to achieve any of its important objectives. By February it was beginning to run out of steam. On 23 February – the 24th anniversary of the foundation of the Red Army – Stalin issued an 'Order of the Day' to all troops. Politically, the main theme of the order was that the Red Army was waging 'not a predatory, not an imperialist war, but a patriotic war, a war of liberation, a just war'. Stalin stressed, too, that the Soviet Union did not aim to exterminate the German people or destroy the German state: 'The experience of history indicates that the Hitlers come and go, but the German people and the German state remain.' Stalin emphasised the anti-racist credentials of the Soviet state and the Red Army which annihilated the invaders 'not because of their German origin, but because they want to enslave our Motherland'. On military matters Stalin was upbeat and confident, claiming that the Soviets now had the initiative and that 'the day is not far distant when the Red Army . . . will thrust back the brutal enemy . . . and the red banners will fly again victoriously over the entire Soviet land'. However, he made no prediction of victory in 1942 but chose instead to introduce the idea that the war would be decided by 'permanently operating factors: stability of the rear, morale of the army, quantity and quality of divisions, equipment of the army, organizing ability of the commanding personnel of the army'[135] – all of which suggested that the war would be won in the medium rather than the short term.

In March 1942 the multi-pronged Soviet offensive became bogged down in the *Rasputitsa* – the spring muds. In April Stavka called the offensive off and the Red Army went over to the defensive. But plans were already being prepared to renew the Soviet counter-offensive in summer 1942. Having tasted victory at Moscow in December 1941 Stalin and his generals were determined to seize the strategic initiative once again and to keep the Germans on the defensive. Hitler, however, had his own ideas and the Wehrmacht was already planning and preparing for another blitzkrieg campaign in Russia.

By the end of 1941 the Red Army had lost nearly 200 divisions in battle and suffered a stunning 4.3 million casualties. Many more men and divisions were lost in the futile counter-offensive of early 1942. But the Soviet regime had survived Hitler's war of annihilation, and had halted and then turned back the German invasion. Stalin was confident that the tide of war would continue to turn his way. But the greatest test of the Soviet system and of Stalin's war leadership was yet to come.

Victory at Stalingrad and Kursk
Stalin and his Generals

For 1942 Hitler was planning another blitzkrieg campaign in Russia. Its scope and aims were to be very different from those of Operation Barbarossa. Notwithstanding its great victories in 1941 the Wehrmacht had taken a severe battering at the hands of the Red Army and was no longer capable of waging a multi-pronged, strategic offensive on the Eastern Front. By March 1942 the Germans had suffered 1.1 million dead, wounded, missing, or captured – some 35 per cent of their strength on the Eastern Front. Only 8 out of 162 divisions were at full strength and 625,000 replacements were needed. The Germans' mobility was severely impaired by the loss of 40,000 trucks, 40,000 motorbikes, nearly 30,000 cars and thousands of tanks. The Wehrmacht's other source of transport was draught animals (mainly horses) and it had lost 180,000 of these as a result of enemy action, with only 20,000 being replaced.[1]

Hitler's only realistic option was an offensive on a single front and his attention focused on the south and on the quest for oil. South of the Caucasus mountains were the Baku oilfields – the source of nearly 90 per cent of Soviet fuel. Hitler's calculation was that the seizure of these fields would deny the Soviets their oil, increase supplies to Germany and its Axis allies, and decrease the Wehrmacht's dependence on the vulnerable Ploesti wells in Romania. Even before the Soviet–German war Hitler had been anxious about his oil supplies: 'Now in the era of air power,' he said in January 1941, 'Russia can turn the Romanian oil fields into an expanse of smoking debris . . . and the very life of the Axis depends on those fields.'[2] Hitler also worried increasingly about the implications of the United States's entry into the war. American economic and military power was seen as crucial in swinging the balance against Germany during the First World War and Hitler was concerned about the danger to his *Festung Europa* (Fortress Europe) from an Anglo-American invasion of France. That invasion did not come until June 1944 but in early 1942 it seemed months rather than years away. It would mean a two-front land war in Europe and Hitler was desperate to settle accounts with Stalin before turning to deal with the British and Americans in the west. Over the long run Hitler needed the means to fight a prolonged war of attrition with the allied coalition on a multiplicity of fronts – in the Atlantic, the Mediterranean, North Africa and the Middle East as well as in Western and Eastern Europe. [3]

The goals of the German summer campaign of 1942 were set out in Führer Directive no. 41, dated 5 April 1942:

> All available forces will be concentrated on the main operations in the Southern sector, with the aim of destroying the enemy before the Don, in order to secure the Caucasian oil fields and the passes through the Caucasian mountains themselves.[4]

Unlike in 1941, Hitler did not necessarily expect to win the war in the east in 1942. His aim was to deal the Red Army a devastating blow by destroying its forces in the Don area and in the Donets basin (the Donbas) and to seize control of oil and other Soviet economic resources in the Ukraine, southern Russia and Transcaucasia. That might lead to victory in the short term, but more important was acquiring the means and securing the position from which to wage a global war over the longer term.

Hitler's generals shared his resource-driven strategic view but their operational priority was the destruction of the Red Army. The plan of campaign was to occupy the Donbas and all the territory west of the Don. Soviet forces in these areas would be encircled and destroyed and a defensive line established along the banks of the Don River. With the Red Army safely in the bag, the Germans could cross the Don south of Rostov and head for the Kuban, the Caucasus and Baku (*see Map 7 on p. 120*).

It was this plan that led in autumn 1942 to the most important turning point of the entire Second World War – the battle of Stalingrad. Stalingrad was located on a bend in the Volga that brought the river to within 50 miles of the most easterly point of the great bend in the Don. From the point of view of defending the line of the Don it made sense for the Germans to occupy key points on the western bank of the Volga in the vicinity of Stalingrad. This would enable them to construct a defensive landbridge between the two rivers. Stalingrad was also a big industrial centre and guarded the flow of oil up the Volga from Astrakhan to northern Russia. According to Hitler's Directive 41, 'every effort will be made to reach Stalingrad itself, or at least bring the city under fire from heavy artillery so that it may no longer be of any use as an industrial or communications centre.'[5] But there was as yet no definite commitment to occupy the city.

The Plan for Operation Blau, April 1942

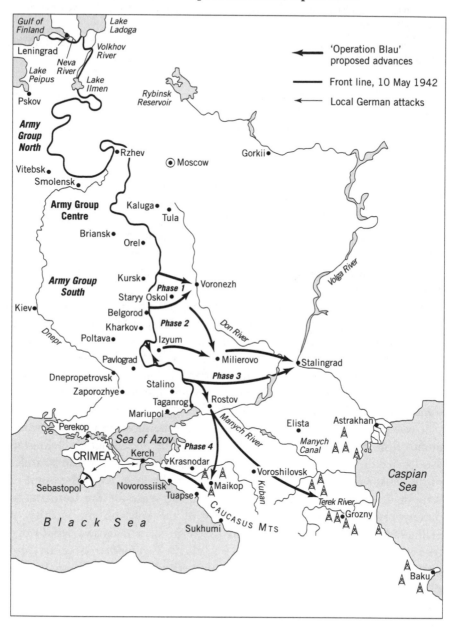

The projected campaign was code-named Operation Blau (Blue) and was to be implemented by Army Group South, consisting of the 6th and 17th Armies and the 1st and 4th Panzer Armies, as well as the 11th Army based in the Crimea. Supporting the German armies were a large number of Axis divisions, including the Hungarian 2nd, Italian 8th and Romanian 3rd and 4th Armies. In total there were 89 divisions, including nine armoured, in this nearly 2-million-strong force.[6]

Before the start of the main campaign the Germans embarked on an operation to complete their conquest of the Crimea. They had conquered virtually all the Crimea in 1941 but had lost control of the Kerch Peninsula in early 1942 – the result of a series of counter-actions by the Red Army designed to relieve the embattled defenders of the city-fortress of Sebastopol.[7] The German 11th Army began its campaign to recapture the Kerch Peninsula on 8 May and within a fortnight had destroyed three Soviet armies with a total of 21 divisions and taken 170,000 prisoners.

Following this débâcle Stalin and Stavka drew up a detailed critique of the performance of the commanders of their Crimean Front. In a document dated 4 June 1942, distributed throughout the senior levels of the Red Army, the leadership of the Crimean Front was criticised, first, because they did not understand the nature of modern warfare; second, because they had lost control of their troops; and, third, because of the indiscipline they had shown in carrying out Stavka instructions. The document also announced the removal and demotion of virtually all the Front's senior officers. Among those demoted was the Front commander General Kozlov; and Lev Mekhlis, the head of the GPU (Main Political Administration of the Red Army), who had been sent to the Crimea as Stavka's representative. Mekhlis lost his post of deputy commissar for defence along with his GPU job and was demoted from army commissar of the first rank to corps commissar. Stalin's ire towards Mekhlis had become evident during the early days of the Wehrmacht's Kerch offensive when the commissar cabled Moscow complaining about the actions of General Kozlov in response to the German attack. In response Stalin dished out a stinging rebuke:

> You are taking a strange position as an outside observer who has no responsibility for the Crimean Front affairs. This position may be convenient but it is utterly disgraceful. You are not some outside observer . . . but the responsible representative of the GHQ, responsible for all the Front's successes and failures and obliged to correct the command's mistakes on the spot.[8]

On another occasion Stalin cabled Kozlov: 'You are the commander of the Front, not Mekhlis. Mekhlis must help you. If he doesn't help, you must report it.'[9] The general lesson of the affair, spelled out in Stavka's 4 June document, was that all commanders should 'master the nature of modern warfare properly', understand the importance of 'coordinated action by all arms' and 'put an end once and for all to harmful methods of bureaucratic leadership . . . they must not confine themselves to issuing orders, but visit the troops, the armies and divisions more often and help their subordinates to carry out the orders. The task is that our commanding staff, commissars and political officers should thoroughly root out elements of indiscipline among commanders of all ranks.'[10]

The Red Army's expulsion from Kerch opened the way for a final German assault on Sebastopol which began on 2 June with a massive aerial and artillery bombardment. During the course of a month-long siege the Luftwaffe flew more than 23,000 sorties and dropped 20,000 tons of bombs on the city. The Germans also transferred from the Leningrad front their very heaviest artillery, including guns which fired 1-ton, 1.5-ton and even 7-ton shells. Following infantry and amphibious assaults Sebastopol fell in early July. Soviet fatalities were in the tens of thousands and the Germans captured another 95,000 prisoners. In turn they suffered 75,000 casualties, including 25,000 dead. The Germans had prevailed but the defenders of Sebastopol had put up an awesome fight and had added to the growing legend and tradition of heroic Red Army defences which had begun at Brest in June 1941 and now ran through Odessa, Smolensk, Leningrad, Tula and Moscow.[11]

The Kharkov Disaster

Meanwhile, major action was also under way in Eastern Ukraine: however, its initiation had come not from the Germans but the Soviets. On 12 May the Red Army launched a major offensive designed to retake Kharkov – the Ukraine's second city. Unfortunately, the Soviet offensive coincided with local German concentration and mobilisation for action preparatory to Operation Blau and the 6th Army and 1st Panzer Army were able to wage an effective defence and mount a devastating counterattack. Not only did the Russians fail to recapture Kharkov but the three Soviet armies involved in the operation were encircled by the Germans and mostly destroyed. The battle was over by 28 May. Soviet casualties were nearly 280,000, including 170,000 killed, missing or captured. Around 650 tanks and nearly 5,000 artillery pieces were also lost by the Red Army.[12]

Kharkov was yet another military disaster subsequently laid at Stalin's door. Leading the charge once again was Khrushchev, who was at the time the political commissar of the South-Western Direction that conducted the Kharkov operation. In 1956 Khrushchev claimed that he had asked Stalin for permission to call off the operation before Soviet forces were encircled by the Germans.[13] Khrushchev's version of events was duly incorporated into the official history of the Great Patriotic War published in the early 1960s when he was still leader of the Soviet Union.[14] But Zhukov flatly denied Khrushchev's story in his memoirs and laid the blame on the South-Western Direction leadership who, he said, had lobbied for the operation and then misled Stalin about the course of the battle.[15] This critique of the local leadership was taken up by Marshal K.S. Moskalenko, one of the army commanders involved in the operation. In his view the South-Western Direction had underestimated the German opposition and exaggerated the capabilities of their own forces.[16] This new version of the affair featured in the official Soviet history of the Second World War published in the 1970s,[17] although a slightly discordant note was struck by Vasilevskii in his memoirs. He went along with the Zhukov–Moskalenko view of events but confirmed Khrushchev's story of his efforts to persuade Stalin to call the whole thing off. Vasilevskii also argued that Stavka might have done more to help the South-Western Direction.[18] This last point was taken up in the memoirs of Marshal Bagramyan, the Chief of Staff of the South-Western Direction, who felt the main problem was Stavka's under-resourcing of the operation.[19]

Stalin's own verdict on the Kharkov failure was delivered in a missive to the South-Western Direction on 26 June announcing that Bagramyan had been sacked as Chief of Staff because of his failure to provide clear and accurate information to Stavka, which 'not only lost the half-won Kharkov operation, but also succeeded in giving 18–20 divisions to the enemy'. Stalin compared the 'catastrophe' to one of the Tsarist army's biggest disasters during the First World War and pointed out that it was not only Bagramyan who had made mistakes but Khrushchev and Timoshenko, the South-Western Direction's Commander-in-Chief. 'If we had reported to the country fully about the catastrophe ... then I fear they would deal with you very sternly.' Stalin, however, treated the guilty parties with kid gloves. While Bagramyan was demoted from a Direction-level to an Army-level Chief of Staff, he later re-emerged as one of the senior Soviet commanders of the whole war – one of only two non-Slavs (he was Armenian, the other was Jewish) to command a multi-army Front.[20] No one else was 'scapegoated'; indeed, many of those involved in the operation later assumed ranking positions in the Soviet High Command; for example, General A.I. Antonov, who became Stalin's Deputy Chief of the General Staff from December 1942. In July 1942 Timoshenko was transferred to Leningrad to become commander of the North-Western Front. This could be seen as a punishment or a demotion, but equally likely it was a case of sending Timoshenko back to the scene of his triumph in the Soviet–Finnish war.[21]

Stalin's lenient treatment of the leadership of the South-Western Direction contrasts sharply with his demotion of the culprits in the Crimean Command reflecting, perhaps, some recognition on his part that the Kharkov catastrophe was a collective responsibility shared by Stavka and the Supreme Commander himself. In this respect the proposals and reports submitted by the South-Western Direction to Stavka in March–May 1942 are highly revealing.[22] These documents show that in proposing the operation the Direction leadership was very confident of success and extremely ambitious, aiming not only to retake Kharkov but to reach the Dnepr. Even when it became clear during the course of the battle that the Germans were much stronger than expected and that goals achieved were falling far short of operational expectations, the Direction's leadership continued to submit optimistic reports to Moscow.

In formulating such plans and maintaining such optimism the Direction – and it was not alone in this respect[23] – reflected Stalin and Stavka's sanguine view of the Red Army's prospects on the Eastern Front in spring 1942: that the renewal of offensive action would achieve the expulsion of German forces from the USSR by the end of the year. Kharkov was only one of a number of ambitious offensive operations authorised by Stalin and Stavka in spring 1942. In the Crimea further offensive action by the Red Army was forestalled only by the launch of the German attack on 8 May. In early May the North-Western Front began an operation against a strong pocket of German forces in the Demyansk area. In mid-May the Leningrad Front began an operation to free a Soviet army trapped in the Lyubon area. In the central sector there was no immediate Red Army action but plans were afoot to launch attacks in the direction of Rzhev, Viazma and Orel.[24]

Arguably, it was Stavka's strategic commitment to the doctrine of the offensive that lay at the root of the Kharkov disaster rather than any operational errors by Stalin or the South-Western Direction. This deeper truth about Kharkov has been obscured by the memoir blame-game and by the widespread acceptance of Zhukov and Vasilevskii's account of discussions within the Soviet High Command in spring 1942. According to them, Stavka's basic plan for 1942 was to remain on the defensive until the summer. In this context the Kharkov operation is presented as an unfortunate deviation from the main plan and as the result of Stalin's predilection for attack and of Timoshenko's lobbying for a big offensive in his area.[25] 'Are we supposed to sit in defence, idling away our time and wait for the Germans to attack first?' Stalin is quoted as saying by Zhukov.[26] Doubtless Stalin was, as usual, gung ho for offensive action, but the picture presented by Zhukov and Vasilevskii of Stavka's basic commitment to strategic defence is unconvincing. According to Zhukov, for example, he favoured a defensive posture but also pushed for an early major offensive against Army Group Centre in the Viazma–Rzhev area, a proposal overruled in favour of the Kharkov operation. This suggests that the discussion within Stavka was about where to deploy resources for attack rather than a debate about whether or not to remain on the defensive. This interpretation is confirmed by Zhukov's subsequent self-serving claim that his Viazma–Rzhev operation – which did actually take place in various forms in July–August 1942 – could have transformed the whole strategic situation in the central sector in front of Moscow had more forces been allocated to it.[27] Vasilevskii's account of the internal discussions within Stavka is equally contradictory. He says that the decision was taken 'simultaneously with the strategic defence to undertake local offensive operations on several sectors which, in Stalin's view, were to consolidate the successes of the winter campaign, improve the operational situation of our troops, help us maintain the strategic initiative and disrupt Nazi plans for a new offensive in the summer of 1942. It was assumed that all combined would set up favourable conditions for the Red Army to launch even greater offensive operations in summer on the entire front from the Baltic to the Black Sea.'[28] This sounds like a rolling programme of offensive action rather than strategic defence and such was the concept embodied in the General Staff's planning documents of spring 1942. These envisaged the local actions mentioned by Vasilevskii, but they were to be followed by ever more ambitious offensives and by an advance to the USSR's western frontier by the end of 1942; the Red Army would *then* assume the defensive.[29] This offensive strategic perspective was propounded by Stalin to Churchill in a message dated 14 March 1942: 'I feel entirely confident that the combined efforts of our troops, occasional setbacks notwithstanding, will culminate in crushing the common enemy and that the year 1942 will see a decisive turn on the anti-Hitler front.'[30] In public, Stalin's Order of the Day on 1 May 1942 defined the current phase of the war as 'the period of the liberation of Soviet lands from Hitlerite scum' and called upon the Red Army 'to make 1942 the year of the final rout of the German-fascist troops and the liberation of the Soviet land from the Hitlerite blackguards!'[31]

Another important aspect of Stavka planning in spring 1942 concerned predictions about the main direction of German offensive action. Whilst there was accurate intelligence that the main German offensive would be in the south and would be aimed at seizing control of Soviet economic resources, the information was not definitive. The fact that Army Group Centre, with its 70 divisions, remained less than 100 miles from Moscow weighed heavily in Stalin's and Stavka's calculations.[32] Although Stalin did not rule out a major German advance in the south, he saw it as aimed mainly at contributing to a flanking attack on Moscow. Defence of those sectors of the front vital to the security of Moscow was given top priority and Stavka's reserves placed in suitable locations. The idea that Hitler aimed above all to capture Moscow prevailed throughout the 1942 campaign and was reinforced actively by a German deception campaign, Operation Kreml, consisting of elaborate faked preparations for an attack on the Soviet capital.[33] In his speech in November 1942 on the 25th anniversary of the Bolshevik Revolution – when the German advance in the south was at its height – Stalin denied that the German summer campaign had been primarily about oil and insisted that the main goal was (still) to outflank Moscow from the east and then to strike at the Soviet capital from the rear. 'In short, the main aim of the Germans' summer offensive was to surround Moscow and end the war this year.'[34]

Not for the first time, Stalin's and Stavka's plans and calculations were upset by the actual course of events. The Red Army's offensive actions at Kharkov and elsewhere not only failed but resulted in large losses and denuded Stavka's reserves. When the German attack came it was directed at Stalingrad and Baku, not Moscow. The decisive engagement between the Red Army and the Wehrmacht in 1942 took place not in front of Moscow but at Stalingrad.

The Road to Stalingrad

Operation Blau was launched on 28 June 1942 [35] and made rapid progress. By the end of July the Germans occupied the whole of the Donbas, much of Don country and were on their way to Stalingrad and the Caucasus. As in summer 1941, the German High Command was soon dizzy with success. On 6 July Halder noted, 'we have overestimated the enemy's strength and the offensive has completely smashed him up'. On 20 July Hitler told Halder: 'The Russian is finished'. Halder replied: 'I must admit that it looks that way.' By the end of August the Germans were on the Volga and Stalingrad was under siege. In the south German forces had reached the foothills of the Caucasus, occupied the Maikop oilfield and were threatening another oilfield at Grozny in Chechnya. On 21 August 1942 the German flag flew on top of Mount Elbruz, the highest peak of the Caucasus (*see Map 8 on p. 127*).[36]

During July and August the Germans took 625,000 prisoners and captured or destroyed 7,000 tanks, 6,000 artillery pieces and more than 400 aircraft. German casualties were high, too: some 200,000 in August alone. The Red Army's losses were significant but not on the scale of summer 1941. Since then the Soviets had learned to withdraw and had become more adept at escaping encirclement. The German strategy of deep penetration and large-scale envelopment worked well, as long as the enemy chose to stand and fight rather than evade encirclement.[37] Although generally adhering to a 'no-retreat' policy, Stalin and Stavka were more willing than previously to authorise withdrawals. Faced with mounting losses and a depletion of their manpower reserves the Soviet High Command was anxious to preserve its forces. During this period

The German Advance in the South, Summer 1942

there were a number of communications from Stalin to front commanders enquiring about the fate of encircled units and demanding to know what was being done to help them escape encirclement.[38] To the Germans, however, it seemed that the relatively small number of enemy prisoners signalled Soviet weakness and full-scale retreat rather than a change of tactics. This mistaken impression had a crucial impact on the strategic reorientation of Operation Blau that took place in July 1942.

In its original conception Blau was a unified and co-ordinated operation whose goals would be achieved on a phased basis. First would come control of the Don and Volga, then a major push south to the Caucasus. On 9 July, however, Army Group South was split into separate commands of Army Groups A and B. Von Bock, the commander of Army Group South, took charge of Army Group B, consisting of the 6th Army, 4th Panzer Army and the various Axis armies. Its task was to strike east from Kursk and Kharkov in the direction of Voronezh and then south-east towards the great bend of the Don River. Army Group A was headed by Field Marshal Wilhelm List, who controlled the 17th Army and the 1st Panzer Army and was tasked to capture Rostov-on-Don and march to Baku. On 13 July Bock was dismissed by Hitler because of operational disagreements and replaced by Field Marshal Baron von Weichs. That same day 4th Panzer was detached from Army Group B and directed to join Army Group A's campaign in the south. Ten days later, on 23 July, Hitler issued Directive 45. This stated that 'in a campaign which has lasted little more than three weeks, the broad objectives outlined by me for the southern flank of the Eastern front have been largely achieved'. Supported by the 11th Army in the Crimea, Army Group A was now tasked to destroy the enemy south of Rostov and then 'to occupy the entire Eastern coastline of the Black Sea' and to reach Baku. What was left of Army Group B would 'thrust forward to Stalingrad to smash the enemy forces concentrating there, to occupy the town, and to block the land communications between the Don and Volga'.[39]

Hitler's decision to split his southern offensive, to pursue two strategic goals simultaneously – the occupation of Baku and the capture of Stalingrad – is widely seen as a fatal mistake. While the Wehrmacht might have been able to achieve one or other of these two goals by concentrating its forces and resources on either Stalingrad or Baku, it was not strong enough to pursue both ambitions. But this was not how it seemed to Hitler at the time and the recapture of Rostov on 23–24 July served only to confirm his optimism.

German forces were now ready to embark on their campaign in Transcaucasia but, as General Alfred Jodl, the operations chief of the German armed forces' High Command, noted paradoxically at the end of July, 'the fate of the Caucasus will be decided at Stalingrad'. The reason was that Stalingrad was the pivot of the defensive block on the Don and Volga that the Germans needed to establish in order to protect their drive to Baku from a flanking Soviet counterattack. But Hitler was confident this would be achieved and when the German 6th Army reached the outskirts of Stalingrad towards the end of August the Führer fully expected the city to be taken by storm.

Stalin's reaction to Operation Blau was coloured by his continuing belief that Moscow would be the Germans' main target in 1942 – a perception confirmed by the initial German attack in the south, which was aimed at Voronezh, located closer to Moscow than Stalingrad. A German break-through at this point would have threatened the capital's communications with the south of the country. The city itself fell to the Germans on 7 July but for weeks after the Red Army mounted counterattack after counterattack in the Voronezh area. The importance Stavka attached to these operations was signalled by the decision to establish a Voronezh Front and the appoint-ment of one of the General Staff's most talented officers, General Nikolai Vatutin, to command it.[40] Another region of persistent Red Army offensive action in summer 1942 was the Rzhev–Viazma area. These operations were conducted by Zhukov's Western Front supported by the Kalinin Front and the Briansk Front. In his memoirs Zhukov says little about these operations, except that they might have succeeded had more forces been allocated. He presents the episode as yet another example of the downgrading of his role because he had dared to argue with Stalin about the priority given to the Kharkov operation. In fact, the Rzhev–Viazma operations were a high priority for Stavka and Zhukov was allocated considerable additional forces at a time when the Soviet position in the south was collapsing and in urgent need of reinforcement.[41]

While the Voronezh battles were covered quite extensively in the Soviet press – at least until Stalingrad took over the headlines – there was little reporting of the Rzhev–Viazma fighting. But both sets of operations featured heavily in the General Staff's daily situation reports and are illustrative of Stavka's continuing commitment to offensive action even in the most dangerous and difficult of circumstances.[42]

Further south the possibilities for offensive action were constrained by the weakness of Timoshenko's South-Western Front following the Kharkov disaster. When the German attack swung south in early July Timoshenko's defences crumbled and Stavka was forced to order a withdrawal towards the Don.[43] The threat to Stalingrad soon became apparent and on 12 July Stavka ordered the establishment of a Stalingrad Front.[44] This was a rebranding of Timoshenko's South-Western Front but with the addition of three reserve armies[45] – the 62nd, 63rd and 64th – which had been deployed to defend Stalingrad. In total Timoshenko had 38 divisions at his disposal, a force of more than half a million, including 1,000 tanks and nearly 750 aircraft.[46] Timoshenko's tenure at the Stalingrad Front did not last long, however; he was replaced by General V.N. Gordov on 22 July.[47] The next day Vasilevskii – who had been appointed Chief of the General Staff on 26 June – arrived in Stalingrad on the first of many trips to the battle zone.[48] Vasilevskii was one of a number of high-ranking military and political figures sent to Stalingrad during the course of the battle to advise and report on the situation on the ground. Stalin's practice of sending Stavka representatives to critical areas of the front was by now well established but its frequency and intensity grew during the battle of Stalingrad.

In Russian and Soviet historiography 17 July 1942 is the 'official' date for the beginning of the so-called '200 days of fire' that were the battle of Stalingrad.[49] On that day forward units of the German 6th Army clashed with the 62nd and 64th armies at the River Chir. Soviet forces were soon driven back to their main defence line along the southern Don and a breakthrough across the river threatened. Stalin's concern about this danger was expressed in a directive to the Southern, North Caucasus and Stalingrad Fronts on 23 July:

> If the Germans succeed in building pontoon bridges across the Don and are able to transfer tanks and artillery to the southern banks of the Don it would constitute a grave threat to [your] Fronts. If the Germans are unable to throw pontoon bridges across to the southern bank they will only be able to send infantry across and this would not constitute a big threat to us . . . In view of this the main task of our forces on the southern bank of the Don and of our aviation is not to allow the Germans to build pontoon bridges across the Don, and if they do succeed they are to be destroyed with all the power of our artillery and air force.[50]

Within a few days the Germans had crossed the southern Don in great numbers and were advancing rapidly towards the Caucasus and to Stalingrad. The most important development was the loss of Rostov at the end of July, an event of symbolic as well as strategic importance. The city guarded the gateway to the Caucasus, which meant the way was now open for the Germans to occupy the Kuban, the rich agricultural zone between the Don and the mountains of Transcaucasia. Equally important was the impact of the loss of Rostov on Soviet morale. The city was first occupied by the Germans in November 1941 and its recapture by the Red Army a few days later had been celebrated as a great turning point in the war, a part of the developing Soviet counter-offensive that culminated in the triumph before Moscow. Now Rostov had fallen to the enemy again and the ease with which the Germans had recaptured the city compared badly with the Red Army and Navy's epic and prolonged defence of Sebastopol.[51]

On 28 July 1942 Stalin issued Order 227, familiarly known as *Ni shagu nazad!* (Not a step back!). The order was not published in the newspapers but the text was distributed throughout the Soviet armed forces. Printed copies were posted up at the front and officers read it out to their men. *Ni shagu nazad!* quickly became the leading slogan of the Soviet press in summer 1942 and numerous articles and editorials disseminated its main themes to the wider population.

The order began frankly by setting out the grave situation facing the country:

> The enemy throws at the front new forces and . . . is penetrating deep into the Soviet Union, invading new regions, devastating and destroying our towns and villages, violating, robbing and killing the Soviet people. The battle rages in the area of Voronezh, in the Don, in the south at the gateway to the Northern Caucasus. The German occupiers are breaking through towards Stalingrad, towards the Volga and want at any price to seize the Kuban and the Northern Caucasus and their oil and bread resources.

But the Red Army, said Stalin, was failing in its duty to the country:

> Units of the Southern Front, succumbing to panic, abandoned Rostov and Novocherkassk without serious opposition and without orders from Moscow, thereby covering their banners with shame. The people of our country . . . are losing faith in the Red Army . . . are cursing the Red Army for giving our people over to the yoke of the German oppressors, while itself escaping to the east.

Underlining the extent of the losses so far, Stalin emphasised that 'to retreat further would mean the ruination of our country and ourselves. Every new scrap of territory we lose will significantly strengthen the enemy and severely weaken our defence, our motherland.' Stalin's solution was to stop the retreat:

> Not a step back! This must now be our chief slogan. It is necessary to defend to the last drop of blood every position, every metre of Soviet territory, to cling on to every shred of Soviet earth and to defend it to the utmost.

The implementation of this policy would require iron discipline, particularly on the part of officers and commissars, who would be treated as traitors if they retreated without orders, said Stalin. More specifically the order decreed the establishment of penal battalions for those guilty of disciplinary offences and called for blocking detachments to be placed behind wavering divisions. The penal battalions would be sent to the most dangerous sections of the front and their members given a chance to atone for their sins of indiscipline, while the blocking detachments would shoot panic-mongers and cowards fleeing to the rear.[52]

There was nothing new in Order 227, although its urgent tone was a telling sign of Stalin's anxiety about the mounting defeats and losses that summer. Iron discipline, harsh punishment and no retreat without authorisation had been Stalin's themes since the very beginning of the war. The proposal to establish penal battalions was presented by Stalin as an idea picked up from the Germans but was, in fact, a revival and reformulation of an earlier Soviet practice of imprisoning in penal units those guilty of disciplinary offences. Between 1942 and 1945 about 600 such penal units were established and some 430,000 men served in them. As Stalin directed, these units were assigned difficult and dangerous missions such as frontal assaults on enemy positions and, consequently, suffered 50 per cent casualties.[53] While blocking detachments already existed on a number of fronts, after Order 227 there was a marked increase in their numbers and activities. According to an NKVD summary report, 193 blocking detachments were formed after Order 227 was issued. Between 1 August and 15 October these detachments detained 140,755 people. Of these detainees 3,980 were arrested, 1,189 were shot, 2,961 were sent to penal battalions or companies and 131,094 were returned to their units.[54]

Order 227 was generally supported by those serving on the front and provided a welcome boost to morale.[55] In fact, the main point of the new disciplinary regime was not to punish offenders but to deter waverers and to reassure those who were determined to do their duty, whatever its costs, that those fighting at their side who broke discipline would be caught and dealt with harshly. Stalin needed heroes much more than he needed an NKVD body count of traitors and his main concern was to bolster those who were willing to sacrifice their lives for the cause.[56]

Deployed alongside the threat of punishment was the appeal to patriotism. The call to patriotic duty had been the main theme of Soviet political mobilisation since the war began but it became even more marked in what Alexander Werth called the 'black summer of 1942', when catastrophic defeat beckoned once again. The crisis atmosphere of this period was intensified by the dashing of popular expectations that the dire circumstances of 1941 would not be repeated. Such optimism was reinforced by official propaganda. On 21 June *Krasnaya Zvezda* (Red Star) the Red Army's main newspaper editorialised that 'the German army of 1942 is still stubborn in defence, but has already been deprived of that offensive drive it had before . . . There can be no question of a German offensive like last summer's.' The next day the Soviet Information Buro (Sovinform) issued a statement reviewing the first year of the war. It reassured readers that 'the German Army of 1942 is not what it was a year ago . . . The German Army cannot carry out offensive operations on a scale similar to last year's.' In *Pravda* the editorial that day stated: '1942 will be the year of the Germans' final defeat, of our final victory.'[57] Hence the rapid German advance in the south came out of the blue for most people and its disillusioning effect contributed to the intense *patrie-en-danger* atmosphere of that summer. Soviet propaganda quickly changed tack, however, and began emphasising the grave dangers of the situation. On 19 July an editorial in *Krasnaya Zvezda* compared the situation in the south with the battles of Moscow and Leningrad in 1941.[58] Anti-German hate propaganda filled the press, exhorting Soviet soldiers to kill as many Germans as they could – or face the extermination of their families, friends and country.[59] After Order 227 was issued the main slogans became 'Not a step back!' and 'Victory or death!'[60]

The key target group of the appeal to patriotic sacrifice was the Soviet officer corps. No group was more dedicated or more important to the Soviet war effort. During the war a million officers were killed and another million were invalided out of the services. On 30 July 1942 Stalin introduced new decorations for officers only: the Orders of Kutuzov, Nevsky and Suvorov. An editorial in *Krasnaya Zvezda* the next day called on readers to 'stand by the motherland like Suvorov, Kutuzov and Alexander Nevsky'.[61] The pages of the Soviet press also began to be filled with articles promoting both the special role of officers in maintaining discipline and the importance to securing victory of their technical expertise and professionalism. Later that year officers were given new distinctive uniforms, complete with epaulettes and gold braid (that had to be specially imported from Britain).[62] Then, in January 1943, the term 'ofitser' was restored to general usage. On 9 October 1942 – at the height of the battle for Stalingrad – a decree was issued abolishing the Institution of Commissars and ending the system of dual command of officers and political officials. The stated rationale for this radical move was that officers had proven their patriotic loyalty during the war and that dual command was impeding the further development of their political as well as their military leadership. The Institution of Commissars was replaced by a number of new organisations devoted to propaganda work within the armed forces and several of the most experienced commissars were transferred to military command positions.[63] The decree was not universally welcomed in the armed forces, not least among commissars. Many felt that the abolition was ill-timed and would undermine the fight to maintain discipline at the front; others felt the commissars had done a good job and that it was lack of ability among military officers that was the main problem, not political interference in command decisions.[64]

While more and more pages of the Soviet press were devoted to glorifying patriotic feats of the pre-Revolutionary era, post-1917 history was not neglected. The civil war theme became particularly prominent, and relevant, as the Germans approached Stalingrad. Parallels were freely drawn between Stalin's successful defence of Tsaritsyn in 1918 and the coming battle to save Stalingrad. The city's defenders pledged to emulate the feat of their illustrious predecessors during the civil war. As Alexander Werth, the *Sunday Times* correspondent in Moscow at the time noted, whilst patriotism predominated in Soviet propaganda, 'the Soviet idea was never quite eclipsed . . . the combination of "Soviet" and "Russia" merely presented, in the danger year of 1942, a different pattern from earlier or later times'.[65]

On Stalin's part there was a growing realisation in summer 1942 that a decisive battle was approaching. In early August Stavka decided to split the Stalingrad Front into two – a Stalingrad Front and a South-Eastern Front. Confusingly, Stalingrad itself came within the remit of the South-Eastern Front, while the Stalingrad Front was deployed north and west of the city along the Don. Yeremenko was appointed commander of the South-Eastern Front, while General Gordov was put in charge of the new Stalingrad Front.[66] To facilitate co-ordination of the defence of Stalingrad, on 9 August Yeremenko was made overall commander of the two fronts. In the directive announcing this new command structure Stalin urged Yeremenko and Gordov to keep in mind that 'the defence of Stalingrad and the defeat of the enemy . . . are of decisive importance to all Soviet Fronts. The Supreme Command mandates you to spare no effort nor to shirk any sacrifice to defend Stalingrad and destroy the enemy.'[67]

Churchill in Moscow

As the Germans approached Stalingrad, Winston Churchill arrived in Moscow in August with some bad news: there was to be no second front in Europe in 1942. Coming on top of Churchill's earlier announcement that because of high losses Britain was suspending its Arctic supply convoys to Russia, this was a bitter blow to Stalin. It meant there was no immediate prospect of relief from German pressure on the Eastern Front.

Stalin had been pressing Churchill for a second front since the beginning of the war. In Britain, the United States and other allied countries the Comintern had mounted a massive campaign for the opening of a second front in France. When Molotov travelled to London and Washington in May–June 1942 one of his main missions was to secure an Anglo-American commitment to open a second front as soon as possible. The outcome was an Anglo-Soviet communiqué on 12 June stating that 'full understanding had been reached on the urgent task of creating a Second Front in Europe in 1942'.[68] This declaration was repeated in a Soviet–American communiqué published that same day.[69] This wording, which was included in both communiqués on Stalin's insistence,[70] generated expectations that a second front in France would indeed be opened in 1942. A *Pravda* editorial of 13 June hailed the declaration as a significant strengthening of the anti-Hitler coalition and called for 1942 to be the year of 'the final defeat of the Hitlerite hordes'.[71] On 18 June Molotov reported to the Supreme Soviet on the results of his trip to Britain and the United States. Molotov said the declaration had 'great importance for the people of the Soviet Union since the creation of a second front will constitute insuperable difficulties for the Hitlerite armies on our front. We hope that our common enemy will soon feel the full weight of the growing military co-operation of the three great powers' – a statement that was greeted with prolonged, stormy applause, according to the official record.[72] In private, however, Molotov was more pessimistic about the prospects for a second front. In agreeing to the declaration the British had entered the caveat that while they were 'making preparations for a landing on the Continent in August or September 1942 . . . we can . . . give no promise in the matter, but provided that it appears sound and sensible, we shall not hesitate to put our plans into effect'. In conversation with Molotov, Churchill had made it plain that this meant at best the landing of six divisions on the Continent, to be followed by a much larger invasion in 1943. Molotov's conclusion in his report to Stalin was that 'the British Government is not undertaking any obligation to open the second front this year, but is saying, and with reservation at that, that it is preparing a trial landing operation'.[73]

When Molotov submitted this report, Stalin was still hoping for a substantial military advance in 1942, notwithstanding the setbacks at Kharkov and in the Crimea. In that context any commitment on the Second Front was welcome: at best, it would happen and contribute to rolling back the Wehrmacht on the Eastern Front by drawing forces to the west; at worst, the threat would deter Hitler from redeploying too many troops from Western Europe. In any event, Stalin believed a public commitment to a second front would add to the political pressure on western governments to go ahead with such an operation. By mid-July, however, the situation on the Eastern Front had deteriorated drastically and Stalin now saw the Second Front as a critical factor in the military equation. The further the Germans advanced in the south the more urgent became Soviet diplomatic efforts to persuade the western allies to implement their promise to open a second front.[74] On 23 July Stalin himself wrote to Churchill that concerning the 'opening of a second front in Europe, I fear the matter is taking an improper turn. In view of the situation on the Soviet–German front, I state most emphatically that the Soviet Government cannot tolerate the second front in Europe being postponed to 1943.'[75] Churchill responded by suggesting a personal meeting at which he could talk to Stalin about Anglo-American plans for military action in 1942. Stalin agreed to meet Churchill but asked the Prime Minister to come to Moscow because neither he nor members of his General Staff could possibly leave the capital at such a critical time.[76]

The prospects for the meeting were not very promising. In the weeks before Churchill's arrival in Moscow Soviet spies in Britain and the United States reported that the Anglo-Americans would not open a second front in Europe in 1942 and were instead planning a major military operation in North Africa.[77] A similarly pessimistic picture was evident in reports from Stalin's ambassador to the United States, Maksim Litvinov, who wrote that while Roosevelt favoured a second front in France, Churchill was opposed to the idea and had persuaded the President of the merits of action in North Africa instead.[78]

On 7 August Ivan Maiskii, Soviet ambassador in London, submitted to Stalin a briefing on the purposes of Churchill's trip to Moscow. These were threefold, wrote Maiskii. First, to pacify public agitation in Britain for a second front. Second, and more positively, to discuss a unified allied strategy to defeat Germany. Third, to convince Stalin that a second front in Europe in 1942 was both impossible and undesirable. Churchill, according to Maiskii, was not confident about the prospects for British military success anywhere and the succession of defeats suffered by Britain in North Africa and the Far East had had a negative impact on his attitude. Maiskii also addressed an issue that continued to trouble Stalin: were the British hoping for a weakening of both Germany *and* the Soviet Union? Yes, said Maiskii, but bourgeois Britain, especially Churchill, feared a Nazi victory and was looking for ways to assist the Soviet Union short of a second front. In conclusion Maiskii argued that since it was unlikely that Churchill's position on the Second Front could be changed, the Soviet side should concentrate on 'second-line' demands, such as increased supplies, and use the visit to begin 'forging a single allied strategy, without which victory would be inconceivable'.[79]

Churchill arrived in Moscow on 12 August, accompanied by Averell Harriman, Roosevelt's lend-lease co-ordinator in London, who had been added to the Prime Minister's party at the President's request. The two had their first meeting with Stalin that same evening.[80] The meeting began with an exchange of views on the military situation. Churchill spoke of the situation in Egypt, while Stalin said that

The news was not good and that the Germans were making a tremendous effort to get to Baku and Stalingrad. He did not know how they had been able to get together so many troops and tanks and so many Hungarian, Italian and Romanian divisions. He was sure they had drained the whole of Europe of troops. In Moscow the position was sound, but he could not guarantee in advance that the Russians would be able to withstand a German attack.

Churchill asked if the Germans would be able to mount a fresh offensive at Voronezh or in the north. Stalin replied that 'in view of the length of the front it was quite possible for Hitler to dispatch 20 divisions and create a strong attacking force'.[81] The discussion then turned to the issue of the Second Front. Churchill explained that it would not be possible to invade France across the Pas-de-Calais in 1942 because there were not enough landing craft to undertake such an operation against a fortified coast. According to the American interpreter's report of the meeting, Stalin began 'to look very glum' and suggested various alternatives, such as an invasion of the Channel Islands. Churchill argued that such actions would do more harm than good and would use up resources that could be better deployed in 1943. Stalin contested Churchill's assessment of German strength in France but the British Prime Minister insisted the 'war was war but not folly, and it would be folly to invite a disaster that would help nobody'. By this time Stalin 'had become restless' and said that 'his view about war was different. A man not prepared to take risks could not win a war.' Stalin further opined that the British and Americans 'should not be so afraid of the Germans' and that they tended to overestimate German strength. Stalin said 'his experience showed that troops must be blooded in battle. If you did not blood your troops you had no idea of their value.' After further exchanges on the possibility of landings in France the conversation turned to the allied bombing campaign over Germany. Here the two leaders found some common ground. Stalin hoped that the population would be bombed as well as the industry as this was the only way to break German morale. Churchill heartily agreed:

As regards the civil population, we looked upon its morale as a military target. We sought no mercy and would show no mercy . . . If need be, as the war went on, we hoped to shatter almost every dwelling in almost every German city.

According to the American report of the conversation, Churchill's 'words had a very stimulating effect upon the meeting, and thenceforward the atmosphere became progressively more cordial'.

Churchill then told Stalin about Operation Torch – the Anglo-American invasion of French North Africa planned for October–November 1942. The aim of Torch was to secure a position from which to attack German and Italian forces in Tunisia and Libya, an operation that would be co-ordinated with a thrust by the British 8th Army from Egypt. To illustrate the value of the operation Churchill drew for Stalin a picture of a crocodile and said that rather than attacking the hard snout of the beast in northern France the Anglo-American intention was to attack its soft underbelly in the Mediterranean. Stalin could be forgiven for thinking that the crocodile's hard snout was pointed at the Eastern Front and that the Red Army was already doing battle with it. As to Torch, Stalin already knew a lot about it from his own sources but he affected great interest and support for the operation. He was concerned that it might antagonise the French but saw four 'outstanding' advantages: (1) it would attack the enemy in the rear; (2) it would make the Germans and French fight each other; (3) it would put Italy out of operation; and (4) it would keep the Spaniards neutral.

By the next day Stalin's enthusiasm for Torch had waned somewhat.[82] He told Churchill and Harriman that while Torch was correct militarily it did not directly concern the Soviet Union. As far as the Second Front was concerned the problem was that for the British and Americans the Russian front was of secondary importance, whereas it was of primary importance for the Soviet government. Stalin then complained about the British and Americans' failure to fulfil their promises of supplies to the Soviet Union and suggested they needed to make higher sacrifices in view of the 10,000 men each day being sacrificed on the Russian front. Churchill responded that it grieved him that the Russians did not think the western allies were doing enough for the common cause. Stalin replied:

> It was not a case of mistrust, but only of a divergence of view. His view was that it should be possible for the British and Americans to land six or eight divisions on the Cherbourg Peninsula, since they had domination of the air. He felt that if the British Army had been fighting the Germans as much as the Russian Army, it would not be so frightened of them. The Russians, and indeed the RAF, had shown that it was possible to beat the Germans. The British infantry could do the same provided they acted at the same time as the Russians.

Stalin also presented Churchill and Harriman with a memorandum which claimed that Soviet military plans for summer and autumn operations had been calculated on the basis of the opening of a second front in Europe in 1942.[83]

On 15 August Churchill met Stalin again, this time without Harriman. It proved to be a much more intimate and friendly encounter than the first two meetings and spilled over into a private dinner in Stalin's Kremlin apartment.[84] Stalin pushed a little more on the Second Front issue suggesting that, if Torch succeeded, the allies would need to occupy southern France as well, a point which Churchill readily conceded. But the main focus of the conversation was on other matters. Of particular interest was Stalin's highly optimistic briefing of Churchill about the situation on the Eastern Front. The Germans, said Stalin, were invading in two streams – one towards the Caucasus and another towards Voronezh and Stalingrad:

> The front had been broken, the enemy had achieved success, but he had not sufficient power to develop it ... They expected to break through to Stalingrad, but they failed to reach the Volga. [He] thought that they would not succeed in reaching it. At Voronezh they wanted to get through to Elets and Riazan, thus turning the Moscow front. Here they had also failed ... At Rzhev the Russians had straightened out the line somewhat and Rzhev would be taken very shortly. Then the Russians would move in a southerly direction in order to cut off Smolensk. At Voronezh the Germans had been driven across the Don. The Russians had large reserves ... north of Stalingrad, and he hoped to undertake an offensive shortly in two directions: (a) towards Rostov, and (b) in a more southerly direction ... The object would be to cut off the enemy forces in the Northern Caucasia ... He concluded by saying that Hitler had not the strength to undertake an offensive on more than one sector of the front at any one time.

At dinner Stalin and Churchill discussed the possibility of a joint operation against northern Norway in order to protect British convoy routes to Murmansk[85] and also exchanged views on the future of Germany. Churchill thought that Prussian militarism and Nazism would have to be destroyed and Germany disarmed after the war, while Stalin said Germany's military cadres would have to be liquidated and the country weakened by detaching the Ruhr. Stalin asked about rumours of an Anglo-German pact not to bomb Berlin or London, which Churchill denied, saying that the bombing would resume when the nights got longer.[86] Churchill said that Maiskii was a good ambassador, but Stalin thought he could be better: 'he spoke too much and could not keep his tongue between his teeth'. Churchill talked about his prewar plan for a 'League of the three Great Democracies: Great Britain, United States and the USSR, which between them could lead the world'. Stalin agreed, and said it would have been a good idea, but for Chamberlain's government. By the end of dinner the text of a joint communiqué on Churchill's visit had been drawn up and signed photographs exchanged by the two leaders. As the British interpreter's report concluded, 'the whole atmosphere was most cordial and friendly'.

After Churchill left Moscow, Molotov wrote to Maiskii, briefing him on the outcome of the visit. 'The negotiations with Churchill were not entirely smooth,' Molotov told Maiskii, but were 'followed by an extensive conversation in Comrade Stalin's private residence, making for a close personal rapport with the guest ... Even though Churchill failed to come up with a satisfactory response on the main question [of the Second Front], the results can nevertheless be regarded as satisfactory.' On a less positive note Molotov informed Maiskii that 'your idea of working out a unified strategy was not discussed. It seems to me that at this stage, when we are the only party at war, this idea is unacceptable to us. You should not put forward this idea to the British. You have not received, and could not have received, such directions from us.'[87]

Throughout his conversations with Churchill and Harriman, Stalin stressed that the controversy over the Second Front was a disagreement between allies, not a matter of bad faith or lack of trust, notwithstanding disputes over supplies or other issues. The personal meeting between the two of them, Stalin told Churchill, was of great significance. Stalin also made it plain to Harriman that he was keen to meet Roosevelt as soon as possible.[88] Stalin's attitude soon soured, however, when the growing crisis at Stalingrad magnified the impact of the absence of a second front in France. Stalin's growing impatience with his allies came to a head publicly on 3 October when he chose to reply to written questions submitted by Henry Cassidy, Associated Press correspondent in Moscow:

Question: What place does the possibility of a Second Front occupy in Soviet estimates of the current situation?

Answer: A very important place: one might say a place of first-rate importance.

Question: To what extent is Allied aid to the Soviet Union proving effective, and what could be done to amplify and improve this aid?

Answer: As compared with the aid which the Soviet Union is giving to the Allies by drawing upon itself the main forces of the German-fascist armies, the aid of the Allies to the Soviet Union has so far been little effective. In order to amplify and improve this aid only one thing is required: that the Allies fulfill their obligations completely and on time.[89]

Stalin's public criticism caused a sensation in the British and American press[90] and signalled that he had given up on a second front for the time being and was now prioritising the issue of supplies. This was consonant with his private communications with the British and Americans which emphasised, above all, the urgent need for aircraft.[91] Stalin returned to the question of the Second Front in his speech on the 25th anniversary of the Bolshevik Revolution on 6 November 1942. He told his audience in Moscow that the absence of a second front in Europe explained the Germans' current military success in Russia since they had been able to concentrate all their reserves on the Eastern Front. Had a second front been launched, the Red Army would now be near Pskov, Minsk, Zhitomir and Odessa and 'the German-fascist army would already have been on the verge of disaster'.[92] Stalin's critique of western policy on the Second Front was repeated in countless newspaper articles and editorials and seems to have been broadly shared by the Soviet public, if NKVD reports on popular opinion are to be believed.[93]

This tension in the Grand Alliance about the Second Front coincided with an inter-allied controversy about the trial and punishment of war criminals. In early October the Soviets were invited by the British and Americans to participate in a war crimes commission. But before Moscow could reply to the invitation the British publicly announced a plan for the *postwar* punishment of war criminals. In response Molotov issued a statement on 'the responsibility of the Hitlerite invaders and their accomplices for the crimes committed by them in the occupied countries of Europe'.[94] The substance of the statement, published on 14 October, was a demand that Nazi leaders apprehended during the war should be arraigned before an international tribunal, not least Rudolf Hess, Hitler's former deputy, who had been languishing in prison since his dramatic flight to Britain in May 1941. On 19 October *Pravda* published an editorial calling for Hess to be tried as a war criminal and commented that 'to recognise that Hess will not be brought to trial until the end of the war, that he will be spared trial by an international tribunal for the whole period of the war, means closing one's eyes to the crimes of one of the bloodiest Hitlerite criminals and looking upon Hess not as a criminal, but as the representative of another state, as Hitler's envoy'.[95]

The war crimes controversy formed the backdrop to an extraordinary telegram from Stalin to Maiskii that same day:

All of us in Moscow have formed the impression that Churchill is intent on the defeat of the USSR in order to then come to terms with . . . Hitler . . . at our expense. Without such a supposition it is difficult to explain Churchill's conduct on the question of the Second Front in Europe, on the question of arms supplies to the USSR, which are progressively reducing, despite the growth in production in England, on the question of Hess, whom Churchill seems to be holding in reserve, on the question of the systematic bombing of Berlin by the English in September, which Churchill proclaimed he would do in Moscow and which he did not fulfil one iota, despite the fact that he could undoubtedly do it.[96]

Maiskii replied to Stalin on 23 October, pointing out that a German victory over the USSR would hardly be welcomed by Churchill since it would leave Hitler dominating not only Europe but Africa and the greater part of Asia, too. There were British advocates of the defeat of the USSR and a deal with Hitler, but they did not enjoy great influence at the present time. Churchill's faults Maiskii ascribed to the fact that he wanted an 'easy war'. Supplies were being reduced because of the demands of Torch. Churchill didn't bomb Berlin because he feared retaliation against London. Hess was not tried because the Germans might retaliate by taking repressive measures against British POWs. Besides, concluded Maiskii, Churchill thought the war would last a long time and Hess might prove to be useful one day.[97] Stalin responded to Maiskii on 28 October:

I still think that as a proponent of an easy war Churchill is easily influenced by those pursing the defeat of the Soviet Union, since the defeat of our country and a compromise with Germany at the expense of the Soviet Union is the easiest form of war between England and Germany.

Of course, the English will later understand that without the Russian front and with France out of action they, the English, are doomed to destruction. But when will they understand this? We will see . . .

Churchill told us in Moscow that by spring 1943 about a million Anglo-American troops would have opened a second front in Europe. But Churchill belongs, it seems, among those leaders who easily make promises in order to forget them or break them. He also promised in Moscow to bomb Berlin intensively in September–October. However, he has not fulfilled his promise and has not even tried to inform Moscow of the motives for non-fulfilment. Well, from now on we will know what kind of allies we are dealing with.

I have little faith in Operation 'Torch'. If, contrary to expectations, the operation finishes successfully, one could reconcile oneself to the fact that aircraft are being taken away from us for the sake of the operation.[98]

Stalin was plainly rattled – by the absence of a second front, by shortages of supplies, by the Hess affair, by the suspicion that many of his so-called allies would like to see the Germans win. Above all, Stalin was feeling the strain of the battle of Stalingrad. Even now the Red Army was preparing a great counter-offensive to defeat the enemy in the Stalingrad area. That action did not depend on holding Stalingrad; strategically the important thing was to keep the Germans at bay along the flanks of the city. But the loss of the city itself would be a devastating blow to Soviet morale, and to Stalin personally. Emotionally and politically he had invested as heavily in the defence of the 'city of Stalin' as Hitler had in its capture.

Siege at Stalingrad

The siege of Stalingrad began with massive air raids on 23 August 1942. For two days the Luftwaffe pounded the city, flying 2,000 sorties and killing at least 25,000 civilians. General Wolfram von Richthofen, head of the Luftwaffe's 8th Air Corps flew over the battered city, noting in his diary that Stalingrad was 'destroyed and without further worthwhile targets'.[99] The day after the air raids began advance units of General Fredrich Paulus's 6th Army reached the Volga at Rynok and Spartakanovka in the northern suburbs of the city. However, the main body of Paulus's forces did not reach the outskirts of central Stalingrad until early September. South of the city Herman Hoth's 4th Panzer Army – now redeployed from the Caucasus campaign to attack Stalingrad – didn't reach the Volga at Kuporosnoye until 10 September but when they did the Soviet defenders were cut off in all directions except east across the Volga.

Defending the city were the 62nd Army in the centre and north of Stalingrad and the 64th Army in the southern suburbs. But they had been separated from each other by the German advance to the Volga. According to Soviet figures, along the 40-mile front of Stalingrad and its environs the Germans deployed 13 enemy divisions, with about 170,000 men, 500 tanks, 3,000 artillery pieces and 1,000 aeroplanes. Facing them was a Soviet force of 90,000, with 2,000 artillery pieces, 120 tanks and fewer than 400 planes.[100]

At first Stalin was confident that he could defend Stalingrad. The city had been preparing for siege since early July and Stavka reserves were flooding into the area. Between mid-July and the end of September Stavka transferred 50 divisions and 33 independent brigades to the Stalingrad area. Among the reinforcements were a number of crack divisions from the Far Eastern command and 100,000 sailors from the navy.[101] On 23 August Stalin issued a directive to Yeremenko stating that the enemy forces breaking through on his front were not very strong and that he had enough strength to deal with them. He was urged to attack the enemy with all his planes and artillery and to harass the enemy day and night. 'The main thing,' said Stalin, 'is not to give in to panic, not to be afraid of the impudence of the enemy and to maintain confidence in our success.'[102] The next day Stalin sent a further directive, ordering Yeremenko to plug gaps in Soviet defences and throw back the Germans from Stalingrad.[103] But Stalin had also learned some caution by now and on 25 August he sent a message to Vasilevskii and Malenkov – visiting Stalingrad as Stavka representatives – to ask them if they thought the 62nd and 64th Armies should be withdrawn to a line along the eastern Don.[104] On 26 August Zhukov was recalled to Moscow and appointed Deputy Supreme Commander.[105] He, too, was sent to Stalingrad to report on the situation. By early September Stalin's confidence was beginning to wane and on the 3rd he instructed Zhukov:

> The situation is getting worse. The enemy is [two miles] from Stalingrad. They can take Stalingrad today or tomorrow . . . Get the commanders of the troops to the north and north-west of Stalingrad to attack the enemy without delay . . . No delay can be tolerated. Delay at this moment is equivalent to a crime. Throw in all aircraft to help Stalingrad. In Stalingrad itself there is very little aviation left.[106]

On 9 September Stavka appointed General Vasilii Chuikov to command the 62nd Army.[107] When Chuikov took over he had about 54,000 troops, 900 artillery pieces and 110 tanks, while Paulus had about twice that strength deployed in the city. Despite being outgunned and outnumbered, it was Chuikov's forces that saved Stalingrad from complete German occupation, although the 63rd, 64th and 66th Armies operating on the flanks of the city also made an indispensable contribution to the defensive battle.

Stalingrad was a long, narrow city that stretched for 30–40 miles along the west bank of the Volga and was divided into three mains sections. In the south was the old town, which bordered on the city's railway stations and the central landing-stage river dock area. In the central section was a modern city centre with wide boulevards, department stores, civic buildings and public amenities. The north of the city was dominated by three huge factories along the river front: the Dzerzhinsky tractor factory (converted during the war to tank production); the Barrikady ordnance works and the Krasnii Oktyabr (Red October) metal plant. The southern section of the city was bisected by the Tsaritsa River (from which derived the city's original name, Tsaritsyn, changed to Stalingrad in 1924 in honour of Stalin's defence of the city during the Russian civil war). The city centre was dominated by a 300-foot hill, Mamayev Kurgan.

In tactical terms the battle for the city was all about control of the riverbank. While the Red Army occupied the riverbank its forces fighting in Stalingrad could be resupplied from the east across the Volga. If the Germans were able to seize control of the riverbank they could liquidate the Soviet bridgehead within the city.

The battle within the city unfolded in four main phases (*see Map 9 on p. 146*).[108] In the first phase, which began on 13 September, the battle concentrated in the south and centre of the city. German aims were to seize control of the city south of the Tsaritsa, to occupy the central landing stage and to split the 62nd Army in two. North of the Tsaritsa the German aims were to occupy the city centre and to capture Mamayev Kurgan. By 26 September Paulus was able to declare that the south and centre of the city had been won. However, whilst the central landing stage was under fire the Germans did not securely occupy it. Similarly, the high ground of Mamayev Kurgan – which consists of several lower peaks as well as the main hill – remained contested territory.

During the second phase of the battle, from 27 September to 7 October, the fight for Mamayev Kurgan continued but the main struggle was waged in the north for control of the factory district. Again the Germans made considerable progress but failed to take the factories or to occupy the crucial river frontage on the west bank of the Volga.

Stalin's increasing anxiety about the tenability of the Soviet position in the city was expressed in an angry directive to Yeremenko on 5 October:

> I think that you do not see the danger threatening the forces of the Stalingrad front. Occupying the city centre and advancing towards the Volga in northern Stalingrad the enemy intends . . . to surround the 62nd Army and take it prisoner and then to surround the 64th Army in the south and take it prisoner. The enemy can accomplish this aim if they can occupy the Volga crossings in the north, centre and south of Stalingrad. To prevent this danger it is necessary to drive the enemy back from the Volga and to occupy the streets and buildings that the enemy has taken from you. To do this it is necessary to turn every street and every building in Stalingrad into a fortress. Unfortunately, you have not managed to do this and continued to give up to the enemy block after block. This speaks of your bad work. The forces you have in the Stalingrad area are greater than those of the enemy, in spite of which the enemy continued to squeeze you out. I am not pleased with your work on the Stalingrad front and demand that you take every measure to defend Stalingrad. Stalingrad must not be yielded to the enemy and every part of Stalingrad occupied by the enemy must be liberated.[109]

Despite Stalin's exhortations, the Red Army was forced to yield yet more ground in the third phase of the battle, which began on 14 October with a renewed assault on the factory district. By the end of the month the Germans had taken the tractor factory and the Barrikady and most of Red October.

The Battle for Stalingrad, September–November 1942

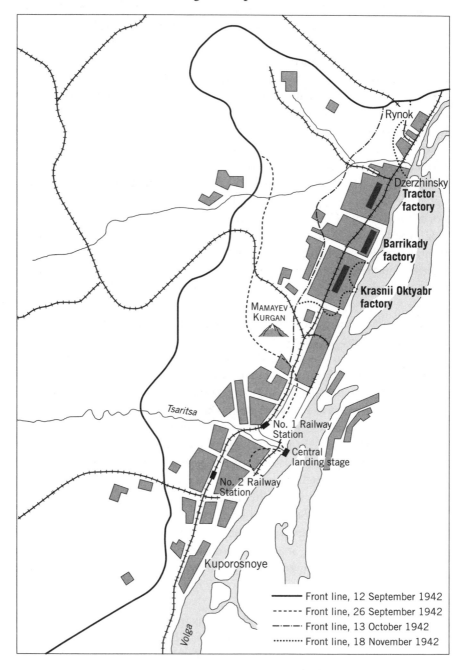

Rynok

Dzerzhinsky
**Tractor
factory**

**Barrikady
factory**

**Krasnii Oktyabr
factory**

MAMAYEV
KURGAN

Tsaritsa

No. 1 Railway
Station

Central
landing stage

No. 2 Railway
Station

Kuporosnoye

Volga

——— Front line, 12 September 1942
------ Front line, 26 September 1942
—·—·— Front line, 13 October 1942
·········· Front line, 18 November 1942

Chuikov's forces were squeezed into a long strip on the west side of the Volga that in places was only hundreds of yards across.

Finally, on 11 November Paulus launched his last major attack in Stalingrad. Again the target was the factory district and the Germans achieved some success in breaking through to the Volga, occupying another section of the west bank of the river, thereby splitting the 62nd Army into three. By mid-November the Germans occupied more than 90 per cent of Stalingrad, but, crucially, Chuikov's troops remained entrenched in a 16-mile-long strip along the Volga's west bank. As long as the Red Army held this bridgehead the Germans could not claim total victory at Stalingrad and remained endangered by a Soviet counterattack. Paulus had also exhausted his forces in getting thus far and the 6th Army was in no condition to mount further offensive action. By hanging on in Stalingrad, by avoiding complete defeat, Chuikov effectively won the strategic battle for control of the city.

Chuikov's success was based on three main factors. First, his employment of some effective street-fighting tactics that involved not only the ferocious defence of fortified positions in the city's rubble but taking the fight to the enemy in hundreds of small battles in the ruined factories and buildings of Stalingrad. The offensive spirit of the Red Army proved to be alive and well at Stalingrad. Second, there was constant resupply from across the Volga. Particularly important were troop reinforcements. Among the units sent across the river was the ill-fated 13th Guards Division commanded by A.I. Rodimtsev. 'Guards' divisions were elite formations, experienced and proven in combat, better paid, and, generally, better supplied. The 13th crossed the Volga on 14 and 15 September and went straight into action in the city centre. On its first day in action the 10,000-strong division suffered 30 per cent casualties, one reason being that many of the men had been sent across the river without ammunition.[110] By the end of the battle for Stalingrad the division had only 320 survivors. In his memoirs Chuikov wrote that 'had it not been for Rodimtsev's division the city would have fallen completely into enemy hands approximately in the middle of September'.[111] Third, there was the air and artillery support for the defenders of Stalingrad. Images of the battle tend to be dominated by pictures of the street and factory fighting, but as important was the fire rained down on the Germans by batteries of Soviet artillery on the eastern bank of the Volga and the contest for air superiority in the skies above Stalingrad.

There was also another reason for the Soviet success at Stalingrad and this was the reason that seemed most obvious to contemporary observers, at least in the allied world: the Red Army's heroic defence of the city. During the course of the battle Chuikov's forces suffered 75 per cent casualties yet the 62nd Army's will to resist did not crack. The Soviet and allied public marvelled at the Red Army's resilience, but were not particularly surprised by it: Stalingrad was the latest in a long line of heroic defences by the Red Army. What was different about this battle was its prolonged and public character as it was played out daily in the pages of western and Soviet newspapers between August and November 1942. Naturally, Soviet propagandists went to great lengths to talk up the Red Army's feats at Stalingrad, and to feed this image of heroism back to those fighting in the city. The legend of heroic Stalingrad was rooted in real heroics but it was amplified by the media coverage. No wonder that for decades afterwards Stalingrad stood as a symbol for do or die defence.

Of course, it wasn't all heroic acts. At Stalingrad, as elsewhere, Stalin's unforgiving and relentless disciplinary regime played its role in steadying the line. Throughout the battle the NKVD submitted reports on its activities in Stalingrad. One report recorded the following incident that took place on 21 September:

> Today, during a breakthrough attack by the enemy, two units of the 13th Guards Division wavered and began to retreat. The commander of one of these units, Lieutenant Mirolubov, also panicked, and ran from the field of battle, leaving his unit. The blocking detachment of the 62nd Army detained the retreating units and stabilized the position. Lieutenant Mirolubov was shot in front of the men.[112]

During the course of the battle the NKVD units in the city and its environs examined the documents of 750,000 people, as a result of which they detained 2,500 deserters and 255 enemy spies, diversionists and parachutists.[113] According to another NKVD summary report, its units operating in the Don and Stalingrad Front areas detained, in the period from 1 August to 15 October, more than 40,000 people: 900 were arrested, 700 shot, 1,300 sent to penal battalions, and the rest returned to their units.[114] However, at Stalingrad even the NKVD was heroic. As well as carrying out its security and counter-intelligence activities, the NKVD was in the thick of the fighting and took a high number of casualties. Its operatives also penetrated enemy lines and committed numerous acts of sabotage.[115]

'Mars', 'Saturn', 'Jupiter' and 'Uranus'

All through the battle in Stalingrad, Stavka had been planning and preparing its riposte. This came on 19 November with the launch of a combined counter-offensive by the Stalingrad, Don and South-Western Fronts. The Stalingrad and Don Fronts had been formed on 28 September when Yeremenko's South-Eastern Front was renamed the Stalingrad Front and

Rokossovskii took command of the old Stalingrad Front, which was renamed the Don Front. The South-Western Front, adjacent to the Don Front, had been set up on 31 October under General Vatutin's command.[116] The basic idea of Operation Uranus was to encircle the enemy at Stalingrad by the armies of all three fronts advancing towards and converging on Kalach (*see Map 10 on p. 150*).

The counter-offensive was prepared in the utmost secrecy and a number of *maskirovka* (deception and disinformation) measures were put into effect.[117] Frontline areas were cleared of civilians[118] and the main assault forces were not deployed until the last moment. Moreover, as the Russian historian V.V. Veshanov has put it, 'this time Stalin did not hurry his commanders, the operation was prepared carefully and efficiently'.[119] To secure the necessary attack forces and reserves, other fronts and armies were placed on the defensive or told to make do with what they had.[120] By mid-November Stavka had assembled an attack force of three-quarters of a million.

Operation Uranus was a stunning success. By 23 November the encirclement of Paulus's forces in Stalingrad was complete. Stavka had expected to trap 100,000 or so enemy troops. In the event, they caught three times that number and Uranus represented the Red Army's first successful grand encirclement manoeuvre. Among the enemy forces pulverised during the encirclement operation were the armies of Germany's Axis allies whose task was to guard Paulus's flanks. After the event the Germans attempted to lay the blame for the débâcle on the weaknesses of their allies, but the Romanians, Hungarians and Italians had been starved of resources by the Wehrmacht and had been given the impossible task of guarding vast swathes of open country with no reserves to counter any enemy breakthroughs.[121]

The origins of Uranus are somewhat contentious. As the Russian proverb has it, while failure is an orphan, success has many fathers. The most widely accepted claim to paternity is that of Zhukov, who wrote in his memoirs that he and Vasilevskii came up with the idea and proposed it to Stalin on 13 September 1942. Vasilevskii subsequently supported Zhukov's account, in his memoirs, although he did not specify a date or repeat Zhukov's dramatic presentation of Stalin as being persuaded to adopt a radical, new plan.[122] However, according to Stalin's appointments diary he had no meetings with Zhukov between 31 August and 26 September. Stalin did meet Vasilevskii during this period but not on any date between 9 and 21 September.[123] Given the number of other dubious claims in his memoirs, it is likely that Zhukov's story is an invention. That is not to say Zhukov was not one of the authors of Operation Uranus. He was, after all, Stalin's deputy and he worked closely with Vasilevskii who, as Chief of Staff, was responsible for drafting the operational plan. Both Zhukov and Vasilevskii spent a lot of

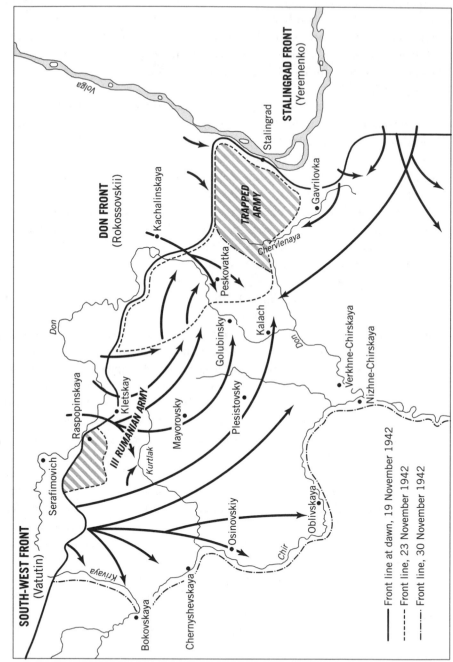

Operation Uranus, November 1942

SOUTH-WEST FRONT
(Vatutin)

DON FRONT
(Rokossovskii)

STALINGRAD FRONT
(Yeremenko)

TRAPPED ARMY

III RUMANIAN ARMY

Volga

Don

Don

Chir

Krivaya

Kurtlak

Chervlenaya

Stalingrad

Gavrilovka

Kachalinskaya

Peskovatka

Kalach

Golubinsky

Plesistovsky

Verkhne-Chirskaya

Nizhne-Chirskaya

Osinovskiy

Oblivskaya

Mayorovsky

Kletskay

Raspopinskaya

Serafimovich

Bokovskaya

Chernyshevskaya

———— Front line at dawn, 19 November 1942

------- Front line, 23 November 1942

-·-·-·- Front line, 30 November 1942

time in the Stalingrad area during the battle and had much first-hand knowledge to contribute.

So the detailed genealogy of Operation Uranus remains unclear but it is likely that it evolved from various plans and ideas to relieve the pressure on the defenders of Stalingrad by attacking the Germans on their flanks. Such counter-offensive thinking and planning was standard operating procedure for the Red Army by this time. At any rate, by early October a decision on a major counter-offensive at Stalingrad had been taken and the Fronts were asked to draw up detailed plans of action.[124]

Another controversy about Operation Uranus concerns its relationship to another offensive – Operation Mars. This was an attack against Army Group Centre by the Kalinin and Western Fronts that aimed to encircle the German 9th Army in the Rzhev salient. Mars was initially scheduled to start before Uranus but because of the weather and other factors was delayed until 25 November. While the forces allocated to Mars were equivalent to those given to Uranus, it was not a great success. By the end of December the operation had been called off, with little to show for the effort but 350,000 Soviet casualties, including 100,000 dead.

In his memoirs Zhukov presented Operation Mars as a largely successful supporting operation to Uranus, designed to make sure that troops from Army Group Centre were not redeployed in the south.[125] Although this account has been accepted by most Russian military historians, in his book *Zhukov's Greatest Defeat*, the American historian David Glantz argued that Mars was the Deputy Supreme Commander's preferred operation and that it was intended to be followed up by another operation called Jupiter or Neptune – a plan for the grand encirclement and destruction of Army Group Centre.[126] Jupiter, in Glantz's view, was a projected companion to Operation Saturn in the south, itself the follow-up to Uranus that aimed to retake Rostov and cut off Army Group A in the Caucasus. As Stephen Walsh has put it, what Stavka had in mind was a breathtakingly 'cosmic strategic design'.[127] As a glance at the operational map shows (*see Map 11 on p. 152*) the planetary nomenclature of Mars–Saturn–Uranus–Jupiter can be seen as a metaphor for the encirclement operations envisaged: relatively small ones in the case of Mars and Uranus; gigantic encirclements in the case of Saturn and Jupiter. More prosaically Glantz and his co-author Jonathan House wrote that 'Soviet strategic aims had expanded far beyond the simple defeat of German forces in southern Russia: the Stavka sought to collapse enemy defences along virtually the entire Eastern Front'.[128] In other words, Mars–Saturn–Uranus–Jupiter was yet another of Stalin's grand designs to destroy the Wehrmacht in one fell swoop. Certainly, it was an ambition that would have appealed to Stalin.

'Mars', 'Jupiter', 'Saturn' and 'Uranus'

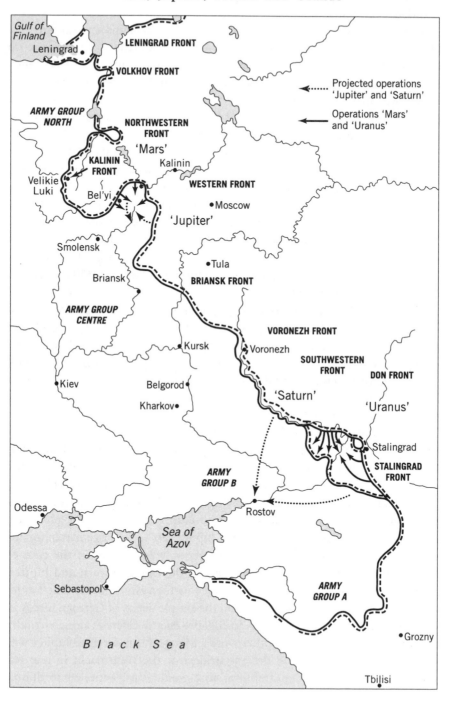

Indeed, even when Mars failed Stalin stuck to the idea of a major rollback of the German army across the Eastern Front.

As to Operation Mars it was probably not so much Zhukov's greatest defeat as his latest setback in the Rzhev–Viazma area. Mars was an operation that grew out of many previous efforts to make headway against Army Group Centre in that area. The difference was that Mars was much better resourced than earlier operations and was conceptually linked to Uranus as one prong of a dual offensive. This, in fact, was how the two operations were presented in the Soviet press until Mars failed and faded from the headlines.[129] Mars did not succeed because Army Group Centre was stronger and entrenched in better-prepared positions than were the German armies in the south; nor had it faced such a tough summer of campaigning. Despite its failure, Mars was a necessary adjunct to Uranus. Stavka could hardly ignore the strong German forces on its doorstep, particularly when Stalin, and probably Zhukov too, continued to believe the Soviet capital was Hitler's main target. As Mikhail Myagkov has argued,[130] from Stavka's point of view a strategic transformation in the south could turn out to be a temporary success if the central sector was not secure as well. Sooner or later the Red Army was going to have to deal with Army Group Centre.

Hitler's response to the encirclement of Paulus's forces in Stalingrad was twofold. First, there was an attempt to keep the 6th Army supplied by air. The problem was that the Luftwaffe needed to fly in 300 tons of supplies a day and it did not have enough planes to do that (half its transport aircraft were busy helping the retreating German armies in North Africa, reeling under the impact of Torch). The weather was also against the German airlift and in the skies above Stalingrad the Red Air Force was growing in strength.[131] Second, there was Operation Wintergewitter (Winter Storm), an attempt to break through to Stalingrad by Army Group Don, a special force set up for this purpose. Commanded by Field Marshal Eric von Manstein, the Germans made some progress but were stopped 25–30 miles short of Stalingrad and Paulus's troops were in no condition to fight their way out to meet them. In any case, Hitler decided that the 6th Army should stand and fight rather than conduct a risky and inglorious retreat. Like Stalin, Hitler saw the value of heroic defeats, particularly when there was little choice in the matter. An important side effect of Operation Wintergewitter was to force the Soviets to revise plans for Operation Saturn. Instead Stavka had to mount Operation Little Saturn to stop Manstein's manoeuvre.[132] Manstein was stopped but Rostov was not retaken until February 1943 – a delay that enabled Army Group A to escape from the Caucasus.

When the Soviets realised the full extent of the force they had trapped in Stalingrad they prepared a major operation to reduce the encirclement ring.

Seven Soviet armies, commanded by Rokossovskii, attacked on 10 January 1943. By the end of the month the battle was won and 90,000 Germans had surrendered. Among them was Paulus, one of 24 German generals at Stalingrad who went into Soviet captivity.

Meanwhile the Red Army had launched a general offensive in the southern sector: Voronezh was retaken on 26 January and Rostov on 14 February. The next day the Germans evacuated Kharkov (but in mid-March they counter-attacked and captured the city again). In early February a major offensive in the Orel, Briansk and Smolensk direction was launched. A few days later Operation Polar Star began – an attempt to lift the blockade of Leningrad. In his Order of the Day on 23 February 1943 Stalin bemoaned the fact that in 'absence of a Second Front in Europe, the Red Army alone bears the whole burden of the war' but claimed that the initiative was now firmly in Soviet hands: 'to-day, in hard winter conditions the Red Army is advancing over a front of 1,500 kilometres and is achieving successes practically every-where'.[133] This was true, but the Soviet advance soon ground to a halt in the *Rasputitsa*. Once again the Red Army's capabilities had not matched Stavka's ambitions and the Germans had proved surprisingly resilient in the wake of the devastating defeat at Stalingrad.

The Victories at Stalingrad and Kursk

While Stavka had failed to achieve its most ambitious goals, the victory at Stalingrad was spectacular enough. The Germans and their Axis allies suffered a million and a half casualties during the course of the 1942 southern campaign and gained nothing. A year after the launch of Operation Blau the Germans were back to the lines they had started from. Nearly 50 divisions had been lost, including the whole of the elite German 6th Army. In Stalingrad alone 150,000 Germans had perished. The armies of all Germany's European Axis allies, except Finland, had been shattered beyond repair. It was the begin-ning of the end for the Axis alliance in Europe, which was to disintegrate entirely in 1943–1944.[134] Resistance movements all over German-occupied Europe took heart from Hitler's defeat at Stalingrad. The psychological boost to Soviet and allied morale was immeasurable. Germany had suffered its first great defeat of the war and victory for the allies now seemed certain.

In retrospect Stalingrad has often been identified as *the* turning point of the war on the Eastern Front. At Stalingrad the Soviets seized the strategic initia-tive and never lost it. After Stalingrad, it was always a question of how and when the Germans would lose the war, no longer if and when. Apart from a last-ditch effort at Kursk in summer 1943 the Wehrmacht was in retreat all the way to Berlin.

Contemporary observers in the allied world were quick to grasp the significance of Stalingrad. In Britain the Soviet victory was hailed in the press as the salvation of European civilisation.[135] Writing in the *Washington Post* on 2 February 1943, Barnet Nover compared Stalingrad to the great battles of the First World War that had saved and delivered victory to the then allied alliance: 'Stalingrad's role in this war was that of the Battle of Marne, Verdun and the Second Marne rolled into one.'

According to the *New York Times* editorial on 4 February 1943:

Stalingrad is the scene of the costliest and most stubborn struggle in this war. The battle fought there to its desperate finish may turn out to be among the decisive battles in the long history of war . . . In the scale of its intensity, its destructiveness and its horror, Stalingrad has no parallel. It engaged the full strength of the two biggest armies in Europe and could fit into no lesser framework than that of a life-and-death conflict which encompasses the earth.

At the time the Soviets themselves had a more restrained view of the significance of Stalingrad. Naturally, the battle was hailed as a great victory,[136] but there were no triumphalist assertions that the war was won. The Soviet High Command knew that great though the victory was it had fallen far short of its hopes for a rout of the German armies across the Eastern Front. It had also been a very hard-won victory for the Soviets, with casualties far in excess of those publicly admitted. Soviet casualties during the course of the Germans' southern campaign were in the order of 2.5 million. These casualties came on top of the colossal losses of 1941, not to speak of the hundreds of thousands incurred elsewhere on the front in 1942. Moreover, Stalin and Stavka also believed that the decisive battle – against Army Group Centre – had yet to come. The road to Berlin lay along the relatively short central axis running through Smolensk, Minsk and Warsaw. While this route remained barred by still substantial German forces there could be no complacency about victory.

As its winter offensive ground to a halt in early spring 1943 Stavka considered its options for future operations. Following various meetings and consultations in March and April a consensus emerged that, for the immediate future, the Red Army should remain on the defensive. Stalin's willingness to countenance a defensive stance seems to have been influenced by three main factors. First, the disappointment that the post-Stalingrad operations had not made greater progress, indeed had been thrown back in a number of sectors, most notably in the Kharkov area. Second, Stavka lacked the reserves necessary to mount offensive operations immediately. On 1 March Stavka had only four reserve armies at its disposal, although by the end of the month this had risen to 10.[137] Third, the Germans' next target could be clearly identified as the outward bulge in the Soviet defensive line near the town of Kursk at the junction of the central and southern theatres of operation. This suggested the possibility of preparing for and absorbing a German attack and then launching a counter-offensive. An early proponent of this strategy was Zhukov, who wrote to Stalin on 8 April:

> The enemy, having sustained heavy losses over the 1942–43 winter campaign, will apparently be unable by spring to build up reserves sufficiently large for a new offensive aimed at seizing the Caucasus and reaching the Volga with the objective of widely enveloping Moscow. Because of limited reserves the enemy will be compelled . . . to open offensive operations on a narrower front and pursue strictly by stages his prime objective of taking Moscow. The present enemy confrontation of our Central, Voronezh and South-Western Fronts leads me to believe that the enemy will strike chiefly against those fronts with the aim of smashing us here in order to secure ground for freely manoeuvring and outflanking Moscow from as close as possible. In the initial stage the enemy is likely to strike in force . . . in a two-pronged movement to envelop Kursk . . . I believe it inexpedient for our forces to launch a preventative offensive in the next few days, it being more to our advantage to wear the enemy down in defensive action, and destroy his tanks. Subsequently by committing fresh reserves, we should assume an all-out offensive completely to destroy the main enemy grouping.[138]

By highlighting the threat to Moscow as well as advocating an all-out offensive at a later stage, Zhukov was pushing the right buttons with Stalin. According to the General Staff's Chief of Operations, S.M. Shtemenko, Stalin's response to Zhukov's proposal was to depart from his long-held principle of 'not being carried away by predictions about the enemy'.[139] He ordered a poll of the opinions of Front commanders and when they responded along much the same lines as Zhukov he was persuaded to prepare for a defensive battle in the Kursk area. In line with this view the main theme of Stalin's Order of the Day on 1 May 1943 was the need to consolidate the successes of the winter battles.[140]

The prediction that Kursk would be the Wehrmacht's next target was confirmed by intelligence reports of German intentions and preparations.[141] In fact, during May there were a number of premature reports of imminent German attack, which prompted Stavka to issue a series of alerts to its front commanders. The failure of the attack to materialise led some in the High Command to conclude that it wasn't coming and that the Red Army needed to take the initiative. One advocate of attack was General Vatutin, now back in command of the Voronezh front. 'We'll miss the boat, let the moment slip,' he reportedly told Vasilevskii. 'The enemy is not going to move, soon it will be autumn and all our plans will be ruined. Let's get off our backsides and begin first. We've enough forces for it.'[142] Zhukov and Vasilevskii managed to persuade Stalin to sit tight and wait for the German attack but the Supreme Commander was anxious about the defensive preparations, particularly the Red Army's ability to withstand a full-scale tank attack. Heightening the tension was the news from Churchill and Roosevelt in June that, although operations were continuing in the Mediterranean, there would definitely be no second front in France in 1943.[143]

The German attack at Kursk came on 4/5 July.[144] Their plan was to pinch out the Kursk salient by combined thrusts from Army Group Centre and the reconstituted Army Group South. Soviet forces trapped inside the encirclement manoeuvre would be destroyed and the Germans' defensive line shortened and consolidated. In effect what the Germans envisaged was a strategic battle of defence, which would wound the Red Army, regain the initiative in the central sector and enable the Wehrmacht to survive the war on the Eastern Front, for the time being at least.

Hitler committed to battle 18 infantry divisions, three motorised divisions and 17 panzer divisions, including large numbers of his new Tiger and Panther tanks, which outgunned anything the Soviets had in their arsenal. The German attack lasted about a week and climaxed in a mass tank battle on 11–12 July – the greatest of the Second World War, which resulted in the loss of hundreds of tanks on both sides. The Red Army's having survived the German attack meant that the defensive battle was won and Stavka now moved into attack mode (*see Map 12 on p. 158*). The Germans were pushed back from the Kursk area and then attacked at a number of other points along the Eastern Front. On 24 July Stalin publicly proclaimed that 'the German plan for a summer offensive can be considered as having failed completely . . . the legend that in a summer offensive the Germans are always successful, and that the Soviet troops are compelled to retreat, is refuted.'[145] Soon the Soviet counterattacks developed into a general offensive. Within a few weeks the Wehrmacht had been driven back to the River Dnepr along a broad front. Among the early reconquests of the Red Army were the cities of Orel and Belgorod in early August. Their recapture was marked by a 120-gun salute in Moscow, the first of 300 such salvoes ordered by Stalin during the remaining years of the war. As Alexander Werth says, the era of Victory Salutes had begun.[146] This was also the period when Stalin began to issue frequent Orders of the Day noting Soviet victories and awarding decorations to the successful commanders. In August Kharkov was retaken, followed by Smolensk in

The Battle of Kursk, July 1943

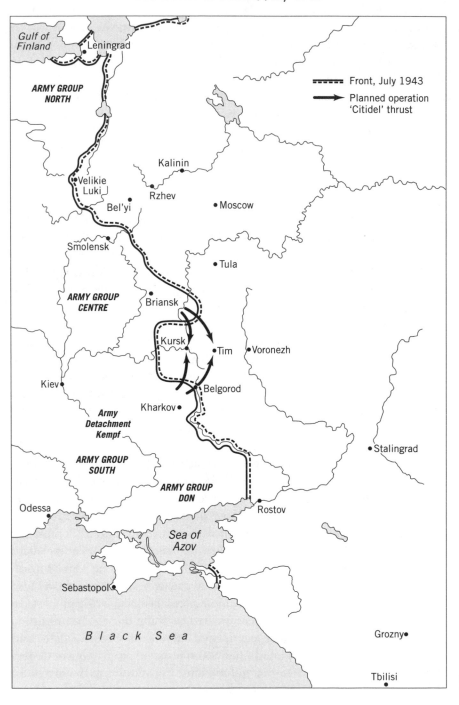

Gulf of Finland

Leningrad

ARMY GROUP NORTH

Front, July 1943

Planned operation 'Citidel' thrust

Kalinin

Velikie Luki

Rzhev

Bel'yi

Moscow

Smolensk

ARMY GROUP CENTRE

Briansk

Tula

Kursk

Tim

Voronezh

Kiev

Belgorod

Kharkov

Army Detachment Kempf

ARMY GROUP SOUTH

ARMY GROUP DON

Stalingrad

Odessa

Rostov

Sea of Azov

Sebastopol

B l a c k   S e a

Grozny

Tbilisi

September, and Kiev in November. By the end of 1943 the Red Army had liberated half the territory occupied by the Germans in 1941–1942. In his November 1943 speech Stalin summed up the year's campaigning as a 'radical turning point in the course of war' which meant that Nazi Germany now faced military and political catastrophe.

Stalin and his Generals

The two main architects of the victory at Kursk were Zhukov and Vasilevskii who, together with Antonov, the Deputy Chief of the General Staff, persuaded Stalin of the merits of a strategic pause in spring 1943. During the Kursk battle Vasilevskii was sent to co-ordinate the Voronezh and South-Western Fronts, while Zhukov looked after the Central, Briansk and Western Fronts. At the same time, Stalin was more inclined than ever to allow Front commanders to take the critical operational decisions and to ask their advice before making up his mind about the best course of action. For example, according to Shtemenko, Stalin thought the Front commanders during the Kursk battle were better placed than Stavka to take the decision about when to make the transition from defensive to offensive action.[147]

Stalin's relationship with his generals during the Kursk battle was illustrative of a broader transformation of relations within the Soviet High Command in 1942–1943. It is often said that Stalin became more willing to listen to professional military advice and to accept the judgement of his generals. The moral of the tale – derived from the memoirs of Zhukov, Vasilevskii and others – is that when Stalin started to heed his generals the Red Army began to win. This somewhat self-serving picture drawn by Stalin's generals is only partly true. In fact, Stalin had always listened to and often taken the advice of his High Command. What happened from Stalingrad onwards was that he listened more, the advice got better and he got better at taking it. The Soviet generals as well as Stalin were on a steep learning curve from day one of the war and it was only through the bitter experience of defeat that they became better commanders and he became a better Supreme Commander. Furthermore, while mistakes are magnified by defeat they tend to be masked by victory. After Stalingrad and Kursk the Soviet High Command continued to make mistakes and to experience many more military setbacks, but none that threatened catastrophe or captured the historical headlines. Arguably, it was victory, more than anything else, that transformed relations between Stalin and his generals and led to a more balanced relationship between his power and their professional expertise. At the same time Stalin remained very much in overall command and continuously asserted his military as well as his political leadership.

Beyond the issue of whether Stalin was as wise, or as foolish, as his generals there is a more important point to make. As Simon Sebag Montefiore has shown very effectively in his portrait of life in Stalin's political court,[148] one of the sources of the Soviet dictator's enduring power was the loyalty and stability of his inner circle. From the late 1920s through to the early 1950s there was remarkable continuity in the Stalinist political grouping that ruled the party and the country. Stalin's closest associates – Molotov, Kaganovich, Voroshilov, Beria, Zhdanov, Malenkov, Mikoyan and Khrushchev – feared him, were overawed by him, were managed and manipulated by him, but they were also charmed by him and seduced by his attention to their personal needs and those of their families. The cumulative result was a leadership clique that stuck together through thick and thin and in which disloyalty to Stalin was *never* an issue even in the most dire of circumstances. During the war Stalin created a similar coherence and loyalty in his closest military associates, and used many of the same techniques to secure it. Marshal Rokossovskii, for example, painted a very flattering picture in his memoirs of Stalin's personal leadership qualities, particularly when compared to those of Zhukov (with whom Rokossovskii often clashed). He wrote that 'the concern displayed by the Supreme Commander was invaluable. The kind, fatherly intonations were encouraging and raised one's self-confidence.'[149] Similarly, in his memoirs Vasilevskii recounted an incident during the battle of Moscow in which Stalin wanted to promote him to general. He declined but asked that some of his assistants should be promoted. Stalin agreed and they were all promoted along with Vasilevskii. 'This attention to us touched us deeply,' wrote Vasilevskii. 'I have already mentioned how Stalin could be very irascible and abrasive; but even more striking was this concern for his subordinates at such a grave time.' In his memoirs Stalin's operations chief, General Shtemenko, told a story which showed that Stalin could be terrifyingly mischievous as well as charming. He had inadvertently left some important maps in Stalin's office after a briefing session. When he went to retrieve them Stalin pretended not to have them and said they must be lost. Shtemenko insisted that he must have left them behind, whereupon Stalin produced them, telling him 'here you are. And don't leave them behind again . . . It's a good thing you told the truth.'[150] Normally, however, Stalin's dealings with his High Command were polite and respectful. While there are examples of acerbity in Stalin's many recorded conversations with his Front commanders, mostly he was businesslike and formally correct in these exchanges, including those conducted amid military disaster, and he rarely forgot to wish his officers success in their missions. It is evident, too, that Stalin did not generally punish or scapegoat his commanders simply for failure. After the purge of Pavlov's Western Front and of the Red Air Force generals in 1941 the Soviet

High Command settled down to a remarkable continuity, notwithstanding the disasters and near defeat of 1941–1942. With the exception of those who were captured or died as a result of combat, Stalin's generals nearly all served in senior command positions throughout the war. According to David Glantz:

Contrary to popular belief . . . command stability was far greater in the Red Army and command turbulence was significantly less damaging than has previously been assumed, not only after November 1942 but also during the first 18 months of war. Furthermore, command was most stable in the Red Army's fronts, key armies, tank and mechanized forces and in its largest supporting air, artillery, and air defence formations . . . More important still, when command instability was the greatest during 1941 and 1942 Stalin was still able to identify and develop the key commanders who would lead the Red Army to victory in the last two years of war . . . In short, most of the marshals and generals who led the Red Army to victory during May 1945 were already serving as generals or colonels in responsible command positions when war began on 22 June 1941. What is surprising is the relatively high percentage of these officers who survived their education at the hands of the Wehrmacht during 1941 and 1942 to emerge as successful commanders in the victorious Red Army of 1945.[151]

Stalin stuck with his generals as long as they were loyal, disciplined and reasonably competent. The first two qualities were a given for all high-ranking Red Army officers, who would never have reached such rank had they not been loyal to Stalin and the party and committed to defend the Soviet system to the utmost. Any doubts were quelled by the experience of the prewar purges and by the exemplary punishment handed out to Pavlov and others in 1941. Stalin was a little more relaxed when it came to competence and inclined to give those loyal to him more than one chance to prove their worth. But there were limits to his patience and if they proved to be too incompetent even the most loyal of cronies were shunted off to safer pastures.

Even more remarkable is how within these inviolable structures of loyalty and discipline Stalin was able to foster a considerable amount of talent and creativity in the upper reaches of the Red Army. A major part of the explanation is the emphasis he personally placed on learning from experience, on experimentation and on adaptation to changing circumstances. During the Great Patriotic War the Red Army was very much a learning organisation. The experience and lessons of combat and command were carefully and systematically collected, and disseminated through documentation and training. Red Army command structures and force organisation were kept under constant review and reformed on many occasions. For example, the large mechanised corps abolished in summer 1941 were reconstituted in 1942 as tank corps and armies. Air armies were formed. 'Shock' armies were formed to spearhead offensives and the combat-proven designation 'Guards' applied to armies as well as divisions and sub-divisional units. The titles and demarcation lines of the 'Fronts' were changed as the military situation demanded and by the end of the war complex, co-ordinated offensive operations by a multiplicity of fronts were the norm. As the war progressed Red Army officers were increasingly encouraged to take risks and to make their own decisions, particularly when they were on the attack. Military doctrine was kept under constant review. Attack remained the priority but the conceptualisation, preparation and implementation of offensive operations became ever more sophisticated. Efforts to improve the effectiveness of propaganda work among the armed forces were as intensive as they were continuous. Of course, Stalin can hardly be credited with all this innovation and dynamism but he did preside over the system and culture that made it possible and none of it could have happened without his assent. Stalin also made one very specific contribution to the Red Army's performance during the war: the priority he attached to supplies and reserves – which he numbered among the 'permanently operating factors' that would determine the outcome of the struggle with Germany in the long run. It is not for nothing that the most noted quality of Stalin's war leadership in both western and Soviet memoirs is his role in organising the materiel foundations of the Red Army's victory over the Wehrmacht.

The transformation in Stalin's military position and standing after the victory at Stalingrad was symbolised by the title Marshal of the Soviet Union bestowed upon him in March 1943. With defeat averted and victory assured it was safe to begin the process of extending the cult of his personality to the realm of military affairs, and from early 1943 the myth of Stalin's strategic genius began to figure increasingly in the Soviet press. But the new title reflected more than propaganda and cult politics. It was a fair reflection of the development of his military abilities and of the positive relationship he had established with his generals since June 1941. Above all, the new title represented the reality of Stalin's supreme commandership, his domination of military decision-making structures, and his central, indispensable position in the Soviet war machine.

The Economic Bases of Victory

The Soviet victories at Stalingrad and Kursk were the result of a number of factors: Stalin's leadership, good generalship, German mistakes, patriotic mobilisation, heroic deeds, harsh discipline, and not a little luck. But overlaying the effects of all these factors was a tremendous economic and organisational achievement.[152]

By the time the battle of Stalingrad commenced the Germans occupied half of European Russia – more than a million square miles of territory containing 80 million people or 40 per cent of the Soviet population. The occupied area accounted for nearly 50 per cent of the USSR's cultivated land and the production of 70 per cent of its pig iron, 60 per cent of its coal and steel and 40 per cent of its electricity. Yet by the end of 1942 Soviet annual output of rifles had quadrupled (to nearly 6 million) compared to 1941, while tank and artillery production had increased fivefold to 24,500 and 287,000 per annum respectively. The number of aeroplanes produced rose from 8,200 to 21,700. This achievement was testimony to the mobilisation power of the Soviet economy but also to the amazing feat of the mass relocation of industrial plant to the eastern USSR in 1941–1942. One of Stalin's first wartime decrees was to order the establishment of an evacuation committee which organised the transfer to the east of more than 1,500 large-scale enterprises in summer 1941. With the plant and machinery went hundreds of thousands of workers. Tens of thousands of trucks were used and up to a million and half railway wagon loads of evacuation cargo. This achievement was replicated on a smaller scale in summer 1942 when 150 big factories were evacuated from the Don and Volga regions. As well as the relocation of industry, the Soviets created 3,500 new factories during the war, most of them dedicated to armaments production.

On the manpower front, by the end of 1941 the original 5-million-strong Red Army had been virtually wiped out by the Germans. However, the Soviets had been preparing for war for a decade or more and there was a civilian pool of 14 million people with basic military training. The Soviet authorities were able to call up 5 million reservists on the outbreak of war and by the end of 1941 the Red Army numbered 8 million. In 1942 the number increased to 11 million, despite the substantial losses of that year. At the time of the Stalingrad counter-offensive the Red Army was able to field an attack force of 90 fully equipped and fresh divisions just for Operation Uranus. The Red Army's 'manpower', it should be noted, included a million Soviet women, about half of whom served at the front in the full range of combat roles.

Did the highly successful Soviet wartime mobilisation of its human and material resources take place because of Stalin or in spite of him? Did the centralised and directive Stalinist state economy deliver the wartime goods or was it the decentralisation of decision-making and the introduction of elements of a market economy that made such a performance possible? Did planning work in wartime or was it improvisation and individual initiative that made the difference between success and failure? Could a better system and better leadership have performed better? The debate continues but one thing is clear: it was within Stalin's power to disrupt the flow of production and undermine the economy's actual performance by bad decisions. Instead, Stalin largely left matters of wartime economic management in the hands of his economic experts, intervening when he deemed it necessary to achieve urgent targets but usually restricting his role to maintaining the priority of supplies for the military, even at the cost of a severe reduction in civilian living standards.

A related controversy concerns the contribution of western aid to the Soviet war effort. Between 1941 and 1945 the USSR's western allies supplied about 10 per cent of Soviet wartime economic needs. For example, the United States under its lend-lease programme supplied 360,000 trucks, 43,000 jeeps, 2,000 locomotives and 11,000 railroad cars – making the Red Army more mobile than the Germans and far less dependent than them on horse-drawn transportation. Canadian and American food shipments fed a third of the Soviet population during the war. Australia supplied thousands of sheepskin coats to keep the Red Army warm in its winter campaigns. The Soviets grumbled constantly about the failure of the west to fulfil its supply commitments and during the early years of the war these complaints spilled over into the public arena, but generally the Soviets were quite fulsome in their thanks for western support. The various supplies agreements were highlighted in the press, as were many individual instances of western aid. Towards the end of the war the Soviet authorities began to reveal to citizens the full extent of the material support they had received.[153] Most of this aid arrived after Stalingrad, so its main role was to facilitate victory rather than stave off defeat. On the other hand, as Mark Harrison has pointed out, the territorial and economic losses of mid-1942 meant the Soviet economy was on a knife-edge of collapse. All support made a crucial difference, including the limited amount of western aid delivered in 1941–1942.[154] As important was the boost to Soviet morale provided by the political alliance with the west which signified that the USSR did not stand alone in its struggle against the Axis. The Anti-Hitler coalition, as the Soviets called it, also represented the hope of a peaceful future. In his wartime speeches Stalin skilfully played on popular hopes and expectations about what peace would bring. Indeed, after the victories at Stalingrad and Kursk, Stalin began to put aside his own fears and disappointments concerning his Anglo-American allies and embraced the idea that after the war there should be a peacetime Grand Alliance to safeguard the postwar world, a new security order that the Soviet Union would play a critical role in shaping and controlling.

6

The Politics of War
Stalin, Churchill and Roosevelt

From the very beginning Stalin saw the war with Hitler as a political and diplomatic contest as well as a military struggle. The war, and the peace that followed, would be won or lost not only on the battlefield but through the political alliances each side formed. For Stalin the Grand Alliance with Britain and the United States was as much a political alliance as a military coalition. Until mid-1943 Stalin's diplomatic efforts within the Grand Alliance focused on ensuring that Hitler, and anti-communist elements within Britain and the US, did not succeed in splitting the Soviet–Western coalition. In his November 1941 speech Stalin spoke at length of the German aim of using the fear of communism and revolution to enlist the British and Americans in an anti-Soviet coalition.[1] In June 1942 the Soviet Information Buro (Sovinform) issued a statement on the first year of the Soviet–German war highlighting the USSR's achievement in averting political isolation and in successfully forging a coalition with its western allies.[2] All major government statements were carefully scrutinised by Stalin and there can be no doubt that Sovinform's view reflected his own. But as shown by his exchange with Ambassador Maiskii about the Hess affair in October 1942, Stalin remained anxious that the British would contemplate a separate peace with Germany should Hitler emerge victorious from the battle of Stalingrad. In this regard the frantic Soviet pressure on the Anglo-Americans to open a second front in France had political as well as military purpose: to get the western allies to commit their troops to a bloody battle that would copper-fasten their commitment to prosecute the war against Germany through to the very end. Even in the darkest days of defeat Stalin was confident the war would be won sooner or later, provided the Soviet Union survived the initial German military onslaught and the coalition with Britain and the United States held together.

But did Stalin ever contemplate an alternative survival strategy: a separate Soviet peace with Germany? There have been many rumours and reports that during the war Stalin sought to entice Hitler into a peace deal. One set of rumours refers to a peace feeler of summer 1941 floated via Ivan Stamenov, the Bulgarian ambassador in Moscow.[3] However, according to Pavel Sudoplatov, the NKVD official entrusted with this approach, Stamenov was a Soviet agent and the object of the exercise was to use him unwittingly to sow disinformation in the Axis camp.[4] Another suggestion is that Stalin was so disturbed by the German approach to Moscow in autumn 1941 that he seriously contemplated a capitulationist peace. But such a scenario does not square with Stalin's comportment during the Moscow crisis or with his plans and preparations for a decisive rebuff of the German threat to the Soviet capital.[5] As Sudoplatov sensibly commented: 'Stalin and the leadership sensed that any attempt at capitulation – in a war that was so harsh and unprecedented – would automatically ruin the leadership's ability to run the country.'[6] In his book *Generalissimus* the Russian historian and war veteran, Vladimir Karpov, reproduced documents that suggest Stalin sought a separate peace with Hitler in early 1942. One of these purported documents is a signed proposal by Stalin dated 19 February 1942 for an immediate armistice, to be followed by a withdrawal of German troops from Russia and then a joint Soviet–German war against 'international Jewry' as represented by England and the US.[7] The fact that in February 1942 Stalin was contemplating the defeat of Germany by the end of the year makes this document an absurd as well as a blatant forgery.

These various stories are such an obvious attempt to discredit Stalin and the Soviet war record that they would barely merit comment were it not for the fact that even serious scholars can be tempted by such speculation. Vojtech Mastny, for example, in his classic study of *Russia's Road to the Cold War*, speculated at length that in 1942–1943 Stalin contemplated using his victories at Stalingrad and Kursk to leverage a good deal with Hitler.[8] Mastny, writing in the 1970s, was repeating wartime rumours of Soviet–German peace negotiations in neutral Sweden in summer 1943. In fact, Moscow was so keen to refute these reports that the official Soviet news agency, Tass, issued two separate denials that the Soviet Union was conducting unofficial peace negotiations with Germany.[9] At the Moscow conference of American, British and Soviet foreign ministers in October 1943 it was agreed to share information about any approaches from the Axis for peace negotiations. For their part, the Soviets were adamant that the only basis for negotiations with any Axis state was its unconditional surrender. At a dinner to mark the end of the conference on 30 October 1943 Stalin told Averell Harriman, the newly appointed American ambassador in Moscow, that he was sure the British and Americans thought 'the Soviets were going to make a separate peace with Germany and he hoped that they had found this was not going to be done'.[10] In line with the agreement made at the conference, on 12 November Molotov sent Harriman a memorandum stating that the Soviet embassy in Stockholm had been approached by the supposed representative of a group of German industrialists, reputedly in close contact with Hitler's Foreign Minister, Ribbentrop, who favoured a separate peace with the Soviet Union. According to Molotov the Soviet embassy staff had rebuffed this approach and refused to conduct any further conversations.[11] These rumours of Soviet–German peace negotiations in Sweden in summer 1943 were revived and repeated in the early years of the cold war[12] but there was no hard evidence to support them then and no such evidence has emerged in the decades since. Indeed, it simply beggars belief that Stalin would even consider such a move when victory was in sight. Nor is it plausible that Stalin would have risked the break-up of the Grand Alliance for the sake of a separate peace with Hitler, who had proved so perfidious in the past. Could any Soviet regime – even Stalin's – have survived the internal opposition that a peace deal with Hitler would have provoked?

In truth, an armistice with Germany was the furthest thing from Stalin's mind after Stalingrad and Kursk. Stalin looked forward to victory with renewed confidence and began to refocus his priorities within the Grand Alliance from war-related issues to problems of the postwar peace. Stalin had begun thinking about Soviet war aims and the shape of the postwar world as early as autumn 1941 and, in his meetings with the British Foreign Secretary Anthony Eden in December of that year, he proposed a wide-ranging programme for the settlement of European frontiers and the maintenance of postwar security. At the forefront of his demands was the restoration of the USSR's June 1941 borders and a Soviet sphere of influence in Europe encompassing military bases in Finland and Romania. In January 1942 Stalin ordered the creation of a 'Commission for the Preparation of Diplomatic Documents', an internal committee of the People's Commissariat of Foreign Affairs, chaired by Molotov, which was charged with the examination of the full range of postwar issues – borders, the postwar economic and political order, the organisation of peace and security in Europe. This commission had a few meetings and generated some materials and reports but did not get very far in its deliberations,[13] probably because Stalin's active interest in postwar questions waned as the military situation worsened in 1942. But after Stalingrad, as victory beckoned once again, the Soviet leader renewed his interest in the settlement of a number of postwar issues. Unlike in 1941–1942, Churchill and Roosevelt were also now keen to arrive at some specific advance agreements about the postwar world. Stalingrad signalled that the Germans would definitely be defeated on the Eastern Front and that the Soviet Union would emerge from the war as the dominant power in continental Europe. The balance of power had shifted to Moscow, leaving London and Washington as the suitors within the Grand Alliance. The Soviet position was also buoyed up by the wave of admiration for the Red Army's heroic deeds at Stalingrad that swept through the allied world.[14] For his part Stalin was happy to explore the possibilities of a peacetime Grand Alliance with Britain and the United States. The more the Big Three talked about the peace, the more likely they were to co-operate and stick together in wartime. Stalin thought it far better to maintain postwar unity with the British and Americans than to have them unite against him, possibly in association with a revived Germany. A peacetime Grand Alliance would offer a framework in which the Soviet Union could attain its security goals, enhance its prestige and secure the time necessary to repair the damages of war.

But how did this diplomatic perspective mesh with Stalin's communist political and ideological perspectives? The answer to this question lies, somewhat paradoxically, in his decision to abolish the Communist International in May 1943.

Abolition of Comintern

The abolition of the Communist International (Comintern) had been on Stalin's personal agenda for quite some time. In April 1941, after a night at the Bolshoi Ballet, Stalin told Dimitrov that he thought the various communist parties should be made independent of Comintern and should concentrate on their national tasks rather than on those of international revolution. Comintern, said Stalin, had been formed in expectation of an international revolution but in today's conditions it had become an obstacle to the development of individual communist parties on a national basis.[15]

When Stalin spoke, even casually and off the cuff, you jumped to it, and Dimitrov and his comrades on the Executive Committee of the Communist International began to discuss how to reform Comintern to make it a more effective support for its constituent parties. However, Stalin did not pursue the idea and any plans he might have been hatching were disrupted by the outbreak of war in June 1941. But Stalin returned to the idea two years later and informed Dimitrov via Molotov that Comintern should be liquidated.[16] Comintern's Executive Committee duly discussed its own abolition and consultations were carried out with a number of foreign communist parties. The proposed passing of the organisation was noted with regret by some, but there was no dissent from the proposal; indeed, the general tenor of the discussion was that the abolition of Comintern would be a positive step forward for the communist movement.[17] On 22 May 1943 the resolution on abolition was published in *Pravda*. The resolution emphasised the deep differences in the historical development of different countries, which required the pursuit of diverse strategies and tactics by national communist parties. The war had accentuated these differences and Comintern had, in any case, increasingly allowed the national parties to decide their own policies.[18] By 8 June the resolution had been approved by 31 national sections and two days later the organisation was formally abolished.[19]

Stalin was closely involved in the internal deliberations leading to Comintern's dissolution, advising Dimitrov on the text of the resolution and on the handling of the process of consultation. At first Stalin advised Dimitrov not to rush the process, but then pushed him to publish the resolution on dissolution even before receipt of all the responses from communist parties abroad.[20] On 21 May 1943 Stalin convened a rare wartime meeting of the Soviet Politburo to discuss Comintern's fate. The resolution passed by that meeting noted the main motive for abolition as the impossibility of directing the activities of all communists from a single international centre during wartime, especially when national parties were confronted by very different tasks: in some countries seeking the defeat of their governments, in others working for victory. Another motive, noted the Politburo resolution, was that it would deny enemies the ability to say that the activities of the communist parties were directed by a foreign state.[21] The text of the resolution was evidently based on remarks made by Stalin at the meeting, who is recorded by Dimitrov in his diary as saying much the same thing. Stalin also exuded confidence about the positive impact of the abolition: 'the step now being taken will undoubtedly strengthen the communist parties as national working-class parties and will at the same time reinforce the internationalism of the popular masses, whose base is the Soviet Union'.[22] Stalin's upbeat assessment was also apparent in a public statement on the proposed abolition of Comintern issued on 28 May. Responding to a written question from Harold King, the Reuters correspondent in Moscow, Stalin said the dissolution of the Communist International would be a good thing for four reasons. First, it would expose the Hitlerite lie that Moscow wanted to 'bolshevise' other countries. Second, it exposed the calumny that communists worked not for the interests of their own people but on orders from outside. Third, it would facilitate the patriotic unity of progressive forces, 'regardless of party or religious faith'.[23] Fourth, it would facilitate the international unity of all freedom-loving peoples and would pave the way for 'the future organisation of a companionship of nations'. Together these four factors, concluded Stalin, would result in a further strengthening of the Grand Alliance against Hitler.[24]

But why did Stalin choose this particular moment – May 1943 – to abolish Comintern? It seems likely that the timing was greatly influenced by the major political development of the preceding month – the 'Katyn' crisis, which had led to the severing of Soviet diplomatic relations with the Polish government in exile in London. The crisis had been provoked by Germany's announcement that it had discovered the mass graves of thousands of Polish officer POWs in the Katyn forest near Smolensk, at that time still under occupation by the Wehrmacht. Moscow responded by claiming that it was a Nazi propaganda ploy and that the Germans themselves must have shot the Poles, not the NKVD, as Berlin claimed. The Polish exile government, however, supported a German proposal for an independent medical commission to examine the graves with a view to determining what had happened to the POWs. The Russians were outraged and *Pravda* and *Izvestiya* both published virulent editorials denouncing the exile Poles as accomplices of Hitler.[25] On 21 April Stalin fired off an indignant telegram to Churchill and Roosevelt deploring the anti-Soviet slander campaign of the Poles.[26] The break in diplomatic relations with the London Poles came four days later.

Behind the Katyn crisis[27] lay events of 1939–1940 when several hundred thousand Polish POWs were captured and imprisoned by the Soviet authorities following the Red Army's invasion of eastern Poland in September 1939. Many of these prisoners were detained only briefly and most of the rest were released after June 1941 under the terms of a wartime treaty of alliance between the USSR and the Polish exile government. By October 1941 the Soviets had released some 400,000 Polish citizens from prison or places of confinement. However, more than 20,000 officers and government officials remained missing and the Poles pressed the Soviet authorities for information on their whereabouts. Even Stalin was probed on this matter by General W. Sikorski, the Polish Prime Minister, and by General W. Anders, the commander of a Polish army being raised on Soviet soil. Stalin insisted, however, that he had no knowledge of their whereabouts and that they must have left the country somehow.

In actuality, the missing POWs had been shot by the NKVD after the adoption of a Politburo resolution on 5 March 1940 that mandated their execution.[28] This decision was as curious as it was chilling and revealed a lot about the dystopian character of Stalin's regime. When the Polish POWs were captured the intention was not to murder them but to segregate them from the population of the newly incorporated territories of Western Belorussia and Western Ukraine and to re-educate them into an acceptance of the new Soviet order in eastern Poland. The NKVD's proselytising in the POW camps made little headway, however, and the Soviets soon concluded that the 'bourgeois' officer POWs were intransigent class enemies who must be liquidated. Accordingly, Beria, the internal affairs commissar, wrote to the Politburo in early March recommending that the POWs be summarily tried by the NKVD and then executed. Bearing down on the Politburo's decision was the Soviets' fear that the war with Finland could escalate into a broader conflict, a context in which the recalcitrant Poles would prove an even greater security problem.

The mass executions were carried out in March–April 1940, not just at Katyn but at a number of other locations in Russia, Belorussia and the Ukraine. At the same time the families of the executed POWs were deported to Kazakhstan.

There is no evidence that Stalin dwelt on this horrific decision, but he must have bitterly regretted the subsequent embarrassment and complications. The Germans' international medical commission found, quite accurately, that the POWs had been shot by the NKVD in spring 1940. When the Red Army recaptured Smolensk the Soviets had to mount an elaborate cover-up operation to convince the world that the Germans were the guilty party. Among the Soviet ploys was an invitation in January 1944 to a group of American journalists to visit the Katyn massacre site. Among those invited was Kathleen Harriman, the daughter of Averell Harriman. On 28 January 1944 Kathleen wrote to her sister Mary about the trip to Smolensk:

The Katyn Forest turned out to be a small measly pine tree woods. We were shown the works by a big Soviet doctor who looked like a chef in white peaked cap, white apron and rubber gloves. With relish he showed us a sliced Polish brain carefully placed on a dinner plate for inspection purposes. And then we began a tour to each and every one of the seven graves. We must have seen a good many thousand corpses or parts of corpses, all in varying degrees of decomposition, but smelling about as bad. (Luckily I had a cold, so was less bothered by the stench than others). Some of the corpses had been dug up by the Germans in the spring of '43 after they'd first launched their version of the story. These were laid in neat orderly rows, from six to eight bodies deep. The bodies in the remaining graves had been tossed in every which way. All the time we were there, the regular work of exhuming continued by men in army uniform. Somehow I didn't envy them! The most interesting thing, and the most convincing bit of evidence, was that every Pole had been shot through the back of the head with a single bullet. Some of the bodies had their hands tied behind their backs, all of which is typically German. Next on the program we were taken into post mortem tents. These were hot and stuffy and smelt to high heaven. Numerous post mortems were going on, each and every body is given a thorough going over, and we witnessed several . . . personally I was amazed at how whole the corpses were. Most still had hair. Even I could recognise their internal organs and they still had a good quantity of red-coloured 'firm' meat on their thighs . . . You see, the Germans say that the Russians killed the Poles back in '40, whereas the Russians say the Poles weren't killed until the fall of '41, so there's quite a discrepancy in time. Though the Germans had ripped open the Poles' pockets, they'd missed some written documents. While I was watching, they found one letter dated the summer of '41, which is damned good evidence.[29]

Another complication of the Katyn crisis was its impact on the Polish Communist Party, or Polish Workers' Party as it was then called. When the crisis broke, Polish communists were in the midst of trying to negotiate a broad national front of resistance to the German occupation of Poland, including unity between themselves and the Polish Home Army – linked to the exile government in London. These negotiations broke down at the end of April 1943 in the face of demands that Polish communists subordinate themselves to the exile government, repudiate Soviet territorial claims on Poland and break their links with Comintern.[30] On 7 May – the day before Molotov spoke to Dimitrov about the abolition of Comintern – Wanda Wasilewska, a leading Polish communist, met with Stalin and, presumably, reported on the failed negotiations with the Home Army.[31] It is quite possible that it was this development that prompted Stalin to abolish Comintern, a move that would help undermine nationalist claims that the Polish communists were not patriots but Soviet agents.

Stalin's dissolution of Comintern has typically been cast as a gesture to Britain and the United States,[32] a signal that he would not be seeking a revolution or a communist takeover in Europe at the end of the war. It may well be that Stalin did want to impress his Grand Alliance partners with his bona fides, but it is more likely that he was seeking to regain the political initiative in the wake of the Katyn crisis. Viewed in the context of the projected struggle for political influence in postwar Poland – by far the most important country on the USSR's western border – a more direct and simple motive suggests itself: Comintern was abolished to enhance the strategic challenge of European communism. In Poland, and in Europe as a whole, communists were seeking influence and political power through the formation of anti-fascist national fronts that would lead the resistance to Nazi occupation and then the struggle for progressive policies after the war. In other words, the European communists would – as the Soviets had done – reinvent themselves as radical patriots dedicated as much to their countries' national interests as to proletarian internationalism. By the middle of the war this process of patriotic reinvention was already far advanced in many countries as communist parties revived and built upon the anti-fascist politics of the prewar popular fronts. Thus, far from being a diplomatic accommodation to the Grand Alliance, the abolition of Comintern represented an ideological and political challenge to the Soviet Union's western allies. Stalin was committed to the maintenance of the Grand Alliance, in peace as well as in war, but that did not mean he believed there could or should be a return to the prewar political status quo in Europe.

At this stage Stalin did not know exactly how European politics would change as a result of the war but he realised that some kind of radical transformation was highly likely and he wanted his communist allies to be in a strong position to exploit any political opportunities as and when they arose.

Another important meaning of the abolition of Comintern was highlighted by the Italian historian Paolo Spriano:[33] Stalin's prestige and myth were now so great that he no longer needed an institution like Comintern to mediate his relationships with the international communist movement. From now on he would personally direct the broad lines of communist strategy and policy and would do so via face to face meetings with foreign party leaders as and when necessary. Stalin had long dominated the international communist movement politically and ideologically, but his power had been balanced to a degree by the collective organisational form of Comintern and by the public prominence of a number of other communist party leaders. Dimitrov, for example, was the hero of the Reichstag Fire trial of 1933 and was widely seen as the personification of the anti-fascist popular front politics of Comintern. In private, Stalin personally dominated Dimitrov but publicly the Comintern leader appeared as a quite independent and charismatic figure, as did other communist leaders such as the French party leader Maurice Thorez, the Italian communist Palmiro Togliatti, and Earl Browder and Harry Pollitt, leaders of the American and British parties. But Soviet success in the war meant that Stalin's figure now cast a huge shadow over the whole international communist movement. At the moment of Comintern's dissolution, the international communist movement became, in effect, the party of Stalin.

Although Comintern as an institution ceased to be in June 1943, many of its constituent organisational elements continued to function much as before. This was particularly true of those structures providing material and financial support to communist parties operating clandestinely and involved in partisan struggles.[34] Dimitrov was transferred to a new 'Department of International Information', a component of the central apparatus of the Soviet communist party that in the postwar years morphed into the party's International Department. Dimitrov's department was to provide information and analyses on international questions to the Politburo and the Central Committee and to liaise and maintain ties with foreign communist parties. At the end of 1944 the department began producing a confidential briefing bulletin *Voprosy Vneshnei Politiki* (Questions of Foreign Policy). A more public version of evolving Soviet views on international relations was provided by *Voina i Rabochii Klass* (War and the Working Class), a fortnightly journal which began publication in June 1943. When the journal was established by the Politburo it was exempted from the formal processes of the Soviet censorship regime.[35] Instead its contents were closely monitored by

Stalin and Molotov. Partly it was a replacement for the Comintern periodical the *Communist International* but it functioned mainly as the public house journal of the People's Commissariat of Foreign Affairs, with much of its content based on internal briefings and on reports produced within the commissariat. Its articles were widely reprinted in the Soviet and communist press and were, quite rightly, viewed as authoritative statements of Moscow's view on current international events and on plans for the postwar world.

Preparing for Peace

The appearance of *Voina i Rabochii Klass* signalled Stalin's growing interest in the project of preparing and planning for the postwar world. In summer 1943 it was decided to replace the Commission for the Preparation of Diplomatic Materials by two new commissions: a *Komissiya po Voprosam Peremiriya* (Commission on Armistice Terms), headed by Marshal Voroshilov, and a *Komissiya po Voprosam Mirnykh Dogovorov i Poslevoennogo Ustroistva* (Commission on Peace Treaties and the Postwar Order) headed by Litvinov, who was recalled from his position as ambassador to the United States in summer 1943. Maiskii – who was under a bit of a cloud because of the failure of the Soviet campaign for a second front – was recalled from London and placed in charge of a Commission on Reparations.[36] Stalin's appointment of Litvinov to head the key commission was highly significant, particularly given the long-standing personal rivalry between Litvinov and Molotov, his replacement as people's commissar for foreign affairs in 1939.[37] Litvinov was by far the most knowledgeable and experienced of Stalin's diplomats and the Soviet leader needed his skills and expertise. Litvinov was also a strong advocate of collaboration with Britain and the United States and had long been urging Stalin to develop the tripartite machinery that would institutionalise Soviet–Western co-operation. After his return from the United States in May 1943 Litvinov wrote a long paper for Stalin and Molotov on 'The Policy of the USA'. In this document he argued that the USSR should 'participate in an American–Anglo-Soviet commission for the discussion of general military-political questions arising from the common struggle against the European Axis'. Such a commission, said Litvinov, would enable the Soviets to influence British and American strategic planning and sway political opinion in the western states.[38] Litvinov's proposal for an allied military-political commission seems to have influenced Stalin's thinking. On 22 August he wrote to Churchill and Roosevelt:

> I think the time is ripe for us to set up a military-political commission of representatives of the three countries . . . for consideration of problems

related to negotiations with various governments falling away from Germany. To date it has been like this: the USA and Britain reach agreement between themselves while the USSR is informed of the agreement between the two Powers as a third party looking passively on. I must say that this situation cannot be tolerated any longer.[39]

Prompted by the allied invasion of Sicily and Italy in summer 1943, this was the first of several messages to Roosevelt and Churchill in the same vein. Mussolini had resigned and a new government headed by the monarchist Marshal Badoglio was negotiating the terms of an armistice with Britain and the United States. Stalin was concerned that the Soviet Union should take part in the negotiations leading to the Italian surrender and in the allied occupation regime to be established there. From Stalin's point of view it made sense to secure an agreement that would facilitate Soviet influence in enemy territories occupied by the British and Americans in exchange for commensurate western influence in lands yet to be invested by the Red Army. Roosevelt, and more particularly Churchill, had a different view: they wanted to hold on to what they had and insisted that the occupation regime in Italy would be the responsibility of their military commanders on the ground. The result was the exclusion of the Soviet Union from any effective say in the allied administration of occupied Italy. Soviet representatives sat on an allied control commission and later on an advisory council but they wielded little, if any, power.[40] The Anglo-American stance on the Italian occupation backfired in the long run since it established a precedent for occupation regimes in the Axis countries of Eastern Europe invaded by the Red Army in 1944–1945: Stalin was able to use the model established in Italy to minimise western influence in the areas of Soviet military occupation.

In 1943, however, Stalin had no idea that the Italian situation would eventually redound to his advantage and he worked to maximise Soviet influence over the occupation regime, sending Deputy People's Commissar for Foreign Affairs, Andrei Vyshinskii to serve on the Advisory Council for Italy. But within a few months the Soviets concluded that the tripartite advisory machinery in Italy was a waste of time. In March 1944 Stalin decided to circumvent inter-allied arrangements by becoming the first of the three great powers to enter into *de facto* diplomatic relations with the Badoglio government (which was now a co-belligerent of the allies and engaged in the battle against the Germans in Italy). A long front-page editorial in *Pravda* on 'The Italian Question' justified Soviet recognition of the Badoglio government by reference to British and American unilateralism in Italy and argued that such a move was necessary to strengthen the anti-fascist struggle.[41] To bolster Soviet influence within the Badoglio government Stalin simultaneously ordered Togliatti to abandon the Italian communists' opposition to serving in a coalition headed by the monarchist Marshal. Stalin told Togliatti:

> The existence of two camps (Badoglio-King and the anti-fascist parties) is weakening the Italian people. This is to the advantage of the English who would like to have a weak Italy in the Mediterranean[42] . . . Communists may join the Badoglio government in the interests of . . . the intensification of the war against the Germans, carrying out the democratization of the country and unifying the Italian people. The essential thing is the unity of the Italian people in its struggle against the Germans for an independent and strong Italy.[43]

Stalin's use of the Italian communist party to bolster his diplomatic and geopolitical position in relation to Italy was also calculated to boost communist influence in the country by the broadening of the communists' political base. Stalin was pessimistic about the prospects for a communist seizure of power in Italy, and adamantly opposed any such adventure while the war against Germany stilled raged.[44] He pursued a similar political and diplomatic strategy in relation to France. In March 1944 French communists were instructed that 'the party must act as the leading force of the nation, expressing its aspirations as a state party capable of arguing and winning over not only its own adherents but broader strata as well'.[45] Stalin did not have a high opinion of de Gaulle but in October 1944 he joined the British and Americans in recognising the General's French Committee for National Liberation as the provisional government of France. At a meeting with the communist leader Maurice Thorez in November 1944, just before the latter's return to liberated France, Stalin urged him to support de Gaulle's government, to seek political allies and not to allow the communists to become isolated. He even suggested the resistance movement in France should change its name to the 'Resurrection Front' and that the programme of the French communist party should be the 'resurrection of industries, granting of jobs for [the] unemployed, defence of democracy, punishment of those who had smothered democracy'.[46]

Another reason for Stalin to push for an agreed approach to the allied occupation regime in Italy in summer 1943 was his forthcoming meeting with Roosevelt and Churchill. Roosevelt had been trying to persuade Stalin to meet him for some time and, in May 1943, sent Joseph Davies the former American ambassador to the Soviet Union, to Moscow with a note suggesting when and where they should get together.[47] Stalin agreed in principle to meet Roosevelt but did not want to commit himself to the specifics until the German summer offensive at Kursk had been dealt with. A date and venue for the meeting were not agreed until September. By then the meeting had been broadened to include Churchill and it had also been agreed that the American, British and Soviet foreign ministers would meet in Moscow in October 1943 as part of the preparations for a conference of the Big Three in Tehran scheduled for the end of November.

Moscow Conference of Foreign Ministers

In preparing for the Moscow conference[48] the British and Americans submitted a large number of agenda items for discussion. The British wanted to discuss Italy and the Balkans; the creation of an inter-allied consultative machinery; the issue of joint responsibilities in Europe (as opposed to separate ones); the Polish question; agreements between big and small powers on postwar questions; the postwar treatment of Germany and the other Axis states; policy towards the partisan movement in Yugoslavia; the formation of a provisional government for France; the formation of federations in Eastern Europe; Iran; and postwar economic co-operation with the USSR. On the American agenda was the establishment of an international security organisation; the treatment of enemy states; postwar reconstruction; and methods of examining political and economic issues arising during the course of the war. In response the Soviets proposed only one item: 'measures to shorten the war against Germany and its allies in Europe'. While the Soviets were prepared to discuss the questions raised by the western allies they asked the British and Americans to table their specific proposals. Moscow also insisted that the conference was only preparatory and could only discuss draft proposals for subsequent consideration by the three governments.[49] This Soviet response to the western agenda proposals reflected Moscow's view that the Anglo-American aim was to distract attention from the issue of the Second Front and to probe the Soviet position on a number of questions, especially in relation to the future of Germany.[50] The Soviet negotiating stance did not augur well but the British and American proposals prompted a major effort by the Soviets to clarify their position on the questions posed. A large number of briefing documents and position papers were produced within the Commissariat of Foreign Affairs and these formed the basis of the Soviet stance at the conference itself.[51] One major contributor to this internal discussion was Litvinov, who wrote a number of documents for Molotov. Unlike some of the Soviet analysts' proposals, Litvinov's were firmly within a tripartite context, although that did not mean that he either neglected specific Soviet interests or too easily conceded to western positions. Indeed, one of the themes of his contributions was the desirability of containing possible future Soviet–Western conflicts by dividing the world into separate zones of security within the framework of an overarching international organisation. Other contributors to the internal discussion – particularly those with a background of work in Comintern – were more suspicious of Britain and the United States and stressed Soviet–Western differences rather than areas of agreement. But no one challenged directly the desirability and possibility of tripartite co-operation. Such a wide-ranging consensus could only have come from the very top of the Soviet decision-making hierarchy – from Stalin – and this pro-tripartite spirit fed into the conference itself, resulting in frank but very friendly discussions with the British and Americans, and in the conclusion of some significant agreements that went far beyond the initial idea of the conference as a preparatory meeting for Tehran.

The Soviet delegation to the conference, which was held in the Spiridonovka Palace, was headed by Molotov, with Litvinov as his deputy. Great Britain was represented by the British Foreign Secretary Anthony Eden and the United States by Secretary of State Cordell Hull. Stalin did not attend but was briefed extensively on its proceedings by Molotov, Litvinov and the other leading members of the Soviet delegation.[52] On 18 October, the day before the conference opened, Stalin was presented with a summary document setting out the Soviet position on the various questions slated for discussion.[53] During the conference Stalin met twice with Eden and once with Hull. He also hosted the closing conference dinner on 30 October.

Stalin's priority for the conference was evident from his talk with Eden on 27 October when he predictably pressed the Foreign Secretary on the question of the Second Front, stressing that the Soviet Union would not be able to mount any more big offensives against the Germans if Hitler was not forced by a substantial threat from the west to divide his forces.[54]

At the conference the western powers reaffirmed their commitment to open a second front in France, this time in spring 1944. Agreement was also reached on the need to persuade Turkey to enter the war against Germany and there was discussion of a Soviet proposal for allied air bases in neutral Sweden. Cordell Hull's priority was an agreement on the establishment of a successor to the discredited League of Nations. A declaration to this effect was issued by the conference. At the Soviets' suggestion it was agreed to hold further trilateral discussions on the proposed new security organisation. Another important decision was the adoption of a British proposal to establish a European Advisory Commission of the three powers with the initial task of examining the armistice terms for Germany. The only specific agreement reached at the conference on the future of Germany was a declaration that Austria would be detached from the Reich and made an independent state again. But in the discussion of the German question it became plain that all three foreign ministers were broadly agreed on the need to disarm, demilitarise, denazify, democratise and dismember Germany. It was also agreed that the major Nazi leaders would be tried as war criminals.[55]

A communiqué issued at the end of the conference declared the three states' commitment to 'continue the present close collaboration and cooperation in the conduct of the war into the period following the end of hostilities' and concluded by noting 'the atmosphere of mutual confidence and understanding which characterised all the work of the Conference'.[56] These sentiments were no mere propagandistic hyperbole. The conference *had* been a resounding success and marked the beginning of a period of extensive tripartite co-operation in planning for the postwar world. Publicly the Soviets lauded the conference as the harbinger of a long and stable peace that would be guaranteed by the co-operation of the Big Three.[57] Internally, the Soviet foreign commissariat instructed its diplomats that the conference was 'a big event in the life of the People's Commissariat of Foreign Affairs' which 'all PCFA workers must study in detail . . . and, if possible, make proposals on the realisation of its decisions'.[58] The British and Americans were no less enthusiastic. The British were particularly gushing about Molotov's performance at the conference, which all agreed had been brilliant. At the end of the conference Eden even proposed that Molotov should chair all future meetings of the three foreign ministers.[59] On his return to London Eden told the House of Commons: 'I have yet to sit under a chairman who showed greater skill, patience and judgement than Mr Molotov, and I must say that it was his handling of a long and complicated agenda that [explains] a large measure of the success we achieved.'[60] Hull told the American Congress that the declaration on the establishment of a new international security organisation meant that 'there will no longer be need for spheres of influence, for alliances, for balance of power, or any other of the special arrangements through which, in the unhappy past, the nations strove to safeguard their security or to promote their interests'.[61] Ambassador Harriman's verdict was that the conference 'came pretty close to the type of intimacy that exists in the discussions between the British and ourselves', while his deputy in the American embassy, Charles Bohlen, thought it 'marked the return of the USSR as a fellow member of the society of nations with the sense of responsibility that carried with it'.[62]

Stalin's verdict on the conference was delivered in his revolution anniversary speech on 6 November 1943, by now an annual event of considerable public importance in setting out the Soviet Union's military and foreign policy. In a section of the speech entitled 'The Consolidation of the Anti-Hitler Coalition and the Disintegration of the Fascist Bloc' Stalin said:

The victory of the allied countries over our common enemy approaches and, notwithstanding the efforts of the enemy, relations between the allies and the military co-operation of their armies is not weakening but strengthening and consolidating. In this regard the historic decisions of the Moscow Conference . . . are eloquent testimony . . . Now our united countries are fully resolved to carry out joint blows against the enemy which will lead to our final victory over them.

Despite the talk about the future of the Grand Alliance Stalin's priority remained a second front in France to draw substantial German forces to the west and ease the Soviet path to victory on the Eastern Front. In his speech, Stalin noted allied military action in North Africa, the Mediterranean and Italy and the impact of the continuing air bombardment of German industry. He also went out of his way to praise western supplies to the USSR, saying that these had greatly facilitated the success of the Soviet summer campaign. The sting in the tail was his observation that allied military action in southern Europe was not the Second Front, which when it was opened would further strengthen the allies' military co-operation and accelerate the victory over Nazi Germany.[63] As the Tehran conference was to show, the realisation of the Second Front remained Stalin's prime goal in his relations with Churchill and Roosevelt. 'The main issue being decided now is whether or not they will help us,' Stalin is reported to have said on the way to Tehran.[64]

The Tehran Conference

Stalin's meeting with Churchill and Roosevelt took place in Tehran because the Soviet leaders insisted on a venue that would enable him to remain in direct telephone and telegraphic contact with his General Staff in Moscow. According to General Shtemenko, his Chief of Operations, on the way to Tehran (by train to Baku and then by plane) he had to report to Stalin three times a day on the situation at the front. Shtemenko carried on briefing Stalin throughout the conference and the Soviet leader continued to authorise military directives telegraphed to him by Antonov, his Deputy Chief of the General Staff.[65]

Iran had been occupied by British and Soviet troops since August 1941 in an operation to oust a pro-German government in Tehran and to secure the supply routes to the southern USSR. By 1943 British and Soviet troops had been formally withdrawn from the Iranian capital but it remained full of allied soldiers and the grounds of the Soviet embassy were considered a safe location for the conference. For security reasons Roosevelt stayed in the Soviet embassy with Stalin, while Churchill resided at the British Legation nearby.

Many stories have been told about the Tehran Conference: about German plots to kidnap or assassinate the Big Three; about Soviet spying on Churchill and Roosevelt; about the spy in the British embassy in Ankara who provided

Berlin with transcripts of the entire conference.[66] But the real drama was the impact of what was said and decided at Tehran on the lives of millions for years to come.

Stalin's first meeting at Tehran was with Roosevelt on 28 November 1943. According to Valentin Berezhkov, one of Stalin's interpreters, the meeting took place in a room adjoining the main conference hall and the Soviet leader was at pains to ensure that the seating arrangements took account of Roosevelt being in his wheelchair.[67] As this was the first ever meeting between the two leaders it was more a social call than anything else. The conversation began with Roosevelt asking about the situation on the Eastern Front and saying that he would like to draw 30–40 enemy divisions away from Stalin's forces. Stalin was naturally gratified and expressed sympathy for the logistical difficulties the United States faced in supporting an army of 2 million located 3,000 miles from the American continent. Roosevelt then said that he intended to talk to Stalin about postwar issues, including the question of trade with the Soviet Union. Stalin said that after the war Russia would be a big market for the US. Roosevelt agreed, noting that the US would have a great demand for raw materials that could be supplied by the USSR. There then followed an exchange about the fighting qualities of China in which both agreed that, while the Chinese were good warriors, they were badly led by the likes of Chiang Kai-shek. An even greater meeting of minds was evident in an exchange about de Gaulle and the French. According to Stalin

In politics de Gaulle is not a realist. He considers himself the representative of the true France which, of course, he doesn't represent. De Gaulle does not understand that there are two Frances: symbolic France, which he represents, and real France, which helps the Germans in the person of Laval, Pétain and others. De Gaulle does not have a relationship with the real France, which must be punished for its aid to the Germans.

Roosevelt's sentiments were similar and the two agreed as well on the need to examine the position of France's colonies after the war. Stalin agreed, too, with an American idea to establish an 'international commission on the colonies', but concurred with Roosevelt that they had better not raise the question of India with Churchill – it was a sore point with the British leader. To Roosevelt's suggestion that India wasn't suited to a parliamentary system and might do better with some kind of Soviet system created from below, Stalin responded that 'this would mean going along the path of revolution. In India there are many different peoples and cultures. There is no force or group in a position to lead the country.' But Stalin agreed with Roosevelt that those – like themselves – with a more detached view of the Indian question were in a better position to examine it objectively.[68]

The rapport established between Roosevelt and Stalin continued during the first plenary session later that day. The main topic of discussion at this first meeting of the Big Three was the cross-Channel invasion of France planned for 1944. In effect, Stalin and Roosevelt ganged up on Churchill and insisted that Operation Overlord, as it was called, should have absolute priority in Anglo-American military operations for 1944. In siding with Roosevelt in this discussion, Stalin was well aware from intelligence reports of the prolonged Anglo-American dispute about the priority of Overlord relative to continuing operations in the Mediterranean area. Although he agreed in principle with Overlord, Churchill doubted the wisdom of a cross-Channel invasion against the well-fortified French coast and instead favoured attacking the 'soft underbelly' of the Axis.[69] In supporting Overlord, as against Churchill's Mediterranean strategy centred on operations in Italy and the Balkans, Stalin was pursuing the long-standing Soviet aim of a second front in France. He wanted a definite end to western procrastination on this issue. Stalin's other major statement during this session was his announcement that the Soviet Union would join the war against Japan in the Far East after Germany had capitulated. This was not exactly a surprise to the Americans since Stalin had revealed his intentions to Harriman and Hull at the earlier Moscow conference. But it still represented a major future military commitment, one that Roosevelt had been seeking from the Soviets ever since Pearl Harbor.[70]

At the tripartite dinner that evening Stalin's main theme was the postwar fate of Germany. According to Bohlen, who acted as American interpreter at Tehran:

> In regard to Germany, Marshal Stalin appeared to regard all measures proposed by either the President or Churchill for the subjugation and for the control of Germany as inadequate . . . He appeared to have no faith in the possibility of the reform of the German people and spoke bitterly of the attitude of the German workers in the war against the Soviet Union . . . He said that Hitler was a very able man, but not basically intelligent, lacking in culture and with a primitive approach to political and other problems. He did not share the view of the President that Hitler was mentally unbalanced and emphasised that only a very able man could accomplish what Hitler had done in solidifying the German people, whatever we thought of the methods.

Stalin also cast doubt on the utility of the principle of unconditional surrender announced by Roosevelt in January 1943, and subsequently accepted by him and Churchill, arguing that it served to unite the German people against the allies.[71] After dinner Stalin had a further exchange on the German question with Churchill. He told Churchill that 'he thought that Germany had every possibility of recovering from this war and might start on a new war within a comparatively short time. He was afraid of German nationalism. After Versailles peace seem assured, but Germany recovered very quickly. We must therefore establish a strong body to prevent Germany from starting a new war. He was convinced that she would recover.' Asked by Churchill how long the Germans would take to recover, Stalin said 15 to 20 years. Stalin agreed with Churchill that the task was to make the world safe from Germany for at least 50 years but did not think the Prime Minister's proposed measures – disarmament, economic controls and territorial changes – went far enough. Judging by later discussions at Tehran, as well as the reports of this particular conversation, Stalin's objection to Churchill's vision of a curtailed and controlled Germany centred on the limited measures of dismemberment proposed by the Prime Minister – basically the detaching and isolating of Prussia from the rest of Germany – which did not go far enough for Stalin. Churchill also raised the Polish question with Stalin, who didn't say much in response but indicated he was ready to discuss the country's postwar borders, including the acquisition by Poland of German territory.[72]

Before the second plenary session, on 29 November, Stalin met Roosevelt again. The main topic of this conversation was Roosevelt's plans for a postwar international security organisation. Stalin knew the President's views since Roosevelt had already, in mid-1942, presented to Molotov his idea of the great powers constituting themselves as an international police force dedicated to maintaining peace. On hearing of Roosevelt's proposal Stalin had cabled Molotov in Washington on 1 June 1942 that the President's 'considerations about peace protection after the war are absolutely sound. There is no doubt that it would be impossible to maintain peace without creating a united military force by Britain, the USA and the USSR capable of preventing aggression. Tell Roosevelt that . . . [he] is absolutely right and that his position will be fully supported by the Soviet Government.'[73] At Tehran Roosevelt outlined to Stalin his plan for an international organisation with three components: a general organisation of all the 'united nations'; an executive committee of 10 or 11 countries; and a 'police committee' of the Big Three plus China. The small states of Europe would not like such an organisation, Stalin observed (referring to the role of China), and suggested instead the foundation of two organisations – one for Europe and one for the Far East. Roosevelt noted this was similar to a proposal put forward by Churchill but added that the US Congress would never agree to membership of a solely European organisation.

Stalin asked that if a world organisation was formed, would the United States send its troops to Europe? Not necessarily, said Roosevelt: in the event of aggression in Europe the US would supply ships and planes but the troops could come from Britain and Russia. Roosevelt enquired about Stalin's views on this and the Soviet leader began by noting that at dinner the previous night Churchill had said Germany would not be able to re-establish its power very quickly after the war. Stalin did not agree. He thought Germany would be able to re-establish itself in 15 to 20 years and then be in a position to launch a new war of aggression. To prevent this aggression the great powers had to be able to occupy key strategic positions in and around Germany. The same was true of Japan, and the new international organisation had to have the right to occupy these strategic positions. Roosevelt said that 'he agreed with Marshal Stalin one hundred percent'.[74]

There was an important, if little known, background to Stalin's evident obsession with the German question at Tehran. Within the People's Commissariat of Foreign Affairs serious work had recently begun on planning the postwar future of Germany. The main thrust of these plans was the long-term military occupation of Germany by the allies and the dismemberment of the German state. At the same time, the Soviets were concerned about pressures from the Germans for reunification and about keeping Germany in a weakened state over the long term. Stalin's idea of being prepared to occupy strategic positions was a natural and logical outgrowth of internal Soviet discussions of the German question.[75]

Stalin's conversation with Roosevelt was interrupted by his need to attend a ceremony to receive the 'Sword of Stalingrad' – a gift from King George VI in honour of the citizens of the heroic city. As was usual on such occasions, a band played the Internationale (still at this time the Soviet national anthem) and God Save the King. After the Soviet dictator and the British Prime Minister had exchanged pleasantries about Anglo-Soviet relations, Stalin took the sword from Churchill, kissed it, and handed it to Voroshilov, who nearly dropped it – an aspect of the ceremony not reported in the allied press.

At the second plenary session the discussion on Operation Overlord continued. Stalin pressed Churchill on a number of connected matters: on the date of the invasion of France (so the Soviets knew where they stood and could plan accordingly); on the appointment of an Anglo-American supreme commander of the operation (necessary for the planning to have any reality, in Stalin's opinion); and on the relationship between Overlord and the other planned military actions by the western allies. The sharpness of the exchanges with Churchill during this session was summed up in Stalin's barb that he 'would like to know whether the English believe in Operation Overlord or simply speak of it to reassure the Russians'.[76]

On the following day, 30 November, Churchill had a bilateral meeting with Stalin, and continued to hesitate about Overlord, arguing that he was not sure an invasion could be sustained if there was a large German force in France. Stalin insisted, however, that the Red Army was counting on an allied invasion of northern France and that he had to know now if the operation would go ahead or not. If it did go ahead the Red Army would be able to mount a multi-pronged offensive to keep the Germans tied down in the east.[77] At the tripartite lunch that followed, Roosevelt announced that it had been agreed to launch Overlord in May 1944, together with a supporting invasion of southern France. With the decision on a second front finally nailed down, the conversation between Churchill and Stalin took an altogether friendlier turn. Churchill started the ball rolling by saying Russia had a right to warm-water ports and Stalin took the opportunity to raise the issue of Turkey's control of the Black Sea Straits and the need to revise the Straits regime in Russia's favour. Stalin also spoke of securing warm-water outlets in the Far East, including the Manchurian ports of Darien and Port Arthur, leased by Tsarist Russia in the nineteenth century but ceded to Japan following defeat in the Russo-Japanese war of 1904–1905. Churchill responded by reiterating that 'Russia must have access to warm waters' and then continued that 'the direction of the world must be concentrated in the hands of those nations who are fully satisfied and have no pretensions . . . our three nations are such countries. The main thing is that after we have agreed between ourselves we will be able to consider ourselves fully satisfied.'[78]

Friendly exchanges on various political matters continued the next day. During lunch there was a long discussion of Churchill's pet project of persuading Turkey to enter the war on the side of the allies. Stalin was sceptical but he committed the Soviet Union to declare war on Bulgaria if Turkey's entry into the war precipitated a Bulgarian–Turkish conflict. This gratified Churchill greatly, and he thanked Stalin for making such a commitment. In a discussion about Finland Churchill expressed sympathy and understanding of the USSR's security needs in relation to Leningrad but hoped the country would not be swallowed up by Russia after the war. Stalin replied that he believed in an independent Finland but there would have to be territorial adjustments in the Soviet Union's favour and that the Finns should pay reparations for war damages. Churchill reminded Stalin of the Bolshevik slogan during the First World War – 'No annexations, no indemnities' – but the Soviet leader quipped, 'I already told you, I have become a conservative.'

After lunch, at the formal plenary session, amicable agreement was soon reached about distribution of the Italian naval and merchant fleet, with Churchill and Roosevelt promising to deliver ships to Stalin as soon as they could. The next subject for discussion was a little trickier: Poland. Churchill and Roosevelt raised with Stalin the question of the re-establishment of Soviet relations with the Polish exile government in London. Stalin was adamant that this would not happen while the Polish exiles continued to collaborate with the Germans. On the territorial question Stalin supported the idea of Poland being compensated at the expense of Germany but insisted that the eastern border must be that established in 1939, i.e. with the incorporation of Western Belorussia and Western Ukraine into the USSR. When Eden suggested that this meant the 'Molotov–Ribbentrop line', Stalin said that he could call it what he liked. Molotov intervened to say that they were talking about the 'Curzon line' and there were no essential differences between the ethnographical frontier established by the British Foreign Secretary Lord Curzon and the Russo-Polish border proposed by the Soviets. Stalin did concede, however, that any area east of the Curzon Line with a majority of ethnic Poles could go to Poland.

The final topic discussed by the Big Three at Tehran was the dismemberment of Germany. The 'German question' was raised by Roosevelt, and Stalin asked him what he had in mind. 'The dismemberment of Germany,' said Roosevelt. 'This is what we prefer,' chipped in Stalin. Churchill also said he favoured the partition of Germany but when questioned by Stalin about his commitment to such a project the British leader explained that he thought Prussia had to be dealt with more severely than the rest of the country and that he favoured a Danubian confederation of Germany's southern provinces, mainly to head off future demands for German reunification. According to the British record of the discussion Stalin's view was that

> It was far better to break up and scatter the German tribes. Of course they would want to unite, no matter how much they were split up. They would always want to reunite. In this he saw great danger, which would have to be neutralized by various economic measures and in the long run by force if necessary. That was the only way to keep the peace. But if we were to make a large combination with Germans in it, trouble was bound to come. We had to see to it that they were kept separate . . . There were no measures to be taken which excluded a movement towards reunion. Germans would always want to reunite and take their revenge. It would be necessary to keep ourselves strong enough to beat them if they ever let loose another war.

Churchill asked if Stalin favoured a fragmented Europe of little states. Not Europe, only Germany, replied Stalin. Roosevelt said Germany had been safer when divided into 107 principalities but Churchill stuck to his view that five or six larger units was better. Stalin reiterated that 'Germany should at all costs be broken up so that she could not reunite' and proposed that the matter be referred to the tripartite European Advisory Commission, established by the Moscow conference to examine the terms of Germany's surrender and occupation.

At the very end of the conference Churchill returned to the question of Poland's frontiers and tabled a formal proposal that they be constituted by the Curzon Line in the east and by the River Oder in the west. Stalin said: 'The Russians have no ice-free ports on the Baltic Sea. Therefore the Russians need the ice-free ports of Königsberg and Memel . . . The Russians need a lump of German territory. If the English agree to transfer to us this territory we will agree to the formula proposed by Churchill.' Churchill said that he would study this very interesting proposal.[79]

On 7 December 1943 the fact that a Big Three meeting had taken place in Tehran was announced to the world and the famous picture of Churchill, Roosevelt and Stalin sitting in front of the conference building was published in the allied press. A communiqué in the name of the three leaders stated that

> we express our determination that our nations shall work together in war and in the peace that will follow. As to war – our military staff have joined in our round table discussions, and we have concerted plans for the destruction of the German forces. We have reached complete agreement as to the scope and timing of operations to be undertaken from the east, west and south . . . And as to peace – we are sure that our concord will win an enduring peace . . . We came here with hope and determination. We leave here, friends in fact, in spirit and in purpose.[80]

Soviet press coverage of the results of Tehran was even more laudatory than its treatment of the Moscow conference. According to *Izvestiya* the Tehran decisions had 'historical importance for the fate of the entire world'; while *Pravda* stated that the conference declaration was 'the harbinger not only of victory but of a long and stable peace'.[81] Stalin himself went to the trouble of changing the headline of the Tass report on Tehran from the neutral 'Conference of the Heads of the Governments of the Soviet Union, USA and Great Britain' to 'Conference of the Leaders of the Three Allied Powers'.[82]

On 10 December a document summarising the discussions at Tehran was prepared for Stalin. Stalin's secretaries were always very careful to compile an accurate record of his conversations and their summary followed the official Soviet records of Tehran very closely. But Stalin's handwritten corrections and annotations indicate that he read this document very carefully and it can, therefore, be taken as a record of what he thought he had said and committed himself to at Tehran.

In relation to Churchill's proposal on Poland's borders the summary document repeated Stalin's offer to accept it, providing there was agreement on the transfer of Memel and Königsberg to the USSR. On Turkey the document cited a statement by Stalin that 'a big country like the USSR must not be locked in the Black Sea and that it was necessary to re-examine the Straits regime'. In relation to Stalin's views on the dismemberment of Germany the document stated:

> Comrade Stalin declared that in relation to the aim of weakening Germany, the Soviet government preferred to dismember her. Comrade Stalin positively favoured Roosevelt's plan but without predetermining the number of states into which Germany is to be split. He came out against Churchill's plan for the creation after the splitting up of Germany of a new, unsustainable state like the Danubian Federation. Comrade Stalin spoke in favour of separate Austrian and Hungarian states.

Regarding the question of a postwar international security organisation the document summarised Roosevelt's views and noted Stalin's counter-proposal of two bodies – one for Europe and one for the Far East. Stalin changed this part of the document to say that he had no objection to Roosevelt's proposal[83] but left unamended the summary of his views on strategic strong points: 'Comrade Stalin indicated that the formation of such an organisation was not sufficient in itself. It was necessary to create an organisation with the right to occupy strategic strong points to prevent Germany and Japan from beginning new aggressions.'[84]

Stalin, Churchill and Roosevelt

Churchill was accompanied to Tehran by Field Marshal Alan Brooke, Chief of the Imperial General Staff. Brooke's assessment of Stalin's performance at Tehran was that 'never once in any of his statements did he make any strategic error, nor did he ever fail to appreciate all the implications of a situation with a quick and unerring eye'.[85] The verdict of Admiral King, the American naval chief, was that 'Stalin knew just what he wanted when he came to Tehran and he got it'.[86] Another Brooke comment was that 'Stalin has the President in his pocket.'[87] Roosevelt himself thought Stalin witty, quick and humorous and a man hewn from granite. To Harry Hopkins the President confided that Stalin was much tougher than expected but he still believed the Soviet leader could be won over to peaceful co-operation after the war if Russia's rights and claims were given due recognition.[88] Churchill was more circumspect in his judgement but even he wrote in January 1944 of 'the new confidence which has grown in our hearts towards Stalin'.[89]

For Stalin the crucial outcome of Tehran was the agreement on Operation Overlord. He no longer saw a second front in France as such a vital military necessity but it remained important that his western allies shared the burden of the land war against Germany. Victory would be Pyrrhic indeed if the Soviet Union was so enfeebled by war that it was unable to win the peace. Anglo-American armies on the Continent also meshed with Stalin's perspective of a prolonged allied military occupation of Germany in order to suppress German power. On the German question Roosevelt had concurred with Stalin in wanting a punitive peace, including the radical dismemberment of the country. Churchill had demurred a little but even he had agreed that harsh measures would be necessary to prevent a resurgence of German power. On Poland Stalin welcomed Churchill and Roosevelt's enthusiasm for shifting its frontiers westward because it legitimised the Soviet–Polish border established as a result of the Nazi–Soviet pact. Roosevelt's perspective on international security promised a prominent role for the USSR in the governance of the postwar world, while Churchill's comments in relation to Russian rights to warm-water outlets augured well for a change in the Straits regime. At a personal level Stalin had established a good working relationship with Roosevelt. There had been some grating moments with Churchill but interpersonal harmony had been restored by the end of the conference.

But what did Stalin really think and feel about Churchill and Roosevelt? As with most questions about Stalin's innermost thoughts, it is difficult to avoid entering the realm of surmise and speculation since he gave little away. In their company Stalin was extremely intimate both politically and personally but, as Spriano noted, he 'was adept at drawing his interlocutors into relations of confidence' and such behaviour was repeated in countless other encounters with western political figures. On the other hand, Churchill and Roosevelt were the only two people he met during the war who could approach him on anything like equal terms. It must have been a relief for Stalin to deal for once with others of equal power and importance, as long as they respected him and he was able to get what he wanted. Separating Stalin from Churchill and from Roosevelt was, of course, a huge ideological gulf. But even that gap was narrower than it might first appear. In Soviet ideological discourse Churchill and particularly Roosevelt were portrayed as the representatives of the progressive sections of the ruling classes of their respective countries: leaders who genuinely wanted to make common cause with the Soviet Union not only during the war but in peacetime, too. Of course, Churchill and Roosevelt's policy was self-interested, but in Stalin's Marxist universe all politics was ultimately driven by real or perceived material interests. Stalin was above all an ideological and political actor and these were the terms on which he judged and related to others. That did not mean that purely personal factors were unimportant to him. Soviet political culture, not least Stalin's own mode of operation, was lubricated by individual and group relations of trust, loyalty and friendship. Stalin was also a great believer in the role of important individuals in history. In an interview in 1931 he had argued that great individuals were those who correctly understood new conditions and how to change them.[90] In this same interview Stalin modestly denied any parallels between his role in Russian history and that of either Peter the Great or the great Lenin, but it is not difficult to divine that, like Hitler, Stalin saw himself as a man of destiny. However, unlike Hitler, Stalin was not an egomaniac and he was prepared to share the historical limelight with two other men of destiny – Churchill and Roosevelt – as long as it continued to suit his purposes and interests.

Two weeks after the Tehran conference Charles Bohlen penned a much-quoted summary assessment of emerging Soviet war aims:

> Germany is to be broken up and kept broken up. The states of eastern and southeastern and central Europe will not be permitted to group themselves into any federations or association. France is to be stripped of her colonies and strategic bases beyond her borders and will not be permitted to maintain any appreciable military establishment. Poland and Italy will remain approximately their present territorial size, but it is doubtful if either will be permitted to maintain any appreciable armed force. The result would be that the Soviet Union would be the only important military and political force on the continent of Europe. The rest of Europe will be reduced to military and political impotence.[91]

Bohlen's assessment was not unfair, although it exaggerated the extent to which Stalin had fixed his war aims beyond the re-establishment of the Soviet Union within its 1941 frontiers. But Bohlen's summary omitted a vital component of Stalin's perspective: Soviet aims would be achieved in co-operation with Churchill and Roosevelt and there would be a quid pro quo regarding British and American goals in their spheres of interest. More importantly, Stalin's emergent goals were political and ideological as well as strategic. The Europe that the Soviet leader sought to dominate would be a continent transformed by social and economic upheavals and by communist political advance. Stalin had every intention of maintaining the Grand Alliance into the indefinite future, but this aim was in tension with his emergent vision of a radical transformation of European politics. Stalin saw no contradiction between a peacetime Grand Alliance and the beginning of a

Europe-wide transition to socialism and communism but this perspective was not shared by Churchill and Roosevelt. Their approach to the postwar world was dominated by a vision of the re-establishment of European capitalism, on a democratic basis and in accordance with British and American economic and strategic interests. While the war continued to rage, this fundamental difference between Soviet and western perspectives on the postwar world could be finessed by the rhetoric of anti-fascist unity. But, as victory approached, the tensions and contradictions within the Soviet–Western coalition began to multiply and to challenge Stalin's commitment to a peacetime Grand Alliance.

7

Triumph and Tragedy
Stalin's Year of Victories

In the annals of Soviet history 1944 became the year of the 'ten great victories'. The original author of this heroic tale was Stalin, who used the ten 'crushing blows' against the enemy as a means of structuring his account of military developments in 1944. The occasion was his speech on the 27th anniversary of the Bolshevik Revolution and it was a good example of Stalin's use of narrative technique in his wartime pronouncements, which typically analysed the course of the war in the form of a sequential story of battles and operations. In this case the events in question were:

1. The lifting of the blockade of Leningrad (January)
2. The encirclement of German troops in south-west Ukraine and the Red Army's entry into Romania (February–March)
3. The liberation of Odessa and the destruction of German forces in the Crimea (April–May)
4. The defeat of Finland at Vyborg (which paved the way for the country's surrender in September 1944) (June)
5. The liberation of Belorussia (June–July)
6. The entry of Soviet forces into Poland (July)
7. The occupation of Romania and Bulgaria (August–September)
8. The liberation of Latvia and Estonia (September)
9. The liberation of Belgrade and the entry of Soviet forces into Hungary and Czechoslovakia (October)
10. The defeat of German forces in northern Finland and northern Norway (October).

(*See Maps 13a and 13b on pp. 193, 194.*)

Apart from Stalin's lauding of the Red Army's military success the speech was significant in signalling a revival of the communist dimension of Soviet propaganda. In previous speeches, most notably those of November 1941,

Soviet Military Operations, 1944

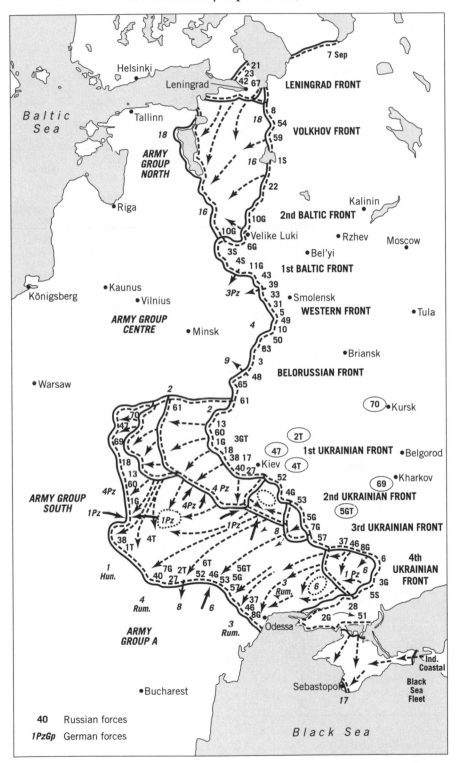

Helsinki

Leningrad

7 Sep

21
23
42 67

LENINGRAD FRONT

Baltic
Sea

Tallinn

8
18 54
59

VOLKHOV FRONT

18

ARMY
GROUP
NORTH

16 1S

22

Kalinin

Riga

16

10G

2nd BALTIC FRONT

10G

Velike Luki

Rzhev

Moscow

6G

3S

Bel'yi

Königsberg

Kaunus

4S 11G

1st BALTIC FRONT

43

Vilnius

39

ARMY GROUP
CENTRE

3Pz

33

31
5
49
10
50

Smolensk

WESTERN FRONT

Tula

Minsk

4

83

Briansk

9

3

48

BELORUSSIAN FRONT

Warsaw

2

65

61

61

2

70

Kursk

1
47
69

13
60
1G

3GT

2T

47

1st UKRAINIAN FRONT

Belgorod

18

18
38 17

4T

40 27

Kiev

52

Kharkov

13
60

4 Pz

4G

53

69

2nd UKRAINIAN FRONT

4Pz

1G

4Pz

1Pz

1Pz

5G

7G

5GT

3rd UKRAINIAN FRONT

1Pz

1Pz →

38

57

37 46
8G

6

4th
UKRAINIAN
FRONT

ARMY GROUP
SOUTH

1T

4T

6T

1 Pz

6

1
Hun.

7G 2T

40 27

52 4G

5GT
5G
53 57

3G

6

5S

28

ARMY
GROUP A

4
Rum.

8

6

3
Rum.

37
46
8G

2G

51

Bucharest

Odessa

Ind.
Coastal

Sebastopol

17

Black
Sea
Fleet

40 Russian forces

1PzGp German forces

Black Sea

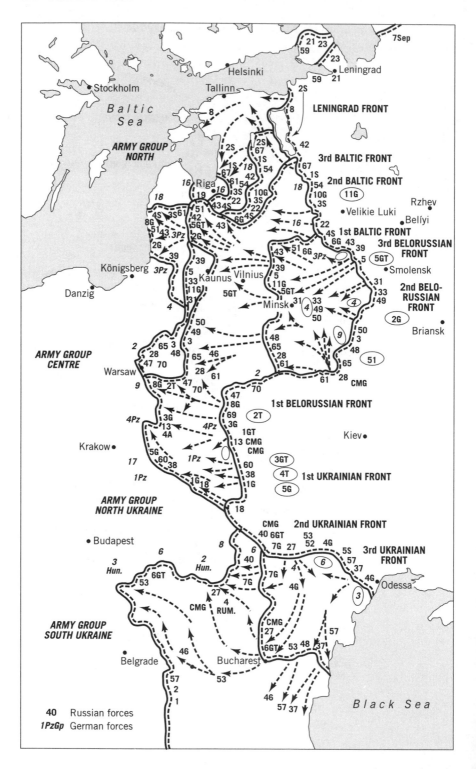

Stalin had located the patriotic war against Germany firmly in the Russian tradition of defence of the motherland. Now he emphasised that 'the Socialist system born in the October Revolution has endowed our people and our Army with a great and unconquerable strength'. When Stalin spoke of the feats of the Soviet people he referred not to Russians or other ethnic groups but used the traditional Bolshevik class categories of workers, peasants and intelligentsia, each seen as playing an important and distinctive role in the wartime struggle – the workers in industry, the peasants on the land, and the intelligentsia in the realm of ideas and organisation. But Stalin brought together the class and ethnic dimensions of the wartime struggle in his definition of Soviet patriotism:

> The strength of Soviet patriotism lies in this, that it is founded not upon racial or nationalist principles, but on profound loyalty and devotion of the people to its Soviet Motherland, the brotherly partnership of the working people of all the nations in our country. In Soviet patriotism are harmoniously combined the national traditions of the peoples and the common vital interests of all the toilers of the Soviet Union. Soviet patriotism does not divide; on the contrary, it welds into a single fraternal family all the nations and nationalities of our country.

The other notable feature of Stalin's November 1944 speech was a long statement in support of the continuation of the Grand Alliance after the war. 'The foundation for the alliance of the USSR, Great Britain and the USSR lies not in chance and passing considerations,' said Stalin, 'but in vitally important and long-term interests.' When the war was won the alliance would face the problem of making 'impossible the outbreak of a new aggression and a new war – if not for ever, then at all events for a very long period'. The danger of a new war arose because, as history showed, it was inevitable that Germany would recover from defeat in 20–30 years and pose a new aggressive threat. The way to avert that threat, said Stalin, was to create an international security organisation endowed with the armed force necessary to protect peace and to deal with any threats posed by aggressive states. At the heart of this new organisation would be those great powers who had borne the burden of the war against Germany and who would, therefore, need to maintain their unity and co-operation in the postwar period.[1]

Dumbarton Oaks

Stalin's pronouncement on the need for an effective replacement for the League of Nations was a response to the outcome of the Dumbarton Oaks conference of August–September 1944, convened to discuss the plan for a new international security organisation that had been announced by the Moscow conference of foreign ministers in October 1943. On the Soviet side preparations for Dumbarton Oaks began early in 1944. Initially, the key figure in Soviet internal discussions was Litvinov. As Chairman of the Commission on the Peace Treaties and the Postwar Order Litvinov wrote a series of reports for his boss Molotov responding to British and American proposals on postwar security and outlining his own vision of the new international organisation. Litvinov's view was that it should be headed by a committee of the great powers, operating on the basis of unanimous decision-making and charged with the prime responsibility for safeguarding international peace and security. Crucially, Litvinov argued, the operations of this leading committee should be underpinned by a series of bilateral commitments and agreements between the great powers. Litvinov's reasoning here was that the experience of the League of Nations showed that the great powers were more likely to stick to specific agreements with each other than to adhere to general commitments relating to collective security. Litvinov also advocated the establishment of a series of regional sub-organisations to provide structure and form to a division of the world into separate zones of great power responsibility and security; in effect, Litvinov's recipe for postwar security was an American–British–Soviet condominium – a division of the world into great power spheres of influence. Litvinov's intention was to form benign spheres of influence that would facilitate the maintenance of peace and security by giving Britain, the United States and the Soviet Union responsibilities as well as power in their own zones of interest. A global division that specified the main sphere of action of each great power would also, in Litvinov's view, separate the competing and potentially conflicting interests of Britain, the United States and the Soviet Union.[2]

Litvinov's ideas played an important part in the formulation of the Soviet position at Dumbarton Oaks but his most radical proposition – that the new organisation should be based on a great power division of the entire world – did not figure in the instructions issued to the USSR's delegation. The Soviet leadership also shied away from the idea of regional sub-organisations and instead adopted the position that the matter required further discussion.[3] The reason for these omissions was indicated in a contribution to the internal Soviet discussion by Yakov Malik, the ambassador in Japan: the problem with dividing the world into zones of responsibility was that it could lead to the USSR's exclusion or marginalisation in the Far East. Malik further pointed out that in a regionally based organisation the British would participate in four sectors (Europe, Asia, Africa and the Americas) and the Americans in three (Europe, Asia and the Americas), while the USSR would only have membership of two (Europe and Asia).[4]

Naturally, the final word in these discussions was Stalin's and in late July/early August Molotov submitted a series of memoranda to him outlining the proposed Soviet negotiating stance at Dumbarton Oaks.[5] One of the most interesting details in this series of notes from Molotov to Stalin is the change in the Soviet position on the question of France's membership of what was later to become the UN Security Council. In the early internal Soviet documentation France was not named as a member of the council of the great powers, only China, Great Britain, the US and the USSR. In the Soviets' final directive to their delegation to Dumbarton Oaks, however, France is included as a member of the future Security Council. Within the People's Commissariat of Foreign Affairs there had been a continuing debate about the future position of France as a great power. Some, like Litvinov, argued for a weak France and for a postwar Soviet–British alliance, while others argued for the restoration of French power as a counter to Great Britain. It may well be that the change in the Soviet position on French membership of the Security Council reflected the ebb and flow of this internal debate. But the reason Molotov gave Stalin was simply the need to keep in step with the Americans, who had changed their minds and agreed to reserve a place on the Security Council for France.[6]

The Soviet delegation at Dumbarton Oaks was led by Andrei Gromyko, who had replaced Litvinov as ambassador to the United States in summer 1943. Conference arrangements were complicated by the fact that the Soviet Union had yet to enter the Far Eastern war and Moscow was reluctant to compromise its neutrality by participating in any formal talks that involved China, which was at war with Japan but not involved in the European theatre. The solution was to hold a two-phase conference. In the first and most important phase, from 21 August to 28 September 1944, the American, British and Soviet delegations held their discussions on the proposed postwar security organisation. When the Soviets departed on the 28th, the British and Americans were joined by the Chinese for a separate, but strictly secondary, discussion.[7]

Like all wartime conferences Dumbarton Oaks was conducted in secret, but there were the inevitable leaks to the press. In many respects the conference was successful and a large measure of inter-allied agreement was reached about the shape of the organisation destined to become the United Nations.[8] Full and final agreement was stymied, however, by two disputes. First there was the question of the founding membership of the organisation. The Soviets wanted membership restricted to those states that had fought as part of the 'United Nations' coalition during the war and were opposed to UN membership for neutral states, many of whom had, in Moscow's view, aided and abetted the Axis during the war. Second, was the question of great power unanimity when it came to agreement on collective security action. The Soviets insisted that all decisions of the Security Council should be agreed unanimously by the great powers. As the internal Soviet report on Dumbarton Oaks noted, the issue of a great power's right to veto decisions of the Security Council 'was the most difficult question discussed at the conference' and Gromyko made it clear to the British and Americans that the Soviets would not agree to a founding conference for the UN until the matter was settled.[9] The British and American position was that unanimity would apply in all cases, but a great power would *not* have the right of veto if it was directly involved in a dispute. Towards the end of the conference Roosevelt appealed to Stalin for an acceptance of this derogation, but the Soviet leader was unmoved and insisted on the complete and consistent application of the unanimity principle which, he argued, was vital to maintaining the great power unity necessary to prevent future aggression.[10]

Failure to reach final agreement on these contentious issues meant the Dumbarton Oaks conference ended on a slightly downbeat note and there was much press speculation about disagreements between the allied powers. Stalin addressed this speculation directly in his November 1944 speech:

There is talk of differences between the three Powers on some questions of security. There are differences, of course, and they will still arise on a number of other questions . . . The surprising thing is not that differences exist but that they are so few, and that as a rule they are settled almost always in the spirit of unity and coordination of action by the three Great Powers. What matters is not that there are differences, but that the differences do not go beyond the bounds of what is tolerable in the interests of the unity of the three Great Powers.[11]

Privately, Stalin was saying much the same thing. In a discussion with members of the communist-controlled Polish Committee of National Liberation on 9 October 1944 he told them: 'The three-power alliance is based on a compromise involving the capitalist powers on the one side and the USSR on the other. This was the source of certain divergences of aims and views. These were, however, subordinate to the fundamental issue of the war against Germany and the establishment of a new set of relationships in Europe. Like any compromise the alliance also contained certain areas of conflict. [But] . . . there have not been any threats of disruption to the basic nature of the alliance. As regards particular current events, each ally had his own point of view.'[12]

In the year since Tehran Stalin's commitment to the Grand Alliance had not weakened and he still saw the shape of the postwar world as being determined by tripartite negotiations between Britain, the Soviet Union and the United

States. Driving this commitment was Stalin's continuing dread of a resurgence of German power after the war. While the Victory Salutes could be heard more and more often in Moscow in 1944, the fighting on the Soviet–German front remained fierce and each battle still had to be won. As Alexander Werth noted, 'the victories of 1944 were spectacular but very few of them were easy victories'.[13] The Red Army was winning the war and advancing towards Berlin but Soviet civilian and military losses were mounting. As the war's end approached the long-term continuation of the Grand Alliance assumed greater, not lesser, importance in the face of the USSR's need for a prolonged period of peace for reconstruction.

Operation Bagration

The biggest Soviet military operation of 1944 was Bagration, named by Stalin after a Georgian hero of the Napoleonic Wars. The plan was to surround and destroy Army Group Centre – the Wehrmacht's last major intact force on the Eastern Front – and expel the Germans from Belorussia. Planning for the Soviet summer campaign of 1944 began early in the year and by mid-April the General Staff had worked out its basic strategy: a campaign to liberate the remaining quarter of the USSR still under German occupation.[14] This goal was proclaimed by Stalin in his Order of the Day on 1 May 1944: 'the objective now is to liberate all our territory from the Fascist invaders and to restore the State frontiers of the Soviet Union in their entirety, from the Black Sea to the Barents Sea'.[15]

As usual there were extensive consultations with Front-level commanders before the final operational plan was adopted on 31 May 1944. What the Soviets had in mind was an ambitious and complex multi-pronged offensive against Army Group Centre. The main attack force consisted of the 1st, 2nd and 3rd Belorussian Fronts and the 1st Ukrainian Front. These four fronts disposed 2.4 million troops, 5,200 tanks, 36,000 artillery pieces and 5,300 military aircraft. They had a two to one superiority over the Germans in personnel, six times as many tanks and four times as many planes and artillery.[16] In a supporting role were the Leningrad and Baltic Fronts, which would pin down Army Group North, as well as pursue secondary goals such as knocking Finland out of the war. Operations were to begin with the Leningrad Front's advance to Vyborg in early June, followed by a surprise attack in Belorussia and then an advance by the 1st Ukrainian Front in the direction of Lvov with the aim of preventing the transfer of enemy forces from the south to the central sector.

Soviet plans for Operation Bagration were closely co-ordinated with Anglo-American preparations for the launch of the long-awaited Second Front in France. The Soviets were informed of the approximate date of D-Day in early

April and, on 18 April, Stalin cabled Roosevelt and Churchill that 'as agreed in Tehran, the Red Army will launch a new offensive at the same time so as to give maximum support to the Anglo-American operation'.[17] Since Tehran there had been a significant increase in the sharing of allied intelligence on the German order of battle and on the Wehrmacht's military technology, particularly that relating to defensive fortifications. There was also extensive co-operation between the Soviets and the British on a deception plan to convince the Germans that an Anglo-Soviet invasion of Norway was in the offing.[18] This false operation, code-named Bodyguard, was part of an elaborate, and highly successful, Soviet *maskirovka* campaign directing the Germans' attention from the planned operation in Belorussia. When Overlord was launched on 6 June 1944 Stalin cabled Churchill and Roosevelt his congratulations and informed them that, in keeping with the agreement reached at Tehran, the Soviet summer offensive would soon be launched on 'one of the vital sectors of the front'.[19] In public Stalin's welcome to the Second Front was nothing less than gushing. The invasion of France, Stalin told *Pravda* on 13 June, was a 'brilliant success for our Allies. One cannot but recognise that the history of warfare knows no other similar undertaking in the breadth of its conception, in its giant dimensions, and in the mastery of its performance . . . History will record this event [as] an achievement of the highest order.'[20]

Belorussia was the main centre of Soviet partisan operations against the Germans and by summer 1944 up to 140,000 partisans were organised into some 200 detachments operating behind the Wehrmacht's lines. On 19–20 June the partisans launched a wave of attacks on German communications, staff headquarters and aerodromes. They also acted as forward observers to guide massive bombing attacks on the Germans on 21–22 June. The main Soviet ground attack began on 23 June and was a stunning success. Attacking across a 500-mile-wide front the Red Army smashed through Army Group Centre's defences and rapidly converged on Minsk. The Belorussian capital was recaptured by the Soviets in early July and, in a poignant reversal of the Red Army's catastrophe at Minsk in June 1941, 100,000 Germans were encircled and trapped east of the city. Vilnius, the Lithuanian capital was recaptured on 13 July and in mid-July the 1st Ukrainian Front commanded by Marshal Konev began its advance towards the West Ukrainian capital, Lvov, which fell to the Red Army on 27 July (*see Map 14 on p. 201*).

Between 22 June and 4 July, Army Group Centre lost 25 divisions and well over 300,000 men; another 100,000 were lost in the weeks that followed.[21] By the end of the July it had ceased to be an effective fighting force. However, the destruction of Army Group Centre did not come cheap. The four main Fronts involved in Operation Bagration suffered three-quarters of a million casualties during the course of the campaign to liberate Belorussia.[22] But there was

Operation Bagration

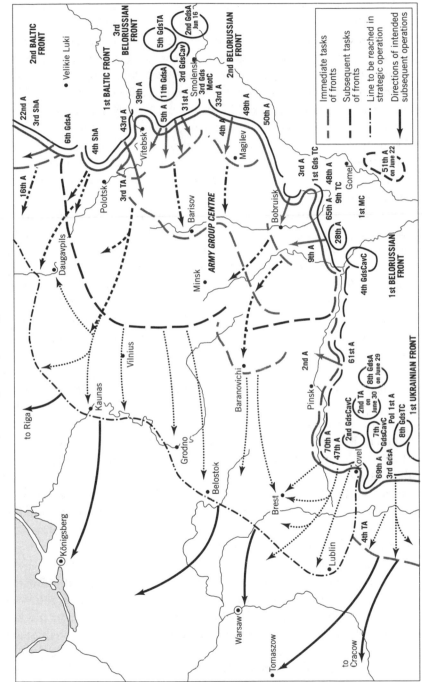

2nd BALTIC FRONT

3rd BELORUSSIAN FRONT

1st BALTIC FRONT

2nd BELORUSSIAN FRONT

• Velikie Luki

22nd A
3rd ShA
6th GdsA
4th ShA
43rd A
39th A
5th A
11th GdsA
3rd GdsCav
31st A
3rd Gds MotC
Smolensk
33rd A
49th A
50th A
4th A
Magilev •
5th GdsTA
2nd GdsA Jun 16
16th A
3rd TA
Polotsk •
Vitebsk •
Barisov •
Minsk •

ARMY GROUP CENTRE

3rd A
1st Gds TC
48th A
9th TC
65th A
28th A
9th A
1st MC
Bobruisk •
Gomel •
51st A on June 22

Daugavpils •

1st BELORUSSIAN FRONT

4th GdsCavC

2nd A
61st A
8th GdsA on June 29
2nd TA on June 30
7th GdsCavC
Pol 1st A
8th GdsTC
2nd GdsCavC
70th A
47th A
69th A
3rd GdsA

1st UKRAINIAN FRONT

Vilnius •
Baranovichi •
Pinsk •

Kaunas •

to Riga

Grodno •
Belostok •

Kovel •

Brest •

Lublin •
4th TA

Königsberg ◉

Warsaw ◉

• Tomaszow

to Cracow

Immediate tasks of fronts

Subsequent tasks of fronts

Line to be reached in strategic operation

Directions of intended subsequent operations

no gainsaying the magnitude of the Soviet victory. By the end of the operation Belorussia and Western Ukraine were back in Soviet hands, Finland was about to capitulate, the Red Army had penetrated deep into the Baltic States and in the south were heading for Belgrade, Bucharest and Budapest. John Erickson went so far as to argue that 'when the Soviet armies shattered Army Group Centre, they achieved their greatest single military success on the Eastern Front. For the German army in the east it was a catastrophe of unbelievable proportions, greater than that of Stalingrad.'[23] At Stalingrad the symbol of Soviet success had been the iconic newsreel footage of the surrender of the 6th Army's commander Field Marshal Fredrich Paulus. In the case of Operation Bagration the symbol of capitulation was the image of 57,000 German POWs led by their generals being marched through the streets of Moscow on 17 July 1944.

The magnitude of the Soviet victory was largely a function of the weakened state of the Wehrmacht by mid-1944 and of the Red Army's decisive superiority in men and materiel, allowing the Soviets to plan and implement offensive action without fear of defeat or even a major counterattack by the Germans. The contribution of the western allies to Soviet successes on the Eastern Front was also a factor of growing importance in 1944. In his May Day statement Stalin paid tribute to 'the United States of America and Great Britain, who hold a front in Italy against the Germans and divert a considerable portion of the German forces from us, supply us with most valuable strategic raw materials and armaments, subject military objectives in Germany to systematic bombardment and thus undermine the latter's military strength'. On 11 June Tass published a statement detailing the deliveries of arms, raw materials, industrial equipment and foodstuffs to the Soviet Union by Britain, Canada and the United States.[24] Allied supplies to the USSR also featured in the Sovinform statement issued on the third anniversary of the outbreak of the Soviet–German war.[25] In his November 1944 speech Stalin estimated that the Second Front in France had tied down as many as 75 German divisions and that without such support the Red Army 'could not in such a short space of time have broken the resistance of the German armies and driven them out of the territory of the Soviet Union'.[26]

Operation Bagration demonstrated the new heights being reached by Soviet operational art. By 1944 Stalin and Stavka had finally learned the lesson that the war would not be won in one fell swoop and that they had to concentrate on the achievement of one strategic goal at a time. Stalin was particularly keen to maintain the focus and priority on Bagration. As Vasilevskii noted, 'Stalin was constantly drawing our attention to preparations for this operation'.[27] By 1944 Stalin was much more realistic about what could be achieved by his armies and had learned the lesson that setting initially modest goals in offensive operations

Ribbentrop, the German Foreign Minister, signing the Nazi–Soviet pact on 23 August 1939. Molotov and Stalin stand in the background.

Stalin and members of the Politburo on their way to a parade in Red Square.

Hitler and his generals.

Text of Stalin's radio broadcast of 3 July 1941, published in *Pravda*.

Stalin giving his speech to the troops in Red Square, 7 November 1941.

Molotov and Eden in Moscow.

Churchill, Averell Harriman, Stalin and Molotov at the Kremlin during Churchill's visit in August 1942.

Victorious Soviet soldiers marching through the ruins of Stalingrad.

Ruins of the factory district in beseiged Stalingrad.

President Franklin Delano Roosevelt and American Secretary of State, Cordell Hull.

Insurgents of the Warsaw uprising surrender to the Germans.

Notes from the Churchill–Stalin percentages agreement.

Soviet soldiers with former prisoners of Auschwitz after the camp's liberation, January 1945.

Churchill, Roosevelt and Stalin at the Yalta conference, February 1945.

Red Army soldiers hoisting the Soviet flag on top of the Reichstag building in Berlin, May 1945.

Soviet troops display captured Nazi banners at the victory parade in Red Square, 24 June 1945.

Stalin and President Harry Truman at the Potsdam conference, July 1945.

Atomic bomb damage in Hiroshima, Japan following the explosion on 6 August 1945.

Berlin children greet the arrival of a 'Raisin Bomber' during the Berlin blockade.

Lavrentii Beria.

Marshal I.S. Konev.

Marshal Zhukov (left) with officials of the Red Army.

Georgi Dimitrov with Stalin on his left and Voroshilov, Kaganovich and Molotov on his right.

Floral tributes to Stalin piled up against the Kremlin wall at the time of his funeral.

Stalin's funeral in March 1953. Beria, Malenkov, Molotov and Bulganin carry Stalin's coffin as it leaves the union building.

paid dividends in the long run. For Bagration the Fronts were limited to an initial advance of no more than 50 miles, the idea being that it was better to consolidate the occupation of a smaller area if that meant the Germans were unable to escape encirclement.[28] The key to the smooth implementation of Operation Bagration was the co-ordination of the Fronts, a problem dealt with by sending Zhukov to co-ordinate the 1st and 2nd Belorussian Fronts and Vasilevskii to the 1st Baltic and 3rd Belorussian Fronts. Later Zhukov and Vasilevskii were given the right to command as well as co-ordinate these Fronts.[29] Unlike in more desperate times, the process of planning and preparation for the operation was characterised by relative harmony in relations between Stalin and his generals and between Stavka and the Front commanders. The usual differences about strategy and tactics and the inevitable gripes about the sharing out of resources were subsumed under a coherent, common purpose. In this respect, Stalin's participation in the formulation and implementation of Bagration was both more restrained and more relaxed than it had been in the past. Although Stalin reserved the last word for himself on all strategic decisions, he had learned to trust his High Command when it came to many operational matters and to concentrate his own energies on troop morale and battle readiness, supplies issues and the work of political officers in the Red Army. This collective and devolved approach to the conduct of operations also meant that Stalin could devote more time to addressing some pressing political problems within the Grand Alliance.

The Warsaw Uprising[30]

The aim of Bagration was to liberate Belorussia, but the collapse of Army Group Centre and the rapid advance of the Red Army propelled Soviet forces to the borders of East Prussia and into central and southern Poland. By the end of July the Red Army was converging on the Polish capital Warsaw from several directions. The extent of the Red Army's penetration westwards raised the question of the future direction of the offensive now that Belorussia had been liberated. On 19 July Zhukov proposed to Stalin a series of operations to occupy East Prussia, or at least cut it off from the main body of Germany. Zhukov's proposals, together with other ideas, were considered at a Stavka meeting with Stalin on 27 July. The meeting decided that East Prussia would be too tough a nut to crack, at least without extensive preparations. The capture of Warsaw was a much more promising prospect, and the decision was made to cross the River Vistula at a number of points and concentrate the Soviet offensive in the direction of the Polish capital.[31] Pride of place in the campaign for Warsaw, which was expected to fall to the Red Army in early August, was given to the 1st Polish Army. Recruited from among Polish citizens who had been deported to the USSR in 1939–1940, the 1st Polish had begun forming up in July 1943. Its leadership was pro-communist and many of its officers were Russian. By July 1944 its total strength was about 20,000 and it formed part of Rokossovskii's 1st Belorussian Front. Its task was to cross the Vistula just south of Warsaw.

Soviet plans soon ran into trouble when the Red Army came up against strong German defences in the Warsaw area. The Wehrmacht was down but not out, and the Germans quickly rebuilt the strength of Army Group Centre by transferring divisions from other sectors of the Eastern Front and from western Europe. Warsaw barred the way to Berlin and was a crucial strategic outpost for the Germans to defend. As the Germans stabilised their defensive position, so the Soviet offensive lost its momentum. Soviet troops were tiring, the Red Army's supply chains were now stretched hundreds of miles long, and the Red Air Force's relocation to forward deployed airfields had disrupted operations and allowed the Luftwaffe to regain some of the initiative in the air. Nonetheless, the Soviets did manage to establish a number of bridgeheads on the western bank of the Vistula and to get as close to Warsaw as Praga, a suburb of the city on the eastern side of the river. But the Red Army had great difficulty in hanging on to its forward positions and was forced to retreat from Praga after the Soviet 2nd Tank Army received a severe mauling at the hands of six German divisions, including five armoured. High casualties were also incurred by the 1st Polish Army in its unsuccessful attempts to cross and establish a bridgehead on the western bank of the Vistula.

In charge of the Warsaw operations were Zhukov, the Stavka co-ordinator of operations on this sector, and Rokossovskii, the commander of the 1st Belorussian Front. On 6 August they reported to Stalin that strong enemy forces in the Warsaw area necessitated the drafting into action of some reserve divisions.[32] On 8 August Zhukov and Rokossovskii submitted to Stalin a detailed plan for the capture of Warsaw which involved securing the attack force's flanks, consolidating the existing bridgeheads on the west bank of the Vistula, and reinforcing the 1st Belorussian Front. They estimated that the operation could begin on 25 August.[33] The go-ahead was given by Stalin, but enemy counter-action in the Warsaw area meant that it was mid-September before the Soviets were ready for another major assault on the city, although local offensive operations continued throughout August and early September.[34] But, as previously, the Red Army's efforts to cross the Vistula in force and advance on Warsaw made little headway in the face of strong German opposition. In early October the Soviet attack was finally called off and the Red Army did not resume offensive operations against Warsaw until January 1945 (*see Map 15 on p. 205*).

The Soviet Advance on Warsaw, Summer 1944

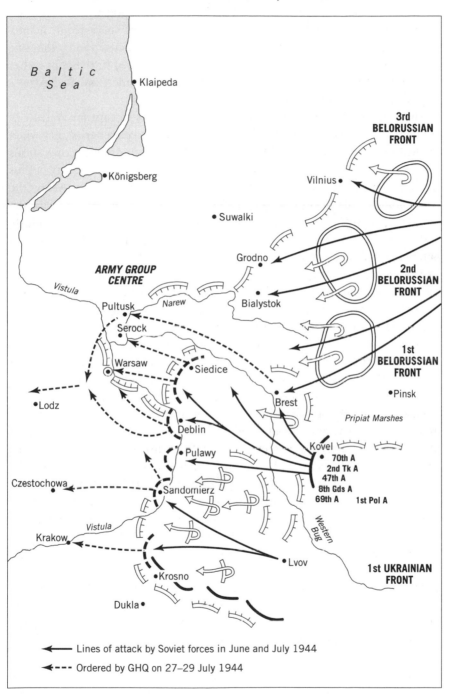

Baltic Sea

Klaipeda

Königsberg

Suwalki

3rd BELORUSSIAN FRONT

Vilnius

Grodno

2nd BELORUSSIAN FRONT

Vistula

ARMY GROUP CENTRE

Pultusk

Narew

Bialystok

Serock

Warsaw

Siedice

1st BELORUSSIAN FRONT

Lodz

Brest

Pinsk

Pripiat Marshes

Deblin

Kovel

70th A
2nd Tk A
47th A
8th Gds A
69th A   1st Pol A

Pulawy

Czestochowa

Sandomierz

Vistula

Krakow

Western Bug

Lvov

1st UKRAINIAN FRONT

Krosno

Dukla

← Lines of attack by Soviet forces in June and July 1944

←--- Ordered by GHQ on 27–29 July 1944

The Soviets had expected to capture the Polish capital quite quickly and easily. When that did not happen they regrouped and prepared for another assault on the city. Again the Soviets were confident of success, but it took much longer to prepare and launch the attack than predicted and by the time it did take place the Germans were even more entrenched in the approaches to Warsaw. The failure of this attack in September ended the Red Army's hopes for the immediate capture of Warsaw.

This picture of consistent, if ill-fated, Soviet efforts to capture Warsaw in summer 1944 runs completely counter to an alternative scenario: that when the Red Army reached the Vistula it deliberately halted its offensive operations to allow the Germans time to crush a popular uprising in the city.[35] This uprising, which began on 1 August, was staged by the Polish Home Army (the AK) – the partisan arm of Poland's government in exile in London. Like the Soviets, the Polish partisans expected Warsaw to fall to the Red Army quickly and easily. The aim was to liberate the city from the Germans and seize control before the Red Army arrived.[36]

Among the many defects of the alternative scenario is that the Red Army did not at any stage voluntarily slacken its efforts to capture Warsaw. Nor does it take into account the Wehrmacht's recovery after its expulsion from Belorussia or the difficulties the Red Army faced in continuing its prolonged offensive. As to Stalin's motives and calculations, the idea that he stood idly by while the Germans finished off the Polish Home Army is way off the mark. If anything, the uprising reinforced Stalin's determination to capture Warsaw as soon as possible. When it began on 1 August Stalin had no idea the uprising would fail; indeed, the collapsing German military position indicated that it might succeed. The anti-Soviet politics of the uprising soon became clear to Stalin, making it even more urgent that the Red Army seize control of Warsaw as soon as possible. It might be supposed that Stalin feared a clash with the Polish Home Army and was, therefore, content to let the Germans crush the AK in Warsaw. But the Red Army had been dealing with the AK ever since it crossed the frontiers of prewar Poland in early 1944, sometimes co-operatively, often conflictually, but at no stage did a few thousand Polish partisans pose a major threat or problem from the military point of view.[37] As Rokossovskii said to Alexander Werth in an off-the-record interview at the end of August 1944: 'And do you think that we would not have taken Warsaw if we had been able to do it? The whole idea that we are in any sense afraid of the AK is too idiotically absurd.'[38] Indeed, that was how the local Polish leaders of the uprising saw the situation themselves. As Jan M. Cienchanowski noted:

The Home Army generals were firmly convinced that the Russians were extremely anxious to capture Warsaw as soon as possible because of its strategic and military importance ... In addition they assumed that the Russians were anxious to take Warsaw because this would enable them to pose as the true 'redeemers of the Polish capital', a role which could be exploited politically.[39]

In his discussion of the motives for the uprising the Polish historian Eugeniusz Duraczynski suggests the uprising was staged not so much in anticipation of the Soviet capture of Warsaw as to force Stalin to prioritise the capture of the city rather than bypass it.[40] If that was their calculation, the uprising's leaders were not far wrong. The uprising did reinforce Stalin's inclination to capture the city; the problem was that he was unable to do so. Stalin could, of course, have ordered the Red Army to concentrate all its available strength on the capture of Warsaw. Even so, it is doubtful that the city would have fallen very quickly given the time it would have taken to redeploy forces from other fronts and such action would have jeopardised other operational goals that were considered by Moscow as important as storming Warsaw. Most important, the Soviets saw no need to take such drastic action. They thought they had enough forces in the Warsaw area to take the city in days rather than weeks.

None of this is to deny Stalin's blatant hostility to the AK, to the uprising, and to the anti-communist and anti-Soviet politics of the Polish government in exile in London – all of which threatened his plans for a postwar Poland friendly to the USSR. If the uprising failed and undermined the nationalist opposition to Soviet and communist influence in Poland, then so much the better from Stalin's point of view. However, a detailed look at Stalin's policy towards Poland at this time reveals that he was not averse to an accommodation with elements of the AK and the Polish exile government, if he could protect the USSR's interests and be assured of Soviet political influence in postwar Poland. The uprising finally convinced him that such an arrangement was not possible, although he continued to be willing to strike deals with those Polish politicians prepared to break with the AK and the exile government.

Ironically, when the uprising began on 1 August the Prime Minister of the Polish government in exile, Stanislaw Mikolajczyk, was in Moscow to discuss with Stalin a Soviet–Polish agreement that would lead to the restoration of diplomatic relations. Mikolajczyk's presence in Moscow was partly the result of pressure from Churchill and Roosevelt for the Soviets to repair relations with the exile Poles. The key issue was the negotiation of an agreement on Poland's postwar borders. At Tehran the understanding reached between Churchill, Roosevelt and Stalin was that Poland's eastern border would run along the Curzon Line (which was very close to the Nazi–Soviet demarcation line of September 1939) but that the country would be compensated for territorial losses by the acquisition of German lands in the west. But no formal agreement had been concluded at Tehran and many details of the proposed Polish–Soviet border remained to be negotiated.

In January 1944 the London Poles issued a statement noting reports that the Red Army had crossed into Poland and asserting their governmental rights in the liberated territories.[41] The territories in question were Western Belorussia and Western Ukraine. On 11 January Moscow issued its reply to the Polish statement, declaring that both territories had joined the USSR of their own free will in 1939. The Soviet statement added that the USSR stood for a strong and independent Poland, one bounded by the Curzon Line in the east and in the west by 'ancient Polish lands' reacquired from Germany. Additionally, the Soviet Union was willing to transfer to Poland any areas in Western Belorussia and Western Ukraine with a majority Polish population.[42]

The Soviets' protestations that they favoured a strong and independent Polish state were not new. There had been many such public statements, including by Stalin himself, and the restoration of an independent Poland after the war was the governing assumption of Soviet internal discussions on its postwar future.[43] Nor was Moscow's insistence that Western Belorussia and Western Ukraine rightly belonged to the USSR at all surprising. But the public commitment to compensate Poland territorially at Germany's expense was a new development, although in private the Soviets had expressed support for such a move on many occasions.[44] While the statement was critical of the Polish exile government it left open the possibility of a reconstruction of relations between it and the Soviet Union, and Moscow's promise to negotiate the ethnic details of the Curzon Line was a definite gesture of conciliation. From the Soviet point of view this was a moderate and positive statement on the Polish question and was presented as such to the American and British ambassadors in Moscow. When Molotov asked Harriman what he thought of the statement the ambassador replied that 'as a statement of the Soviet position of the Polish question it was most friendly in tone'.[45]

On 15 January the London Poles replied to the Soviets, reasserting their rights in relation to Western Belorussia and Western Ukraine and reiterating their desire to co-operate with the USSR in the struggle against Germany. This was not acceptable to the Soviets, who issued a rebuttal statement two days later emphasising that the key issue for them was recognition of the Curzon Line as the Polish–Soviet frontier.[46] In presenting a preview of this statement to the British and American ambassadors Molotov signalled a hardening of the Soviet position: Moscow was willing to negotiate with the London Poles, but only if their government was reconstructed and the anti-Soviet elements were excluded.[47] At a further meeting with Harriman and Clark Kerr, the British ambassador, on 18 January Molotov clarified that the reconstructed Polish government he had in mind would include Poles living in Britain, the

United States and the Soviet Union as well as those active in anti-German resistance in Poland.[48]

Acceptance of the Curzon Line and reconstruction of the exile government – these were the constant themes of the Soviet position on the Polish question, repeatedly stated by Stalin and Molotov in their meetings with the two ambassadors and by Stalin in his correspondence with Churchill and Roosevelt. Stalin made no effort to hide his exasperation that the London Poles refused to negotiate on these terms. 'Again the Poles. Is that the most important question?' Stalin impatiently asked Harriman when he came to see him on 3 March 1944.[49] Churchill's efforts to broker a deal acceptable to both sides Stalin dismissed as a waste of time, even accusing the British Prime Minister of making threats to force the Soviets to settle the Polish question on terms unfavourable to the USSR.[50] At a meeting with Clark Kerr on 29 February Stalin snorted and sniggered at the British compromise solution and reiterated that he wanted a reconstructed Polish exile government and acceptance of the Curzon Line. 'This dreary and exasperating conversation lasted for well over an hour. No argument was of any avail,' reported the British ambassador.[51]

The one positive constant in Stalin's and Molotov's statements on the Polish question was that they were prepared to contemplate a reconstructed government that included the exile Poles' Prime Minister, Mikolajczyk. As leader of the Polish peasant party, the biggest political party in prewar Poland, Mikolajczyk was seen as an important bridge to the formation of a broad-based government in liberated Poland with which the Soviets could work. For this reason Stalin resisted pressure from Polish communist circles to establish a provisional government for Poland based on a purely left-wing alliance.[52] Although highly desirable, a leftist government was not seen as strong enough to rule effectively over a Polish population that remained staunchly nationalist, notwithstanding the wartime political gains made by the communists and their socialist allies. When Stalin finally agreed to the establishment by the communists and their allies of a Polish Committee of National Liberation (PCNL) on 22 July 1944, part of the motivation was that he needed an organisation that could be entrusted with the administration of Polish territories liberated by the Red Army. This was how he presented the decision to Churchill and Roosevelt on 23 July. But while Stalin said that he did not consider the PCNL to be 'a Polish Government', he noted that it could become 'the core of a Polish Provisional Government made up of democratic forces'. The door remained open to a reconstructed government including Mikolajczyk, but the threat to bypass him remained. In the same message Stalin said that he would not refuse to see the Polish leader if he came to Moscow, as Churchill and Roosevelt had been suggesting.[53]

Stalin was encouraged in his approach to the Polish question by Oscar Lange, a Polish-American Marxist economist who in January 1944 suggested to the Soviets the formula of a reconstructed Polish government based on the London Poles, pro-Soviet Poles in Moscow and Poland, and independent Polish political figures from the Polish émigré communities of Britain and the United States. In spring 1944 Lange travelled to Moscow with the pro-Soviet Polish-American Catholic priest Stanislaw Orlemanksi to discuss with Stalin the way forward.[54] Stalin's conversations with these two intermediaries were highly significant for what they revealed of his strategic thinking about Polish–Soviet relations. Stalin wanted a friendly Poland with a left-leaning government that included his communist allies, but he also wanted a united country that was strong enough to participate in a long-term alliance of Slavic states against the future German threat.

The idea that the war with Hitler was a pan-Slavic struggle against the traditional German enemy had long figured in Soviet propaganda. As early as August 1941 the Soviets had formed a Pan-Slav committee and convened an all-Slav congress in Moscow. Many more such gatherings followed, not just in the Soviet Union but in other allied countries as well.[55] This was a natural tactic for Moscow to adopt given that the main victims of German aggression were the predominantly Slav states of Czechoslovakia, Poland, Yugoslavia and the Soviet Union. In 1943 Stalin began moves to create a formal political and diplomatic alliance of these Slavic states. In December 1943 a Soviet–Czechoslovak Treaty of Friendship, Mutual Aid and Postwar Co-operation was concluded with the Czech exile government headed by President Eduard Beneš. The treaty, signed in Moscow on 12 December, contained a protocol providing for a third country to join in the arrangement – a clause specifically aimed at facilitating a Czechoslovak–Polish–Soviet pact.[56] Stalin was not long back from Tehran and his continuing obsession with the postwar re-emergence of the German threat was evident in his talks with Beneš. In his conversation with the Czech President on 18 December Stalin opined that two countries threatened peace in the long run – Japan and Germany. 'The Germans are a very powerful and talented people and they would be able to recover very quickly after the war. From the Tehran conference [he] had formed the impression that this view was fully shared by all the allies.' At the final reception for Beneš on 22 December Stalin spoke of the 'necessity for Slavic co-operation after the war' and noted that 'up to now the Germans had been able to divide the Slavs, co-operating with some Slavs against others and then turning against them. From now on the Slavs must be united.'[57]

Stalin returned to the Slavic unity theme in his talk with Father Orlemanski on 28 April 1944:

Germany will be able to renew itself in some 15 years. That is why we must think not only about how to end this war . . . but also about what would happen in 20 years, when Germany revives itself. This is why an alliance between Russia and Poland is absolutely necessary in order not to let the Germans become an aggressor once again . . . [He] could give the example of the Grunwald[58] battle during which the Slavic peoples united against the members of the German order of Knights of the Sword. The united Poles, Russians, Lithuanians, Ukrainians, and Belorussians then defeated the Germans . . . we should revive the policy of Grunwald on a broad basis. This is his dream.[59]

In his talk with Lange on 17 May Stalin emphasised that the USSR needed a strong Poland in order to be able to deal with German aggression in the future. Stalin also made clear his opposition to a 'half-hearted' punitive peace like the Versailles treaty. If that happened again there would be another war in 15 years' time. Germany had to be kept weak for 50 years, Stalin told Lange, and since he was talking to a Marxist economist he took the opportunity to make the point that capitalist Britain and the United States would support the destruction of German and Japanese industry because this would eliminate two of their trade competitors.[60]

The third partner in Stalin's projected Slavic alliance was Yugoslavia. Unlike Poland, the dominant force in the partisan movement in Yugoslavia were the communists led by Marshal Tito. Even in 1944 it was clear that Tito's communists would emerge as the major political players in Yugoslavia's postwar politics. But Stalin was more pessimistic than Tito about the communists' postwar prospects. 'Be careful,' he reportedly told Tito in September 1944: 'the bourgeoisie in Serbia is very strong.' 'Comrade Stalin, I do not agree with your view. The bourgeoisie in Serbia is very weak,' replied Tito.[61] In April 1945 Stalin warned Tito that Germany would recover from the war very quickly: 'Give them twelve to fifteen years and they'll be on their feet again. And this is why the unity of the Slavs is important. The war shall soon be over. We shall recover in fifteen to twenty years, and then we'll have another go at it.'[62]

In relation to the postwar government of Yugoslavia, Stalin's policy was to broker a deal between Tito and the Yugoslav government in exile, including provision for the continuation of the monarchy. In Yugoslavia, as in Poland, Stalin's preferred formula was a reconstruction of the exile government and then its combination with his own supporters to form a provisional government inclusive of a broad range of political opinion. In the case of Poland, however, Stalin's patience was wearing pretty thin by the time Mikolajczyk arrived in Moscow at the end of July 1944.

Stalin's first meeting with Mikolajczyk was on 3 August. At the start of the meeting Mikolajczyk raised three questions for discussion: joint action in the struggle against the Germans; the agreement the Soviets had reached with the PCNL about the administration of liberated Polish territory; and the Polish–Soviet border issue. Mikolajczyk mentioned that an uprising in Warsaw had broken out and that he would like to be able to go to the Polish capital very soon to form a government that would combine the parties of the London Poles and those of the Polish communists. Stalin replied that the questions he had raised were of great political and practical importance but that Mikolajczyk had to negotiate those issues with the PCNL with a view to forming a united provisional government – a point that the Soviet leader repeatedly came back to in the ensuing conversation. When Mikolajczyk spoke of the role of the AK in Poland Stalin pointed out that its units were very weak and lacked guns, let alone artillery, tanks and planes. When Mikolajczyk suggested that the AK should be armed, Stalin replied that the most effective aid to the Soviet campaign to liberate Poland would be the formation of a unified government. When the conversation turned to the border issue Stalin restated the Soviet position that the Polish border should run along the Curzon Line in the east and the Oder River in the west; Poland would get Danzig but Königsberg would go to the Soviet Union. Responding to Polish claims to Lvov in Western Ukraine and Vilnius in Lithuania, Stalin said that 'according to Leninist ideology, all peoples were equal' and that he 'did not want to offend the Lithuanians, the Ukrainians or the Poles'. He went on to point out that the greatest territorial losses would be suffered by the Soviet Union, which was giving up that part of Poland that had once belonged to the Russian empire. Stalin also returned to the theme of Slavic unity, using the Grunwald analogy again: 'the first time the Poles and Russians united . . . together they beat the Germans. Then the Russians and Poles quarrelled. In the 17th century under Tsar Aleksei Mikhailovich there was a minister of foreign affairs, Ordin-Nashchekin, who proposed the conclusion of a union with the Poles. For this he was sacked. Now a return is necessary. The war has much to teach our people.' At the end of the talk Mikolajczyk asked Stalin how he envisaged the frontier issue being resolved. Stalin's answer – that it would be negotiated with a united Polish government – was yet another signal that he was prepared to work with Mikolajczyk.[63]

The next day the British ambassador in Moscow sent Eden a very positive report of the Mikolajczyk–Stalin meeting:

Although from time to time the talk was lively and direct, the atmosphere throughout was friendly . . . There were no recriminations from the Russian side . . . The Poles were impressed by the great 'wisdom' and apparent willingness of Stalin and his readiness to listen. They felt that he in his turn was impressed and even surprised by the simplicity and liberalism of Mikolajczyk.[64]

Mikolajczyk's talks with the PCNL leaders were less successful, the sticking points being the Polish Premier's insistence that his exile government should form the basis of a new provisional government and that the communist-led partisans should be assimilated into the AK.[65] While Mikolajczyk was talking to the PCNL, Churchill and Stalin exchanged messages about aid to the Warsaw uprising. On 4 August Churchill told Stalin the British intended to drop 60 tons of equipment and ammunition in the south-west section of the city. In his reply to Churchill the next day Stalin doubted the AK would be able to take Warsaw, because it was defended by four German divisions.[66]

On 8 August Stalin wrote to Churchill about his talk with Mikolajczyk: 'It has convinced me that he has inadequate information about the situation in Poland. At the same time I had the impression that Mikolajczyk is not against ways being found to unite the Poles.' Although the talks between the PCNL and Mikolajczyk had not been successful they had been useful, Stalin told Churchill, because they had provided an opportunity for an exchange of views. This was the first stage in the development of relations between the PCNL and Mikolajczyk and 'let us hope that things will improve', Stalin concluded.[67]

In Mikolajczyk's second talk with Stalin on 9 August the Polish Premier raised the question of Soviet aid to the Warsaw uprising. Stalin responded that he did not consider the uprising a 'realistic affair when the insurgents had no guns whereas the Germans in the Praga area alone had three tank divisions, not to speak of infantry. The Germans will simply kill all the Poles.' Stalin explained that the Red Army had advanced to within a few kilometres of Warsaw but the Germans then brought up reinforcements. The Red Army would continue its attack and take Warsaw, said Stalin, but it would take time. He was willing to supply the insurgents with munitions but worried about the supplies falling into German hands and asked Mikolajczyk if there were safe places to drop guns. After being reassured that there were such areas Stalin promised to give Rokossovskii the necessary orders and to pursue all possibilities. Towards the end of the conversation Stalin once again aired his fears of a German revival after the war and emphasised the need for a Polish–Soviet alliance to meet this threat.[68]

Mikolajczyk left Moscow the next day. According to Harriman, he departed the Soviet capital 'much more hopeful of the possibility of a settlement than when he arrived. He was impressed by his cordial reception and his frank discussions with Stalin and Molotov. At the meeting last night Stalin agreed to undertake to drop arms in Warsaw . . . Stalin told him that he had expected to take Warsaw on August 6 but that because the Germans had brought in four new Panzer divisions and two other divisions to hold the bridgehead [on the east bank of the Vistula], the taking of the city had been delayed but he was confident that the new difficulties could be overcome.'[69]

All these signs of a potentially amicable development of Polish–Soviet relations were shattered by the onset of intense inter-allied acrimony about aid to the Warsaw uprising. The British had begun airlifting supplies to the Warsaw insurgents in early August, using their bases in Italy. On 13 August the Americans decided to drop supplies, using planes flying from Britain, but that required landing on Soviet airfields for refuelling before returning home. On 14 August Harriman forwarded to Molotov the request for landing and re-fuelling facilities. The response, a letter from Deputy Foreign Commissar Andrei Vyshinskii the next day, shocked British and American sensibilities. The Soviets would not co-operate with American air drops to Warsaw, announced Vyshinskii, because 'the outbreak in Warsaw into which the Warsaw population has been drawn is purely the work of adventurers and the Soviet Government cannot lend its hand to it'.[70] In a face to face meeting with Harriman and Clark Kerr later that day Vyshinskii was equally obdurate, pointing out that the Soviets had sent a liaison officer to the rebels in Warsaw but he had been killed.[71] The next day Vyshinskii clarified the Soviet position: they would not co-operate with Anglo-American air drops but they would not object to them.[72]

This negative turn in the Soviet attitude to the Warsaw uprising seems to have been provoked by western press reports that the AK's action had been co-ordinated with the Red Army, which was now refusing to aid the insurgents. On 12 August Tass issued an angry denial and blamed the London Poles for the tragedy that was unfolding in Warsaw as the Germans moved to crush the uprising.[73] On 16 August Stalin wrote to Churchill pointing out that after seeing Mikolajczyk he had ordered supply drops to Warsaw but the liaison officer parachuted into the city had been captured and killed by the Germans:

> Now, after probing more deeply into the Warsaw affair, I have come to the conclusion that the Warsaw action is a reckless and fearful gamble, taking a heavy toll of the population. This would not have been the case had Soviet headquarters been informed beforehand about the Warsaw action and had the Poles maintained contact with them. Things being what they are, Soviet headquarters have decided that they must dissociate themselves from the Warsaw adventure.[74]

Stalin refused to see Harriman and Clark Kerr on 17 August. Instead he deputed Molotov to convey his intransigent position that there would be no

Soviet supplies to the Warsaw insurgents.[75] Harriman was angered by these exchanges with the Soviets and reported to Washington: 'my recent conversations with Vyshinskii and particularly with Molotov tonight lead me to the opinion that these men are bloated with power and expect that they can force their will on us and all countries'.[76] Harriman's mood communicated itself to others in the American embassy. On 17 August Harriman's personal assistant, R.P. Meiklejohn wrote in his diary:

It is just a case of cold-blooded murder, but there is nothing we can do about it. When the full story of this incident comes out it will certainly go down in history as one of the most infamous deeds of war. Beneath all their veneer of civilisation, the ruling elements here are nothing but a highly intelligent and ruthless gang of thugs and murderers. They have shown their hand in this case too clearly to leave any doubt about their character.[77]

The Warsaw uprising was an emotional event for the Soviets, too. They had lost millions of troops reaching Warsaw, and would suffer another half-million casualties in liberating Poland from the Germans; they did not take kindly to suggestions that they had provoked the uprising and then abandoned the Warsaw population to their fate. Equally important was the fact that the Red Army was preparing further assaults on the Polish capital and the Soviet expectation was that Warsaw would fall to them within days, thus making redundant any question of supplying the uprising.

On 20 August Churchill and Roosevelt appealed jointly to Stalin to drop supplies to Warsaw, if only to propitiate world opinion. Stalin replied on 22 August:

Sooner or later the truth about the handful of power-seeking criminals who launched the Warsaw adventure will out . . . From the military point of view the situation . . . is highly unfavourable both to the Red Army and to the Poles. Nevertheless, the Soviet troops . . . are doing all they can to repulse the Hitlerite sallies and go over to a new large-scale offensive near Warsaw. I can assure you that the Red Army will stint no effort to crush the Germans at Warsaw and liberate it for the Poles. That will be the best, really effective, help to the anti-Nazi Poles.[78]

By September, however, the Soviets were beginning to worry about the public relations aspect of the affair. On 9 September the People's Commissariat for Foreign Affairs sent a memorandum to the British embassy proposing the establishment of an independent commission to investigate who was responsible for launching the uprising and why it had not been co-ordinated with the

Soviet High Command. The memo also announced a change in policy on supplies to the insurgents, pointing out that the Soviets had already made several air drops but that each time the food and munitions had ended up in German hands. However, if the British and Americans insisted on such air drops the Soviets would co-operate and facilitate the operation.[79]

In mid-September the Soviets also began to step up their own air drops to Warsaw – a move which coincided with the launch of the Soviet attack on the city. Between 14 September and 1 October the 1st Belorussian Front made 2,243 flights to Warsaw and dropped 156 mortars, 505 anti-tank guns, 2,667 sub-machine-guns and rifles, 3 million cartridges, 42,000 hand grenades, 500 kilos of medicines and 113 tons of food.[80] This compared with British supplies during August and September of 1,344 pistols and revolvers, 3,855 machine pistols, 380 light machine-guns, 237 bazookas, 13 mortars, 130 rifles, 14,000 hand grenades, 3,000 anti-tank grenades, 8.5 tons of plastic explosive, 4.5 million rounds of ammunition and 45 tons of food.[81] Most of these supplies ended up in the hands of the Germans, although the Soviets claimed their low-level air drops were more accurate and effective than the high-altitude drops made by the RAF.

By the end of September inter-allied harmony had been restored and Harriman was messaging to Roosevelt that he had had 'a most satisfactory talk with Stalin . . . For the first time Stalin spoke with sympathy for the insurgents.'[82]

The Warsaw uprising was a disaster for all concerned except the Germans. For the Warsaw Poles it was a catastrophe. The AK incurred about 20,000 fatal- ities and many thousands more wounded, while the civilian population, caught in the crossfire, suffered somewhere between 150,000 and 200,000 dead. When the uprising came to an end on 2 October the Germans finished the demolition job they had begun during the course of military operations against the AK by razing the entire city centre to the ground and deporting the surviving popula- tion to concentration camps. For the Polish government in exile the failure of the uprising represented a critical weakening of its ability to influence the postwar politics of Poland. The communist left was, with Soviet help, able to capitalise on the undermining of the nationalist power base in Poland but the suspicion lingered that they and their Red Army allies had not done enough to aid the uprising. The Red Army was blamed for not capturing Warsaw sooner and the British and Americans were accused of appeasing their Soviet ally by not going public on their differences with Stalin over Poland. Within the Grand Alliance the diplomatic damage caused by differences over the uprising was limited and temporary, but in years to come the Warsaw controversy came to be seen as an important negative turning point in Soviet–Western relations and as an early harbinger of the cold war. During the cold war the blame game over the

Warsaw uprising became one of the touchstones of east–west ideological polemics. The west laid the blame on the Red Army's refusal to aid the uprising until it was too late, while the Soviets accused the anti-communist AK of recklessness and adventurism. Neither side devoted much time or energy to blaming Germany, surely the real villain of the piece. But when set beside the Holocaust and the mass murder of Soviet citizens, the crushing of the Warsaw uprising was just another German atrocity.

The Churchill–Stalin Percentages Agreement

Although in retrospect it is the drama of the Warsaw uprising that has attracted the historical attention, at the time it was only one item among many on Stalin's crowded military and political agenda. Poland was not the only country invaded by the Red Army in summer 1944. On 20 August the Red Army began a major invasion of Romania. This sparked an internal crisis in the country and a coup that led to the overthrow of the pro-German government and a switching of the country to the allied side of the war. On 31 August the Red Army entered the country's capital, Bucharest. Within days a Romanian delegation arrived in Moscow to negotiate the terms of an armistice, and a truce treaty was signed on 12 September. Because of pan-Slavic sentiment and pro-Russian popular attitudes Bulgaria had remained formally neutral during the Soviet–German conflict, although it had supported the Wehrmacht's campaign in a number of material ways and had fulfilled its Axis commitments by declaring war on Britain and the United States. On 5 September, however, the Soviet Union declared war on Bulgaria. Again there was an internal coup, this time led by the pro-communist Fatherland Front. By 9 September Bulgaria had ceased military operations against the Red Army and on 26 September ended hostilities with Britain and the United States. The Bulgarian armistice treaty was signed in Moscow on 28 October. Like Romania, Bulgaria switched sides in the war, opening the way for Red Army operations in Yugoslavia. Most of that country was liberated by Tito's partisans but the Red Army did conduct a campaign that led at the end of September to the capture of the Yugoslav capital, Belgrade. In Slovakia a communist-led national uprising broke out at the end of August. Like Warsaw, the insurgents appealed for Soviet aid but, unfortunately, the Red Army was bogged down on the other side of the Carpathian mountains and was able to offer only limited aid. The uprising was crushed by the Germans and it was not until May 1945 that the Red Army entered the Czechoslovak capital, Prague. Hungary sued for peace, too, but a German takeover of the country prevented Soviet capture of Budapest until January–February 1945.[83]

These unfolding events formed the backdrop to Churchill's second trip to Moscow and to the infamous 'percentages agreement' of October 1944.

Churchill arrived in Moscow on 9 October and went straight to the Kremlin, where he met and dined with Stalin.[84] Churchill's celebrated account of the meeting was published in the final volume of his history of the Second World War in 1954:

> The moment was apt for business, so I said [to Stalin], 'Let us settle about our affairs in the Balkans. Your armies are in Romania and Bulgaria. We have interests, missions, and agents there. Don't let us get at cross-purposes in small ways. So far as Britain and Russia are concerned, how would it do for you to have ninety percent predominance in Romania, for us to have ninety per cent of the say in Greece, and go fifty-fifty about Yugoslavia?' While this was being translated I wrote out on a half-sheet of paper:

	%
Rumania	
Russia	90
The others	10
Greece	
Great Britain	90
(in accord with U.S.A.)	
Russia	10
Yugoslavia	50–50
Hungary	50–50
Bulgaria	
Russia	75
The others	25

> I pushed this across to Stalin, who had by then heard the translation. There was a slight pause. Then he took his blue pencil and made a large tick upon it, and passed it back to us. It was all settled in no more time than it takes to set down . . . After this there was a long silence. The pencilled paper lay in the centre of the table. At length I said, 'Might it not be thought rather cynical if it seemed we had disposed of these issues so fateful to millions of people, in such an offhand manner? Let us burn the paper.' 'No, you keep it', said Stalin.[85]

It's a good story but, like so many of Churchill's tales, the lily was somewhat gilded.[86] While Churchill emphasised the drama of the moment, the British ambassador's report verged on the comic. Churchill had produced what he called a 'naughty document' showing a list of Balkan countries and the proportion of interest in them of the Great Powers. He said that the Americans would be shocked if they saw how crudely he had put it. Marshal Stalin was a realist. He himself was not sentimental while Mr Eden was a bad man. He had not consulted his cabinet or Parliament.[87]

More solemn was the Soviet record which said that Churchill announced 'he had prepared a table. The thought which was expressed in this table might be better stated in diplomatic language because, for example, the Americans, including the President, would be shocked by the division of Europe into spheres of influence.' Later in the conversation Churchill returned to this issue, saying that he 'had prepared a rather dirty and rough document, which showed the division of influence of the Soviet Union and Great Britain in Romania, Greece, Yugoslavia and Bulgaria'. In response, Stalin said 'that the 25 per cent envisaged for England in Bulgaria did not harmonise with the other figures in the table. He . . . considered that it would be necessary to enter an amendment envisaging 90 per cent for the Soviet Union in Bulgaria and 10 per cent for England.' The conversation then wandered off, but Stalin later reiterated that the figures for Bulgaria should be amended and it was agreed that Molotov and Eden would consider the matter further.[88]

Eden and Molotov discussed the so-called percentages deal at meetings on 10 and 11 October and agreed to adjust the percentage of influence in Bulgaria and Hungary to 80/20 in favour of the Soviets.[89] From the records of these two discussions it is clear that Eden and Molotov had little or no idea what their bosses meant when they talked about a spheres of influence deal expressed in terms of percentages. In the end their conversations boiled down to an exchange on the role of their respective countries in the Allied Control Commissions that were to be established to oversee the military occupation of Bulgaria, Hungary and Romania. In effect the Churchill–Stalin percentages came to reflect the amount of control Britain and the Soviet Union were each to have within these control commissions. This was largely an academic discussion since the Soviets were, or would be, the sole military occupiers of Bulgaria, Hungary and Romania, and the pattern of allied occupation regimes in Axis states had been established by the Italian precedent – control would rest with the allied armed forces occupying the country and the Allied Control Commission would act as an advisory and consultative body.

For all the retrospective hype of Churchill's presentation, the percentages deal was not mentioned in his extensive correspondence with Stalin in the months that followed or, with one exception, in their future face to face meetings at Yalta and Potsdam.[90]

In popular historical mythology the percentages deal is depicted as a cynical Anglo-Soviet carve-up; condemned as Churchill's betrayal of Eastern Europe to Stalin by right-wing commentators and characterised as Stalin's betrayal of the revolution in Greece and Yugoslavia by their left-wing counterparts. In truth the Churchill–Stalin exchange about spheres of influence was important only for one country – Greece. Securing British freedom of action in Greece was by far Churchill's most important priority in his conversation with Stalin. What Churchill feared was the takeover of Greece by ELAS-EAM – the communist-led partisan movement which already controlled large tracts of the country, acquired during the course of its struggle against German occupation. What Churchill sought from Stalin was an assurance that the Soviet Union would not involve itself in Greek affairs and would lay a restraining hand on the local communists. Churchill achieved this goal in the percentages agreement, but even before he produced his naughty document, Stalin had 'agreed that England must have the right of decisive voice in Greece'.[91]

The alacrity with which Stalin gave up Greece reflected established Soviet policy. Soviet policy-makers had begun to locate Greece within a British sphere of interest in the eastern Mediterranean as early as summer 1943. Internal briefing papers prepared for the Moscow Conference of Foreign Ministers of October 1943 noted the importance of British interests in Greece, including the strong ties between London and the Greek government in exile. Soviet interests, on the other hand, lay in extending Moscow's influence in the Slavic states of the Balkans.[92] These themes were taken up by Ivan Maiskii in a memorandum he submitted to Molotov in January 1944. The memo, a wide-ranging survey of the USSR's postwar prospects and perspectives, noted in relation to Greece:

> The USSR is interested in Greece much less than in other Balkan countries, whereas England, in contrast, is seriously interested in Greece. In relation to Greece, therefore, the USSR should observe great caution. If democratic Greece, following the example of other Balkan countries, would also like to conclude a pact of mutual assistance with the USSR, we would have no reason to discourage it. However, if the conclusion of a bilateral Greek–Soviet pact caused some complications with England, one could try to deal with the problem by way of the conclusion of a trilateral mutual assistance pact between England, Greece and the USSR (as in the case of Iran).[93]

When in summer 1944 a Soviet military mission was dispatched to the communist-led partisan army its officers went with instructions not to involve themselves in Greek internal affairs.[94] When British troops attempted to disarm ELAS-EAM in December 1944 and thereby provoked an armed revolt in Athens, Stalin refused to support the Greek communists. Dimitrov asked Molotov if the Greek comrades could expect assistance 'in order to oppose armed intervention by England'. The reply was that 'our Greek friends will not be able to count on active assistance from here [Moscow]'.[95] In January 1945 Stalin himself pronounced on Greek developments to Dimitrov:

> I advised not starting this fighting in Greece ... They've taken on more than they can handle. They were evidently counting on the Red Army's coming down to the Aegean. We cannot do that. We cannot send our troops into Greece, either. The Greeks have acted foolishly.[96]

In the Soviet policy community the governing assumption was that Greece was and would remain in the British sphere of influence. In November 1944 Litvinov wrote a report 'On the Prospects and Basis of Soviet–British Co-operation' that envisaged an Anglo-Soviet division of postwar Europe into spheres of security and allocated Greece to the British sphere along with Holland, Belgium, France, Spain and Portugal.[97] On the eve of the Big Three's Yalta conference in February 1945 Ambassador Gromyko wrote a briefing paper that considered recent events in Athens and noted British and American opposition to the coming to power of progressive forces in Greece, especially the communists. Gromyko noted that this raised the issue of great power interference in the internal affairs of small states but recommended that the Soviet side should not take any initiative in relation to Greece, except to make clear that they sympathised with progressive elements.[98]

At the Yalta conference Stalin raised the question of Greece during the plenary session on 8 February 1945. While there was allied support for a unified government in Yugoslavia, he wondered what was going on in Greece. But, Stalin added:

> He was by no means getting ready to criticise British policy in Greece ... *Churchill,* interrupting ... Stalin, states that he is very grateful to him for the restraint shown by the Soviet side during the Greek events ... *Stalin,* continuing, says that he would like to ask Churchill simply to inform us about what is going on in Greece.

Having listened to Churchill's explanation Stalin politely repeated that he didn't mean to interfere in the internal affairs of Greece, he just wanted to know what was going on.[99]

Churchill's retrospective view was that the percentages deal saved Greece from communism.[100] Stalin, however, had no intention of communising the country or of involving himself in a political project to that end. As he told

Churchill at their meeting on 14 October 1944, the 'Soviet Union did not intend to organise a Bolshevik Revolution in Europe'. [101] That did not mean he was averse to radical political change, especially if it served Soviet interests. But in Greece, as in other countries in Europe, he saw such change as coming about peacefully and democratically. In states that the Soviet Union occupied or exercised direct influence over Stalin would work to facilitate change. In countries such as Greece, which lay within the western allied sphere of occupation and influence, his advice to local communists was to co-operate with the British and Americans, particularly while the war continued; to adopt a long-haul strategy; and to seek the gradual transformation of their societies.

Despite all the subsequent attention lavished on the spheres of influence deal it was by no means the most discussed topic in Moscow. By far the greater part of Stalin and Churchill's time was taken up by the Polish question. This was the very first issue raised by Churchill at the meeting on 9 October, when he suggested that Mikolajczyk, who was in Cairo, should again be invited to Moscow. The Polish leader did go to Moscow and Stalin and Churchill met him on 13 October, but the discussion got nowhere. Stalin wanted Mikolajczyk to work with the PCNL to form a reconstructed Polish provisional government and to accept the Curzon Line as Poland's eastern border. The best Mikolajczyk could offer was the Curzon Line without Lvov, and that only as a demarcation line pending final negotiation of the Polish–Soviet frontier. This was unacceptable to Stalin, who emphasised that under no circumstances would he agree to the partition of Belorussia and the Ukraine.[102] Mikolajczyk then met the PCNL leader Boleslaw Bierut, who offered him a quarter of the ministerial posts in a reconstructed Polish government, a figure that Stalin increased to one third, including the position of Prime Minister.[103] Churchill also met Bierut and was charmed by his intelligence, but it is doubtful that he believed Stalin's protestations that the Pole was not a communist.[104] Stalin's growing impatience with Mikolajczyk was reflected in his comment to Churchill on 16 October that the Pole had 'not a word of thanks to the Red Army for liberating Poland . . . He thinks that the Russians are in service to him.'[105] Meanwhile Mikolajczyk was beginning to think that the deal on offer was the best the exile Poles could hope for. Indeed, after failing to persuade his colleagues of the merits of the Soviet terms he resigned as premier of the exile government at the end of November 1944.

Among the other topics discussed by Churchill and Stalin was the question of Turkey and the revision of the Montreux Convention on the control of the Black Sea Straits. This came up at the meeting on 9 October and Stalin told Churchill that 'under the Montreux Convention Turkey has all the rights to the Straits, while the Soviet Union has very few rights . . . it was necessary to discuss the question of revising the Montreux Convention, which did not correspond to the current situation at all.' Churchill reiterated his support for warm-seas access for Russia but asked what exactly Stalin had in mind. Stalin was unable to say what specific changes to Montreux he wanted but he successfully pressed Churchill to agree that revision was necessary.[106] According to the British record of this discussion Stalin also said:

> It was quite impossible for Russia to remain subject to Turkey, who could close the Straits and hamper Russian imports and exports and even her defence. What would Britain do if Spain or Egypt were given this right to close the Suez Canal, or what would the United States Government say if some South American Republic had the right to close the Panama Canal?[107]

At their final meeting on 17 October Churchill and Stalin exchanged views on the future of Germany. Once again Stalin expressed his fear of a revival of German power and made plain his preference for the dismemberment of the country. Asked by Churchill if he supported the formation of a federation of East European states to protect against German aggression, Stalin gave an interesting reply. The Soviet leadership thought that for the

> first three or four years after the war there will be a nationalistic atmosphere in Hungary, Czechoslovakia and Poland. The first desire of the peoples of these countries will be to organise their national life . . . To a degree the Hitler regime developed national feelings, as shown for example in Yugoslavia . . . where everyone wants their autonomy. In the first years after the war the predominant feeling will be the desire to live a full national life without interference. After the last war a number of untenable states were formed that had little basis and they suffered bankruptcy. Now there is the danger of going to the other extreme and forcing small peoples to unite together. It is difficult to see the Czechs and Hungarians, even the Czechs and Poles, finding a common language. Hence it is not possible to think about such associations, although they are not excluded in the future.[108]

Stalin was being a little disingenuous here. Soviet opposition to federations or confederations of East European states was of long standing and was based on the fear that such associations would take on an anti-Soviet character, even to the extent of reviving the cordon sanitaire around Bolshevik Russia established by the British and French after the First World War.[109] Stalin's remarks also reflected his growing consciousness of ethnic issues during this period and his preference for ethnic unification where possible. Hence his support for the return of Transylvania to Romania, a region inhabited mainly by Romanians, albeit with a significant Hungarian minority.[110] In relation to the

Soviet Union's own ethnic integrity this outlook led Stalin in 1945 to negotiate the transfer from Czechoslovakia to the USSR of sub-Carpathian Ukraine, a sparsely populated region of no great economic or strategic importance. As he explained later:

> In their times, in the thirteenth century, the Russians lost the trans-Carpathian Ukraine and from that time they always dreamt of recovering it. Thanks to our correct policy, we succeeded in recovering all Slavic – Ukrainian and White Russian – lands and to realize the age-old dreams of the Russian, Ukrainian and White Russian people.[111]

At the end of Churchill's trip to Moscow a communiqué was issued that spoke of an open and sincere exchange of views and of progress in negotiations about the Polish question and about the formation of a united government for Yugoslavia.[112] This was not much to show for an 11-day visit by the British Prime Minister. On the other hand, the talks had been very friendly and there was none of the rancour that had punctuated Churchill and Stalin's previous negotiations in Moscow in 1942 and at Tehran in 1943. When Churchill left Moscow on 19 October Stalin presented him with a commemorative vase decorated with a picture entitled appropriately enough 'With bow against Bear'. Stalin was in a good mood throughout the Prime Minister's visit and he agreed to dine at the British embassy – the first time he had attended such a function there.[113] Stalin also accompanied Churchill to the Bolshoi Ballet. It was here that Kathleen Harriman, daughter of the American ambassador, met Stalin for the first time. On 16 October she wrote to her friend Pamela Churchill (at that time married to Randolph, Winston's son):

> Stalin hadn't been to the theater since the war started, and for him to go with a foreigner was even more amazing. Between the acts, we went into a sit down dinner at which Molotov presided ... There were toasts to everyone and Stalin was very amusing when Moly got up and raised his glass to Stalin with a short conventional phrase about 'our great leader'. Stalin, after he'd drunk came back with a 'I thought he was going to say something new about me!' Moly answered with a rather glum, 'It's always a good one', which I thought very funny. Ave[rell] said that Stalin was exceptionally gay. He did have a good wit and looked as though he was enjoying his task as host to the P.M.[114]

In political terms the percentages deal had little practical significance but Churchill's willingness to negotiate such a wide-ranging deal and to demarcate vital interests must have been psychologically reassuring to Stalin. Of importance, too, for Stalin's calculations were the tensions in Anglo-American relations revealed by Roosevelt's response to the British Premier's trip to Moscow. On the eve of Churchill's departure for the Soviet capital Roosevelt wrote to Stalin asking that Ambassador Harriman be allowed to observe proceedings, pointedly stating that 'in this global war there is literally no question, military or political, in which the United States is not interested. I am firmly convinced that the three of us, and only the three of us, can find the solution to the questions unresolved. In this sense, while appreciating Mr Churchill's desire for the meeting, I prefer to regard your forthcoming talks with the Prime Minister as preliminary to a meeting of the three of us.' It was a point that needed no labouring for Stalin. He knew where power lay in the western half of the Grand Alliance and he wrote back reassuring Roosevelt that the meeting was Churchill's idea and that he would report to him on its progress.[115] Stalin was a little peeved at Roosevelt's intervention, or pretended to be, and said so to Churchill at their first meeting, noting that the US President was demanding too many rights for himself and allowing too few to Britain and the Soviet Union which were, after all, bound together by a formal treaty of alliance whereas the USSR and the United States were not. Churchill defused the situation by joking that they would discuss the Dumbarton Oaks negotiations but not tell Roosevelt![116]

Stalin and de Gaulle

The next important foreigner to visit Stalin was General de Gaulle, who arrived in Moscow in early December 1944. At Tehran Stalin had been very disparaging about de Gaulle and at the Yalta conference two months *after* de Gaulle's visit to Moscow he was not much kinder. At a meeting with Roosevelt on 4 February Stalin said that

> De Gaulle does not fully understand the position of France. Americans, English and Russians have spilt blood in order to liberate France. The French suffered defeat and now have only eight divisions. Nevertheless, de Gaulle wants France to have the same rights as the USA, England and Russia.[117]

At the Yalta plenary session on 5 February Stalin came out against French participation in the control of occupied Germany and remarked that 'it was impossible to forget the past. In this war France opened the gates to the enemy. This cost the allies colossal sacrifices in Europe. This is why we cannot place France on the same level as the three great allies.'[118]

But face to face with de Gaulle in December 1944 Stalin oozed personal charm and expressed full understanding of France's position and aspirations. At his first meeting with the General on 2 December Stalin emphasised that he supported the restoration of France as a great power.[119] Stalin was not being wholly disingenuous. In April 1944 the French communists had joined de Gaulle's French Committee of National Liberation and then agreed to serve in the provisional government that the General now headed. The Soviets were also genuinely grateful for the contribution of the Free French air regiment Normandie, which took part in some of the fiercest aerial combat on the Eastern Front. On the other hand, Moscow suspected that as a conservative de Gaulle had anti-communist and anti-Soviet tendencies.[120]

De Gaulle's trip to Moscow was at his request.[121] His purpose was to enhance liberated France's prestige by the conclusion of a Franco-Soviet pact similar to the Anglo-Soviet treaty of alliance of 1942. Stalin was happy to sign such a treaty, although he first made sure that Churchill and Roosevelt had no objections.[122] Stalin also decided to try to leverage some support from de Gaulle for the Soviet position on the Polish question. Molotov suggested to his French counterpart, Georges Bidault, that France should exchange representatives with the PCNL. For this reason the Polish question loomed large in Stalin's second conversation with de Gaulle on 6 December. In defence of the Soviet position on Poland Stalin reminded de Gaulle that the Curzon Line had been supported by the French Prime Minister Clemenceau after the First World War and pointed out that twice in the last 30 years Poland had been used as a corridor for a German invasion of Russia. Stalin also defended Soviet actions in relation to the Warsaw uprising, saying that by the time the Red Army reached the Polish capital its offensive had penetrated to a depth of 600 kilometres and its artillery shells had to be shipped 400 kilometres to the front.[123]

At their third and final meeting on 8 December de Gaulle raised the German question and Stalin warmed to his pet theme of the need to keep the Germans down, telling the General that he thought the British would take a hard line against Germany. When de Gaulle suggested that, judging by Versailles, Britain's commitment to a punitive peace would not last long, Stalin told him that this time around it would be possible to dismantle German industry and that the British understood the importance of this. The question of French relations with the PCNL also came up and Stalin offered de Gaulle a deal. Churchill had raised with Stalin the possibility of a tripartite pact involving Britain, rather than just a bilateral Franco-Soviet pact. De Gaulle did not like this idea; he wanted a bilateral agreement with Stalin on a par with the Anglo-Soviet pact. Stalin said that he would sign such a pact if de Gaulle would agree to exchange official representatives with the PCNL. 'Let the French do us a favour and we will do them one,' Stalin told the General. At the end of the conversation de Gaulle came back to the Polish question and expressed great sympathy for the Soviet position. In relation to the PCNL he said that the French had already suggested an exchange of representatives with the Poles.[124]

On 9 December Bidault told Molotov that de Gaulle was willing to exchange representatives with the PCNL in return for a Franco-Soviet pact. However, Molotov also wanted the French to publish a statement to this effect in the form of an exchange of letters between de Gaulle and the Chairman of the PCNL. This would have been tantamount to the diplomatic recognition of the Lublin government – a step the Soviets had yet to take formally themselves. Bidault told Molotov that his proposal was unacceptable.[125] It seems that discussions continued that night at the farewell dinner for the French delegation. Perhaps to oil the wheels of negotiation Stalin suggested to de Gaulle that they should 'bring out the machine guns. Let's liquidate these diplomats!'[126] Such drastic action was not necessary, however, and the Franco-Soviet treaty of mutual aid was signed the next day.[127] The French got their way on the non-publication of a statement on the exchange of representatives with the PCNL and were able to present the deal to the British and Americans as a decision to exchange low-level representatives.[128] Stalin, on the other hand, told the PCNL that it had been a hard-won concession and lambasted de Gaulle as a died-in-the-wool reactionary.[129]

As might be expected, the Soviet press devoted lavish coverage to de Gaulle's visit and hailed the Franco-Soviet pact as a milestone in the development of relations between France and the USSR. A particular theme of the Soviet public assessment of the pact was its importance for dealing with the German danger, not just at the time but in the future. An editorial in Izvestiya noted: 'this enemy is not only the present Hitlerite army, which will be totally routed; this enemy is German imperialism, which aspires to world supremacy, invariably and consistently giving birth to Bismarcks, Wilhelms and Hitlers'.[130]

The underlying reason for Soviet pressure on the French over the Polish question became apparent on 4 January 1945 when Moscow announced it was officially recognising the PCNL as the provisional government of Poland.[131] This statement ended the prospect of any further negotiations with the exile Poles in London about the formation of a united Polish government, although it did not rule out talks with the likes of Mikolajczyk. With the Red Army about to resume its march on Warsaw, Stalin had evidently decided to pursue his political goals in Poland through the pliable offices of the PCNL.

Liberation, Conquest, Revolution
Stalin's Aims in Germany and Eastern Europe

After de Gaulle left Moscow Stalin's next big diplomatic assignment was the Yalta conference of February 1945. It was Roosevelt's idea to hold a second meeting of the Big Three and he originally hoped to hold the conference in Scotland in September 1944, but Stalin demurred about the date because of military commitments and then suggested a Black Sea port as a venue. Stalin hated flying and he could travel to the Black Sea coast by train. By this stage, however, the American presidential election was in progress and it was decided to postpone the conference until after Roosevelt's inauguration for his fourth term in January 1945. Eventually agreement was reached on Yalta as the conference venue.[1]

Stalin's mood and outlook on the eve of Yalta – the most important tripartite conference of the Second World War – may be gleaned from two sources: indirectly via an examination of Soviet diplomatic preparations for the conference; and by an analysis of some striking private statements by Stalin in January 1945.

Curiously, Soviet diplomatic preparations for Yalta were not as extensive and systematic as for the Moscow conference of foreign ministers of October 1943. This was probably because the Soviet position on most questions was fixed by this time and implementation issues were the responsibility of the various internal policy and planning commissions established in 1943. As at Tehran, there was no fixed, formal agenda for Yalta and Stalin, the complete master of his foreign policy brief, could be relied upon to give nothing away to Britain and the United States.

Like the boss, in the run-up to Yalta the officials of the People's Commissariat of Foreign Affairs were preoccupied with the German question. First, there was the work of the Armistice Commission headed by Voroshilov. As the name suggests, the commission's brief was to prepare policy on the terms of surrender for Germany and the other Axis states. Its work paralleled the discussions and negotiations of the tripartite European Advisory

Commission (EAC), established by the Moscow foreign ministers' conference. The EAC was based in London with Moscow's ambassador to Great Britain, Fedor Gusev, serving as the Soviet representative on the commission. By the end of 1944 agreement had been reached within the EAC on the unconditional surrender of Germany; on the division of the country into American, British and Soviet zones of military occupation; and on the establishment of an Allied Control Commission to co-ordinate allied policy during the occupation. It had also been agreed to divide Berlin into separate zones of allied occupation – notwithstanding the fact that the German capital was located deep inside the proposed Soviet occupation zone in the east of the country. In November 1944 France joined the EAC and later received a share in the occupation of Germany and Berlin. The point to note about Soviet preparations for the occupation of Germany is the assumption that it would be prolonged and could be achieved and sustained only in co-operation with Britain and the United States.[2]

The second strand of Soviet policy work on Germany was embodied in the Reparations Commission headed by Ivan Maiskii. That the Soviet Union would receive reparations from Germany was beyond question, from Moscow's point of view; it could hardly be otherwise given the extent of the damage caused by the German invasion. Maiskii's commission was to formulate policy on how much and in what form reparations would be paid to the Soviet Union. The problem was that the British and Americans were sceptical about reparations payments. They feared a repetition of the experience after the First World War when Germany, unable to pay its reparations, secured foreign loans to service its debts and then reneged on the repayments. To circumvent this objection the Soviet proposal was for reparations in kind rather than in money, i.e. German plant and machinery would be confiscated and what was left of the country's industry would then supply goods on an annual basis to the USSR. One argument used by Maiskii and the Soviets in support of this approach to reparations was that it would also serve to weaken Germany's capacity to rearm.[3]

The third strand of the Soviets' German policy work concerned dismemberment, an issue within the remit of Litvinov's Commission on Peace Treaties and the Postwar Order. The policy of breaking up Germany after the war had been stated time and again by Stalin, most notably in his conversations and correspondence with Churchill and Roosevelt. It is no surprise, then, that Litvinov's commission spent a great deal of time in 1943 and 1944 discussing various schemes of dismemberment. No firm conclusions were reached about how many states Germany should be broken up into but by January 1945 Litvinov was proposing a maximum of seven – Prussia, Hanover, Westphalia, Württemberg, Baden, Bavaria, and Saxony – and arguing that this should constitute the negotiating position of the Soviets in their discussions with the British and Americans. Again, the underlying assumption was that such a radical policy – essentially a proposal to turn the clock back to the time in the nineteenth century when Germany was not a unitary state – could only be achieved in co-operation with Britain and the United States.[4]

In the pre-Yalta period Litvinov also speculated on some grander themes. In November 1944 he wrote a paper for Molotov 'On the Prospects and Possible Basis of Soviet-British Cooperation'.[5] According to Litvinov the fundamental basis for postwar Anglo-Soviet co-operation would be containment of Germany and the maintenance of peace in Europe. However, the war would bequeath a dangerous power imbalance arising from the Soviet defeat of Germany and from French and Italian decline. But that problem could be resolved by the demarcation of British and Soviet security spheres in Europe. Specifically, Litvinov suggested a maximum Soviet security zone of Finland, Sweden, Poland, Hungary, Czechoslovakia, Romania, the Balkans (but not Greece) and Turkey. The British security zone would encompass Western Europe, but with Norway, Denmark, Germany, Austria and Italy constituting a neutral zone. According to Litvinov:

> This delimitation will mean that Britain must undertake not to enter into specifically close relations with, or make any agreements against our will with the countries in our sphere, and also not to have military, naval or air-force bases there. We can give the corresponding undertaking with regard to the British sphere, except for France which must have the right to join an Anglo-Russian treaty directed against Germany.

Litvinov linked the prospects for such an Anglo-Soviet accord to Britain losing its global power struggle with the Americans which, he believed, would encourage London to consolidate its position in continental Europe. Litvinov returned to the question of postwar Anglo-Soviet co-operation on 11 January 1945 in a note to Molotov on 'On the Question of Blocs and Spheres of Influence'.[6] Litvinov reiterated his proposal for a division of Europe into British and Soviet spheres of interest, pointing out that tripartite discussions involving the Americans did not preclude bilateral arrangements and agreements between the great powers. Litvinov also commented on an idea put forward by the American journalist Walter Lippmann that not just Europe but the whole world be divided into spheres of influence. This proposal, said Litvinov, was too fantastic and unrealistic to merit serious discussion. In particular Litvinov derided Lippmann's concept of an all-embracing western community of interest consisting of North and South America, Britain and the British Commonwealth, and Western Europe. Litvinov did not see any reason why the United States should be involved in Anglo-Soviet discussions about zones of security, especially in view of the antipathy of the American press and public opinion to the notion of blocs and spheres of influence. Litvinov pointed out, too, that when objecting to spheres of influence in Europe the Americans chose to forget about the Monroe Doctrine and the US sphere in Latin America. Litvinov concluded that any agreement on British and Soviet security zones in Europe should be the result of bilateral agreement and not be dependent on the establishment of the regional structures of a future international security organisation.

The problem with Litvinov's approach was that the British had given no indication that they were willing to go any further than the vague and limited spheres of influence agreement embodied in the percentages deal. Furthermore, it was clear that US opposition to spheres of influence would carry a lot of weight within the Grand Alliance and that the kind of grand bargain advocated by Litvinov was not a practical proposition. That did not rule out an implicit Soviet–Western spheres of influence arrangement and that, indeed, was the policy pursued by Stalin and Molotov in 1945. The problem was that because the limits and character of the Soviet and western spheres of influence remained unstated some serious misunderstandings and frictions developed between the two sides. Matters were further complicated by Stalin's pursuit of his ideologically driven communist political goals in postwar Europe. Stalin did not see his ideological policy as incompatible with his security policy, but decision-makers in London and Washington came to view the Soviet and communist political advance in postwar Europe as threatening and as a form of 'ideological *Lebensraum*'.[7]

Litvinov was not the only one indulging in grand speculation. As early as January 1944 Maiskii had sent Molotov a long memorandum setting out his views on the coming peace and the possible character of the postwar order.[8] Maiskii's starting point was Moscow's postwar goal of a prolonged period of peace – between 30 and 50 years – during which time Soviet security would be guaranteed. To achieve that goal the Soviet Union had to pursue a number of policies. The USSR's borders would be those extant in June 1941, while Finland and Romania would conclude mutual assistance pacts with the Soviet Union and permit Soviet military bases on their territory. French and Polish independence would be restored but neither country would be allowed to become strong enough to pose a threat to the Soviet Union in Europe. Czechoslovakia would be bolstered as a key Soviet ally and mutual assistance treaties signed with Yugoslavia and Bulgaria. Germany had to be ideologically and economically disarmed as well as militarily weakened with the aim of rendering the country harmless for 30 to 50 years. The Soviet Union wanted

Japan defeated but had no interest in becoming embroiled in the Far Eastern war when it could achieve its territorial goals (the acquisition of South Sakhalin and the Kuril Islands) at the peace conference. Providing there was no proletarian revolution in Europe Maiskii did not foresee any sharp conflicts with Britain or the United States after the war. Maiskii thought the US would be a dynamic and expansionist imperial power after the war whereas Britain would be a conservative imperialist state interested in preservation of the status quo. This meant there was a good basis for close postwar co-operation between Britain and the USSR. Both countries would be interested in postwar stability and the Soviets needed to keep Britain strong as a counterbalance to American power. As to Soviet–American relations, the prospects were equally rosy. There were no direct conflicts between American and Soviet interests and, in the context of its imperial rivalry with Great Britain, Washington would be concerned to keep Moscow neutral. Overall there was no reason why the Soviet Union should not be able to maintain good relations with both Britain and the United States.

Most of what Maiskii had to say in this memorandum was a gloss on existing Soviet policies and perspectives. The most innovative point was his advocacy of a long-term Anglo-Soviet alliance, which was akin to Litvinov's perspective of a Soviet–British spheres of influence agreement in Europe. The two men had worked very closely when Maiskii was ambassador in London and Litvinov was the foreign commissar and they remained close during the war. Both could be fairly described as Anglophiles (Litvinov had an English wife), although that did not stop either of them from adopting a hard-nosed view of British foreign policy. Where Maiskii differed from Litvinov was in his greater sensitivity to the ideological dimension of Soviet foreign policy and how this might impact on relations with Britain and the United States. In common with other Soviet analysts Maiskii detected both reactionary and progressive trends in British and American domestic politics and saw the complications this could cause should elements hostile to the new democratic order the Soviets wished to see established in Europe gain the ascendancy.

Of a younger generation in the Soviet diplomatic corps was the future Soviet Foreign Minister, Andrei Gromyko. On 14 July 1944 Gromyko submitted a long document to Molotov entitled 'On the Question of Soviet–American Relations',[9] one of a number of such communications to Molotov on the theme of the wartime Soviet–American *détente* and its durability.[10] Gromyko's outlook on Soviet–American relations was generally positive. He argued that Roosevelt's policy of co-operation with the Soviet Union had majority support in Congress, in both Democratic and Republican parties, and among the public. In terms of opposition to Roosevelt's policy he highlighted the role of the reactionary, anti-communist elements of the press and of the Catholic Church. There were 23 million Catholics in the US, Gromyko pointed out, including 5 million Polish-Americans. Gromyko also highlighted American fears of communist revolution and sovietisation, particularly in Eastern Europe. Nevertheless, he still believed that Soviet–American co-operation would continue after the war. Isolationist foreign policies had been abandoned in favour of involvement in European and international affairs. The US had a common interest with the Soviets in dealing with the German threat and in securing the conditions for a prolonged peace. Gromyko also identified significant economic and trade reasons for postwar Soviet–American co-operation and concluded that 'notwithstanding the difficulties which will probably arise from time to time . . . without doubt the conditions exist for the continuation of collaboration between the two countries . . . To a large degree relations between the two countries in the postwar period will be determined by the relations shaped and continuing to be shaped in wartime.'

In another letter to Molotov ten days later Gromyko analysed the reasons for the replacement of Vice-President Henry Wallace by Harry Truman as Roosevelt's running mate in the 1944 American presidential election. In Gromyko's view Wallace was replaced because he was too radical and had offended business circles, as well as right-wing conservative elements in the Democratic Party and among the 'southern bloc' of Democratic senators and congressmen. But, Gromyko concluded, as far as foreign policy was concerned, Truman 'always supported Roosevelt. He is a supporter of co-operation between the United States and its allies. He stands for co-operation with the Soviet Union. He speaks positively of the Tehran and Moscow conferences.'[11]

As ambassador to the United States, Gromyko was charged with briefing Moscow on the issues likely to come up at the Yalta conference. In his documents Gromyko identified a number of issues that might prove to be controversial – Poland, Greece, Yugoslavia, Dumbarton Oaks, the role of the EAC – and made suggestions about the tactics the Soviets should pursue to protect their interests in these spheres. But there was no hint in Gromyko's analyses that he thought any of the difficulties were insurmountable or could not be resolved by agreement. On Poland he thought that Roosevelt would eventually recognise the Lublin provisional government. On Greece he said that the Soviets must not get involved in the struggle between the British and the communist partisans in ELAS-EAM but should make clear their sympathy for the progressive elements. On Yugoslavia he thought it would be possible to garner more support for Tito from the British and Americans. As the head of the Soviet delegation to the Dumbarton Oaks conference Gromyko had a particular interest in the veto controversy. This was the one issue on which he advocated a hard line – under no circumstances should the Soviets surrender the principle of unanimous decision-making; without a veto the Soviet Union could be outvoted by Britain and the United States in the EAC and in the future UN Security Council.[12]

What Gromyko, Litvinov and Maiskii were saying and proposing were not necessarily what Stalin was thinking. But in Stalin's Russia the terms of discussion were highly restrictive and usually set by the Soviet dictator himself. Even as independent a figure as Litvinov had to be careful not to overstep the mark of what it was permissible to say. Like future historians these three mid-level policy-makers were faced with the task of trying to deduce what was on Stalin's mind by reading the runes of his public statements, interpreting what was being said in the Soviet press and making use of the confidential information at their disposal. One advantage they had over the historians who followed them was that all three had personal dealings with Stalin, and even more so with their immediate boss, Molotov, who could always be relied upon to stick closely to the Great Leader's views. In the case of Litvinov, his personal interactions with Stalin had historically been quite extensive, but were in severe decline during the war as Molotov, his long-time personal rival, manoeuvred to isolate him. Maiskii continued to have some direct dealings with Stalin during the war, particularly after his recall to Moscow from London. Gromyko's personal contact with Stalin was more limited but he was one of the rising stars of the foreign commissariat and well in with Molotov. In short, it is reasonable to assume that the speculations of Gromyko, Litvinov and Maiskii on the shape of the postwar world were not idiosyncratic but reflected the language and terms of the internal discourse on foreign policy and international relations that was taking place at the highest levels of decision-making. Their documents tell us that in the diplomatic sphere, at least, the Soviets saw the future in terms of the long-term continuation of tripartite collaboration. It was in this spirit that they approached the Yalta conference.

More direct evidence of Stalin's thinking on the eve of Yalta comes from some conversations he had in January 1945 with a delegation from Tito's Yugoslav Committee of National Liberation. The delegation was headed by Andrija Hebrang, a member of the Politburo of the Yugoslav communist party. At his first meeting with Stalin on 9 January the conversation dealt mainly with Balkan matters. Hebrang outlined to Stalin various Yugoslav territorial claims. Stalin was sympathetic but said territorial transfers should be based on the ethnic principle and that it would be best if the demand to join Yugoslavia came from the local populations themselves. When Hebrang mentioned claims to Greek Macedonia and Saloniki Stalin warned that the

Yugoslavs were creating hostile relations with Romania, Hungary and Greece and seemed intent on going to war with the whole world, which did not make much sense. Stalin also reined in Yugoslav ambitions to incorporate Bulgaria into their Federation, saying that a confederation uniting the two countries on equal terms would be better. On the crisis in Greece, Stalin noted that the British had feared a Red Army advance into the country. That would have created a very different situation there, Stalin told Hebrang, but nothing could be done in Greece without a navy. 'The British were surprised when they saw the Red Army was not moving into Greece. They cannot understand a strategy that forbids the army to move along divergent lines. The strategy of the Red Army is based on the movement along convergent lines.' In relation to the governmental issue in Yugoslavia Stalin said it would be premature for Tito to proclaim a provisional government. The British and Americans would not recognise it and the Soviets had their hands full with the same issue in Poland. Stalin also strongly advised the Yugoslavs not to give Churchill any excuse to do in their country what he was doing in Greece and asked that they consult with Moscow before taking any important decisions since they might put the Soviets in a 'stupid position'. This remark led Stalin to his final contribution to the discussion:

> In relation to bourgeois politicians you have to be careful. They are . . . very touchy and vindictive. You have to keep a handle on your emotions; if emotions lead – you lose. In his time Lenin did not dream of the correlation of forces we have achieved in this war. Lenin thought that everyone would attack us . . . whereas it turns out that one group of the bourgeoisie was against us but the other with us. Lenin did not think it would be possible to ally with one wing of the bourgeoisie and fight with the other. But we managed it; we are led not by emotion but by reason, analysis and calculation.[13]

Talking to Dimitrov about the meeting the next day, Stalin said he did not like the way the Yugoslavs were behaving, although Hebrang himself seemed a sensible man.[14] In his telegram to Tito on 11 January summarising the outcome of the meeting, Hebrang noted that Stalin considered it 'necessary to be circumspect in relation to foreign policy questions. Our basic task is to strengthen the achievement of victory. It is necessary to avoid big demands on neighbouring countries in order not to provoke negative relations or clashes with us.'[15]

On 28 January Hebrang had a further meeting with Stalin. This time a Bulgarian delegation was present and one of its members, the communist V. Kolarev, made some notes of Stalin's comments at the meeting. Its main purpose was to discuss relations between Bulgaria and Yugoslavia and Stalin repeated his view that unification of the two countries should be gradual and equitable. More generally Stalin stated:

> The capitalist world is divided into two hostile blocs – democratic and fascist. The Soviet Union takes advantage of this in order to fight against the most dangerous [country] for the Slavs – Germany. But even after the defeat of Germany the danger of war/invasion will continue to exist. Germany is a great state with large industry, strong organisation, employees, and traditions; it shall never accept its defeat and will continue to be dangerous for the Slavonic world, because it sees it as an enemy. The imperialist danger could come from another side.
>
> The crisis of capitalism today is caused mainly by the decay and mutual ruin of the two enemy camps. This is favourable for the victory of socialism in Europe. But we have to forget the idea that the victory of socialism could be realised only through Soviet rule. It could be presented by some other political systems – for example by a democracy, a parliamentary republic and even by constitutional monarchy.[16]

Another version of Stalin's remarks at this meeting, which took place at his dacha, is provided in Dimitrov's diary:

> Germany will be routed, but the Germans are a sturdy people with great numbers of cadres; they will rise again. The Slavic peoples should not be caught unawares the next time they attempt an attack against them, and in the future this will probably, even certainly, occur. The old Slavophilism expressed the aim of tsarist Russia to subjugate the other Slavic peoples. Our Slavophilism is something completely different – the unification of the Slavic peoples as equals for the common defense of their existence and future . . . The crisis of capitalism has manifested itself in the division of the capitalists into two factions – one fascist, the other democratic. The alliance between ourselves and the democratic faction came about because the latter had a stake in preventing Hitler's domination, for that brutal state would have driven the working class to extremes and to the overthrow of capitalism itself. We are currently allied with one faction against the other, but in the future we will be allied against the first faction of capitalists, too.
>
> Perhaps we are mistaken when we suppose that the Soviet form is the only one that leads to socialism. In practice, it turns out that the Soviet form is the best, but by no means the only, form. There may be other forms – the democratic republic and even under certain conditions the constitutional monarchy.[17]

Stalin's remarks about the two wings of capitalism have often been interpreted to mean that he believed conflict with the democratic faction of capitalism was inevitable. But, as both quotations show, what was really on Stalin's mind was the long-term German threat and the need for Slavic unity to confront it. Stalin's message to the Bulgarian and Yugoslav comrades was that the Slavs could only rely on themselves to deal with the Germans, not an enduring alliance with democratic capitalism: he hoped the Grand Alliance with Britain and the United States would last, but it might not. Equally, it is clear that in terms of communist strategy Stalin was advocating a moderate political course, one that focused on gradual reform rather than on a revolutionary upheaval on the model of Russia in 1917. This remained Stalin's policy for the communist movement for another two or three years; it was only when the strategy of gradual communist political advance was deemed to have failed that he embraced a more militant and leftist politics, and unleashed the radical tendencies of the Yugoslav and other European communist parties.

But as the Yalta conference approached the auguries for tripartite co-operation were good. Neither Stalin's diplomatic nor his political strategy presaged any major conflicts with Britain and the United States, at least not in the immediate future. The scene was set for serious negotiations with Churchill and Roosevelt to resolve a number of current controversies and create the basis for a durable, peacetime Grand Alliance.

The Crimean Conference

The Yalta, or Crimean conference as the Soviets called it, was an altogether grander affair than Tehran. The delegations were larger and included more key personnel. Stalin, for example, was accompanied to the conference by Molotov, by Antonov, the Deputy Chief of the General Staff, by the naval commissar Admiral Kuznetsov, Deputy Foreign Commissar Vyshinskii, and by Gromyko, Gusev and Maiskii. Discussions ranged further and wider and many more decisions were taken than at Tehran. At the previous meeting of the Big Three the main focus of discussion had been the war; at Yalta the three leaders were firmly focused on the emergent postwar order.

The setting was a little unreal: Tsar Nicholas II's magnificent 50-room Livadia Palace in the spa town of Yalta on the Black Sea. It had been badly damaged by the Germans during their occupation of the Crimea, but the Russians repaired the palace as best they could. One problem with the venue was an acute shortage of bathrooms, much to the disgruntlement of the American delegation.[18] This shortage of facilities impacted on the Big Three as well. Kathleen Harriman, who accompanied her father to the conference, wrote to Pamela Churchill that one day, during a break in proceedings Stalin came out of the conference hall very quickly, searching for a toilet:

> U.J. [Uncle Joe] was shown to one & came out quickly – washroom without toilet. By that time the P.M. was occupying the next nearest John so one of our embassy boys took Stalin 'way the hell down the hall to the next nearest toilet. In the shuffle, Stalin's NKVD generals got separated. Then there was havoc – everyone meleeing around whispering. I think they thought the Americans had pulled a kidnapping stunt or something. A few minutes later a composed U.J. appeared at the door & order was restored![19]

As at Tehran, there were bilateral meetings among the Big Three as well as the tripartite plenary sessions. Stalin's first port of call on 4 February 1945 was Churchill. Both Soviet and western forces were by now fighting in Germany and the two leaders had a brief exchange about the progress of the battle there.[20] Stalin next met Roosevelt and had a more extensive conversation with the President, during which the two continued to carp about de Gaulle, as they had at Tehran.[21] The first plenary session began at 5.00 p.m. that day with Stalin inviting Roosevelt to open proceedings, which he did by saying the participants already had a good understanding of each other and should be frank in the discussions at the conference. The plenary then turned to an exchange of information and views about the military situation on the various fronts.[22]

The first real political discussion at Yalta took place at the second plenary session on 5 February. The topic was the future of Germany, and Stalin pushed very hard for a definite commitment to dismember Germany. 'Evidently, we are all for the dismemberment of Germany,' he said to Churchill and Roosevelt. 'But it is necessary to shape this into the form of decisions. He, comrade Stalin, proposes to take such decisions at today's session.' Referring to his discussions with Churchill in Moscow in October 1944, Stalin noted that because of Roosevelt's absence it had not been possible to take a decision on the dismemberment of Germany, but 'had not the time come for decision on this question?' As the conversation developed, Stalin interrupted Churchill to ask 'when the question of the dismemberment of Germany would be put before the new people in Germany? The thing is this question is not in the conditions of capitulation. Perhaps a clause on the dismemberment of Germany should be added to the terms of surrender?' Responding to Roosevelt's suggestion that the matter should be referred to the three foreign ministers who should be charged with drawing up a plan for the study of the project, Stalin said that while one could accept this 'compromise proposal', 'it was necessary to say directly that we consider it necessary to dismember Germany and that we are all for this'. Stalin continued:

The second point of decision must be the inclusion in the surrender terms of a point concerning the dismemberment of Germany, but without indicating [into] how many parts. He, comrade Stalin, would like the decision on the dismemberment of Germany made known to groups of persons who will be shown the terms of unconditional surrender. It is important for the allies that groups of people, be they generals or other persons, know that Germany will be dismembered. To comrade Stalin, Churchill's plan not to tell the leading groups of Germans about the dismemberment of Germany seems risky. It would be expedient to speak of this beforehand. It would be to the advantage of us allies if the military groups or the government not only signed the surrender terms drawn up in London [by the EAC] but also signed terms about the dismemberment of Germany in order to bind the population to it. Then the population will be more easily reconciled to dismemberment.

Eventually Stalin conceded that it would be unwise to publicise dismemberment too far in advance but continued to urge clarity on the allied position and the inclusion of dismemberment in the terms of surrender:

Comrade Stalin further stated that one could take a decision on the first point which would read: 'the dismemberment of Germany and the establishment of a commission to work out a concrete plan for dismemberment'. The second point of decision would read: 'to add to the terms of unconditional surrender a point about the dismemberment of Germany without mentioning the number of parts into which it will be dismembered'.[23]

The discussion then moved on to the question of whether or not France should be given a zone of occupation in Germany. Stalin opposed the move, arguing that the French did not deserve it and that such a decision would lead to demands from other allied countries for a share in the occupation. Stalin relented only when it was made clear that the French zone would be carved out of territories to be occupied by the British and Americans. But he continued to oppose the inclusion of France on the Allied Control Commission for Germany, notwithstanding British arguments that it was illogical to allow the French an occupation zone but to deny them representation on the ACC. Stalin was evidently not prepared to continue that discussion so he switched the debate to the more comfortable topic of reparations and announced that Maiskii, who was sitting beside him, would make a presentation on the Soviet behalf. This was news to Maiskii, who whispered to Stalin that they had yet to put a figure on Soviet reparations demands. Molotov, who was sitting on the other side of Stalin, intervened in this huddle and it was agreed on the spot to demand $10 billion in reparations rather than $5 billion, the low-end figure that had featured in Soviet internal discussions before the conference.[24]

Maiskii duly gave his report outlining the principles of the Soviet reparations plan. First, reparations would be paid by Germany in kind, not money. Second, Germany would pay reparations in the form of lump withdrawals of factories, machinery, vehicles and tools from its national wealth at the end of the war and annual deliveries of goods thereafter. Third, Germany would be economically disarmed by reparations, leaving only 20 per cent of its prewar heavy industry intact. Fourth, reparations would be paid over a 10-year period. Fifth, to implement the reparations policy the German economy would have to be strictly controlled by Britain, the United States and the USSR for a prolonged period. Sixth, all allied countries damaged by Germany would be compensated by reparations, applying the principle that those that had suffered the most would receive the biggest payments, although in no case could there be full restitution. When it came to the compensation figure for the Soviet Union, Maiskii played safe and spoke of *at least* $10 billion. He concluded by proposing the establishment of an Anglo-American-Soviet Reparations Commission that would meet in Moscow and negotiate the details of the plan.

In the ensuing discussion both Churchill and Roosevelt argued that the experience of the First World War cast doubt on the wisdom of trying to extract reparations from Germany, but they agreed to establish the Reparations Commission. At the end of the session Churchill quipped that he thought the reparations plan should be based on the principle of 'each according to their needs, and in Germany's case according to her abilities [to pay]'. Stalin replied that he 'preferred another principle: each according to their deserts'.[25] The final protocol of the conference incorporated the substance of the Soviet reparations plan but, on Churchill's insistence, remained noncommittal on the figures, mentioning $20 billion as an overall figure (with the Soviets getting half) but only as a basis for discussion by the Reparations Commission.

At the third plenary session on 6 February the Big Three discussed the issue of the voting rights of the great powers in the proposed United Nations organisation. Stalin stressed that the agreed procedure had to be designed to avoid divergences among the great powers and the aim was to construct an organisation that would ensure peace for at least another 50 years. This first discussion was inconclusive, but the voting issue was resolved amicably later in the conference by adoption of the great power veto principle that the UN Security Council retains to this day. It was also agreed that the states invited to the founding conference of the UN in San Francisco would include any country that declared war on Germany by the end of the month, a device designed by Churchill to allow Turkey to attend (Ankara declared war on Germany on

23 February 1945) but to exclude neutral states such as Ireland that had not been as co-operative as the British Prime Minister thought they should have been.[26]

A much thornier issue, raised by Churchill at the session on 6 February, was the question of Poland; specifically the question of recognising the pro-Soviet 'Lublin Poles' as the Polish Provisional Government (a misnomer, as by this time the PCNL had moved to Warsaw). Both Churchill and Roosevelt wanted the so-called Lublin government replaced by a broad-based provisional government that would reflect Polish public opinion. In response Stalin strongly defended the Soviet Union's Polish policy, pointing out that the re-establishment of a strong and independent but friendly Poland was a vital matter of security for the USSR. He argued, too, that 'the new Warsaw Government . . . has no less a democratic basis than, for example, the government of de Gaulle'[27] – a point that Churchill contested, saying that it had the support of less than a third of the Polish population.[28]

After the third plenary session Roosevelt wrote Stalin a note making it clear that the United States would not recognise the Lublin government, proposing instead the formation of a new government consisting of Poles based in Poland and those living abroad, including former members of the London exile government such as Mikolajczyk.[29] In response, at the fourth plenary session on 7 February the Soviets tabled a proposal on Poland consisting of three main components: (a) recognition of the Curzon Line; (b) Poland's western border to run along the Oder–Neisse line; and (c) the enlargement of the Lublin government to include 'democratic leaders' from Poles living abroad.[30] This proposal was essentially a variation on the position the Soviets had been pushing for a year or more. It provoked much discussion, extending over several plenary sessions both of the Big Three and of the three foreign ministers – Eden, Molotov and Edward Stettinius (who had replaced Hull as American Secretary of State) – who were meeting separately as well as attending the plenaries. Eventually it was agreed that 'the Provisional Government which is now functioning in Poland' would be 'reorganised on a broader democratic basis with the inclusion of democratic leaders from Poland itself and from Poles abroad. This new Government should then be called the Polish Provisional Government of National Unity.' The Curzon Line was agreed as Poland's eastern frontier but the details of its western frontier with Germany were left open for further discussion at a future peace conference.

Agreement on a government formula for liberated Yugoslavia proved much easier to reach and the decision was quickly taken that Tito and the Yugoslav exile politicians should form a united government.

Equally congenial was the discussion about Soviet participation in the Far Eastern war, the subject considered by Stalin and Roosevelt at a bilateral meeting on 8 February.[31] The agreement reached was that the USSR would abrogate the Soviet–Japanese neutrality pact of April 1941 and join the war in the Far East two or three months after the defeat of Germany. In return the Soviet Union would regain the territories and concessions Imperial Russia had lost to Japan as a result of defeat in the Russo-Japanese war of 1904–1905. South Sakhalin would be returned, and the Kuril Islands handed over to the Soviet Union as well. Port Arthur on the Chinese mainland would be leased to the USSR as a naval base, while nearby Dairen would be internationalised and Soviet interests in the port safeguarded. A joint Soviet–Chinese company would be established to safeguard Moscow's railway transit rights through Manchuria. The only proviso on this deal was that concessions concerning China would also have to be negotiated and agreed with the Chinese. But neither Stalin nor Roosevelt foresaw any great difficulty about that and both assumed the Chinese would be sufficiently grateful for Soviet entry into the war for any deal to be unproblematic.

On 11 February 1945 the Big Three met for the last time to agree the communiqué issued at the end of the conference. Agreeing the text posed no great difficulties and the statement was issued the same day in the names of Churchill, Roosevelt and Stalin. It announced the Big Three's policy on Germany, the United Nations, Poland and Yugoslavia. It also contained the text of a Declaration on Liberated Europe that committed Britain, the Soviet Union and the United States to the destruction of Nazism and fascism and the establishment of a democratic Europe based on free elections. In conclusion the three leaders pledged to maintain wartime unity and to create the conditions for a secure and lasting peace. As well as this statement of policy there was a confidential protocol setting out the decisions of the conference the Big Three did not want to make public, for example in relation to the USSR's entry into the Far East war.[32]

Stalin had every reason to be pleased with the results of Yalta. On almost every policy issue the Soviet position had prevailed. The Big Three had got on well once again and Stalin had proved to be as effective a negotiator as he had been at Tehran. The only major concession to western wishes was the Declaration on Liberated Europe. But the Soviet interpretation of this document emphasised its anti-fascist rather than its democratic character and, anyway, Stalin was confident that his communist allies across Europe would form part of the broad-based coalition governments the declaration spoke of and would do very well in the elections that followed. Soviet press coverage of the conference was predictably ecstatic.[33] Maiskii drafted for Molotov a confidential information telegram to be sent to Soviet embassies that concluded: 'in general the atmosphere at the conference had a friendly character and the feeling was one of striving for agreement on disputed questions. We assess the conference as highly positive, especially in relation to the Polish and Yugoslav questions and also the question of reparations.'[34] In a private letter to Alexandra Kollantai, the Soviet ambassador in Sweden, Maiskii wrote that the 'Crimean Conference was very interesting. Especially impressive was that our influence in general and that of Stalin personally was extraordinarily great. The decisions of the conference were 75 per cent our decisions . . . The co-operation of the "Big Three" is now very close and Germany has nothing to celebrate, neither during the war nor after it.'[35]

Yet barely six weeks after Yalta Stalin was in a sombre mood when it came to relations with his western allies. At a reception for a visiting Czechoslovak delegation at the end of March 1945 Stalin spoke yet again about the need for Slavic unity in the face of the German threat but was distinctly pessimistic when he spoke of the role of Britain and the United States in this project:

> We are the new Slavophile-Leninists, Slavophile-Bolsheviks, communists who stand for the unity and alliance of the Slavic peoples. We consider that irrespective of political and social differences, irrespective of social and ethnic differences, all Slavs must ally with one another against the common enemy – the Germans. The history of the Slavs teaches that an alliance between them is necessary to defend Slavdom. Take the last two world wars. Why did they begin? Because of the Slavs. The Germans wanted to enslave the Slavs. And who suffered most because of these wars? In the First World War as well as the Second World War the Slavic peoples suffered most: Russia, Ukraine, Belorussia, Serbia, the Czechs, the Slovaks, the Poles . . .
>
> Now we are beating the Germans and many think the Germans will never be able to threaten us again. This is not so. I hate the Germans. But that must not cloud one's judgement of the Germans. The Germans are a great people. Very good technicians and organisers. Good, naturally brave soldiers. It is impossible to get rid of the Germans, they will remain. We are fighting the Germans and will do so until the end. *But we must bear in mind that our allies will try to save the Germans and come to an arrangement with them. We will be merciless towards the Germans but our allies will treat them with kid gloves.* Thus we Slavs must be prepared for the Germans to rise again against us. That is why we, the new Slavophile-Leninists, are so insistent on calling for the union of the Slavic peoples. There is talk that we want to impose the Soviet system on the Slav peoples. This is empty talk. We do not want this because we know that the Soviet system cannot be exported abroad as you wish; certain conditions are necessary. We can't establish the Soviet system in Bulgaria if they don't want it there. But we don't want to do that. In friendship with the Slavic countries we want genuine democratic governments. [emphasis added][36]

Stalin's reference to his allies' kid gloves treatment of the Germans reflected his disappointment about Churchill and Roosevelt's resistance at Yalta to the policy of dismembering Germany. After Yalta Stalin reassessed his own position and in the light of western reluctance dropped the idea of dismemberment. On 24 March Molotov telegraphed Gusev, Soviet representative on the tripartite Commission on Dismemberment in London, saying that Moscow did not consider binding the Yalta decision on the dismemberment of Germany. Molotov's telegram was sent in response to a report from Gusev that the British were proposing to downgrade dismemberment to one option among many possible policies. This was not satisfactory, Gusev quite rightly pointed out, because it undermined the in-principle agreement at Yalta to dismember Germany. Molotov, however, instructed Gusev to raise no objections to the British proposal, explaining that Britain and the United States were trying to saddle the USSR with the blame for dismemberment.[37] Stalin had evidently decided that if dismemberment was not going to happen, then he was not going to be blamed for pushing for it. Henceforth Stalin spoke publicly and privately only of a united Germany – disarmed, demilitarised, denazified and democratised, but not dismembered.

Another cause of Stalin's sombre mood was the post-Yalta acrimony in relation to Poland. At Yalta it had been decided that a Polish commission consisting of Molotov, Harriman and Clark Kerr would implement the decision to reorganise the Lublin government and establish a new provisional government for Poland. The commission held its first meeting in Moscow on 23 February and the talks were quite friendly at first, but in subsequent meetings the discussions degenerated into prolonged procedural wrangles.[38] From the Soviet point of view what had been agreed at Yalta was that the so-called Lublin government would be enlarged by the inclusion of other Polish political leaders. The Soviets also insisted that only Poles who accepted the Yalta decisions on Poland could serve in the new government. This ruled out politicians like Mikolajczyk who refused to accept the Curzon Line as the Soviet–Polish frontier, at least not without further negotiation. For their part the British and Americans chose to interpret the Yalta declaration on Poland as meaning that a completely new provisional government would be established and they sought to level the negotiating playing field for the pro-western Polish politicians they favoured. By early April the commission's talks had reached an impasse. Roosevelt appealed to Stalin to break the log jam but the Soviet leader was unmoved. He was determined that Poland would have a government friendly to the Soviet Union and made it clear that the only way forward was acceptance by the British and Americans of Moscow's interpretation of the Yalta agreement. If that was accepted, Stalin told Roosevelt, 'the Polish question can be settled in a short time'.[39]

Another country experiencing a governmental crisis at this time was Romania.[40] At the end of February 1945 Deputy Foreign Commissar Andrei Vyshinskii travelled to Bucharest to demand that the existing government be replaced by one based on the communist-led National Democratic Front. This latest in a series of domestic crises in Romania resulted, at Vyshinskii's behest, in the formation of the country's fourth government since its surrender in summer 1944. The Soviets believed they had acted with restraint in Romania, seeking to stabilise the internal situation, secure implementation of the terms of the armistice agreement, and maximise the country's contribution to the continuing war with Germany. In pursuing this moderate course the Soviets were handicapped by constant demands from their communist allies in the country for a more decisive intervention and by the parallel intrigues of Romanian politicians determined to draw on British and American diplomatic support. Making matters worse were British and American protests that Vyshinskii's intervention was not in accordance with the Declaration on Liberated Europe. In reply Molotov pointed out that the Romanian government had failed to carry out the terms of the armistice agreement and had not taken action to root out fascist and Nazi elements in the country.[41] Stalin did not become directly embroiled in the dispute although he was kept well informed of events in Romania by Soviet intelligence services.[42]

Stalin's Aims in Eastern Europe

But what were Stalin's longer-term aims in relation to Poland, Romania and the other East European states liberated, conquered and occupied by the Red Army? Time and again during the war Stalin denied that his aim was revolution or the imposition of communism. Much the same message was given privately to his communist supporters. For example, in April 1944 Stalin and Molotov sent the following telegram to Tito and the Yugoslav communists:

> We regard Yugoslavia as an ally of the Soviet Union, and Bulgaria as an ally of the Soviet Union's enemies. In the future, we would like Bulgaria to dissociate itself from the Germans and become the Soviet Union's ally. In any event, we would like Yugoslavia to become our chief mainstay in Southeastern Europe. And we deem it necessary to explain that we do not plan the sovietisation of Yugoslavia and Bulgaria, but instead, prefer to maintain contacts with democratic Yugoslavia and Bulgaria, which will be allies of the USSR.[43]

While Stalin's priority was to establish friendly regimes in Eastern Europe, he also wanted to create a geo-ideological buffer zone along the USSR's western borders to protect Soviet territorial security by the maintenance of an adjacent friendly political space. The character of that political space was defined ideologically and labelled 'new democracy'. A good guide to Soviet thinking about 'new democracy' may be found in a wide-ranging article on 'The Development of Democracy in the Liberated Countries of Europe' published in the October 1945 issue of *Bol'shevik*, the theory journal of the Soviet communist party.[44]

The article's starting point was that Soviet and communist aims in Europe grew out of Stalin's designation of the war as a liberation struggle that would result in the smashing of fascism, the restoration of national independence and sovereignty, and the replacement of the Nazis' 'New Order' in Europe with a democratic one. Such goals cast the communists in the role of patriots leading 'national fronts' of anti-fascists and democrats who were working to construct a new democratic order in their countries. Under these new people's democratic regimes the old elites, particularly those with fascist connections, would be displaced from power, the political role and influence of the working class and peasantry would predominate, land would be redistributed and many industries nationalised. The state, including the army, would be democratised and come under working-class control. Ethnic divisions would be subsumed in Soviet-style friendships of the nations that respected difference and protected minority rights.

Needless to say, these new democracies were aligned politically and diplomatically with the USSR and the article was very frank about the role of the Soviet Union in the process of socio-economic transformation and democratisation. Indeed, it argued that in Eastern Europe where the Red Army was in a position to support the struggles of the communist-led national fronts, the new democracies had achieved their most developed form. West European countries liberated from fascism, on the other hand, had not progressed as far along the road to new democracy because Britain and the United States tolerated elements of the old reactionary elites that continued to wield substantial influence.

While the article said nothing about the connection between 'new democracy' and socialism and communism or even about the struggle against capitalism, it did not really need to. The communist movement had begun formulating the idea of transitional regimes of popular democracy back in the 1930s. An important model was Spain of the civil war period, when communists had participated in a left Republican government and had attempted to construct a radical anti-fascist regime that pursued the social and political transformation of Spanish society while at the same time conducting an anti-Franco military struggle. The radical transformation of Republican-controlled Spain through land redistribution and state control of industry was seen by the Spanish communists, and by their mentors in the Comintern in Moscow, as laying the basis for further progress in the direction of socialism.[45]

Many arguments and analyses similar to those in the *Bol'shevik* article could be found in the Soviet press, in *Voina i Rabochii Klass* (renamed *Novoe Vremya* – New Times – in 1945) and in *Voprosy Vneshnei Politiki* (Questions of Foreign Policy) a confidential briefing bulletin of the Soviet party's Central Committee that began publication at the end of 1944.[46]

Stalin made his views known in a series of confidential conversations with East European communist leaders in 1945–1946. In March 1945 Stalin told Tito that 'today socialism is possible even under the English monarchy. Revolution is no longer necessary everywhere . . . Yes, socialism is possible even under an English king.' When a member of the Yugoslav delegation interjected that there was already a Soviet government in Yugoslavia because the communist party held all the key positions, Stalin retorted that 'no, your government is not Soviet – you have something in between de Gaulle's France and the Soviet Union'.[47] In a conversation with Polish communist leaders in May 1946 Stalin expounded at length on his view of 'new democracy':

In Poland there is no dictatorship of the proletariat and you don't need it there. It is possible that if in the USSR we had had no war the dictatorship of the proletariat would have taken on a different character . . . We had strong opponents . . . the Tsar, landowners, and strong support from Russian capitalists from abroad. In order to overcome these forces it was necessary to use power, to lean on the population, that is to say, dictatorship. You have a completely different situation. Your capitalists and landowners have been so compromised by their ties with the Germans they could be dealt with without great difficulty. They could not flaunt patriotism. This 'sin' they could not commit. Undoubtedly, removing the capitalists and landowners in Poland was aided by the Red Army. That is why you have no basis for the dictatorship of the proletariat in Poland. The system established in Poland is democracy, a democracy of a new type. It has no precedent . . . Your democracy is special. You have no class of big capitalists. You have nationalised industry in a 100 days, while the English have been struggling to do that for the past 100 years. Don't copy western democracy. Let them copy you. The democracy that you have established in Poland, in Yugoslavia and partly in Czechoslovakia is a democracy that is drawing you closer to socialism without the necessity of establishing the dictatorship of the proletariat or the Soviet system. Lenin never said there was no path to socialism other than the dictatorship of the proletariat, he admitted that it was possible to arrive at the path to socialism utilising the foundations of the bourgeois democratic system such as Parliament.[48]

According to Clement Gottwald, the Czechoslovak communist leader, in July 1946 Stalin told him:

Experience shows, and the classics of Marxism-Leninism teach, there is not one path to the Soviet system and the dictatorship of the proletariat, under certain conditions another path is possible . . . Actually, after the defeat of Hitler's Germany, after the Second World War, which cost so much, but which destroyed the ruling classes in a number of countries, the consciousness of masses of people was raised. Under these historical conditions, there appeared many possibilities and paths open to the socialist movement.[49]

In August 1946 Stalin returned to the theme of the inappropriateness of the dictatorship of the proletariat in another conversation with his Polish allies:

Must Poland go along the path of the establishment of the dictatorship of the proletariat? No it must not. It is not necessary. More than that, it would be harmful. For Poland, as for the other countries of Eastern Europe, the results of the war have opened up an easier, less bloody path of development – the path of socio-economic reform. As a result of the war there has arisen in Yugoslavia, Poland, Czechoslovakia, Bulgaria and other countries of Eastern Europe new democracy, a special kind of democracy . . . a more complex democracy. It affects the economic as well as the political life of the country. This democracy has carried out economic transformation. In Poland, for example, the new democratic government has implemented agrarian reform and nationalised big industry and this is an entirely sufficient basis for further development in a socialist direction, even without the dictatorship of the proletariat. As a result of this war the communist party has changed its outlook, changed its programme.[50]

In September 1946 Stalin advised the Bulgarian communists to form a 'Labour' party:

You have to unite the working class with the other toiling masses on the basis of a minimalist programme; the time for a maximalist programme has yet to come . . . In essence, the party would be Communist, but you would have a broader basis and a better mask for the present period. This would help you to achieve Socialism in a different way – without the dictatorship of the proletariat. The situation has changed radically in comparison with our revolution, it is necessary to apply different methods and forms . . . You should not be afraid of accusations of opportunism. This is not opportunism but the application of Marxism to the present situation.[51]

As these remarks show, Stalin was actively rethinking the universal validity of the Soviet model of revolution and socialism. There was nothing novel or surprising about this. The communist movement had been revising its views and ideas on this fundamental issue since its early days. When Comintern was founded in 1919 the communist expectation was that a revolution along Bolshevik, insurrectionist lines would soon sweep the whole of Europe. When that didn't happen, the strategy and tactics of communist revolution were rethought and adapted to the aim of strengthening the role and influence of communists within the capitalist system. Initially this was a tactical adaptation, seen as part of the preparation for an eventual seizure of power when the revolutionary crisis of capitalism resumed. But the longer the revolution was delayed the more the policy of increasing the political power of communists within the capitalist system became an end in itself. In the 1930s the priority of combating fascism led Comintern to view the virtues of bourgeois democracy more positively and to consider the transitional role that democratic anti fascist regimes could play in the struggle for socialism. From there it was a short ideological step to the wartime strategy of broad-based anti-fascist national fronts and then to the postwar perspective of new democracy and people's democracy.[52]

But to what extent was new democracy a point of arrival and to what extent was it a point of departure? What came after new democracy, and when and how? What route would the communists take to a socialist society if not via a brutal proletarian dictatorship, as had happened in the Soviet case? In one of his conversations with the Poles, Stalin reminded them that the USSR was no longer a dictatorship but a Soviet democracy (as proclaimed by the new Soviet Constitution of 1936). According to Rakosi, the Hungarian communist leader, in 1945 Stalin told him that the party's assumption of total power in Hungary would have to wait 10 to 15 years.[53] It seems, then, that what Stalin had in mind was a long, slow transition to Soviet-style socialism and democracy; this transition would be peaceful and would be achieved by democratic reforms rather than a revolutionary upheaval, but it was not clear whether and for how long western-style democracy – parliament, parties, contested elections, oppositional politics – would persist in these transitional regimes. It is worth bearing in mind, too, that at the end of the Second World War Stalin was already in his mid-sixties and could not expect to live to see the long-term outcome of the people's democracy experiment. Maybe this played a part in the vagueness of his strategic perspective.

In the event, people's democracy proved to be a short-lived experiment and the new regimes sponsored by Stalin did not long retain their democratic character. By 1947–1948 'people's democracy' had become a synonym for Soviet-type systems under complete communist party domination, and the broad-based national fronts that had come to power in Eastern Europe at the end of the Second World War had been liquidated in all but name. One reason for the abrupt change in Stalin's thinking and priorities has been highlighted by Eduard Mark: the failure, contrary to the Soviet leader's expectations, of new democracy to establish itself as a popular form of regime in Eastern Europe. As Mark argues, Stalin fully expected his 'revolution by degrees' to succeed in Eastern Europe on the basis of popular support and consent for new democracy and he anticipated that communists would win their leadership role in free and open elections.[54] This was the tenor of Stalin's conversations with the leaders of the East European communist parties in the early postwar period, conversations that were devoted more to immediate political tactics than to musings about the nature of people's democracy. It is evident that Stalin was convinced that, given the right policies, the right tactics and sufficient willpower, the communists would prevail over their political opponents and command overwhelming public support for the radical regime of new democracy. Publicly, Stalin's confidence in the people's democracy project and in the political prospects for communist parties found expression in his reply to Churchill's 'Iron Curtain' speech of March 1946. After denouncing Churchill as an anti-Bolshevik and a warmonger, Stalin went on to say:

Mr Churchill comes somewhat nearer the truth when he speaks of the increasing influence of the Communist parties in eastern Europe. It must be remarked, however, that he is not quite accurate. The influence of the Communist parties has grown not only in eastern Europe, but in nearly all the countries of Europe which were previously under fascist rule . . . or which experienced . . . occupation . . . The increased influence of the Communists cannot be considered fortuitous. It is a perfectly logical thing. The influence of the Communists has grown because, in the years of the rule of fascism in Europe, the Communists showed themselves trusty, fearless, self-sacrificing fighters against the fascist regime for the liberty of the peoples . . . plain people have views of their own, and know how to stand up for themselves. It was they . . . who defeated Mr Churchill and his party in Britain . . . It was they . . . who isolated the reactionaries and advocates of collaboration with fascism in Europe, and gave their preferences to the left democratic parties. It was they . . . who . . . came to the conclusion that the Communists were fully deserving of the people's confidence. That was how the influence of the Communists grew in Europe.[55]

Stalin's belief in the growing strength of European communism was by no means misplaced, as this table of party membership figures published in *Voprosy Vneshnei Politiki* in May 1946 shows:[56]

COUNTRY	PREWAR MEMBERSHIP	POSTWAR MEMBERSHIP
Albania	1,000	12,000
Austria	16,000	132,000
Belgium	10,000	100,000
Britain	15,000	50,000
Bulgaria	8,000	427,000
Czechoslovakia	80,000	1,292,000
Denmark	2,000	60,000
Finland	1,000	25,000
France	340,000	1,000,000
Germany	300,000	805,000
Greece	n/a	100,000
Holland	10,000	50,000
Hungary	30,000	608,000
Italy	58,000	1,871,000
Norway	5,000	22,000
Poland	20,000	310,000
Romania	1,000	379,000
Spain	250,000	35,000
Sweden	11,000	48,000
Yugoslavia	4,000	250,000

This impressive postwar performance by European communism was replicated in the results of postwar elections. To give just the East European figures, in the November 1945 election in Bulgaria the communist-led Fatherland Front scored 88 per cent of the vote; in Czechoslovakia in May 1946 the communists won 38 per cent of the vote; in Hungary the communists managed to win only 17 per cent of votes in November 1945 but in the August 1947 election this increased to 22 per cent and the left bloc headed by the party obtained 66 per cent of the seats in parliament; in the Polish elections of January 1947 the communist-led Democratic Bloc received 80 per cent of the vote; in November 1946 in Romania the communist-led Bloc of Democratic Parties recorded 80 per cent of the vote; and in Yugoslavia in November 1945, 90 per cent of the electorate voted for communists' Popular Front although, since the opposition boycotted the elections there were no alternative candidates.[57]

But the communist advance was not sufficiently strong or deep to achieve Stalin's postwar project of a people's democratic Europe under Soviet influence. While the communist vote in Czechoslovakia, Yugoslavia, and even Hungary, was fairly, if roughly, won, in the three states of most importance to Soviet security – Bulgaria, Poland and Romania – the communist majorities were secured only with the aid of a good deal of ballot rigging, violence and intimidation. Another problem for Stalin's postwar political strategy was that the relatively liberal regimes of people's democracy he wished to introduce had few deep-rooted democratic traditions on which to base themselves in Eastern Europe. Apart from Czechoslovakia, the political history of interwar Eastern Europe was mainly one of authoritarianism, demagogic nationalist politics, and anti-communist repression. The corollary of this political history was that the communist parties of Eastern Europe, again except for Czechoslovakia, had little experience of democratic politics and little inclination to embrace its ways. This drawback was compounded by Stalin's own roughhouse notions of democratic politics. While he lectured the East European communists on the virtues of new democracy he also tutored them on the ruthless tactics necessary to isolate and marginalise their opponents and to maximise their own political domination. Particularly provocative to Stalin were the constant efforts of the communists' opponents in Eastern Europe to internationalise their internal struggles and difficulties by involving Britain and the United States. Any interference or involvement by the British and Americans was unacceptable to Stalin, who defined Eastern Europe as a sphere of influence free from all great power meddling except his own. Interestingly, one defeated country that escaped the fate of Soviet-style people's democracy was Finland, a state whose leaders studiously refrained from appealing for American and British intercession on their behalf. Instead they relied on their own political resources to deal with the Soviet occupation regime and with their Finnish communist coalition partners. Stalin had no reason to fear that Finland would slip into the western sphere if it wasn't controlled by the communists and he was content to allow the country to remain strictly neutral when the cold war broke out.[58]

Stalin's concerns about western interference in his sphere of influence in Eastern Europe became increasingly entangled with fears that the progressive deterioration of Soviet relations with Britain and the United States in 1946–1947 was leading to the formation of an anti-communist western bloc. Although the communist abandonment of new democracy in Eastern Europe took place at different times and was very much influenced by the course of domestic developments, ultimately Stalin's radical change of strategy and tactics in the region was prompted by the outbreak of the cold war in 1947. With the Grand Alliance collapsing, Stalin opted for a tightly controlled sphere in Eastern Europe that he could weld into a foreign policy bloc that would sternly resist any western encroachment into a political and territorial space that he considered absolutely vital to Soviet security.

As the Second World War came to a close Stalin had two strategic-political aims: first, to continue the Grand Alliance with Britain and the United States in order to maintain the great power co-operation necessary to contain the long-term threat of a resurgent Germany; second, to pursue his long-term ideological goals in Europe through transitional regimes of people's democracy, a political device which guaranteed that the USSR's western borders would be buffered by friendly regimes. Stalin saw no inherent contradiction between these two strategic goals. He believed that western interests favoured a peacetime Grand Alliance and he calculated that people's democracy was not immediately threatening to western-style democratic capitalism in Britain and the United States, both countries that in any case had become more social democratic and state capitalist as a result of the war and had moved closer to the Soviet and people's democratic models. Stalin was also prepared to accept Anglo-American predominance in their spheres of interest and to restrain West European communists by encouraging them to pursue a more moderate version of the people's democracy project, one that emphasised the priority of postwar reconstruction and the maintenance of national unity.

But not for the first time in his political career Stalin mistakenly projected his own rationality and calculations on to others. After the war his Grand Alliance partners increasingly viewed Germany as an ally in the struggle against communism rather than as a potential threat that required a continuing coalition with the Soviets. Neither did the Anglo-Americans accept their complete exclusion from the Soviet sphere in Eastern Europe, particularly when Stalin was self-evidently meddling in their sphere in Western Europe through the good offices of the western communist parties. They also saw the postwar rise of communism and Soviet influence in Europe as an immediate, not a long-term threat. They saw people's democracy as a ruse and anticipated a radical change in Stalin's postwar policy that would threaten their most crucial interests. It was a classic case of the self-fulfilling prophecy: the west's overly defensive actions and reactions in response to a perceived threat provoked a counter-reaction in the form of a tightly controlled Soviet-communist bloc in Eastern Europe and a militant communist challenge in Western Europe – the very thing London and Washington had feared all along.

A postwar political struggle with the west was not Stalin's preferred choice but it was a challenge he was prepared to face if the alternative was to accept a loss of Soviet influence and control in Eastern Europe. Having won the struggle against Hitler at such great cost, Stalin had no intention of losing the peace, even if that meant waging a dangerous cold war.

9

Last Battles
Stalin, Truman and the End
of the Second World War

The Red Army resumed its advance to Berlin in January 1945. In an offensive known as the Vistula–Oder operation Soviet armies swept through Poland and into East Prussia and eastern Germany. By the time the offensive petered out in February 1945 advance units of the Red Army were within 50 miles of the German capital. The Vistula–Oder operation was the largest single Soviet offensive of the Second World War. The two main fronts involved in the operation deployed 2.2 million troops and possessed more tanks and aircraft – 4,500 and 5,000 respectively – than the whole of the Red Army in May 1942. With an eleven to one superiority in infantry, seven times more tanks and 20 times more airpower and artillery, the Red Army was able to advance at a rate of 15 to 20 miles a day, taking a total of 147,000 prisoners and destroying or nearly destroying over 50 German divisions (*see Map 16 on p. 255*).[1]

Planning for the Vistula–Oder operation began in autumn 1944 during a lull in offensive action in the central sector after the Red Army's failure to take Warsaw. The General Staff's calculation was that it would be better to regroup and take the time to prepare a major offensive rather than to continue attacking with exhausted troops and overstretched supply lines. In the meantime, offensive operations would be conducted on the flanks – in the south in Hungary and Austria, and in the north in East Prussia towards Königsberg – with the aim of drawing German forces away from the central axis from Warsaw to Berlin. The General Staff's plan was for a two-phase operation in the New Year that would last 45 days in total, culminating in the capture of Berlin. While the General Staff's concept was that there would be a seamless transition from the first to the second phase of the operation, no decisions on a final thrust to Berlin would be taken until the progress of the operation had been reviewed.[2]

The operation was to be conducted by the 1st Belorussian Front and the 1st Ukrainian Front with support from the 2nd Belorussian and 3rd Belorussian Fronts. In charge of the 1st Ukrainian was Marshal Konev. Heading the 1st

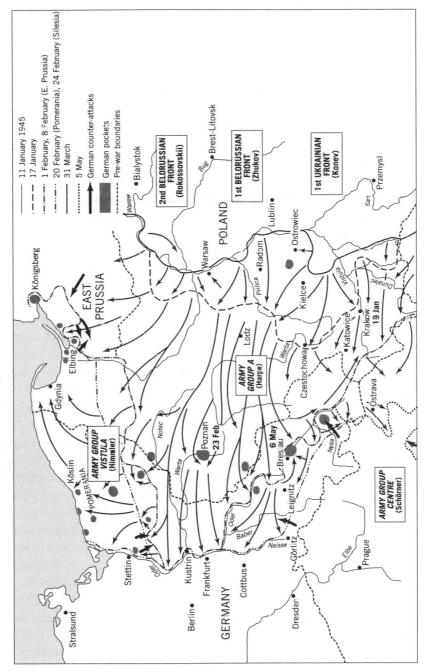

The Vistula–Oder Operation, January–February 1945

11 January 1945
17 January
1 February, 8 February (E. Prussia)
20 February (Pomerania), 24 February (Silesia)
31 March
5 May
German counter-attacks
German pockets
Pre-war boundaries

2nd BELORUSSIAN FRONT (Rokossovskii)

1st BELORUSSIAN FRONT (Zhukov)

1st UKRAINIAN FRONT (Konev)

ARMY GROUP VISTULA (Himmler)

ARMY GROUP A (Harpe)

ARMY GROUP CENTRE (Schörner)

Brest-Litovsk
Bialystok
Warew
Bug
POLAND
Warsaw
Pritica
Lublin
Radom
Ostrowiec
Kielce
Lodz
Katowice
Krakow
19 Jan
Czestochowa
Warta
Ostrava
San
Przemysl
Dunajec
Vistula
Vistula

Königsberg
EAST PRUSSIA
Elbing
Gdynia
Köslin
POMERANIA
Notec
Warta
Poznan
23 Feb
6 May
Bres au
Leignitz
Oder
Baber
Neisse
Görlitz
Nysa
Prague
Elbe
Dresden
Cottbus
Frankfurt
Kustrin
Stettin
Oder
Berlin
GERMANY
Stralsund

Belorussian Front was Marshal Rokossovskii, replaced in November 1944 by Zhukov. The 1st Belorussian's task was to advance in the centre and capture Berlin – a responsibility and honour that Stalin felt should go to Zhukov, his Deputy Supreme Commander. Rokossovskii was transferred to the 2nd Belorussian Front but Stalin assured him that this was not a secondary sector of the front but part of the main offensive. 'If you and Konev don't advance,' Stalin told him, 'neither will Zhukov.'[3] Marshal Vasilevskii's projected role in these events was somewhat marginal. He was Stavka co-ordinator of the 1st and 2nd Baltic Fronts and because of his absence from Moscow his role as Chief of the General Staff had been taken over by his deputy, General Aleksei Antonov, and it was Antonov who accompanied Stalin to the Yalta conference in February 1945. These were not signs that Vasilevskii had fallen into disfavour (although Stalin's mood in relation to his generals did wax and wane). Rather, Stalin valued Vasilevskii's skills as a co-ordinator on difficult sectors of the front; more importantly, the Soviet leader had earmarked him for a transfer to the Far East to head up the coming assault on Japanese forces in Manchuria. Stalin's plans were disrupted, however, by the death of General Chernyakhovskii, the (Jewish) commander of the 3rd Belorussian Front, in February 1945. Vasilevskii was his replacement and so came to play an unanticipated role in the final Soviet conquest of Germany.

The basic plan of the Vistula–Oder operation was to cover and occupy the ground between the two great rivers that bisected eastern Poland and eastern Germany respectively. Rokossovskii's task was to strike out across northern Poland in the direction of Danzig. In the south Konev was to head for Breslau and the important industrial area of Silesia, which Stalin was keen to capture for economic as well as strategic reasons. (He described the area as 'gold' to Konev and instructed him to take care not to damage its industrial resources.)[4] Zhukov's role was to capture Warsaw then advance to Poznan and on to Berlin. Chernyakhovskii's goal was to destroy the strong German forces in East Prussia, capture Königsberg and link up with Rokossovskii's forces in a joint advance along the Baltic coastal lands. In the absence of Zhukov and Vasilevskii from Moscow, the Stavka co-ordinator of this complex, multi-front offensive was Stalin – the first time he had undertaken such a role; he was ably assisted by Antonov and by General S.M. Shtemenko, his Chief of Operations.

The start time of the Vistula–Oder operation is a matter of some minor controversy. On 6 January 1945 Churchill wrote to Stalin asking if he could expect a Soviet offensive in Poland to relieve the pressure on the western front created by the Germans' Ardennes counter-offensive of December 1944 (the so-called 'Battle of the Bulge'). Stalin replied the next day saying that, notwithstanding unfavourable weather conditions, the Soviet offensive would be launched early. Churchill was suitably effusive in his thanks and in his Order of the Day in February 1945 Stalin made great play of the fact that the Vistula–Oder operation helped save the day in the west.[5] It seems, however, that the operation was originally timed to begin on 8–10 January but was delayed by bad weather.[6] It may be, therefore, that Stalin was claiming undeserved credit for favours to his western allies. On the other hand, Konev is quite specific in his memoirs that his Front's offensive was timed to begin on 20 January but that on 9 January he was asked by Antonov to speed up preparations and launch his attack as soon as possible.[7]

Konev began his offensive on 12 January and on the 14th Zhukov and Rokossovskii unleashed their forces. Zhukov and Konev made rapid progress. On 17 January Warsaw fell to the 1st Belorussian Front, while Konev captured Kracow on the 19th. By the end of the month Zhukov's and Konev's forces had reached their initial goal of the line of the Oder. Rokossovskii's 2nd Belorussian Front was less fortunate. On 20 January he was ordered to turn his right flank north into East Prussia to assist the advance on Königsberg of Chernyakhovskii's 3rd Belorussian Front. The result was a slowing down of Rokossovskii's own advance towards the northern Oder and the opening of a gap on his left flank with Zhukov's rapidly advancing armies in the central sector.[8] This exposed Zhukov's drive towards Berlin to a counterattack by strong Wehrmacht forces stationed in Pomerania (the north German province adjacent to East Prussia). At first neither Zhukov nor Stavka were too worried by this. When at the end of January both Zhukov and Konev submitted proposals to continue their offensives, with the aim of capturing Berlin by mid-February, Stalin gave the go-ahead and continued to endorse such plans even as he attended the Yalta conference. By mid-February, however, it had become obvious that the only sure way to deal with the Pomeranian threat was to task significant elements of 1st Belorussian to support Rokossovskii's efforts in the area. This meant the end of any hope Zhukov had of taking Berlin on the march. Meanwhile in the south, Konev's advance was also slowing. In early February his forces penetrated Lower Silesia west of the Oder but progress was slow and the 4th Ukrainian Front protecting Konev's left flank was also experiencing difficulties. All along the front there were the by now familiar problems of these gigantic Soviet offensives: tired troops, short supplies and strained logistics. By the end of February the Vistula–Oder operation had ended, although fierce fighting continued in East Prussia and Pomerania.

The Red Army's failure to reach Berlin in February 1945 was the latest in a long line of over-optimistic grand schemes that had gone awry. To paraphrase Clausewitz, no Soviet strategic plan ever survived contact with the enemy. But not everyone accepts that Stalin and Stavka tried but failed to capture Berlin. One theory is that Stalin deliberately forwent the possibility of an early capture of Berlin for political reasons: he did not want to add to tensions within the Soviet–Western alliance, particularly while the Yalta conference was in progress from 4 to 11 February. Besides, there were political gains to be made from advancing on the flanks – towards Hungary, Czechoslovakia, Austria and Denmark rather than Berlin.[9] Such speculation is not warranted by the documents: it was only *after* the Yalta conference that the idea of an immediate capture of Berlin was finally abandoned. Nor were there any great tensions in the Soviet–Western alliance at this particular time. Another view was put forward by General Chuikov in his memoirs published in 1964. Chuikov, the hero of Stalingrad, was commander of the 8th Guards Army (the renamed 62nd Army) and served with Zhukov in the 1st Belorussian Front during the march to Berlin. Chuikov claimed that Zhukov wanted to take Berlin in February but was overruled by Stalin. Zhukov, along with many of the other principals involved, refuted Chuikov's claims and insisted that the delay in the advance to Berlin was the result of logistical problems and the threat posed by the strong German forces in Pomerania and East Prussia.[10] In subsequent editions of his memoirs Chuikov excised the offending passages and acquiesced in the official line that Berlin could *not* have been taken in February 1945.[11]

These differing views of Soviet strategic decision-making in early 1945 raise the issue of Stalin's evolving view of the military situation. Some clues are provided by his interactions with western military and political leaders in this period. In mid-December 1944 Stalin had a long discussion with Ambassador Harriman about the military situation on the Eastern and Western Fronts. Harriman told Stalin about Anglo-American plans for offensive action in the west and asked what support they could expect in the form of Soviet attacks in the east. Although Stavka's plans for the Vistula–Oder operation were well advanced Stalin was coy about revealing Soviet intentions. He reassured Harriman that there would be a major Soviet offensive soon but stressed that the Red Army's superiority lay in air power and artillery rather than troop numbers and that good weather was required to utilise those arms effectively. While the weather remained bad 'the Russians considered it unwise to undertake large operations', said Stalin. Prospects in the southern sector were better, however, and he invited the British and Americans to join in an advance on Vienna.[12] This conversation took place just before the Germans' Ardennes counter-offensive, an event that cast a cloud over the prospects for an early crossing of the Rhine by western allied forces. The Anglo-American military difficulties had important implications for the ambitions of the coming Soviet offensive, which was predicated on the pinning down of large German forces in the western theatre. These considerations were evident in a conversation Stalin had with Air Chief Marshal Tedder on 15 January 1945 during which the Soviet leader enquired anxiously about German claims that their

Ardennes action had frustrated the western allied offensive by a minimum of two months and a maximum of six. Tedder was in Moscow as the envoy of the Supreme Allied Commander in the west, General Eisenhower, and his mission was to seek information on Soviet strategic plans. Stalin told Tedder about the Soviet offensive that had just started, saying the objective was to reach the Oder, although he wasn't sure if this would be achieved. He also stated that because of weather conditions (i.e. the spring rains and muds) large-scale offensive action on the Eastern Front would grind to a halt from mid-March to late May. Stalin did not think the war would end until the summer, most likely because by that time the Germans would be starving. He continued:

> The Germans can produce lots of potatoes but, in his opinion, they would require grain (which will not be available) to fight a prolonged war . . . we must not forget, however, that the Germans are frugal and enduring. They have more stubbornness than brains. In fact, they should not have under-taken the Ardennes offensive; that was very stupid of them. In his opinion, even now the Germans must be moving forces from the west. If they do not they cannot resist in the east. The weight of the present Red Army offensive is such that there is no possible local shuttle of reserves in the east.[13]

From these two conversations it is evident Stalin had a somewhat cautious view of the prospects for Soviet offensive action. He did not anticipate an early German collapse, nor did he give any hint that Berlin was a feasible target in the short term. A point made by Shtemenko in his memoirs should also be borne in mind. At this stage in the war the defeat of Germany was not equated with the fall of Berlin. The Germans had strong forces in Hungary, Western Europe and East Prussia/Pomerania and there was plenty of talk about Hitler retreating to an 'Alpine stronghold' that would prove a very tough nut to crack.[14]

At the Yalta conference a report on the progress of the Soviet offensive was presented to the Big Three by General Antonov at the first plenary session on 4 February. He went to great lengths to stress that the offensive had started early because of western allied requests and emphasised that there had been a significant transfer of German forces from the west to the east, including the transfer of troops to defend Berlin along the line of the Oder. From this Antonov drew the conclusion that the western allies should begin their offensive in mid-February and that they should take steps to prevent the transfer of German forces to the Eastern Front. In his contribution to the ensuing discussion Stalin made the point that in launching their offensive early the Soviets had gone far beyond the obligations they had entered into at Tehran to co-ordinate military action with the western allies, implying, but not stating, that he expected Churchill and Roosevelt to reciprocate.[15]

According to the American minutes of that first plenary, Stalin said 'he felt it would be most useful for the [military] staffs to discuss the question of a summer offensive against Germany because he was not so sure that the war would be over before summer'. During his discussion with the British and American chiefs of staff Antonov was quite explicit that he believed the current Soviet offensive would be disrupted by the spring weather, which would make the roads impassable, and that major offensive action would not resume until the summer.[16] It is possible that Antonov was engaged in a conspiracy with Stalin to fool the western allies about Soviet intentions in relation to Berlin but it makes more sense to assume that the two of them really thought the Red Army's offensive would peter out. That after all had been the pattern of Soviet offensive action in 1942, 1943 and 1944: a winter offensive that went well but lost momentum in the spring and had to be resumed in the summer.

Stalin's relative pessimism about the likely course of military events must have been reinforced by the faltering of the Red Army's march to Berlin in mid-February. Publicly Stalin's restrained view of the military situation found expression in his Order of the Day on 23 February – the 27th anniversary of the foundation of the Red Army. Naturally, Stalin lauded his troops' achievement in marching so rapidly from the Vistula to the Oder. However, he made no claims about the timetable for final victory except to say that it would be soon and to caution that it would be a hard fight right to the end:

Complete victory over the Germans approaches. But victory never comes of its own accord – it is achieved by hard battles and persistent effort. The doomed enemy is throwing into battle his last forces, desperately resisting, trying to avoid severe retribution. He is taking up and will take up the most extreme and foul forms of struggle. It is necessary to remember, therefore, the nearer our victory the higher must be our vigilance, the more powerful our blows against the enemy.[17]

During March, while the Red Army ground down the Germans in East Prussia and Pomerania, it is likely that Stalin was preoccupied with pressing political matters, such as the wrangle with the west over the reconstruction of the Polish government and the governmental crisis in Romania. At the end of March Stalin received a communication from Eisenhower informing him of Anglo-American strategic plans. Eisenhower told Stalin that his immediate objective was to destroy German forces defending the Ruhr. He would then head for Erfurt, Dresden and Leipzig and link up with Soviet forces in that area. It was possible that western forces would conduct a secondary advance towards Regensburg–Linz, with the aim of foiling German plans to establish a redoubt in the south of the country. Eisenhower concluded by asking Stalin for information on his plans so that actions east and west against Germany could be co-ordinated.[18]

Eisenhower's message to Stalin was delivered to him in his office on the evening of 31 March by Harriman, Clark Kerr, the British ambassador, and General Deane, the American military representative in Moscow. Twenty minutes after they left, Stalin called in Zhukov, Antonov and Shtemenko, presumably to consult them about its contents.[19] The next day Stalin replied to Eisenhower. He told the American commander that western and Soviet strategic plans coincided. He agreed that Soviet and western forces would link up in the Erfurt–Leipzig–Dresden area and said that the Red Army's main attack would be in that direction. As for Berlin, Stalin said it 'has lost its former strategic significance. Therefore the Soviet Supreme Command is thinking of setting aside only secondary forces for Berlin.' The main Soviet attack, Stalin informed Eisenhower, would begin in the second half of May, including, if circumstances did not change, a secondary blow south in the direction of Linz and Vienna.[20] On 2 April Stalin met Zhukov, Antonov and Shtemenko again. Joined by Konev, the meeting lasted two hours. The four generals returned on 3 April for a shorter meeting.[21] That same day Stalin signed directives to Zhukov and Konev. Zhukov's task was to launch an offensive to capture Berlin and to reach the Elbe river (the agreed Soviet–Western military demarcation line in Germany) within 12 to 15 days of the beginning of the operation. Konev's task was to rout the Germans south of Berlin and to advance to Dresden within 10 to 12 days and then to consider an attack on Leipzig. The demarcation line between the 1st Belorussian and the 1st Ukrainian Fronts was fixed at Lubben about 50 miles south-east of Berlin, effective from 15 April – an indication that the dual offensive was to commence on the 16th.[22] So the basic plan was for Zhukov to strike out directly for the German capital and to envelop the city from the north, while Konev's forces were to surround the city from the south. A supporting role was to be played by Rokossovskii's 2nd Belorussian Front, which was to open its offensive towards Berlin on 20 April with the aim of protecting Zhukov's right flank from a northern counterattack by the Germans (see Map 17 on p. 262).[23]

Many historians have argued that Eisenhower was misled by Stalin and that Berlin was the primary Soviet target, which the Soviet dictator was desperate to capture before the western allies. However, that was not necessarily how Stalin saw events. In 1948 he got into an argument about the Berlin operation with Walter Bedell Smith, the then American ambassador, who had been Eisenhower's chief of staff dring the war. According to Stalin, Berlin was a secondary target and that is why only Zhukov's forces were tasked to take the German capital. But Zhukov's advance was held up by the Germans, so Konev

The Berlin Operation, April 1945

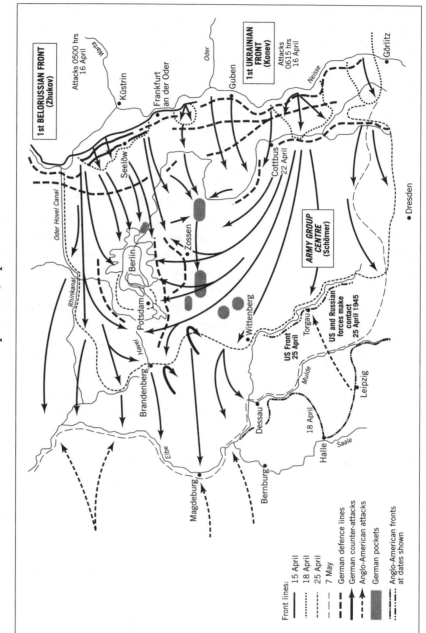

1st BELORUSSIAN FRONT (Zhukov)

Attacks 0500 hrs 16 April

1st UKRAINIAN FRONT (Konev)

Attacks 0615 hrs 16 April

ARMY GROUP CENTRE (Schörner)

Werra
Küstrin
Frankfurt an der Oder
Oder
Guben
Neisse
Görlitz
Seelöw
Cottbus 22 April
Oder Hovel Canal
Zossen
Dresden
Rhinkanal
Berlin
Potsdam
Wittenberg
Torgau
US and Russian forces make contact 25 April 1945
US Front 25 April
Havel
Brandenberg
Mulde
Leipzig
Elbe
Dessau
18 April
Halle
Saale
Magdeburg
Bernburg

Front lines:
— 15 April
········· 18 April
– – – 25 April
– · – 7 May
▬▬▬ German defence lines
⟶ German counter-attacks
⟶ Anglo-American attacks
▬ German pockets
··-··- Anglo-American fronts at dates shown

and Rokossovskii had to help out. This transformed Berlin from a secondary to a primary target. An indignant Stalin even offered to go with Smith to the military archives there and then and show him the orders he had given for the Berlin operation. Stalin added that since Berlin was in the agreed Soviet zone of occupation in Germany it was morally and strategically right for the Red Army to take the city.[24]

Stalin's version of events broadly corresponds with the course of operations. The original plan was for Zhukov's forces to take Berlin alone but the 1st Ukrainian Front made more rapid progress and on 17 April an opportunity arose to redirect some of Konev's forces to attack Berlin from the south.[25] As Soviet troops fought their way to the top of the ruined Reichstag building in the centre of Berlin to plant the red flag, Hitler committed suicide in his bunker. Happily for Stalin, the three soldiers who made it to the top of the Reichstag on 30 April 1945 were a Georgian, a Russian and a Ukrainian. Later, the Soviet photographer Yevgeni Chaldei re-enacted the scene with two other soldiers, aiming to create as iconic a picture of the Red Army's conquest of Berlin as the hoisting of the Stars and Stripes by US troops over Iwo Jima a couple of months earlier.

Victory did not come cheap. The Red Army suffered 300,000 casualties, including nearly 80,000 dead during the final assault on Berlin. The most costly fighting took place on the approaches to Berlin rather than in the city itself. So there was no repeat of the extensive street fighting that had taken place in Stalingrad in 1942 or, for that matter, in Budapest in February 1945 when it fell to the Red Army after a fierce, prolonged battle.[26]

Apart from the massive casualties (with German losses even higher than those of the Soviets) a shadow was cast over the Red Army's triumphal march to Berlin by the atrocities and looting committed by a significant minority of Soviet soldiers. Particularly appalling was the large number of rapes by members of the Red Army. Estimates of the extent of this crime range from tens of thousands to the low millions.[27] The true figure probably lies somewhere in between, with the vast majority of rapes taking place in greater Berlin, a city that by 1945 was largely a city of women.[28] Berliners were not the only ones to suffer mass rape. In Vienna there may have been as many as 70,000–100,000 rapes.[29] In Hungary the estimates range from 50,000 to 200,000.[30] Women were raped by Red Army soldiers in Romania and Bulgaria, and in the liberated countries of Poland, Yugoslavia and Czechoslovakia, although in much smaller numbers.

It is difficult to know whether Stalin was aware of the full extent of what was going on but he had a good inkling and made suitable excuses for the behaviour of his men. In March 1945 he told a visiting Czechoslovak delegation:

Everyone praises our Red Army, and, yes, it deserves this praise. But I would like our guests not to be disappointed by the Red Army's charms in the future. The point is that there are now nearly 12 million people in the Red Army. These people are far from being angels. These people have been hardened by war. Many of them have travelled 2,000 kilometres in battle, from Stalingrad to the middle of Czechoslovakia. On the way they have seen much grief and many atrocities. Don't be surprised therefore if some of our people in your country do not behave themselves as they should. We know that some soldiers of little intelligence pester and insult girls and women and behave disgracefully. Let our Czechoslovak friends know this now so that their praise of the Red Army does not turn into disappointment.[31]

Stalin was even more explicit when talking with Tito and the Yugoslav comrades about this matter in April 1945:

You have, of course, read Dosteoevsky? Do you see what a complicated thing is man's soul, man's psyche? Well, then, imagine a man who has fought from Stalingrad to Belgrade – over thousands of kilometres of his own devastated land, across the dead bodies of his comrades and dearest ones. How can such a man react normally? And what is so awful in his having fun with a woman, after such horrors? You have imagined the Red Army to be ideal. And it is not ideal, nor can it be . . . The important thing is that it fights Germans . . .[32]

But Stalin's indulgence had its limits, particularly when the Red Army's running amok damaged what little was left of Germany's valuable economic infrastructure, a bounty the Soviets hoped to extract as part of their reparations payments. One way Stalin chose to signal a halt to the retribution was by the publication of an article in *Pravda* on 14 April 1945 attacking the Soviet writer Ilya Ehrenburg, who had become famous during the war for his powerful anti-German hate propaganda, much of it published in *Krasnaya Zvezda*, the Red Army newspaper. Under the headline 'Comrade Ehrenburg Simplifies', the Soviet propaganda chief, Georgii Alexandrov wrote that it was a mistake to see all Germans as the same and that it was necessary to distinguish Hitler and the Nazis from the German people. The Soviet people, stated Aleksandrov, were not hostile to Germans and to suggest otherwise played into the hands of Nazi propaganda, which was trying to split the Soviet–Western alliance.[33] Ehrenburg was unrepentant and wrote in private to Alexandrov:

Reading your article anybody might come to the conclusion that I have been calling for the complete annihilation of the German people. Whereas, naturally, I never issued any such call: it was German propaganda that ascribed this to me. I cannot write a single line until I have cleared up this misunderstanding, one way or the other . . . It is my integrity as a writer and an internationalist, to whom the racialist theory is an abomination, that has been challenged.[34]

While appalling, the contemporary public and political impact of the Red Army rapes should not be exaggerated. In 1945 the Red Army was almost universally admired in the allied world as the saviour of Europe from Nazi barbarism. It had fought a savage war against a cruel enemy but for this most people were thankful, not critical. What captured public attention were not accusations of mass rape by Nazi propagandists, who were predicting such events even before the Red Army crossed into Germany, but the newsreel footage of SS extermination camps and of their pitiful survivors, 'liberated' by the Soviets as they swept through Poland in early 1945. The first Nazi death camp had been overrun by the Red Army at Majdenak in July 1944. At the end of January 1945 Auschwitz fell to the Red Army, and then the camps at Belzec, Chelmno, Sobibor and Treblinka – surely the darkest roll call of horror in the annals of human existence.

Without doubt, it was a time of great personal triumph for Stalin but, never satisfied, when Harriman congratulated him on reaching Berlin he reminded the ambassador that 'Czar Alexander got to Paris'.[35]

On 7 May the Germans finally surrendered, although it wasn't until the next day that Zhukov signed the treaty of capitulation in Berlin. Consequently, VE Day was celebrated in the Soviet Union a day later than in Britain and the United States. Alexander Werth recalled the scene in Moscow in 1945:

May 9 was an unforgettable day in Moscow. The spontaneous joy of the two or three million people who thronged the Red Square that evening . . . was of a quality and depth I had never yet seen in Moscow before. They danced and sang in the streets; every soldier and officer was hugged and kissed . . . they were so happy they did not even have to get drunk, and under the tolerant gaze of the militia, young men even urinated against the walls of the Moskva Hotel, flooding the wide pavement. Nothing like *this* had ever happened in Moscow before. For once Moscow had thrown all reserve and restraint to the winds. The fireworks display that evening was the most spectacular I have ever seen.[36]

In his pronouncement on the great victory Stalin emphasised that the defeat of Hitler meant freedom and peace between peoples, pointing out that the German aim had been to dismember the Soviet Union by detaching the

Caucasus, the Ukraine, Belorussia, the Baltic States and other areas.[37] Stalin's reference to the threat the war had posed to the USSR as a multinational state may be contrasted with his next public statement on the war in which he specifically highlighted the contribution of the Russian people to victory. At a military reception in the Kremlin on 24 May 1945 Stalin proposed a toast to the health of the Soviet people but 'above all to the Russian people', a statement that was followed by prolonged applause and cheers. Stalin continued:

> I drink above all to the health of the Russian people because they are the most prominent of the nations that make up the Soviet Union . . . I drink to the health of the Russian people not only because they are the leading people but because they have common sense, social and political common sense, and endurance. Our government made not a few mistakes, we were in a desperate position in 1941–1942 . . . Another people would have said: go to hell, you have betrayed our hopes, we are organising another government, which will conclude peace with Germany and give us rest . . . But the Russian people did not do that, did not go for compromise, they showed unconditional trust in our government. I repeat, we made mistakes, our army was forced to retreat, appearing to lose control of events . . . But the Russian people had faith, persisted, waited and hoped we had things under control. For this trust in our government shown by the Russian people we say a big thank you.[38]

Much discussed in retrospect, Stalin's singling out of the Russian role in the Soviet war effort occasioned little comment at the time. It was self-evidently true that the Russians had been the loyal bulwark of the Soviet state during the war and Stalin's public recognition of this was part of a discourse extolling the Russians' human and political virtues that extended back to the 1930s. Wartime propaganda had typically utilised Russian as well as Soviet patriotic themes. When the Soviets adopted a new national anthem in January 1944 (to replace the communist 'Internationale') the key verse was:

> The unbreakable union of free republics
> Has been joined for ever by Great Russia
> Long live the united and mighty Soviet Union
> Created by the will of the peoples

On 24 June a victory parade was held in Red Square, led by Zhukov mounted on horseback. Stalin reviewed the parade atop Lenin's Mausoleum and watched as thousands of German military banners were piled up in front of him. That night Stalin entertained 2,500 generals and officers at a reception in the Kremlin, but the message he had for them was a little unexpected. In his toast, published in the newspapers, Stalin praised not his generals but the millions of little people, the cogs in the great state machine, upon whom he and his marshals had depended to win the war.[39]

From Roosevelt to Truman

One of the slogans shouted by the crowd that gathered outside the US embassy on Victory Day was 'Hurray for Roosevelt'. But the President had died a month earlier. Harriman telephoned Molotov with news of Roosevelt's death in the early hours of 13 April 1945. Molotov immediately went to the American embassy – this was 3a.m. – to express his condolences. According to Harriman, Molotov 'seemed deeply moved and disturbed. He stayed for some time talking about the part President Roosevelt had played in the war and in the plans for peace, of the respect Marshal Stalin and all the Russian people had for him and how much Marshal Stalin had valued his visit to Yalta.' With regard to new President Harry Truman, Molotov expressed confidence in him because he had been selected as Vice-President by Roosevelt. 'I have never heard Molotov talk so earnestly,' commented Harriman in his telegram to Washington.[40]

Harriman saw Stalin later that day: 'When I entered Marshal Stalin's office I noticed that he was obviously deeply distressed at the news of the death of President Roosevelt. He greeted me in silence and stood holding my hand for about 30 seconds before asking me to sit down.' Harriman told Stalin that he had come to see him because he thought the Soviet leader might have some questions about the situation in the United States following Roosevelt's death. Stalin, however, expressed confidence that there would be no change in US policy. 'President Roosevelt has died but his cause must live on,' Stalin told Harriman. 'We shall support President Truman with all our forces and all our will.' In response Harriman suggested that to smooth Truman's path and reassure American public opinion Stalin should send Molotov to the United States, to meet the new President and to attend the founding conference of the United Nations in San Francisco. This was a personal suggestion of Harriman's but Stalin agreed on the spot to send Molotov to the US if an official invitation was forthcoming.[41] The Soviet report of this meeting is much the same as Harriman's, but it contains one important additional detail: Stalin specifically asked if there would be any 'softening' of American policy towards Japan. When Harriman replied that a change of policy was out of the question, Stalin said Soviet policy towards Japan remained as before – based on the agreement reached at Yalta.[42]

As well as commiserating with Harriman, Stalin wrote that day to Truman to express his 'deep regret' at Roosevelt's death and to state his confidence that wartime co-operation would continue in the future.[43] Stalin also arranged for Moscow Radio to broadcast a message of personal condolence to Eleanor Roosevelt that characterised the President as a 'great organiser of freedom-loving nations against the common enemy and a leader who stood for safe-guarding the security of the whole world'.[44] On 15 April a memorial service for Roosevelt in Moscow was attended by Molotov and all his deputy foreign commissars (except for Litvinov, who was ill) as well as representatives of other government ministries and the armed forces.[45]

On the eve of Molotov's trip to the United States, Andrei Gromyko, the Soviet ambassador in Washington, telegraphed his assessment of the new presidency. He reported that the general view in the US was that Truman was a Rooseveltian New Dealer who would continue the dead President's foreign and domestic policies, including co-operation with the Soviet Union. But at the end of his telegram Gromyko struck a note of caution: 'How far he will continue the policy of co-operation with the Soviet Union and to what extent he will come under the influence of isolationist anti-Soviet groups is difficult to say at the moment.' This was a question, Gromyko concluded, that would be clarified by Molotov's forthcoming talks with Truman.[46]

In the United States Molotov had two meetings with Truman, on 22 and 23 April. This first encounter between Truman and Molotov has a somewhat famous history. According to Truman's memoirs, published in 1955, at the end of the second meeting Molotov blurted out: 'I have never been talked to like that in my life.' To which Truman supposedly replied: 'Carry out your agreements and you won't get talked to like that'. However, neither the American nor the Soviet record of the Molotov–Truman talks contains any mention of this supposedly acerbic exchange.[47] It seems, then, that Truman spiced up his memoirs with a little cold war rhetoric designed to show that he had talked tough with the Russians right from the beginning of his presidency. It is likely, too, that the source of this reported exchange with Molotov was not Truman's memory but press gossip of what supposedly happened between the two men. According to Carl Marzani's 1952 book on the origins of the cold war, 'Washington gossip had it that Molotov had walked out on Truman. According to foreign correspondent Edgar A. Mowrer, Molotov had said "no one has ever talked to me like this before".'[48]

There was indeed some tough talking at the two meetings between Molotov and Truman and the debate centred on the continuing inter-allied row about the government of postwar Poland. On one side were the Soviets, sticking to their interpretation of the Yalta agreement that the existing pro-communist regime in Warsaw should be broadened and reconstructed. On the other side were the British and Americans, insisting that the Yalta agreement meant there must be a new government in Poland and that members of the existing regime could expect no special treatment in the negotiations on its formation. This argument had been going on in Moscow in a Polish Commission established by the Yalta conference, and the tough talking continued in the United States not only with Truman but in Molotov's meetings with British Foreign Secretary Eden and the American Secretary of State Edward Stettinius. Molotov's personal irritation about these discussions bubbled to the surface during a petty incident in San Francisco when he forbade Pavlov, his interpreter, from comparing translation notes with his British counterpart.[49]

The Polish dispute notwithstanding, the impression Molotov gained from his two meetings with Truman was far from negative. Their first meeting, on 22 April, was quite friendly. At the end of the meeting Truman proposed a toast, saying that since the two of them spoke the same language he would like to meet Stalin and hoped the Soviet leader would visit the United States one day. From the Soviet point of view the crucial moment in this first meeting was Truman's response to Molotov's question of whether the President knew about the Yalta agreement on Soviet entry into the Far Eastern war. Truman replied that he entirely stood by the Yalta decision and Molotov thanked him for such a clear answer, saying that he would report it to Stalin. At their second meeting Truman – acting under the influence of some hard-line advice from his policy circle[50] – took a much firmer position on the Polish question than he had during his first encounter with Molotov. But the President's comments were simply a restatement of the Anglo-American position, including what Truman had directly messaged to Stalin on 18 April.[51] What mattered to Molotov and Stalin was not Truman's predictable attempt to pressurise them over Poland but his firm commitment to continue Roosevelt's policy of co-operation with the Soviet Union and to stand by existing agreements.

Truman's tough talking with Molotov was to no avail. Stalin stuck to the Soviet interpretation of the Yalta agreement on Poland and insisted in no uncertain terms that Moscow would not allow the formation in Warsaw of a government unfriendly to the USSR. On 23 April Stalin wrote to Truman:

> You evidently do not agree that the Soviet Union is entitled to seek in Poland a Government that would be friendly to it, that the Soviet Government cannot agree to the existence in Poland of a Government hostile to it . . . I do not know whether a genuinely representative Government has been established in Greece, or whether the Belgian Government is a genuinely democratic one. The Soviet Union was not consulted when those Governments were being formed, nor did it claim the right to interfere in those matters, because it real-izes how important Belgium and Greece are to the security of Great Britain. I cannot understand why in discussing Poland no attempt is made to consider the interests of the Soviet Union in terms of security as well.[52]

Truman blinked first over Poland. When the European war ended he decided that Harry Hopkins, Roosevelt's trusted confidant and a favourite with the Soviets, should go to Moscow to broker a deal with Stalin.[53] Hopkins arrived in the Soviet capital on 25 May and the next day began a series of meetings with Stalin. He told Stalin that American public opinion was disturbed by recent developments in US–Soviet relations, particularly the failure to implement the Yalta agreement on Poland. But, Hopkins reassured Stalin, Truman intended to continue Roosevelt's policy of co-operation with the USSR. In response Stalin employed one of his favourite debating tactics, blaming a third party, saying the problem was that while the Soviets wanted a friendly government in Poland, Great Britain was trying to revive the anti-Bolshevik cordon sanitaire of the post-First World War years. Towards the end of this conversation Stalin expressed the rather paranoid view that Hitler was not dead but in hiding somewhere and perhaps had escaped by submarine to Japan. In fact, by this time Soviet military and medical authorities had already conducted an investigation and carried out autopsies that proved beyond reasonable doubt that Hitler and Goebbels had committed suicide. But Stalin still suspected that evidence had been planted to cover up the Nazi dictator's escape from Berlin.[54]

At their meeting on 27 May Stalin expounded to Hopkins his own gripes about Soviet–American relations. As well as the Polish dispute, Stalin resented American manoeuvres to gain UN membership for Argentina – a neutral state that the Soviets saw as a wartime collaborator of the Germans. Then there was France's involvement in allied discussions about reparations from Germany – which Stalin opposed – and the abrupt manner in which the United States had cut lend-lease shipments to the Soviet Union as soon as Germany surrendered. Stalin was also keen to secure a share of the German navy and merchant fleet and suspected the British and Americans might oppose this. Later in the conversation Stalin adopted a more conciliatory tone. He told Hopkins that the United States was a world power with worldwide interests and for this reason he accepted that the Americans had a right to be involved in the resolution of the Polish question. Stalin admitted that the Soviet Union had acted unilaterally in Poland but asked Hopkins to understand the reasons why. As to the future, Stalin proposed that four or five of the ministers in a reorganised Polish government could be chosen from the lists of favoured politicians drawn up by the British and Americans. This suggestion of Stalin's soon led to a resolution of the Polish dispute. During the course of June 1945 a deal was struck that the communist-dominated Polish provisional government would be reorganised to include four pro-western cabinet ministers, including Mikolajczyk who became one of two deputy premiers (the other was the Polish communist leader, Gomulka) serving under a left-wing socialist prime minster,

Edward Osobka-Morawski. This reorganised government was recognised by the British and Americans on 5 July.

Another important topic of conversation between Hopkins and Stalin was Soviet entry into the Far Eastern war. Hopkins wanted to know about the Red Army's preparations for war, particularly the proposed date of Soviet entry into the war. At their third meeting on 28 May Stalin told Hopkins the Red Army would be ready to attack by 8 August, in accordance with the Yalta agreement, which specified that the Soviet Union would declare war on Japan two or three months after the end of the war in Europe. However, implementation of the Yalta agreement was tied to China agreeing to recognise the independence of Outer Mongolia and to concede to the Soviet Union various port and railway facilities in Manchuria. Stalin told Hopkins that he did not want to start talking to the Chinese until the secret redeployment of Soviet forces to the Far East was well advanced. He also made it clear to Hopkins that he thought Japan should, like Germany, be jointly occupied after the war and divided into American, British and Soviet zones of military occupation. Stalin's attitude to the treatment of Japan was similar to the one he held in relation to Germany – he favoured a punitive peace:

> Marshal Stalin said that war such as the present could only happen once in a hundred years and it was better to take advantage of it and utterly defeat Japan and cope with the military potential and in that manner assure fifty or sixty years of peace.

Hopkins was gravely ill when he went on his last mission to Moscow (he died in January 1946) but he performed a very important service. His meetings with Stalin paved the way for a resolution of the Polish dispute and made possible the airing of grievances about a number of other issues in Soviet–American relations. Both sides signalled their intention to continue relations in the co-operative tradition established by Roosevelt. The scene was set for the repetition at Potsdam of the triumphal tripartism of Yalta, leading to a strengthening of relations between the Soviet Union and its wartime allies.

This rosy post-Yalta, pre-Potsdam scenario is not one that finds favour with all historians. Some prefer to emphasise the differences and divergences within the Grand Alliance at this time. Such interpretations tend to reflect the later impact of the cold war and the influence exercised by protagonists such as Truman and Churchill who subsequently sought to distance themselves from the co-operative spirit of Yalta and Potsdam. A similar distancing from the Grand Alliance took place on the Soviet side after the outbreak of the cold war, but Stalin's contemporaneous view of relations with the west was quite optimistic and the Soviet delegation set off for Potsdam confident that tripartite co-operation between Britain, the US and the USSR to achieve postwar security and a durable peace remained by far the best option for all.

The Potsdam Conference

Stalin's armies did not get as far as Paris but they had reached Berlin. When France capitulated in 1940 Hitler had made a triumphal – and much photographed – tour of central Paris; both Churchill and Truman took time to drive around the ruins of Berlin. Stalin displayed no such interest. He arrived quietly by train, even ordering Zhukov to cancel any plans he might have had to welcome him with a military band and a guard of honour.[55]

The conference venue was one of the few large buildings left intact in the greater Berlin area – the Cecilienhof Palace, built for Kaiser Wilhelm II's son and named after his wife. More Tudor country house than classical European palace, the 176-room residence sat in a wooded park by Lakes Jungfern and Heiliger. Among the improvements made by the Soviets in preparation for the conference was the shipping in from Russia of a suitable round table for the participants to deliberate around and a flower bed arrangement in the central courtyard with blooms in the colour and shape of a Red Star.[56]

The Potsdam conference lasted for two weeks (17 July to 2 August), far longer than the four days of Tehran and the week Churchill, Roosevelt and Stalin spent at Yalta. One reason for the length of the conference was a break at the end of July when Churchill flew home for the results of the British general election. He lost the election by a landslide and never returned to Potsdam; his and Eden's places at the conference table were taken by the new Labour Prime Minister, Clement Attlee, and his Foreign Minister, Ernest Bevin (although Attlee, as Deputy PM, had accompanied Churchill to Potsdam). Another reason for the duration of the conference was the number and type of issues discussed at Potsdam. At Tehran the main theme had been the co-ordination of military action against Germany while at Yalta it was general perspectives on the postwar world that dominated the discussions. Potsdam was more like the Moscow conference of foreign ministers of October 1943 in that it focused on the resolution of specific issues: the future of Germany; peace treaties with enemy states; the revision of the Montreux Convention on access to the Black Sea; the formation of territorial trustee-ships to govern Italy's former colonies; and the establishment of procedures for the future conduct of Soviet–Western relations within the Grand Alliance, as well as a number of other issues. Stalin was keen to deal with all these ques-tions as soon as possible because he worried that the benevolent glow of the common victory over Germany would not last much longer and that relations with his Anglo-American allies would become progressively more difficult after the war. Stalin also thought he had a trump card to play in the negotiations: the Red Army was needed to help finish off Japan.

In personal terms the relations between Churchill, Stalin and Truman never achieved the intimacy of Churchill, Roosevelt and Stalin at Tehran and Yalta. But the new Big Three were pretty friendly with each other. The Prime Minister was 'again under Stalin's spell', complained Eden. 'He kept repeating "I like that man".'[57] At the time Truman thought that Stalin was 'straight-forward' and 'knows what he wants and will compromise when he can't get it'. Later, Truman recalled that he had been a 'Russophile' and thought he could live with Stalin; indeed he 'liked the little son of a bitch'.[58] According to Charles Bohlen, Truman's interpreter, 'while everyone was outwardly friendly there was a certain reserve on both sides that symbolized basic mistrust'.[59] But the conference records are full of good humour, jokes, laughter and much effort all round to avoid confrontation and deadlock in negotiations. Stalin was his usual charming self at the banquet he hosted. After a piano concert by leading Soviet artistes Truman got up and played some Chopin. According to the British interpreter, Major A.H. Birse, 'Stalin applauded with enthusiasm, remarking that he was the only one of the three with no talents; he had heard that Churchill painted, and now the President proved that he was a musician.'[60]

There were, of course, sharp political differences at Potsdam, prolonged negotiations and hard bargaining. Stalin also had to contend with the ever more marked tendency of the British and Americans to line up together against the Soviets in negotiations. But there were Anglo-American differences too. As James F. Byrnes, Truman's foreign minister, joked at the conference: 'one gets the impression that when we agree with our Soviet friends, the British delegation withholds its agreement, and when we agree with our British friends, we do not obtain the agreement of the Soviet delegation. (*Laughter*).'[61]

Stalin's first meeting at Potsdam was with Truman on 17 July. Stalin began by apologising for arriving a day late at the conference. He had been detained in Moscow by negotiations with the Chinese and his doctors had forbidden him to fly to Berlin. After an exchange of pleasantries Stalin listed the issues he would like discussed at the conference: the division of the German fleet, reparations, Poland, territorial trusteeships, the Franco regime in Spain. Truman was happy to discuss these issues but said the United States had its own items for the agenda, although he did not specify what these were. To Truman's statement that there were bound to be difficulties and differences of opinion during the negotiations, Stalin responded that such problems were unavoidable but the important thing was to find a common language. Asked about Churchill, Truman said he had seen him yesterday morning and that the

Prime Minister was confident of victory in the British general election. Stalin commented that the English people would not forget the victory in the war, in fact they thought the war was over already and expected the Americans and Soviets to defeat Japan for them. This provided Truman with an opening to remark that while there was active British participation in the war in the Far East, he still awaited help from the USSR. Stalin replied that Soviet forces would be ready to launch their attack on the Japanese by the middle of August. This led to the final exchange of the conversation in which Stalin indicated that he was sticking to the agreement at Yalta on the terms of Soviet participation in the Far Eastern war and did not intend to demand anything more.[62]

Stalin's conversation with Truman was friendly enough although it did not match the bonhomie he had achieved with Roosevelt at Tehran and Yalta. But Truman was new to the job, was still feeling his way with Stalin and, unlike his predecessor, had not engaged in a long wartime correspondence with the Soviet leader prior to meeting him.

As might be expected, Stalin's chat with Churchill over dinner the next evening was much cosier and, as usual, ranged far and wide. Stalin was confident Churchill would win the British general election and predicted a parliamentary majority of 80 for the Prime Minster. Stalin also evinced admiration for the role of King George in unifying the Empire, saying that 'no one who was a friend of Britain would do anything to weaken the respect shown to the Monarchy'. Churchill was equally effusive, saying that he would 'welcome Russia as a great power on the sea' and that the country had a right of access to the Mediterranean, the Baltic Sea and the Pacific Ocean. On Eastern Europe, Stalin repeated previous promises to Churchill that he would not seek its sovietisation, but expressed disappointment at western demands for changes to the governments in Bulgaria and Romania, especially when he was refraining from interfering in Greek affairs. Churchill spoke of difficulties in relation to Yugoslavia, pointing to the 50–50 arrangement he had made with Stalin in October 1944, but the Soviet leader protested that the share of influence in Yugoslavia was 90 per cent British, 10 per cent Yugoslavian and 0 per cent Russian. Stalin continued that Tito had a 'partisan mentality and had done several things that he ought not to have done. The Soviet Government often did not know what Marshal Tito was about to do.' The positive tenor of the conversation was summed up by Churchill's remark towards the end of dinner that 'the Three Powers gathered round the table were the strongest the world had ever seen, and it was their task to maintain the peace of the world'.[63]

The first plenary session at Potsdam was held on 17 July[64] and on Stalin's proposal Truman was elected Chairman for the duration of the conference. The main item on the agenda was an exchange of views on what issues the three leaders wanted to discuss at the conference. Stalin's list was similar to the one he had presented to Truman at their bilateral meeting earlier that day. Again, the division of the German navy and merchant fleet was number one on his list, followed by reparations, the resumption of diplomatic relations with Germany's former satellites, and the position of the Franco regime in Spain. Stalin's order of priorities was interesting for a number of reasons. First, it reflected his always keen desire to get a fair share of war booty and he suspected that the British, in particular, were trying to deny the Soviets their share of German shipping. Second, Stalin had asserted on a number of occasions during the war that one of the defining features of a great power was a big fleet and he was planning a significant postwar build-up of the Soviet navy. This required a share of the German as well as the Italian fleet (already agreed at Yalta) and port facilities in various parts of the world.[65] The demand for a share of the German fleet reflected Stalin's view that now the war in Europe was over the Soviet Union should get its just rewards. 'We want no gifts,' Stalin told Truman and Churchill later in the conference, 'but wish to know whether or not the principle is recognised, whether or not the Russian claim to a part of the German navy is considered legitimate.'[66] Stalin displayed a similar attitude in relation to a number of other questions that came up at the conference. Justifying the Soviet demand for Königsberg he said:

> We consider it necessary to have at the expense of Germany one ice-free port in the Baltic. I think that this port must serve Königsberg. It is no more than fair that the Russians who have shed so much blood and lived through so much terror should want to receive some lump of German territory which would give some small satisfaction from this war.[67]

A more serious issue of national pride concerned Soviet demands in relation to Turkey. In June 1945 the Soviet Union had demanded the return of the provinces of Kars and Ardahan to the USSR. These were areas of eastern Turkey with Armenian and Georgian populations and had been part of the Tsarist empire from 1878 to 1921, when a Soviet–Turkish treaty returned the two districts to Turkey. These Soviet territorial demands were prompted by a suggestion from the Turkish ambassador that the Soviet Union and Turkey should sign a treaty of alliance. Molotov responded that before such an agreement could be concluded the frontier dispute about Kars and Ardahan needed to be resolved and there had to be negotiations about the revision of the Montreux Convention and the establishment of Soviet military bases on the Dardanelles.[68] At Potsdam the USSR tabled a demand for joint control of the Black Sea Straits with Turkey, including provisions for Soviet military bases.[69] At the plenary session on 23 July Stalin defended the Soviet position on Kars and Ardahan on ethnic grounds, and in relation to the straits said:

For a great power such as Russia the question of the Straits has great significance. The Montreux Convention was directed against Russia, it was an
agreement hostile to Russia. Turkey was given the right not only to close the
Straits to our shipping during war but when there exists a threat of war, as
defined by Turkey. An impossible position! Turkey can always show that
such a threat exists and she can always close the Straits. We Russians have
the same rights in relation to the Straits as the Japanese Empire. This is
laughable but it is a fact . . . Imagine the uproar there would be in England
if such an agreement existed in relation to Gibraltar, or in America if such
an agreement existed in relation to the Panama Canal . . . You consider
that a naval base on the Straits is unacceptable. Very well, then give me
some other base where the Russian fleet would be able to carry out repairs
and re-equip and where, together with its allies, it would be able to defend
Russia's rights.[70]

Stalin's allusion to a naval base elsewhere was a reference to another issue of
prestige raised by the Soviets at Potsdam: the demand for Soviet participation
in the administration of the Trusteeship Territories that were to supersede
Italy's colonies in North Africa. The background to the Soviets' demand was a
long-standing American proposal that the League of Nations' mandate system
for overseeing the transition of former colonies to independence should be
replaced by a trusteeship system. At the San Francisco conference in June 1945
there was correspondence between Gromyko and Stettinius, the American
Secretary of State, which indicated that the United States would support Soviet
participation in the proposed trusteeship system.[71] This was very encouraging
for Moscow and at Potsdam the Soviets proposed there should be a discussion
about whether territories taken into trusteeship should be managed collectively by the Big Three or by individual countries responsible for separate territories. Stalin and Molotov pressed for a discussion of this matter but it was
agreed to refer the issue to the first meeting of the newly created Council of
Foreign Ministers, scheduled to meet in London in September.[72] After Potsdam
Moscow hardened its position on the trusteeship issue and decided to demand
that Tripolitania (western Libya) should become a Soviet trust territory, which
meant Stalin would have been able to establish port facilities in the
Mediterranean. The Soviets were quite open about their self-interested aims in
relation to Tripolitania and saw nothing wrong with them, although they did
stress that their intention was to establish merchant fleet facilities.[73]

At Potsdam a number of questions were raised and then tabled for future
discussion by the Big Three's foreign ministers. But there were some issues
that had to be discussed and decided upon by the conference. First and fore-
most was Germany's future. This was a matter considered over several plenary

sessions and by the foreign ministers and specialist working commissions of less senior officials. The most difficult issue was that of reparations. At Yalta it had been agreed in principle that the Soviet Union would receive reparations from Germany, the ball-park figure being $10 billion. The reparations were to be extracted in kind by the dismantling of German industry and infrastructure and by deliveries from current production. The difficulty was that German industry was mostly located in the western-occupied areas of the country such as the Ruhr. The British and Americans, none too keen on reparations anyway, feared they would end up having to meet Soviet reparations demands by deliveries from their zones. Their preference was for the Soviets to extract reparations exclusively from their own zone of occupation in Germany and, if there were to be reparations deliveries from the west, these should be in exchange for agricultural products from the east. In the end agreement was reached that 10 per cent of German industry would be removed from the western zones in part payment of Soviet reparations and another 15 per cent would be dismantled and shipped east in exchange for food and raw materials. As important, from Stalin's point of view, was that the agreement provided for Germany's 'complete disarmament and demilitarization' and the elimination of its war potential. Stalin's views on the long-term danger of a German revival were well rehearsed and they came to the fore once again in an exchange with Truman on 21 July about the utility of shifting Poland's border with Germany as far west as possible:

Stalin: Of course the proposal . . . to shift the frontier westwards will create difficulties for Germany. I do not object to the claim that it will create difficulties for Germany. Our task consists in creating more difficulties for Germany . . .

Truman: But it is not good to create difficulties for the allies as well.

Stalin: The less industry in Germany, the greater the outlets for your goods. Germany will not be competing with your goods. Is that so bad? It seems very good to me. We put on its knees the state which threatens peace and peaceful competition . . . There are difficulties for Germany here, but we must not be afraid of them.[74]

Alongside the German question, the issue of Poland's western border with Germany gave rise to the most protracted discussion at Potsdam. At Yalta it had been agreed that Poland would be compensated for territorial losses to the Soviet Union by gains at Germany's expense. But no agreement had been reached on the precise frontier and there were differences about how far west the German–Polish border should be pushed. Those differences were compounded by the fact that the Soviets controlled all the German territory in question and they had handed it over to Polish administrative control. The Poles began resettling the area in anticipation that it would become part of Poland and there was a consequent mass exodus of Germans westwards, causing problems for the British and Americans in their zones of occupation in Germany.

The discussion of this issue at Potsdam provides a rare example of Stalin being tactically outsmarted in a diplomatic negotiation. Early in the conference both Truman and Churchill raised the question of how the concept of 'Germany' was to be defined. Stalin said that Germany should be considered either as a purely geographical concept or should be taken 'as she is in 1945'. But the Soviet leader made the mistake of agreeing that 'Germany' referred to the state that existed before 1937 (i.e. before Hitler annexed Austria and seized the Sudetenland from Czechoslovakia). This concession enabled Truman and Churchill to argue later that what was going on in the German territories handed over to the Poles was an inter-allied matter, not a bilateral issue in Soviet–Polish relations, since Germany was under joint allied occupation. Stalin countered that this territory had come under *de facto* Polish control because the Germans had fled west, but he had no real answer to the argument that the German–Polish border was a matter to be determined by a peace conference. However, by the end of the conference a demarcation line between Germany and Poland had been agreed and Polish administration of the German territories in question had been accepted by the British and Americans, 'pending the final determination of Poland's western frontier' at a future peace conference.

A third area of contention at Potsdam concerned Big Three relations with Germany's erstwhile allies during the Second World War – Italy, Bulgaria, Finland, Hungary and Romania. The scenario was that the British and Americans sought special treatment for Italy, while Stalin strove to protect the interests of those countries that fell within his sphere of influence in Eastern Europe. The argument began with a western proposal that Italy be admitted as a member of the United Nations. The Soviets did not object but Stalin did not see why the other four ex-enemy states should not be treated in the same way. The British and Americans said they did not have diplomatic relations with those states and so could not consider their admission to the UN until peace treaties had been signed. The compromise finally agreed was to prioritise the negotiation and signing of a peace treaty between the Big Three and Italy that would lead to the country's admission to the UN. Soviet sensibilities were assuaged by a commitment from the British and Americans to consider recognising the governments of Bulgaria, Finland, Hungary and Romania.

At the conclusion of the Potsdam conference on 2 August 1945 the participants solemnly declared that it had 'strengthened the ties . . . and extended the scope of their collaboration and understanding' and had renewed their confidence in their ability to deliver 'a just and enduring peace'. The conference communiqué went on to announce, first, the establishment of a Council of Foreign Ministers that would constitute a permanent forum of tripartite collaboration and, second, plans for postwar Germany, including policy on reparation payments. There followed the announcement of various other decisions such as the transfer of Königsberg to the USSR and the agreement on Poland's western border. The final communiqué also paved the way for the admission of more states to the United Nations, including countries that had remained neutral throughout the war. Explicitly excepted from this provision was Franco's Spain on the grounds that his regime had been founded with the support of the aggressor states and had maintained a close association with them during the war. With a view to undermining Franco's regime Stalin and the Soviets had proposed much stronger action but this was as far as the British and Americans were prepared to go.[75] As well as the public communiqué an unpublished conference protocol dealt with matters such as the tripartite disposal of the German navy and merchant marine and the need to revise the regime governing the Black Sea Straits.[76]

The Soviet assessment of Potsdam was very positive, and not only in the press, where the conference received the same adulatory treatment that had greeted Tehran and Yalta.[77] Particularly interesting are the confidential statements recorded by the Yugoslav ambassador in Moscow: 'According to Molotov and Vyshinskii at the conference it was possible to see, and to see in its results, that the English and Americans accept that they have lost Eastern Europe and the Balkans . . . Molotov said that throughout the conference there was a good atmosphere, albeit not without harsh polemics and sharp words. Everyone tried to ensure that all questions were resolved by compromise decisions . . . About Truman they said he was quite cultured and shows much understanding of European problems.'[78] In his diary Georgi Dimitrov recorded the following: 'spoke with Molotov about the Berlin conference, and in particular about decisions affecting Bulgaria and the Balkans. Basically, these decisions are to our advantage. In effect, this sphere of influence has been recognised as ours.'[79] In a report circulated to Soviet ambassadors Molotov wrote that 'the conference ended with quite satisfactory results for the Soviet Union'.[80]

Stalin and the Far Eastern War

After Potsdam Stalin turned his attention to the last Soviet campaign of the Second World War – the attack on Japanese forces in Manchuria in August 1945. It was not only another military victory that beckoned but a substantial increase in Soviet power and influence in the Far East.[81]

The United States had begun angling for Soviet involvement in the Far Eastern war as early as December 1941, but Stalin had resisted these American overtures and Roosevelt did not press the point. Stalin's policy towards Japan was to stick to the terms of the Soviet–Japanese Neutrality Pact of April 1941 in the hope that Tokyo would do the same. The attack on Pearl Harbor had signalled a course of southern Japanese expansion, so Stalin could reasonably expect that Japan would remain neutral in the Soviet–German war, assuming that the Red Army was able to halt and turn back the Nazi attack. But Stalin could not afford to be complacent. The Japanese military establishment in Manchuria and Korea increased to more than a million troops after June 1941 and remained at comparable levels thereafter. To counter this potential threat the Red Army maintained a force some 700,000 strong in the Far East. A deputy Chief of the General Staff for the Far East was established in 1942 and Stavka issued a stream of directives to its Far Eastern commanders on what to do in the event of a Japanese attack. After the victories at Stalingrad and Kursk, Stalin could be fairly certain the Japanese would not be so foolhardy as to initiate military hostilities against the Soviet Union. However, a pre-emptive strike against targets such as the strategically important and vulnerable Far Eastern port of Vladivostok could not be ruled out if the Japanese suspected the Soviets were preparing for war against them. Stalin had to tread very carefully. Unlike Roosevelt in relation to Britain in 1940–1941, Stalin made no declarations of political solidarity with the struggle of his western allies in the Far East. Soviet press coverage of the Pacific War was sympathetic to the western allies but not particularly hostile to Japan. The only significant deviation from this restrained public stance was a comment made by Stalin in his November 1944 Revolution anniversary speech that classified Japan as an aggressor nation. But this statement was made in the context of an argument in favour of an effective postwar international security organisation to replace the League of Nations and was not interpreted by the Japanese as signalling any change in Soviet policy.[82] When the Soviets denounced the neutrality pact with Japan in April 1945, they went to great lengths to assure the Japanese that they harboured no aggressive intentions towards them.

Even so, there could be little doubt the Soviet Union would involve itself in the war against Japan if the opportunity arose. From Stalin's point of view Japan represented a military threat second only to Germany, and he had stated this publicly and privately on numerous occasions. There was a long history behind Stalin's hostility towards Japan. During the Russian civil war the Japanese had dispatched a huge army to invade Siberia and it took several years to secure its departure from the USSR. Japan's invasion of Manchuria in 1931 provoked intense security concerns in Moscow, especially when combined with the rise of fascism and Nazism in Europe.[83] Japanese expansion into Manchuria and then northern China in 1937 had led to several large-scale military clashes with Japanese forces on disputed sections of the Soviet–Mongolian and Sino-Soviet borders.[84] In 1936 Japan had signed the Anti-Comintern Pact with Germany and Moscow well knew there were powerful Japanese military and political factions that preferred an anti-communist war to a military clash with the Americans and the British. During the Sino-Japanese war Stalin resisted the efforts of the Chinese nationalist leader, Chiang Kai-shek, to involve the Soviet Union directly in the conflict but, from the late 1930s, the USSR was a major military supplier to China and this relationship continued during the Great Patriotic War.[85]

Japan's defeat by the United States was inevitable but its potential to re-emerge as a threatening military and industrial power was reason enough for Soviet involvement in the Far Eastern war. Soviet entry into the war would ensure a decisive and devastating defeat of Japan; would cement Stalin's relations with his western allies; and would open the door to Soviet involvement in the Far Eastern peace settlement. In terms of specific Soviet war aims in the Far East, Stalin's agenda combined patriotic sensibilities with strategic interests. In the 1904–1905 war with Japan, Tsarist Russia had suffered a humiliating defeat and had been forced by the Treaty of Portsmouth to give up port facilities and territorial concessions in China and to concede to Japan the southern half of the island of Sakhalin. In Soviet times Moscow lost control of the Chinese Eastern Railway that ran through Manchuria to Vladivostok and became embroiled in long-running disputes with Japan about fishing rights and Japanese mining concessions in North Sakhalin. But while war with Japan offered the possibility of reversing these losses, Stalin did not formulate or articulate his demands until quite late in the day. As so often with Stalin, his policy demands emerged and evolved in response to the initiatives of others.

Stalin's road to war with Japan began in October 1943 at the Foreign Ministers' conference in Moscow when he told Cordell Hull, the American Secretary of State, and Harriman, the newly arrived American ambassador, that the Soviet Union would enter the Far Eastern war as soon as Germany was defeated. Stalin's linking of Soviet entry into the war against Japan to the termination of hostilities in Europe may have been a tactic to encourage the British and Americans to fulfil their promise of opening a second front in France, but it may also have been a simple reflection of the military realities of planning, preparing and implementing a major campaign in the Far East. Stalin's promise to join in the struggle against Japan was firmed up in conversations with Churchill and Roosevelt at Tehran.

After Tehran, Harriman raised the question of Soviet participation in the Far Eastern war on a number of occasions. In February 1944 he discussed with Stalin the question of Soviet co-operation with the American bombing campaign against Japan, including the establishment of US air bases on Soviet territory. Stalin replied that the Soviet Union was unable to participate in such operations against Japan because its forces in the Far East were too weak and it would take two to three months to build them up to strength, and that was out of the question while the Red Army was busy in the west. However, when German resistance weakened, divisions could be transferred to the Far East and 'as soon as these forces are transferred the Soviet Government will cease to fear Japanese provocation and may even provoke the Japanese itself'. Stalin was not averse to establishing American air bases on Soviet territory but emphasised that if Japan was provoked into attacking first that could lead to the loss of coastal territory and of areas earmarked for US bases.[86] In June 1944 Harriman took advantage of the warm afterglow of the D-Day landings in France to raise again the issue of American bomber bases in the Soviet Far East. As before, Stalin was amenable to the idea in general but Harriman could not pin him down on a date to begin specific discussions.[87] In September 1944 Harriman and Clark Kerr went to see Stalin to report the results of the Churchill–Roosevelt meeting in Quebec. Harriman used the opportunity to raise the question of joint military operations in the Pacific theatre. Stalin asked Harriman what he had in mind – the formulation of plans or the fixing of a date for action. Harriman replied that he was thinking of plans and that the date for Soviet involvement could only be fixed after the end of the war in Europe. When he mentioned the issue of bombing again, it seemed to annoy Stalin, who said that if Churchill and Roosevelt wanted Soviet participation in the war they had to appreciate that it would necessitate the transfer of 25 to 30 divisions to the Far East. Stalin wanted to know if there had been any change in Roosevelt's plans regarding Soviet participation in the war and wondered if the idea was that its role would be restricted to the provision of air bases. 'At Tehran Roosevelt demanded or, more accurately, requested Soviet participation in the war against Japan,' Stalin told Harriman. 'The Russians gave their agreement. The position of the Russians remains the same. He would like to know if the intention of America and England was to bring Japan to its knees without the aid of the Soviet Union.' Both Clark Kerr and Harriman assured Stalin that this was not the case but the Soviet leader pointed out that he needed to know about Anglo-American plans for Soviet participation if he was to proceed with his own preparations.[88]

The next Harriman–Stalin conversation about Soviet participation in the Far Eastern war took place in October 1944. The occasion was Churchill's trip to Moscow and on 14 October the two leaders discussed military issues. Harriman was in attendance, accompanied by General Deane, who gave a presentation on the Pacific War. Deane responded to Stalin's question to Harriman the previous month and outlined the American Chiefs of Staff's concept of Soviet participation in the Far Eastern war. The aims of such participation, said Deane, would be: to safeguard the Trans-Siberian Railway and the port of Vladivostok; the formation of Soviet and American strategic air bases for operations against Japan; severing Japan's communications with mainland Asia; the destruction of Japanese forces in Manchuria; and, finally, the safeguarding of Pacific supply lines. At the end of his presentation Deane posed some questions to the Soviets: how soon after the defeat of Germany would the USSR enter the war against Japan; how long would it take for the Soviets to concentrate their forces in the Far East; how many supplies could the Trans-Siberian railway carry to strategic air forces; and how quickly could the Soviet government move to establish such forces?[89] General Antonov replied to Deane's questions at a meeting the next day. It would take two and half to three months to concentrate sufficient Soviet forces, said Antonov. Stalin chipped in to say that it wasn't just a question of transporting forces to the Far East but of sufficient supplies to keep them going and on the supply side the Soviets would need American help. Asked by Harriman when the Soviet Union would enter the war against Japan, Stalin said three months after Germany's defeat.[90]

On 16 October Stalin met Harriman and Deane again and gave the ambassador a list of supplies the Soviets would need if they were to participate in the Far Eastern war. Deane repeated in summary form what he had said at the previous meeting and Stalin responded that he thought the most important task for the Red Army would be to destroy the Japanese forces in Manchuria.[91] According to Harriman, Stalin made it clear he would have political demands to make in relation to Soviet participation in the Far Eastern war since the Soviet people had to know what they were fighting for.[92] But it was only when the ambassador asked Stalin what his demands were at a further meeting on 14 December that the Soviet leader revealed his hand. Basically, Stalin wanted a reversal of the Treaty of Portsmouth: South Sakhalin would return to Russia and Port Arthur and Darien on the Liaotung Peninsula in Manchuria would be leased to the USSR, as would the railway lines connecting these two ports to the Soviet Union. Stalin also wanted the status quo in relation to Outer Mongolia to be preserved, which meant *de facto* Chinese recognition of the independence of the People's Republic of Mongolia – a Soviet client state since the 1920s. Finally, Stalin wanted to annex the Kuril Islands to the USSR.[93] This was a chain of islands that ran from the USSR's Kamchatka Peninsula to the northernmost tip of the Japanese home island of Hokkaido. Mostly uninhabited, their status was uncertain until Russia conceded them to Japan in an agreement signed in 1875. However, as a matter of principle the USSR did not accept that it was bound by the agreements of its Tsarist predecessor, so there was a legal and historical case to be made for Soviet possession of what the

Japanese called their Northern Territories. Legal disputes aside, the strategic rationale for Stalin's plan to seize the Kurils was that they controlled the mouth of the Sea of Okhotsk and blocked access to the Pacific Ocean from Vladivostok. As Stalin said to the Chinese ambassador in July 1945, 'if the Kuril Islands were Soviet and Formosa and other territories were returned to China, we will always be able to keep Japan hemmed in from the east, south and west'.[94] It may be, too, that the Kurils were to Stalin the Far Eastern equivalent of Königsberg in Germany – a 'lump' of Japanese territory in part payment for the Soviet blood that would be spilt in the Far Eastern war.

One of Stalin's themes in many of his conversations with Harriman was the vital need to keep the Soviet intention to attack Japan a secret and he pointedly told the ambassador that this question would only be discussed at the very highest levels of Moscow's political and military decision-making. Stalin even kept the secret from his top diplomats, including Yakov Malik, Soviet ambassador in Tokyo and S.A. Lozovskii, the deputy foreign commissar with special responsibility for the Far East. Both Malik and Lozovskii operated under the assumption that the USSR would seek to keep out of the war with Japan and argued in their policy briefings that Soviet aims in the Far East, including overturning the Portsmouth treaty, could be achieved by negotiations at the postwar peace conference. Stalin knew, however, that his political and territorial demands in China and in relation to Japan would not be taken seriously in the absence of an active Soviet role in the Far Eastern war.[95]

At the Yalta conference in February 1945 Stalin got what he wanted in relation to the Far East. In a secret agreement that, at Stalin's insistence, was personally signed by the Big Three, Churchill and Roosevelt agreed to the demands Stalin had detailed to Harriman in December, with two provisos: Darien would be internationalised as a commercial port rather than being leased to the USSR as a naval base, and all the Soviet demands in relation to Manchuria were subject to Chinese assent. Stalin also promised that the USSR would negotiate and conclude a Sino-Soviet treaty of alliance.[96]

After Yalta preparations for Soviet participation in the Far Eastern war began in earnest.[97] Plans were drawn up, key personnel appointed and a start made on the transfer of Soviet forces to the east. In charge of the campaign was Marshal Vasilevskii who began work on the operational plans at the end of April 1945. For security reasons no announcement was made about his appointment; indeed, he wasn't formally named overall Soviet commander in the Far East until the end of July. He had arrived in the area a few weeks earlier but under an assumed name and he did not wear his Marshal's uniform. A number of other experienced senior officers from the European theatre were transferred along with Vasilevskii, including Marshal R.Y. Malinovskii, who was appointed commander of the Transbaikal Front in Outer Mongolia – the main Soviet Far Eastern front – and Marshal Meretskov of Finnish war fame to command the Primorye (1ˢᵗ Far Eastern) Front.

Apart from planning the operation, the key task was the concentration of Soviet forces in the Far East. This involved a doubling of Soviet forces in the Far East and, between April and August 1945, three infantry armies and one tank army, a total of 39 divisions, were transferred from the western military districts of the USSR some 10,000 kilometres away. By the time of the Soviet attack Red Army forces in the Far East consisted of a million and a half troops, 26,000 artillery pieces and mortars, 5,500 tanks and self-propelled guns and 3,900 combat aircraft.

The first Stavka orders in preparation for the campaign were issued at the end of March 1945.[98] Interestingly, these were instructions about what to do in the event of a Japanese attack. This was partly an updating of previous directives on defensive action and partly a precautionary move in case of pre-emptive Japanese action following the renunciation of the Soviet–Japanese neutrality pact. But these directives also showed that the Soviet General Staff had learned from the experience of 22 June 1941 and they were determined not to get caught on the hop again while preparing for offensive action. According to General Shtemenko's memoirs, the calculation was that 'any plan for war in the Far East should provide some safeguard against a surprise attack . . . the defence element was included in the plan, provision for defence was made and the documentary records reflect this peculiarity of the General Staff's thinking on our major tactics and strategy'.[99]

On 28 June Stalin issued orders to the Transbaikal and the 1ˢᵗ Far Eastern Fronts to be ready to attack by 25 July, and to the 2ⁿᵈ Far Eastern Front to be ready by 1 August.[100] The main plan of campaign was to destroy the Japanese Kwantung Army in Manchuria, with the main blows coming from the Transbaikal Front. In support would be the 1ˢᵗ and 2ⁿᵈ Far Eastern Fronts as well as the Soviet Pacific Navy, which would take action to split and isolate the Japanese forces in Manchuria (*see Map 18 on p. 286*).

Running parallel to these military preparations was diplomatic action to secure favourable conditions for Soviet entry into the Far Eastern war. The most important task was to convince the Japanese they had nothing to fear from the Soviet Union, at least in the short term. This became a particularly pressing task after Moscow announced on 5 April 1945 that it would not be renewing the Soviet–Japanese neutrality pact when its initial five-year term ran out.[101] Few of Japan's decision-makers thought the USSR would attack in the near future, so they continued to approach Moscow with proposals that the Soviets should mediate a negotiated end to the Pacific War. As David Holloway points out, 'the Soviet Union gave no sign of being tempted by the

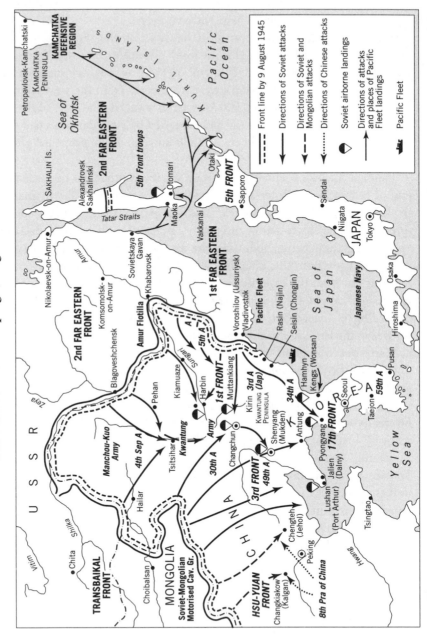

The Manchurian Campaign, August 1945

Japanese approaches. It showed not the slightest inclination to help Japan negotiate a peace agreement with the United States; nor was it interested in staying out of the war in return for Japanese offers of greater Soviet influence in Asia . . . Stalin consistently supported the goal of unconditional surrender, which he interpreted in the harshest terms.'[102]

The other task of Soviet diplomacy at this time was to negotiate a treaty of alliance with China, as had been agreed at Yalta. Stalin was reluctant, however, to enter negotiations with the Chinese too soon because he did not trust their ability to keep secrets and feared they would give the game away about the coming Soviet attack on Japan. Talks did not begin, therefore, until the end of June, although when they did Stalin took a very active part in them. Between 30 June and 12 July Stalin met the Chinese representative T.V. Soong six times.[103] The Chinese were happy to sign a treaty with the USSR and were eager to see the Red Army attack the Japanese, but they were reluctant to recognise Outer Mongolian independence or accept Soviet control of Darien and Port Arthur.[104] By the time Stalin left for the Potsdam conference in mid-July, agreement had still not been reached on these issues.

Stalin's conversations with Soong were laborious, tedious to read in retrospect, and doubtless very frustrating for the Soviet leader. As Stalin complained to Harriman after one meeting, he 'couldn't make out exactly what Soong had suggested. Soong had talked a lot and wasted a lot of time making notes but they had not understood exactly what he was proposing. They had asked him to put his proposals in writing but he had not yet done so . . . they had put their own proposals to Soong in writing, both in Russian and English. From Soong they had only words.'[105] Nevertheless, the Stalin–Soong talks provide a fascinating window on the Soviet dictator's global thinking at the end of the Second World War. Stalin's main theme was the parallel between the long-term Japanese threat and that emanating from the Germans. On 2 July he told Soong:

> Japan will not perish, even if it is forced to surrender unconditionally. History shows that the Japanese are a powerful nation. After the Versailles Treaty everyone thought that Germany would not rise again. But after some 15–17 years, it had restored its strength. If Japan is forced to its knees, then it too will in time be able to repeat what Germany did.

Stalin went on to explain to Soong that his main aim in signing the Yalta agreement on the Far East was to strengthen the Soviet strategic position in order to fight a future war with Japan.[106] On 7 July Stalin said to Soong that 'the Soviet Union is thinking about the future, about the long-term, not six months or a year. Japan will recover some 20 years after she is defeated. The

Soviet Government wants to construct a Chinese–Soviet relationship not just for the present but for the future, the long term.'[107] On 11 July Stalin returned to the German analogy, pointing out to Soong that if German heavy industry was not dismantled it would be easy for the country to rearm. In relation to Japan his fear was that the British and Americans 'would forget about the sufferings inflicted by the present war and would begin to give Japan various privileges, as happened with Germany after the First World War ... in America and England there were people who would help Japan. Soong did not know ... how hard Soviet representatives had fought at Tehran and Yalta for acceptance of the demand for the unconditional surrender of Germany ... they [the British and Americans] want to preserve Germany for a political game, for balancing. Without doubt there will be people in the US and England who will help Japan.'[108]

As David Holloway argues:

> Stalin's vision of the postwar world was very much coloured by the revival of German power after World War I, and by the dual threat posed to the Soviet Union in the 1930s by Germany in the west and Japan in the east. He foresaw the eventual emergence of Japanese and German power after World War II but wished to postpone it for as long as possible. He feared that Britain and the United States would seek to restore the power of those countries in order to balance the Soviet Union. That was why it was important to secure positions that would make it possible to prevent, delay or counter the restoration of German and Japanese power and to ensure a dominant Soviet position in Europe and in Asia.[109]

In Europe Stalin's solution to the dilemma posed by German power and his fears about the inconstancy of his western allies was to build a long-term alliance of Slavic states. In the Far East his solution was a strong Sino-Soviet alliance. Another parallel with Europe concerned the role of the Chinese communists in Stalin's postwar schema for the Far East. In China, as in Europe, the communists were urged by Stalin to construct a national front against the common enemy – in this case the Japanese – and to adopt the perspective of a postwar democratic progressive regime. For Mao and the Chinese communist party this line was a little hard to swallow since they had been involved in an intermittent civil war with Chiang Kai-shek's nationalist government for nearly two decades. But the evidence is that Mao accepted Stalin's strategic direction, if not all his tactical advice, and, like the communists of Eastern Europe, saw numerous benefits accruing from eventual Soviet military intervention in the war against Japan.[110] Naturally, this prospect worried Chiang but he was reassured by Stalin's commitment to recognise his regime as the sole legitimate government of China. In one conversation with Harriman, Stalin jokingly referred to Mao and his comrades as 'margarine communists', which the ambassador took to mean that they were not real communists but patriots whose main concern was their country's national interests. In Asia, as in Europe, Stalin's consistent message to his western allies was that 'sovietisation' no longer figured on the communists' political agenda.

At Potsdam Stalin told Truman that he would be ready to attack Japan by the middle of August. This pleased Truman. 'I've gotten what I came for,' he confided to his wife on 18 July. 'Stalin goes to war August 15 with no strings on it . . . I'll say that we'll end the war a year sooner now, and think of the kids who won't be killed. That's the important thing.'[111] According to the British record of Stalin's conversation with Churchill on 18 July: 'it was evident that Russia intends to attack Japan soon after August 8. (The Marshal [i.e. Stalin] thought it might be a fortnight later.'[112] In his discussion with the British and American Chiefs of Staff on 24 July Antonov stated that Soviet forces would be 'ready to commence operations in the last half of August'.[113] These indications were consistent with the commitment the Soviets had given at Yalta to enter war two or three months after the defeat of Germany, with Soviet military plans and preparations in the Far East (which had yet to be finalised), and with Stalin and Antonov's practice of giving their western allies conservative estimates about the timing of Red Army offensive action, both for security reasons and to allow for unpredictable contingencies such as the weather.

While Antonov had some quite detailed discussions with his western counterparts at Potsdam about Soviet participation in the Far Eastern war, it hardly figured at all in the conference's political discourse. Stalin had little to say; the political deal had been done and the wheels of military planning and preparation were grinding their way towards offensive action. He might have raised the issue of the postwar occupation of Japan but it was self-evident the Americans would not countenance a Soviet zone of occupation in advance of Soviet participation in the war itself. At Potsdam both Stalin and Antonov stuck to the line that Soviet entry into the war was conditional on an alliance with China that would underwrite the deal agreed at Yalta, but this was not an essential precondition. If the Chinese would not concede Stalin's demands in relation to Darien and Port Arthur, the Red Army would just take them. For Truman, the picture was complicated by the fact that American interest in Soviet participation in the war against Japan was fading by the time of Potsdam. Militarily, it was no longer seen as vital as it had been. This view was reinforced by the successful A-bomb test on 17 July and by the accumulating signs that the Japanese were getting ready to sue for peace. The changing American attitude to the Soviets in the Far Eastern context was indicated by Truman's handling of the Potsdam Proclamation of 26 July 1945. This was a public statement by Britain, China and the United States calling upon Japan to surrender unconditionally or face 'prompt and utter destruction'. In the original American draft of the declaration the Soviet Union was included among the signatories and there was a reference to the 'vast military might of the Soviet Union' having been added to the arsenals of Britain, China and the US.[114] But on 26 July Byrnes sent Molotov a copy of a new text of the declaration that omitted these references.[115] The Soviets immediately got to work producing their own draft declaration, which read:

> The time has come when the governments of the allied democratic countries, the USA, China, Great Britain and the Soviet Union, have recognized the necessity of declaring their attitude to Japan.
>
> Eight years ago Japan attacked China and since then has conducted a bloody war against the Chinese people. After that Japan treacherously attacked the United States and Great Britain, beginning a war of brigandage in the Pacific. And this time Japan used the same method of perfidious surprise attack as forty years ago when it attacked Russia.
>
> Throwing itself into war, Japan tried to exploit the situation created as a result of Hitler's aggression in Europe. The tenacious resistance of the Chinese people and the courageous struggle of the American and British armed forces upset the predatory plans of Japanese militarists.
>
> Like Hitler's Germany in the West, bellicose Japan has caused, and continues to cause, countless disasters to peace-loving peoples. In spite of the defeat of Germany and the end of the war in Europe, Japan continues to drag out the bloody war in the Far East. The calamities of peoples and the victims of war continue to grow, in spite of the futility of prolonging the war. It is impossible to tolerate this situation any longer.
>
> Throughout the world the peoples are full of a desire to put an end to a war that has dragged on. The United States, China, Great Britain and the Soviet Union consider it their duty to come forward with joint decisive measures that ought to lead to an end to the war.
>
> Japan should understand that further resistance is futile and presents the greatest danger for the Japanese people itself. Japan must end the war, lay down its arms and surrender unconditionally.[116]

Just before midnight the Soviets rang the American delegation to ask them to postpone publication of the Proclamation for three days. Fifteen minutes later, however, the Soviets were informed it had already been released to the press.[117] The subsequent American explanation for this lack of consultation was that since the Soviet Union was still neutral it would not want to get involved in such a statement. This was a pretty lame excuse and Stalin showed his annoyance by pointedly referring at the plenary session on 28 July to the fact that 'he had not been informed beforehand of the call to surrender published by the British and American governments'.[118] Even so, Stalin did not give up the idea of a public show of allied solidarity in advance of the Soviet attack on Japan. He suggested to Truman that Britain and the United States should issue a statement inviting the Soviet Union to enter the war in the Far East. Truman responded by suggesting that the Moscow declaration on general security issued in October 1943 and the as yet unratified Charter of the United Nations provided sufficient formal grounds for Soviet entry into the war.[119] This was hardly satisfactory from Stalin's point of view and when the Soviets did declare war on 8 August they used the pretext of Japan's failure to comply with the Potsdam Proclamation to justify their action.[120]

The significance of this sequence of events for an assessment of Stalin's policy in relation to the Far Eastern war is summed up by David Holloway:

> One striking aspect of Stalin's policy . . . is his persistence in seeking the agreement of the Allies for what he wanted to do. He was very pleased . . . when Roosevelt at Yalta agreed to his political conditions for entering the war. He very much wanted the Yalta agreement to be signed by Roosevelt and Churchill. He tried to conclude the treaty with China in time to enter the war as China's ally. He prepared an alternative to the Potsdam Proclamation to be signed by himself as well as his allies. He asked Truman for a public invitation to join the war; when that was denied he nevertheless portrayed Soviet entry into the war as a response to the Allies' request for help.[121]

When Stalin returned to Moscow from Potsdam he received a report from Vasilevskii dated 3 August informing him that the Far Eastern fronts would be ready for action by 5 August. Vasilevskii proposed the attack should begin no later than 9–10 August and pointed out to Stalin that the weather would be good from 6–10 August. On the 7th, Stalin and Antonov issued a directive to Vasilevskii ordering him to attack on 8/9 August.[122] This directive was issued in the absence of a pact with China. Indeed, Stalin did not even bother to see Soong again before giving the final go-ahead for war. Stalin had evidently decided to attack Japan first and conclude the treaty of alliance with China later. It has been suggested that the decisive factor in prompting Stalin to action was the atomic bombing of Hiroshima on 6 August and fear that Japan would surrender before the USSR entered the war and grabbed what it wanted in Manchuria, South Sakhalin and the Kurils. Stalin knew all about the American atomic bomb programme from his extensive intelligence apparatus in the US, which had penetrated the Manhattan Project at the very highest levels.[123] He could not have been very surprised at Potsdam on 24 July, when Truman told him about the successful Trinity test. According to Truman's account, Stalin did not evince a great deal of interest in the news and other western memoirs back up this story. Soviet memoirists, on the other hand, suggest that Stalin reacted very strongly to the news and saw it as the beginning of American nuclear blackmail tactics, which he sought to counter by a dramatic speeding up of the Soviets' own atom bomb programme.[124]

It is most unlikely that Stalin realised the full significance of the bomb as a new weapon in advance of its use against Japan. While he may indeed have been impressed by the atomic power displayed at Hiroshima and responded by entering the war as quickly as possible, it is just as likely that he had tired of the endless tedious negotiations with the Chinese and decided to shock Chiang Kai-shek into an agreement. The Soviet entry into the war certainly did the trick with the Chinese, who quickly agreed terms with Moscow and concluded the pact of alliance on 14 August – the day the Japanese announced they were surrendering unconditionally. The most notable feature of the Sino-Soviet pact was its anti-Japanese character and under its terms Stalin achieved most of what he wanted in Manchuria, but not full control of Darien.[125]

On the day the Soviet Union declared war on Japan Stalin had a conversation with Harriman in which the ambassador asked him what effect he thought the Hiroshima bombing would have. Stalin replied that he thought it might give the Japanese a pretext to replace their government with one that would undertake to surrender. Later in the conversation Stalin said that the atomic bomb would 'mean the end of war and aggressors. But the secret would have to be well kept.' Stalin further informed Harriman that Russian scientists had been working on the same project but had not achieved any results and neither had the Germans, whose laboratory the Soviets had captured. When Harriman said the British and Americans had pooled their knowledge but that it had taken enormous installations to conduct the experiments, Stalin commented that it must have been very expensive. Harriman agreed, saying that it had cost over $2 billion and that Churchill had played an important role in encouraging the project. 'Churchill was a great innovator, persistent and courageous,' said Stalin in response.[126]

As this exchange with Harriman shows, Stalin had somewhat modest expectations about the immediate impact of the Hiroshima bomb but was not slow to grasp the potential long-term significance of the new weapon. Indeed, on 20 August, not long after that meeting, Stalin signed an order authorising a massive, high-priority programme to produce a Soviet atom bomb. In charge of the project was Lavrentii Beria, who was given full authority to secure the resources he needed to complete research and development in the shortest time possible.[127]

While impressed by the bomb, Stalin did not underrate the impact of Soviet military intervention in bringing the Far Eastern war to a swift conclusion. On 10 August he told Soong that Japan had announced it was capitulating. 'Japan is preparing to capitulate,' said Stalin, 'as a result of the united effort of all the allies . . . Japan wants to capitulate with conditions but for us it is necessary that it capitulates unconditionally.'[128] Later, in a different context, Stalin told Gomulka, the Polish communist leader, 'not atomic bombs, but armies decide about the war'.[129] This assessment by Stalin has been endorsed by many historians and the current consensus is that the atomic bombs alone did not shock the Japanese into a speedy surrender. The added shock of the Soviet attack was as important, and perhaps more so. The point about the Soviet attack was that it was not only a massive military blow, it also blew away the last Japanese hope for a negotiated end to hostilities in which they could avoid the shame of unconditional surrender.[130]

The Manchurian campaign in many ways represented the peak of Soviet operational art during the Second World War. In an operation that combined armour, infantry, close air support and airborne drops, the Red Army's task was to attack across a 5,000-kilometre-wide border, penetrate to a depth of 300 to 800 kilometres and conduct operations in a territory of 1.5 million square kilometres. In the case of Malinovskii's Transbaikal Front that meant crossing arid desert, scaling high mountains and bridging formidable rivers. By the time Japan announced its unconditional surrender on 14 August the Soviets had penetrated to the centre of Manchuria and split the Kwantung Army into several pieces. Fighting carried on for several days, both in Manchuria and on Sakhalin and the Kuril Islands, where combat continued until the end of August. For once Soviet losses were relatively light – 36,500 casualties, including 12,000 dead. Japanese casualties were much higher, with as many as 80,000 killed and half a million taken prisoner.

From a political point of view the most interesting episode of the Soviet war in the Far East is Stalin's attempt to secure occupation rights in the northern half of the Japanese home island of Hokkaido.[131] On 16 August Stalin wrote to Truman suggesting the Japanese surrender in northern Hokkaido should be accepted by the Red Army and saying that this would be an act of 'special importance to Russian public opinion. As is known, in 1919–1921 the Japanese occupied the whole of the Soviet Far East. Russian public opinion would be gravely offended if the Russian troops had no occupation area in any part of the territory of Japan proper.' Whilst the Americans had previously considered offering the Soviets an occupation zone in Japan, they had no intention of doing so now. On 18 August Truman wrote back to Stalin to say that the United States would accept the Japanese surrender on all the main home islands, including Hokkaido. Adding insult to injury, Truman asked

Stalin to concede US air and naval bases in the Kurils. Stalin did not reply for four days, and during this time he had to make a critical decision: whether or not to rescind orders for a Soviet invasion of Hokkaido. On 22 August Stalin replied to Truman, acquiescing in his refusal of the Soviet request to occupy northern Hokkaido but saying that 'I and my colleagues had not anticipated that such would be your reply'. Stalin then rejected Truman's request for bases in the Kurils, complaining that it was a kind of demand 'laid either before a vanquished country or before an allied country that is unable to defend a particular part of its territory . . . I must tell you in all frankness that neither I nor my colleagues understand the circumstances in which this claim on the Soviet Union could have been conceived.' In response to this last missive, Truman beat a rapid retreat, saying that he only wanted landing rights on one of the Kurils in order to facilitate the American occupation of Japan. This seemed to satisfy Stalin, who agreed to Truman's request and said that he was 'glad that the misunderstandings that had crept into our correspondence have been dispelled'. [132]

Although he was stung by Truman's refusal to concede to the Soviet Union occupation rights in Japan, Stalin evidently decided to back away from confrontation with the US over Hokkaido. One reason might have been that operations on Sakhalin and the Kurils had shown that the Japanese could put up a hard fight and might do so again to stop the Red Flag being planted on Hokkaido. But the priority of maintaining good relations with the United States is likely to have been more important in Stalin's calculation. Stalin still wanted a peacetime Grand Alliance and in that context hoped it would be possible to negotiate a substantial Soviet role in the occupation of postwar Japan.

On 2 September 1945 Japan formally surrendered and Stalin cabled his congratulations to Truman on the brilliant victory of the United States and its people. That same day Stalin addressed his own people and sought to justify to them Soviet involvement in the Far Eastern war. Japan, Stalin told them, had not only been a member of an aggressive fascist bloc but had attacked Russia a number of times in the past and sought to keep the country bottled up in the Far East. Now that South Sakhalin and the Kurils had been recovered, the Soviet Union had direct access to the Pacific and possession of the bases necessary to contain future Japanese aggression. 'We the people of the old generation have waited forty years for this day,' said Stalin.[133]

Notwithstanding Stalin's dual appeal to patriotic sentiment and strategic self-interest, his 'broadcast that day left people with a strangely unsatisfactory impression', recalled Alexander Werth.[134] There were firework displays and parades but none of the popular enthusiasm and relief that had greeted victory in Europe. The Soviet war with Japan was Stalin's war, not that of the

Soviet people, who would probably have preferred to let events in the Far East run their course and let the western allies bear the burden and the casualties for a change. During the Great Patriotic War the Soviet people had given their all for victory and suffered an unprecedented national trauma. Their expectations of what the peace would bring were as much a part of the complex political reality facing Stalin in the postwar period as the diplomatic manoeuvres and ideological tensions of the emerging cold war with the west.

10

The Lost Peace
Stalin and the Origins of the Cold War

As the Second World War drew to a close Stalin foresaw a great future for the Grand Alliance. The success of Potsdam augured well for the first meeting of the Council of Foreign Ministers (CFM), the body established by the Big Three to negotiate the postwar peace settlement. Its first task was to draw up peace treaties for the minor Axis states – Bulgaria, Finland, Hungary, Italy and Romania. The Soviets prepared for the CFM confident that the tripartite spirit of co-operation displayed at Yalta and Potsdam would be sustained and that negotiations with their Grand Alliance partners would result in further diplomatic gains for the USSR.[1]

But already in summer 1945 there were ominous signs of the tensions and disputes that would eventually tear the Grand Alliance apart. The most contentious issue was diplomatic recognition of the pro-Soviet governments of Bulgaria and Romania. Stalin began lobbying Churchill and Truman for western recognition of Bulgaria and Romania in May 1945 but to no avail.[2] London and Washington considered the communist-dominated Bulgarian and Romanian coalition governments as neither democratic nor favourable to western interests. At Potsdam the problem was glossed over by an Anglo-American promise to consider recognition as part of a package leading to membership of the United Nations for all the minor Axis states. After Potsdam, however, there was a sharp divergence of Soviet and western policies.[3] On 8 August 1945 Moscow recognised the Romanian government headed by Petru Groza and a few days latter announced that it would recognise the Bulgarian regime after the elections were held there on 26 August. The Anglo-Americans responded by making it clear that they would not recognise the Groza government until free elections had been held. This prompted the Romanian King Michael to ask for Groza's resignation on the grounds that the country would not be able to negotiate a peace treaty with the allied powers until it had a recognised democratic regime. With strong support from Moscow, Groza refused the king's repeated requests that he resign. Stalin was planning a military alliance with Romania and was determined to keep a firm grip on the country. In Bulgaria events took a somewhat different course when British and American demands for postponement of the elections were combined with threats from the opposition to boycott them. Moscow buckled under this dual pressure and on 25 August agreed to postpone the elections. The signs are that this decision was taken on the hoof and caught even the Bulgarian communists by surprise.[4] In his diary on 24 August Dimitrov described the request from the Bulgarian Foreign Minister to postpone the elections as 'outrageous', 'scandalous' and 'capitulationist'.[5] A few days later Stalin explained to a Bulgarian communist delegation that the decision to postpone the elections was a minor concession and that the important thing was to stand firm in resisting demands for changes in the composition of the government. Stalin then proceeded to lecture the Bulgarians on the need to devise an electoral system that would facilitate the existence of an independent opposition and insisted that they should work to normalise relations with the British and Americans.[6]

In this conversation Stalin seemed unperturbed by developments in Bulgaria and Romania but he must have been more than a little peeved at Anglo-American interference in his sphere of influence. It certainly seems to have coloured his perception of events at the CFM, which opened in London on 11 September 1945. The conference began in a friendly spirit but soon ran into problems. An early point of contention was Soviet support for Tito in the Italian–Yugoslav conflict over the Trieste area – an ethno-territorial dispute that had led in May 1945 to a military confrontation between Tito's partisans and western allied forces rushing to occupy the area.[7] Then there was the western refusal of the Soviet demand for the trusteeship of the former Italian colony of Tripolitania (western Libya). Molotov was under strict instructions from Stalin to obtain this concession and at the plenary session on 15 September he made an impassioned plea:

The Soviet Government considered the future of Tripolitania as of primary importance to the Soviet people and they must press their request to assume the trusteeship of that territory. The Soviet government claimed the right to active participation in the disposal of the Italian colonies because Italy had attacked, and had inflicted enormous damage upon, the Soviet Union ... The territory of the Soviet Union was vast, stretching from the extreme east far into the west. It had a sea outlet in the north; it must also have use of ports in the south, especially since it now had the right to use Darien and Port Arthur in the Far East ... Britain should not hold a monopoly of communications in the Mediterranean. Russia was anxious to have bases in the Mediterranean for her merchant fleet. World trade would develop and the Soviet Union wished to share in it ... the Soviet Government possessed wide experience in establishing friendly relations between various nationalities and was anxious to use that experience in Tripolitania. They would not propose to introduce the Soviet system in Tripolitania. They would take steps to promote a system of democratic government.[8]

As far as the Soviets were concerned they had been promised a share of Italy's colonies by the Americans at the San Francisco conference in June 1945 and all that had to be negotiated were the practicalities. But there was no sign at the CFM that either the Americans or the British were prepared to concede to Soviet control Tripolitania or any other Italian colony. When it came to Bulgaria and Romania, the Anglo-Americans were even more obdurate, making it clear that there would be no recognition of the two governments before free and fair elections conducted under the scrutiny of western observers. In their pre-conference preparations the Soviets had anticipated this problem and resolved to pursue two tactics: first, to raise the situation in Greece, a country under British control that was plunging into civil war as communist-led partisans clashed with the monarchists and conservatives backed by London; and, second, to link the signature of a peace treaty with Italy with the simultaneous conclusion of peace treaties with Bulgaria, Finland, Hungary and Romania – which would require western diplomatic recognition of those states. The Soviet calculation was that the Anglo-American desire to finalise the peace treaty with their Italian ally would encourage them to compromise in relation to Bulgaria and Romania. If that proved not to be the case Stalin was prepared to face the collapse of the multilateral approach to the negotiation of peace treaties with the minor Axis states. 'It might happen that the Allies could sign a peace treaty with Italy without us,' Stalin wrote to Molotov in London. 'So what? Then we have a precedent. We would get the possibility in our turn to reach a peace treaty with our satellites without the Allies. If such a development would mean that the current session of the Council of Ministers winds up without taking decisions on major issues, we should not be afraid of such an outcome either.'[9]

Stalin's speculation that the CFM might fail to produce any results turned into a self-fulfilling prophecy when he decreed an abrupt change of negotiating tactics on 21 September. Stalin felt that Molotov had been too concessionary in the negotiations, particularly on the procedural issue of who had the right to participate in CFM discussions. When the CFM was established at Potsdam it was envisaged as primarily a tripartite body that would also involve the Chinese and French foreign ministers in discussion of issues that directly concerned them. For example, France had been at war with Italy and so would have the right to be involved in the Italian peace treaty negotiations but had no such rights in relation to Bulgaria and Romania. However, at the first session of the CFM, Molotov, acting in a co-operative spirit, agreed that the French and Chinese could participate in all the CFM's discussions.[10] As might be expected, the Chinese and particularly the French took an active part in the council's deliberations, generally lining up with the British and the Americans, much to Stalin and Molotov's annoyance. Stalin instructed Molotov to withdraw his consent for Chinese and French participation in all CFM discussions and to return to the Potsdam formula of mainly tripartite negotiations.[11]

On 22 September Stalin's decision was relayed by Molotov to Ernest Bevin, the British Foreign Secretary, and James F. Byrnes, the American Secretary of State.[12] Molotov was quite explicit that he was acting on Stalin's instructions but the British and Americans decided to appeal directly to the Soviet dictator over the foreign commissar's head. Both Truman and Attlee cabled Stalin an appeal to break the log jam. But Stalin insisted the Potsdam decision on the organisation of the CFM remained in force. 'I think we shall deprecate the Berlin Conference decisions if we for a single moment grant the Council of Foreign Ministers the right to revoke them,' Stalin told Attlee.[13] Since the British and Americans were unwilling to revert to the Potsdam formula the CFM meeting was effectively over, although discussions continued for several days on issues that the French and Chinese were entitled to comment on.

Behind Stalin's obstructionist tactics was his deep dissatisfaction with the western refusal to recognise his client regimes in Bulgaria and Romania, all the more annoying since he was sticking to the promise he had made to Churchill in October 1944 not to interfere in Greek affairs. At the CFM the Soviets tabled a mild resolution of protest at events in Greece, saying that they could not 'accept any moral responsibility whatsoever for the political situation' in the country,[14] but generally they maintained a hands-off approach and expected the same of the British and Americans in relation to Eastern Europe. 'Why does the American government,' an exasperated Molotov asked Byrnes, 'only want to reform the government in Romania before elections and not in Greece? It seems that the United States does not want to interfere with the English in Greece, but it does with the Russians in Romania.'[15]

Actually, Bevin and Byrnes were prepared to allow the Soviets quite a lot of latitude in Eastern Europe but they were not prepared to accept the complete exclusion of western influence from Bulgaria and Romania. From their point of view what defined a great power was its general geopolitical interests and rights, not simply the exercise of power in its own particular sphere.[16] When it suited him this was precisely the great power standard that Stalin himself applied, a case in point being his attitude to the Far Eastern peace settlement.

The USSR had entered the Far Eastern war in August 1945 in return for a number of territorial concessions but Stalin also expected to share in the postwar occupation of Japan. On 21 August the United States established a Far Eastern Advisory Commission (FEAC) to assist the American occupation of Japan. The Soviets accepted an invitation to join the FEAC but wanted to see the establishment of an Allied Control Council (ACC) for Japan along the lines of those that existed in Europe. At the CFM the Soviets tabled a motion calling for the immediate creation of an ACC for Japan.[17] Although the resolution envisaged an ACC with wide-ranging powers (similar to those exercised by its counterpart in Germany), Stalin's instructions to the Soviet delegation indicated that he was prepared to accept an Italian-type occupation regime in which the role of the council would be restricted to advising the American Commander-in-Chief in Japan, General Douglas MacArthur. Similarly, while the resolution called for a Soviet role in the garrisoning of Tokyo Stalin did not really expect such a concession to be granted by the Americans.[18]

Although Stalin's aims in relation to the postwar occupation of Japan were more symbolic than substantive, he accorded them a high priority. This was evident in his response to a proposal by Byrnes for a 25-year pact on the disarmament and demilitarisation of Germany. Molotov was interested in Byrnes's proposal,[19] but Stalin's response was negative. The aim of the Byrnes proposal, Stalin wrote to Molotov, was 'first, *to divert our attention from the Far East*, where America assumes a role of tomorrow's friend of Japan, and to create thereby a perception that everything is fine there; second, to receive from the USSR a formal sanction for the US playing the same role in European affairs as the USSR, so that the US may hereafter, in league with England, take the future of Europe into their hands; third, to devalue the treaties of alliance that the USSR has already reached with European states; fourth, to pull out the rug from under any future treaties of alliance between the USSR and Romania, Finland, etc.'[20] Despite this damning litany Stalin did not reject the Byrnes proposal outright but instructed Molotov to propose the simultaneous conclusion of an anti-Japanese pact between the Soviet Union and the United States as a precondition for an anti-German treaty.

One of the themes running through the CFM discussions was the Soviet belief that its entitlements as a great power and as the major victor of the Second World War were being denied or obstructed by Britain and the United States. The sense of indignation this provoked was summed up by Molotov in a statement to Bevin on 23 September 1945:

> Hitler had looked upon the USSR as an inferior country, as no more than a geographical conception. The Russians took a different view. They thought themselves as good as anyone else. They did not wish to be regarded as an

inferior race. He would ask the Secretary of State to remember that our relations with the Soviet Union must be based upon the principle of equality. Things seemed to him like this: there was the war. During the war we had argued but we had managed to come to terms, while the Soviet Union was suffering immense losses. At that time the Soviet Union was needed. But when the war was over His Majesty's Government had seemed to change their attitude. Was that because we no longer needed the Soviet Union? If this were so it was obvious that such a policy, far from bringing us together, would separate us and end in serious trouble.[21]

Stalin's particular bugbear was that the Soviet contribution to the war in the Far East was not sufficiently recognised by the United States. 'The Soviet Government had its self-respect as a sovereign state,' he told Ambassador Harriman at a meeting on 25 October. 'No decisions made by MacArthur were being transmitted to it. In point of fact the Soviet Union had become an American satellite in the Pacific. This was a role it could not accept. It was not being treated as an Ally. The Soviet Union would not be a satellite of the United States in the Far East or elsewhere.'[22]

The CFM talks finally collapsed and the conference closed without agreement on 2 October. In his press conference Molotov tried to put as positive a spin as possible on the failure of the conference. No agreements had been reached but much good work had been done, he said. Yes, there had been a procedural dispute but it could be resolved by returning to the Potsdam decision that had established the CFM. In conclusion Molotov stated, 'the Soviet Union has emerged a victor from the last World War and occupies a fitting place in international relations. This is the result of the enormous efforts which were exerted by the Red Army and the whole Soviet people . . . It is also the result of the fact that in those years the Soviet Union and the Western Allies marched side by side and collaborated successfully. The Soviet delegation looks ahead confidently and hopes that all of us will strive to consolidate the collaboration of the Allies.'[23] After his return to Moscow, Molotov exchanged public messages with Bevin, thanking him for British hospitality in London and expressing the hope that Anglo-Soviet co-operation would continue, recent difficulties notwithstanding.[24] Privately, however, the Soviets were quite disturbed by the experience of the CFM. An internal briefing drawn up by the Foreign Commissariat noted western efforts, aided by a hostile Anglo-American press, to undermine the decisions of Yalta and Potsdam. Truman's Democratic administration was castigated for allowing reactionary Republican elements to influence its foreign policy in an anti-Soviet direction, while the English Labourites were accused of being more conservative than the Conservatives in their defence of British imperial interests. The document concluded that the CFM had witnessed the 'failure of the first postwar diplomatic attack by American and English circles on the foreign policy gains made by the Soviet Union during the war. Further pressure on the USSR by the English and Americans is not excluded but we have every possibility of defending and consolidating the Soviet Union's foreign policy positions. We must display skilfulness, resourcefulness, steadfastness and persistence, as the interests of the USSR demand.'[25]

Stalin aired his disgruntlement about relations with his British and American allies in a conversation with Wladyslaw Gomulka, the Polish communist leader, on 14 November:

> Do not believe in divergences between the English and the Americans. They are closely connected to each other. Their intelligence conducts lively operations against us in all countries . . . everywhere their agents spread information that the war with us will break out any day now. I am completely assured that there will be no war, it is rubbish. They are not capable of waging war against us. Their armies have been disarmed by agitation for peace . . . Not atomic bombs but armies decide about the war. The goals of their intelligence activities are the following. First of all, they are trying to intimidate us and force us to yield in contentious issues concerning Japan, the Balkans and reparations. Secondly, [they want] to push us away from our allies – Poland, Romania, Yugoslavia and Bulgaria . . . Whether in thirty years or so they want to have another war is another issue. This would bring them great profit, particularly in the case of America, which is beyond the oceans and couldn't care less about the effects of war. Their policy of sparing Germany testifies to that. He who spares the aggressor wants another war.[26]

Balancing this private mood of hostility to the Anglo-Americans was the publicly expressed faith in the future of the Grand Alliance. When Molotov spoke at the 28th anniversary celebration of the Bolshevik Revolution on 6 November he emphasised that while the failure of the CFM was worrying, in the past there had been differences in the Anglo-American-Soviet coalition but these had been overcome.[27] Even Stalin had indicated to Gomulka that there would be a Soviet–American agreement and when at the end of November Byrnes proposed a tripartite meeting to iron out the problems that had cropped up at the CFM, the Soviet leader accepted with alacrity. The conclusion Stalin drew from this development was that his firm negotiating tactics had won the day. On 9 December he wrote to his inner circle analysing foreign policy events since the CFM. Steadfastness, he told them, had won the battle over the involvement of France and China in tripartite discussions that did not concern them. A similar policy had won out in the Balkans, as shown by communist success in the postponed elections in Bulgaria, and in Yugoslavia which had also gone to the polls in November 1945. In dealing with the British and Americans, concluded Stalin, there could be no giving in to intimidation and a policy of firmness and tenacity should guide further negotiations with them.[28] It should be noted, however, that Stalin did not always display the steadfastness in negotiations with the west that he demanded of his lieutenants. When Harriman went to see him while he was on holiday on the Black Sea at the end of October Stalin displayed quite a lot of give and take in discussions with the ambassador about Japan and in relation to the procedural wrangling at the CFM.[29]

Stalin adopted a similar attitude when Bevin and Byrnes arrived in Moscow for the conference of the three foreign ministers. The conference took place from 16 to 26 December in the Spiridonovka Palace, the usual Moscow venue for such gatherings. Despite Stalin's homily to his comrades on the virtues of hardball negotiating tactics, the conference was very constructive and proved to be a breakthrough in Soviet–Western discussions of the postwar peace settlement. Indeed, the Soviets approached the conference as an opportunity to return to the days of the Big Three and were prepared to compromise on a number of issues. In relation to setting limits to France and China's participation in the CFM the Soviets got their way but agreed in turn to convene a broader peace conference to consider the draft peace treaties for the minor Axis states. The log jam on Bulgaria and Romania was broken by an agreement to broaden the two governments by the inclusion of opposition politicians. Soviet demands in relation to Japan were satisfied by the abolition of the FEAC and its replacement by a Far Eastern Commission and an ACC for Japan, although the country's occupation regime remained under American control.[30] Stalin contributed to proceedings by hosting the conference dinner and by meeting Bevin and Byrnes on two occasions each. Byrnes recalled, shortly after, that 'my talks with the Generalissimo [at dinner] that night, like those during the two earlier interviews, were marked by their encouraging combination of frankness and cordiality'.[31] At his meeting with Stalin on 24 December Byrnes took the opportunity to mention his proposal for a pact on the disarmament of Germany. Stalin replied that such a pact could be signed but there would have to be a similar agreement in relation to Japan.[32] At his meeting with Bevin that same day Stalin was keen to discuss a Soviet trusteeship for Tripolitania and complained that if the CFM had agreed to this demand 'Great Britain would have lost nothing because she already had plenty of bases all over the world, more even than the United States. Could not the interests of the Soviet Government also be taken into account?' Later in the conversation Stalin said that 'as he saw the situation, the United Kingdom had

India and her possessions in the Indian Ocean in her sphere of interest: the United States had China and Japan, but the Soviet [Union] had nothing'.[33]

In a message to Truman on 23 December Stalin expressed himself well satisfied with the progress of the conference and optimistic about future relations with the United States.[34] To his Bulgarian and Romanian communist allies Stalin insisted that he had conceded very little and that the Moscow agreements represented an opportunity to undermine the opposition. 'The main thing is to demoralise the opposition,' Stalin told a visiting Bulgarian governmental delegation on 7 January. 'The decisions of the Moscow conference on Romania and Bulgaria are already undermining the opposition in those two countries.'[35] On the other hand the Soviets did work to implement the conference's decisions on changes to the Bulgarian and Romanian governments in a way that would at least assuage Anglo-American sensibilities.[36] Molotov's overall assessment of the conference was that 'we managed to reach decisions on a number of important European and Far Eastern issues and to sustain development of the cooperation among the three countries that emerged during the war'.[37]

At the Moscow conference Stalin and the Soviets signalled their intention to revive the CFM and to negotiate the terms of the European peace settlement within the framework of the Grand Alliance. As far as Molotov was concerned his main task in the months ahead would be to negotiate the terms of the peace treaties with Bulgaria, Finland, Hungary, Italy and Romania. Progress was slow, tedious and not a little dispiriting for the foreign commissar. The CFM reconvened in Paris for three weeks in April–May 1946 for 18 sessions of negotiations and again in June–July for a further 24 meetings. Then came the Paris Peace Conference of July–October 1946, when the 21 states that had fought against the Axis in Europe met to consider the drafts of the peace treaties prepared by the CFM. Predictably, consensus proved impossible to achieve in Paris, with significant splits occurring between a Soviet-led bloc of countries and a western alliance. In November–December the CFM had to hold another six-week session in New York to negotiate the outstanding differences and it was not until February 1947 that the peace treaties with Bulgaria, Finland, Hungary, Italy and Romania were finally signed.[38]

Acting under strict instructions from Stalin, Molotov had adopted an intransigent negotiating stance, refusing to compromise on any issue considered vital to Soviet interests.[39] There were endless procedural wrangles as Molotov insisted that everything had to be agreed by unanimous resolution of the Big Three. Much of the debate was acrimonious and spilled over into the public domain, with intense media coverage of the Paris Peace Conference heightening the polarisation of differences. In terms of substance, a lot of the arguments concerned the peace treaty with Italy, a document that was three times longer than the other treaties. The Soviets wanted reparations, a fair share of war booty and a resolution of the Trieste territorial dispute that favoured Yugoslavia. Molotov also persisted with the demand for Soviet trusteeship of Tripolitania. Another important issue for Moscow was the withdrawal of Anglo-American military forces from Italy, a demand that formed part of a pattern of Soviet complaints in 1945–1946 about the establishment of a global chain of American military bases. In May 1946 Molotov complained bitterly to Byrnes:

> There is no corner of the world in which the USA cannot be seen. The US has air bases everywhere: in Iceland, Greece, Italy, Turkey, China, Indonesia and other places and an even greater number of air and naval bases in the Pacific Ocean. The US maintains its troops in Iceland despite the protests of the Icelandic government, also in China, while the USSR's troops have been withdrawn from China and other foreign territories. This is evidence of a real expansionism and expresses the striving of certain American circles towards an imperialist policy.[40]

Molotov made this statement to Byrnes on instruction from Stalin, who also tutored his foreign minister on the importance of symbolism. During the Paris Peace Conference there was a military parade which Molotov attended but then abruptly left when he found himself seated in the second row among the representatives of small countries. 'You behaved absolutely correctly,' Stalin told him. 'The dignity of the Soviet Union must be defended not only in big matters, but also in minutiae.' As the Russian historian Vladimir Pechatnov commented, this incident was 'a vivid example of how zealously Stalin defended and promoted the newly-won image of the Soviet Union as a great power'.[41]

Stalin thought Molotov did well in the CFM negotiations and commended him for his performance at the Paris Peace Conference. When the peace treaties were signed they were welcomed by the Soviet press but presented as the result of a long struggle with reactionary forces in Britain and the United States striving to undermine the postwar democratic peace.[42] The idea that reactionary forces were on the rise in the west had been a developing theme of Soviet public and internal discourse since the failure of the London CFM. This trend in Soviet analysis was boosted by Stalin's public riposte to Churchill's 'Iron Curtain' speech of March 1946. Stalin linked Churchill's speech to the growth of anti-Soviet forces in the west and to the threat of a new war. This theme was developed in a document of September 1946 drawn up by N.V. Novikov, the Soviet ambassador to the United States (his predecessor,

Gromyko, had been posted to the United Nations). Novikov was a member of the Soviet delegation to the Paris Peace Conference and Molotov asked him to compile a broad survey of the main trends in American foreign policy. Novikov's main contention was that under the influence of reactionary forces the United States was striving for world supremacy politically, economically and militarily. Roosevelt's policy of Big Three co-operation had been abandoned, said Novikov, and the Americans were now seeking to undermine the position of the Soviet Union because it was the main obstacle to their supremacist plans. Within the United States a vicious anti-Soviet campaign was being conducted with a view to a possible war against the USSR.[43]

Novikov's document has often been compared with a much more famous dispatch of February 1946 penned by George Kennan, the American chargé d'affaires in Moscow. The fame of what would otherwise have been an obscure diplomatic document stemmed from its publication in July 1947 in the influential American journal *Foreign Affairs* under the title 'The Sources of Soviet Conduct' and its attribution to the author 'X'. In a mirror-image of Novikov's analysis Kennan painted a picture of a messianic, expansionist Soviet state that could only be contained by the adroit deployment of countervailing power.[44] Kennan's analysis is widely credited with setting the cold war course of American foreign policy in 1946–1947. Novikov's document had no such impact on the Soviet side for the simple reason that there was nothing original about it; all its different elements could be found in the Soviet press and in other confidential briefings produced for the Soviet leadership around the same time. What distinguished Novikov's document was its relentless pessimism about the future of Soviet–American relations, which reflected not just the author's views but the low point the CFM negotiations had reached after months of inconclusive wrangling at the Paris Peace Conference. However, by the time Molotov arrived in New York in November 1946 for the next CFM session the atmosphere had improved somewhat and he had some quite friendly chats with Truman and Byrnes, encouraged perhaps by the pilgrimage he made to Roosevelt's house at Hyde Park. In his talk with Truman, Molotov harked back to the businesslike atmosphere of Yalta and Potsdam that had produced such good results in wartime negotiations.[45] During the CFM negotiations in New York Stalin instructed Molotov to make a deal: 'I advise you to make all possible concessions to Byrnes so that we can finally get the peace treaties over with.'[46]

Kennan's anonymously published article did not use the term 'cold war' but the journalist Walter Lippmann wrote a series of newspaper pieces in response to it that were later published in booklet form under the title *The Cold War*. It was Lippmann's publication that popularised the concept of cold war – shorthand for the growing tensions in postwar Soviet–Western relations which, said Lippmann, were the result of the expansion of Stalin's military power rather than his ideological impulses.[47]

War Scares of 1946

Despite its reputation as the first declaration of the cold war Churchill's 'Iron Curtain' speech in Fulton, Missouri on 5 March 1946 did not use the term and it was by no means uniformly hostile to the Soviet Union. Churchill's lecture was actually entitled 'The Sinews of Peace' and he spoke of the life of the Anglo-Soviet treaty of alliance of 1942 being extended from 20 to 50 years (a proposal Bevin had put to Stalin in December 1945). 'We aim at nothing but mutual assistance and collaboration with Russia,' said Churchill. Later Churchill expressed 'strong admiration and regard for the valiant Russian people and for my wartime comrade, Marshal Stalin. There is deep sympathy and goodwill in Britain . . . towards the people of all the Russias and a resolve to persevere through many differences and rebuffs in establishing lasting friendships. We understand the Russian need to be secure on her western frontiers by the removal of all possibility of German aggression. We welcome Russia to her rightful place among the leading nations of the world. We welcome her flag upon the seas.' But the section of the speech that captured the headlines – both contemporary and historical – was the following:

> From Stettin in the Baltic to Trieste in the Adriatic an *iron curtain* has descended across the Continent. Behind that line lie all the capitals of the ancient states of Central and Eastern Europe. Warsaw, Berlin, Prague, Vienna, Budapest, Belgrade, Bucharest and Sofia, all these famous cities . . . lie in what I must call the Soviet sphere, and all are subject in one form or another, not only to Soviet influence, but to a very high and, in some cases, increasing measure of control from Moscow . . . The Communist parties . . . have been raised to pre-eminence and power far beyond their numbers and are seeking everywhere to obtain totalitarian control.

Churchill went on to talk about the communist threat in Western Europe and to highlight the anxieties provoked by Soviet policies in relation to Turkey, Iran and the Far East. The moral that Churchill drew from this was that the western democracies had to stick together and take a strong stand in defence of their principles. The Russians had no respect for weakness, Churchill told his audience, and he drew a parallel with the appeasement that had allowed Hitler to unleash war. To prevent that happening again 'a good understanding' had to be reached with Russia.[48]

Churchill was no longer British Prime Minister but his high status as a western political leader was beyond question. Indeed, the former PM was invited to Fulton by Truman (Missouri was his home state) and the American President shared the platform with him at Westminster College, where Churchill delivered the speech and was awarded an honorary degree. The first Soviet reply came in the form of a hostile editorial in *Pravda* on 11 March and an equally hostile article the next day in *Izvestiya*, penned by Evgenii Tarle, a leading Soviet historian. Both papers carried long summaries and extracts from Churchill's speech, including the offending remarks about the 'Iron Curtain' – a concept, as Tarle pointed out, that Goebbels had used during the war to characterise the Red Army's liberation of Eastern Europe from German occupation.[49] On 14 March Stalin entered the fray with the publication of a long 'interview' with *Pravda*. As in all such texts, the questions as well as the answers were carefully composed by the Soviet dictator himself. Churchill, according to Stalin, was trying to provoke a new war and was an advocate of English-speaking domination of the world. Stalin did not mention the 'Iron Curtain' but frankly asserted the USSR's right to friendly regimes in Eastern Europe, given the role those states had previously played in providing a platform for German aggression against the Soviet Union. In conclusion Stalin alluded to Churchill's role in the anti-Bolshevik coalition that had intervened in the Russian civil war many years before and promised that if 'Churchill and his friends' succeeded in organising a 'new march against "Eastern Europe"' they 'will be beaten again as they were beaten in the past'.[50]

In the midst of the uproar over the Fulton speech, Alexander Werth, the *Sunday Times* correspondent in Moscow, returned to Russia after a trip to Finland and 'found people badly rattled by the talk about "the next war"'.[51] As Werth noted, the Fulton episode caused genuine alarm in the Soviet Union and was an important psychological turning point in the drift to cold war. Adding to the intensity of the crisis atmosphere were a series of other Soviet–Western confrontations in 1946, among which were the crisis over the withdrawal of Soviet troops from Iran in the spring and the Soviet–Turkish confrontation over the Black Sea Straits in the summer.

The crisis over Iran arose from the British-Soviet occupation of the country during the Second World War.[52] British and Soviet forces had entered the country in August 1941 with the aim of overthrowing German influence on the Iranian government, protecting oil supplies, and securing supply routes to the USSR. In a treaty with Iran signed in January 1942 the British and the Soviets agreed to withdraw their forces six months after the end of the war with Germany. Later, at Moscow's behest, the agreement was reinterpreted to refer to the end of the war with Japan, which meant a withdrawal deadline of 2 March 1946. There is no evidence that Stalin intended anything other than withdrawal of Soviet forces but two complicating factors caused a delay in full implementation of the agreement. The first was Moscow's desire to sign an agreement with Tehran on the exploitation of oilfields in northern Iran. The second was the emergence in 1945 of a communist-led nationalist movement in Azerbaijani Iran demanding autonomy and the development of links with their compatriots in the Soviet Republic of Azerbaijan. As well as appealing to Stalin's predisposition to support ethnic autonomy and unity when it suited him, the independence movement promised the possibility of an extension of Soviet political influence within Iran. As the March 1946 deadline approached, Moscow announced that because of the unstable situation in parts of Iran they would make only a partial withdrawal of their forces. In private the Soviets continued efforts to negotiate an oil deal with the Iranians. In the meantime, however, the Iranians had brought the matter of Soviet troop withdrawal before the United Nations and did so again in March 1946 after the agreed deadline had passed. Moscow's response was to order Gromyko to walk out of the UN discussions on the grounds that it was a matter for bilateral negotiation between the Soviet Union and Iran. In fact, by early April the outstanding issues had been settled by Moscow and Tehran and all Soviet troops were withdrawn by early May. The Soviets got their oil concessions, although the Iranians later reneged on the deal when the Tehran parliament refused to ratify it. In truth, the Iranian affair was a minor crisis, blown out of all proportion by contemporary press coverage and again by western cold war historians seeking evidence of Soviet postwar expansionism.

In May 1946 Stalin wrote a revealing letter to the communist leader of the Azerbaijani autonomy movement explaining why he felt he had to withdraw Soviet troops when he did:

> We could no longer keep them in Iran, mainly because the presence of Soviet troops in Iran undercut the foundations of our liberationist policies in Europe and Asia. The British and Americans said to us that if Soviet troops could stay in Iran, then why could not British troops stay in Egypt, Syria, Indonesia, Greece, and also the American troops – in China, Iceland, in Denmark. Therefore we decided to withdraw troops from Iran and China in order to seize this tool from the hands of the British and Americans, to unleash the liberation movement in the colonies and thereby render our liberationist policy more justified and efficient. You as a revolutionary will certainly understand that we could not have done otherwise.[53]

Stalin's combination of geopolitical calculation and ideological aspiration was typical of his thinking in this period, although it was not often that the two elements were so neatly brought together in a single statement.

There was an ethno-nationalist component to the Soviet–Turkish crisis as well, but the main cause was Stalin's long-standing strategic demand for control of the Black Sea Straits. Soviet dissatisfaction with the 1936 Montreux Convention, which gave Turkey full control of the Straits, had surfaced a number of times during the war and Stalin was fond of the parallel with American and British control of the Panama and Suez canals. In summer 1945 the Soviets began to exert pressure on Turkey, including demanding the return of the districts of Kars and Ardahan to Armenia and Georgia. When the matter was raised at the London CFM, Molotov pointed out to Bevin that during the First World War Britain had been prepared to concede not just the straits to Russian control but Constantinople itself.[54] In December 1945 Stalin reiterated the Soviet demands to Bevin but said that 'all talk of war against Turkey was rubbish'.[55] In April 1946 Stalin told the new US ambassador to Moscow, Walter Bedell Smith: 'I have assured President Truman and have stated publicly that the Soviet Union has no intention of attacking Turkey . . . but Turkey is weak, and the Soviet Union is very conscious of the danger of foreign control of the Straits, which Turkey is not strong enough to protect. The Turkish Government is unfriendly to us. That is why the Soviet Union has demanded a base in the Dardanelles. It is a matter of our own security.'[56]

The 'crisis' over the straits began on 7 August 1946 when the USSR sent the Turkish government a diplomatic note on revision of the Montreux Convention. Following a critique of Turkey's operation of the straits regime during the war, the note proposed that the Straits should: (1) always be open to merchant shipping; (2) always be open to the warships of Black Sea powers; (3) be closed to the warships of non-Black Sea powers, except in special circumstances; (4) be under the control of Turkey and other Black Sea powers; and (5) be jointly defended by the Soviet Union and Turkey. Significantly, there was no mention in the note of the demand for the return of Kars and Ardahan.[57]

The August diplomatic note was presented as building on existing American, British and Soviet proposals for the revision of Montreux – a point emphasised in a moderate and conciliatory *Izvestiya* article on the subject.[58] Indeed, the first three points of the Soviet proposal bore a close resemblance to an American diplomatic note on the revision of Montreux that had been issued in November 1945.[59] On 19 August 1946, however, the United States challenged Moscow's assertion that the straits regime was an exclusive concern of Black Sea powers and called for a multilateral conference to revise Montreux. The British conveyed a similar view to Moscow two days later. On 22 August Turkey replied to Moscow, echoing the British and American responses and stating in addition that the Soviet demand for joint defence of the straits was incompatible with the maintenance of Turkish sovereignty and security.[60] On 24 September Moscow responded with a memorandum that reiterated the special rights of Black Sea powers in relation to the straits and denied that the Soviet proposals threatened or undermined Turkish sovereignty or security.[61] On 9 October the British and Americans reiterated their position and on 18 October the Turks restated theirs.[62] A classic impasse had been reached. The only diplomatic way forward was a multilateral conference on Montreux, but that was unacceptable to Moscow. Both publicly and privately the Soviet view was, and remained, that the straits regime was primarily a matter for Black Sea powers and that any multilateral conference should be preceded by direct negotiations between the USSR and Turkey.[63]

There has been some speculation on how far Stalin was prepared to go to get his way in the Black Sea, with some suggesting that only strong western support for Turkey averted a Soviet attack. The idea that Stalin was prepared to go to war with Turkey over this issue seems far-fetched, although it is quite possible that he rattled a few sabres on the Soviet–Turkish border as part of his pressure tactics on Ankara.[64] In the event, Moscow never replied to the final Turkish note and the diplomatic 'crisis' over the straits petered out.

What the Iranian and Turkish incidents showed was that Stalin was prepared to push hard for strategic gains but not at the expense of a break in relations with Britain and the United States. Stalin was anxious to avert a split in the Grand Alliance, not provoke one through confrontations on the periphery. Soviet Black Sea bases were close to Stalin's Georgian heart and, as always, he accorded high priority to control of vital economic resources such as oil. But much more important to him was the overall situation in Europe and he continued to feel that negotiations within the Grand Alliance were the best way both to protect his sphere of influence in Eastern Europe and to avert the rise of a hostile anti-Soviet bloc in Western Europe. Apart from intemperate attacks on Churchill after Fulton the consistent message of Stalin's public statements was that tensions in east–west relations could be reduced, that problems within the Grand Alliance could be resolved by negotiation, and that peace and security could be preserved.

In March 1946 Stalin was asked about the 'war danger' by Eddie Gilmore of the Associated Press. He replied that neither nations nor their armies were striving for a new war; that was just provocative propaganda promoted by some political groups. In September 1946 Alexander Werth asked Stalin the same question and was told that the Soviet leader did not believe in the danger of a new war. In the same interview Stalin denied that the United States and Great Britain were engaged in the capitalist encirclement of the USSR and affirmed his faith in further possibilities of peaceful coexistence with the west. Werth also asked Stalin if he thought the American monopoly of the atomic bomb constituted a threat to peace: 'I do not believe the atomic bomb to be as serious a force as certain politicians are inclined to regard it. Atomic bombs are intended to intimidate the weak-nerved, but they cannot decide about the outcome of the war, since such bombs are by no means sufficient for this purpose.' In October it was the turn of Hugh Bailey of United Press to ask the questions. Asked if he agreed with a recent speech by Byrnes that said tensions were rising in Soviet–American relations, Stalin replied no. Asked if he thought the negotiations about the peace treaties would succeed, Stalin said he hoped so. On the war danger Stalin repeated his view that 'Churchill and his friends' were to blame for current fears and said their efforts to instigate a new war had to be exposed and restrained. All these responses by Stalin were in the form of written answers to written questions submitted by the journalists. In December 1946, however, Stalin granted a live interview to Elliott Roosevelt. Naturally, Roosevelt was interested to know if Stalin thought there had been a weakening of friendship and co-operation between the United States and the Soviet Union since his father's death. Stalin replied that while relations between the Soviet and American people continued to improve, some misunderstandings had arisen between the two governments. But Stalin did not think there would be a further deterioration in relations and ruled out a military conflict, for which there was no basis: 'I think the threat of a new war is unreal,' said Stalin.[65]

In April 1947 Stalin gave another personal interview, this time to Republican Senator Harold Stassen. Again, Stalin's mood was upbeat. He pointed out to Stassen that despite the differences in their economic systems the Soviet Union and the United States had co-operated during the war and there was no reason why they could not continue to do so in peacetime. In support of his belief in the possibility of the peaceful coexistence of the socialist and capitalist systems Stalin invoked Lenin's teachings. When Stassen pointed out that before the war Stalin had talked about 'capitalist encirclement' the Soviet leader replied that he had never denied the possibility of co-operation with other states, only spoken of the existence of actual threats from countries such as Germany. Each side supported its own social system, Stalin told Stassen, and which was the better would be decided by history. In the meantime both sides should stop sloganising and name-calling. He and Roosevelt had never called each other 'totalitarian' or 'monopoly capitalists'. 'I am not a propagandist,' said Stalin, 'I am a man of business.'[66] After a text was agreed by the two men the interview was published in *Pravda*, on 8 May – two years after the end of the war in Europe – and viewed in context it represented a determined effort by Stalin to return to the spirit of the Grand Alliance. By this time, however, a big cloud was hanging over Soviet–Western relations in the form of a famous speech by President Truman to the American Congress in March 1947.

The Truman Doctrine and the Marshall Plan

The President's speech later became known as the Truman Doctrine. Its ostensible purpose was to persuade Congress to vote financial aid for Greece and Turkey. Truman mentioned neither the Soviets nor the communists in his speech but there could be no doubt about the target of his comments:

> The peoples of a number of countries . . . have recently had totalitarian regimes forced upon them . . . The Government of the United States has made frequent protests against coercion and intimidation . . . At the present moment in world history nearly every nation must choose between alternative ways of life . . . One way of life is based on the will of the majority, and is distinguished by free institutions, representative government, free elections, guarantees of individual liberty, freedom of speech and religion and freedom from political oppression. The second way of life is based on the will of a minority forcibly imposed upon the majority. It relies upon terror and oppression, a controlled press and radio, fixed elections and the suppression of personal freedoms. *I believe it must be the policy of the United States to support free peoples who are resisting attempted subjugation by armed minorities or by outside pressures.* I believe we must assist free peoples to work out their own destinies in their own way.[67]

Truman's speech was even more provocative to the Soviets than Churchill's 'Iron Curtain' lecture. Unlike Churchill, Truman was in power, and was proposing to aid Greece, a regime battling a communist insurgency, and Turkey, a country in confrontation with the Soviet Union over the straits. Yet the Soviet response was surprisingly muted. On 14 March *Pravda* carried a Tass report of Truman's speech that concentrated on the proposal to aid Greece and Turkey rather than on the more general delineation of US foreign policy. The paper's editorial next day launched a strong attack on Truman, accusing him of using the defence of freedom as a cover for American expansionism. A week later *Novoe Vremya* (New Times) editorialised that Truman's speech had announced a foreign policy based on force and power.[68] But there was no riposte from Stalin himself. Perhaps he thought it unwise to engage in a direct polemic with a serving American President and, anyway, the Truman speech made no direct reference to the Soviet Union. More importantly, Stalin's attention was directed elsewhere. Two days before Truman's speech a meeting of the CFM began in Moscow. Having dealt with the minor Axis states, the council turned to the peace treaties for Germany and Austria. The CFM session lasted for six weeks and ended with few discernible results but publicly the Soviets evaluated its work very highly and refuted suggestions that no progress had been made.[69] In another sign of conciliation the Soviets used the conference to pursue a British suggestion to extend the Anglo-Soviet Treaty of Alliance of 1942 from 20 to 50 years' duration. This idea, raised by Bevin in December 1945, had been further discussed by Stalin and Field Marshal Bernard Montgomery when he visited Moscow in January 1947. As a sidebar to the CFM the Soviets presented the British delegation with a new draft of the Anglo-Soviet treaty.[70]

On 15 April Stalin met George Marshall, Byrnes's successor as American Secretary of State, and had a very friendly discussion about the CFM conference. Using an analogy that General Marshall, formerly US Chief of Staff, might appreciate, Stalin described the CFM session as like 'the first battle, a reconnaissance battle. When the partners have exhausted themselves then will come the possibilities of compromise. It is possible that the present session will not achieve any significant results. But don't despair. The results can be achieved at the next session. On all the main questions – democratisation, political organisation, economic unity and reparations – it is possible to achieve compromise. Only have patience and don't despair.'[71]

Stalin's conversations with Marshall and with Stassen took place within a few days of each other and indicate he was in an optimistic mood. The peace treaties with the minor Axis states had been completed in February and now progress was being made in relation to Germany and Austria. The peacetime Grand Alliance that Stalin desired had proved to be more problematic and elusive than he had hoped at the end of the war but two years later it was still intact, if a little tattered. Within a very short time, however, Stalin was to abandon active pursuit of *détente* with the west and embrace a cold war rhetoric and policy that was almost the mirror-image of the Truman Doctrine. The key event in precipitating this change in policy was the Soviet response to the Marshall Plan.[72]

The so-called 'Marshall Plan' was launched by the American Secretary of State in a speech at Harvard University on 5 June 1947.[73] Basically, Marshall proposed a large-scale American aid programme for war-torn Europe with the funds being distributed on a co-ordinated basis by the Europeans themselves. Marshall's proposal was taken up by Britain and France. The British and French foreign ministers met in Paris and on 19 June issued an invitation to the USSR to attend a tripartite conference there to discuss a co-ordinated European recovery programme backed by US aid.

The Soviet response to these developments was mixed. The initial response in the form of press articles was negative, with the Marshall Plan being linked to the Truman Doctrine as an instrument for American interference in European affairs.[74] On 21 June, however, the Politburo endorsed a positive reply to the Anglo-French proposal for a meeting to discuss the Marshall Plan.

Meanwhile, behind closed doors the Soviet leadership was considering the advice it was getting on the meaning of the plan. An early contribution came from Ambassador Novikov in Washington on 9 June who cabled that 'in this American proposal are the clear contours of a West European bloc directed against us'.[75] In a further dispatch on 24 June Novikov affirmed that 'a careful analysis of the Marshall Plan shows that in the end it amounts to the creation of a West European bloc as an instrument of US policy ... Instead of the previous uncoordinated actions directed towards the economic and political subjection of European countries to American capital and the formation of an anti-Soviet grouping, the Marshall Plan envisages more extensive action aimed at resolving the problem in a more effective way'.[76] Different policy advice came from another quarter. Eugene Varga, a prominent Soviet economist who had long operated on the fringes of Stalin's inner circle, was asked to provide an analysis of the Marshall Plan. Varga's view was that the plan was primarily a response to America's postwar economic problems, particularly a lack of demand for its exports in Europe. The purpose of the plan was to provide dollars to Europeans so that they could afford to buy American goods and services. Varga also pointed out the drawbacks of the Soviet Union not participating in the plan: it would facilitate American domination of Europe, strengthen the US hand in relation to the economic future of Germany, and allow reactionaries to blame the USSR if the plan failed.[77]

The implication of Varga's analysis was that it might suit the Americans to give loans and grants to the Soviet bloc countries. Moscow had long been hoping for a large-scale loan from the Americans to help Soviet postwar reconstruction[78] and the Marshall Plan could provide the framework to receive such funds. On the other hand, there were the political drawbacks highlighted by Novikov and others. Was the Marshall Plan a threat or an opportunity? Stalin's response to this conundrum was to keep an open mind and see what happened. The Soviet delegation to the talks with the British and French was instructed (a) to find out what American aid was on offer; (b) to block any move that threatened interference in the internal affairs of aid recipients; and (c) to make sure that discussion of the German question remained the prerogative of the CFM.[79]

The Anglo-Franco-Soviet conference on the Marshall Plan was held in Paris at the end of June and the beginning of July 1947.[80] Molotov arrived with a large party of technical advisers – a sign that Moscow was serious about the negotiations. In line with his brief Molotov made it clear that the Soviet Union was opposed to a programme co-ordinated by a central body; instead, each country should draw up a list of its needs which would be received by a series of committees and then transmitted to the Americans. The British and French insisted, however, on a highly co-ordinated programme which, they said, accorded with Marshall's own wishes. Negotiations quickly reached deadlock. On 2 July Molotov made his final statement to the conference:

> The question of American economic aid . . . has . . . served as a pretext for the British and French governments to insist on the creation of a new organisation standing above the European countries and intervening in the internal affairs of the countries of Europe . . . There are two roads to international cooperation. One is based on the development of political and economic relations between states with equal rights . . . another . . . is based on the dominating position of one or several strong Powers in relation to other countries, which thereby fall into the position of some kind of subordinated states, deprived of independence.

Following the collapse of the talks with the Soviets, the British and French issued an invitation to European states to a conference in Paris that would establish an organisation to supervise Marshall Aid. The Soviets responded to this initiative on 5 July by sending a note to European governments explaining their differences with the British and French.[81] That same day they sent a message to their communist allies in Eastern Europe informing them that for tactical reasons they were not against other states participating in the Anglo-French conference:

> Some countries friendly to the Soviet Union . . . are considering refusing participation in the conference, on the grounds that the USSR has decided not to participate. We think it would be better not to refuse participation in this conference but to send delegations to it, in order to show at the conference itself the unacceptability of the Anglo-French plan, not to allow the unanimous adoption of this plan and then withdraw from the meeting, taking with them as many delegates from other countries as possible.[82]

Two days later, however, Moscow changed its mind about this tactic and sent another message advising against participation since in some East European countries the 'friends' (i.e. the local communists) had declared against the conference. The problem was that Czechoslovakia – keen to obtain some Marshall money – had already declared that it would participate in the conference. Stalin himself took the lead in 'persuading' the Czechoslovaks to change their decision. At a meeting with a Czechoslovak government delegation on 9 July he explained that Marshall Plan credits were very uncertain and were being used as a pretext to form a western bloc and isolate the USSR. Czechoslovak participation in the forthcoming Paris conference was a matter of fundamental importance to the Soviet Union: 'If you go to Paris, you will show that you want to cooperate in an action aimed at isolating the Soviet Union. All the Slav states refused, even Albania was not afraid to refuse, and that is why we believe you should withdraw your decision.'[83] Needless to say, Czechoslovakia along with all the Soviet bloc states (and Finland, too) boycotted the Marshall Plan discussions.

Alongside the boycott the Soviets launched a major propaganda campaign against the Marshall Plan. In September 1947 Deputy Foreign Minister Andrei Vyshinskii denounced the Marshall Plan in a speech to the UN:

> The Marshall Plan constitutes in essence merely a variant of the Truman Doctrine . . . the implementation of the Marshall Plan will mean placing European countries under the economic and political control of the United States and direct interference in the internal affairs of those countries . . . this plan is an attempt to split Europe into two camps . . . to complete the formation of a bloc of several European countries hostile to the interests of the democratic countries of Eastern Europe and most particularly to the interests of the Soviet Union.[84]

For Stalin the Marshall Plan was the breaking point in postwar relations with the United States. It indicated that co operation with the Americans was no longer possible without putting in jeopardy the Soviet sphere of influence in Eastern Europe. The Marshall Plan and the Truman Doctrine foretold the formation of an anti-Soviet western bloc, one which Stalin sought to counter by consolidating the Soviet and communist position in Eastern Europe. Isolating the Soviet bloc from subversive outside influences now set Stalin's agenda for postwar Europe rather than the maintenance of the Grand Alliance.

Cominform and the Cold War

Stalin's new approach was unveiled at the founding conference of the Communist Information Buro (Cominform) in September 1947.[85] The idea of creating a successor to Comintern had been in the air for some time. The catalyst for action was not so much the Truman Doctrine and the Marshall Plan as Moscow's desire to exercise more direct control over European communist parties.[86] Of particular concern was the failure of the French and Italian communist parties to keep the Soviets informed about their expulsion from their national governing coalitions in May 1947.[87] This explains the peculiar composition of the Cominform, which consisted of the governing communist parties of Eastern Europe plus the French and Italian communists. Much of the Cominform's founding conference, a private meeting held in Poland, was devoted to criticism of the 'reformist politics' and 'parliamentary illusions' of the French and Italian communist parties. Leading this criticism was Edvard Kardelj, Tito's representative at the conference; the Yugoslavs had long been advocating a more militant, leftist line for the communist movement. The Yugoslav role in the foundation of the Cominform was reflected in the location of the organisation's headquarters in Belgrade.[88]

As well as directing the communist movement to adopt a leftist political strategy of opposition to capitalism and bourgeois institutions, the inaugural Cominform conference provided Stalin with an opportunity for a major pronouncement on foreign policy and international relations. His spokesman at the conference was A.A. Zhdanov, the former Leningrad party boss who was now Stalin's ideology chief. Throughout the summer Zhdanov worked on his speech, composing and amending many drafts following consultation with Stalin. The key moment in this process came when Zhdanov introduced into his draft the notion that the postwar world had split into 'two camps'.[89] Until now the Soviets had spoken of two trends or two lines in postwar world politics. For example, in his speech on the 29th anniversary of the Bolshevik Revolution in November 1946 Zhdanov had referred to the Paris Peace Conference as demonstrating 'two tendencies in postwar policy . . . One policy conducted by the Soviet Union is . . . to consolidate peace and prevent aggression . . . The other . . . opening the path for the forces of expansion and aggression'.[90] A year later at the Cominform conference Zhdanov propounded what became known as the 'two-camps doctrine':

> The further we are removed from the end of the war, the more clearly do the two basic orientations in postwar international politics stand out, corresponding to the division . . . into two basic camps: the imperialist and anti-democratic camp . . . and the anti-imperialist and democratic camp . . . The principal leading force in the imperialist camp is the USA . . . The fundamental aim of the imperialist camp is to strengthen imperialism, prepare a new imperialist war, fight against socialism and democracy, and give all-round support to reactionary and anti-democratic, pro-fascist regimes and movements. For the performance of these tasks the imperialist camp is ready to rely on reactionary and anti-democratic elements in all countries and to back former war-enemies against its own wartime allies. The anti-imperialist and anti-fascist forces constitute the other camp, with, as their mainstay, the USSR and the countries of new democracy . . . The aim of this camp is to fight against the threat of new wars and imperialist expansion, to consolidate democracy and to uproot what remains of fascism.[91]

Zhdanov's speech was a signal for the European communist movement to execute a sharp 'left turn' in its strategy and policy. In Western Europe communists abandoned the policy of national unity and participation in the postwar reconstruction of their countries. The reformist strategy that Stalin had advocated at the end of the Second World War was replaced by a rhetorical if not real return to the revolutionary perspective of the communist movement's early days.[92] In Eastern Europe the change in communist policy was equally radical and far-reaching. After the Cominform conference the pace of 'communisation' – the establishment of single-party communist control – began to accelerate. This process involved communist control of all the levers of government; state control of the press; the dissolution and repression of opposition parties; and an end of independent left-wing parties by forced socialist–communist party mergers (hence the curious fact that in the people's democracies the ruling communist parties were often called workers' and socialist parties). The extension of communist power provided the springboard for the 'sovietisation' of Eastern Europe. This meant imposing a Soviet model of socialism on the East European states: state-owned and controlled economies; centralised state planning; collectivised agriculture; and communist totalitarian intrusion into civil society. An element of 'Stalinisation' was also introduced in the form of personality cults of the local party leaders and mimicking of the political terrorism of the prewar Stalin regime in the form of purges, arrests, show trials and executions.

The communisation, sovietisation and Stalinisation of Eastern Europe did not take place all at once or according to a single timetable. Even before the Cominform conference the process of transforming people's democracy into full-blown communist regimes on the Soviet model was far advanced in several countries (Bulgaria, Romania and Yugoslavia), while in others (Hungary, Poland and East Germany) there were apparent distinct tendencies in that direction. The trend was least marked in Czechoslovakia, the one East European country with an established tradition of parliamentary democracy and where the communists and their socialist allies had won a majority in the 1946 elections. However, a government crisis in Prague in February 1948 resulted in the ousting from power of liberal and centre parties and the end of the Czechoslovak experiment in coalitionist people's democracy.[93]

Zhdanov's espousal of the two-camps doctrine signalled the final breakdown of the Grand Alliance and the onset of the cold war. Like Truman, Stalin had decided the time for diplomacy and compromise was over and the time had come to use his power resources to defend what the USSR had gained as a result of the war.

The political distance Stalin had travelled since the war was summed up in a discussion he had with the French communist leader Maurice Thorez in

November 1947. The last time Stalin had spoken to Thorez was in November 1944, just before the Frenchman returned home from wartime exile in Moscow. On that occasion Stalin had urged Thorez to co-operate with de Gaulle and to work for the economic rehabilitation of France and the reinforcement of the country's democracy. By contrast in November 1947 Stalin speculated whether the French communists could have seized power at the end of the war, although he agreed with Thorez that the presence of British and American forces in France made that impossible. Of course, the situation would have been different if the Red Army had reached Paris, Stalin told Thorez, who enthusiastically agreed. Stalin also wondered if the French communists had armaments and offered to supply them from Soviet sources, if necessary. 'One must have armaments and organisation if one does not want to become disarmed before the enemy. Communists can be attacked and then they should fight back. There can be all kinds of situations.'[94] This was more a case of Stalin playing the militant Bolshevik than a serious proposition, but it does reveal his sense of the sharpness of struggle he now thought he was involved in with the west. That struggle, it should be emphasised, was not conceived as a forthcoming armed conflict. As G.M. Malenkov, Stalin's second spokesman at the Cominform conference, said, the desire of the imperialists to unleash war was one thing, their ability to do it quite another.[95] Indeed for Stalin the purpose of waging the cold war was not only to protect Soviet interests but to inflict a political and ideological defeat on warmongers in the west. Even at the very height of cold war in the late 1940s and early 1950s – as Europe became polarised, as armed camps formed, as confrontations developed – Stalin continued to struggle for the lasting peace that he saw as his legacy.

11

Generalissimo at Home
The Domestic Context of
Stalin's Postwar Foreign Policy

'We won because we were led to victory by our great chief and genius of a commander, Marshal of the Soviet Union – Stalin!' declared Zhukov at the Victory Parade in Red Square on 24 June 1945.[1] Four days later a decree was published announcing that Stalin had been promoted to Generalissimo – the first person to hold such rank in Russia since Alexander Suvorov, the great Tsarist commander of the Napoleonic Wars. At the Potsdam conference, however, Stalin told Churchill that he hoped he would continue to call him Marshal. Neither did Stalin like the Generalissimo's uniform and he continued to wear his Marshal's uniform whenever he appeared in public. But the title of Generalissimo stuck. 'If we defeated Hitlerism,' said G.F. Aleksandrov, the Soviet propaganda chief, at the Lenin memorial meeting in January 1946, 'it is because the Soviet people had at its head the greatest commander-in-chief, Generalissimo Stalin.'[2]

Stalin usually kept his distance from the excesses of his eponymous personality cult. Supremely confident, he saw the political utility of deifying his image but, unlike some dictators, did not suffer from the delusion that it was actually true. As he famously scolded his son, Vasilii, for trying to take advantage of the family name: 'you're not Stalin and I'm not Stalin. Stalin is Soviet power. Stalin is what he is in the newspapers and the portraits, not you, no not even me!'[3] But in the aftermath of the great victory over Nazi Germany Stalin was tempted to believe his own propaganda. In March 1947, for example, he allowed the publication of an exchange of letters between himself and Colonel Razin, an instructor at the Frunze Military Academy, who had written to ask if Lenin's positive appraisal of Clausewitz, the great nineteenth-century German military strategist, remained valid. Stalin replied that Lenin was not an expert in military affairs (unlike his successor, of course) and Clausewitz's views on strategy had been outmoded by developments in military technology. Stalin eschewed the cult content of Razin's letter, saying that its panegyrics to his name pained him, but concluded his reply by drawing an implicit comparison between himself and the great military commanders of the past who understood the importance of the 'counter-offensive' in war.[4]

The concept of the 'counter-offensive' referred to the idea of absorbing an enemy's attack and then launching a massive counterattack to secure a decisive victory. It was one of the key ideas in early postwar Soviet discussions of the military lessons of the Great Patriotic War and it served to explain away the Red Army's defeats and setbacks in the early years of the war. After publication of Stalin's exchange with Razin the concept of the counter-offensive became even more entrenched in the Soviet story of the war, a narrative that glossed over the military catastrophes of 1941–1942, presenting the Red Army's defeats and retreats as part of a carefully calculated strategy to wear the enemy down.[5]

The apogee of the cult of Stalin's military genius came with the publication in 1951 of a book on 'Stalin and the Armed Forces of the USSR' by the Soviet dictator's long-time crony, Marshal Kliment Voroshilov. In the section on the Great Patriotic War, Soviet military success was presented as entirely due to Stalin. The Red Army's victory in the war, concluded Voroshilov, represented a triumph for Stalinist military science and the leadership genius of the great Stalin.[6]

Ever loyal, Stalin's generals accepted their reduced role in the limelight. One exception was Zhukov, happy to join in the praise of Stalin but not reticent about his own contribution and achievements as the Deputy Supreme Commander. Immediately after the war Zhukov's star was still shining brightly and in 1945–1946 he served as commander of the Soviet armed forces in occupied Germany. In March 1946 he was recalled to Moscow and appointed commander of all Soviet land forces. But shortly after returning home he fell victim to an intrigue that revolved around accusations that he had highlighted his own leadership role during the war and claimed credit for all the major offensive operations, including those that had nothing to do with him.[7] Zhukov's position was complicated by the fact that his new command had resulted in turf conflicts with other generals jockeying for position in the postwar hierarchy of the Red Army. Even more damaging was the arrest in April 1946 of General A.A. Novikov, the former head of the Red Air Force and a good friend of Zhukov.[8] Novikov was arrested as part of the so-called 'Aviators Affair' – a purge of the Soviet aircraft industry following accusations that during the war the fighter planes had been of poor quality. Zhukov was not directly implicated in the affair and his great prestige and wartime service to Stalin meant there was little chance he would suffer Novikov's fate of imprisonment. But in June 1946 Zhukov was demoted to chief of the Odessa military district and then, in February 1947, stripped of his candidate membership of the party Central Committee on grounds that he had displayed anti-party attitudes.[9] This latter move prompted him to write to Stalin to ask for a personal meeting to clear up the slanders being spread about him. A few days later Zhukov wrote a grovelling letter of apology to the Soviet leader in which he admitted that during the war he had been egotistical, tact-less and disrespectful in dealings with his colleagues in the High Command, including Stalin. Although Zhukov's letter concluded with a plea for the restoration of trust in him,[10] Stalin did not even bother to reply; Zhukov remained in exile and in 1948 was transferred to the even lowlier post of head of the Urals military district. In a 1949 poster tableau depicting Stalin and his generals plotting and planning the great counter-offensive at Stalingrad, Zhukov was nowhere to be seen. On the other hand, he did retain the rank of Marshal and there were signs of his rehabilitation in the early 1950s. In June 1951 Zhukov accompanied Molotov on a fraternal delegation to Poland and delivered a speech in Warsaw on Polish–Soviet unity, a declaration in which Stalin's virtues as a military and political leader featured prominently.[11] In 1952 Zhukov was restored to candidate membership of the Central Committee. Other Soviet generals were not so fortunate. In December 1946 General Gordov (who had commanded the Stalingrad Front in 1942) and General Rybalchenko, his Chief of Staff in the Volga Military District, were recorded exchanging dissident remarks about Stalin. Both men were arrested and later shot.[12]

Stalin's treatment of Zhukov after the war was typical of his brutal disdain for any sign or scintilla of disloyalty. There was also an obvious element of *pour encourager les autres*: if Stalin's Deputy Supreme Commander – the saviour of Leningrad and Moscow, the liberator of Poland, the conqueror of Berlin, and the leader of the 1945 Victory Parade – could fall from grace for transgressing the norms of conformity to the dictator's cult of personality, it could happen to anyone. But it was not simply a question of keeping the generals in their place; Stalin had to define a postwar role for the military that would acknowledge its continuing importance but not threaten his and the communist party's domination of Soviet society. He did this in an edict published in February 1946 on the 28th anniversary of the founding of the Red Army. Although Stalin began by hailing the Red Army's victories and sacri-fices, he pointed out that the war could not have been won without the full support of the Soviet people or the leadership of the communist party. The Red Army's prime task in peacetime, said Stalin, was to safeguard the country's peaceful reconstruction and facilitate the rebuilding of the Soviet state's economic and military power. He finished with the usual slogan, 'Long live the victorious Red Army', but his overall message was unmistakable: for the military there would be no basking in the glories of the war or claims to special status in Soviet society.[13]

In a further signal of his intention to maintain full civilian control over the armed forces, Stalin retained the post of defence commissar and appointed a political commissar, General Nikolai Bulganin, as his deputy. In 1947 Bulganin succeeded Stalin as Defence Minister and was promoted to Marshal. In 1949 Marshal Vasilevskii took over as Defence Minister but Bulganin remained in overall control of the armaments industry.[14]

Stalin's adoption of a military persona during and after the war was one aspect of his changing public identity; another was the building of his image as an international statesman. After the war Stalin did not attend any international conferences but he continued to receive and negotiate directly with a stream of foreign diplomats and politicians. During the early postwar years he was very prominent at diplomatic receptions and treaty-signing ceremonies and gave a number of interviews on foreign affairs issues. The most striking feature of Stalin's postwar diplomatic persona was his close identification with the leaders of the people's democracies of Eastern Europe. While Stalin often spoke of his earnest desire for postwar co-operation with Britain and the United States, the constant flow of meetings, pictures and communiqués shared with his communist allies in Eastern Europe told another story – that the Grand Alliance was being downgraded in favour of the emerging Soviet bloc.

After the war Stalin was preoccupied mainly with foreign policy decision-making and was content to leave the day-to-day running of the economy to others. Stalin's continuation of his wartime practice of non-interference in economic affairs led to a much more orderly and structured running of the economy after the war. He had the power to intervene but mostly he chose not to and, as a substitute for his will and whimsy, there developed committee systems, administrative procedures and a high degree of technocratic rationality. Soviet party and state institutions gained greatly from Stalin's forbearance as the prewar pattern of constant crises, emergencies and upheavals spurred on by purges and terror was replaced by routinism, professionalisation, and a growing bureaucracy. In this new economic order the middle stratum of technicians, managers and state officials continued to expand and entrench itself within the Soviet system, providing a vital source of support and stability for Stalin's postwar regime.[15]

While Stalin's personal postwar priorities were keeping an eye on the military and conducting diplomacy, the country's priorities were reconstruction and the transition to a peacetime social and economic regime. These postwar domestic processes were designed to achieve a degree of normality in social and economic life – a vital task in a country that had not only been devastated and traumatised by war but had suffered decades of upheaval during the course of successive national emergencies in the 1920s and 1930s.

In October 1945 Stalin went on holiday to the Black Sea – the first in a series of prolonged postwar vacations which meant that he was absent from Moscow for up to five months at the end of each year.[16] The war had exacted a physical toll on Stalin, now aged 66. He continued to work hard, even on holiday, but at nowhere near the level of wartime intensity. Stalin's new work regime meant more delegation to his subordinates but it also gave him more time and leisure to snipe at their efforts on his behalf. Indeed, the most striking feature of Stalin's postwar relations with his Politburo colleagues is the disrespectful tone of his dealings with them. In the traditional Bolshevik manner, he had always been rough, tough and rude but now he scolded his comrades in the bullying manner of a senior manager dealing with junior clerks who were not performing as well as expected. As Alexander Werth noted, by the late 1940s Stalin had a reputation for being an 'angry old man' – a perception amply confirmed by Stalin's postwar correspondence with Politburo members, which is full of petty personal put-downs of his comrades.[17]

Postwar Reconstruction[18]

Stalin's absence from Moscow in autumn 1945 meant the task of speaking on the 28th anniversary of the Bolshevik Revolution fell to Molotov. One of the main themes of Molotov's speech was the impact of the war. According to Molotov, the 'German-Fascist invaders' had destroyed 1,710 towns and 70,000 villages, demolished 6 million buildings, demolished or damaged 31,850 industrial enterprises, ruined or ransacked 98,000 collective farms, and made 25 million people homeless.[19] Grim though these figures were, they actually understated the country's war damage and reconstruction burden. According to Mark Harrison's calculations the war cost the Soviet Union some 25 per cent of its physical assets and about 14 per cent of its prewar population.[20] Molotov did not cite casualty figures in his speech, but the official Soviet figure was 7 million fatalities. In truth, the USSR's military fatalities alone were higher than this and there were another 15 to 16 million civilian deaths to be counted. Those suffering physical injury or psychological trauma numbered tens of millions more.

Complicating the task of postwar reconstruction was the fact that in the western borderlands of Belorussia, the Ukraine and the Baltic States – territories incorporated into the USSR only in 1939–1940 – the authorities faced not only the task of completing the process of sovietisation that had been interrupted by the war but the waging of a counter-insurgency campaign against tens of thousands of nationalist partisans. In Western Ukraine, for example, it is estimated that anti-communist partisans killed 35,000 Soviet military and party cadres between 1945 and 1951, while in Lithuania up to 100,000 people took part in the struggle to prevent the restoration of communist power.[21] In retaliation the Soviet authorities killed, imprisoned and deported tens of thousands of resisters. In other parts of the country ethnic groups of suspect loyalty continued to be targeted for persecution and deportation. During the war the NKVD had deported 2 million Volga Germans, Crimean Tatars, Cossacks, Chechens and other Turkic peoples to the eastern interior of the USSR. The rationale was that these ethnic groups had collectively collaborated with the enemy. But the deportations did not stop with victory. Among the hundreds of thousands of postwar victims of deportation were Balts, Finns, Greeks, Moldovans, Ukrainians and Belorussians.[22] Another stream of forced ethnic migration arose from the border change between Poland and the USSR, which resulted in 2 million Poles leaving Western Belorussia and Western Ukraine, while half a million Ukrainians, Russians, Belorussians and Lithuanians moved in the other direction.[23]

One of the most pressing priorities facing the regime was the reintegration into Soviet society of millions of returning war veterans. Between 1945 and 1948, 8 million Soviet soldiers were demobilised. All had to be rehoused, re-employed and absorbed into social, cultural and political life. Many of the so-called *frontoviki* were members of the communist party as during the war 6 million members of the armed forces had joined the party and by the end of the conflict two-thirds of communist party members were wartime recruits. The postwar party membership was younger, better educated and more representative of white-collar occupations than before, although the party remained male-dominated, with female membership increasing only from 14.5 per cent to 18.3 per cent of the total. After the war the young, educated and mainly male *frontoviki* came to play a prominent role in the organisation and life of the party.[24] One consequence of this generational shift was a party less prone to political and ideological activism and more inclined to respect managerial and technical expertise and to define its own role as the supervision of state and economic managers rather than, as in the 1930s, populist campaigning to control the bureaucracy. This 'depoliticisation' of communists was not entirely welcomed by the Soviet party leadership, which took steps to counter it by launching numerous campaigns of ideological education, but it did mirror and harmonise with the change in Stalin's own leadership style after the war. In both instances – the Leader and the led – the change reflected the wartime experience of allowing individuals and groups more autonomy in finding local solutions to local problems and in seeking different ways of meeting prescribed goals.[25]

Demobilisation began with the release, in June 1945, of the oldest classes of conscripts. By the end of 1945 nearly 5 million members of the armed forces had been demobilised. Veterans were given new clothing, free food and transport home, and severance pay. Returnees had the right to be re-employed in their old jobs but many hundreds of thousands resettled elsewhere, including large numbers of peasants who moved to towns, thereby adding to urban housing shortages and the demand for jobs.

In September 1945 the military emergency was declared officially terminated and various powers were restored to the civil administration and the civil courts. On 4 September the GKO (State Defence Committee) was abolished and its economic functions transferred to the Council of People's Commissars. Within the council various structural changes and reorganisations culminated in the establishment in 1947 of a number of sectoral bureaus with responsibility for different areas of the economy.[26] In March 1946 the commissariats were renamed ministries and the people's commissars became ministers. This change was approved by a plenum of the party's Central Committee in March 1946 – the first such gathering since January 1944. The plenum was chaired by Stalin, who explained the change in nomenclature in the following terms:

> The name people's commissar . . . reflects the period of instability, the period of civil war, a period of revolutionary fracture . . . This period has passed. The war has shown that our social order is very strong and no longer reflects such a name, which relates to the period of an unstable social order, which had still not been established and become normal . . . It is time to change the name people's commissar to minister. The people will understand very well because there are commissars here, there and everywhere. It confuses people. God only knows who is higher. (*Laughter in the hall*.)[27]

In October 1945 a decree was issued on elections to the Supreme Soviet. The elections were held in February 1946 and a month later the newly elected Supreme Soviet met and adopted the new five-year plan. The initial aim of restoring the economy to prewar levels of production was achieved by the late 1940s, although only at the cost of a continued squeeze on living standards and the maintenance of a strict disciplinary regime at work. Wartime rationing was not abolished until December 1947. Simultaneously, the authorities introduced a currency reform that radically reduced the value of the rouble and soaked up surplus cash in the economy before excess demand could cause inflation.

The famine and food crisis of 1946–1947 was perhaps the greatest challenge faced by the regime. In summer 1946 there was a drought, the harvest failed, and the winter that followed was one of the worst on record. Lend-lease food supplies that had fed a third of the population during the war had stopped in 1945 and only a limited amount of aid was forthcoming from the United

Nations Relief and Rehabilitation Administration. Germany and other former enemy states were stripped for reparations but there was little in the way of food imports. The result was that an estimated 1–1.5 million Soviet people (mainly peasants) died as a result of starvation or famine-induced diseases.

As Donald Filtzer has argued, the deprivations of the early postwar period had the paradoxical effect of strengthening the stability of Stalin's regime. On one hand, the population was so exhausted by the daily struggle for survival that it had little time or energy for organised social protest and tended towards passive acceptance of dashed hopes for a healthier, wealthier and freer future after the war. On the other, when conditions did get better in the late 1940s and early 1950s the regime received some of the credit for the improvement and there was widespread popular relief that a semblance of normality had finally been achieved.[28]

The 1946 Elections

The most important act of political 'normalisation' was the holding of elections to the Supreme Soviet, an occasion that returned the communist party to centre stage and gave the population a chance to pass their verdict on the regime's performance during the war. Although these were single-party and single-candidate elections, contested only by the communist party or its nominees and with only one candidate per constituency, 'the atmosphere of the election', according to Elena Zubkova, was 'something like a national holiday' and 'demonstrated that the people's faith in the authorities was real, not imaginary'.[29] According to official statistics, of the 101,717,686 registered voters, 99.7 per cent voted. Of these voters, 818,955 crossed out the name of the nominated candidate on the ballot paper and thereby cast a negative vote. In the Baltic States the combined figures for abstentionist and negative voters were much higher, amounting to 10 per cent in Lithuania. No doubt levels of dissidence would have been much higher throughout the USSR in any freely contested election but the available evidence on public opinion does suggest that popular support for the Stalin regime was quite high immediately after the war. Stalin had led the country to a great victory and the Soviet people were optimistic about the future, despite the massive task of postwar reconstruction. Among the intelligentsia there was widespread hope that the wartime cultural relaxation of the Stalinist regime would continue. The cult of Stalin's personality was absurd but its propagation over many years had its impact on popular consciousness. Among the general population he was mostly worshipped as a god or viewed as a benign authoritarian figure.[30]

The Supreme Soviet election campaign culminated on 9 February 1946 in Stalin's address to the electors of his Moscow constituency, delivered with all pomp and circumstance in the theatre of the Bolshoi Ballet. In keeping with the effort to revive and reassert the role of the communist party Stalin began his speech with the ideologically orthodox point that the Second World War had been caused by the economic contradictions of capitalism and imperialism. However, because the war had pitted fascist states against freedom-loving countries like Britain and the United States it had taken on a liberating and anti-fascist hue from the very beginning, a characteristic strengthened by the USSR's entry into the conflict and by the formation of the Soviet–Western alliance. Stalin made much of the test the war had set the Soviet social system, arguing that it showed 'the Soviet social system is a truly popular system, issued from the depths of the people and enjoying its mighty support'. The war also demonstrated, said Stalin, the success of the Soviet system as a multi-national state in which there was friendship and collaboration between its constituent peoples. As far as the communist party was concerned, Stalin highlighted its prewar role in preparing the country for war by prioritising heavy industry and building up national defences. As to the future, Stalin noted the new five-year plan's targets in relation to production but also emphasised the efforts that would be made to raise mass consumption and living standards. He concluded by talking about relations between the communist party and 'non-party' people. In the past communists had been suspicious of non-party people, said Stalin, because they feared bourgeois influences. Now, however, communists and non-party people were members of a strong Soviet social system: 'Living together in one common collective, they fought together for the strengthening of the might of our country. Together they fought and shed their blood . . . for the sake of the freedom and greatness of our motherland. Together they forged and shaped the victory over the enemies of our country. The only difference between them is that one is in the party, while the other is not. But this is a formal difference. The important thing is that both have a common aim.'[31]

The Campaign against the West

Stalin's election speech was a typically assured performance that exuded confidence in the strength and future of the Soviet system. Similar sentiments were expressed in the election speeches of Stalin's key lieutenants.[32] However, another theme of Soviet discourse in the early postwar period augured less well for the future: the belief that the USSR's role in winning the war was not recognised sufficiently abroad and that efforts were afoot internationally to deprive the Soviet Union of the fruits of its victory. The most explicit statement of these concerns during the election campaign was made by Georgii Malenkov, Stalin's deputy within the party apparatus: 'There were cases in history when the fruits of victory slipped out of the victor's hands. This must not happen to us ... We must, in the first place, consolidate and strengthen still further our Soviet socialist states ... And we must remember that our friends will respect us only so long as we are strong.' In his election speech Andrei Zhdanov, Stalin's ideology chief, warned that 'even amongst the peace-loving nations, there are reactionary elements who are hostile to the Soviet Union ... you know that our policy of peace and security ... does not please everybody. No, we can't please everybody, but we've got to be extremely vigilant.'[33] Zhdanov returned to this theme in November 1946 when he gave the Revolution anniversary speech. He also commented bitterly on the treatment of the Soviet Union and the Soviet people in the western press:

> One reads and wonders how quickly the Russians have changed. When our blood streamed in the battlefields they admired our courage, bravery, high morale and boundless patriotism. And now that we wish, in co-operation with other nations, to make use of our equal rights to participation in international affairs, they begin to shower us with abuse and slander, to vilify and abuse us, saying at the same time that we possess an unbearable and suspicious character.[34]

What Zhdanov was saying in public was expounded with equal vigour in Soviet internal discussions. At the end of the war Sovinform, the government's propaganda arm, prepared a series of reports on its activities and those of its western counterparts. According to Sovinform, now the war was over Soviet propaganda abroad faced an uphill task because reactionary circles in the west were waging a massive anti-communist slander campaign. In this anti-Soviet campaign, supported and sponsored by the information agencies of Britain and the United States, a particularly pernicious role was being played by social democratic elements in the labour movement.[35] Similar themes were evident in the Central Committee's confidential bulletin on international affairs, *Voprosy Vneshnei Politiki* (Questions of Foreign Policy), which commenced publication at the end of 1944. Article after article noted the re-emergence and growth of reactionary circles in western countries and commented on the developing struggle between pro and anti-Soviet forces, especially within the European labour movement. Much the same analyses could be found in *Novoe Vremya* (New Times – the postwar successor to *War and the Working Class*) and elsewhere in the Soviet press. In March 1946 Stalin himself entered the fray when he published a lengthy reply to Churchill's 'Iron Curtain' speech that depicted the former British premier as an anti-Bolshevik reactionary who was advocating war with the USSR.[36] The Soviet people needed little prompting to cheer on their own side in these polemics. As the Czechoslovak communist Zdenek Mlynar recalled from his time studying in the Soviet Union after the war:

> The most fundamental conviction was that the Soviet Union had at the price of enormous sacrifices decided the fate of mankind during the war, and it was thus entitled to the special respect of all nations. These people regarded any criticism as an insult to the memory of the dead. In this respect they were at one with the government, however critical they were of it in other questions.[37]

Domestically, the cultural and political counterpart of growing Soviet resentment and suspicion of the west was an ultra-patriotic and nationalistic campaign to promote the unique virtues of the USSR. Behind this campaign was Stalin's hubris about the place that victory should accord the USSR in the postwar world. Stalin expected far more recognition and concessions from his partners in the Grand Alliance than he actually received. Particularly irksome to Stalin was the USSR's exclusion from the postwar occupation of Japan and the signs that Britain and the United States were reneging on their acceptance at Yalta and Potsdam of the Soviet sphere of influence in Eastern Europe. Stalin responded by playing hardball in postwar negotiations with the Anglo-Americans and by berating his close associates about any signs of 'servility' to the west. In the front line of these admonitions was the long-suffering Molotov, who had the most dealings with foreigners and the most opportunities to make mistakes. In November 1945, for example, Stalin criticised Molotov for allowing a speech by Churchill to be published in the USSR:

> I think the publication of Churchill's speech eulogizing Russia and Stalin was a mistake. Churchill needs these eulogies to soothe his guilty conscience and to camouflage his hostile attitudes towards the USSR, and in particular to camouflage the fact that he and his pupils from the Labour Party are the organizers of the Anglo-American-French bloc against the USSR. We only help these gentlemen by publishing these kinds of speeches. We now have quite a lot of high-ranking functionaries who burst into foolish raptures when praised by Churchills, Trumans, Byrneses . . . I regard such a mood as dangerous, as it develops foreign figures in this country. Hard struggle should be waged against servility towards foreigners. But if we continue to publish speeches like this we will only cultivate servility and fawning. I do not mention the fact that Soviet leaders have no need to be praised by foreign leaders. As for myself, this kind of praise only jars upon me.[38]

It may be, as some suggest, that outbursts like this were designed by Stalin to discipline his Politburo colleagues and to reassert his domination of them after the war. However, Stalin's indignation seems genuine and it is doubtful that he felt threatened in any way by the likes of Molotov. The war had strengthened Stalin's dictatorial power within the Politburo and his role in the Soviet victory placed him in an unchallengeable political position. If there was an element of calculation in Stalin's campaign against servility to the west it related to his genuine concern about the impact on Soviet society of contacts with the capitalist world. The war and the Grand Alliance had opened the Soviet Union to a myriad of foreign political, cultural and economic influences and there were great expectations that these would continue in peacetime. In summer 1944, for example, the Soviet writer Vsevolod Vyshnevksii presented a glowing portrait of cultural coexistence after the war:

> When the war is over, life will become very pleasant. A great literature will be produced as result of our experiences. There will be much coming and going, and a lot of contacts with the West. Everybody will be allowed to read whatever he likes. There will be exchanges of students, and foreign travel for Soviet citizens will be made easy.[39]

At the war's end Stalin was confident in the Soviet system and in his own power but that did not mean he had given up on his prewar view that the class struggle continued under socialism or his fear of the negative impact on the Soviet people of capitalist influences. One expression of these concerns was the severe treatment of Soviet citizens and POWs repatriated from Nazi-occupied Europe. All returnees were required to report to transit camps for screening by the NKVD. Of the approximately 4 million to be repatriated 2,660,013 were civilians and 1,539,475 were former POWs. Of those, 2,427,906 were sent home; 801,152 were reconscripted into the armed forces; 608,095 were enrolled in the work battalions of the defence ministry; 272,867 were found guilty of some crime or misdemeanour and transferred to the authority of the NKVD for punishment; 89,468 remained in the transit camps as reception personnel until the repatriation process was finally wound up in the early 1950s.[40]

The screening process was designed to root out traitors and spies – a genuine concern given that a million Soviet citizens served in Axis armed forces during the war, half in a military capacity, the rest as civilian auxiliaries – and to make sure that those captured by the Germans or conscripted as slave labourers had not given themselves up too easily. As far as higher-ranking officers were concerned, the only acceptable circumstance of capture was if they had been wounded and unable to fight on.[41] But the main purpose of the transit camps was not to punish traitors but to probe the loyalty of citizens returning from foreign lands.

Zhdanovshchina

In summer 1946 Stalin's campaign against western capitalist influences took a new and radical turn when the party Central Committee issued an edict attacking the Leningrad-based monthly journals *Zvezda* and *Leningrad* for publishing works 'that cultivate the spirit, alien to the Soviet people, of servility before the modern bourgeois culture of the West'. Two days later, on 16 August, Zhdanov delivered a speech to the Leningrad branch of the Soviet writers' union condemning the satirist Mikhail Zoshchenko and the poet Anna Akhmatova. Zoshchenko was pilloried for depicting Soviet people as 'idlers and moral monsters and as generally stupid and primitive'. Akhmatova was fingered as an individualist who represented a 'mixture of nun and harlot'. Needless to say, the two writers were soon expelled from their union, while the *Zvezda* editorial board was reorganised and the *Leningrad* journal closed down altogether. In September 1946 the Central Committee issued a decree on ideologically incorrect films, including among them Sergei Eisenstein's *Ivan the Terrible Part 2*, which was attacked for misrepresenting the fearsome Tsar's progressive role in Russian history. In due course this cultural purge was extended to the theatre and to music. In February 1948 Shostakovich was criticised for the un-Soviet formalism of his compositions. A year later Soviet theatre critics were attacked as a group for being unpatriotic. One of the main forums for these attacks was a new journal published by Zhdanov's department in the Central Committee: *Kul'tura i Zhizn'* (Culture and Life).[42]

Although it became known as the *Zhdanovshchina* this turn in cultural policy was initiated and orchestrated by Stalin, who vetted and edited all the major public statements on the matter. Stalin's motives were evident in one version of Zhdanov's August 1946 speech:

> Some of our literary people have come to see themselves not as teachers but as pupils [and] ... have slipped into a tone of servility and cringing before philistine foreign literature. Is such servility becoming of us Soviet patriots, who are building the Soviet system, which is a hundred times higher and better than any bourgeois system? Is it becoming of our vanguard Soviet literature ... to cringe before the narrow-minded and philistine bourgeois literature of the West?[43]

In his memoirs Konstantin Simonov recounted an episode from May 1947 when he and some other officials from the Soviet writers' union went to see Stalin, ostensibly about royalty payments, but the Soviet leader's mind was on the inadequate education of the intelligentsia in patriotism. 'If you take our middle intelligentsia – the scientific intelligentsia, professors and doctors – they don't exactly have developed feelings of Soviet patriotism. They engage in an unjustified admiration of foreign culture ... This backward tradition began with Peter [the Great] ... there was much grovelling before foreigners, before shits.'[44]

It was not only artists who came under attack for such alleged servility. In 1947 there was public discussion of a book on the history of western philosophy by Aleksandrov, the propaganda chief. He was accused of underestimating the Russian contribution in the history of philosophy and of failing to emphasise Marxism's ideological break with the western tradition. In his contribution to the discussion Zhdanov noted that it was Stalin himself who had drawn attention to the book's flaws. (Zhdanov did not explain why in that case the book had been awarded a Stalin Prize when it was published in 1946.) Another Soviet intellectual who came under attack in 1947 was the economist Eugene Varga. His sin was to publish a book which argued that there had been radical changes in the character of capitalism as a result of the war, particularly an increased role for the state in economic management, and that these changes augured well for the gradual transformation of western states in a socialist direction. When the book was published in 1946 Varga's views were fully in accord with Stalin's own concept of a postwar people's democratic Europe achieved by socio-economic reforms and peaceful political struggle. But the growing cold war atmosphere of 1947 provided Varga's hard-line opponents in the communist party and the Soviet academy with openings to attack his writings. Eventually, Varga was forced to recant his heterodox views, while his research institute and the journal it published were closed down.[45]

In the natural sciences the campaign against pernicious western influences took the peculiar form, among others, of the 'honour court'. The first victims of this process were the medical scientists Nina Kliueva and her husband Grigorii Roskin. In summer 1946 their lab was visited by the new US ambassador to Moscow, Walter Bedell Smith. Subsequently, Klieuva and Roskin arranged for a copy of the manuscript of their book on the treatment of malignant cancers to be passed to American doctors. In early 1947 this came to Stalin's attention. On his initiative the government passed a resolution on the formation of honour courts throughout the central apparatus of the Soviet state with a view to examining cases of anti-patriotic, anti-state and anti-social actions by officials and employees. The issue at stake in the Ministry of Health honour court that examined the case of Klieuva and Roskin was whether or not they had acted correctly in sharing the secrets of Soviet medical science with foreigners. In his submission to the court Zhdanov stressed that the two scientists had acted individualistically and without consulting the relevant authorities.[46]

No criminal sanctions were imposed on Klieuva and Roskin. The point of the so-called honour court was to administer a public political and ideological lesson about the dangers of relations with foreigners. (Their 'trial' was actually a public meeting attended by 800 people.) To ram the point home the Central Committee issued a confidential circular to party members, 'On the case of Professors Kliueva and Roskin'. The document criticised 'slavishness and servility before things foreign', urged the 'education of the Soviet intelligentsia in the spirit of Soviet patriotism' and warned against 'kowtowing and servility before the bourgeois culture of the West'.[47]

The patriotic imperative was also evident in the so-called Lysenko affair.[48] Trofim Lysenko, a Soviet biologist who specialised in plant science, believed that acquired characteristics could be inherited and hence influenced by environmental changes. His view brought him into conflict with Soviet geneticists who contended that inheritance was a function of genes, not the influence of the environment or the scientific manipulation of nature. The long-standing debate between these two factions within Soviet biology took a new turn in April 1948 when Yuri Zhdanov, son of Andrei, who was in charge of the science section of the Central Committee, gave a lecture which criticised Lysenko's views. Lysenko wrote to Stalin to complain. The result was an official endorsement of Lysenko's position via the publication in *Pravda* of the proceedings of a conference of July–August 1948 that expounded Lysenko's views and trounced those of his geneticist critics. Lysenko may have been a poor scientist but he was politically astute and he took pains to couch his position in terms of 'Soviet' versus 'western' science, and of 'materialist, progressive and patriotic' biology versus 'reactionary, scholastic and foreign' biology.

Lysenko triumphed because Stalin backed his views and upbraided Yuri Zhdanov for expressing his personal opinion on the heredity versus genetics debate. 'In the party we have no personal opinions or personal points of view,' Stalin told him. 'There are only the views of the party.'[49] Stalin supported Lysenko's views because of their appeal to Soviet patriotism and because they chimed with his own voluntaristic Marxist philosophy that the natural world could be radically transformed by active human intervention. In line with this modernist vision the Soviet press announced in October 1948 'The Great Stalinist Plan to Transform Nature', a project for the mass planting of trees and grasslands and the creation of 44,000 new ponds and reservoirs. 'Capitalism,' editorialised *Pravda*, 'is incapable not only of the planned transformation of nature but of preventing the predatory use of its riches.'

In his February 1946 election speech Stalin had said that he was 'confident that if we give our scientists the help they need, they will soon catch up with and even surpass the achievements of science abroad'. Two years later the tone of public discourse had shifted to the triumphalist assertion that Soviet, and indeed Russian, scientific achievements already surpassed those of the west. 'Throughout its history, the Great Russian People have enriched national and world technology with outstanding discoveries and inventions,' claimed a *Pravda* columnist in January 1949. The occasion for this comment was a session of the Soviet Academy of Sciences devoted to the history of Russian science. That same month in *Komsomol Pravda* (the newspaper of the Young Communist League) a headline read 'The Aeroplane Is a Russian Invention'. According to the author of this article:

> It is impossible to find one area in which the Russian people have not blazed new paths. A.S. Popov invented radio. A.N. Lodygin created the incandescent bulb. I.I. Pozunov built the world's first steam engine. The first locomotive, invented by the Cherepanovs, moved on Russian land. The serf Fedor Blinov flew over Russian land in a plane heavier than air, created by the genius Aleksandr Fedorovich Mozhaiskii, twenty-one years before the Wright Brothers.[50]

As this quotation shows, there was also strong element of Russification in the postwar Soviet patriotic campaign. In keeping with this trend, Stalin's image in official portraits obliterated all physical traces of his Georgian origins. The classic postwar portrait of Stalin in full dress military uniform, for example, was modelled on a photograph of an illustrious Russian explorer and geographer.[51] Stalin also continued to show special regard for the Russian people and their culture as a bulwark against the west. The 110th anniversary of Pushkin's death was commemorated with great fanfare in 1947. In September 1947 Stalin issued greetings to Moscow on the 800th anniversary of the city's foundation: 'The greatness of Moscow consists not only in liberating our country three times from foreign oppression – from the Mongol yoke, from the Polish–Lithuanian invasion, and from the French encroachment. The greatness of Moscow consists above all in the fact that it was the basis for the unification of a divided Russia into a single state with one government and a united leadership.'[52] In 1950 Stalin published a series of articles in *Pravda* on Marxism and linguistics that defended the special virtues of the Russian language.[53]

The Return of Repression

The *Zhdanovshchina* grew in intensity as Soviet–Western relations worsened. The initial campaign against the west was inspired by Stalin's disgruntlement about relations with Britain and the United States and concerns about the penetration of Soviet society by western influences. The cultural purge of

1946–1947 coincided with fears in Moscow that the future of the Grand Alliance was threatened by the growing influence of anti-Soviet forces in western countries. The development of Soviet and Russian ultra-patriotism intersected with the outbreak of the cold war in 1947–1948 and with the onset of ideological competition with the west. Finally, in the late 1940s and early 1950s, when the cold war conflict reached its peak, Soviet domestic politics underwent a pronounced xenophobic turn. Citizens were banned from contact with foreigners, western journalists working in Moscow were subject to harsh censorship, foreign travel was severely restricted even for Soviet officials, and draconian penalties were introduced for betraying state secrets. In effect, there was a return to the isolationism and siege mentality that had characterised Soviet society in the 1930s. It was in this context that Stalin unleashed a new wave of trials, arrests and repressions. The scale of Stalin's postwar terror in no way matched the scale and intensity of the *Yezhovshchina* of 1937–1938 but it was a bitter blow to the hope of the intelligentsia that victory would bring an era of liberalisation.

At the leadership level the most notable event was the so-called 'Leningrad affair' of 1949.[54] This refers to a purge of the Leningrad party leadership following accusations that it had distanced itself from the Central Committee and operated its own networks of patronage. Caught up in the affair was Nikolai Voznesenskii, head of the state planning organisation, Gosplan. He had personal connections with the Leningrad leaders and came under fire for providing the Council of Ministers with misleading information and for losing secret state documents. Very quickly the charges against the accused escalated into claims that they had been involved in espionage. The Leningrad leaders were arrested in August 1949 and Voznesenskii in October. In a secret trial in Leningrad a year later all were convicted and then executed. The repression extended to mid-level officials in the Leningrad area and more than 200 people were sentenced to death, imprisonment or exile as a result.

Stalin's precise motives for this purge remain a little murky but it seems he was genuinely annoyed by the independence shown by the Leningrad leaders and punished them as an example to other party leaders who might be tempted into unauthorised actions. It may be, too, that Stalin was concerned about proposals and plans emanating from the Leningraders to establish a Russian communist party along the lines of the national parties in the other Soviet republics. Such a move had always been resisted in the Soviet communist party because of the dangers of encouraging Great Russian chauvinism. Stalin was all in favour of Russian nationalism and patriotism, providing they remained strictly under his control.[55] In the case of Voznesenskii there was a strong element of caprice in Stalin's decision to throw him to the wolves. Voznesenskii had established himself as one of Stalin's 'chief truth tellers' on economic matters. When Stalin decided that Voznesenskii had breached that trust by providing misleading information he was expelled from the party and handed over to the security people, regardless of his pitiful pledges of eternal loyalty.[56]

It is highly unlikely that Stalin believed that Voznesenskii and the others actually were spies and traitors. Rather, as in the 1930s, Stalin probably thought that they and others might go over to the enemy camp if preventative action was not taken. Feeding this fantasy was the cold war with the west, and the activities of western intelligence agencies engaged in espionage and sabotage operations. In the Western Ukraine and the Baltic States such activities meshed with local armed resistance to Soviet rule.[57]

The fear of western penetration featured even more strongly in the purge of the Jewish Anti-Fascist Committee (JAFC). The JAFC was one of a number of anti-fascist organisations set up by the Soviets during the Great Patriotic War.[58] Its job was to rally support for the USSR among Soviet Jews and among Jews abroad. The committee was chaired by Solomon Mikhoels, a famous actor and director, and included many prominent Soviet-Jewish artistes, intellectuals and scientists. The committee organised public rallies in Moscow, sponsored Yiddish publications, raised money abroad, and sought to highlight the plight of the Jews in the face of the Nazi onslaught. Within the Soviet Union it sought to encourage Jewish culture and identity, publicised the Nazi massacre of the Jews, and lobbied for the establishment of a Jewish Soviet Socialist Republic in the Crimea. As a result of their activities abroad committee members developed extensive connections with Jewish organisations, including Zionists working to establish the State of Israel. After the war Mikhoels argued for the development of the JAFC into a progressive Jewish organisation campaigning abroad in support of the Soviet Union. Within the communist party apparatus, however, various resolutions were tabled to wind the committee up after the war. The apparatchiks' complaint was that while the organisation had played an important role during the war it had become too nationalistic and too Zionist. The committee, its critics argued, highlighted Jewish life in the USSR but not the culture of other nationalities, such as the Russians, and did not display a sufficient degree of Soviet patriotism. The JAFC vigorously refuted these allegations, stressing its loyalty to the Soviet Union. In January 1948, however, Mikhoels was killed in Minsk, apparently as a result of a hit-and-run road accident but probably at the hands of the Soviet security forces.[59] In March 1948 events took a further ominous turn with the submission of a report to Stalin by V.S. Abakumov, the head of the Soviet Security Ministry, stating that 'the leaders of the Jewish Anti-Fascist Committee, being active nationalists with pro-American leanings, in essence are conducting an anti-Soviet nationalistic campaign'. After providing extensive details of this alleged campaign Abakumov concluded by noting that his ministry had uncovered a number of American and English spies among recently arrested Jewish nationalists.[60]

Despite this dire warning from his security chief, Stalin made no immediate move to close the committee down. Some analysts have suggested that the committee was protected by Zhdanov until his death in August 1948 but others have highlighted the restraining influence of Stalin's own postwar alliance with Zionism.[61]

After the war a *de facto* alliance developed between the Soviet Union and the nascent Israeli state. Although there was some sympathy for the calamity that had befallen European Jewry at the hands of the Nazis, the main Soviet motive was self-interest. The Soviets did not trust Arab nationalism, which they identified as being overly influenced by the British and Americans, and they saw Zionism as a useful counter to western influence in the Middle East. Moscow's preferred option for the settlement of the Palestine problem was the establishment of an independent, multinational state that would respect the interests of both Jews and Arabs. When it came to the crunch, however, the Soviets were prepared to vote for the partition of Palestine into Jewish and Arab states. Andrei Gromyko's speech to the United Nations in May 1947 announcing the Soviet position was almost textbook Zionist propaganda:

> During the last war, the Jewish people experienced exceptional sorrow and suffering . . . The Jews in territories where the Hitlerites held sway were subjected to almost complete physical annihilation . . . Large numbers of the surviving Jews of Europe were deprived of their countries, their homes, and their livelihood . . . Past experience . . . shows that no Western European state was able to provide adequate assistance for the Jewish people in defending its rights and its very existence . . . This . . . unpleasant fact . . . explains the aspirations of the Jews to establish their own state. It would be unjust not to take this into consideration and to deny the right of the Jewish people to realize this aspiration.[62]

The foundation of Israel in May 1948 was quickly followed by the establishment of diplomatic relations with the Soviet Union. In September Tel Aviv's first ambassador arrived in Moscow. Golda Meyerson (better known as Golda Meir and later became Prime Minister of Israel) reported home on 12 September that 20,000 people had celebrated the declaration of the State of Israel at a Moscow synagogue. On 6 October Meyerson reported that on Rosh Hashanah (Jewish New Year) huge crowds packed the Great Synagogue in Moscow and that in the street she was met by thunderous cheers and 'cries' in Hebrew. Other reports by her testify to the developing contacts between the

Israeli embassy and members of the JAFC.[63] In all probability it was these events that finally turned Stalin against the JAFC. Under no circumstances would he countenance independent political activity. The only displays of nationalism and patriotism allowed were those approved and sponsored by the Soviet state. In November 1948 the Politburo finally resolved to disband the JAFC on the grounds that it was a centre of anti-Soviet propaganda that regularly submitted anti-Soviet information to foreign intelligence agencies.[64] Although the resolution specified that 'nobody should be arrested yet' it wasn't long before the leading members of the JAFC were rounded up. In the spring and summer of 1952 a secret trial was held of 15 JAFC officials and activists. Among those accused of Jewish nationalism, Zionism and espionage was S.A. Lozovskii, a former deputy commissar for foreign affairs, who had the misfortune to be given responsibility for the JAFC after the war, although he personally favoured winding up the committee. At the trial Lozovskii, whose political career as a Bolshevik included a spell as the head of the Comintern's trade union section, retracted his confession and staunchly refuted the charges levelled against him. Lozovskii's status and eloquence had its impact on the trial judge, Alexander Cheptsov, who attempted to get the investigation into the JAFC reopened. Even after he was pressured to sentence Lozovskii and 12 others to death (one of the accused had already died in prison, while another was found guilty and sentenced to three and a half years in a labour camp followed by five years in exile) Cheptsov allowed appeals for clemency – something that would have been unthinkable for a Stalinist judge to do in the 1930s.[65]

One JAFC activist who got off relatively lightly was Polina Zhemchuzhina, Molotov's Jewish wife. She was arrested along with all the others in January 1949 but Soviet investigators eventually decided to separate her case from the main JAFC trial and her punishment was a period of exile in Kazakhstan. When the issue of his wife's expulsion from the party came up at the Politburo Molotov abstained, but he soon recanted[66] and acceded to Stalin's request that he divorce her. (The two were not reunited until after Stalin's death.) Molotov's punishment was his dismissal in March 1949 as Minister for Foreign Affairs but it was more of a sideways move than anything else. He continued to play a central role in the formulation of Soviet foreign policy and was placed in charge of a Politburo commission on foreign affairs. Molotov's successor as Foreign Minister, former Deputy Foreign Minister Andrei Vyshinskii, frequently sought advice and input from his predecessor. Among the other important tasks allocated to Molotov during this period was the preparation of Stalin's wartime correspondence with Churchill, Roosevelt, Truman and Attlee for publication.[67]

The purge and repression of the JAFC coincided with the onset of a Soviet domestic campaign against 'rootless cosmopolitanism' whose main theme was the necessity of combining proletarian internationalism with Soviet patriotism and a respect for Russian culture. Although not specifically aimed at Jews, the anti-cosmopolitan campaign had anti-Semitic connotations and took place in the context of virulent anti-Zionist propaganda that climaxed with a break in Soviet diplomatic relations with Israel in 1952. The campaign against Zionism and its alleged links with western imperialist sabotage and espionage activities within the USSR soon spread to the rest of the Soviet bloc. In November 1952, 14 former leaders of the Czechoslovak communist party, including its General Secretary, Rudolph Slansky, were tried publicly in Prague as members of an anti-state conspiracy with Zionist connections. Eleven of the 14 defendants, including Slansky, were Jewish. Three of the defendants received life imprisonment; the rest were executed, among them Slansky.[68]

Stalin's personal attitude towards the Jews is a matter of continuing controversy but the available evidence points towards Zhores Medvedev's conclusion that he was not so much anti-Semitic as politically hostile to Zionism and Jewish nationalism, which he saw as threats to his power.[69] Officially the Soviet state was opposed to all forms of racism, including anti-Semitism, and Stalin made many public statements to this effect. In his birthplace of Georgia there was no Jewish ghetto and the predominant tradition there was the assimilation of Jews, a policy Stalin favoured when he came to power in the USSR. Stalin was surrounded by Jewish officials, or officials with Jewish wives, and he continued to fête Jewish writers and artists even at the very height of the anti-Zionist campaign of the early 1950s. In December 1952 Stalin made the following highly revealing statement to the plenum of the Central Committee:

> The more successful we are the more our enemies will try to damage us. Because of our great success our people have forgotten this and become complacent, thoughtless and conceited.
>
> Every Jew-Nationalist is an agent of American intelligence. Jew-Nationalists think that their nation was saved by the USA (there they can get rich, become bourgeois, etc). They consider themselves obligated to the Americans.
>
> Among the doctors there are many Jew-Nationalists.[70]

As this quotation shows, Stalin's political hostility to Zionism and Jewish nationalism tended to assume an ethnic dimension: some Jews were classified as enemies because of their politics but all Jews were politically suspect because of their race unless proven otherwise. This was evident in the 'Doctors affair' alluded to by Stalin – the last of the mythical conspiracies foiled by his security police.

The so-called 'Doctors affair' – some would call it a plot[71] – began in July 1951 when a senior investigator of the Ministry of State Security, Lieutenant Colonel M.D. Ryumin, wrote to Stalin alleging that Dr Yakov Etinger – 'a confirmed Jewish nationalist' – had confessed that in 1945 he had used the cover of medical treatment to murder A.A. Shcherbakov, a much-loved member of the Politburo. Ryumin further stated that Etinger was involved in a broader terrorist conspiracy with a number of other doctors. Crucially, Ryumin claimed that his boss, Abakumov, had intervened during the interrogation of Etinger and closed the case. (Actually, Etinger had died during interrogation by Ryumin in March 1951 and it seems likely that he was attacking Abakumov as a means of covering his own back.)

Stalin responded by establishing a commission headed by Malenkov to investigate Ryumin's allegations. Included among the commission's members was Beria, Abakumov's predecessor as Minister of State Security. The commission rapidly concluded that Abakumov was culpable. On 13 July 1951 the Central Committee issued a 'closed' letter to party organisations announcing that Abakumov had been removed from office and expelled from the party for failing to investigate Etinger's confession. The letter further pointed out that in January 1951 the members of a Jewish anti-Soviet youth organisation had been arrested but Abakumov had hidden their terrorist plots from the government. Abakumov was soon arrested and his ministry purged, with more than 40,000 people losing their jobs.

In November 1951 state security officials submitted further reports to the Central Committee on the Doctors affair claiming that Zhdanov, who had died of heart failure in 1948, and other leading communists had been the victims of a murderous medical conspiracy. A year later this 'plot' scenario blossomed into a full-blown conspiracy theory. On 4 December 1952 the party Central Committee issued a declaration that a group of doctors working for British and American intelligence had conspired to use medical treatment to shorten the lives of leading members of the party and government. Only some of the accused doctors were identified as Jewish and the supposed conspiracy uncovered by the Central Committee was characterised as capitalist and imperialist rather than Zionist. However, when the plot was unveiled to the Soviet public by *Pravda* in January 1953 a distinctly anti-Jewish spin was put on the affair. The *Pravda* article, hand-corrected by Stalin prior to publication, claimed the doctors had been recruited to American intelligence via a Jewish bourgeois nationalist organisation and had received their instructions to assassinate Soviet leaders from Mikhoels, 'the well-known Jewish bourgeois nationalist'.[72]

Hundreds of Soviet physicians were arrested in 1952–1953. Among them was a core group of 37 doctors and their wives, including 17 Jews, who were implicated in the central conspiracy against the top Soviet leaders. Happily, all survived and were exonerated after Stalin's death. The executed members of the JAFC were posthumously rehabilitated, too, as were those caught up in the Leningrad affair.

Jonathan Brent and Vladimir Naumov consider 'The Doctors' Plot: Stalin's Last Great Criminal Conspiracy'[73] and paint a picture of a grand plot manipulated to the predetermined end of creating the conditions for a final cataclysmic confrontation in which all the Soviet dictator's enemies would be eliminated. In other words, Stalin had in mind a re-enactment of the Great Terror of the 1930s; only this time he would finish the job. Brent and Naumov wax lyrical about Stalin's abilities as a grand conspirator: 'Stalin is Godot, absent from an empty landscape. We wait, we guess, we attribute motives, receive incomprehensible communications, but in the end he will not reveal himself, and there is no direct way toward understanding him as a "person".'[74] This credits Stalin with a subtlety and foresight which he never possessed. What was actually revealed by the Leningrad, the JAFC and the Doctors affairs was the extent to which Stalin remained liable to believe in criminal conspiracies directed against his power and the dysfunctional impact his political paranoia had on his own regime. Whilst the repressions frightened people into passivity and compliance they also resulted in the murder or imprisonment of some of the most talented and loyal servants of the system. In December 1952, for example, Stalin dismissed A.N. Poskrebyshev, his long-time private secretary, for 'passing secret documents' and had his own bodyguard arrested. One of Stalin's last victims was Ivan Maiskii, who was arrested on 19 February 1953 as a foreign spy and not released from prison for two years.

In general terms the level of repression in the USSR remained quite high after the war, taking into account the postwar ethnic deportations, the counter-insurgency campaigns in the western borderlands and treatment of returning POWs and labour conscripts. The Soviet regime also remained prone to imprisoning large numbers of citizens for criminal wrongdoing, although in 1945 Stalin amnestied a million ordinary criminals as part of the victory celebrations.[75] Political prisoners were excluded from this amnesty but the postwar trend was towards a significant decline in arrests for alleged counter-revolutionary crimes. In 1946 the number convicted of political offences was 123,294; in 1952 it was just 28,800. In 1946 there were 2,896 political executions and 1,612 in 1952.[76] These figures compare to the millions arrested and the hundreds of thousands of political prisoners executed in the 1930s.

Despite the Leningrad, JAFC and Doctors affairs, the postwar Soviet regime was in transition from a system based on purges and terror. This analysis is strengthened by the fact that even at the height of the hysteria about foreign spies and sabotage in the early 1950s only a few hundred people were arrested.

Moreover, alongside this relatively limited repression ran a reversal of some of the more extreme aspects of the *Zhdanovshchina*. The so-called 'harlot-nun' poet Akhmatova was rehabilitated and allowed to publish again. In literature and theatre there was a backlash against over-politicisation and a reassertion of the value of depicting the drama and complexities of human life. As Timothy Dunmore argued, the much-lauded cultural thaw after Stalin's death actually began, albeit hesitantly, in the early 1950s.[77] Much the same was true in relation to the Gulag – the vast system of punitive labour camps run by Beria's Ministry of Internal Affairs. By the last years of Stalin's reign there was an established trend towards converting prisoner slave labour into a civilian workforce spurred on by economic incentives. When Stalin died the gates of the Gulag were prised open and the whole system soon dismantled, but the preliminary steps had been taken while he was still alive.[78]

The 19th Party Congress

Symptomatic of the process of transition from the late Stalin era to post-Stalin times was the 19th party congress held in October 1952 – the first such gathering since 1939 and the last of Stalin's reign.[79] According to party rules congresses were supposed to be held every three years. It was not possible to hold a congress during the war but one was planned for 1947 or 1948, with the major item on the agenda a new party programme and changes to the party's constitution. The congress was delayed, probably because Zhdanov, who had the job of drafting the new party programme, fell ill and died. After Zhdanov's death Stalin had more pressing matters on his mind – such as the Leningrad affair and the deteriorating international situation – and the convening of a party congress dropped off his agenda. It was not until December 1951 that the Politburo, at Stalin's behest, passed a resolution to hold a congress the following year. Discussion of the party constitution remained on the agenda but the idea of revising the party programme was dropped. In its place was a discussion of the five-year plan for 1951–1955. Significantly, the main political report was to be delivered by Malenkov, not Stalin. The job of presenting the five-year plan was given to M.Z. Saburov, Voznesenkii's successor at Gosplan, and the item on revising the party's rules was entrusted to Nikita Khrushchev, who had been appointed Secretary of the Central Committee in 1949. Molotov was tasked to open the congress and Voroshilov to give the closing speech.

Stalin's absence from the list of main speakers presumably reflected his declining health – he was nearly 73 by the time the congress convened and only six months away from the stroke that would kill him. His appearances at the congress were met with rapturous applause but he made only one brief contribution to the discussion in the form of greetings to the fraternal delegates of foreign communist parties.[80] However, Stalin was not inactive in preparations for the congress. On the eve of the congress he published a booklet called *Economic Problems of Socialism in the USSR*. Although mainly an arcane treatment of the workings of economic laws in a socialist economy, Stalin's pronouncements were much discussed at the congress. All the major speeches to the congress were vetted and edited by Stalin. He paid particular attention to Malenkov's report, which went through a number of drafts and was subject to detailed correction by the Soviet dictator. Most interesting was the fact that Malenkov's report was also submitted for comment to all the other members of the Politburo. Stalin's word was final, of course, but Malenkov's report was to some degree the product of collective deliberation by the Soviet leadership as a whole. There were no surprises in Malenkov's speech. Much of it was devoted to international economic and political developments since the end of the war, in particular the continuing crisis in the capitalist countries and the Soviet struggle for a lasting peace.

In practical terms the most important outcomes of the congress were changes to the party's rules. The name of the party was changed from All-Union Communist Party (Bolsheviks) to Communist Party of the Soviet Union. The position of General Secretary was abolished and Stalin became one of a number of First Secretaries of the party (another was Khrushchev). The Politburo was replaced by the Presidium, a larger body than its predecessor with 25 full members and 11 candidate members, although after the congress a smaller Buro of the Presidium was also established. Meetings of party structures at lower levels were regularised, with the aim of injecting an element of democracy into the party and increasing rank and file control over officials.[81]

It is not clear exactly what Stalin hoped to achieve by these changes but at the October 1952 plenum of the Central Committee, held immediately after the congress, he explained them as a means of introducing new and younger blood into the top party leadership. He also highlighted the complicated and dangerous international situation and launched into a personal attack on Molotov and Anastas Mikoyan, his long-time trade minister, as cowards and capitulationists. Although both men continued to hold important government positions they were demoted politically and excluded from Stalin's inner circle during the last few weeks of the Soviet dictator's life.[82]

Stalin's attack on Molotov and Mikoyan can be linked to the much-quoted statement about his comrades on the Politburo recorded in Khrushchev's memoirs: 'you are blind like kittens, without me the imperialists will throttle you.'[83] If Stalin did say and believe this, he had only himself to blame. Having cultivated a supine leadership circle he had left no obvious successor, and Stalin displayed little confidence in the ability of his colleagues to substitute their collective leadership for the cult of his personality. It turned out, however, that Stalinism without Stalin was entirely feasible and his reconstructed postwar regime was to endure for nearly 40 years after his death.

The domestic backdrop to Stalin's foreign policy was of critical importance in shaping his response to the postwar world. The Soviet Union emerged from the war militarily victorious, as a dominant power in Europe, and as a signifi- cant player in the postwar peace settlement. But the USSR had been damaged extensively and traumatised by the war; its western borderlands were in revolt against the re-imposition of Soviet rule; and the growth of patriotism and nationalism both challenged and complicated the country's communist iden- tity. In these difficult circumstances it was a great disappointment to Stalin that his Grand Alliance partners were not prepared to accommodate Soviet security needs nor to concede what he considered to be the USSR's just rewards for securing victory.

Stalin was suspicious about what the future held and his response was to close the country to foreign influences and to adopt a more strident foreign policy. The outbreak of the cold war in 1947 confirmed Stalin's worst fears and he sought to intensify the USSR's campaign against the west on the domestic and international fronts. But the polarisation of international politics and the break up of the Grand Alliance brought with it other dangers and by the late 1940s Stalin was beginning to draw back from cold war confrontation and to seek a new *détente* with the west. But the international situation remained tense and there was no relaxation in Soviet domestic politics. Stalin's postwar repression of party and state officials reached its peak in the early 1950s, driven by his conviction that the more powerful the socialist system was the more intense became the struggle of its enemies against it.

Stalin's notion that class struggle intensified under socialism carried little conviction with the rest of the Soviet leadership and they dropped this ideo- logical tenet as soon as Stalin died. But, while Stalin lived, it was his percep- tions and preferences that held sway. In domestic politics, as in foreign policy, Stalin was the Generalissimo. Those in the Soviet leadership who served under him jostled for position, pursued their personal rivalries and protected their institutional interests, but the main lines of policy were set by Stalin, who also took all the major decisions.[84]

The war had served to profoundly reinforce Stalin's power and he remained unchallenged and unchallengeable at home. Abroad it was a different story. In the international arena he faced a powerful American rival and an emerging anti-Soviet western bloc – threats magnified in Stalin's mind by the complica- tions of his domestic situation. Stalin continued nonetheless to strive for a *modus vivendi* with the west that would curtail the cold war and establish a durable peace with his erstwhile allies.

12

Cold War Confrontations
Stalin Embattled

Soviet foreign policy during the last five years of Stalin's reign was a kaleidoscope of seemingly contradictory elements. The collapse of the Grand Alliance in 1947 provoked widespread fear that the cold war would soon develop into a 'hot war'. Stalin's own public statements warned of nefarious activities by western warmongers, especially 'Churchill and his friends'. But he also talked down the war danger and insisted on the possibility of the peaceful coexistence of communism and capitalism. As the cold war intensified Stalin welded the Soviet sphere of influence in Eastern Europe into a tightly controlled bloc. But he faced a major challenge to his authority when Tito's Yugoslavia separated from the communist movement in 1948. As Europe in the late 1940s split into the cold war blocs that divided the continent for the next 40 years, Stalin continued to seek ways to attenuate the polarisation and to find an agreed solution to the German question. In 1949 the Soviet Union tested its first atomic bomb and in the early 1950s began to develop the much more powerful hydrogen bomb – a programme that coincided with an intense Soviet-sponsored peace campaign demanding disarmament and the abolition of nuclear weapons. In 1950 North Korea invaded South Korea with the aim of unifying the country under the communist leadership of Kim Il Sung. The invasion had Stalin's blessing and support but when the United States intervened on South Korea's behalf he quickly backed away from direct confrontation with the Americans.

The unifying theme of these disparate events was Stalin's effort to control the consequences of the cold war. Stalin saw the cold war struggle as necessary to protect Soviet security and communist gains after the Second World War but feared that escalation of the conflict would result in an even greater danger: the revival of German militarism and its combination with an American-led western bloc. It cannot be overemphasised that for Stalin the resolution of the German question – the problem of how to contain or tame German power and aggression in Europe – was the key to Soviet postwar security. It was an issue he returned to again and again during the postwar period, including one last effort in 1952 to secure an agreement to neutralise and pacify Germany, even at the cost of sacrificing communist-controlled East Germany.

The Stalin–Tito Split

On the face of it Stalin's split with Tito in 1948 was about Moscow's right to lead and control the people's democracies of Eastern Europe – a right the Yugoslavs challenged by asserting their own national interests over Soviet interests. Certainly this is the image of the dispute cultivated by Tito's supporters in the 1950s. They depicted Yugoslavia standing up for its rights as a small nation against the Great Russian bear. But closer inspection reveals a more complex picture in which Stalin's treatment of Tito had as much to do with his fears about the intensifying cold war with the west as it did with regulating internal relations in the Soviet-communist bloc.

The events which precipitated the split were twofold. First, moves to form a federation between Yugoslavia and Bulgaria, a project linked to a broader concept of a Balkan federation involving a provisional government proclaimed by communist partisans in Greece in December 1947. Second, Yugoslavia's desire to dominate Albania (also a member of the Soviet bloc), including the establishment of a military base there that would aid the struggle of the communist partisans in the Greek civil war.[1] Stalin did not object in principle to such plans but he did expect to be consulted about their formulation and implementation. He was particularly annoyed by an unauthorised public statement made in January 1948 by the former Comintern leader, Georgi Dimitrov – back now in his native Bulgaria – about the projected Bulgarian–Greek–Yugoslav federation. On 10 February 1948 Stalin met a Bulgarian–Yugoslav delegation headed by Dimitrov and by Edvard Kardelj, Tito's representative. From various records of this meeting it is clear that Stalin's main concern was that the premature formation of a Balkan communist federation would provide ammunition for reactionary elements in the west and aid their efforts to consolidate an anti-Soviet bloc. Stalin pointed out to the Bulgarians and Yugoslavs that there were elections forthcoming in the United States (he was referring to Presidential and Congressional elections) and their actions could result in the victory of an even more reactionary American administration than the existing one. In relation to Greece, Stalin thought the partisan struggle was hopeless, at least for time being, and that the British and Americans would use it as an excuse to establish military bases in the country. For the same reasons he also opposed the deployment of Yugoslav troops in Albania. Stalin's message to

Dimitrov and Kardelj was: go slowly, consult with Moscow at every stage, and consider the complications of the international situation.[2]

The Soviets expected the Yugoslavs and Bulgarians to toe the line after their meeting with the 'boss'. While the ever-loyal Dimitrov did so, Tito rebelled. On 1 March 1948 the Yugoslav Politburo resolved to defy the Soviets and to act in accordance with what they saw as Yugoslavia's national interests. Tito did not intend to precipitate an open split with Stalin but, unfortunately for him, Soviet supporters in the Yugoslav leadership told Moscow what was going on. Stalin retaliated by ordering the preparation of a political and ideological critique of the Yugoslav party and by withdrawing Soviet military and civilian technicians and advisers from Yugoslavia. On 27 March Stalin and Molotov sent a letter to Tito accusing Yugoslavia of embarking on an anti-Soviet course. The Yugoslav communists were accused of nationalism and opportunism and parallels were drawn between their politics and those of Stalin's arch-enemy Trotsky. Adding insult to injury, the Yugoslavs were also accused of harbouring an English spy in their Ministry of Foreign Affairs.[3]

The Stalin–Molotov letter was circulated to other communist leaders in Europe and an increasingly acrimonious correspondence developed between Moscow and Belgrade, despite Yugoslav denials of the Soviet charges and proclamations of their fidelity to communism. The scene was set for the exclusion of the Yugoslav party from the Communist Information Buro at the organisation's second conference in June 1948. The Cominform resolution excluding Tito's party held out the hope that it would return to the fold once a new leadership was installed in Yugoslavia,[4] but the dispute continued to escalate. At the height of the ideological spat the 'Titoites' were accused by Stalin's supporters of being imperialist spies carrying out a restoration of capitalism in Yugoslavia. Throughout the European communist movement there was a hunt for Titoite heretics.[5] In the people's democracies a number of alleged 'nationalists', 'spies' and 'right-wing deviationists' were unmasked in the upper reaches of the communist leadership. Among the victims was Gomulka, the Polish communist leader, who lost his position in the party hierarchy at the end of 1948 following accusations of nationalist deviationism. Later he was arrested and imprisoned. A more drastic fate befell a number of Czechoslovak party leaders who in 1952 suffered the ultimate indignity of a show trial and then execution for anti-communist treachery.

As the split with Tito began to develop, the politics, policies and leadership of all the ruling communist parties in Eastern Europe came under Soviet scrutiny. In 1948 the Soviet Communist Party's international department drew up a number of reports for Stalin criticising the ideological and political errors of the East European communist parties, the main theme being a critique of nationalist deviations from communist ideology and departures from the Soviet model of socialism.[6]

The aim of the anti-Tito campaign was not just to discipline and unify the communist bloc at a time of growing international tensions, but to absolutise Stalin's leadership. No repeat of the Yugoslav rebellion could be allowed in the ever more dangerous and complex international situation created by the cold war.

The German Question

The consolidation of the Soviet and communist position in Eastern Europe was one element of Stalin's cold war strategy; another was a more aggressive approach to the German question. Stalin's most dramatic act was the imposition in June 1948 of a land blockade of West Berlin. In response the British and Americans launched their celebrated airlift to supply the western sectors of the German capital that had been cut off by the Soviets. Notwithstanding the drama of this first great crisis of the cold war, Stalin's goal was pretty mundane: to force the western powers to resume negotiations with the Soviet Union about the future of Germany.

During the war the Grand Alliance had agreed to divide Germany into zones of military occupation including – for symbolic and political reasons – the capital Berlin, even though it lay deep in the occupation zone in eastern Germany allocated to the Soviet Union (*see Map 19 on p. 351*). Each country would control its own occupation zone and sector of Berlin and an Allied Control Council (ACC) would co-ordinate the implementation throughout Germany of the 'four Ds' – demilitarisation, disarmament, denazification and democratisation. During the war Stalin had been a strong supporter of a fifth 'D' – the dismemberment of Germany – but he dropped that policy when the British and Americans began dragging their feet over it. Instead he embraced the alternative perspective of a united but peace-loving and democratic Germany.

Stalin's political strategy in postwar Germany was a variation of his more general project for a people's democratic Europe. The hope was that postwar Germany would evolve into a left-wing, democratic and anti-fascist state ruled by a coalition including Stalin's communist allies. While Stalin was optimistic that the people's democratic project could succeed in Germany, he could not guarantee that the politics of a future German state would be to his liking. But he could control developments in his own zone where the Soviet occupation authorities, in alliance with the East German communists, pursued people's democracy with the aim of extending this model to the rest of Germany when reunification took place.[7] Stalin's economic aim in relation

The Postwar Division of Germany

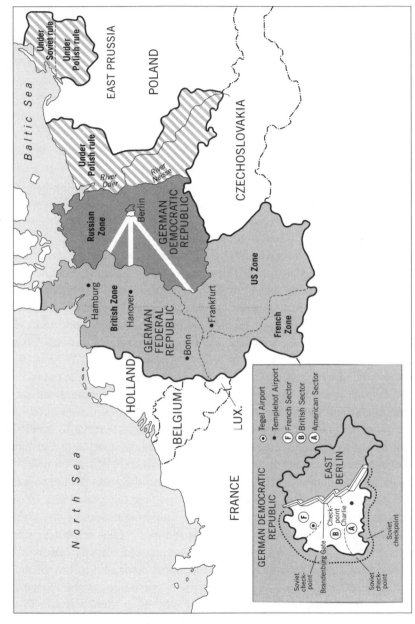

to Germany was the implementation of the Yalta and Potsdam decisions on the payment of $10 billion worth of reparations to the Soviet Union, which was vital to Russia's postwar reconstruction.

Stalin's political and economic aims in Germany brought him into conflict with the British and Americans. They did not like reparations – which Stalin expected to receive from the western zones as well as his own. In the western view reparations would hinder Germany's economic recovery, seen as central to a more general revival of the European economy after the war. Nor did the Anglo-Americans like the idea of a united Germany falling under communist and Soviet sway. Hence, while Stalin favoured German unity, albeit in a form and under conditions that would suit Soviet interests, the British and Americans increasingly preferred to divide Germany politically and economically and to retain control over the destiny of the western zones of occupation. As Soviet and western policies on Germany increasingly diverged, the mistrust between the two sides grew. The state of mistrust on the Soviet side was highlighted by Moscow's response to an American proposal for a Soviet–Western treaty on the long-term disarmament and demilitarisation of Germany, an idea that should have appealed to Stalin given his oft-stated belief in the inevitable revival of the German threat. This proposal was first broached by James F. Byrnes, the American Secretary of State, at the London meeting of the Council of Foreign Ministers in September 1945. Byrnes mentioned it again when he met Stalin in December 1945. At the Paris CFM meeting in April 1946 he tabled a formal proposal for a 'Twenty-Five Year Treaty on the Disarmament and Demilitarisation of Germany'.[8] When Molotov returned to Moscow there was a detailed discussion of the so-called Byrnes Plan within the Soviet Foreign Ministry. The main tenor of this discussion – which was replicated in the Soviet press – was that the Byrnes Plan was a device to secure the premature end of the allied occupation of Germany and was conceived as a substitute for full implementation of the 'four Ds'.[9] When Molotov returned to the Paris CFM in July he told Byrnes the proposed treaty did not 'correspond to the interests of ensuring the peace and security of nations' and insisted on the complete implementation of the Yalta and Potsdam decisions on the German question.[10] This response infuriated Byrnes, who insisted his plan was a genuine attempt to address Soviet concerns about postwar security. But Molotov remained unmoved and took the same unbending position in subsequent discussions of the Byrnes Plan.

Apart from these exchanges over the Byrnes Plan there was no substantive discussion of the German question at the CFM until the Moscow meeting of the council in March–April 1947. In Moscow the Soviets pushed hard for an agreement on the establishment of a central German government. That this was a private as well as a public preference is shown by the Soviet internal documents in preparation for the conference and by Stalin's remarks at a long meeting with German communist leaders in January 1947. Stalin told them that it could prove difficult to reach an agreement on German unity since the British and Americans preferred a weak Germany, a country they could dominate economically and exclude from world markets. On the other hand, Stalin was optimistic about political prospects in Germany. In the Soviet zone of occupation the communist and social democratic parties had recently merged to form a Socialist Unity Party. Stalin looked forward to its extension to West Germany and used the analogy of the Bolsheviks in 1917 to show how a minority party could rapidly grow in support and then win power.[11]

At the Moscow CFM much of the discussion centred on the question of reparations and concerned the interpretation and renegotiation of the Yalta and Potsdam agreements on German payments to the Soviet Union. Naturally, the Soviets sought to maximise their position while the west sought an end to reparation deliveries from their zones of occupation. The other main issue was the establishment of a central German administration. The western representatives argued that various economic issues had to be sorted out before there could be political unity. The western powers also favoured a German central government with relatively weak powers and devolution of most decision-making to the German regions – a policy that suited their aim of excluding Soviet and communist influence from as much of Germany as they could. When Stalin met George Marshall, who had replaced Byrnes as US Secretary of State, on 15 April 1947 the Soviet leader argued that German political unity had to precede economic unity and he explained his preference for a unified German state as opposed to some kind of federal solution:

> The allies don't want to make the same mistake as Napoleon when he formed scores of states in Germany . . . the result of this dismemberment was . . . that the idea of German unity became a weapon in the hands of German chauvinists and revanchists, bred Bismarck, the Franco-Prussian war etc.[12]

From the western point of view the Moscow CFM was quite problematic and the weeks of discussion wholly unproductive. As one of Marshall's advisers said shortly after the conference: 'It is a mistake to underestimate the extent and significance of the failure at Moscow. With respect to Germany the conference ended with the participants further apart than they had been at Potsdam.'[13] From the Soviet point of view, however, there had been some progress in the discussions. This was the tenor of remarks made by Deputy Foreign Minister Vyshinskii at a press conference on 12 April and, in closing the conference on 24 April, Molotov spoke of the great preparatory work that had been done and looked forward to the next round of negotiations. The *Pravda* editorial on the results of the conference echoed this line and reiterated that the basic issue remained implementation of the Yalta and Potsdam agreements on Germany.[14]

The CFM reconvened in London six months later, in November–December 1947, to continue discussing the terms of a peace treaty for Germany, but by this time the international atmosphere had worsened considerably. In July the Soviets had rejected participation in the Marshall Plan and in September they had established the Cominform and proclaimed the two-camps doctrine – a direct counter to Truman's doctrine of an American global campaign in defence of the free world. A fortnight before he left for London Molotov gave the speech on the 30th anniversary of the Bolshevik Revolution. It bristled with hostility to the western powers. Britain and the United States were accused of surrounding the Soviet Union with a global chain of air and naval bases. 'It is obvious,' said Molotov, 'that the creation of military bases in various parts of the world is not designed for the purposes of defence, but as preparation for aggression.'[15] Molotov continued in this tone at the London CFM, claiming in his opening statement that the choice facing the postwar world was between a democratic peace and an imperialist peace.[16] Not surprisingly, the London CFM failed to reach any agreement. Soviet proposals for the establishment of a central German government were countered by western demands that the economic principles of the new regime be agreed first and that meant fundamental changes to the reparations deal struck at Potsdam, which Moscow was not prepared to accept. When the CFM ended on 15 December there were no plans to reconvene the council.[17] Despite this, Stalin continued to hope for a deal on German unity. In a meeting with East German communist leaders in March 1948 Stalin urged them to draft a German constitution and to sponsor widespread discussion of it in West Germany. Stalin saw this move as both a counter to British and American efforts to buy off the West German population economically and as part of the preparations for German unity: 'All the people must be drawn into discussion of the constitution. This will form the psychological basis for the realisation of a united Germany.'[18]

In 1948 the western states began moves to force an East–West division of Germany. On 7 June Britain, France and the United States issued a communiqué from London announcing their intention to establish a federal German state in the western zones of occupation.[19] A few days later a new currency was issued in the western zones, an initiative that threatened to undermine the much weaker Soviet-backed currency in East Germany. These events precipitated the Soviet blockade of West Berlin at the end of June. Although termed a 'blockade' by the west, the Soviet action consisted of a limited set of restrictions on land access to the western sectors of Berlin from West Germany. It did not preclude supplies to West Berlin from the Soviet zone of occupation – which continued to flow into the city – nor was air access prohibited; hence the famous airlift.[20] The aim of Stalin's pressure tactics was to force the western states to rescind their London communiqué and return to the CFM negotiating forum. Stalin was quite frank about his aim in two conversations he had with the British, French and American ambassadors in August 1948[21] and, in January 1949, he made this position public when he agreed with a western interviewer that the blockade would be lifted if the west agreed to convene another CFM session devoted to the German question.[22]

In May 1949 the blockade was lifted following an agreement to reconvene the CFM in Paris at the end of the month. The Soviet representative at the Paris meeting was Vyshinskii, who had replaced Molotov as Foreign Minister in March 1949. Vyshinskii's brief was to secure a return to the Yalta and Potsdam agreements, including the restoration of four-power control of Germany. It seems the Soviets were not unoptimistic about achieving some progress but the CFM closed on 20 June without any agreement.[23] In September 1949, the Federal Republic of Germany formally came into existence when the West German parliament was convened. Stalin responded in October by establishing the German Democratic Republic (GDR) in the east, a somewhat problematic move given his commitment to a united Germany. Now he would have to deal with an even more entrenched local communist regime in East Germany and with the complications of conducting negotiations about the future of Germany with two German governments as well as with the western powers.

Ultimately, the Berlin blockade tactic backfired on Stalin. It allowed anti-Soviet critics in the west to paint him as the aggressor and did not play well with German public opinion, which the Soviets and their East German allies were trying to win over on the basis that they stood for a united Germany. What Stalin had underestimated were both the possibilities of supplying West Berlin by air and western determination to proceed with their plans for the establishment of a West German state.

When the North Atlantic Treaty Organisation (NATO) was established in April 1949 the anti-Soviet western bloc long feared by Stalin assumed a more definite form. When the US announced in January 1949 the forthcoming formation of NATO, Moscow issued a statement linking the proposed North Atlantic Pact with the Marshall Plan and with Anglo-American plans to establish their domination not only of Europe but of the whole world. In March 1949 when the text of the NATO treaty was published the Soviet Foreign Ministry issued another statement condemning the organisation as an aggressive alliance directed against the USSR and the people's democracies. The formation of NATO was also said to be incompatible with the Anglo-Soviet and Franco-Soviet wartime pacts of alliance, which forbade the signatories from entering coalitions directed against each other. Responding to accusations that the Soviet Union's own mutual defence pacts with Romania, Hungary, Bulgaria and Finland (all signed in 1949) were as threatening to the west as NATO was to the east, the statement pointed out that these treaties were explicitly directed against a revival of German aggression. In July 1949 the Soviets protested strongly against Italy's accession to NATO, claiming that the Italians were infringing their peace treaty commitment not to enter into any arrangements that threatened other signatories (the USSR, for example).[24] Despite these various protestations Moscow did not see NATO as an immediate military threat. As Stalin reportedly told a leading Chinese communist in mid-1949:

> A third world war was improbable, if only because no one had the strength to start it. The revolutionary forces were growing, the people were more powerful than before. If the imperialists wanted to start a world war, preparations for it would take at least twenty years. If the peoples did not want war, there would be no war. How long the peace lasted depended on how hard we worked for it and how events would develop . . . The thing to do was to safeguard peace for as long as possible. But who could be sure no madmen appeared on the scene?[25]

Madmen apart, it was the political coalescence of the western bloc that concerned Stalin, not the immediate prospect of war with the NATO alliance.[26] In the early 1950s, however, a much more disturbing prospect came into view: the rearmament of West Germany and its integration into western defence structures. Stalin's response to this threatening development was to renew calls for the demilitarisation of Germany and for the CFM to meet to negotiate a peace treaty. In March 1952 Moscow launched a major new initiative on the German question when it issued and published a diplomatic note to the western powers setting out the principles on which to base a peace treaty with Germany. Often referred to as the 'Stalin Note', this document was actually issued in the name of the Soviet government; if anyone was the main author it was Molotov, who worked closely with Vyshinskii in preparing the draft for Stalin's approval. The most significant formulation in the Soviet note was that the German peace treaty could only be negotiated with the representatives of an all-German government 'expressive of the will of the German people'. This opened the door for negotiations about holding all-German elections – the key western demand in relation to the resolution of the German question. But the Soviet note went on to make it clear that negotiations with an all-German government – whatever its political complexion – must result in a 'democratic and peaceloving Germany', and that meant guarantees about German neutrality and its non-participation in military blocs.[27] While Moscow hoped for a good showing by the communists and their allies in all-German elections there could be little doubt that such a contest would be won by pro-western politicians. It seemed, then, that the deal on offer was that the Soviets were prepared to relinquish control of East Germany, provided Germany remained neutral, non-aligned and non-threatening for the foreseeable future. Was Stalin serious about this proposal or was it just a propaganda ploy designed to impress gullible Germans that he was sincere about wanting German unity? This was the question people asked themselves at the time and historians have debated it ever since. Some historians argue that the Soviet note of March 1952 should be taken at face value as simply a restatement of Stalin's commitment to the reunification of Germany under acceptable conditions. Other historians have drawn attention to evidence from Soviet archives that Moscow's main eye was on the propaganda value of such an initiative.[28]

One of the most important pieces of evidence bearing on this debate is the record of Stalin's meetings with a delegation from the GDR in April 1952. These conversations took place in the wake of western rejection of the Soviet note on 25 March. The western counter-proposal was all-German elections, to be followed by negotiations about the peace treaty with a democratically elected German government that would make its own decisions about the country's alignment in foreign policy, including Germany's participation in NATO. Such a proposal was self-evidently unacceptable to Moscow since the whole aim of Soviet policy was to prevent German rearmament and Germany's participation in NATO.

If the March note was a propaganda ploy, the GDR leaders were not privy to the conspiracy. At their first meeting with Stalin on 1 April they wanted to know what the prospects for a peace treaty were, when the CFM would meet and how they should prepare for all-German elections. Stalin did not reply directly but the next day *Pravda* published an interview with him in which he said that the present moment was opportune for the unification of Germany.[29] On 7 April Stalin met the East Germans again and replied to their question about his perspectives on Germany. He told them:

> Whatever proposals we make on the German question the western powers won't agree with them and they won't withdraw from West Germany. To think that the Americans will compromise or accept the draft peace treaty would be a mistake. The Americans need an army in West Germany in order to keep control of Western Europe. They say the army is directed against us. Actually, the army stays to control Europe. The Americans are drawing West Germany into the [NATO] pact. They will form West

German forces . . . In West Germany an independent state is being formed. And you must organise your own state. The demarcation line between West Germany and East Germany should be considered a frontier, and not just any frontier but a dangerous frontier. It is necessary to strengthen the security of this frontier. In the first line of security will be the Germans, in the second line Russian forces.

On the basis of this evidence it is reasonable to conclude that while Stalin was genuine about the German unity proposal in the March note he did not rate its prospects for success very high, a presupposition confirmed by the rapid western rejection of his proposal. However, that did not mean an end to the Soviet campaign for a united Germany. When the conversation on 7 April drew to a close and the Germans asked Stalin if they should change their policy on German unity, Stalin replied in the negative: 'it is necessary to continue propaganda for a united Germany all the time. This has great significance for the education of the West German people. At the present time this is a weapon in your hands and it is necessary that at all times it remains in your hands. We will also continue to make proposals on German unity, in order to expose the Americans.'[30]

On 9 April Moscow issued another note indicating that all-German elections could be held in the near future under the right conditions.[31] This note was followed by several further public exchanges with the western powers in which the sticking point was Soviet insistence that holding all-German elections had to be linked to prior agreement on German neutrality in the cold war. Stalin might be prepared to give up East Germany but it would have a high price and he would do everything possible to strengthen the Soviet position in Germany as a whole. In September 1952 he complained to Chou En-lai, the Prime Minister of communist China, that 'America will not support German unification. They plundered Germany; if West Germany and East Germany unite, then it will not be possible to plunder Germany any longer. That is why America does not want German unification.'[32]

It is difficult to say what would have happened if the west had responded positively to Stalin's last initiative on the German question. It might have led to German reunification some time in the 1950s and to a considerable easing of cold war tensions in Europe. On the other hand, it might have led to greater uncertainty and instability as there was no guarantee Germany would have remained neutral or disarmed for long. As western diplomats and politicians often pointed out to the Soviets in the 1950s, there were advantages for Moscow in West Germany's inclusion in the western bloc. As the old saying has it: NATO was established to keep the Americans in, the Russians out, and the Germans down! But that sanguine perspective was not shared by Stalin or by his successors as Soviet leader, whose view of the German question was formed by their experience of the Great Patriotic War and by their continuing dread of the re-emergence of a powerful and aggressive Germany.

Stalin's Peace Campaign

Even as the cold war raged, the idea of a revival of the Grand Alliance to contain Germany still had its allure in Moscow, not least for Stalin who had been very reluctant to relinquish the project of postwar co-operation with the west. In January 1949 Stalin responded positively to a question from an American journalist about whether he would be prepared to meet Truman to discuss a 'peace pact' – an American–Soviet non-aggression agreement.[33] A few months later, at a meeting of the United Nations in September, Vyshinskii proposed that the five great powers – Britain, China, France, the Soviet Union and the United States – should sign a pact for the strengthening of peace.[34] Vyshinskii's proposal was somewhat undercut by his simultaneous demand that Britain and the United States be condemned by the UN as warmongering states. But the peace pact was one of a number of such Soviet initiatives at the UN in the early postwar years. In 1946 the USSR proposed that all nuclear weapons should be banned. In 1947 the Soviets sponsored a UN resolution on the prohibition of war propaganda. In 1948 they called for the conventional armed forces of the five great powers to be reduced by a third.[35] At the 19th party congress in October 1952 Malenkov drew the threads of these policies together when he spoke of 'prohibiting war propaganda ... prohibiting nuclear and bacteriological weapons, progressive reductions in the armed forces of the great powers, the conclusion of a Peace Pact between the powers, the growth of trade between countries, the restoration of a single international market, and other such measures in the spirit of strengthening peace'.[36]

The wider context of these various Soviet peace proposals was a massive communist-sponsored peace campaign in the west. Soviet and communist agitation for peace dated back to the early postwar years when Moscow first began to worry about the influence of Churchill and other western 'warmongers'. But the campaign took more definite form with the convening in the late 1940s and early 1950s of a series of world peace congresses involving a number of prominent western intellectuals. The peak of the peace movement's success came with the Stockholm Appeal, a petition launched in the Swedish capital in March 1950 that called for a ban on the use of nuclear weapons. Some 560 million signatures were gathered in support of the appeal. The majority of the signatories were from the Soviet bloc, including communist China, but many millions signed in Western Europe and North America as well.

How serious was Stalin about these 'peace proposals'? Did he really believe it possible to restore some semblance of the Grand Alliance or was he just playing propaganda games? In his study of Soviet foreign policy in the late Stalin era,[37] Marshall Shulman suggested that like all such communist campaigns the aims were multi-dimensional and had their power-political, propaganda and ideological (or doctrinal) aspects. In power-political terms the aim of the peace campaign was to bring political pressure to bear within western states that would block or disrupt plans for the formation of a US-led western bloc against the USSR. Particular emphasis was laid on the political influence that could be wielded by Moscow in France and Italy, where there were mass communist parties. In Britain the communist party was small but not without influence in the labour movement. Even in the United States the political situation was not without hope. In May 1948 Stalin exchanged open letters with Henry Wallace, Roosevelt's Vice-President from 1940 to 1945, who was running a third party presidential campaign against Truman under the banner of the Progressive Party. Stalin welcomed as a good basis for discussion Wallace's proposals for overcoming problems in American–Soviet relations and said that differences of economics and ideology did not preclude the peaceful resolution of disputes between the two countries.[38]

In terms of propaganda the main theme of the Soviet peace campaign was the USSR's identity as a peace-loving state. Promotion of this self-image dated back to the 1920s when the Soviet leadership first began to talk about peaceful coexistence with capitalism. It had its cynical and manipulative element, but there is no reason to suppose that Stalin and the Soviet leadership did not believe their own propaganda about the essentially peace-loving policy of the USSR. Soviet self-conceptions of the USSR as a peaceful state were reinforced by the ideological rationalisation for the peace campaign. Within Soviet ideology there was a strong belief that the economic contradictions and rivalries of capitalism and imperialism inevitably led to war.[39] Stalin himself pronounced on this topic in his last major theoretical work – *Economic Problems of Socialism in the USSR*, published in 1952. In a section of the booklet entitled the 'Inevitability of Wars between Capitalist Countries' Stalin reaffirmed the traditional Soviet doctrine that intra-capitalist wars were inevitable. He noted postwar America's economic domination of the capitalist world but was confident that eventually the US position would be challenged by Britain and France and by a revived Germany and Japan. In relation to communist–capitalist relations Stalin denied that the contradictions between the USSR and the capitalist world were necessarily stronger or sharper than those between the capitalist states. Again, he utilised the traditional Soviet belief that war with the USSR was deemed more dangerous by the capitalists (the intelligent ones, at least) because defeat in such a war could threaten the very existence of capitalism itself. The peace movement's role in this scenario was to wage a broad-based campaign to preserve peace by preventing specific wars. It could not succeed in eliminating war in general while capitalism and imperialism still existed but it could prevent particular wars in particular circumstances and preserve a particular peace, said Stalin.[40]

The point of Stalin's convoluted reasoning was fourfold: to reaffirm the traditional Soviet doctrine of the inevitability of inter-capitalist wars; to encourage the continuation of the political activism that powered the peace movement; to question the permanency of American hegemony in the capitalist world; and to deny that war between communism and capitalism was inevitable, notwithstanding the high tensions of the cold war. For Stalin the struggle for peace was a serious business; it was an indispensable part of the process of ameliorating the warlike tendencies of the capitalist states, not least to protect the USSR from attack by extremist anti-communist elements in the western camp who might wish to resolve imperialism's internal contradictions at the Soviet expense. Not that Stalin relied on the peace movement to protect the Soviet Union. He had more conventional means available for that purpose.

Stalin's War Machine

As the cold war intensified, Stalin called a halt to the postwar demobilisation of Soviet armed forces. By the late 1940s numbers in the armed forces had stabilised at a little under 3 million (down from the 11 million of 1945), organised in 175 divisions (as compared with 500 during the Great Patriotic War). Between 1948 and 1955, however, the Soviet armed forces doubled in size and were supplemented by increases in the armies of the people's democracies which by 1953 numbered over a million. Poland alone provided 400,000 troops, headed by the Polish-born Marshal K.K. Rokossovskii, who was appointed Polish defence minister in October 1949. Soviet forces in the GDR were bolstered and plans hatched to create an East German army. In January 1951 Stalin convened a secret meeting of the Soviet–East European bloc in Moscow to discuss counter-measures to the growing threat of NATO and German rearmament. Soviet defence spending increased by 20 per cent and in the five-year plan for 1951–1955 there was provision for a 2.5-fold increase in defence production. In early 1951 the Council of Ministers established a new bureau to supervise the military-industrial complex. It was headed by Stalin's latest protégé, Marshal Nikolai Bulganin. Two years later ambitious plans were drawn up for a substantial increase in the size and capabilities of the Soviet air force and navy.[41]

The purpose of these measures was not to prepare for war in the short or even the medium term. Rather, they were a precautionary response to an emergent long-term threat from the western bloc (especially in the form of German rearmament) and a means of offsetting any attempt by the United States to use the threat of military power to extract political concessions or gain diplomatic advantage.

The highest priority of the Soviet defence industry was the programme to develop an atomic bomb that had been established by Stalin in August 1945 and was headed by Lavrentii Beria, his Minister for Internal Affairs. The first Soviet bomb was tested on 29 August 1949 and there were two more tests while Stalin lived, both in 1951. By the time Stalin died in 1953 the Soviets possessed something like 50–100 bombs (as opposed to nearly a thousand in American hands). After Stalin died there were many more Soviet nuclear tests, thousands of atomic bombs were produced, and Moscow was never shy of publicising and boasting of the USSR's technological achievements in this sphere. Curiously, Moscow remained silent about the first test, which took the world by surprise and should have been a cause for celebration in the USSR. In the west the expectation had been that it would take the Soviets many years to develop a bomb, notwithstanding their success in stealing western atomic secrets. The news of the Soviet test was, in fact, broken to the world by Truman on 23 September. The next day the Soviet news agency Tass issued a statement claiming that the USSR had possessed the bomb since 1947 and that the recent explosion was connected to 'large-scale blasting' necessary for infra-structural building works such as mines, canals, roads and hydroelectric power stations.[42] Such coyness may have reflected the Soviet obsession with secrecy or it may have been calculated to avoid provoking the Americans too much. It may also have been connected to Vyshinskii's imminent address to the UN about Soviet proposals for disarmament, the prohibition of nuclear weapons, and the control of atomic energy. Indeed, on 23 November 1949 Vyshinskii claimed at the UN that, in contrast to the aggressive US nuclear tests, those of the Soviet Union were peaceful because they were being used to level mountains and move rivers – a claim described by one incredulous American author as 'one of the most nonsensical statements ever perpetrated on an international organisation'.[43]

So where did the atomic bomb fit into Stalin's postwar military and polit-ical perspectives? The difficulty, as David Holloway noted, is that 'Stalin said little about the bomb between 1946 and 1953, and what he did say was intended to create a particular impression'.[44] The impression Stalin wished to convey was that the bomb was not as important as some people made it out to be. Stalin began playing down the significance of the bomb in November 1945 when he told Gomulka that 'not atomic bombs, but armies decide about the war' and he continued in this vein for the remainder of his life. For example, in July 1952 he told the Italian Socialist leader, Pietro Nenni, that the

US had the technological power to wage a third world war but not the human capital. 'It is not enough for America to destroy Moscow, just as it is not enough for us to destroy New York. We want armies to occupy Moscow and to occupy New York.'[45]

There is no reason to believe that Stalin did not mean what he said, and it was not an unrealistic perspective. Before development of the hydrogen bomb in the early 1950s the United States did not have the capacity to atom bomb the Soviet Union to destruction. At best the Americans would have been able to inflict as much damage as the Germans had when they invaded the Soviet Union in 1941. This meant the Soviets would retain the capacity for a substantial counter-offensive because while the atomic weapons of the 1940s could be used against cities they could not be deployed effectively against dispersed armies. On the other hand, the fact that Stalin did not see the bomb as a self-sufficient war-winning weapon did not mean that he underestimated the importance of possessing one. He had been impressed by the impact of the allied strategic bombing campaign on Germany and Japan during the war and appreciated the qualitative difference that nuclear weapons could make in future to such campaigns. In his postwar defence programme Stalin accorded high priority to the Soviet air force. In July 1948 the air force was established as a separate service on an equal footing with the army and the navy and Stalin pushed hard for better air defence capacity, the development of long-range strategic bombers, and the establishment of a rocket force. According to one source, at a meeting with military leaders and rocket scientists in April 1947 Stalin said, 'do you realise the tremendous strategic importance of machines of this sort? They could be an effective straitjacket for that noisy shopkeeper Harry Truman. We must go ahead with it, comrades. The problem of the creation of transatlantic rockets is of extreme importance to us.'[46] It is probably another one of those *post hoc* apocryphal stories, but it is not difficult to imagine Stalin saying such things.

David Holloway, author of the classic *Stalin & the Bomb*, summarises the situation as follows:

> The atomic bomb occupied a central place in postwar military policy. Stalin gave high priority to defense against atomic attack and to the development of delivery vehicles for Soviet nuclear weapons. He did not, however, regard the bomb as a decisive weapon . . . he saw the bomb as a strategic weapon to be used against targets in the rear, and did not regard it as an effective counterweight to ground forces or sea power . . . Stalin did not think that the atomic bomb had ushered in a revolution in military affairs. Soviet military strategy drew heavily on the experience of the war with Germany. There was no radical shift in the Soviet conception of war.[47]

Stalin's balanced view of the utility of nuclear weapons had two further implications. First, he did not allow American monopoly of the bomb to affect his
foreign policy and diplomacy. Fear of the bomb had no impact on his
handling of the Iranian and Turkish crises in 1946 nor did it deter him from
declaring the cold war in 1947 or from provoking the Berlin crisis in 1948.
Second, all those Soviet proposals on banning nuclear weapons were not
simply propaganda. Stalin was perfectly prepared to enter into serious discussions about controlling and limiting nuclear weapons even after the USSR had
acquired its own bomb. For Stalin the bomb was a very important addition to
his military arsenal but it did not define the Soviet Union's postwar defence
posture, which relied on the country's capacity to absorb a NATO attack and
then launch a counter-offensive in the form of a land invasion of Western
Europe.

The Korean War

In Europe Stalin sought peace and a resolution of the German question. In
military competition with the United States his policies were reactive and
restrained. Although on occasion he rattled his sabres, he talked constantly and
consistently about peaceful coexistence with capitalism. The one exception to
this pattern of restraint was the Korean War of 1950–1953.

The war began with a North Korean invasion of South Korea in June 1950.
By the end of the summer most of the country was in communist hands. The
South Koreans managed, however, to hang on to the south-east corner of their
country around the port of Pusan. This gave the United States time to intervene on their behalf and to launch a series of counter-offensives that halted
and then repelled the North Korean advance. In September General Douglas
MacArthur carried out an amphibious operation at Inchon that outflanked
the North Korean forces and recaptured the South Korean capital of Seoul.
MacArthur's forces advanced north across the 38th parallel that marked the
border of the two countries and it was the turn of the North Koreans to
retreat. By November MacArthur was approaching the Korean–Chinese
border and it was only the intervention of large numbers of Chinese communist 'volunteers' that saved the North Korean regime from total defeat. By July
1951 the war was stalemated along the 38th parallel and peace negotiations
began. Two years later a ceasefire was signed and military operations ended,
although the two countries remained in a theoretical state of war for decades
to come (*see Map 20 on p. 365*).

The roots of the Korean conflict lay in the postwar division of the country.[48]
Until 1945 Korea was a Japanese colony. When Japan surrendered in August
1945 the country was divided along the 38th parallel by the USSR and the US.

The Korean War, 1950–1953

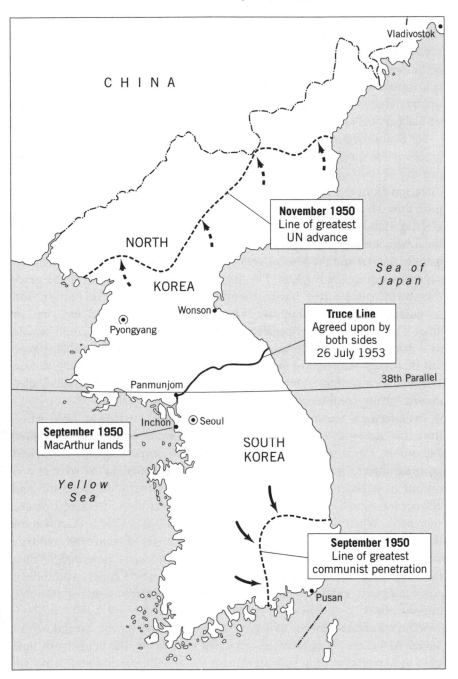

As in the case of Germany, the original intention was to hold elections and reunite the country but when Soviet and American troops evacuated Korea in 1948–1949 they left behind two governments-cum-states: an authoritarian communist regime in the North headed by Kim Il Sung and an authoritarian capitalist regime in the south headed by Syngman Rhee. Both leaders had ambitions to reunite the country under their rule, by force if necessary. Each side threatened the other with invasion and there were numerous small-scale military clashes on the border. In the event it was Kim who struck first after he had persuaded Stalin to support his invasion plans.

For Stalin the Korean War was a very costly miscalculation; its only saving grace was the survival, with China's help, of Kim's regime. When the war broke out the Soviets were boycotting the UN in protest at communist China's exclusion from the organisation; this gave an opening to the Americans to push through a resolution that authorised an intervention in Korea under the UN flag. Hence a number of other countries' troops fought in Korea alongside the Americans and the South Koreans. Stalin was seen in the west as the instigator of the war and the North Korean attack as part of a programme of Soviet expansionism in the Far East. The war undermined the efforts of the peace movement, complicated Soviet attempts to resolve issues in Europe, and encouraged massive programmes of rearmament by the United States and its allies. The war itself was expensive and distracting for Stalin. It could be sold as a determined rebuff to imperialist encroachments on the socialist zone but that claim rang hollow even in communist circles. Above all, the Korean War led to an almost complete breakdown of what the Russians called *doverie* – trust, confidence, good faith – in east–west relations.

To understand Stalin's failure in Korea it is necessary to look at the situation from his strategic and ideological point of view. Strategically a united communist Korea was attractive to Stalin as an outpost against a renewed Japanese threat. Stalin expected Japan as well as Germany to recover and resume its aggressive ways. When the Sino-Soviet treaty of friendship and alliance was signed in August 1945 it was directed against a revival of Japanese aggression. When the Soviet representative to the Allied Control Council for Japan was dispatched to Tokyo his prime directive was to secure the country's disarmament and the destruction of its military-industrial potential.[49] When the Sino-Soviet treaty was renegotiated with the new Chinese communist government in 1950 it remained directed against a revival of Japanese imperialism.[50]

Stalin's fears in relation to Japan were intensified by the breakdown of Soviet–American negotiations about a peace treaty for the country. In June 1946 the Americans proposed a treaty on the demilitarisation and democratisation of Japan – in effect, a Byrnes Plan for the Far East. Like its German treaty counterpart, this proposal was rejected by the Soviets as providing no long-term guarantees that Japan would remain pacific. For its part the US increasingly bypassed the ACC and moved towards signing a separate peace treaty with Japan. In January 1950, Dean Acheson, the American Secretary of State, declared that Japan would be a bastion of anti-communism in the Far East.[51] These developments resembled those in relation to the German question and in Stalin's mind the projected revival of Germany and of Japan were linked. In this context the incorporation of the whole of Korea into the Soviet bloc had its attractions, particularly when it seemed that Acheson had drawn a strategic frontier that included Japan but excluded Korea from the western bloc.

In ideological terms developments in Korea were seen by Stalin as part of the general expansion of communism after the Second World War. The victory of the communists in the Chinese civil war in 1949 had a particularly strong impact on Stalin's ideological view of the Korean situation. At first, Stalin had been sceptical about the prospects for Mao's communists in their fight with Chiang Kai-shek's nationalists and for a while after the Second World War he continued to favour the formation of some kind of national progressive government in China. But under the dual impact of communist military successes and nationalist China's alignment with the US in the cold war, Stalin changed his mind and began to support Mao more actively. In June 1947 he invited Mao to Moscow for talks. Mao couldn't come, ostensibly because of the rapidly changing military situation in China (an excuse that may have rung a few bells with Stalin, who had often said the same thing to Churchill and Roosevelt when meeting them didn't suit) but there developed a lengthy correspondence between the two men and in January 1949 Stalin sent Politburo member Anastas Mikoyan to China for extensive conversations with Mao and the communist leadership.[52] Mao finally arrived in Moscow in December 1949 – two months after he had proclaimed the People's Republic of China in Peking – to discuss the terms of a new Sino-Soviet treaty of alliance. At their first meeting on 16 December Stalin told Mao that China faced no immediate threats militarily: 'Japan has yet to stand up on its feet and is thus not ready for war; America though it screams war, is actually afraid of war more than anything; Europe is afraid of war; in essence, there is no one to fight with China, not unless Kim Il Sung decides to invade China!'[53] Stalin also counselled Mao to avoid unnecessary conflicts with the British and Americans and take time to consolidate the communist position in China.

Yet despite the caution of his advice to Mao, Stalin drew two radical conclusions from developments in China. First, as he had told another visiting Chinese communist leader in summer 1949, 'the centre of revolution . . . has moved to China and East Asia'.[54] Second, the United States was either unwilling or incapable of intervening to stop further communist advance. Nevertheless, as Kathryn Weathersby has shown, Stalin hesitated to provoke a military conflict in Korea and when war did break out drew back from any steps that would precipitate a major confrontation with the United States.[55]

Kim Il Sung began pressing Stalin for permission to attack South Korea in March 1949, trying to persuade the Soviet leader that an invasion would be welcomed by the South's population and supported by a communist guerrilla army already fighting there. Stalin told him:

> You should not advance to the South. First of all, the Korean People's Army does not have an overwhelming superiority of troops . . . Second, there are still American troops in the south . . . Third, one should not forget that the agreement on the 38th parallel is in effect between the USSR and the United States. If the agreement is broken by our side, it is more of a reason to believe the Americans will interfere . . . If the adversary has aggressive intentions, then sooner or later it will start the aggression. In response to the attack you will have a good opportunity to launch a counterattack. Then your move will be understood and supported by everyone.

In June 1949 the last American forces withdrew from Korea and in September Kim proposed a limited offensive against the South to improve North Korea's defensive position along the border. Stalin gave this proposal serious consideration but in the end rejected it on the grounds that it would be difficult to keep such an attack limited to one section of the border and it could result in serious international complications. In January 1950, however, Stalin began to change his mind about the feasibility of such an attack and when he met Kim again in March he was ready to give the go-ahead for an invasion, if the idea was endorsed by the Chinese. Stalin explained his change of mind as the result of two main considerations. First, the communist victory in China meant that Mao would be able to assist the Koreans if necessary. Second, the Sino-Soviet treaty of alliance meant the Americans were less likely to interfere and the mood in the US was, in any case, against intervention – a mood reinforced by Soviet possession of the atomic bomb. But Stalin made it clear to Kim that he 'should not count on direct Soviet participation in the war because the USSR had serious challenges elsewhere to cope with, especially in the West . . . the USSR was not ready to get involved in Korean affairs directly, especially if the Americans did venture to send troops to Korea'.

After seeing Stalin, Kim travelled to Peking in May to obtain Mao's approval for his plan of campaign. It should be noted that Kim's plan at this stage was still for localised offensive operations that would later develop into a more general offensive. However, the plan changed and, with Stalin's blessing, the

North Koreans launched a broad attack across the 38th parallel. After the war began Stalin was anxious that the South be 'liberated' before the Americans had a chance to intervene. Stalin's forebodings proved prescient when the Americans launched their successful counter-offensive in September. In October Stalin appealed to Mao to send Chinese troops into Korea to support Kim. At first Mao refused, prompting Stalin to send him a long message arguing for Chinese intervention. Stalin pointed out that Chinese comrades had repeatedly promised to intervene if necessary and he scorned the idea that such action would provoke a wider conflict with the United States. The Americans, he told Mao, are 'not ready at present for a big war'. Stalin conceded that the US might be drawn into a big war for the sake of prestige but argued that the Soviet Union and China should not fear this prospect because 'together we will be stronger than the USA and England, while the other European capitalist states . . . do not present serious military forces. If a war is inevitable, then let it be waged now, and not in a few years when Japanese militarism will be restored as an ally of the USA and when the USA and Japan will have a ready-made bridgehead in the form of the entire Korea run by Syngman Rhee.' There was more than a little bravado in this statement for when the Chinese remained unmoved Stalin ordered Kim to prepare for evacuation. The Chinese did intervene, however, and mounted a counter-offensive that pushed MacArthur's forces back across the 38th parallel. Stalin supplied material military aid to North Korea and China but refrained from any direct involvement in war, although Soviet pilots did take part in the air battle above the 38th parallel. While there was still a chance of gaining military advantage Stalin favoured a continuation of the war, but by mid-1951 he had accepted the necessity of armistice negotiations.[56]

In August 1952 Chou En-lai travelled to Moscow to meet Stalin. In his talks with the Chinese Prime Minister, Stalin put a positive spin on the war. 'The war is getting on America's nerves,' he told him. 'The war in Korea has shown America's weakness. The armies of 24 countries cannot continue the war in Korea for long, since they have not achieved their goals and cannot count on success in this matter.' This was typical Stalin bombast in the face of failure, and he continued in the same vein:

Americans are not capable of waging a large-scale war at all, especially after the Korean war. After all their strength lies in air power and the atom bomb . . . America cannot defeat little Korea. One must be firm when dealing with America . . . It's been already two years, and the USA has still not subdued little Korea . . . They want to subjugate the world, yet they cannot subdue little Korea. No, the Americans don't know how to fight. After the Korean war, in particular, they have lost the capability to wage large-scale war. They are pinning their hopes on the atom bomb and air power. But one cannot win a war with that. One needs infantry, and they don't have infantry; the infantry they do have is weak. They are fighting little Korea, and already people are weeping in the USA. What will happen if they start a large-scale war? Then, perhaps, everyone, will weep.[57]

Perhaps Stalin believed this rhetoric but it did not take much insight to appreciate that the Americans were not the only ones unable to win in Korea. For all Stalin's disavowals of the nuclear factor, America's atomic superiority must have encouraged caution in relation to direct involvement in the Korean conflict. American prestige, on the other hand, was running high because of their leadership of the UN intervention in Korea. It was the Soviets, the Chinese and the North Koreans who were under international pressure to end their military adventure and accept a compromise peace. When the war ended in 1953 casualties were in the order of 10 million, the North Koreans were back where they started when they launched their invasion, South Korea's independence was guaranteed by a massive American military presence, and Japan had been established as the mainstay of the US strategic position in East Asia. Stalin's differences with the Chinese about the conduct of the war fed resentments that precipitated the Sino-Soviet split in the late 1950s.[58] Stalin's last war was one of his most abject failures.

The Last Days

Stalin died in March 1953 at the age of 73. There are many conspiracy theories about his death but the simple truth is that he had a brain haemorrhage on 2 March and died three days later.[59] Until the last few days of his life he remained very active and in full control of events. His appointments diary for the three months before his death records many meetings. In December 1952 he issued his last public statement when he replied to the questions of an American newspaper correspondent about his response to the new Eisenhower administration in the United States. He told the journalist that war between the Soviet Union and the United States was not inevitable and that the two countries could live in peace. He denounced the cold war and welcomed the possibility of diplomatic negotiations with Eisenhower, including an end to the war in Korea.[60]

One of the very last foreigners to see Stalin alive was K.P.S. Mennon, the Indian ambassador, who was called to the Kremlin on the evening of 17 February 1953. The meeting lasted only half an hour but it had quite an impact on the ambassador. The next day he wrote a long entry in his diary pondering the meaning of his meeting with the great man. He recalled what others had said about Stalin. Joseph E. Davies, the American ambassador in Moscow before the war: 'His demeanour is kindly, his manner almost deprecatingly simple . . . he gave me the impression of being sincerely modest.' And Winston Churchill: 'Premier Stalin left upon me an impression of deep, cool wisdom and the absence of illusions . . . a man direct, even blunt, in speech . . . with that saving sense of humour which is of high import.' For Mennon it was Stalin's 'simplicity, shrewdness and ruthlessness' that impressed:

> Everything about him is simple – his dress, his room, his manners, his modes of speech . . . This is the man whose will . . . saved Russia for communism and communism for the world; but for him neither Russia nor communism would have been able to resist the assault of Hitler. This is the man held not only in his own country but by millions all over the world as the 'leader and teacher of all progressive mankind'; whose portraits have taken the place of holy icons in every Russian home; and at the mention of whose name, every audience in Russia rises to its feet with prolonged applause amounting to ovation. Yet adulation left no more mark on him than does water on a duck's back; there is not a trace of ostentation or affectation about him. When Voltaire returned to Paris after many years in exile, he was greeted by a crowd of admirers. When a friend asked him whether or not he was pleased to be the people's idol, he replied, 'Yes, but an equally large crowd would have turned up if my head appeared on a scaffold'. That is a sentiment which Stalin himself would not hesitate to express. This leads me to the second quality . . . his shrewdness, which was shown as much by his silence as his speech. He declined to be drawn into a discussion of our Korean resolution or even of the Korean problem generally . . . Perhaps he feels that he has come to the stage when he can devote his thoughts exclusively to fundamentals, leaving details to the henchmen . . . I was also struck by his ruthlessness. Twice he spoke of the futility of preaching morals to an evil person. Gandhi's phrase, 'a change of heart' would mean nothing to Stalin. Perhaps it was to Gandhi's preoccupation with moral considerations that Stalin was referring when he drew the metaphor of the peasant's refusal to moralize with the wolf. I telegraphed to my government that this represented the essence of Stalin's philosophy.[61]

Charming and disarming, revealing and mysterious, alluring and disturbing; to the very end Stalin presented many faces to the world.

13

Conclusion
Stalin in the Court of History

In the Soviet Union the re-evaluation of Stalin's leadership began soon after his body was laid to rest in the Lenin Mausoleum in March 1953. In May 1954 Marshal V.D. Sokolovskii, Chief of the Soviet General Staff, published an article in *Pravda* on the ninth anniversary of victory in the Great Patriotic War. It did not even mention Stalin except in a passing reference to the 'banner of Lenin and Stalin'.[1] In December 1954 *New Times*, the Soviet journal of international affairs, published an article on the 75th anniversary of Stalin's birth that emphasised the extent to which he had been a pupil of Lenin. A year later an article in the same journal on the 76th anniversary of Stalin's birth was devoted mainly to Lenin. Stalin was not criticised directly but his importance was significantly downgraded as the centrality of Lenin to the identity of the communist party was asserted.[2] Then came Khrushchev's secret speech to the 20th party congress in February 1956 and the sluice gates of criticism of Stalin were prised open, eventually leading to a flood of condemnation in the 1980s and 1990s.

As far as the war was concerned, Khrushchev's theme was that victory had been secured by the collective efforts of the communist party and its leadership, not by Stalin who had played a mainly malign role. According to the accounts of military memoirists and historians who took up the cudgels of Khrushchev's critique, the war was won in spite of Stalin by the Soviet armed forces and its generals. Later, under the impact of the more positive assessments of Stalin as a supreme commander by Zhukov, Vasilevskii and Shtemenko, the Great Patriotic War became a victory for Stalin *and* his generals. For many among the intelligentsia, however, the Great Patriotic War was a victory for the Soviet people whose great sacrifices had been betrayed by Stalin after the war when he reimposed his and the party's dictatorship.

In the west the revision of Stalin's wartime reputation was well under way while he was still alive. First, there were the cold war polemicists who depicted him and his regime as no better than, and morally equivalent to, Hitler and the Nazis. According to them, Stalin's victory over Hitler should rather be seen as a defeat for the half of Europe that became subsumed under his totalitarian rule. Then there was the more subtle downgrading of Stalin's role by Winston Churchill and other western memoirists and historians who sidelined the strategic importance of the Soviet–German conflict and reduced its role in the overall narrative of the Second World War.[3] Lastly, there were the memoirs written by Hitler's surviving generals, who told the story of a certain victory thrown away by the mistakes of the German dictator. The Second World War was lost by Hitler not won by Stalin, they argued.[4]

In the decades that followed, more balanced and rounded views of Stalin's war record were put forward by some historians in the Soviet Union and in the west. To an extent those works represented a return to the contemporary, commonsense narrative of Stalin's war leadership. At the time it seemed obvious to most people that Stalin, as the Soviet leader, was crucial to the Soviet war effort. Without him the efforts of the party, the people, the armed forces and their generals would have been considerably less effective. He was a great war leader not because he had won but because he had done so much to achieve victory. Even Hitler appreciated Stalin's significance in determining the outcome of the war. 'Compared with Churchill, Stalin is a gigantic figure,' confided Hitler to Goebbels on the eve of the battle of Stalingrad. 'Churchill has nothing to show for his life's work except a few books and clever speeches in parliament. Stalin on the other hand has without doubt – leaving aside the question of what principle he was serving – reorganised a state of 170 million people and prepared it for a massive armed conflict. If Stalin ever fell into my hands, I would probably spare him and perhaps exile him to some spa; Churchill and Roosevelt would be hanged.'[5] Stalin's view of Hitler was less forbearing and he made clear on innumerable occasions that he wanted the Führer and all other Nazi leaders shot. As for Churchill and Roosevelt, Stalin retained a great personal affection and respect for their war leadership. Roosevelt's death was mourned by him and he continued to hold Churchill in high regard even when their political relationship broke down after the war. In January 1947 Stalin told Field Marshal Montgomery, who visited him in Moscow, that 'he would always have the happiest memories of his work with [Churchill] as the great war leader of Britain' and that 'he had the greatest respect and admiration for what [Churchill] had done during the war years'. Churchill was equally effusive, writing back to Stalin that '[your] life is not only precious to your country, which you saved, but to the friendship between Soviet Russia and the English-speaking world'.[6]

This book has tried to show that the contemporaneous perception of Stalin's war leadership was closer to the truth of the matter than many of the layers of historical interpretation that followed. The problem with the light of historical perspective is that it can be shone from an ideological angle to dazzle as well as to illuminate. In the case of Stalin's war leadership, to show the truth it is necessary to look beyond both the cold war polemics of the west and the contingencies of destalinisation in the USSR. This book has also tried to show that the real depth of Stalin's ability to cope with an unprecedented emergency in 1941–1942 was actually masked by the personality cult view of Stalin as a military genius who could do no wrong. To make so many mistakes and to rise from the depths of such defeat to go on to win the greatest military victory in history was a triumph beyond compare.

Stalin's failure to make better use of that victory from a democratic point of view was undoubtedly a function of the political limitations of his dictatorial regime. But it also occurred because western politicians such as Churchill and Truman were unable to see that beyond the alleged communist threat was an opportunity to arrive at a postwar settlement that could have averted the cold war and avoided the ideological warfare that obscured the paradoxical truth that Stalin was the dictator who defeated Hitler and helped save the world for democracy.

History can be a kind of court. The prosecution wants us to condemn Stalin outright for his crimes or for his inadequate leadership. But as jurors it is our duty to review all the evidence, including that for the defence, and to see the whole picture. This may not make it easy to arrive at a verdict but it will enhance our historical understanding and equip us with the knowledge that could enable us to do better in the future. History *can* make us wiser, if we allow it to.

Notes

Preface and Acknowledgements

1. G. Roberts, *Victory at Stalingrad: The Battle That Changed History*, Longman: London 2002.
2. M. Harrison, 'Stalin and Our Times' in G. Roberts (ed.), *Stalin – His Times and Ours*, IAREES: Dublin 2005.
3. R.H. McNeal, *Stalin: Man and Ruler*, Macmillan: London 1998 p.312.
4. L. Strachey, *Eminent Victorians*, Penguin Books: London 1986 p.9.
5. G. Gorodetsky, *Grand Delusion: Stalin and the German Invasion of Russia*, Yale University Press: New Haven and London 1999.

1 Introduction: Stalin at War

1. C. Merridale, *Night of Stone: Death and Memory in Twentieth Century Russia*, Penguin Books: London 2002 pp. 257–63.
2. Cited by J. Brent and V.P. Naumov, *Stalin's Last Crime: The Plot against the Jewish Doctors, 1948–1953*, HarperCollins: New York 2003 p. 328. There is a widespread presumption in the literature that the funeral tributes to Stalin were less than fulsome and that even at this early stage his acolytes had begun to desert him. However, that interpretation is not borne out by the texts of the tributes published in the Soviet press or by the film of the funeral proceedings and speeches.
3. For an outstanding biography of Stalin that stresses the significance of the personality cult see R.H. McNeal, *Stalin: Man and Ruler*, Macmillan Press: London 1998.
4. The speech is reproduced in a number of publications, including in the first version of Khrushchev's memoirs: *Khrushchev Remembers*, Sphere Books: London 1971 pp. 503–62.
5. The resolution represented a retreat from the radical critique of Stalin propounded by Khrushchev and was an attempt to control the discussion that erupted within the party following the secret speech, which wasn't published, but was read out at party meetings throughout the Soviet Union. See P. Jones, 'From Stalinism to Post-Stalinism: Demythologising Stalin, 1953–1956' in H. Shukman (ed.), *Redefining Stalinism*, Frank Cass: London 2003.
6. Cited by J. Brooks, *Thank You, Comrade Stalin! Soviet Public Culture from Revolution to Cold War*, Princeton University Press: Princeton NJ 2000 p. 241
7. On the post-1956 development of the discussion on Stalin in the Soviet Union see S.F. Cohen, 'The Stalin Question since Stalin' in his *Rethinking the Soviet Experience: Politics and History since 1917*, Oxford University Press: Oxford 1985.

8. See R.W. Davies, *Soviet History in the Glasnost Revolution*, Macmillan: London 1989; A. Nove, *Glasnost' in Action*, Unwin Hyman: London 1989; and W. Laqueur, *Stalin: The Glasnost Revelations*, Scribners: New York 1990.

9. For a highly critical view of the 1990s transition in Russia see S.F. Cohen, *Failed Crusade: America and the Tragedy of Post-Communist Russia*, Norton: New York 2000.

10. For example: F. Chuev, *Sto sorok besed s Molotovym*, Moscow 1991 (in English: *Molotov Remembers*, ed. A. Resis, Ivan R. Dee: Chicago 1993); L. Kaganovich, *Pamyatnyye Zapiski*, Moscow 1996; A. Mikoyan, *Tak Bylo*, Moscow 1999; A. Malenkov, *O Moyom Ottse Georgii Malenkove*, Moscow 1992; and S. Beria, *Beria, My Father: Inside Stalin's Kremlin*, Duckworth: London 2001.

11. 'More Than Half of All Russians Positive About Stalin', Radio Free Europe/Radio Liberty *Newsline*, 5/3/03. Cited by M. Harrison, 'Stalin and Our Times' in G. Roberts (ed.), *Stalin – His Times and Ours*, IAREES: Dublin 2005 p. 67.

12. See A.J.P. Taylor, 'Is Stalin a Statesman?' reprinted in his *Europe: Grandeur and Decline*, Penguin Books: London 1967.

13. I. Deutscher, *Russia after Stalin*, pb edition, Jonathan Cape: London 1969 p. 55.

14. Although unpublished, the speech was read out at party meetings all over the USSR. In June 1956 the US Department of State released the text of the speech. See: *The Anti-Stalin Campaign and International Communism*, Columbia University Press: New York 1956 pp. 1–2.

15. One of the more notorious examples of the Khrushchev personality cult was the legend that he was one of the main authors of the great Red Army counter-offensive at Stalingrad in November 1942, widely regarded as the most important turning point of the Second World War. Hitherto the plan to outflank and surround the German 6th Army in Stalingrad had been attributed to Stalin's military genius. Now the credit went to Khrushchev, a political commissar at Stalingrad during the battle, and to Marshal A.I. Yeremenko, one of the Front commanders in the area. In fact, while the Stalingrad counter-offensive had many authors, Khrushchev and Yeremenko did not rank very high among them. The claim about Khrushchev's and Yeremenko's role in originating the plan for the counter-offensive at Stalingrad was put forward in 1957 and repeated in the latter's memoirs published in 1961: A.I. Yeremenko, *Stalingrad*, Moscow 1961 pp. 325–37. Initially, this claim was met with silence from others involved in the decision-making process. After Khrushchev's fall from power in 1964, however, Yeremenko's claims were criticised and contested from a number of quarters. See for example the memoirs published in *Stalingradskaya Epopeya*, Moscow 1968.

16. For an extensive collection of excerpts from Soviet military memoirs published in the 1960s see S. Bialer (ed.), *Stalin and his Generals: Soviet Military Memoirs of World War II*, Souvenir Press: New York 1969. Works substantially based on these and subsequently published memoirs include: A. Seaton, *Stalin as a Military Commander*, Combined Publishing: Pennsylvania 1998; H. Shukman (ed.), *Stalin's Generals*, Phoenix Press: London 1997; and A. Axell, *Stalin's War through the Eyes of his Commanders*, Arms and Armour Press: London 1997.

17. *Khrushchev Remembers* p. 537. Cf. the comments of Stalin's deputy, Marshal Zhukov ('the widespread tale that the Supreme Commander studied the situation and adopted decisions when toying with a globe is untrue') and his Chief of Operations during the war, General Shtemenko ('the talk of fronts being directed by reference to a globe is completely unfounded'). Cited by Axell, *Stalin's War* p. 167.

18. The term Great Patriotic War was first used in an article published in *Pravda* on 23 June 1941. In July 1943 the first edition of Stalin's war speeches was published under the title *O Velikoi Otechestvennoi Voine Sovetskogo Souza* (On the Great Patriotic War of the Soviet Union).

19. I. Stalin, *Sochineniya*, vol. 16 (1946–1952), Moscow 1997 pp. 6–7. An English translation of this speech may be found in an appendix to J.P. Morray, *From Yalta to Disarmament*, Monthly Review Press: New York 1961.

20. See G. Roberts, *The Soviet Union in World Politics: Revolution, Coexistence and the Cold War, 1945–1991*, Routledge: London 1998.

21. N. Voznesenky, *War Economy of the USSR in the Period of the Great Patriotic War*, Foreign Languages Publishing House: Moscow 1948 pp. 126–33.

22. See J. Erickson, 'Soviet War Losses' in J. Erickson and D. Dilks (eds), *Barbarossa: The Axis and the Allies*, Edinburgh University Press: Edinburgh 1994.

23. I have argued extensively for this interpretation of the origins of the Nazi–Soviet pact including in G. Roberts, *The Unholy Alliance: Stalin's Pact with Hitler*, I.B. Tauris: London 1989 and *The Soviet Union and the Origins of the Second World War*, Macmillan: London 1995.

24. The main phase in this debate began with the publication of Victor Suvorov's *Icebreaker: Who Started the Second World War?*, Hamish Hamilton: London 1990. 'Suvorov' was the pseudonym of V.B. Rezun, a member of the Soviet intelligence services who defected to the west in 1978. A Russian edition of Suvorov's book was published in 1992 and its arguments were subsequently taken up and elaborated by a number of Russian historians. For a summary of the debate – from a point of view critical of Suvorov and his supporters – see T.J. Uldricks, 'The Icebreaker Controversy: Did Stalin Plan to Attack Hitler?' *Slavic Review*, vol. 58, no. 3, Fall 1999.

25. On the war–revolution nexus see M.J. Carley, *1939: The Alliance That Never Was and the Coming of World War II*, Ivan R. Dee: Chicago 1999.

26. See *The Tehran, Yalta and Potsdam Conferences: Documents*, Progress Publishers: Moscow 1969.

27. *Stalin's Correspondence with Churchill, Attlee, Roosevelt and Truman, 1941–1945*, Lawrence & Wishart: London 1958. On the background to the publication of this correspondence from the Soviet archives: G. Roberts, 'Stalin, the Pact with Nazi Germany and the Origins of Postwar Soviet Diplomatic Historiography', *Journal of Cold War Studies*, vol. 4, no. 3, Summer 2002.

28. See J. Barber, 'The Image of Stalin in Soviet Propaganda and Public Opinion during World War 2' in J. and C. Garrard (eds), *World War 2 and the Soviet People*, St. Martin's Press: New York 1993.

29. I. Deutscher, *Stalin: A Political Biography*, Pelican: London 1966 pp. 456,457.

30. 'Posetiteli Kremlevskogo Kabineta I.V. Stalina', *Istoricheskii Arkhiv*, no. 6, 1994; nos 2, 3, 4, 5–6, 1995; nos 2, 3, 4, 5–6, 1996; and no. 1, 1997.

31. The most important source of evidence on Stalin's private thinking is the diary of the leader of the Communist International, Georgi Dimitrov: I. Banac (ed.), *The Diary of Georgi Dimitrov, 1933–1949*, Yale University Press: New Haven 2003. Also important is Stalin's correspondence with Molotov, his Foreign Minister, when the latter was abroad. See: O.A. Rzheshevsky (ed.), *War and Diplomacy: The Making of the Grand Alliance (Documents from Stalin's Archive)*, Harwood Academic Publishers: Amsterdam 1996; V.O. Pechatnov, 'The Allies are Pressing on You to Break Your Will': Foreign Policy Correspondence between Stalin and Molotov and other Politburo Members, September 1945–December 1946, Cold War International History Project, Working Paper no. 26, September 1999; and the diary of Stalin's minister for tank production, V.A. Malyshev published in *Istochnik* no. 5, 1997. There is also a limited amount of correspondence between Stalin and his inner circle in the postwar period published in *Politburo TsK VKP(b) i Sovet Ministrov SSSR, 1945–1953*, Moscow 2002. Some of this correspondence is translated in A.O. Chubaryan and V.O. Pechatnov (eds), 'Molotov "the Liberal": Stalin's 1945 Criticism of his Deputy', *Cold War History*, vol. 1, no. 1, August 2000.

32. W. Averell Harriman, 'Stalin at War' in G.R. Urban (ed.), *Stalinism: Its Impact on Russia and the World*, Wildwood House: Aldershot 1982 pp. 41, 42. In his memoirs Harriman described Stalin as 'better informed than Roosevelt, more realistic than Churchill, in some ways the most effective of the war leaders'. W. Averell Harriman and E. Abel, *Special Envoy to Churchill and Stalin, 1941–1946*, Random House: New York 1975 p. 536.

33. Ibid. p. 43.

34. R. Overy, *Why the Allies Won*, Jonathan Cape: London 1995 p. 259.

35. Statistical analysis of Stalin's appointments diary reveals that Stalin's most constant companions during the war were his security chief, Lavrentii Beria, his Foreign Minister, Vyacheslav Molotov, and the secretary of the party's central committee, Georgii Malenkov, who also served on the State Defence Committee and acted as Stalin's personal political emissary to the front line. Other frequent visitors to Stalin's office during the war were the trade minister Anastas Mikoyan, the war economy supremo, Nikolai Voznesenskii, and transport minister Lazar Kaganovich. See: 'Posetiteli Kremlevskogo Kabineta I.V. Stalina: Alfavitnyi Ukazatel'', *Istoricheskii Arkhiv*, no. 4, 1998.

36. The most detailed picture of Stalin's routine during the war is in the memoirs of his Chief of Operations for most of the war, General S.M. Shtemenko, *The Soviet General Staff at War, 1941–1945*, 2 vols, Progress Publishers: Moscow 1970, 1973.

37. Bialer, *Stalin and his Generals* pp. 33–6.

38. J. Erickson, *The Road to Berlin*, Weidenfeld & Nicolson: London 1983 p. ix.

39. See Erickson, 'Soviet War Losses', also: the discussion in Laqueur, *Stalin*, pp. 216–19.

40. *Marshal Zhukov comments on the Soviet High Command at War*, Soviet Weekly Booklet, London 1970 p. 18.

41. J. Stalin, *On the Great Patriotic War of the Soviet Union*, Hutchinson: London 1943 p. 17

42. Malyshev diary, p. 128.

43. Copies of many of the archive documents collected by Volkogonov are deposited in his papers in the Manuscript Division of the Library of Congress.

44. D. Volkogonov, *Stalin: Triumph and Tragedy*, Phoenix Press: London 2000 p. 451.

45. For contrasting views see M.A. Gareev, *Polkovodtsy Pobedy i ikh Voennoe Naslediye*, Moscow 2004 and L. Mlechin, *Iosif Stalin, Ego Marshaly i Generaly*, Moscow 2004.

46. On Stalin's activities during the civil war: Seaton, *Stalin* chaps 1–3. Stalin was also witness to the Bolshevik débâcle in relation to the Brest-Litovsk treaty of March 1918. When they came to power in 1917 the Bolsheviks were determined to avoid signing a predatory peace deal with Germany whereby they would concede vast tracks of territory. This is exactly what happened, however, when German offensive action in early 1918 threatened the Bolshevik regime and forced them to sue for peace on highly unfavourable terms.

47. Volkogonov, *Stalin* p.474.

48. A.M. Vasilevsky, *A Lifelong Cause*, Progress Publishers: Moscow 1981 pp. 447–50. Originally published in Russian as *Delo vsei zhizni*, Moscow 1974.

49. See H.E. Salisbury (ed.), *Marshal Zhukov's Greatest Battles*, Sphere Books: London 1969. The articles collected in this volume were published originally in *Voenno-Istoricheskii Zhurnal*.

50. *The Memoirs of Marshal Zhukov*, Jonathan Cape: London 1971 pp. 284–5. There are various versions of Zhukov's and Vasilevskii's memoirs but none that changes the balance of their assessment of Stalin cited here.

51. The literature on Tukhachevskii and his arrest is vast. In English see: N. Abramov, 'The New Version of the Tukhachevsky Affair', *New Times*, no. 13, 1989; D.C. Watt, 'Who Plotted Against Whom? Stalin's Purge of the Soviet High Command Revisisted', *Journal of Soviet Military Studies*, vol. 3, no. 1, 1990; I. Lukes, 'The Tukhachevsky Affair and President Edvard Benes', *Diplomacy & Statecraft*, vol. 7, no. 3, 1996; S.J. Main, 'The

Arrest and "Testimony" of Marshal of the Soviet Union M.N. Tukhachevsky', *Journal of Slavic Military Studies*, vol. 10, no. 1, 1997; and S. Naveh, 'Tukhachevsky' in Shukman (ed.), *Stalin's Generals*. See also the books by Spahr and Stoecker cited in notes 52 and 64 below.

52. W.J. Spahr, *Stalin's Lieutenants: A Study of Command under Stress*, Presidio Press: Novato, Calif. 1997 p. 174.

53. On the purge statistics see R. R. Reese's 'The Impact of the Great Purge on the Red Army', *Soviet and Post-Soviet Review*, vol. 19, nos 1–3, 1992; 'The Red Army and the Great Purges' in J.A. Getty and R.T. Manning (eds), *Stalinist Terror: New Perspectives*, Cambridge University Press: Cambridge 1993; and R. Reese, *Stalin's Reluctant Soldiers*, University Press of Kansas: Lawrence, Kansas 1996 chap. 5. Reese points out that earlier estimates suggested that 25–50 per cent of the officer core were purged. However, these calculations underestimated the number of officers in the Soviet armed forces, which was about 300,000, which meant that the proportion purged was substantially less than 10 per cent.

54. Figures calculated from the tables appended to O.F. Suvenirov, *Tragediya RKKA, 1937–1938*, Moscow 1998, pp. 373–485. My figures include only those arrested in 1937–1938. Another major, detailed study of these purges, based on Soviet military archives now closed to researchers, is that by the Polish historian P.P. Wieczorkiewicz, *Lancuch Smierci: Czystka w Armii Czerwonej, 1937–1939*, Warsaw 2001.

55. Suvenirov, *Tragediya* based much of his research on the records of the rehabilitation commissions of the mid-1950s and gives the dates of individual rehabilitations in his tables.

56. Stalin ordered the execution of 20 of his generals during the war. The main batch of executions occurred in July 1941 when General Dmitrii Pavlov, the commander of the Western Front, and several members of his staff were shot, as were several air force generals in October 1941, blamed by Stalin for the loss of thousands of planes during the first few days of the war. All were exonerated after the war. Between 1941 and 1945 421 Soviet admirals and generals died in action. See R. Woff, 'Stalin's Ghosts' in Shukman (ed.), *Stalin's Generals*.

57. M. Harrison and R.W. Davies, 'The Soviet Military-Economic Effort during the Second Five-Year Plan (1933–1937)', *Europe–Asia Studies*, vol. 49, no. 3, 1997. Also: R.W. Davies et al., *The Economic Transformation of the Soviet Union, 1913–1945*, Cambridge University Press: Cambridge 1994 pp. 143–7.

58. There is a long-standing debate about whether Stalin was complicit in the assassination of Kirov. For a summary and assessment of the discussion see N. Baron, 'The Historiography of the Kirov Murder', *Slovo*, vol. 11, 1999.

59. M. Reiman, 'Political Show Trials of the Stalinist Era', *Telos*, 1982–1983, no. 54.

60. According to O.V. Khlevnuk 'in 1930–1940 at least 726,000 people were shot, most of them in 1937–1938' (*The History of the Gulag: From Collectivisation to the Great Terror*, Yale University Press: New Haven 2004 p. 306). There is an extensive debate about the origins and character of the Great Terror, including about the numbers killed and imprisoned. Khlevnuk's figure is among the lowest quoted but is based on extensive first-hand research in the relevant Russian archives. A good collection of primary documents on the Great Terror is J. Arch Getty and O.V. Naumov (eds), *The Road to Terror: Stalin and the Self-destruction of the Bolsheviks, 1932–1939*, Yale University Press: New Haven 1999.

61. For a summary see G. Roberts, 'The Fascist War Threat and Soviet Politics in the 1930s' in S. Pons and A. Romano, *Russia in the Age of Wars, 1914–1945*, Feltrinelli: Milan 2000. On popular attitudes towards the terror see: S. Davies, *Popular Opinion in Stalin's Russia: Terror, Propaganda and Dissent, 1934–1941*, Cambridge University Press: Cambridge 1997 and S. Fitzpatrick, *Everyday Stalinism: Ordinary Life in Extraordinary Times*, Oxford University Press: Oxford 1999.

62. R.V. Daniels, *A Documentary History of Communism*, vol. 1, I.B. Tauris: London 1985 pp. 258–61.

63. *Molotov Remembers* p. 254. Molotov's view has been endorsed by many historians. For example, O. Khlevnuk, 'The Objectives of the Great Terror, 1937–1938' in J. Cooper et al. (eds), *Soviet History, 1917–1953*, Macmillan: London 1993 and idem, 'The Reasons for the "Great Terror": the Foreign-Political Aspect' in Pons and Romano (eds), *Russia.*

64. See S.W. Stoecker, *Forging Stalin's Army, Marshal Tukhachevsky and the Politics of Military Innovation*, Westview Press: Oxford 1998; D.R. Stone, 'Tukhachevsky in Leningrad: Military Politics and Exile, 1928–31', *Europe–Asia Studies*, vol. 48, no. 8, 1996; L. Samuelson, 'Mikhail Tukhachevsky and War-Economic Planning', *Journal of Slavic Military Studies*, vol. 9, no. 4, December 1996; R.R. Reese, 'Red Army Opposition to Forced Collectivisation, 1929–1930: The Army Wavers', *Slavic Review*, vol. 55, no. 1, 1996; and S.J. Main, 'The Red Army and the Soviet Military and Political Leadership in the Late 1920s', *Europe–Asia Studies*, vol. 47, no. 2, 1995.

65. T. Martin, 'The Origins of Soviet Ethnic Cleansing', *Journal of Modern History*, December 1998.

66. G. Roberts, 'Stalin and the Katyn Massacre' in Roberts (ed.), *Stalin: His Times and Ours.*

67. R. Overy, *The Dictators: Hitler's Germany and Stalin's Russia*, Allen Lane: London 2004 chap. 13. A number of documents on the Stalin era deportations are contained in *Stalinskiye Deportatsii 1928–1953*, Moscow 2005. The volume also contains a chronological table of the different deportations, together with estimates of the numbers involved.

68. D. Brandenberger, *National Bolshevism: Stalinist Mass Culture and the Formation of Modern Russian National Identity, 1931–1956*, Harvard University Press: Cambridge, Mass. 2002.

69. E. van Ree, *The Political Thought of Joseph Stalin: A Study in Twentieth Century Revolutionary Patriotism*, Routledge: London 2002.

70. See A.J. Rieber, 'Stalin: Man of the Borderlands', *American Historical Review*, no. 5, 2001.

71. Cited by R. Service, *Stalin: A Biography*, Macmillan: London 2004 pp. 272–3.

72. For a summary of Lenin and Stalin's policy on the national question see: T. Martin, 'An Affirmative Action Empire: The Soviet Union as the Highest Form of Imperialism' in R.G. Suny and T. Martin (eds), *A State of Nations: Empire and Nation-Making in the Age of Lenin and Stalin*, Oxford University Press: Oxford 2001.

73. J.V. Stalin, 'Marxism and the National Question' in J.V. Stalin, *Works*, vol. 2, Foreign Languages Publishing House: Moscow 1953.

74. S. Blank, *The Sorcerer as Apprentice: Stalin as Commissar of Nationalities, 1917–1924*, Greenwood Press: London 1994.

75. T. Martin, *The Affirmative Action Empire: Nations and Nationalism in the Soviet Union, 1929–1939*, Cornell University Press: Ithaca, NY 2001 chaps 10–11.

76. Brandenberger, *National Bolshevism* p. 55.

77. Cited by A.I. Vdovin, 'Natsional'nyi Vopros i Natsional'naya Politika v SSSR v gody Velikoi Otechestvennoi Voiny', *Vestnik Moskovskogo Universiteta: Seriya 8: Istoriya*, no. 5, 2003.

78. See ibid; G. Hosking, 'The Second World War and Russian National Consciousness', *Past & Present*, no. 175, 2002; and T.K. Blauvelt, 'Military Mobilisation and National Identity in the Soviet Union', *War & Society*, vol. 21, no. 1, May 2003.

79. *Documents on British Policy Overseas*, series 1, vol. 2, HMSO: London 1985 p. 317.

80. Y. Gorlizki and O. Khlevniuk, *Cold Peace: Stalin and the Soviet Ruling Circle, 1945–1953*, Oxford University Press: Oxford 2004 pp. 31–8.

81. See Chubar'yan and Pechatnov, 'Molotov'.

82. Brandenberger, *National Bolshevism* p. 191.

83. V. Pechatnov, 'Exercise in Frustration: Soviet Foreign Propaganda in the Early Cold War, 1945–47', *Cold War History*, vol. 1, no. 2, January 2001.

84. 'Otvet Korrespondentu "Pravdy"' in Stalin, *Sochineniya*, vol. 16, Moscow 1997 pp. 25–30. There is an English translation of Stalin's interview in W. LaFeber (ed.), *The Origins of the Cold War, 1941–1947*, John Wiley: New York 1971 doc. 37.

85. Stalin, *Sochineniya* p. 57.

86. A. Resis, *Stalin, the Politburo, and the Onset of the Cold War, 1945–1946*, The Carl Beck Papers in Russian and East European Studies no. 701, April 1998 p. 27.

87. For overviews of Stalin's strategy after the war: V.O. Pechatnov, *The Big Three after World War II: New Documents on Soviet Thinking about Postwar Relations with the United States and Great Britain*, Cold War International History Project Working Paper no. 13, 1995; G. Roberts, 'Ideology, Calculation and Improvisation: Spheres of Influence in Soviet Foreign Policy, 1939–1945', *Review of International Studies*, vol. 25, October 1999; S. Pons, 'In the Aftermath of the Age of Wars: the Impact of World War II on Soviet Foreign Policy' in Pons and Romano (eds), *Russia*; E. Mark, *Revolution by Degrees: Stalin's National-Front Strategy for Europe, 1941–1947*, Cold War International History Project Working Paper no. 31, 2001; and N.M. Naimark, 'Stalin and Europe in the Postwar Period, 1945–53', *Journal of Modern European History*, vol. 2, no. 1, 2004.

88. *Cold War International History Project Bulletin*, no. 11, Winter 1998, p. 136.

89. On the Soviet turn to cold war in 1947: G. Roberts, 'Moscow and the Marshall Plan: Politics, Ideology and the Onset of Cold War, 1947', *Europe–Asia Studies*, vol. 46, no. 8, 1994. Zhdanov's 'two camps' speech was delivered to the founding conference of the Communist Information Buro (Cominform) held in Poland. See G. Procacci (ed.), *The Cominform: Minutes of the Three Conferences 1947/1948/1949*, Milan 1994.

90. For an overview of the Soviet domestic scene after the war: E. Zubkova, 'The Soviet Regime and Soviet Society in the Postwar Years: Innovations and Conservatism, 1945–1953', *Journal of Modern European History*, vol. 2, no. 1, 2004.

91. *Politburo TsK VKP(b) i Sovet Ministrov SSSR, 1945–1953*, Moscow 2002 doc. 299 details Stalin's vacation schedule between 1945 and 1941.

92. Y. Gorlizki, 'Ordinary Stalinism: The Council of Ministers and the Soviet Neopatrimonial State, 1945–1953', *Journal of Modern History*, vol. 74, no. 4, 2002.

93. But Malenkov's speech to the congress was heavily edited by Stalin. See: Rossiiskii Gosudarstvennyi Arkhiv Sotsial'no-Politicheskoi Istorii (RGASPI), F.592, Op.1, D.6.

94. Stalin, *Sochineniya* p. 229.

95. Cited by E. Mawdsley, 'Stalin: Victors Are Not Judged', *Historically Speaking: The Bulletin of the Historical Society*, 2006.

2 Unholy Alliance: Stalin's Pact with Hitler

1. W.S. Churchill, *The Gathering Storm*, Cassell: London 1964 p. 346; *Ciano's Diary 1939–1943*, Heinemann: London 1947 pp. 131, 132; and W.L. Shirer, *The Nightmare Years, 1930–1940*, Bantam Books: New York 1984 pp. 425, 430.

2. On the triple alliance negotiations from the Soviet point of view: G. Roberts, 'The Alliance that Failed: Moscow and the Triple Alliance Negotiations, 1939', *European History Quarterly*, vol. 26, no. 3, 1996; A. Resis, 'The Fall of Litvinov: Harbinger of the German–Soviet Non-Aggression Pact', *Europe–Asia Studies*, vol. 52, no. 1, 2000; and D. Watson, 'Molotov's Apprenticeship in Foreign Policy: The Triple Alliance Negotiations in 1939', *Europe–Asia Studies*, vol. 52, no. 4, 2000.

3. This is the version of Stalin's remarks recorded by Churchill's interpreter A.H. Birse at the meeting in Moscow on the night of 15–16 August 1942 (Harriman Papers, Container 162, Chronological File 14–15 August 1942). A slightly different version is cited in W.S. Churchill, *The Second World War*, vol. 1, Cassell: London 1948 p. 344: 'We

formed the impression that the British and French Governments were not resolved to go to war if Poland were attacked, but that they hoped the diplomatic lineup of Britain, France and Russia would deter Hitler. We were sure it would not.'

4. 'Captain H.H. Balfour Moscow Diary 1941', Library of Congress Manuscript Division Harriman Papers, Container 164.

5. *Nazi–Soviet Relations, 1939–1941*, Didier: New York 1948 (hereafter NSR) p. 38. For Astakhov's record of the same meeting: *Dokumenty Vneshnei Politiki 1939 god* (hereafter: DVP 1939) Moscow 1992, vol. 22, book 1, doc. 445.

6. NSR pp. 68–9.

7. NSR pp. 72–6.

8. NSR pp. 76–8.

9. J. Degras (ed.), *Soviet Documents on Foreign Policy*, vol. 3 (1933–1941), Oxford University Press: London 1953 pp. 363–71.

10. J. Stalin, *Leninism*, Allen & Unwin: London 1942 p. 526.

11. See for example, A.L. Weeks, *Stalin's Other War: Soviet Grand Strategy, 1939–1941*, Rowman & Littlefield: Oxford 2002, which contains an appendix with a translation of one version of the text of the speech.

12. S.Z. Sluch, 'Rech' Stalina, Kotoroi ne Bylo', *Otechestvennaya Istoriya*, no. 1, 2004. This article contains an exhaustive analysis of the speech, its provenance and its citation in the historical literature.

13. Degras, *Soviet* p. 406. The publication of the 'speech' by the French press was reported to Moscow by the Soviet ambassador in Paris, Yakov Suritz, on 28 November 1939 (DVP 1939 vol. 22 book 2, doc. 813).

14. NSR p. 86.

15. Ibid. p. 87.

16. I. Banac (ed.), *The Diary of Georgi Dimitrov*, Yale University Press: New Haven 2003 pp. 115–16.

17. Degras, *Soviet*, pp. 374–6; A. Werth, *Russia at War, 1941–1945*, Pan Books: London 1964 pp. 73–7.

18. Churchill, *Second World War* p. 353. Churchill's view was shared by his boss, Neville Chamberlain: 'I take the same view as Winston,' he wrote to his sister, 'to whose excellent broadcast we have just been listening. I believe that Russia will always act as she thinks her own interests demand, and I cannot believe she would think her interests served by a German victory followed by a German domination of Europe.' Cited by M. Gilbert, *Winston S. Churchill*, vol. 6, Heinemann: London 1983 p. 51.

19. Dimitrov diary pp. 120–1.

20. The record of Stalin's discussions with Ribbentrop on 27–28 September 1939 was published in I. Fleischhauer, 'The Molotov–Ribbentrop Pact: The German Version', *International Affairs*, August 1991.

21. NSR pp. 105–7.

22. Degras, *Soviet* pp. 379–80.

23. Ibid. pp. 388–400.

24. See M.J. Carley, '"A Situation of Delicacy and Danger": Anglo-Soviet Relations, August 1939–March 1940', *Contemporary European History*, vol. 8, no. 2, 1999 and Dzh. Roberts, 'Cherchil' i Stalin: Epizody Anglo-Sovetskikh Otnoshenii (Sentyabr' 1939–Iun' 1941 goda)' in A.O. Chubar'yan (ed.), *Voina i Politika, 1939–1941*, Moscow 1999.

25. On Soviet–German relations in the 1930s: G. Roberts, *The Soviet Union and the Origins of the Second World War: Russo-German Relations and the Road to War, 1939–1941*, Macmillan: London 1995.

26. DVP 1939, vol. 22, book 2, p. 609.

27. See G. Roberts, 'The Fascist War Threat in Soviet Politics in the 1930s' in S. Pons and A. Romano (eds), *Russia in the Age of Wars, 1914–1945*, Feltrinelli: Milan 2000.

28. For a detailed analysis of Soviet–German economic negotiations and relations in this period see E.E. Ericson, *Feeding the German Eagle: Soviet Economic Aid to Nazi Germany, 1933–1941*, Praeger: Westport, Conn. 1999. This book contains the texts of the three German–Soviet trade agreements and tables detailing the imports and exports. Further analyses and statistics may be found in A.A. Shevyakov, 'Sovetsko–Germanskiye Ekonomicheskiye Otnosheniya v 1939–1941 godakh', *Voprosy Istorii*, nos 4–5, 1991; V.Ya. Sipols, 'Torgovo-Ekonomicheskie Otnosheniya mezhdu SSSR i Germaniei v 1939–1941 gg v Svete Novykh Arkhivnykh Dokumentov', *Novaya i Noveishaya Istoriya*, no. 2, 1997; and Kh.P. Shtrandman, 'Obostryaushchiesya Paradoksy: Gitler, Stalin i Germano-Sovetskie Ekonomicheskie Svyazi, 1939–1941' in Chubar'yan (ed.), *Voina i Politika*.

29. Werth, *Russia at War* p. 125.

30. *Vneshnyaya Torgovlya SSSR za 1918–1940*, Moscow 1960 pp. 558–62.

31. Ericson, *German Eagle* p. 182.

32. On Soviet–German military co-operation: G. Weinberg, *Germany and the Soviet Union, 1939–1941*, Leiden 1954 pp. 76–85 and B. Newman, *The Captured Archives*, Latimer House: London 1948 pp. 135–6.

33. *Report of the Select Committee to Investigate Communist Aggression and the Forced Incorporation of the Baltic States into the USSR: Third Interim Report of the Select Committee on Communist Aggression (House of Representatives)*, Washington DC 1954 pp. 225–6.

34. 'The Baltic Countries Join the Soviet Union: Documents on the USSR's Relations with the Baltic Countries in 1939 and 1940', *International Affairs*, March 1990, pp. 141–2.

35. *Polpredy Soobshchayut: Sbornik Dokumentov ob Otnosheniyakh SSSR s Latviei, Litvoi i Estoniei, Avgust 1939g–Avgust 1940g*, Moscow 1990 doc. 58.

36. Ibid. doc. 59.

37. *Report . . . Committee on Communist Aggression* p. 316.

38. J. Urbsys, 'Lithuania and the Soviet Union, 1939–1940', *Litaunus*, vol. 35, no. 2, 1989, p. 4.

39. The relevant documents are in *Polpredy Soobshchayut* and 'The Baltic Countries Join . . .' For citations see G. Roberts, 'Soviet Policy and the Baltic States, 1939–1940: A Reappraisal', *Diplomacy & Statecraft*, vol. 6, no. 3, 1995.

40. *Dimitrov diary* p. 120.

41. *DVP 1939*, vol. 22, book 2, doc. 536.

42. J.T. Gross, *Revolution from Abroad: The Soviet Conquest of Poland's Western Ukraine and Western Belorussia*, Princeton University Press: Princeton NJ 1988.

43. See G. Roberts, 'Stalin and the Katyn Massacre' in G. Roberts (ed.), *Stalin: His Times and Ours*, IAREES: Dublin 2005.

44. V.N. Zemskov, 'Prinuditelnye Migratsii iz Pribaltiki v 1940–1950-kh godakh', *Otechestvennyi Arkhiv*, no. 1, 1993, p. 4.

45. *DVP 1939*, vol. 22, book. 2, docs 769, 783; *Sovetsko–Bolgarskie Otnosheniya i Svyazi, 1917–1944*, Moscow 1976 doc. 504–6, 510.

46. *DVP 1939*, vol. 22, book 2, doc. 654.

47. O. Manninen and N.I. Baryshnikov, 'Peregovory Osen'u 1939 goda' in O.A. Rzheshevskii and O. Vekhvilyainen (eds), *Zimnyaya Voina 1939–1940*, vol. 1, Moscow 1999 pp. 119–21.

48. The course of the Soviet–Finnish negotiations is documented in *The Development of Soviet–Finnish Relations*, London 1940 and 'The Winter War (Documents on Soviet–Finnish Relations in 1939–1940)', *International Affairs*, nos 8 & 9, 1989. The most recent book-length study of the war in English is C. van Dyke, *The Soviet Invasion of Finland, 1939–1940*, Frank Cass: London 1997.

49. K. Rentola, 'The Finnish Communists and the Winter War', *Journal of Contemporary History*, vol. 33, no. 4, 1998, p. 596. Most of those arrested were released after a short detention.
50. N.I. Baryshnikov, 'Sovetsko–Finlyandskaya Voina 1939–1940gg', *Novaya i Noveishaya Istoriya*, no. 4, 1991, p. 33.
51. V. Mitenev, 'Archives Reopen Debate on the Winter War', *Soviet Weekly*, 3/6/89.
52. Baryshnikov, 'Sovetsko . . .' p. 34.
53. Degras, *Soviet* pp. 401–3.
54. 'Posetiteli Kremlevskogo Kabineta I.V. Stalina', *Istoricheskii Arkhiv*, nos 5–6, 1995, p. 60.
55. *Khrushchev Remembers*, Sphere Books: London 1971 pp. 135–6.
56. DVP 1939, vol. 22, book 2, doc. 821.
57. Degras, *Soviet*, pp. 407–10. Attached to the published treaty was a confidential protocol giving the Soviets the right to station up to 15,000 troops to protect their bases on the leased island of Hanko and adjacent islands in the Gulf of Finland. See *Zimnyaya Voina* p. 181.
58. See T. Vihavainen, 'The Soviet Decision for War against Finland, 30 November 1939: A Comment', *Soviet Studies*, April 1987 and M.I. Mel'tukov, '"Narodny Front" dlya Finlyandii? (K Voprosy o Tselyakh Sovetskogo Rukovodstva v Voine s Finlyandiei 1939–1940gg', *Otechestvennaya Istoriya*, no. 3, 1993.
59. Dimitrov diary p. 124.
60. Ibid.
61. On the Soviet–Finnish War: van Dyke, *The Soviet*; D.M. Glantz and J. House, *When Titans Clashed: How the Red Army Stopped Hitler*, University Press of Kansas: Lawrence, Kansas 1995 pp. 18–23; W.J. Spahr, *Stalin's Lieutenants*, Presidio Press: Novato, Calif. 1997 pp. 216–26; and A.F. Upton, 'The Winter War' in Purnell's *History of the Second World War*, 1966 pp. 122–40. Recent Russian work on the war includes *Sovetsko–Finlyandskaya Voina, 1939–1940*, 2 vols, St Petersburg 2003.
62. Degras, *Soviet* pp. 421–3.
63. I. Maisky, *Memoirs of a Soviet Ambassador*, Hutchinson: London 1967 p. 40.
64. Cited by Carley 'Situation', pp. 195–6.
65. *Sotsialisticheskie Revolutsii v Estonii 1917–1940 i yeyo Vkhozhdeniye v Sostav SSSR: Dokumenty i Materialy*, Tallin 1987 doc. 94.
66. 'Finnish historian says Stalin agreed to end Winter War based on inaccurate intelligence', *Helsingin Sanomat: International Edition* 15/10/02.
67. L. Woodward, *British Foreign Policy in the Second World War*, vol. 1, HMSO: London 1970 chaps 2–4; Churchill, *Second World War*, chap. 30; and Gilbert, *Churchill*, chap. 6.
68. A.J.P. Taylor, *English History, 1914–1945*, Penguin: London 1975 pp. 571–2.
69. DVP 1939, vol. 22, book 2, doc. 886.
70. Degras, *Soviet* pp. 436–49. Soviet casualties may have been much higher than those announced by Molotov, with perhaps as many as 70,000 dead, 40,000 missing and 180,000 wounded. See P.A. Altekar', 'Opravdany li Zhertvy? (O Poteryakh v Sovetsko–Finlyandskoi Voine)' in A.E. Taras (ed.), *Sovetsko–Finskaya Voina, 1939–1940gg*, Minsk 1999 and *Zimnyaya Voina* pp. 324–5.
71. Dimitrov diary pp. 127–9.
72. *Zimnyaya Voina* vol. 2, pp. 272–82. An English translation of the proceedings of the conference may be found in A.O. Chubaryan and H. Shukman (eds), *Stalin and the Soviet–Finnish War, 1939–1940*, Frank Cass: London 2002.
73. 'Zimnyaya Voina': *Rabota nad Oshibkami Aprel'–Mai 1940g (Materialy Komissii Glavnogo Voennogo Soveta Krasnoi Armii po Obobshcheniu Opyta Finskoi Kampanii)*, Moscow 2004.
74. *Istoriya Velikoi Otechestvennoi Voiny Sovetskogo Souza 1941–1945*, vol. 1, Moscow 1960 pp. 463–8; J. Erickson, *The Road to Stalingrad*, Harper & Row: New York 1975 pp. 16–24; Glantz and House, *Titans* pp. 23–4.

75. D.M. Glantz, *Colossus Reborn: The Red Army at War, 1941–1943*, University Press of Kansas: Lawrence, Kansas 2005 pp. 216–19. As Glantz points out, these corps proved to be too large and unwieldy in battle, but the idea of an armoured counter to the German panzer columns was the right one.

76. See S. Bialer (ed.), *Stalin and his Generals*, Souvenir Press: New York 1969 pp. 152–75 and Erickson, *Road to Stalingrad* pp. 31–7.

77. Stalin's statement is as recollected by General M.I. Kazakov in Bialer (ed.), *Stalin and his Generals* p. 145.

78. Degras, *Soviet*, pp. 457–8.

79. G. Gorodetsky, *Grand Delusion: Stalin and the German Invasion of Russia*, Yale University Press: New Haven 1999 pp. 31 ff.

80. See Roberts, 'Soviet Policy and the Baltic States'.

81. DVP 1940–1941, vol. 23, book 1, Moscow 1995 doc. 240.

82. NSR pp. 166–8.

83. Degras, *Soviet* p. 463.

84. M.Yu. Myagkov (ed.), *Mirovye Voiny XX Veka: Vtoraya Mirovaya Voina (Dokumenty i Materialy)*, vol. 4, Moscow 2002, doc. 91. For a sustained argument that Hitler's calculations in relation to Britain played a crucial role in his decision to invade Russia see S. Berthon and J. Potts, *Warlords*, Politico's Publishing: London 2005.

85. G.T. Waddington, 'Ribbentrop and the Soviet Union, 1937–1941' in J. Erickson and D. Dilks (eds), *Barbarossa*, Edinburgh University Press: Edinburgh 1994.

86. NSR pp. 255–8.

87. Ibid. p. 213.

88. Ibid. p. 216.

89. These directives were hand-written by Molotov and appear to have been dictated by Stalin. See: 'Direktivy I.V. Stalina V.M. Molotovu pered Poezdkoi v Berlin v Noyabre 1940g', *Novaya i Noveishaya Istoriya*, no. 4, 1995. See also: L.A. Bezymenskii, 'Vizit B.M. Molotova v Berlin v Noyabre 1940g. v Svete Novykh Dokumentov', *Novaya i Noveishaya Istoriya*, no. 6, 1995. An English translation of the document may be found in G. Roberts, 'From Non-Aggression Treaty to War: Documenting Nazi–Soviet Relations, 1939–1941', *History Review*, December 2001.

90. NSR pp. 252–4.

91. For an interview with Chadaev see G.A. Kumanev, *Ryadom so Stalinym*, Moscow 1999 pp. 392–420.

92. NSR pp. 258–9.

93. J. Erickson, 'Threat Identification and Strategic Appraisal by the Soviet Union, 1930–1941' in E.R. May (ed.), *Knowing One's Enemies*, Princeton University Press: Princeton NJ 1984 p. 414.

94. DVP 1940–1941, vol. 23, book 2, part 1, Moscow 1998 doc. 599.

95. NSR pp. 260–4.

96. Werth, *Russia at War* p. 89.

3 Grand Illusions: Stalin and 22 June 1941

1. I. Banac (ed.), *The Diary of Georgi Dimitrov*, Yale University Press: New Haven 2003 p. 137.

2. G. Gorodetsky, *Grand Delusion: Stalin and the German Invasion of Russia*, Yale University Press: New Haven 1999 pp. 65–6; *Dokumenty Vneshnei Politiki 1940–1941* (hereafter: DVP) vol. 23, book 2, part 1, Moscow 1998 doc. 549.

3. DVP 1940–1941, vol. 23, book 2, part 1 doc. 564.

4. *Sovetsko–Ugoslavskie Otnosheniya, 1917–1941*, Moscow 1992 docs 303, 304.

5. Ibid. docs 305, 307.

6. DVP 1940–1941, vol. 23, book 2, part 2, doc. 745.
7. Ibid. doc. 746.
8. *Sovetsko–Ugoslavskie Otnosheniya* doc. 320.
9. N.N. Novikov, *Vospominaniya Diplomata,* Moscow 1989 pp. 78–9.
10. See the remarks of Milan Gavrilovic, the Yugoslav ambassador to Moscow, 1940–1941, recorded in *Foreign Relations of the United States 1941,* vol. 1, pp. 301–2 and 312–15.
11. Gorodetsky, *Grand Delusion* p. 204.
12. *Nazi–Soviet Relations, 1939–1941,* Didier: New York 1948 (hereafter NSR) p. 324. Krebs later became Hitler's last Chief of the General Staff. For another eyewitness account see H.C. Cassidy, *Moscow Dateline, 1941–1943,* Riverside Press: Cambridge, Mass. 1943. For further details: Gorodetsky, *Grand Delusion* pp. 198–9.
13. *Rossiiskii Gosudarstvennyi Arkhiv Noveishei Istorii* (RGANI) F.2, Op. 1, D. 1. The Politburo resolution also made Zhdanov Stalin's deputy within the party. Zhdanov's job as propaganda chief was taken over by A.S. Shcherbakov.
14. NSR p. 336.
15. NSR p. 344.
16. J. Degras (ed.), *Soviet Documents on Foreign Policy,* vol. 3 (1933–1941), Oxford University Press: London 1953 p. 489.
17. DVP 1940–1941, vol. 23, book 2, part 2, doc. 772
18. NSR pp. 330–2.
19. DVP 1940–1941, vol. 23, book 2, part 2 docs 814, 823, 828. In connection with these meetings there is an oft-told story that Schulenburg actually warned Dekanozov that Hitler was going to attack and asked him to pass this information to Stalin. One source of this story is the memoirs of Stalin's trade minister, Anastas Mikoyan (*Tak Bylo,* Moscow 1999 p. 377). Dekanozov's reports show that this story is entirely without foundation. Indeed, since Schulenburg's purpose was to help improve Soviet–German relations it would have been extraordinary if he had told Dekanozov that he thought Hitler was going to attack Russia. See also Gorodetsky's treatment of this episode, *Grand Delusion* pp. 211–17.
20. 'Posetiteli Kremlevskogo Kabineta I.V. Stalina', *Istoricheskii Arkhiv,* no. 2, 1996, p. 47.
21. Gorodetsky, *Grand Delusion,* pp. 181–6.
22. Ibid. chap. 12.
23. *Vestnik Ministerstva Inostrannykh Del SSSR,* 30/4/90 pp. 77–8.
24. *1941 god,* vol. 1, Moscow 1998 doc. 327.
25. *1941 god,* vol. 2 docs 393, 413, 472, 525, 528.
26. *Organy Gosudarstvennoi Bezopasnosti SSSR v Velikoi Otechestvennoi Voine,* vol. 1, book 2, Moscow 1995 doc. 201.
27. Ibid. doc. 273. This is a tabulation of the reports these two sources submitted in the period September 1940–June 1941.
28. *Lubyanka: Stalin i NKVD–NKGB–GUKR 'Smersh', 1939–1946,* Moscow 2006 doc. 173.
29. Gorodetsky, *Grand Delusion* pp. 296–7.
30. *1941 god,* vol. 2 docs 488, 513, 514, 566, 567, 590 and *Sovetsko–Yaponskaya Voina 1945 goda: Istoriya Voenno-Politicheskogo Protivoborstva Dvukh Derzhav v 30–40-e gody* (in the series Russkii Arkhiv), Moscow 1997 docs 14, 148, 150, 151, 152, 154.
31. DVP 1940–1941, vol. 23, book 2, part 2 doc. 853.
32. *Vestnik Ministerstva Inostrannykh* pp. 76–7.
33. B. Whaley, *Codeword Barbarossa,* MIT Press: Cambridge, Mass. 1973 chap. 7 and D. Murphy, *What Stalin Knew: The Enigma of Barbarossa,* Yale University Press: New Haven 2005 chap. 17.
34. Cited by A. Seaton, *Stalin as Military Commander,* Combined Publishing: Conshohocken, PA 1998 p. 154.
35. L. Rotundo, 'Stalin and the Outbreak of War in 1941', *Journal of Contemporary History,* vol. 24, 1989 p. 283.

36. *1941 god*, vol. 2, doc. 550
37. Ibid. doc. 605.
38. E. Mawdsley, *Thunder in the East: The Nazi–Soviet War, 1941–1945*, Hodder Arnold: London 2005 p. 34.
39. This section owes a great deal to the following works: J. Erickson, 'Barbarossa: June 1941: Who Attacked Whom', *History Today*, July 2001; C.A. Roberts, 'Planning for War: The Red Army and the Catastrophe of 1941', *Europe–Asia Studies*, vol. 8, no. 47, 1995; E. Mawdsley, 'Crossing the Rubicon: Soviet Plans for Offensive War in 1940–1941', *International History Review*, December 2003; Gorodetsky, *Grand Delusion*, and Rotundo, 'Stalin'.
40. 'Zakluchitel'naya Rech' Narodnogo Komissara Oborony Souza SSR Geroya i Marshala Sovetskogo Souza S.K. Timoshenko na Voennom Soveshchanii 31 Dekabrya 1940g' p. 12. Copy in Volkogonov Papers.
41. G.K. Zhukov, 'Kharakter Sovremennoi Nastupatel'noi Operatsii' in *Nakanune Voiny: Materialy Soveshchaniya Vysshego Rukovodyashchego Sostava RKKA 23–31 Dekabrya*, Moscow 1993 (in the series Russkii Arkhiv) pp. 129–51.
42. Mawdsley, 'Crossing the Rubicon', pp. 826–7.
43. J. Stalin, *Works*, vol. 12, Foreign Languages Publishing House: Moscow 1955 p. 269.
44. In 1936 Stalin told the American journalist Roy Howard: 'We Marxists believe that revolution will occur in other countries as well. But it will only come when it is considered possible or necessary by the revolutionaries in those countries. Export of revolution is nonsense. Each country, if it so desires, will make its own revolution, and if no such desire exists, no revolution will occur.' Degras, *Soviet* p. 166.
45. M. Djilas, *Wartime*, Secker & Warburg: London 1977 p. 437. Albert Resis points out, however, that Stalin's statement to Djilas was not always borne out by Soviet actions. On many occasions the Red Army withdrew from territories it occupied: Denmark, Norway, Iran, China, Manchuria. See his *Stalin, the Politburo, and the Onset of the Cold War, 1945–1946*, The Carl Beck Papers in Russian and East European Studies no. 701, April 1998 p. 25.
46. In this connection see M. von Hagen, 'Soviet Soldiers and Officers on the Eve of the German Invasion' in J.L. Wieczynski (ed.), *Operation Barbarossa*, Charles, Schlacks: Salt Lake City 1993.
47. *1941 god*, vol. 2 pp. 557–571.
48. Ibid. vol. 1 doc. 95.
49. Ibid. doc. 117.
50. Ibid. doc. 134.
51. Ibid. doc. 315.
52. Gorodetsky, *Grand Delusion* pp. 121–4.
53. M.V. Zakharov, *General'nyi Shtab v Predvoennye Gody*, Moscow 1989 pp. 220–4. Zakharov, who died in 1972, worked on this book in the 1960s. Its publication was deferred for 20 years because of his critical arguments and because of the secret materials he refers to. A new edition of the book was published in 2005.
54. *1941 god*, vol. 1 doc. 224.
55. Mawdsley, 'Rubicon'.
56. *1941 god*, vol. 2 doc. 473.
57. The document first came to light in Dmitri Volkogonov's biography of Stalin published in the Soviet Union in 1989. Volkogonov's source was a three-page typescript that he found in the Soviet military archives (copy in the Volkogonov Papers in the Library of Congress Manuscripts Division). This typescript was then published in the journal *Voenno-Istoricheskii Zhurnal* ('Upryamye Fakty Nachala Voiny', no. 2, 1992). However, this text was only a section from a much longer, handwritten document (L.A. Bezymenskii, 'O 'Plane Zhukova' ot 15 May 1941g', *Novaya i Noveishaya Istoriya*, no. 3, 2000). On the use of this document by those who argue that Stalin was

planning a preventative war and a pre-emptive strike in 1941 see T.J. Uldricks, 'The Icebreaker Controversy: Did Stalin Plan to Attack Hitler?', *Slavic Review*, vol. 58, no. 3, Fall 1999.

58. There are various third-hand reports that Stalin was shown or told about the document, but the problem with all these sources is that they post-date knowledge of the existence of the document itself. The various sources are detailed and discussed in Mawdsley, 'Rubicon'.

59. Roberts, 'Planning for War' p. 1320.

60. A. Werth, *Russia at War, 1941–1945*, Pan Books: London 1964 p. 132.

61. See the discussion in the Mawdsley, 'Rubicon'.

62. 'Posetiteli Kremlevskogo Kabineta I.V. Stalina', *Istoricheskii Arkhiv*, no. 2, 1996 pp. 48–9.

63. A.M. Vasilevsky, *A Lifelong Cause*, Progress Publishers: Moscow 1981 p. 84.

64. G.A. Kumanev, *Ryadom so Stalinym*, Moscow 1999 p. 233. See also Mawdsley, 'Rubicon', pp. 864–5.

65. Gorodetsky, *Grand Delusion* p. 240. Zhukov's comment was written on the text of an unpublished interview by Vasilevskii.

66. K.K. Rokossovskii, *Soldatskii Dolg*, Moscow 2002 pp. 50–4. This passage from Rokossovskii's memoirs was, along with a number of others, excluded from the original edition published in 1968.

67. G.K. Zhukov, *Vospominaniya i Razmyshleniya*, 10th edn, vol. 1, Moscow 1990 p. 289. This statement was censored from pre-glasnost era editions of Zhukov's memoirs.

68. Mawdsley, *Thunder* pp. 86–7.

4 War of Annihilation: Stalin versus Hitler

1. D.M. Glantz and J. House, *When Titans Clashed: How the Red Army Stopped Hitler*, University Press of Kansas: Lawrence, Kansas 1995 p. 31.

2. D. Glantz, *Barbarossa: Hitler's Invasion of Russia 1941*, Tempus Publishing: Stroud 2001 p. 234.

3. *1941 god*, vol. 2, Moscow 1998 doc. 612

4. Preparations for a German attack on the Soviet Union are covered in detail in the various essays in H. Boog et al., *Germany and the Second World War: The Attack on the Soviet Union* (vol. 4 of *Germany and the Second World War*), Clarendon Press: Oxford 1998. Unless otherwise stated, the material in this section is from that volume.

5. J. Keegan, *The Second World War*, Arrow Books: London 1989 p. 186.

6. A. Clark, *Barbarossa: The Russian–German Conflict, 1941–1945*, Phoenix: London 1996 p. 43.

7. Ye. N. Kul'kov, 'Napadeniye Germanii na SSSR' in *Mirovye Voiny XX Veka*, vol. 3, Moscow 2002 p. 138.

8. M.U. Myagkov (ed.), *Mirovye Voiny XX Veka*, vol. 4, Moscow 2002 doc. 199.

9. Glantz, *Barbarossa* p. 55.

10. L. Dobroszycki and J.S. Gurock (eds), *The Holocaust in the Soviet Union*, M.E. Sharpe: New York 1993.

11. See J. Matthaus, 'Operation Barbarossa and the Onset of the Holocaust' in C. Browning, *The Origins of the Final Solution*, University of Nebraska Press: Lincoln, NB 2004 and the contributions of J. Förster, C. Streit, O. Bartov, and C. Browning to D. Cesarini (ed.), *The Final Solution*, Routledge: London 1994.

12. C. Streit, 'Partisans–Resistance–Prisoners of War' in J.L. Wieczynski (ed.), *Operation Barbarossa*, Charles, Schlacks: Salt Lake City 1993.

13. A graphic description of Soviet soldiers fighting their way out of encirclement may be found in Konstantin Simonov's novel *The Living and the Dead*, Raduga Publishers: Moscow 1989.

14. Myagkov, *Mirovye*.
15. G.A. Kumanev, 'The USSR's Degree of Defense Readiness and the Suddenness of the Nazi Attack' in Wieczynski (ed.), *Barbarossa*; M.N. Ramanichev, 'Nevidannoye Ispytaniye' in G.N. Sevost'yanov (ed.), *Voina i Obshchestvo, 1941–1945*, vol. 1, Moscow 2004.
16. A. Werth, *Russia at War*, Pan Books: London 1964 p. 249.
17. W.E.D. Allen and P. Muratoff, *The Russian Campaigns of 1941–1943*, Penguin Books: London 1944 p. 53.
18. *Khrushchev Remembers*, Sphere Books: London 1971 pp. 535–6.
19. R. and Z. Medvedev, *The Unknown Stalin*, Overlook Press: Woodstock and New York p. 242.
20. A. Mikoyan, *Tak Bylo*, Moscow 1999 pp. 390–1.
21. R. and Z. Medvedev, *Unknown Stalin* p. 244. Constantine Pleshakov has pointed out that while Mikoyan claims that Voroshilov was involved in the visit to the dacha he was, in fact, at the front and out of Moscow at this time (*Stalin's Folly*, Houghton Mifflin: Boston 2005 p. 300 n. 219).
22. Chadaev's memoir is unpublished but extensive extracts may be found in E. Radzinsky, *Stalin*, Hodder & Stoughton: London 1997 pp. 445–55. Another book that cites extensively from the Chadaev memoirs is S. Berthon and J. Potts, *Warlords*, Politico's Publishing: London 2005.
23. G.A. Kumanev, *Ryadom so Stalinym*, Moscow 1999 p. 413.
24. A Resis (ed.), *Molotov Remembers*, Ivan R. Dee: Chicago 1993 p. 39.
25. *The Memoirs of Marshal Zhukov*, Jonathan Cape: London 1971 p. 268.
26. *Organy Gosudarstvennoi Bezopasnosti SSSR v Velikoi Otechestvennoi Voine*, vol. 2, book 1, Moscow 2000 p. 107.
27. 'Posetiteli Kremlevskogo Kabineta I.V. Stalina: 1940–1941', *Istoricheskii Arkhiv*, no. 2, 1996 pp. 51–4.
28. R. and Z. Medvedev, *Unknown Stalin* p. 243.
29. *Organy Gosudarstvennoi* docs 293, 306, 306.
30. Ibid. doc. 337. The connection with the 3 July radio address was brought to my attention by Zhukov, *Memoirs* p. 270.
31. *1941 god*, vol. 2, Moscow 1998 doc. 608.
32. Resis (ed.), *Molotov Remembers* p. 38.
33. '"Nashe Delo Pravoe": Kak Gotovilos' Vystupleniye V.M. Molotova po Radio 22 Iunya 1941 goda', *Istoricheskii Arkhiv*, no. 2, 1995. This article contains a photocopy of Molotov's handwritten draft. For a partial English translation of Molotov's broadcast speech, see J. Degras (ed.), *Soviet Documents on Foreign Policy*, vol. 3, Oxford University Press: London 1953 pp. 490–1.
34. I. Banac (ed.), *The Diary of Georgi Dimitrov, 1933–1949*, Yale University Press: New Haven 2003 pp. 166–7.
35. *Dokumenty Vneshnei Politiki 1941–1942*, vol. 24, Moscow 2000 doc. 2 (hereafter DVP).
36. W.S. Churchill, *War Speeches, 1940–1945*, Cassell: London 1946 pp. 67–9.
37. *Sovetsko–Amerikanskie Otnosheniya 1939–1945*, Moscow 2004 p. 134. On Roosevelt's policy towards the Soviet Union during the war: M.E. Glantz, *FDR and the Soviet Union: The President's Battles over Foreign Policy*, University Press of Kansas: Lawrence, Kansas 2005.
38. *Sovetsko–Amerikanskie* doc. 102.
39. Ibid. doc. 135 and nn. 16–17 pp. 576–83.
40. Ibid. doc. 145.
41. Ibid. docs 227–30.
42. For the texts of the three directives see *1941 god*, vol. 2, docs 605, 607, 617. For English translations see appendix 2 of Glantz, *Barbarossa* pp. 242–3.

43. In his memoirs Zhukov distanced himself from the third directive ordering counter-offensive action by claiming that Stalin rang him up at 1 p.m. on 22 June and ordered him to go immediately to Kiev (p. 238). However, Stalin's office diary records that Zhukov was meeting him from 2 to 4 p.m. Further, as Boris Sokolov correctly points out, the memoirs of Marshal I.Kh. Bagramyan record that Zhukov arrived at the South-Western Front a while after the receipt of the third directive (B.V. Sokolov, *Georgii Zhukov*, Moscow 2004 p. 220).

44. S.M. Shtemenko, *The Soviet General Staff at War, 1941–1945*, vol. 1, Progress Publishers: Moscow 1970 p. 32.

45. J. Barber, 'Popular Reactions in Moscow to the German Invasion of June 22, 1941' in Wieczynski (ed.), *Barbarossa*. See also: M.M. Gorinov, 'Muscovites' Moods, 22 June 1941 to May 1942' in R.W. Thurston and B. Bonwetsch (eds), *The People's War: Responses to World War II in the Soviet Union*, University of Illinois Press: Urbana and Chicago 2000.

46. Zhukov, *Memoirs* p. 250.

47. G.K. Zhukov, *Vospominaniya i Razmyshleniya*, vol. 2, Moscow 1990 p. 38.

48. Glantz, *Barbarossa* p. 40.

49. *Organy Gosudarstvennoi* doc. 340

50. J. Stalin, *On the Great Patriotic War of the Soviet Union*, Hutchinson: London 1943/4 pp. 5–9. For an analysis of Stalin's early wartime speeches see E. Mawdsley, 'Explaining Military Failure: Stalin, the Red Army, and the First Period of the Patriotic War, 1941–1942' in G. Roberts (ed.), *Stalin: His Times and Ours*, IAREES: Dublin 2005.

51. *Moskva Voennaya, 1941–1945*, Moscow 1995 docs 19–20.

52. Ramanichev, 'Nevidannoye' p. 62.

53. Yu. Gor'kov, *Gosudarstvennyi Komitet Oborony Postanovlyaet (1941–1945)*, Moscow 2002 p. 20.

54. *Organy Gosudarstvennoi* doc. 423.

55. D. M. Glantz, *Colossus Reborn: The Red Army at War, 1941–1943*, University Press of Kansas: Lawrence, Kansas 2005 chap. 11.

56. *Organy Gosudarstvennoi* doc. 384.

57. *1941 god*, vol. 2 doc. 634.

58. *Stavka VGK: Dokumenty i Materialy 1941 god*, Moscow 1996 (series Russkii Arkhiv) doc. 106. The Institution of Commissars was re-established in the Soviet navy on 20 July.

59. *Glavnye Politicheskiye Organy Vooruzhennykh Sil SSSR v Velikoi Otechestvennoi Voine 1941–1945gg*, Moscow 1996 (series 'Russkii Arkhiv') doc. 42.

60. *Organy Gosudarstvennoi* doc. 413.

61. Ibid. doc. 490.

62. Ibid. doc. 550.

63. *1941 god*, vol. 2 doc. 635.

64. *Organy Gosudarstvennoi* docs 379, 436, 437, 438. In 1956 Pavlov and a number of others were rehabilitated. Copies of some of the rehabilitation documents may be found in the Volkogonov Papers. The authors of these materials argued that while Pavlov committed many mistakes as a commander this was due to his inexperience rather than negligence or cowardice. For an evaluation of Pavlov's mistakes see E. Mawdsley, *Thunder in the East: The Nazi–Soviet War 1941–1945* Hodder Arnold: London 2005 pp. 60–2 and V.A. Anfilov, *Doroga k Tragedii Sorok Pervogo Goda*, Moscow 1997.

65. O.F. Suvenirov, *Tragediya RKKA, 1937–1939*, Moscow 1998 p. 381.

66. G. Jukes, 'Meretskov' in H. Shukman (ed.), *Stalin's Generals*, Phoenix Press: London 1997.

67. *Organy Gosudarstvennoi* doc. 424.

68. Ibid. doc. 454. According to Zhukov (*Memoirs* pp. 287–9) he met Stalin on 29 July and told him that he would have to give up Kiev and that it was after this meeting that he was replaced as Chief of the General Staff. However, according to Stalin's appointments diary there were no meetings with Zhukov between 21 July and 4 August. In connection with Zhukov's departure from the General Staff it should be borne in mind that the creation of Stavka upon the outbreak of war had downgraded the General Staff's position in the military hierarchy.

69. Zhukov, *Vospominaniya* vol. 2, p. 132.

70. Glantz, *Barbarossa* pp. 86–90.

71. Werth, *Russia at War* pp. 188–95.

72. Glantz, *Barbarossa* p. 90.

73. Ramanichev, 'Nevidannoye' p. 67.

74. Glantz, *Barbarossa* p. 96.

75. A.J.P. Taylor, *The War Lords*, Penguin Books: London 1978 p. 107.

76. A.M. Vasilevsky, *A Lifelong Cause*, Progress Publishers: Moscow 1981 pp. 97–104.

77. *Stavka VGK: Dokumenty i Materialy 1941 god* doc. 168.

78. A.M. Vasilevskii, *Delo Vsei Zhizni*, Moscow 1974 p. 145. This and the following quoted passage were omitted from the English translation of Vasilevskii's memoirs.

79. Ibid. p. 146.

80. Vasilevsky, *A Lifelong Cause* pp. 106–7.

81. Ibid. p. 107.

82. Zhukov, *Vospominaniya*, vol. 2 pp. 132–3. This sentence was omitted from the English edition of the memoirs.

83. I. Kh. Bagramyan, *Tak Shli My k Pobede*, Moscow 1998 p. 180.

84. *Stavka VGK: Dokumenty i Materialy 1941 god* doc. 255.

85. Ibid. doc. 254.

86. Vasilevsky, *A Lifelong Cause* p. 110.

87. *Stavka VGK: Dokumenty i Materialy 1941 god* doc. 280.

88. Glantz, *Barbarossa*, p. 132.

89. Bagramyan, *Tak Shli* p. 188.

90. DVP vol. 24 pp. 577–83 n.17.

91. *Stalin's Correspondence with Churchill, Attlee, Roosevelt and Truman, 1941–1945*, Lawrence & Wishart: London 1958 docs 3, 10, 12, pp. 12–25.

92. Vasilevsky, *A Lifelong Cause* p. 108.

93. Mawdsley, *Thunder* p. 74.

94. Ibid. p. 110. The view of Allen and Muratoff, *Russian Campaigns* was that 'in the balance of the whole campaign, the sacrifice made at Kiev [by the Red Army] was worth it' (p. 46).

95. The military overview in this section is based on D. M. Glantz, *The Battle for Leningrad, 1941–1944*, University Press of Kansas: Lawrence, Kansas 2002.

96. Ibid. pp. 54–5.

97. Ibid. pp. 85–6.

98. For an account of Zhdanov's activities in Leningrad during the war see H.E. Salisbury, *The 900 Days: The Siege of Leningrad*, Avon Books: New York 1970.

99. N.A. Lomagin, *Neizvestnaya Blokada*, vol. 1, St Petersburg: 2002 pp. 58–61.

100. N.Ya Komarov and G.A. Kumanev, *Blokada Leningrada: 900 Geroicheskikh Dnei, 1941–1944*, Moscow 2004 pp. 72–6.

101. Cited by D. Watson, 'Molotov, the War and Soviet Government' (unpublished paper). See also Lomagin, *Blokada* p. 63.

102. Stavka directive in Volkogonov Papers. According to a Politburo resolution of April 1942 Voroshilov was relieved of his command because of the Leningrad Military Council episode and because he had concentrated on the creation of workers'

battalions rather than conventional defence issues. See Volkogonov's essay in Shukman (ed.), *Stalin's Generals* p. 318.

103. Glantz, *Battle for Leningrad*, pp. 81–2; see also Komarov and Kumanev, *Blokada* p. 113 who date this order 21 September and Lomagin, *Blokada* p. 69 who says it was issued on 22 September.

104. Mawdsley, *Thunder* p. 136.

105. The unsurpassed popular history of the Leningrad blockade is Salisbury's book. My figures in this paragraph are taken from Glantz, *Battle for Leningrad* p. 468.

106. *Stavka VGK: Dokumenty i Materialy 1941 god* doc. 504.

107. Mawdsley, *Thunder* p. 95.

108. Glantz, *Barbarossa* p. 157.

109. Vasilevsky, *A Lifelong Cause* p. 112.

110. For further discussion of the reasons for the Viazma-Briansk débâcle see Mawdsley, *Thunder*, pp. 97–100.

111. *G.K. Zhukov v Bitve pod Moskvoi: Sbornik Dokumentov*, Moscow 1994 docs 1, 3, 5, 7.

112. Vasilevsky, *A Lifelong Cause* p. 119.

113. V. Gavrilov and E. Gorbunov, *Operatsiya 'Ramzai'*, Moscow 2004 chap. 9.

114. *Organy Gosudarstvennoi Bezopasnosti SSSR v Velikoi Otechestvennoi Voine*, vol. 2, book 2, Moscow 2000 doc. 611; Mawdsley, *Thunder* pp. 96–7.

115. *Moskva Voennaya* docs 56 and 63.

116. A good description of the panic may be found in Werth, *Russia at War*, pp. 224–33. *Moskva Voennaya* contains a number of relevant documents.

117. See Gorinov, 'Muscovite Moods'.

118. *Marshal Zhukov's Greatest Battles*, Sphere Books: London 1971 pp. 53–4.

119. Ibid. p. 63.

120. Stalin, *Great Patriotic War* pp. 10–21.

121. Ibid. pp. 21–3.

122. *Moskva Voennaya* doc. 7.

123. Gorinov, 'Muscovite Moods' p. 126.

124. Lomagin, *Neizvestnaya Blokada*, vol. 2 doc. 1 p. 359.

125. DVP vol. 24 doc. 305 p. 473.

126. Mawdsley, *Thunder* p. 121.

127. J. Erickson, *The Road to Stalingrad*, Harper & Row: New York 1975 pp. 277–342; Glantz, *Colossus Reborn* pp. 17–24; Glantz, *Battle for Leningrad* pp. 149–56.

128. In his memoirs Zhukov makes various claims about how he tried to persuade Stalin to forgo offensive operations in this period. There is no contemporary evidence to support his assertions and every reason to doubt his account since it forms part of a persistent pattern of distancing himself from failed Soviet offensives while as the same time taking most of the credit for the successful ones. In reality, Zhukov was the greatest hawk among Stalin's generals and it is likely that he was an enthusiast of the winter offensive of 1941–1942 not its detractor.

129. O.A. Rzheshevsky (ed.), *War and Diplomacy*, Harwood Academic Publishers: Amsterdam 1996 doc. 4.

130. Ibid. doc. 7.

131. Ibid. docs 5–6. On the diplomatic background to Eden's trip to Moscow V.V. Sokolov, 'I.M. Maiskii Mezhdu I.V. Stalinym i U. Cherchillem v Pervye Mesyatsy Voiny', *Novaya i Noveishaya Istoriya*, no. 6, 2001.

132. *Stalin's Correspondence* doc. 40.

133. Rzheshevsky, *War and Diplomacy* docs 37–8.

134. Vasilevsky *A Lifelong Cause* p. 152.

135. Stalin, *Great Patriotic War* pp. 23–8.

5 Victory at Stalingrad and Kursk: Stalin and his Generals

1. B. Wegner, 'The War against the Soviet Union, 1942–1943' in H. Boog et al. (eds), *Germany and the Second World War*, vol. 6, Clarendon Press: Oxford 2001. This is by far the best account of Hitler's 1942 campaign. See also the same author's 'The Road to Defeat: The German Campaigns in Russia, 1941–1943', *Journal of Strategic Studies*, vol. 13, no. 1, March 1990.
2. J.S.A. Hayward, *Stopped at Stalingrad: The Luftwaffe and Hitler's Defeat in the East, 1942–1943*, University Press of Kansas: Lawrence, Kansas 1998 p. 4
3. On Hitler's motives for the 1942 campaign: J. Hayward, 'Hitler's Quest for Oil: The Impact of Economic Considerations on Military Strategy, 1941–1942', *Journal of Strategic Studies*, vol. 18, no. 4, December 1995.
4. H. R. Trevor-Roper, *Hitler's War Directives, 1939–1945*, Sidgwick & Jackson: London 1964 p. 117.
5. Ibid. p. 119.
6. G. Jukes, *Stalingrad: The Turning Point*, Ballantine Books: New York 1968.
7. On the Soviet Kerch operations see E. Mawdsley, *Thunder in the East: The Nazi–Soviet War, 1941–1945*, Hodder Arnold: London 2005 pp. 136–41.
8. A.M. Vasilevsky, *A Lifelong Cause*, Progress Publishers: Moscow 1981 p. 159. A copy of the full text of this document may be found in the Volkogonov Papers.
9. P.P. Chevela, 'Novye Ispytaniya' in V.A. Zolotarev et al. (eds), *Velikaya Otechestvennaya Voina 1941–1945*, vol. 1, Moscow 1998 p. 332.
10. Vasilevsky, *A Lifelong Cause* p. 161. The full text of the 4 June Stavka document may be found in the Volkogonov Papers.
11. For a graphic description of the defence of Sebastopol: A. Werth, *Russia at War*, Pan Books: London 1964 pp. 363–9.
12. D.M. Glantz, *Kharkov 1942: Anatomy of a Military Disaster through Soviet Eyes*, Ian Allan Publishing: Shepperton, Surrey 1998. This invaluable book not only contains a detailed narrative of the battle but an extensive account of the Soviet discussion of the disaster and a number of important Stavka documents.
13. *Khrushchev Remembers*, Sphere Books: London 1971 pp. 536–7. Khrushchev repeated and elaborated on his claim in his memoirs (pp. 160–7).
14. Glantz, *Kharkov 1942* p. 240.
15. *The Memoirs of Marshal Zhukov*, Jonathan Cape: London 1971 p. 368.
16. K.S. Moskalenko, *Na Ugo-Zapadnom Napravlenii*, vol. 1, 2nd edn, Moscow 1975 pp. 168–213.
17. Glantz, *Kharkov 1942* p. 241.
18. Vasilevsky, *A Lifelong Cause* pp. 163–4.
19. I. Kh. Bagramyan, *Tak Shli My k Pobede*, Moscow 1998 pp. 305–53.
20. Glantz, *Kharkov 1942* pp. 224–5. A copy of the original Russian document may be found in the Volkogonov Papers.
21. Ibid. pp. 275–9 for an account of the subsequent careers of the senior commanders involved in the Kharkov operation. Timoshenko was appointed commander of the newly formed Stalingrad Front on 12 July but relieved of this position a few days later and then sent to Leningrad. The relevant Stavka directives may be found in the Volkogonov Papers.
22. Ibid. pp. 252–72.
23. It seems that in spring 1942 frontline commanders bombarded Stavka with proposals for offensive action, provided they could have additional forces. See M.N. Ramanichev, 'Nevidannoe Ispytaniye' in G.N. Sevast'yanov (ed.), *Voina i Obshchestvo, 1941–1945*, vol. 1, Moscow 2004 p. 88.
24. D. Glantz, *Colossus Reborn: The Red Army at War, 1941–1943*, University Press of Kansas: Lawrence, Kansas 2005 pp. 30ff.

25. Timoshenko died in 1970, i.e. shortly after the publication of Zhukov's memoirs and three years before the appearance of Vasilevskii's.
26. Zhukov, *Memoirs* p. 366.
27. Ibid. p. 275.
28. Vasilevsky, *A Lifelong Cause* p. 157.
29. Chevela, 'Novye Ispytaniya' pp. 325–7. See also Ramanichev, 'Nevidannoe Ispytaniye'.
30. *Stalin's Correspondence with Churchill, Attlee, Roosevelt and Truman, 1941–45*, Lawrence & Wishart: London 1958 doc. 36 p. 41.
31. J. Stalin, *On the Great Patriotic War of the Soviet Union*, Hutchinson: London 1943 pp. 32, 34
32. A.M. Samsonov, *Stalingradskaya Bitva*, 4th edn, Moscow 1989 p. 52.
33. See E.F. Ziemke and M.E. Bauer, *Moscow to Stalingrad: Decision in the East*, Center of Military History, US Army: Washington DC 1987 pp. 328–30.
34. Stalin, *On the Great Patriotic War* p. 38.
35. The name of the operation was changed to 'Braunschweig' after an operations officer carrying plans for Blau was involved in a plane crash in enemy territory.
36. Traditionally the ascent of Mount Elbrus has been cited as marking the maximum extent of the German advance into the Caucasus, but in October 2003 it was reported that the bodies of a number of German soldiers had been found buried further south, at Digara. T. Parfitt, 'Graves Mark Peak of Nazis' Reach', *The Times*, 6/10/03.
37. See Ziemke and Bauer, *Moscow to Stalingrad* pp. 343–4, 510–12.
38. For example, *Stavka VGK: Dokumenty i Materialy 1942*, Moscow 1996 (Russkii Arkhiv series) doc. 379.
39. Trevor-Roper, *War Directives* pp. 129–30. See further G. Jukes, *Hitler's Stalingrad Decisions*, University of California Press: Berkeley 1985 pp. 36–46.
40. *Stalingradskaya Bitva*, 2 vols, vol 1, Moscow 2002 pp. 160, 169.
41. *Stavka VGK: Dokumenty i Materialy 1942* doc. 359, 423. Also: V.V. Beshanov, *God 1942 – 'Uchebnyi'*, Minsk 2002 pp. 300ff.
42. Extensive extracts from the Soviet General Staff's daily briefing reports may be found in *Stalingradskaya Bitva*. The volumes also contain reprints of many articles from the Soviet press as well Stavka directives, Front and Army reports and many other documents.
43. Ziemke and Bauer, *Moscow to Stalingrad* p. 343.
44. *Stalingradskaya Bitva*, vol. 1, p. 184.
45. Originally the 7th, 5th and 1st Reserve Armies, they were deployed in the Stalingrad area in June 1942 and redesignated the 62nd, 63rd and 64th respectively on 9 July 1942. *Stalingrad, 1942–1943: Stalingradskaya Bitva v Dokumenakh*, Moscow 1995 docs 67,68, 72.
46. Beshanov, *God 1942* p. 473.
47. Volkogonov Papers.
48. Vasilevsky, *A Lifelong Cause* p. 177.
49. *Khronika Ognennykh Dnei, 17 Iulya 1942–2 Fevralya 1943*, Volgograd 2002. The date derives from the Soviet General Staff's study of the Stalingrad battle prepared in 1943. This divided the defensive stages of the battle into four: (1) the defensive battle on the distant approaches to Stalingrad, 17 July–17 August; (2) the second stage of the defensive battle on the near approaches to Stalingrad, 17 August–2 September; (3) the battle for the inside lines of Stalingrad, 2–13 September; and (4) the street-fighting stage of the battle from 14 September to 19 November. The offensive stage of the battle began, from the Soviet point of view, on 19 November 1942 with the launch of the counter-offensive which trapped the German 6th Army inside the city. See L. Rotundo (ed.), *Battle for Stalingrad: The 1943 Soviet General Staff Study*, Pergamon-Brassey's: London 1989 pp. 12–13.
50. *Stalingrad, 1942–1943* doc. 95.

51. Werth, *Russia at War* pp. 375–6.
52. A full English translation of Order 227 is appended to G. Roberts, *Victory at Stalingrad: The Battle That Changed History*, Pearson/Longman: London 2002.
53. Glantz, *Colossus Reborn* pp. 570–9.
54. *Stalingradskaya Epopeya*, Moscow 2000 doc. 50
55. Ibid. docs 28–9, 31–3. These are NKVD reports on reactions in the armed forces to Order 227. From the NKVD's point of view the order was also useful in identifying dissenting voices – those critical of the order or expressing other 'anti-Soviet' views being arrested.
56. On the role of discipline on the Eastern Front see J. Barber and M. Harrison, 'Patriotic War, 1941–1945' in R.G. Suny (ed.), *The Cambridge History of Russia*, vol. 3, Cambridge University Press: Cambridge 2006.
57. A. Werth, *The Year of Stalingrad*, Hamish Hamilton: London 1946 pp. 97–8.
58. 'Na Uge', *Krasnaya Zvezda*, 19/7/42.
59. Werth, *Year of Stalingrad* pp. 80–1, 130–3, 170–1.
60. For example the editorial 'Stoiko Zashchishchat' Rodnuyu Zemlu', *Krasnaya Zvezda*, 30/7/42.
61. 'Postoyat za Rodinu kak Suvorov, Kutuzov, Alexandr Nevskii', *Krasnaya Zvezda* 31/7/42.
62. Werth, *Russia at War* pp. 382–94.
63. 'Ob Ustanovlenii Polnogo Edinonachaliya I Uprazdnenii Instituta Voennykh Komissarov v Krasnoi Armii', *Krasnaya Zvezda*, 10/10/42.
64. *Stalingradskaya Epopeya* docs 49, 51, 53.
65. Werth, *Year of Stalingrad* p. 82.
66. *Stalingrad, 1942–1943* docs 109–10.
67. Ibid. doc. 120
68. *Sovetsko–Angliiskiye Otnosheniya vo Vremya Velikoi Otechestvinnoi Voiny 1941–1945*, vol. 1, Moscow 1983 doc. 114.
69. *Sovetsko–Amerikanskiye Otnosheniya vo Vremya Velikoi Otechestvennoi Voiny, 1941–1945*, vol. 1, Moscow 1984 doc. 109.
70. Ibid. doc. 102
71. 'Krepnushchaya Moshch' Antigitlerovskoi Koalitsii', *Pravda*, 13/6/42.
72. *Vneshnyaya Politika Sovetskogo Souza v period Otechestvennoi Voiny*, vol. 1, Moscow 1944 p. 260.
73. O.A. Rzheshevsky (ed.), *War and Diplomacy: The Making of the Grand Alliance*, Harwood Academic Publishers: Amsterdam 1996 docs 112, 119.
74. I. N. Zemskov, *Diplomaticheskaya Istoriya Vtorogo Fronta v Evrope*, Moscow 1982 pp. 110–20. This book contains citations from a number of Soviet diplomatic documents that have yet to be published or made accessible in the archives.
75. *Stalin's Correspondence* doc. 57 p. 56.
76. Ibid. docs 58, 60 pp. 57–8.
77. *Organy Gosudarstvennoi Bezopasnosti SSSR v Velikoi Otechestvennoi Voine*, vol. 3, book 2, Moscow 2003 docs 1005, 1022, 1024, 1031, 1037, 1041.
78. *Sovetsko–Amerikanskie Otnosheniya* docs 113, 123, 124, 125.
79. 'New Documents about Winston Churchill from Russian Archives', *International Affairs*, vol. 47, no. 5, 2001 pp. 131–4
80. The summary that follows derives from the American interpreter's report in the Harriman Papers, Library of Congress Manuscript Division, Container 162, Chronological File 16–23/8/42. The Soviet report of the meeting is in *Sovetsko–Angliiskiye Otnosheniya* doc. 130. The American report is longer but does not conflict in any essential way with the Soviet report.
81. In Harriman's handwritten notes of the meeting Moscow is specifically mentioned by Churchill as a possible target. Stalin replied: 'I don't know. But in view of the length

of the front, it is quite possible to take 20 divisions to create a striking force, thus creating a threat to Moscow or elsewhere . . . Moscow is safer but can't guarantee the unexpected surprise.' Harriman Papers, c.162, cf. 14–15/8/42.

82. The summary that follows is based on the American interpreter's report in Harriman Papers, c.162, cf. 16–23/8/42. The Soviet report of the meeting may be found in *Sovetsko–Angliiskie Otnosheniya* doc. 131.

83. *Sovetsko–Amerikanskiye Otnosheniya* doc. 132.

84. The summary that follows is based on the report of the British interpreter at the meeting, Major A.H. Birse, in Harriman Papers, c.162, cf. 14–15/8/42. The Soviet report of the meeting, but not of the conversation at dinner, may be found in *Sovetsko–Angliiskie Otnosheniya* doc. 137.

85. The idea of such an operation had first been raised by Stalin in a message to Churchill on 18 July 1941. See: *Stalin's Correspondence* doc. 3 p. 12.

86. These exchanges about Germany and bombing Berlin were omitted from the Birse notes of the dinner conversation but recorded in those made by V. Pavlov, Stalin's interpreter. See O.A. Rzheshevskii, *Stalin i Cherchill'*, Moscow 2004 doc. 152.

87. 'New Documents about Winston Churchill from Russian Archives' pp. 137–8.

88. See Harriman's notes on his talks with Stalin during the official dinner on 14 August in Harriman Papers, c.162, cf. 14–15/8/42.

89. Stalin, *On the Great Patriotic War* pp. 34–5. For Cassidy's account of the background to this statement see H. C. Cassidy, *Moscow Dateline*, The Riverside Press: Cambridge, Mass 1943 chap. 16.

90. R. Ivanov, *Stalin i Souzniki, 1941–1945 gg*, Smolensk 2000 pp. 240–1.

91. For example, Stalin's conversation with Wendell Wilkie, Roosevelt's Republican opponent in the 1940 presidential election, on 23 September 1942. *Sovetsko–Amerikanskiye Otnosheniya* doc. 93.

92. Stalin, *On the Great Patriotic War* pp. 39–41.

93. *Stalingradskaya Epopeya* docs 46 and 55; N.A. Lomagin (ed.), *Neizvestnaya Blokada*, Moscow 2002 pp. 380–2, 389–91.

94. *Vneshnyaya Politika Sovetskogo Souza v period Otechestvennoi Voiny* pp. 273–7. This whole episode was drawn to my attention by Cassidy, *Moscow Dateline* chap. 17. For an NKVD report on popular reactions in Leningrad to this statement, the Hess business and the *Pravda* editorial cited below see Lomagin (ed.), *Neizvestnaya Blokada* pp. 386–8.

95. Cited by J. Haslam, 'Stalin's Fears of a Separate Peace, 1942', *Intelligence and National Security*, vol. 8, no. 4, October 1993, p. 98. Also: Cassidy, *Moscow Dateline* p. 286 for a further citation from the same editorial. On this whole issue see A.J. Kochavi, 'Anglo-Soviet Differences over a Policy towards War Criminals', *SEER*, vol. 69, no. 3, July 1991.

96. *Sovetsko–Angliiskie Otnosheniya* doc. 147.

97. O.A. Rzheshevskii, *Stalin i Cherchill'* doc. 157.

98. Ibid. doc. 158. See also 'New Documents about Winston Churchill from Russian Archives' p. 138 for an alternative translation.

99. Hayward, *Stopped at Stalingrad* p. 189.

100. Samsonov, *Stalingradskaya* p. 178.

101. Mawdsley, *Thunder* p. 170.

102. *Stalingrad, 1942–1943* doc. 146.

103. Ibid. doc. 147.

104. *Stavka VGK: Dokumenty i Materialy 1942* doc. 527.

105. Ibid. doc. 529.

106. J. Erickson, *The Road to Stalingrad*, Harper & Row: New York 1975 p. 384; ibid. doc. 552.

107. *Stavka VGK: Dokumenty i Materialy 1942* doc. 559. In his directive to Yeremenko on 24 August, cited in n. 105 above, Stalin criticised the then commander of the 62nd Army

General A.I. Lopatin as 'clumsy and inept'. Lopatin, however, went on to command a number of other armies during the war and was made a Hero of the Soviet Union in 1945.

108. On Stalingrad see G. Roberts, *Victory at Stalingrad*. The book contains a guide to the literature on the battle.

109. *Stalingrad, 1942–1943* doc. 220.

110. *Stalingradskaya Epopeya* doc. 40.

111. V. Chuikov, *The Beginning of the Road*, MacGibbon & Kee: London 1963 p. 205.

112. *Organy Gosudarstvennoi Bezopasnosti SSSR v Velikoi Otechestvennoi Voine* doc. 1116.

113. Ibid. doc. 1233

114. Rounded figures calculated from *Stalingradskaya Epopeya* doc. 50.

115. *Organy Gosudarstvennoi Bezopasnosti SSSR v Velikoi Otechestvennoi Voine* docs 1199 and 1233. For an overview of the NKVD's role during the war see Glantz, *Colossus Reborn* pp. 446–9.

116. *Stalingradskaya Bitva* pp. 635, 782–3.

117. D.M. Glantz, *Soviet Military Deception in the Second World War*, Frank Cass: London 1989 chap. 5.

118. *Stalingradskaya Bitva* pp. 742–3.

119. Beshanov, *God 1942* p. 570.

120. *Stavka VGK: Dokumenty i Materialy 1942* docs 564, 577

121. See M. Fenyo, 'The Allied Axis Armies and Stalingrad', *Military Affairs*, vol. 29, no. 2, 1965.

122. Zhukov, *Memoirs* pp. 381–4; Vasilevsky, *A Lifelong Cause* p. 189.

123. 'Posetiteli Kremlevskogo Kabineta I.V. Stalina', *Istoricheskii Arkhiv*, no. 2, 1996 pp. 35–8.

124. According to the 1943 Soviet General Staff study of Stalingrad (Rotundo, *Battle* p. 415) planning for Uranus began in the second half of September and on 4 October Zhukov held a conference with front commanders to discuss the coming counter-offensive. The conference was followed by the submission of various proposals from the fronts about their particular role in the counter-offensive. See *Stalingrad, 1942–1943* docs 221, 225, 227, 228, 229, 231, 258.

125. Zhukov, *Memoirs* pp. 413–16.

126. D.M. Glantz, *Zhukov's Greatest Defeat: The Red Army's Epic Disaster in Operation Mars, 1942*, University Press of Kansas: Lawrence, Kansas 1999. For further discussion of Mars: Mawdsley, *Thunder* pp. 152–5.

127. S. Walsh, *Stalingrad, 1942–1943*, St. Martin's Press: New York 2000 p. 111. Mawdsley (*Thunder* pp. 174–5) points out that the code names were chosen by Stalin and speculates that the Soviet leader's youthful experience of working in the Tiflis observatory might have influenced his choices.

128. D.M. Glantz and J.M. House, *When Titans Clashed: How the Red Army Stopped Hitler*, University Press of Kansas: Lawrence, Kansas 1995 p. 143.

129. Various articles, editorials and Sovinform statements published in *Izvestiya*, *Pravda* and *Krasnaya Zvezda* from 29 November 1942 onwards.

130. M. Myagkov, ' Operatsiya "Mars" i ee Znachenie v Khode Stalingradskoi Bitvy', paper presented to the conference on the 60th anniversary of Operation Uranus, Volgograd, November 2002.

131. See Hayward, *Stopped at Stalingrad* chaps 8–9.

132. *Stalingradskaya Bitva* vol. 2 pp. 204–5.

133. Stalin, *Great Patriotic War* pp. 50–5.

134. J. Förster, *Stalingrad: Risse in Bundis 1942/3*, Freiburg 1975.

135. P.M.H. Bell, *John Bull and the Bear: British Public Opinion, Foreign Policy and the Soviet Union 1941–1945*, Edward Arnold: London 1990.

136. For example, M. Bragin, 'Velikoe Spazheniye pod Stalingradom', *Pravda*, 5/2/43.

137. S. Shtemenko, *The Soviet General Staff at War*, vol. 1, Progress Publishers: Moscow 1970 p. 151
138. Zhukov, *Memoirs* pp. 433–4.
139. Shtemenko, *Soviet General Staff* p. 153.
140. Stalin, *Great Patriotic War* pp. 56–60.
141. V.V. Korovin, *Sovetskaya Razvedka i Kontrrazvedka v gody Velikoi Otechestvennoi Voiny*, Moscow 2003 pp. 113–22.
142. Vasilevsky, *A Lifelong Cause* p. 272.
143. *Stalin's Correspondence* docs 90, 92, 97 pp. 67–76.
144. On the Kursk battle: J.M. House and D.M. Glantz, *The Battle of Kursk*, University Press of Kansas: Lawrence, Kansas 1999. For further treatment and discussion see Mawdsley, *Thunder* pp. 262–70.
145. Stalin, *Great Patriotic War* p. 63.
146. Werth, *Russia at War* p. 619.
147. Shtemenko, *Soviet General Staff* p. 156.
148. S. Sebag Montefiore, *Stalin: The Court of the Red Star*, Weidenfeld & Nicolson: London 2003.
149. K. Rokossovsky, *A Soldier's Duty*, Progress Publishers: Moscow 1970 p. 86.
150. Shtemenko, *Soviet General Staff* pp. 174–6.
151. Glantz, *Colossus Reborn* pp. 534–5.
152. In relation to the Soviet economy during the war and the role of lend-lease aid my main source has been the work of Mark Harrison, in particular: *Soviet Planning in Peace and War 1938–1945*, Cambridge University Press: Cambridge 1985; *The Economics of World War II: Six Great Powers in International Comparison*, Cambridge University Press: Cambridge 1998; and *Accounting for War: Soviet Production, Employment, and the Defence Burden, 1940–1945*, Cambridge University Press: Cambridge 1996.
153. For example, 'Dva goda Sovetsko–Amerikanskogo Soglasheniya ', *Pravda*, 11/6/44.
154. M. Harrison, 'The USSR and the Total War: Why Didn't the Soviet Economy Collapse in 1942?' in R. Chickering et al. (eds), *A World at Total War: Global Conflict and the Politics of Destruction, 1939–1945*, Cambridge University Press: Cambridge 2005.

6 The Politics of War: Stalin, Churchill and Roosevelt

1. J. Stalin, *On the Great Patriotic War of the Soviet Union*, Hutchinson: London 1943 p. 12.
2. 'Politicheskiye i Voennye Itogi Goda Otechestvennoi Voiny', *Izvestiya*, 23/6/42.
3. D. Volkogonov, *Stalin: Triumph and Tragedy*, Phoenix Press: London 2000 pp. 412–13.
4. P. Sudoplatov, *Special Tasks*, Warner Books: London 1995 pp. 145–7. See also the interview with Sudoplatov: 'Stalin Had No Intention of Surrendering', *New Times*, no. 15, 1992.
5. In an interview with the Soviet writer Konstantin Simonov in 1965 Marshal I.S. Konev recalled that during the battle of Moscow Stalin had been so nervous that he lapsed into the third person and said: 'Comrade Stalin is not a traitor. Comrade Stalin is an honest person. Comrade Stalin will do everything to correct the situation that has been created.' These words were supposedly uttered by Stalin during a telephone call to the headquarters of the Western Front. See K. Simonov, *Glazami Cheloveka Moego Pokoleniya: Razmyshleniya o I.V. Staline*, Moscow 1990 p. 351.
6. Sudoplatov, *Special Tasks* pp. 147–8.
7. V. Karpov, *Generalissimus*, vol. 1, Moscow 2003 pp. 458–62.
8. V. Mastny, *Russia's Road to the Cold War*, Columbia University Press: New York 1979 pp. 73–85. See also the following article by Mastny in which he speculates at even

greater length but to no more effect: 'Stalin and the Prospects of a Separate Peace in World War II', *American Historical Review*, vol. 77, 1972.

9. *Vneshnyaya Politika Sovetskogo Souza v period Otechestvennoi Voiny*, vol. 1, Moscow 1944 pp. 395–6.

10. Harriman Papers, Library of Congress Manuscripts Division, Container 170, Chronological File 29–31/10/43. Hull's version of these remarks was that Stalin 'proceeded on his own initiative to elaborate in the most sarcastic terms about those who have been circulating reports in the past to the effect that the Soviet Union and Germany might agree on peace terms. He wound up his repeated sarcasm by ridiculing all phases of the matter in unequivocal terms with the idea of effectively disposing of that report.' *Foreign Relations of the United States 1943*, vol. 1 p. 687.

11. Ibid. cf. 8–17/11/43.

12. W.H. McNeill, *America, Britain and Russia: Their Co-operation and Conflict, 1941–1946*, Oxford University Press: London 1953 p. 324.

13. G.P. Kynin and I. Laufer (eds), *SSSR i Germanskii Vopros*, vol. 1, Moscow 1996 docs 15, 18, 38.

14. See W.F. Kimball, 'Stalingrad: A Chance for Choices', *Journal of Military History*, no. 60, January 1996.

15. I. Banac (ed.), *The Diary of Georgi Dimitrov*, Yale University Press: New Haven 2003 pp. 155–6.

16. Ibid. p. 270.

17. *Komintern i Vtoraya Mirovaya Voina*, vol. 2, Moscow 1998 docs 134, 136, 137. These documents, which record the Comintern's EC's discussions on abolition, are translated into English in A. Dallin and F.I. Firsov (eds), *Dimitrov & Stalin, 1934–1943*, Yale University Press: New Haven 2000 docs 51, 52, 53. A file containing the responses of the communist parties to abolition may be found in the Comintern archives in Rossiiskii Gosudarstvennyi Arkhiv Sotsial'no-Politicheskoi Istorii (RGASPI) F.495, Op.18, D.1340, Ll.105–81.

18. J. Degras (ed.), *The Communist International, 1919–1943*, vol. 3, Frank Cass: London 1971 pp. 476–9.

19. Ibid. pp. 480–1; *Komintern i Vtoraya Mirovaya Voina* doc. 143.

20. Dimitrov diary pp. 271–7. Stalin's hurrying of Dimitrov may have been prompted by press reports that Comintern was going to be abolished.

21. RGASPI, F.17, Op.3, D.1042 L. 58.

22. Dimitrov diary pp. 275–6.

23. Stalin's reference to 'religious faith' presaged a major shift in Soviet policy towards extensive wartime co-operation with the Russian Orthodox Church. Stalin's policy on religion during the war and the motives behind his desire to co-operate with church leaders are examined in detail in S. Merritt Miner, *Stalin's Holy War: Religion, Nationalism and Alliance Politics, 1941–1945*, University of North Carolina Press: Chapel Hill NC 2003.

24. Stalin, *Great Patriotic War* pp. 61–2.

25. 'Otvet SSSR Pol'skim Posobnikam Gitlera', *Izvestiya* 27/4/43; 'Protiv Pol'skikh Soobshchnikov Gitlera', *Pravda*, 28/4/43.

26. *Stalin's Correspondence with Churchill, Atlee, Roosevelt and Truman, 1941–1945*, Lawrence & Wishart: London 1958 doc. 150 pp. 120–1.

27. I have explored the Katyn affair in detail in 'Stalin and the Katyn Massacre' in G. Roberts (ed.), *Stalin: His Times and Ours*, IAREES: Dublin 2005. My article and the summary in the present book are based mainly on two collections of documents from the Russian/Soviet archives: *Katyn': Plenniki Neob'yavlennoi Voiny*, Moscow 1997 and *Katyn': Mart 1940g.-Sentyabr' 2000g.*, Moscow 2001. See also G. Sanford, 'The Katyn Massacre and Polish–Soviet Relations, 1941–1943', *Journal of Contemporary History*, vol. 21, no. 1, 2006.

28. The relevant documentation is widely available in English translation on the internet, including at http://www.katyn.org
29. Harriman Papers c.171, cf.22–31/1/44. On 25 January 1944 Harriman's father, Averell, reported to Washington that Kathleen and a member of the embassy staff had returned from Smolensk and 'although inconclusive, from the general evidence and the testimony Kathleen and the Embassy staff member believe that in all probability the massacre was perpetrated by the Germans'. Harriman Papers, c.187 (Katyn Forest Massacre File).
30. A. Polonsky and B. Drukier, *The Beginnings of Communist Rule in Poland*, Routledge & Kegan Paul: London 1980 pp. 7–8.
31. 'Posetiteli Kremlevskogo Kabineta I.V. Stalina: 1942–1943', *Istoricheskii Arkhiv*, no. 3, 1996 p. 66.
32. N. Lebedeva and M. Narinksy, 'Dissolution of the Comintern in 1943', *International Affairs*, no. 8, 1994.
33. P. Spriano, *Stalin and the European Communists*, Verso: London 1985 chap. 16.
34. G.M. Adibekov, E.N. Shakhnazarov and K.K. Shirinya, *Organizatsionnaya Struktura Kominterna, 1919–1943*, Moscow 1997 pp. 233–41.
35. RGASPI, F.17, Op.3, D.1047, Ll.63–4. After the war the journal's name was changed to *Novoe Vremya* (New Times) and it was published in French, German and English as well as Russian. Formally the journal was published by the Soviet trade unions and this allowed Stalin to disavow its contents when it suited.
36. *SSSR i Germanskii Vopros* p. 665
37. On Litvinov's role during the war see G. Roberts, 'Litvinov's Lost Peace, 1941–1946', *Journal of Cold War Studies*, vol. 4, no. 2, Spring 2002.
38. Arkhiv Vneshnei Politiki Rossiiskoi Federatsii (AVPRF) F.06, Op.5, Pap.28, D.327, Ll.5–28. This is the archive copy of Litvinov's document that was read by Molotov and it is replete with underlinings and annotations that indicate Molotov's querying of Litvinov's views. The document (minus the Molotov markings) was published in *Vestnik Ministerstva Inostrannykh Del SSSR*, no. 7, 1990 pp. 55–63. An English translation of the document may be found in A. Perlmutter, *FDR and Stalin: A Not So Grand Alliance, 1943–1945*, University of Missouri Press: Columbia, 1993 pp. 230–46.
39. *Stalin's Correspondence* doc. 174 p. 149.
40. M. Gat, 'The Soviet Factor in British Policy towards Italy, 1943–1945', *Historian*, vol. 1, no. 4, August 1988.
41. 'Ital'yanskii Vopros', *Pravda*, 30/3/44.
42. Ironically, as Gat, 'Soviet Factor' notes, it was the Soviet and communist challenge in Italy that led the British to abandon their aim of hegemonising the country and instead support its independence.
43. Dimitrov diary p. 304.
44. On Soviet policy towards Italy: O.V. Serova, *Italiya i Antigitlerovskaya Koalitsiya, 1943–1945*, Moscow 1973 and S. Pons, 'Stalin, Togliatti, and the Origins of the Cold War in Europe', *Journal of Cold War Studies*, vol. 3, no. 2, Spring 2001.
45. Dimitrov diary p. 305.
46. 'Anglichane i Amerikantsy khotyat vezde sozdat' reaktsionnye pravitel'stva', *Istochnik*, no. 4, 1995. This document is translated into English in *Stalin and the Cold War, 1945–1953: A Cold War International History Project Documentary Reader*, 1999 pp. 81–6.
47. E. Kimball MacLean, 'Joseph E. Davies and Soviet–American Relations, 1941–1943', *Diplomatic History*, vol. 4, no. 1, 1980.
48. On the Moscow conference: K. Sainsbury, *The Turning Point*, Oxford University Press: Oxford 1986; V. Mastny, 'Soviet War Aims at the Moscow and Tehran Conferences of 1943', *Journal of Modern History*, no. 47, September 1975; and D. Watson, 'Molotov et La Conférence du Moscou Octobre 1943', *Communisme*, no. 74/75, 2003.

49. *Moskovskaya Konferentsiya Ministrov Inostrannykh Del SSSR, SShA i Velikobritanii,* Moscow 1984 docs 10, 11, 14.
50. 'K Predstoyashchemu Soveshchaniu v Moskve Trekh Ministrov', AVPRF, F.6, Op.5b, Pap.39, D.6, Ll.52–8. This document, dated 3/10/43 and entitled 'Towards the Forthcoming Conference of the Three Ministers in Moscow', was written by Deputy Commissar for Foreign Affairs, Vladimir Dekanozov. A copy is printed in *SSSR i Germanskii Vopros* doc. 59.
51. AVPRF F.6, Op.5b, Pap.39, Dd.1–2, 4–6 and Pap.40, D.11. A number of these documents are reproduced in *SSSR i Germanskii Vopros.*
52. 'Posetiteli Kremlevskogo Kabineta I.V. Stalina: 1942–1943' pp. 82–4.
53. AVPFR F.6, Op.5b, Pap.39, D.6, Ll.16–27.
54. *Sovetsko–Angliiskie Otnosheniya vo Vremya Velikoi Otechestvennoi Voiny 1941–1945,* vol. 1, Moscow 1983 doc. 295.
55. *Moskovskaya Konferentsiya* contains the Soviet record of the conference proceedings, the protocol of decisions and the resolutions and declarations of the conference. The equivalent American records may be found in *Foreign Relations of the United States 1943,* vol. 1 and the British in PRO F0371/37031.
56. *Foreign Relations of the United States 1943,* vol. 1 pp. 742–4.
57. 'Znacheniye Moskovskoi Konferentsii', *Izvestiya,* 2/11/43; 'Vazhnyi Vklad v Obshchee Delo Souznikov', *Pravda,* 2/11/43; and 'K Itogam Moskovskoi Konferentsii', *Voina i Rabochii Klass,* no. 11, 1943.
58. AVPRF F.0511, Op.1, D.1, L.72.
59. H. Feis, *Churchill–Roosevelt–Stalin,* Princeton University Press: Princeton NJ 1957 p. 237.
60. Cited by Watson, 'Molotov'.
61. Feis, *Churchill . . .* p. 238.
62. Harriman Papers c.170, Cf. 8–17/11/1943.
63. I. Stalin, *O Velikoi Otechestvennoi Voine Sovetskogo Souza,* Moscow 1946 pp. 108–9.
64. *International Affairs,* no. 2, 2004 p. 149.
65. S.M. Shtemenko, *The Soviet General Staff at Work, 1941–1945,* vol. 1, Progress Publishers: Moscow 1970 chap. 9.
66. For example, L. Havas, *Hitler's Plot to Kill the Big Three,* Corgi Books: London 1971.
67. V. Berezhkov, *History in the Making: Memoirs of World War II Diplomacy,* Progress Publishers: Moscow 1983 p. 254. This story is probably apocryphal. Berezhkov claims that only he, Roosevelt and Stalin were present at this meeting. However, Roosevelt's interpreter, Charles Bohlen, was also present, as one would expect, and wrote a report of the meeting. Moreover, according to Bohlen, Pavlov, Stalin's chief interpreter, was present at the meeting, not Berezhkov.
68. *Tegeranskaya Konferentsiya Rukovoditelei Trekh Souznykh Derzhav – SSSR, SShA i Velikobritanii,* Moscow 1984 doc. 52. This volume contains the officially published Soviet record of the Tehran conference. However, a comparison between this volume and the conference transcripts in the Russian Foreign Ministry archive reveals a number of omissions and discrepancies between the published and unpublished record, including the absence of Stalin's statement on de Gaulle cited here and the second sentence of Stalin's comment regarding India (AVPRF F.0555, Op.1, Pap.12, D.24, Ll.5–7). The American record of this discussion may be found in *Foreign Relations of the United States: The Conferences of Cairo and Tehran 1943,* Washington DC 1961 pp. 483–6. See also the summary by Bohlen, the American interpreter, of Stalin's comments on France at the tripartite dinner on 28 November: 'throughout the evening Marshal Stalin kept reverting to the thesis that the French nation, and in particular its leaders and ruling classes were rotten and deserved to be punished for their criminal collaboration with Nazi Germany.' Ibid. p. 512.

69. For a masterly analysis of Churchill's views on Overlord and the nature of his alternative 'Mediterranean strategy' see D. Reynolds, *In Command of History: Churchill Fighting and Writing the Second World War*, Penguin Books: London 2005 espec. chap. 24.

70. *Tegeranskaya Konferentsiya* doc. 53. A partial English translation of the Soviet transcripts of the plenary sessions at Tehran may be found in *The Tehran, Yalta & Potsdam Conferences*, Progress Publishers: Moscow 1969. However, the section of the transcript which records Stalin's statement on Soviet entry into the Far Eastern war is omitted in this volume.

71. *The White House Papers of Harry L. Hopkins*, Eyre & Spottiswoode: London 1949 p. 777. See also *Tegeranskaya Konferentsiya* doc. 54.

72. PRO Prem 3/136/11/75892.

73. O.A. Rzheshevsky (ed.), *War and Diplomacy: The Making of the Grand Alliance (Documents from Stalin's Archive)*, Harwood Academic Publishers: Amsterdam 1996 doc. 82.

74. *Tegeranskaya Konferentsiya* doc. 56.

75. *SSSR i Germanskii Vopros* docs 58, 59, 63, 64, 65

76. *Tegeranskaya Konferentsiya* doc. 57.

77. Ibid. doc. 58; PRO Prem 3/136/11/75892.

78. *Tegranskaya Konferentsiya* doc. 59. Cf. *Foreign Relations of the United States: The Conferences of Cairo and Tehran 1943* pp. 565–681.

79. *Tegeranskaya Konferentsiya* doc. 62; PRO Prem 3/136/11/75892; *Foreign Relations of the United States: The Conferences of Cairo and Tehran 1943* pp. 596–604; and AVPRF F.0555, Op.1, Pap.12, D.24, LL.50–101. The references to Stalin's explicit support for dismemberment, the Molotov–Ribbentrop pact and the Russian need for a lump of German territory were all excised from the published Soviet record of the Tehran conference.

80. *The Tehran, Yalta & Potsdam Conferences* pp. 51–2.

81. 'Znamenatel'naya Vstrecha Rukovoditelei Trekh Souznykh Dezhav', *Izvestiya*, 7/12/43; 'Istoricheskoe Resheniye', *Pravda*, 7/12/43.

82. *Mezhdunarodnaya Zhizn'*, no. 2, 2004 p. 121 has a facsimile of Stalin's hand correction.

83. This correction was in accordance with Stalin's statement to Roosevelt, at a third meeting of the two on 1 December, that he now supported the President's proposal for a single international organisation. The other topic of this discussion was the Soviet occupation of the Baltic States in 1940 and Roosevelt's explanation of the political difficulties this posed for him at home because of the influence of Baltic-American groups. *Tegeranskaya Konferentsiya* doc. 63.

84. 'Izlozheniye Otdel'nykh Voprosov Obsuzhdavshikhsya na Konferentsii v Tegerane', RGASPI, F.558, Op.11, D.234, LL.99–104.

85. Cited by R. Edmonds, *The Big Three*, Penguin Books: London 1991 p. 341.

86. Cited by R. Nisbet, *Roosevelt and Stalin: The Failed Courtship*, Regnery Gatway: Washington DC 1988 p. 50.

87. Ibid.

88. D.J. Dunn, *Caught between Roosevelt and Stalin: America's Ambassadors to Moscow*, University Press of Kentucky: Lexington 1998 p. 221.

89. Cited by D. Carlton, *Churchill and the Soviet Union*, Manchester University Press: Manchester 2000 p. 109. On the Churchill–Stalin relationship during the war see: Lord Moran, *Winston Churchill: The Struggle for Survival, 1940–1965*, Sphere Books: London 1968.

90. 'Talk with the German Author Emil Ludwig, December 13, 1931', in J. Stalin, *Works*, vol. 13, Foreign Languages Publishing House: Moscow 1955 pp. 106–25.

91. Cited by Mastny, *Russia's Road* p. 132.

7 Triumph and Tragedy: Stalin's Year of Victories

1. *Soviet Foreign Policy during the Patriotic War: Documents and Materials*, vol. 2, Hutchinson: London 1945 pp. 25–33.
2. Arkhiv Vneshnei Politiki Rossiiskoi Federatsii (AVPRF) F.06, Op.6, Pap.3, D.133–4. See further G. Roberts, 'Litvinov's Lost Peace, 1941–1946', *Journal of Cold War Studies*, vol. 4, no. 2, Spring 2002.
3. 'Sovetskii Souz i OON: Direktivy Politburo TsK VKP (b) Sovetskoi Delegatsii na Konferentsii v Dumbarton-Okse 1944g.', *Istoricheskii Arkhiv*, no. 4, 1995 pp. 52–8.
4. AVPRF F.06, Op.6, Pap.3, D.134, Ll.44–50.
5. Ibid. D.135.
6. Ibid. L.33. On the internal Soviet debate about the postwar role of France: S. Pons, 'In the Aftermath of the Age of Wars: The Impact of World War II on Soviet Security Policy' in S. Pons and A. Romano (eds), *Russia in the Age of War, 1914–1945*, Feltrinelli: Milan 2000.
7. For a summary of the discussions at Dumbarton Oaks see W.H. McNeill, *America, Britain and Russia: Their Co-operation and Conflict, 1941–1946*, Oxford University Press: London 1953 pp. 501–11. For the Soviet record of the conference: *Konferentsiya Predstavitelei SSSR, SSha i Velikobritanii v Dumbarton-Okse*, Moscow 1984. The Soviet position on the new international organisation is set out in a memorandum to the American and British governments on 12 August 1944. See doc. 26 in the aforementioned volume.
8. The name 'United Nations' derived from the Declaration of the United Nations issued by the allied states in January 1942. This was a public statement pledging complete commitment to fight the war to the very end and to the principles of the Atlantic Charter issued by Churchill and Roosevelt in August 1941. At Dumbarton Oaks Gromyko suggested that because of this association of the name United Nations with the allied alliance it should be called the World Council or something similar. Gromyko's proposal did not fly, however, and the UN name stuck.
9. AVPRF F.6, Op.6, Pap.12, D.125, Ll.27, 69.
10. *Stalin's Correspondence with Churchill, Attlee, Roosevelt and Truman, 1941–1945*, Lawrence & Wishart: London 1958 doc. 227 p. 160. Message from Stalin to Roosevelt dated 14/9/44.
11. *Soviet Foreign Policy*, p. 30.
12. A. Polonsky and B. Drukier, *The Beginnings of Communist Rule in Poland*, Routledge & Kegan Paul: London 1980 p. 297.
13. A. Werth, *Russia at War, 1941–1945*, Pan Books: London 1964 p. 688.
14. As well as the specific references below I have relied mainly on the following texts for my treatment of Bagration: J. Erickson, *The Road to Berlin*, Weidenfeld & Nicolson: London 1983 pp. 191–247; D.M. Glantz and J. House, *When Titans Clashed: How the Red Army Stopped Hitler*, University Press of Kansas: Lawrence, Kansas 1995 chap. 13; R. Overy, *Russia's War*, Allen Lane: London 1997 pp. 237–46; S.M. Shtemenko, *The Soviet General Staff at War, 1941–1945*, Progress Publishers: Moscow 1970 chap. 11; A.M. Vasilevsky, *A Lifelong Cause*, Progress Publishers: Moscow 1981 pp. 356–88; and I.V. Timokhovich, 'Operatsiya "Bagration"' in *Velikaya Otechestvennaya Voina, 1941–1945*, vol. 3, Moscow 1999. The Soviet General Staff's daily situation reports during the battle may be found in the documentary collection *Operatsiya 'Bagration'*, Moscow 2004.
15. *Soviet Foreign Policy*, p. 24.
16. Timokhovich, 'Bagration' p. 58.
17. *Stalin's Correspondence* doc. 260 p. 215.
18. B.F. Smith, *Sharing Secrets with Stalin: How the Allies Traded Intelligence, 1941–1945*, University Press of Kansas: Lawrence, Kansas 1996 espec. chap. 9.

19. *Stalin's Correspondence* doc. 274 p. 224.
20. *Soviet Foreign Policy* p. 25.
21. Glantz and House, *Titans* p. 209.
22. Timokhovich, 'Bagration' p. 77.
23. Erickson, *Road to Berlin* p. 228.
24. *Soviet War News*, 12/6/44.
25. Ibid. 27/6/44.
26. *Soviet Foreign Policy during the Patriotic War*, vol. 2 pp. 23, 28.
27. Vasilevsky, *A Lifelong Cause* p. 360.
28. Shtemenko, *Soviet General Staff* p. 253.
29. *SSSR i Pol'sha, 1941–1945: K Istorii Voennnogo Souza*, Terra: Moscow 1994 (series Russkii Arkhiv) doc. 9 p. 202.
30. The account of Soviet military action in this section is based on Erickson, *Road to Berlin* pp. 247–90; Werth, *Russia at War* part 7, chap. 8; Overy, *Russia's War* pp. 246–9; Timokhovich, 'Bagration'; S.M. Shtemenko, *The Soviet General Staff at War, 1941–1945*, book 2, Progress Publishers: Moscow 1986 chaps. 2 & 3; K. Rokossovsky, *A Soldier's Duty*, Progress Publishers: Moscow 1970 pp. 254–63; and M.I. Mel'tukhov, 'Operatsiya "Bagration" i Varshavskoe Vosstaniye 1944 goda', *Voprosii Istorii*, no. 11, 2004.
31. Shtemenko, *Soviet General Staff* book 2 pp. 71–81; *Stavka VGK, 1944–1945*, Moscow 1999 doc. 160.
32. Ibid. p. 92.
33. *SSSR i Pol'sha, 1941–1945* doc. 29 pp. 218–19. A translation of this document may be found ibid. pp. 93–4.
34. See the situation reports in *Operatsiya 'Bagration'*.
35. For an overview of the uprising and of the controversies surrounding it, see N. Davies, *Rising '44: The Battle for Warsaw*, Pan Books: London 2004.
36. On the motives for the uprising: J.M. Ciechanowski, *The Warsaw Rising of 1944*, Cambridge University Press: Cambridge 1974 espec. chap. 9.
37. On Soviet policy and action in relation to the Polish Home Army in 1944–1945 see the documents in *NKVD i Pol'skoe Podpol'e, 1944–1945*, Moscow 1994.
38. Werth, *Russia at War* p. 786.
39. Ciechanowski, *Warsaw Rising* pp. 244–5.
40. E. Duraczynski, 'The Warsaw Rising: Research and Disputes Continue', *Acta Poloniae Historica*, no. 75, 1997.
41. A. Polonsky (ed.), *The Great Powers and the Polish Question, 1941–1945*, Orbis Books: London 1976 doc. 82
42. *Vneshnyaya Politika Sovetskogo Souza v Period Otechestvennoi Voiny*, vol. 2, Moscow 1946 pp. 59–61. A translation of this statement may be found in *Soviet War News* 12/1/44.
43. See Stalin's reply to journalists' questions on Poland on 4 May 1943 in J. Stalin, *On the Great Patriotic War of the Soviet Union*, Hutchinson: London 1943 pp. 60–1. In terms of internal Soviet discussions on the Polish question, the policy of a strong and independent Poland, but one friendly to the USSR, was formulated most explicitly during preparation for the Moscow conference of foreign ministers of October 1943. For example: AVPRF, F.6, Op.5b, Pap.41, D.20, Ll.31–3.
44. In December 1941 Stalin told Eden that he 'believed Poland should be given all lands up to the Oder'. In one version of the secret protocol that Moscow wished to attach to the British–Soviet treaty of alliance the proposal was 'to increase the territory of Poland at the expense of the western part of East Prussia', but in another version of the proposed protocol the frontier question was left open to discussion. See O.A. Rzheshevskii (ed.), *War and Diplomacy*, Harwood Academic Publishers: Amsterdam 1996 docs 4–6. For a treatment of the public discussion of Poland's

western border during the war years see W. Wanger, *The Genesis of the Oder–Neisse Line*, Brentano-Verlag: Stuttgart 1957.

45. Harriman Papers, Library of Congress Manuscript Division, Container 171, Chronological File 1–15/1/44.
46. *Vneshnyaya Politika Sovetskogo Souza v Period Otechestvennoi Voiny* vol. 2 pp. 339–40.
47. Harriman Papers, c.171, cf 16–21/1/44
48. Ibid..
49. Ibid. cf 1–8/3/44.
50. *Stalin's Correspondence*, doc. 257 pp. 212–13.
51. Harriman Papers, c.175, cf. 22–29/2/44.
52. See A. Polonsky and B. Drukier, *The Beginnings of Communist Rule in Poland* pp. 14–23.
53. *Stalin's Correspondence* doc. 310 pp. 241–2.
54. On Lange: A.M. Cienciala, 'New Light on Oskar Lange as an Intermediary between Roosevelt and Stalin in Attempts to Create a New Polish Government', *Acta Poloniae Historica*, no. 73, 1996.
55. *Pravda*, 11/8/41 and 12/8/41 (editorial on 'Vse Slavyane na bor'bu protiv obshchego vraga.'); H. Kohn, 'Pan-Slavism and World War II', *American Political Science Review*, vol. 46, no. 3, September 1952.
56. *Vneshnyaya Politika Sovetskogo Souza v Period Otechestvennoi Voiny*, vol. 1, Moscow 1944 pp. 372–6.
57. 'Peregovory E.Benesha v Moskve (Dekabr' 1943g.)', *Voprosy Istorii*, nos 1 & 3, 2001. This two-part article contains Russian translations of the Czechoslovak notes of Beneš's talks with Stalin and Molotov. An English translation of most but not all of this documentation may be found in V. Mastny, 'The Benes–Stalin–Molotov Conversations in December 1943', *Jahrbücher für Geschichte Osteuropas*, vol. 20 1972.
58. Stalin may have picked up the Grunwald analogy from a statement issued by a group of Polish emigrants in London that featured in a *Pravda* editorial of June 1943. See 'Unity of Slavs' in *Soviet War News*, 19/6/43. Grunwald was also mentioned in passing in Stalin's conversation with Sikorski and Anders in December 1941.
59. *Stalin and the Cold War, 1945–1953: A Cold War International History Project Documentary Reader*, 1999 p. 3.
60. Ibid. pp. 9, 15–16.
61. V. Deijer, *Tito Speaks*, Weidenfeld & Nicolson: London 1953 p. 234.
62. M. Djilas, *Wartime*, London; Secker & Warburg 1977 p. 438. Another remark by Stalin at this meeting, as recorded by Djilas was: 'This war in not as in the past. Whoever occupies a territory also imposes on it his own social system. Everyone imposes his own system as far as his army can reach' (ibid. p. 437). This statement is often interpreted as signalling Stalin's intention to sovietise the countries of Eastern Europe occupied by the Red Army. However, the remark should be interpreted as Stalin laying a restraining hand upon the leftist Yugoslav communists by pointing out to them that they had to accept the realities imposed by military power, in their case the reality of the western allied occupation of disputed Trieste and the role being played by British forces in putting down a communist insurrection in Greece.
63. *Sovetskii Faktor v Vostochnoi Evrope, 1944–1953*, vol. 1, Moscow 1999 doc. 9.
64. *The Great Powers and the Polish Question, 1941–1945* doc. 102.
65. Ibid.; *Sovetskii Faktor v Vostochnoi Evrope* doc. 10; and Polonsky and Drukier, *The Beginnings of Communist Rule in Poland* doc. 27.
66. *Stalin's Correspondence* docs 311, 313 pp. 248–9.
67. Ibid. doc. 315 pp. 250–1.
68. *Sovetskii Faktor v Vostochnoi Evrope* doc. 11.
69. *The Great Powers and the Polish Question, 1941–1945* doc. 102 p. 211. For Mikolajczyk's memoir account of his trip to Moscow, which presents a view radically different from

that in the contemporary documentation see S. Mikolajczyk, *The Pattern of Soviet Domination*, Sampson, Low & Marston: London 1948 chap. 6.

70. Ibid. doc. 106.
71. Harriman Papers, c.173, cf. 13–15/8/44. For Vyshinskii's record of this conversation: *Sovetsko–Amerikanskie Otnosheniya, 1939–1945*, Moscow 2004 doc. 251.
72. Harriman Papers, cf.16–18/8/44; *Sovetsko–Amerikanskie Otnosheniya, 1939–1945* doc. 252.
73. Ibid. doc. 103.
74. *Stalin's Correspondence* doc. 321 p. 254.
75. Harriman Papers c.173 cf16–18/8/44; *Sovetsko–Amerikanskie Otnosheniya, 1939–1945* doc. 253.
76. *The Great Powers and the Polish Question, 1941–1945* doc. 107.
77. Meiklejohn diary p. 543 in Harriman Papers, c.165.
78. *Stalin's Correspondence* docs 322–3 pp. 254–5.
79. Harriman Papers, c.174, cf.1–5/9/44.
80. *The Soviet General Staff at War, 1941–1945*, book 2 pp. 102–4. See also Timokhovich, 'Bagration' p. 75.
81. A. Chmielarz, 'Warsaw Fought Alone: Reflections on Aid to and the Fall of the 1944 Uprising', *Polish Review*, vol. 39, no. 4, 1994 p. 421. Also: R.C. Lukas, 'The Big Three and the Warsaw Uprising', *Military Affairs*, vol. 39, no. 3, 1975.
82. Cited by S. Berthon and J. Potts, *Warlords*, Politico's Publishing: London 2005 p. 265.
83. On the Soviet liberation/conquest of Bulgaria, Romania, Hungary and Czechoslovakia: Erickson, *Road to Berlin* chap. 6 and Mawdsley, *Thunder in the East* chap. 12.
84. Because the Stalin–Churchill meeting of 9 October 1944 took the form of a dinner in the Kremlin there is no record of it in Stalin's appointments book, which recorded visitors to his office. Stalin's meetings with Churchill on 14, 16 and 17 October are recorded in the appointments diary, however. See: 'Posetiteli Kremlevskogo Kabineta I.V. Stalina', *Istoricheskii Arkhiv*, no. 4, 1996 p. 87.
85. W.S. Churchill, *The Second World War*, vol. 6, Cassell: London 1954 pp. 194–5.
86. For a fascinating and detailed dissection of Churchill's history of the Second World War see D. Reynolds, *In Command of History: Churchill Fighting and Writing the Second World War*, Penguin Books: London 2005. For detailed studies of the so-called percentages agreement see: K.G.M. Ross, 'The Moscow Conference of October 1944 (Tolstoy)' in W. Deakin, E. Barker and J. Chadwick (eds), *British Political and Military Strategy in Central, Eastern and Southern Europe in 1944*, London: Macmillan 1988; A. Resis, 'The Churchill–Stalin Secret "Percentages" Agreement on the Balkans, Moscow, October 1944', *American Historical Review*, April 1978; P. Tsakaloyannis, 'The Moscow Puzzle', *Journal of Contemporary History*, vol. 21, 1986; P.G.H. Holdich, 'A Policy of Percentages? British Policy and the Balkans after the Moscow Conference of October 1944', *International History Review*, February 1987; and G. Roberts, 'Beware Greek Gifts: The Churchill–Stalin "Percentages Agreement" of October 1944', *Mir Istorii*, www/historia.ru/2003/01/roberts.htm.
87. G. Ross (ed.), *The Foreign Office and the Kremlin: British Documents on Anglo-Soviet Relations 1941–1945*, Cambridge University Press: Cambridge 1984, doc. 30. The quote is from a paragraph in a draft report which was omitted by Clark Kerr in his final, official record of the meeting.
88. 'Zapis' Besedy Tov. I.V. Stalina s Cherchillem 9 Oktyabrya 1944 g. v 22 chasa', Rossiiskii Gosudarstvennyi Arkhiv Sotsial'no-Politicheskoi Istorii (RGASPI), F.558, Op.11, D.283, Ll.6–9, 13. This document, together with most of the Soviet records of the other Stalin–Churchill conversations in October 1944, has now been published in O.A. Rzheshevskii, *Stalin i Cherchill'*, Moscow 2004. The greater part of the record of the 9 October meeting is translated in O.A. Rzheshevsky, 'Soviet Policy in Eastern Europe 1944–1945: Liberation or Occupation' in G. Bennett (ed.), *The End of the War in*

Europe, 1945, HMSO: London 1996 pp. 162–8. This was the first publication of the Soviet record of the percentages discussion.

89. The British records of these two meetings are reproduced in J.M. Siracusa, 'The Meaning of Tolstoy: Churchill, Stalin and the Balkans, Moscow, October 1944', *Diplomatic History*, Fall 1979. The Soviet record of the meeting on 10 October may be found in Rzheshevskii, *Stalin i Cherchill'* doc. 162.

90. The exception was a meeting at the Potsdam conference in July 1945 where Churchill complained that he was not getting his 50 per cent influence in Yugoslavia. Stalin replied that the Soviet Union had no influence and that Tito was his own man.

91. RGASPI F.558, Op.11, D.283, L.6.

92. AVPRF F.6, Op.5b, Pap.39, D1.

93. G.P. Kynin and J. Laufer (eds), *SSSR i Germanskii Vopros*, vol. 1, Moscow 1996 doc. 79.

94. P.J. Stavrakis, *Moscow and Greek Communism, 1944–1949*, Cornell University Press: New York 1989 pp. 28–9.

95. *The Diary of Georgi Dimitrov 1933–1949*, Yale University Press: New Haven 2003 p. 345 (diary entries for 8 and 9 December 1944).

96. Ibid. pp. 352–3.

97. Litvinov's report is cited in detail in V.O. Pechatnov, *The Big Three after World War II: New Documents on Soviet Thinking about Postwar Relations with the United States and Great Britain*, Cold War International History Project, 1995, Working Paper no. 13.

98. AVPRF F.06, Op.7a, D.5, Ll.11–12.

99. This exchange on Greece was omitted completely from the Soviet records of Yalta published in the 1960s. It was included in a revised version published in the 1980s, but still minus the directly quoted sentences, which come from the typed transcript of the conference proceedings in the Russian Foreign Ministry archive. Cf. *Krymskaya Konferentsiya Rukovoditelei Trekh Souznykh Derzhav – SSSR, SShA i Velikobritanii*, Moscow 1984 p. 145 and AVPRF F.06, Op.7a, D.7, L.105.

100. D. Carlton, *Churchill and the Soviet Union*, Manchester University Press: Manchester 2000 p. 120.

101. RGASPI F.558, Op.11, D.283, L.21.

102. Rzheshevskii, *Stalin i Cherchill'* doc. 164.

103. Polonsky and Drukier, *The Beginnings of Communist Rule in Poland* doc. 56

104. Rzheshevskii, *Stalin i Cherchill'* doc. 165; RGASPI F.558, Op.11, D.283, L.20.

105. RGASPI F.558, Op.11, D.283, L.64.

106. Ibid., Ll.10–11.

107. Siracusa, 'The Meaning of Tolstoy' p. 449.

108. RGASPI F.558, Op.11, D.283, L.84.

109. See for example Molotov's conversation with Eden on 21 May 1942 in O.A. Rzheshevsky (ed.), *War and Diplomacy*, Harwood Academic Publishers: Amsterdam 1996 doc. 16.

110. Transylvania was annexed from defeated Hungary by Romania in 1920. In 1940, however, Transylvania was partitioned under the terms of the so-called Vienna arbitration award of Germany and Italy, with the bulk of it going to Hungary. The territory reverted to Romania after the Second World War. See Y. Lahav, *Soviet Policy and the Transylvanian Question (1940–1946)*, Research Paper no. 27, The Hebrew University of Jerusalem, July 1977. A number of the Soviet documents are collected in *Transil'vanskii Vopros Vengero-Rumynskii Territorial'nyi Spor i SSSR 1940–1946*, Moscow 2000.

111. Cited by E. van Ree, *The Political Thought of Joseph Stalin*, Routledge: London 2002 p. 232. A detailed study of the transfer, with documents, is V. Mar'ina, *Zakarpatskaya Ukraina (Podkarpatskaya Rus') v Politike Benesha i Stalina*, Moscow 2003.

112. Rzheshevskii, *Stalin i Cherchill'* doc. 173.

113. A.H. Birse, *Memoirs of an Interpreter*, Michael Joseph: London 1967 p. 173.

114. Harriman Papers, c.174, cf.15–16/10/44.
115. *Stalin's Correspondence* docs 230–1 pp. 162–3.
116. RGASPI F.558, Op.11, D.283, Ll.7–8.
117. AVP RF F.06, Op.7a, D.7, L.18
118. Ibid. L.30. This and the preceding quotation were omitted from the published Soviet record of the Yalta conference as it appears in *Krymskaya Konferentsiya Rukovoditelei Trekh Souznykh Derzhav – SSSR, SShA i Velikobritanii*, Moscow 1979. When these records were first published in 1961 the Soviets were actively seeking *détente* with a French government headed by de Gaulle, and all such disparaging remarks were omitted.
119. *Sovetsko–Frantsuzskie Otnosheniya vo Vremya Velikoi Otechestvennoi Voiny, 1941–1945*, Moscow 1959 doc. 197. This was one of the very first volumes of Soviet diplomatic documents to contain confidential records from the Soviet archives.
120. On Soviet relations with de Gaulle during the war: G-H. Soutou, 'Le General de Gaulle et L'URSS, 1943–1945', *Revue d'histoire diplomatique*, no. 4, 1994; N. Narinskii, 'Moscou et le Gouvernement provisoire du général de Gaulle', *Relations internationales*, no. 108, 2001; M.Ts. Arzakanyan, 'Pochemu Sharl' de Goll' stal "bol'shim drugom SSSR"', *Voenno-Istoricheskii Zhurnal*, no. 2 1995; and I. Chelyshev, 'Marshal Stalin vsegda mozhet rasschityvat' na de Gollya', *Istochnik*, no. 2, 2002.
121. *Sovetsko–Frantsuzskie Otnosheniya vo Vremya Velikoi Otechestvennoi Voiny, 1941–1945*, vol. 2, Moscow 1983 docs 69, 75, 76. This two-volume set is a revised edition of the collection cited in n. 119 above, but with many new documents.
122. *Stalin's Correspondence* docs 360, 364, 365, 366, 370 pp. 227–84; docs 243, 244, 245, 246 pp. 170–2.
123. *Sovetsko–Frantsuzskie Otnosheniya* (1959 edition) doc. 202.
124. Ibid. doc. 209
125. *Sovetsko–Frantsuzskie Otnosheniya* (1983 edition) doc. 101.
126. Harriman Papers, c.175, cf.8–14/12/44.
127. *Sovetsko–Frantsuzskiye Otnosheniya* (1983 edition) doc. 102.
128. Harriman Papers, c.175, cf.8–14/12/44.
129. *Stalin and the Cold War, 1945–1953: A Cold War International History Project Documentary Reader* p. 103.
130. 'Resurgent France', *Soviet War News*, 20/12/44.
131. *Vneshnyaya Politika Sovetskogo Souza v Period Otechestvennoi Voiny*, vol. 3, Moscow 1947 pp. 61–2.

8 Liberation, Conquest, Revolution: Stalin's Aims in Germany and Eastern Europe

1. D.S. Clemens, *Yalta*, Oxford University Press: Oxford 1970 pp. 63–73. Despite its venerability and the author's lack of access to confidential Soviet sources this book remains a very valuable general study of the Yalta conference.
2. Soviet records of the Armistice Commission: Arkhiv Vneshnei Politiki Rossiiskoi Federatsii (AVPRF) F.0511, Op.1, Dd.1–4 and the EAC: AVPRF F.0425, Op.1, Dd.1–5, 11–12. A number of documents from these and other files are printed in G. Kynin and J. Laufer (eds), *SSSR i Germanskii Vopros*, vol.1, Moscow 1996. For analyses of the work of the EAC in relation to Germany based on western sources see T. Sharp, *The Wartime Alliance and the Zonal Division of Germany*, Clarendon Press: Oxford 1975 and D.J. Nelson, *Wartime Origins of the Berlin Dilemma*, University of Alabama Press: Tuscaloosa 1978. For a participant's account see P.E. Mosley, *The Kremlin in World Politics*, Vintage Books: New York 1960 chaps 5–6.

3. On the work of the Maiskii commission: *SSSR i Germanskii Vopros* docs 114, 129, 136, 138, 137, 142.
4. Ibid. docs 64, 65, 91, 92, 141.
5. I am relying on the summary and quotes from this document in S. Pons, 'In the Aftermath of the Age of Wars: The Impact of World War II on Soviet Foreign Policy' in S. Pons and A. Romano (eds), *Russia in the Age of Wars, 1914–1945*, Feltrinelli: Milan 2000; A.M. Filitov, 'Problems of Post-War Construction in Soviet Foreign Policy Conceptions during World War II' in F. Gori and S. Pons (eds), *The Soviet Union and Europe in the Cold War, 1943–1953* Macmillan: London 1996; V.O. Pechatnov, *The Big Three after World War II: New Documents on Soviet Thinking about Post-War Relations with the United States and Great Britain*, Cold War International History Project, Working Paper no.13, 1995; and A.M. Filitov, 'V Kommissiyakh Narkomindela' in O.A. Rzheshevskii (ed.), *Vtoraya Mirovaya Voina* Moscow 1995.
6. *SSSR i Germanskii Vopros* doc. 140.
7. K. Hamilton, 'The Quest for a Modus Vivendi: The Daubian Satellites in Anglo–Soviet Relations 1945–6', *FCO Historical Branch Occasional Papers*, no. 4, April 1992 p. 6.
8. *SSSR i Germanskii Vopros* doc.79.
9. *Sovetsko–Amerikanskie Otnosheniya, 1939–1945*, Moscow 2004 doc. 244. See also Pechatnov, *Big Three* pp. 6–9.
10. See also ibid doc. 81 and *Sovetsko–Amerikanskie Otnosheniya vo Vremya Velikoi Otechestvennoi Voiny, 1941–1945*, vol. 1, Moscow 1984 doc. 131. The archive copy of this document is in AVPRF, F.06, Op.4, Pap.22, D.232, Ll.1–11. Also: AVPRF, F.06, Pap.22, D.235, Ll.118–20.
11. *Sovetsko–Amerikanskie Otnosheniya* (2004) doc. 246.
12. AVPRF, F.06, Op.7a, D.5, Ll.7–22. Moscow was also briefed by Gusev (Ll.23–28) but, typically, he committed himself on very little and expressed few opinions of his own. For a discussion of Gusev's role as Soviet ambassador in London see V.V. Sokolov, 'Posol SSSR F.T. Gusev v Londone v 1943–1946 godax', *Novaya i Noveishaya Istoriya*, no. 4, 2005.
13. *Vostochnaya Evropa v Dokumentakh Rossiiskikh Arkhivov, 1944–1953*, vol. 1, Moscow 1997 doc. 37. A translation of the relevant section of this document may be found in G.P. Murashko and A.F. Noskova, 'Stalin and the National-Territorial Controversies in Eastern Europe, 1945–1947 (Part 1)', *Cold War History*, vol. 1, no. 3, 2001.
14. I. Banac (ed.), *The Diary of Georgi Dimitrov, 1933–1949*, Yale University Press: New Haven 2003 pp. 352–3.
15. *Otnosheniya Rossii (SSSR) s Yugoslaviei, 1941–1945gg*, Moscow 1998 doc. 517.
16. *Stalin and the Cold War, 1945–1953: A Cold War International History Project Documentary Reader*, 1999 p. 130.
17. Dimitrov diary pp. 357–8.
18. Clemens, *Yalta* p. 114.
19. Letter from Kathleen Harriman to Pamela Churchill dated 7/2/45, in the Pamela Harriman Papers, Library of Congress Manuscript Division. I am grateful to W.S. Churchill for allowing me access to his mother's papers.
20. *Krymskaya Konferentsiya* doc. 3.
21. Ibid. doc. 4. Stalin's critical comments about de Gaulle were excised from this published document but may be found in the archive record: AVPRF F.06, Op.7a, D.7, L.30.
22. Ibid. doc. 5. At the end of this session Churchill raised the question of Germany's future 'if it had one'. Stalin responded that Germany would have 'some future'. However, the qualifying particle 'some' (*kakoe-libo*), recorded in the archive record, is omitted from this published document (AVPRF F.06, Op.7a, D.7, L.12). For an English translation of the Soviet records of the plenary sessions at Yalta see *The Tehran, Yalta and Potsdam Conferences*, Progress Publishers: Moscow 1969.

23. AVPRF F.06, Op.7a, D.7, Ll.21–26. The quoted statements by Stalin were all omitted from the published Soviet record, ibid. doc. 6. For the British and American records of this discussion on dismemberment: see PRO CAB 99/31 pp. 119–20 and FRUS: Yalta pp. 611–15, 624–7.
24. This incident is recounted in Maiskii's diary entry for 5 February 1945, reproduced in O. A. Rzheshevskii (ed.), *Stalin i Cherchill'* Moscow 2004 doc. 175. Maiskii's memoir of Yalta makes no mention of this incident and rather downplays his own role in the proceedings. See I. M. Maiskii, *Vospominaniya Sovetskogo Diplomata*, Moscow 1987 pp. 747–64.
25. *Krymskaya Konferentsiya* doc.6.
26. On Irish neutrality during the Second World War see B. Girvin, *The Emergency: Neutral Ireland, 1939–1945*, Macmillan: London 2005.
27. AVPRF F.06, Op.7a, D.7, L.33. The quoted statement by Stalin was omitted from the published Soviet record.
28. *Krymskaya Konferentsiya* doc. 8.
29. *Stalin's Correspondence with Churchill, Attlee, Roosevelt and Truman, 1941–1945*, Lawrence & Wishart: London 1958, doc. 266 pp. 187–9.
30. *Krymskaya Konferentsiya* doc.10.
31. Ibid. doc. 12.
32. Ibid. docs 25, 28.
33. 'Istoricheskie Resheniya Krymskoi Konferentsii', *Pravda*, 13/2/45; 'Krymskaya Konferentsiya Rukovoditelei Trekh Souznykh Derzhav', *Izvestiya*, 13/2/45.
34. *SSSR i Germanskii Vopros* doc. 144.
35. *Ivan Mikhailovich Maiskii: Izbrannaya Perepiska s Rossiiskimi Korrespondentami*, vol. 2, Moscow 2005 doc. 550.
36. Diary of V.A. Malyshev, published in *Istochnik*, no. 5, 1997 p. 128.
37. *SSSR i Germanskii Vopros* docs 146–54.
38. The American records of the Polish Commission's discussions may be found in the Harriman Papers in Containers 177–8, chronological files for February–March 1945. The Soviet record of the first meeting on 23 February is printed in *Sovetsko–Amerikanskie Otnosheniya* (2004) doc. 274.
39. *Stalin's Correspondence* docs 284, 289 pp. 201–13.
40. On the Romanian crisis of February 1945 see A.J. Rieber, 'The Crack in the Plaster: Crisis in Romania and the Origins of the Cold War', *Journal of Modern History*, no. 76, March 2004. A number of Soviet documents on the crisis may be found in *Tri Vizita A.Ya Vyshinskogo v Bukharest, 1944–1946*, Moscow 1998.
41. *Sovetsko–Amerikanskie Otnosheniya, 1939–1945* (2004) docs 275, 276, 278, 279, 280, 283, 284.
42. Gosudarstvennyi Arkhiv Rossiiskoi Federatsii, F.9401 Op.2, D.93–7.
43. Cited by V. Volkov, 'The Soviet Leadership and Southeastern Europe' in N. Naimark and L. Gibianskii (eds), *The Establishment of the Communist Regimes in Eastern Europe, 1944–1949*, Westview Press: Boulder Col. 1997 p. 56.
44. F. Oleshchuk, 'Razvitiye Demokratii v Osvobozhdyonnykh Stranakh Evropy', *Bol'shevik*, nos 19–20, October 1945.
45. See G. Roberts, 'Soviet Foreign Policy and the Spanish Civil War, 1936–1939' in C. Leitz (ed.), *Spain in an International Context*, Berghahn Books: Oxford 1999.
46. For example, from *Voprosy Vneshnei Politiki*: 'O Polozhenii v Bolgarii', no. 10, 15/5/45; 'O Vnutripoliticheskom Polozhenii Vengrii', no. 19, 1/10/45; 'O Vnutripoliticheskom Polozhenii Finlyandii', no. 20, 15/10/45; and 'K Sovremennomu Vnutripolitcheskomu Polozheniu Rumynii', no. 22, 15/11/45. All in Rossiiskii Gosudarstvennyi Arkhiv Sotsial'no-Politicheskoi Istorii (RGASPI), F.17, Op.128, D.12.
47. M. Djilas, *Wartime*, Secker & Warburg: London 1980 p. 437.
48. *Vostochnaya Evropa v Dokumentakh Rossiiskikh Arkhivov, 1944–1953* doc. 151.

49. Ibid. p. 579 n. 3.

50. Ibid. doc.169.

51. Cited by V. Dimitrov, 'Revolution Released: Stalin, the Bulgarian Communist Party and the Establishment of Cominform' in Gori and Pons (eds), *Soviet Union and Europe* p. 284.

52. On the popular front strategy in the 1930s: K. McDermott and J. Agnew, *The Comintern*, Macmillan: London 1996 chap. 4.

53. W.O. McCagg, *Stalin Embattled, 1943–1948*, Wayne State University Press: Detroit 1978 p. 26. This book is an important early study of Stalin's policy of new democracy.

54. E. Mark, *Revolution by Degrees: Stalin's National-Front Strategy for Europe, 1941–1947*, Cold War International History Project Working Paper no. 31, 2001. See also: N.M. Naimark, 'Post-Soviet Russian Historiography on the Emergence of the Soviet Bloc', *Kritika*, vol. 5, no. 3, Summer 2004. My own views on Stalin's postwar political strategy in Eastern Europe – which emphasise the authenticity of the people's democracy project for the short time that it lasted – parallel the views of T.V. Volokitina and her colleagues at the Institute of Slavic Studies of the Russian Academy of Sciences. The Volokitina group edited and published the documents in *Vostochnaya Evropa v Dokumentakh Rossiiskikh Arkhivov* and *Sovetskii Faktor v Vostochnoi Evrope*. A further volume of documents produced by the group is *Moskva i Vostochnaya Evropa*, 1949–1953, Moscow 2002.

55. W. Lafeber, *The Origins of the Cold War, 1941–1947*, John Wiley: New York 1971 doc.37.

56. RGASPI F.17, Op.128, D.94, *Voprosy Vneshnei Politiki*, no. 10(34), 15 May 1946. I have simplified this table somewhat. For example, the 'prewar' party membership figure for Germany dates from 1933 while that for Hungary is from March 1945 (i.e. the eve of the final liberation of the country by the Red Army). The table also records postwar party membership figures of 20,000 in Japan, 60,000 in Korea, 80,000 in the US and 1,210,000 in China.

57. Figures drawn from J. Tomaszewski, *The Socialist Regimes of Eastern Europe: Their Establishment and Consolidation, 1944–1967*, Routledge: London 1989 *passim*.

58. See A.J. Rieber, *Zhdanov in Finland*, The Carl Beck Papers in Russian and East European Studies, no. 1107, University of Pittsburgh, February 1995.

9 Last Battles: Stalin, Truman and the End of the Second World War

1. S. Bialer (ed.), *Stalin and his Generals: Soviet Military Memoirs of World War II*, Souvenir Press: London 1970 p. 617 n. 22. My other sources on the Vistula–Oder operation, apart from those cited below, are: A. Werth, *Russia at War, 1941–1945*, Pan Books: London 1964 part 8, chap. 1; J. Erickson, *The Road to Berlin*, Weidenfeld & Nicolson: London 1983 chap. 7; D.M. Glantz and J. House, *When Titans Clashed: How the Red Army Stopped Hitler*, University Press of Kansas: Lawrence, Kansas 1995 pp. 241–50; and E. Mawdsley, *Thunder in the East: The Nazi–Soviet War, 1941–1945*, Hodder Arnold: London 2005 chap. 13.

2. S.M. Shtemenko, 'In the General Staff' in Bialer, *Stalin* pp. 472 and 472–80 and Shtemenko, *The Soviet General Staff at War, 1941–1945*, Progress Publishers: Moscow 1970 chap. 13.

3. K. Rokossovsky, *A Soldier's Duty*, Progress Publishers: Moscow 1970 p. 267.

4. I. Konev, *Year of Victory*, Progress Publishers: Moscow 1969 pp. 5, 67–8.

5. Werth, *Russia at War* pp. 849–850.

6. The main proponent of this argument is the Russian military historian V.N. Kisilev, for example in his article 'Padeniye Berlina' (p. 256) in G.N. Sevost'yanov, *Voina i Obshchestvo, 1941–1945*, vol.1, Moscow 2004.

7. Konev, *Year of Victory* p. 14.
8. Rokossovsky, *Soldier's Duty* pp. 281–2.
9. V. Mastny, *Russia's Road to the Cold War*, Columbia University Press: New York 1979 pp. 242–3.
10. For the exchange between Chuikov and Zhukov see Bialer, *Stalin* pp. 500–15.
11. For example: V.I. Chuikov, *Konets Tret'ego Reikha*, Moscow 1973 and idem, *Ot Stalingrada do Berlina*, Moscow 1980.
12. Harriman Papers, Library of Congress Manuscripts Division, Container 175, Chronological File 15–20/12/44 and the Soviet version of this conversation in *Sovetsko–Amerikanskiye Otnosheniya vo Vremya Velikoi Otechistvennoi Voiny, 1941–1945*, vol. 2, Moscow 1984 doc. 164.
13. Ibid. c176, cf 11–16–1/45.
14. Shtemenko, *Soviet General Staff* p. 307.
15. *The Tehran, Yalta and Potsdam Conferences*, Progress Publishers: Moscow 1969 pp. 54–65.
16. *Foreign Relations of the United States: The Conferences at Malta and Yalta 1945*, Government Printing Office: Washington 1955 pp. 580, 597, 645–6.
17. I. Stalin, *O Velikoi Otechestvennoi Voine Sovetskogo Souza*, Moscow 1946 p. 158.
18. Cited by C. Ryan, *The Last Battle*, New English Library: London 1968 p. 142.
19. 'Posetiteli Kremlevskogo Kabineta I.V. Stalina: 1944–1946', *Istoricheskii Arkhiv*, no. 4 1996 p. 96.
20. Text of Stalin's message reproduced in O.A. Rzheshevskii, 'Poslednii Shturm: Zhukov ili Konev', *Mir Istorii* http://gpw.tellur.ru.
21. 'Posetiteli Kremlevskogo Kabineta I.V. Stalina', 1996 p. 96. In the literature 1 April is the date mentioned for the beginning of this conference. However, according to the diary Stalin met, as he often did, only with Antonov and Shtemenko (for two hours in the evening) that day.
22. Konev, *Year of Victory* pp. 87–8.
23. Rokossovsky, *Soldier's Duty* p. 316.
24. *Sovetsko–Amerikanskie Otnosheniya, 1945–1948*, Moscow 2004 doc. 287.
25. Konev, *Year of Victory* pp. 104–108. In his memoirs Shtemenko (*Soviet General Staff* p. 320) presents Stalin's determination of the demarcation line as setting up a competition between Konev and Zhukov as to who would reach Berlin first. 'Let the one who is first to break in take Berlin,' Shtemenko cites Stalin as saying. This quote and theme have been taken up in much of the authoritative literature on the Berlin operation. However, neither Konev nor Zhukov remembers it that way.
26. On the Berlin battle see the treatments of Mawdsley, Erickson and Ryan cited above. Also: A Read and D. Fisher, *The Fall of Berlin*, Pimlico: London 1993, 2002, A. Beevor, *Berlin: The Downfall 1945*, Viking: London 2002 and J. Erickson, 'Poslednii Shturm: The Soviet Drive to Berlin, 1945' in G. Bennett (ed.), *The End of the War in Europe 1945*, HMSO: London 1996.
27. The most balanced and authoritative treatment of the Red Army rapes in Germany may be found in N.M. Naimark, *The Russians in Germany: A History of the Soviet Zone of Occupation, 1945–1949*, Harvard University Press: Cambridge, Mass. 1995.
28. Ryan, *Last Battle* p.23
29. G. Bischof, *Austria in the First Cold War, 1945–1955*, Macmillan: London 1995 pp. 30–4.
30. M. Mevius, *Agents of Moscow: The Hungarian Communist Party and the Origins of Socialist Patriotism, 1941–1953*, Oxford University Press: Oxford 2005 pp. 60–3.
31. V.A. Malyshev diary entry, 28/3/45 *Istochnik*, no. 5, 1995 pp. 127–8.
32. Cited by R. Overy, *Russia's War*, Penguin Books: London 1998 pp. 261–2.
33. G. Aleksandrov, 'Tovarishch Ehrenburg Uproshchaet', *Pravda*, 14/4/1945. The article was specifically a response to an article by Ehrenburg published in *Krasnaya Zvezda* on

11 April under the headline 'Khvatit!' (i.e. grab/snatch/seize). Aleksandrov's article was also published in *Krasnaya Zvezda*.

34. I. Ehrenburg, *The War, 1941–1945*, MacGibbon & Kee: London 1964 p. 177.
35. W. Averell Harriman, *America and Russia in a Changing World*, Doubleday: New York 1971 p. 44.
36. Werth, *Russia at War* pp. 867–8.
37. I. Stalin, *O Velikoi Otechestvennoi Voine Sovetskogo Souza*, Moscow 1946 pp. 170–1.
38. This quotation is from the stenographic record of Stalin's toast published in V.A. Nevezhin, *Zastol'nye Rechi Stalina*, Moscow–St Petersburg 2003 doc. 107. The stenographic text was edited and corrected by Stalin before the toast was published in the Soviet press (see doc. 108). A number of changes were made but none that alters the essential meaning of what Stalin said.
39. Ibid. doc. 111.
40. Harriman Papers, c.178, cf. 10–13/4/45.
41. Ibid.
42. *Sovetsko–Amerikanskie Otnosheniya* (1984), vol. 2, doc. 219.
43. *Stalin's Correspondence with Churchill, Attlee, Roosevelt and Truman, 1941–1945*, Lawrence & Wishart: London 1958 doc. 291 p. 214.
44. Cited by V.O. Pechatnov, 'Stalin i Ruzvel't' in G.N. Sevost'yanov (ed.), *Voina i Obshchestvo, 1941–1945*, vol. 1, Moscow 2004 p. 418. Pechatnov doesn't cite this text as that of the radio broadcast, but I think that is what it is.
45. Harriman Papers, c.178, cf. 14–16/4/45
46. *Sovetsko–Amerikanskie Otnosheniya* (1984), vol. 2, doc. 224.
47. Arkhiv Vneshnei Politiki Rossiiskoi Federatsii (AVPRF) F.6, Op.7b, Pap. 60, D.1, Ll.6–8, 11–13; *Foreign Relations of the United States 1945*, vol. 5, Government Printing Office: Washington DC 1967 pp. 237–41. I have examined this whole episode in detail in G. Roberts, 'Sexing up the Cold War: New Evidence on the Molotov–Truman Talks of April 1945', *Cold War History*, vol. 4, no. 3, April 2004. This article contains translations of the Soviet reports on the Molotov–Truman talks.
48. C. Marzani, *We Can Be Friends: Origins of the Cold War*, Topical Book Publishers: New York 1952 p. 187.
49. A.H. Birse, *Memoirs of an Interpreter*, Michael Joseph: London 1967 p. 200.
50. D.S. Clemens, 'Averell Harriman, John Deane, the Joint Chiefs of Staff, and the "Reversal of Cooperation" with the Soviet Union in April 1945', *International History Review*, vol. 14, no. 2, 1992 and W.D. Miscamble, 'Anthony Eden and the Truman–Molotov Conversations, April 1945', *Diplomatic History*, Spring 1978.
51. *Stalin's Correspondence with Churchill, Attlee, Roosevelt and Truman, 1941–1945*, Lawrence & Wishart: London 1958, doc. 293 pp. 215–17.
52. Ibid. doc. 298 p. 220.
53. This section on the Hopkins mission is based on the reports of his conversations with Stalin published in *Foreign Relations of the United States: The Conference of Berlin 1945*, vol. 1, US Government Printing Office: Washington 1960 pp. 21–63. Additionally, the record of Hopkins's meeting with Stalin on 6 June may be found in R.E. Sherwood, *The White House Papers of Harry L. Hopkins*, vol. 2, Eyre & Spottiswoode: London 1949 pp. 900–2. There are published Soviet reports of the meetings on 26 and 28 May but these do not differ in any essentials from the American records. See *Sovetsko–Amerikanskie Otnosheniya* (1984), vol. 2, docs 258, 260.
54. See L. Bezymenski, *The Death of Adolf Hitler: Unknown Documents from the Soviet Archives*, Michael Joseph: London 1968. Also, S.M. Shtemenko, *The Soviet General Staff at War*, vol. 2, Progress Publishers: Moscow 1986 pp. 424–6. The statement by Stalin claiming that Hitler was still alive was omitted from the published Soviet record of his conversation with Hopkins (see *Sovetsko–Amerikanskiye Otnosheniya* (1984) doc. 258) but its existence is indicated by the inclusion of ellipses.

55. *The Memoirs of Marshal Zhukov*, Jonathan Cape: London 1971 p. 668.
56. C.L. Mee, *Meeting at Potsdam*, André Deutsch: London 1975 pp. 40, 283. According to the tourist brochure at Potsdam (dated 1991) the Red Star flower arrangement was in accordance with an inter-allied agreement before the conference.
57. Cited by Mastny, *Russia's Road to the Cold War* p. 293
58. Cited by M. Trachtenberg, *A Constructed Peace: The Making of the European Settlement, 1945–1963*, Princeton University Press: Princeton NJ 1999 p. 37.
59. Cited by V. Berezhkov, *History in the Making: Memoirs of World War II Diplomacy*, Progress Publishers: Moscow 1983 p. 458.
60. Birse, *Memoirs of an Interpreter* p. 208.
61. *The Tehran, Yalta and Potsdam Conferences*, Progress Publishers: Moscow 1969 p. 265.
62. *Berlinskaya (Potsdamskaya) Konferentsiya Rukovoditelei Trekh Souznykh Derzhav – SSSR, SShA i Velikobritanii*, Moscow 1984 doc. 2. An English translation of the Soviet records of the plenary sessions at Potsdam may be found in *The Tehran, Yalta and Potsdam Conferences* but the transcripts published in this volume are not complete and the Soviet records of the other meetings at Potsdam are only available in Russian. There is no American record of this Truman–Stalin conversation, apparently because Stalin's remark about Soviet participation in the war against Japan led to the report being given a high security classification and a filing fate from which it never emerged. See *Foreign Relations of the United States: The Conference of Berlin 1945*, vol. 1, p. 43.
63. *Documents on British Policy Overseas*, series 1, vol. 1, HMSO: London 1984 pp. 386–90. I know of no Soviet record of this conversation.
64. *Berlinskaya (Potsdamskaya) Konferentsiya* doc. 3.
65. See the memoirs of the Soviet naval commissar, N.G. Kuznetsov, 'Ot Yalty do Postdama' in A.M. Samsonov (ed.), *9 Maya 1945 goda*, Moscow 1970.
66. *The Tehran, Yalta and Potsdam Conferences* p. 173.
67. AVPRF F.07, Op.10–12, Pap.49, D.2, L.20. This statement of Stalin's is omitted from the published Soviet record of the conference. Cf. *Berlinskaya (Potsdamskaya) Konferentsiya* p. 152.
68. N.V. Kochkin, 'SSSR, Angliya, SShA i "Turetskii Krizis" 1945–1947gg', *Novaya i Noveishaya Istoriya*, no. 3, 2002.
69. *Berlinskaya (Potsdamskaya) Konferentsiya* doc. 63.
70. Ibid. p. 149.
71. The details of this exchange are as follows. On 9 June 1945 Gromyko had meetings with both Stettinius and Harold Stassen, another member of the US delegation to the San Francisco conference, which indicated that the Americans would support the Soviet desire to administer a trusteeship territory. On 20 June Gromyko wrote to Stettinius to confirm the content of these conversations and to propose further discussions before the end of the conference. On 23 June Stettinius replied to Gromyko's letter confirming that the US 'supported in principle the Soviet proposal that [the USSR] had the right to be considered a potential [trusteeship adminis-trator]'. However, Stettinius pointed out that the Yalta agreements did not provide for a concrete discussion of this question at the San Francisco conference. Gromyko raised the matter again with the new American Secretary of State, James Byrnes, at the Potsdam conference on 20 July 1945. Byrnes, however, stated that he had no knowledge of the Gromyko–Stettinius correspondence and stressed that the US government had not yet arrived at a specific policy on this matter. See *Sovetsko–Amerikanskie Otnosheniya* (2004) docs 324, 326 and 342.
72. *Berlinskaya (Potsdamskaya) Konferentsiya* pp. 131–4, 442, 461; docs 50, 107, 155.
73. AVPRF, F.0431/1, Op.1, Pap.5, D.33, Ll.1–30; AVPRF F.0431/1, Op.1, D.1, Ll.1–16. See also S. Mazov, 'The USSR and the Former Italian Colonies, 1945–1950', *Cold War History*, vol. 3, no. 3, April 2003.

74. AVPRF F.07, Op.10–2, Pap.49, D.2, Ll.16–17. This statement by Stalin was omitted from the published Soviet record of the conference. Cf. *Berlinskaya (Potsdamskaya) Konferentsiya* p. 152.

75. See E. Moradiellos, 'The Potsdam Conference and the Spanish Problem', *Contemporary European History*, vol. 10, no. 1, 2001 and G. Swain, 'Stalin and Spain, 1944–1948' in C. Leitz and D.J. Dunthorn (eds), *Spain in an International Context, 1936–1959*, Berghahn Books: Oxford 1999.

76. *The Tehran, Yalta and Potsdam Conferences* pp. 317–41.

77. For example, the editorials published in *Pravda* and *Izvestiya* on 3 August 1945, both under the headline 'Berlinskaya Konferentsiya Trekh Derzhav'.

78. Cited by L. Ya. Gibianskii, 'Doneseniya Ugoslavskogo Posla v Moskve o Otsenkak Rukovodstvom SSSR Potsdamskoi Konferentsii i Polozheniya v Vostochnoi Evrope', *Slavyanovedeniye*, no. 1, 1994.

79. I. Banac (ed.), *The Diary of Georgi Dimitrov, 1933–1949*, Yale University Press: New Haven 2003 p. 377.

80. Cited by R.B. Levering, V.O. Pechatnov et al., *Debating the Origins of the Cold War: American and Russian Perspectives*, Rowman & Littlefield: Lanham, Maryland 2002 p. 105.

81. Apart from the specific references below, this section owes a great deal to T. Hasegawa, *Racing the Enemy: Stalin, Truman, and the Surrender of Japan*, Harvard University Press: Cambridge, Mass. 2005 and D. Holloway, 'Jockeying for Position in the Postwar World: Soviet Entry into the War with Japan in August 1945' in T. Hasegawa (ed.), *Reinterpreting the End of the Pacific War: Atomic Bombs and the Soviet Entry into the War*, Stanford University Press: Stanford forthcoming. I am grateful to Professor Holloway for providing me with a copy of his article in advance of publication.

82. Stalin, *O Velikoi Otechestvennoi Voine Sovetskogo Souza* p. 147. The Japanese reaction to the speech was noted by the Soviet ambassador to Moscow on 25 November 1944. See p. 56 of the Slavinskii book cited in n. 94 below.

83. On Soviet–Japanese relations before the Second World War see J. Haslam, *The Soviet Union and the Threat from the East, 1933–1941*, Macmillan: London 1992.

84. O.E. Clubb, 'Armed Conflicts in the Chinese Borderlands, 1917–1950' in R.L. Garthoff (ed.), *Sino-Soviet Military Relations*, Praeger: New York 1966.

85. See J.W. Garver, 'Chiang Kai-shek's Quest for Soviet Entry into the Sino-Japanese War', *Political Science Quarterly*, vol. 102, no. 2, 1987.

86. *Foreign Relations of the United States 1944* vol. 4, Government Printing Office: Washington DC 1966 pp. 942–4. The published Soviet record of this conversation omits this exchange between Stalin and Harriman but it does record the former's preceding statement that there had been negotiations with Tokyo about Japanese mining and oil concessions in North Sakhalin and that an agreement settling the dispute about these would be signed soon. He also told Harriman of an approach in Tokyo by the Chief of the Japanese General Staff who had said he would like to go to Moscow and meet Stalin. According to Stalin this approach showed how afraid the Japanese were. *Sovetsko–Amerikanskiye Otnosheniya* (1984) doc. 9.

87. FRUS ibid. pp. 965–6.

88. *Sovetsko–Amerikanskie Otnosheniya* (1984) doc. 119.

89. O.A. Rzheshevskii, *Stalin i Cherchill'*, Moscow 2004 doc. 167.

90. Ibid doc. 168.

91. Ibid. doc. 170

92. Hasegawa, *Racing the Enemy* p. 31.

93. *Sovetsko–Amerikanskie Otnosheniya* (1984) doc. 164.

94. *Russko–Kitaiskie Otnosheniya v XX Veke*, vol. 4, part 2, Moscow 2000 doc. 657 p. 77. The earliest known mention of the idea of acquiring the Kuril Islands in Soviet internal documentation is in Maiskii's long memorandum to Molotov in January 1944 on

perspectives on the postwar world. Maiskii mentioned the idea of acquiring the Kurils in the context of strengthening the strategic borders of the USSR for the foreseeable future. It may be that this is where Stalin got the idea from, directly or indirectly via Molotov. The Kuril Islands remain an issue of territorial dispute between Russia and Japan. For differing historical-political views on this topic among Russian historians see B.N. Slavinskii, *Yaltinskaya Konferentsiya i Problem 'Severnykh Territorii'*, Moscow 1996 and A. Koshkin, *Yaponskii Front Marshala Stalina*, Moscow 2004.

95. See Holloway, 'Jockeying for Position'.
96. *The Tehran, Yalta and Potsdam Conferences* pp. 145–6.
97. On Soviet preparations for war with Japan: Shtemenko, *Soviet General Staff* chap. 14; Vasilevsky, *A Lifelong Cause* pp. 453–82; and M. Zakharov, *Final: Istoriko-Memuarnyi Ocherk o Razgrome Imperialisticheskoi Yaponii v 1945 gody*, Moscow 1969.
98. *Sovetsko–Yaponskaya Voina 1945 goda*, Moscow 1997 (series Russkii Arkhiv), Moscow 1997 docs 312–13.
99. Shtemenko, *Soviet General Staff* p. 328.
100. *Sovetsko–Yaponskaya Voina 1945 goda* docs 314–16.
101. *Vneshnyaya Politika Sovetskogo Souza v Period Otechestvennoi Voiny*, vol. 3, Moscow 1947 pp. 166–7.
102. Holloway, 'Jockeying for Position'.
103. The Soviet records of Stalin's conversations with Soong in summer 1945 may be found in *Russko-Kitaiskie Otnosheniya v XX Veke*. English translations of the Chinese records of most of these conversations may be found in *Stalin and the Cold War, 1945–1953, A Cold War International History Project Documentary Reader*, Washington DC 1999.
104. For an analysis of these negotiations: A.M. Ledovskii, *SSSR i Stalin v Sud'bakh Kitaya*, Moscow 1999 pp. 295–320. This section of the book is in English.
105. *Stalin and the Cold War, 1945–1953* p. 217.
106. *Russko–Kitaiskie Otnosheniya v XX Veke* doc. 657.
107. Ibid. doc. 660.
108. Ibid. doc. 674.
109. Holloway, 'Jockeying for Position'.
110. On the Stalin–Mao relationship in this period see Nui Jun, 'The Origins of the Sino-Soviet Alliance' in O.A. Westad, *Brothers in Arms: The Rise and Fall of the Sino-Soviet Alliance, 1945–1963*, Stanford University Press: Stanford 1998.
111. Cited by M. Leffler, *For the Soul of Mankind: The United States, the Soviet Union and the Cold War* (forthcoming).
112. *Documents on British Policy Overseas*, HMSO: London 1985 doc. 185.
113. *Foreign Relations of the United States: The Conference of Berlin 1945* vol. 2, Government Printing Office: Washington DC 1960 p. 345.
114. *Documents on British Policy Overseas*, doc. 231.
115. *Berlinskaya (Potsdamskaya) Konferentsiya* doc. 97
116. Cited by Holloway, 'Jockeying for Position'.
117. *Russko–Kitaiskie Otnosheniya v XX Veke* doc. 685.
118. *Documents on British Policy Overseas* p. 959.
119. *Stalin's Correspondence* doc. 358, pp. 258–9.
120. *Vneshnyaya Politika Sovetskogo* vol. 3 pp. 362–3.
121. Holloway, 'Jockeying for Position'.
122. *Sovetsko–Yaponskaya Voina 1945 goda* doc. 324. That same day Vasilesvksii informed his front commanders (docs 325–7) that the date of the attack had been moved forward from 1800 Moscow time on 10 August to 1800 Moscow time on 8 August (i.e. 2400 in the Far Eastern time zone, which meant the Soviets could commence hostilities on the 9th). Stalin's directive makes no mention of bringing forward the date of the attack by a couple of days so it may be that the directive to attack on the 10th was

provisional or may even have emanated from Vasilevskii himself as a contingency plan while he awaited instructions from Moscow in response to his report of 3 August.

123. See D. Holloway, *Stalin & the Bomb*, Yale University Press: New Haven 1994.

124. See 'Truman Tells Stalin, July 24, 1945', www.dannen.com/decision/potsdam.html.

125. English language text of the Sino-Soviet treaty of 1945 in Garthoff, *Sino-Soviet* Appendix A.

126. *Stalin and the Cold War, 1945–1953* pp. 221–2.

127. For a translation of this directive and a commentary on its content and significance see M. Kramer, 'Documenting the Early Soviet Nuclear Program', *Cold War International History Project Bulletin*, nos 6–7, Winter 1995/1996.

128. *Russko-Kitaiskie Otnosheniya v XX Veke* doc. 699.

129. Ibid. p. 272.

130. See Hasegawa's discussion, *Racing the Enemy* pp. 290–330.

131. See ibid. pp. 267–74.

132. *Stalin's Correspondence* pp. 266–9.

133. Stalin, *O Velikoi Otechestvennoi Voine Sovetskogo Souza* pp. 180–3.

134. Werth, *Russia at War* p.928.

10 The Lost Peace: Stalin and the Origins of the Cold War

1. Arkhiv Vneshnei Politiki Rossiiskoi Federatsii (AVPRF) F.0431/1, Op.1, Dd 1–4. These are the files on Soviet preparations for the CFM, including the Politburo directive to the delegation. For an analysis of the Soviet position at the CFM based on these and other files see G.A. Agafonova, 'Diplomaticheskii Krizis na Londonskoi Sessii SMID' in I.V. Gaiduk and N.I. Egorova (eds), *Stalin i Kholodnaya Voina*, Moscow 1997. See further: J. Knight, 'Russia's Search for Peace: The London Council of Foreign Ministers, 1945', *Journal of Contemporary History*, vol. 13, 1978.

2. *Stalin's Correspondence with Churchill, Attlee, Roosevelt and Truman, 1941–1945*, Lawrence & Wishart: London 1958 doc. 476 p. 361.

3. See L. E. Davis, *The Cold War Begins: Soviet–American Conflict over Eastern Europe*, Princeton University Press: Princeton NJ 1974 chap. 9.

4. Some of the paper trail leading to the Soviet decision to postpone the elections may be found in *Vostochnaya Evropa v Dokumentakh Rossiiskikh Arkhivov, 1944–1953*, vol. 1, Moscow 1997 docs 85, 87, 90, 91, 92. The decision to postpone the elections was within the remit of the Allied Control Commission established under the terms of the armistice agreement with Bulgaria. The ACC was controlled by the Soviets and the decision was taken by General Biruzov on instructions from Moscow. Malcolm Mackintosh, who was British liaison officer with the ACC, recalled that Stalin himself called from Moscow and said that 'Biruzov and his colleagues were shaken to the core: one officer who had taken the call actually fainted. But Stalin's orders were obeyed, and jubilant Bulgarians took to the streets convinced that the Western powers had forced the Soviets to give in.' M. Mackintosh, *Eastern Europe 1945–1946: The Allied Control Commission in Bulgaria*' FCO Historical Branch Occasional Papers, no. 4, 1992. The memoirs of the Soviet chair of the Bulgarian ACC glosses over the whole episode. S.S. Biruzov, *Sovetskii Soldat na Balkanakh*, Moscow 1963.

5. I. Banac (ed.), *The Diary of Georgi Dimitrov, 1933–1949*, Yale University Press: London 1993 pp. 379–80.

6. Ibid. p. 381 and *Stalin and the Cold War, 1945–1953: A Cold War International History Project Documentary Reader* 1999 pp. 247–9.

7. On the Trieste crisis R.S. Dinardo, 'Glimpse of an Old War Order: Reconsidering the Trieste Crisis of 1945', *Diplomatic History*, vol. 21, no. 3, 1997; L.Ya Gibianskii, 'Stalin

i Triestskoe Protivostoyanie 1945g.' in Gaiduk and Egorova *Stalin*; and G. Valdevit, 'The Search for Symmetry: A Tentative View of Trieste, the Soviet Union and the Cold War' in F. Gori and Silvio Pons (eds), *The Soviet Union and Europe in the Cold War, 1943–1953*, Macmillan: London 1996.

8. *Documents on British Policy Overseas* (hereafter: DBPO), series 1, vol. 2, HMSO: London 1985 p. 177. On Soviet policy on the trusteeship question: S. Mazov, 'The USSR and the Former Italian Colonies, 1945–1950', *Cold War History*, vol. 3, no. 3, April 2003. For an overview: S. Kelly, *Cold War in the Desert: Britain, the United States and the Italian Colonies, 1945–1950*, Macmillan: London 2000.

9. Cited by V.O. Pechatnov, *'The Allies are Pressing on You to Break Your Will . . .': Foreign Policy Correspondence between Stalin and Molotov and Other Politburo Members, September 1945–December 1946*, Cold War International History Project, Working Paper no. 26, 1999 p. 2. The Russian version of this important article may be found in *Istochnik*, nos 2 & 3 1999.

10. *Sessiya Soveta Ministrov Inostrannykh Del v Londone 11 Sentyabrya–2 Oktyabrya 1945 goda: Stenograficheskiye Zapisi Zasedanii*, AVPRF F.0431/1, Op.1, D.5, L.3

11. Pechatnov, '*Allies*' p. 4. It should be noted that at the session on 20 September i.e. before the instructions from Stalin about returning to the Potsdam agreement that only directly interested parties would take part in CFM discussions, Molotov had raised this question himself on the practical grounds of the time it was taking for the five foreign ministers to discuss everything. *Stenograficheskiye Zapisi Zasedanii* L.41.

12. AVPRF F.0431/1, Op.11, D.18, Ll.32–39. These documents are published in *Sovetsko–Amerikanskie Otnosheniya, 1945–1948*, Moscow 2004 docs 13–14.

13. *Stalin's Correspondence* doc. 512 p. 378.

14. *Stenograficheskiye Zapisi Zasedanii* L.8.

15. AVPRF F.0431/1, Op.11, D.18, L.24. This document is published in *Sovetsko–Amerikanskie Otnosheniya, 1945–1948* doc. 9.

16. See K. Hamilton, 'The Quest for a *Modus Vivendi*: The Danubian Satellites in Anglo-Soviet Relations 1945–1946', *FCO Historical Branch Occasional Papers*, no. 4, 1992; E. Mark, 'American Policy towards Eastern Europe and the Origins of the Cold War, 1941–1946', *Journal of American History*. vol. 68, no. 2, September 1981; and E. Mark, 'Charles E. Bohlen and the Acceptable Limits of Soviet Hegemony in Eastern Europe', *Diplomatic History*, vol. 3, no. 3, Summer 1979.

17. *Stenograficheskiye Zapisi Zasedanii* L.57.

18. AVPRF F.0431/1, Op.1, D.1, Ll.6–7, 15.

19. Ibid. Op.11. D.18, Ll.25–27; *Sovetsko–Amerikanskie Otnosheniya, 1945–1948* doc. 10.

20. Pechatnov, '*Allies*' p. 5. Emphasis added.

21. DBPO doc. 108 p. 317.

22. *Stalin and the Cold War, 1945–1953* pp. 264–5.

23. 'V.M. Molotov's Press Conference', *Soviet News*, 5/10/45.

24. *Vneshnyaya Politika Sovetskogo Souza, 1945 god*, Moscow 1949 p. 81.

25. AVPRF F.0431/1, Op.1, D.26, Ll.22–4.

26. *Stalin and the Cold War, 1945–1953* p. 272.

27. 'Report by V.M. Molotov', *Soviet News*, 8/11/45.

28. *Politburo TsK VKP (b) i Sovet Ministrov SSSR, 1945–1953*, Moscow 2002 doc. 177. A translation of this document may be found in R.B. Levering et al., *Debating the Origins of the Cold War*, Rowman & Littlefield: Lanham, Maryland 2002 pp. 155–6.

29. *Stalin and the Cold War, 1945–1953* pp. 254–69.

30. The text of the decisions of the Moscow conference may be found at www.yale.edu/lawweb/avalon/decade/decade19.htm.

31. J. F. Byrnes, *Speaking Frankly*, Harper & Brothers: New York 1947 p. 118.

32. G.P. Kynin and J. Laufer (eds), *SSSR i Germanskii Vopros*, vol. 2, Moscow 2000 doc. 71.

33. DBPO doc. 340 p. 868.

34. *Stalin's Correspondence* doc. 384 pp. 280–1.
35. *Vostochnaya Evropa v Dokumentakh Rossiiskikh Arkhivov* doc. 127. An English translation of this document may be found in *Stalin and the Cold War, 1945–1953* pp. 281–6.
36. See for example the documents on the implementation of the Moscow agreement in Romania in *Tri Vizita A.Ya. Vyshinskogo v Bukharest, 1944–1946*, Moscow 1998.
37. Cited in Levering et al., *Debating* p. 114.
38. The Soviet records of the Paris sessions of the CFM may be found in AVPRF F.431/II Op.2, Dd.1–2. The Soviet records of the Paris Peace Conference, which consist of 1,200 pages of typescript, are in AVPRF F.432, Op.1, Dd.1–4, although the main proceedings of the conference were published in the press. The Russian texts of the peace treaties are in *Vneshnyaya Politika Sovetskogo Souza, 1947 god*, Moscow 1952 pp. 64–360.
39. For Stalin's correspondence with Molotov during these negotiations see Pechatnov, 'Allies'. For a further treatment of Molotov's role in the CFM negotiations see D. Watson, *Molotov: A Biography*, Palgrave Macmillan: London 2005 chap. 13.
40. *SSSR i Germanskii Vopros* doc. 114. On the Soviet campaign against foreign military bases in 1945–1946 see C. Kennedy-Pipe, *Stalin's Cold War: Soviet Strategies in Europe, 1943–1956*, Manchester University Press: Manchester 1995 pp. 101–9.
41. Pechatnov, 'Allies', p. 20.
42. 'Mirnye Dogovory s Byvshimi Souznikami Germanii', *Pravda*, 16/2/47; 'Vazhnyi Shag na Puti Ukrepleniya Mira i Bezopasnosti', *Izvestiya*, 16/2/47; 'K Podpisanniu Mirnykh Dogovorov s Byvshimi Souznikami Germanii', *Novoe Vremya*, no. 7, 14/2/47.
43. *Sovetsko–Amerikanskie Otnosheniya, 1945–1948* doc. 138. This document is translated and commented upon in a symposium on 'The Soviet Side of the Cold War' in *Diplomatic History*, vol. 15, no. 4, Fall 1991. See also: K.M. Jensen (ed.), *Origins of the Cold War: The Novikov, Kennan and Roberts 'Long Telegrams' of 1946*, Washington DC 1991.
44. Kennan's widely available article is reproduced together with a number of commentaries in C. Gati (ed.), *Caging the Bear: Containment and the Cold War*, Bobbs-Merrill: Indianapolis 1974. The collection includes an interview with Kennan on the 25th anniversary of his article's publication, which he describes as misunderstood and misinterpreted.
45. Ibid. docs 144, 145, 148, 151, 152.
46. Pechatnov, 'Allies' p. 21.
47. W. Lippmann, *The Cold War: A Study in US Foreign Policy*, Hamish Hamilton: London 1947.
48. Full text of Churchill's speech: www.historyguide.org/europe/churchill.html.
49. *Pravda* 11/3/46 (with details of Churchill's speech on the back page); E. Tarle, 'Po Povodu Rechi Cherchilliya', *Izvestiya* 12/3/41 (with report on Churchill's speech on p. 4).
50. I. Stalin, *Sochineniya*, vol. 16, Moscow 1997 pp. 26–30. For an English translation: W. LaFeber (ed.), *The Origins of the Cold War, 1941–1947*, John Wiley & Sons: New York 1971 doc. 37.
51. A. Werth, *Russia: The Postwar Years*, Robert Hale: London 1971 p. 112.
52. On the Iranian crisis: see B.R. Kuniholm, *The Origins of the Cold War in the Near East*, Princeton University Press: Princeton NJ 1980; F.S. Raine, 'Stalin and the Creation of the Azerbaijan Democratic Party in Iran, 1945', *Cold War History*, vol. 2, no. 2, October 2001; N.I. Yegorova, *The 'Iran Crisis' of 1945–1946: A View from the Russian Archives*, Cold War International History Project Working Paper no. 15, May 1996; S. Savrankaya and V. Zubok, 'Cold War in the Caucasus: Notes and Documents from a Conference', *Cold War International History Project Bulletin*, nos 14–15; and 'From the Baku Archives', idem. nos 12–13; R.K. Ramazani, 'The Autonomous Republic of Azerbaijan and the Kurdish People's Republic: Their Rise and Fall' in T.T. Hammond (ed.), *The*

Anatomy of Communist Takeovers, Yale University Press: New Haven 1975; and S.L. McFarland, 'A Peripheral View of the Origins of the Cold War: The Crises in Iran, 1941–1947', *Diplomatic History*, vol. 4, no. 4, Fall 1980.

53. The text of Stalin's letter is reproduced in Yegorova, '*Iran Crisis*'.
54. DBPO pp. 317–18.
55. Ibid. p. 781.
56. W. Bedell Smith, *Moscow Mission, 1946–1949*, Heinemann: London 1950 pp. 41–2.
57. *Vneshnyaya Politika Sovetskogo Souza, 1946 god*, Moscow 1952 pp. 167–70.
58. 'The Problem of the Black Sea Straits', *Izvestiya* article translated and published in *Soviet News*, 22/8/46.
59. Kuniholm, *Origins* p. 266.
60. A.R. De Luca, 'Soviet–American Politics and the Turkish Straits', *Political Science Quarterly*, vol. 92, no. 3, Autumn 1977 p. 519.
61. *Vneshnyaya Politika Sovetskogo Souza, 1946* pp. 193–202.
62. Kuniholm, *Origins* pp. 372–3.
63. N.V. Kochkin, 'SSSR, Angliya, SShA i "Turetskii Krizis" 1945–1947gg', *Novaya i Noveishaya Istoriya*, no. 3, 2002
64. See E. Mark, 'The War Scare of 1946 and Its Consequences', *Diplomatic History*, vol. 21, no. 3, Summer 1997.
65. I. Stalin, *Sochineniya* pp. 32–3, 37–43, 45–8. The Bailey, Werth and Roosevelt interviews are translated in *Stalin and the Cold War, 1945–1953*.
66. Ibid. pp. 57–67. A translation of the Stassen interview may be found in *Stalin and the Cold War, 1945–1953*. While in Moscow Stassen also talked to Molotov and Zhdanov, who said much the same thing to him as Stalin.
67. LaFeber, *Origins* doc. 40. Emphasis added.
68. 'Vystuplenie Trumena . . .', *Pravda*, 14/3/47; 'Poslanie Trumena Kongressu', *Pravda*, 13/3/47; 'O Vneshnei Politike Soedinennykh Shtatov', *Novoe Vremya*, no. 12, 21/3/47.
69. See the *Pravda* and *Izvestiya* editorials published in *Soviet News* 29/4/47, 1/5/47 and 7/5/47.
70. N.V. Kochkin, 'Anglo-Sovetskii Souznyi Dogovor 1942 goda i Nachalo "Kholodnoi Voiny"', *Voprosy Istorii*, no. 1, 2006.
71. *Sovetsko–Amerikanskie Otnosheniya, 1945–1948* doc. 185.
72. On the Soviet response to the Marshall Plan: S.D. Parrish and M.M. Narinsky, *New Evidence on the Soviet Rejection of the Marshall Plan, 1947*, Cold War International History Project Working Paper no. 9, March 1994; G. Roberts, 'Moscow and the Marshall Plan: Politics, Ideology and the Onset of Cold War, 1947', *Europe–Asia Studies*, vol. 46, no. 8, 1994; and M. Cox and C. Kennedy-Pipe, 'The Tragedy of American Diplomacy: Rethinking the Marshall Plan', *Journal of Cold War Studies*, Spring 2005.
73. LaFeber, *Origins* doc. 41.
74. 'Novoe Izdanie "Doktriny Trumana"', *Pravda* 16/6/47; K. Gofman, 'Mr Marshall's "New Plan" for Relief to European Countries', *New Times*, 17/6/47.
75. *Sovetsko–Amerikanskie Otnosheniya, 1945–1948* doc. 198.
76. The Novikov document is reproduced in G. Takhnenko, 'Anatomy of the Political Decision: Notes on the Marshall Plan', *International Affairs*, July 1992.
77. *Sovetsko–Amerikanskie Otnosheniya, 1945–1948* doc. 200.
78. See T.G. Paterson, *Soviet-American Confrontation: Postwar Reconstruction and the Origins of the Cold War*, Johns Hopkins University Press: Baltimore 1973. Paterson's research was based mainly on US sources but his finding that the Soviets were serious about accepting an American loan, provided the terms were right, has been amply borne out by the new evidence from Russian archives.
79. Directive to the Soviet delegation to the Paris conference, reproduced in Takhnenko, 'Anatomy'.

80. The public documents of the conference, including Molotov's speeches, may be found in *French Yellow Book: Documents of the Conference of Foreign Ministers of France, the United Kingdom and the USSR held in Paris from 27 June to 3rd July 1947*.

81. *Sovetsko–Amerikanskie Otnosheniya, 1945–1948* doc. 203.

82. Document in Takhnenko, 'Anatomy'. This document may also be found in Levering et al., *Debating* pp. 167–69.

83. The quotation is from the Czechoslovak record of this meeting reproduced in 'Stalin, Czechoslovakia, and the Marshall Plan: New Documentation from Czechoslovak Archives', *Bohemia Band* no. 32 1991. The Soviet record is in *Vostochnaya Evropa v Dokumentakh Rossiiskikh Arkhivov* doc. 227 (translation in Levering et al., *Debating* pp. 169–72).

84. M. McCauley, *The Origins of the Cold War*, Longman: London 2003 doc. 27.

85. The key text on the Cominform is G. Procacci (ed.), *The Cominform: Minutes of the Three Conferences, 1947/1948/1949*, Feltrinelli: Milan 2004. This volume contains a number of very valuable analyses of the history of the Cominform as well as the conference minutes. The Russian edition of this book contains additionally a number of reports from the conference sent to Stalin: *Soveshchaniya Kominforma, 1947, 1948, 1949: Dokumenty i Materialy*, Moscow 1998.

86. See A.D. Biagio, 'The Cominform as the Soviet Response to the Marshall Plan' in A. Varsori and E. Calandri (eds), *The Failure of Peace in Europe, 1943–48*, Palgrave: London 2002.

87. Rossiiskii Gosudarstvennyi Arkhiv Sotsial'no-Politicheskoi Istorii (RGASPI) F.77, Op.3, D.89, Ll.7–13.

88. See G. Swain, 'The Cominform: Tito's International?', *Historical Journal*, vol. 35, no. 3 1992.

89. RGASPI F.77, Op.3, D.91, Ll.13, 84–5.

90. Zhdanov's speech was published in *Izvestiya*, 7/11/46. A translation may be found in *Soviet News*, 8/11/46.

91. Procacci, *Cominform* pp. 225–7.

92. D. Sassoon, 'The Rise and Fall of West European Communism, 1939–1948', *Contemporary European History*, vol. 1, no. 2 1992.

93. On the communist takeover in Eastern Europe after the war: N. Naimark and L.Gibianskii (eds), *The Establishment of Communist Regimes in Eastern Europe, 1944–1949*, Westview Press: Boulder, Col. 1997. A detailed study of the later stages of the process is T.V. Volokitina et al. (eds), *Moskva i Vostochnaya Evropa: Stanovlenie Politicheskikh Rezhimov Sovetskogo Tipa, 1949–1953*, Moscow 2002. On the events in Prague in Fenruary 1948: G.P. Murashko, 'Fevral'skii Krizis 1948g v Chekhoslovakii i Sovetskoe Rukovodstvo', *Novaya i Noveishaya Istoria*, no. 3, 1998.

94. Stalin's two conversations with Thorez are in *Stalin and the Cold War, 1945–1953* pp. 81–6, 403–7.

95. Procacci, *Cominform* p. 91.

11 Generalissimo at Home:
The Domestic Context of Stalin's Postwar Foreign Policy

1. *Moskva Poslevoennaya, 1945–1947*, Moscow 2000 doc. 18.

2. Cited by A. Werth, *Russia: The Postwar Years*, Robert Hale: London 1971 p. 81.

3. Cited by S. Sebag Montefiore, *Stalin: The Court of the Red Tsar*, Weidenfeld & Nicolson: London 2003 p. 4.

4. Razin's letter and Stalin's reply may be found in P.M. Kober, 'Clausewitz and the Communist Party Line: A Pronouncement by Stalin', *Military Affairs*, vol. 13, no. 2,

Summer 1949. Because of his positive appraisal of Clausewitz, Razin was arrested and imprisoned. However, he was later rehabilitated by Stalin and returned to his researches on the history of military strategy. See: R. Medvedev, 'Generalissimo Stalin, General Clausewitz and Colonel Razin' in R. and Z. Medvedev, *The Unknown Stalin*, The Overlook Press: Woodstock NY 2004.

5. M.P. Gallagher, *The Soviet History of World War II*, Frederick A. Praeger: New York 1963 espec. chap. 3.

6. K.E. Voroshilov, *Stalin i Vooruzhennye Sily SSSR*, Moscow 1951 p. 129. The book was the postwar successor of prewar articles by Voroshilov on the same topic.

7. *Georgii Zhukov*, Moscow 2001 doc. 3.

8. See B. V. Sokolov, *Georgii Zhukov*, Moscow 2004 pp. 478ff. and O.P. Chaney, *Zhukov*, University of Oklahoma Press: London 1996 chap. 13.

9. Rossiiskii Gosudarstvennyi Arkhiv Noveishei Istorii (RGANI) F.2, Op.1, D.11, Ll.2–3.

10. *Georgii Zhukov* docs 6, 8.

11. Ibid. docs 11–12.

12. E. Radzinsky, *Stalin*, Hodder & Stoughton: London 1997 pp. 502–3. It was routine for Stalin to bug the conversations of members of the Soviet military and political leadership.

13. I.V. Stalin, *Sochineniya*, vol. 16, Moscow 1997 pp. 17–20.

14. *Politburo TsK VKP (b) i Sovet Ministrov SSSR*, 1945–1953, Moscow 2002 doc. 58.

15. See J. Eric Duskin, *Stalinist Reconstruction and the Confirmation of a New Elite, 1945–1953*, Palgrave: London 2001 and Y. Gorlizki and O. Khlevniuk, *Cold Peace: Stalin and the Soviet Ruling Circle, 1945–1953*, Oxford University Press: Oxford 2004.

16. The dates of Stalin's postwar holidays may be found in *Politburo TsK VKP (b) i Sovet Ministrov SSSR* doc. 299.

17. Werth, *Russia* p. 283. The documents in ibid. contain a number of Stalin's letters to Politburo members in the 1940s. On Stalin's relations with the Politburo: N.M. Naimark, 'Cold War Studies and New Archival Materials on Stalin', *Russian Review* no. 61, January 2002.

18. For overviews of social and economic postwar developments see J.N. Hazard, 'The Soviet Government Organizes for Reconstruction', *Journal of Politics*, vol. 8, no. 3, August 1946; S. Fitzpatrick, 'Postwar Soviet Society: The "Return to Normalcy", 1945–1953' in S.J. Linz (ed.), *The Impact of World War II on the Soviet Union*, Rowman & Allanheld 1985; and E. Zubkova, 'The Soviet Regime and Soviet Society in the Postwar Years', *Journal of Modern European History*, vol. 2, no. 1, 2004.

19. A translation of Molotov's November 1945 speech may be found in *Soviet News*, 8/11/45.

20. M. Harrison, *Accounting for War: Soviet Production, Employment and the Defence Burden, 1940–1945*, Cambridge University Press: Cambridge 1996 pp. 141, 159–61.

21. J. Burds, *The Early Cold War in Soviet West Ukraine*, The Carl Beck Papers in Russian and East European Studies, no. 1505, January 2001 p. 8 and A.J. Rieber, 'Civil Wars in the Soviet Union', *Kritika*, vol. 4, no. 1, Winter 2003 p. 160. A number of documents on NKVD counter-insurgency activities may be found in *Lubyanka: Stalin i NKVD–NKGB–GUKR 'Smersh', 1939–1946*, Moscow 2006.

22. *Stalinskie Deportatsii, 1928–1953: Dokumenty*, Moscow 2005 pp. 789–98 (table of Soviet deportation operations).

23. See T. Snyder, '"To Resolve the Ukrainian Problem Once and for All": The Ethnic Cleansing of Ukrainians in Poland, 1943–1947', *Journal of Cold War Studies*, vol. 1, no. 2. Spring 1999.

24. For a study of how this worked in practice in the Western Ukraine after the war see A. Weiner, *Making Sense of War: The Second World War and the Fate of the Bolshevik Revolution*, Princeton University Press: Princeton NJ 2001. Also: M. Edele 'Soviet Veterans as an Entitlement Group, 1945–1955', *Slavic Review*, vol. 65, no. 1, 2006.

25. On the party during and immediately after the war: C.S. Kaplan, 'The Impact of World War II on the Party' in Linz, *Impact* and S. Pons, 'Stalinism and Party Organization (1933–1948)' in J. Channon (ed.), *Politics, Society and Stalinism in the USSR*, Macmillan: London 1998.

26. Gorlizki and Khlevniuk, *Cold Peace* pp. 52–7.

27. RGANI F.2, Op.1, D.28, Ll.23–4. The previous CC plenum was in January 1944 and the main item was changing the status of the commissariats of defence and foreign affairs from 'all-union' to 'union-republic', an arcane change that was rationalised by reference to the development of the republics during the war and the need for them to develop their independent role. In the event the only concrete result was that the Ukraine and Belorussia established and ran their own foreign ministries for a while, although in political and policy terms they remained strictly subordinate to the central foreign commissariat. RGANI F.2, Op.1, Dd.3–4.

28. D. Filtzer, *Soviet Workers and Late Stalinism*, Cambridge University Press: Cambridge 2002 p. 13.

29. E. Zubkova, *Russia after the War*, M.E. Sharpe: New York 1998 p. 74.

30. Ibid., espec. chap. 8. A range of documentation on public attitudes in postwar USSR may be found in *Sovetskaya Zhizn' 1945–1953*, Moscow 2003. *Moskva Poslevoennaya, 1945–1947* contains a number of documents on public opinion in Moscow after the war, including during the election period.

31. Stalin, *Sochineniya* pp. 5–16. An English translation of this speech may be found in J.P. Morray, *From Yalta to Disarmament*, Monthly Review Press: New York 1961 Appendix B.

32. For further analysis of the election campaign speeches: A. Resis, *Stalin, the Politburo and the Onset of the Cold War, 1945–1946*, The Carl Beck Papers in Russian and East European Studies, no. 701, April 1988 and D. Allen, 'The International Situation, 1945–1946: The View from Moscow', SIPS Paper, University of Birmingham 1986

33. Werth, *Russia*, pp. 84, 88.

34. Zhdanov's speech in *Soviet News*, 9/11/46.

35. RGASPI F.17, Op.125, Dd.296, 315, 386, 387, 388. For a detailed discussion based on these Sovinform files see V. Pechatnov, 'Exercise in Frustration: Soviet Foreign Propaganda in the Early Cold War, 1945–1947', *Cold War History*, vol. 1, no. 2, January 2001.

36. Stalin, *Sochineniya* pp. 25–30. An English translation of Stalin's reply to Churchill may be found in LaFeber (ed.), *The Origins of the Cold War, 1941–1947* doc. 37.

37. Cited by Zubkova, *Russia* p. 84. Mlynar was one of the leaders of the 'Prague Spring' of 1968.

38. This citation is from a document translated in A.O. Chubar'yan and V.O. Pechatnov, 'Molotov "the Liberal": Stalin's 1945 Criticism of his Deputy', *Cold War History*, vol. 1 no. 1, August 2000.

39. Werth, *Russia* p. 99.

40. V.N. Zemskov, 'Repatriatsiya Peremeshchennykh Sovetskikh Grazhdan' in G.N. Sevost'yanov (ed.), *Voina i Obshchestvo, 1941–1945*, vol. 2, Moscow 2004 pp. 341–2. See also M. Dyczok, *The Grand Alliance and the Ukrainian Refugees*, Macmillan: London 2000 pp. 166–7. Dyczok cites higher figures than Zemskov but these include over a million citizens and POWs displaced within the borders of the USSR and who therefore cannot be classed as foreign repatriatees.

41. See A.A. Maslov, 'Forgiven by Stalin – Soviet Generals Who Returned from German Prisons in 1941–45 and Who Were Rehabilitated', *Journal of Slavic Military Studies*, vol. 12, no. 2, June 1999.

42. Werth, *Russia* chaps 11 and 16 and T. Dunmore, *Soviet Politics, 1945–53*, Macmillan: London 1984 chap. 6.

43. Cited by Gorlizki and Khlevniuk, *Cold Peace* pp. 34–5.

44. *Moskva Poslevoennaya, 1945–1947* doc. 124. This episode was brought to my attention by R. Service, *Stalin: A Biography*, Macmillan: London 2004 pp. 561–2.

45. On the Varga discussion: G. D. Ra'anan, *International Policy Formation in the USSR: Factional 'Debates' during the Zhdanovshchina*, Archon Books: Hamden, Conn. 1983 chap. 6; J. Hough, 'Debates about the Postwar World' in Linz (ed.), *Impact* and R.B. Day, *Cold War Capitalism: The View from Moscow, 1945–1975*, M.E. Sharpe: London 1995.

46. *Politburo TsK VKP (b) i Sovet Ministrov SSSR* n. 1 pp. 229–30 and doc. 201; Gorlizki and Khlevniuk, *Cold Peace* pp. 36–8.

47. Ibid.

48. Gorlizki and Khlevniuk, *Cold Peace* pp. 38–42 and Z. Medvedev, 'Stalin and Lysenko' in R. and Z. Medvdev, *The Unknown Stalin*.

49. Malyshev diary, *Istochnik*, no. 5, 1997 p. 135.

50. This quotation and the preceding quotations from *Pravda* are cited in J. Brooks, *Thank You, Comrade Stalin! Soviet Public Culture from Revolution to Cold War*, Princeton University Press: Princeton NJ 2000 pp. 213–14.

51. Z. Medvedev, 'Stalin as a Russian Nationalist' in R. and Z. Medvdev, *The Unknown Stalin*.

52. Stalin, *Sochineniya* p. 68.

53. J.V. Stalin, *Concerning Marxism in Linguistics*, Soviet News Booklet, London 1950.

54. I follow the treatment of Gorlizki and Khlevniuk, *Cold Peace* pp. 79–89. Documentation on Voznesenskii's fall may be found in *Politburo TsK VKP (b) i Sovet Ministrov SSSR* docs 238–53 and on the purge of the Leningrad party in *TsK VKP (b) i Regional'nye Partiinye Komitety 1949–1953*, Moscow 2004 docs 84–104.

55. See D. Brandenberger, 'Stalin, the Leningrad Affair and the Limit of Postwar Russocentrism', *Russian Review*, no. 63, April 2004. See also the response to Brandenberger's article by Richard Bidlack in the January 2005 issue of the *Russian Review*, which appears together with a brief reply by the former.

56. Gorlizki and Khlevniuk, *Cold Peace* p.83.

57. See J. Burds, *Early Cold War*.

58. The history of the JAFC is documented and analysed in detail S. Redlich (ed.), *War, Holocaust and Stalinism: A Documentary History of the Jewish Anti-Fascist Committee in the USSR*, Harwood Academic Publishers: Luxembourg 1995. A Russian study of the wartime activities of the committee is N.K. Petrovka, *Antifashistskie Komitety v SSSR: 1941–1945gg*, Moscow 1999, who stresses that that the JAFC was, above all, a Soviet patriotic organisation.

59. For the argument and evidence that Stalin had Mikhoels killed see G.V. Kostyrchenko, *Tainaya Politika Stalina*, Moscow 2001. It should be noted, however, that Mikhoels's death was met with a laudatory obituary in *Pravda* and a huge funeral in Moscow attended by many party and government dignitaries.

60. Redlich, *War* doc. 180.

61. See G. Gorodetsky, 'The Soviet Union and the Creation of the State of Israel', *The Journal of Israeli History*, vol. 22, no. 1, 2003 and L. Rucker, *Moscow's Surprise: The Soviet–Israeli Alliance of 1947–1949*, Cold War International History Project Working Paper no. 46. A number of documents on Soviet–Israeli relations during this period have been published in Russian and English: *Sovetsko–Izrail'skie Otnosheniya*, vol. 1 (1941–1953), Moscow 2000 and *Documents on Israeli–Soviet Relations, 1941–1953*, Frank Cass: London 2000.

62. Cited by Rucker, *Moscow's Surprise* p. 17.

63. *Documents on Israeli–Soviet Relations* docs 160, 173, 180, 195.

64. Redlich, *War* doc. 181.

65. J. Rubenstein and V.P. Naumov (eds), *Stalin's Secret Pogrom: The Postwar Inquisition of the Jewish Anti-Fascist Committee*, Yale University Press: New Haven 2001. This volume contains an edited transcript of the trial. Its contents are very illuminating but have

been criticised for making the defendants appear less Soviet and more Jewish than they actually were.

66. *Politburo TsK VKP (b) i Sovet Ministrov SSSR* docs 254–255.

67. RGASPI, F.82, Op.2, Dd.1091–112. See G. Roberts, 'Stalin, the Pact with Nazi Germany, and the Origins of Postwar Soviet Diplomatic Historiography', *Journal of Cold War Studies*, vol. 4, no. 3, 2002.

68. J. Pelikan (ed.), *The Czechoslovak Political Trials, 1950–1954*, Macdonald: London 1970.

69. Z. Medvedev, *Stalin i Evreiskaya Problema*, Moscow 2003. Cf. G. Kostyrchenko, *Out of the Shadows: Anti-Semitism in Stalin's Russia*, Prometheus Books: New York 1995.

70. Malyshev diary pp. 140–1.

71. My treatment is based on the documentation, but not the interpretation, of J. Brent and V.P. Naumov, *Stalin's Last Crime: The Plot against the Jewish Doctors, 1948–1953*, HarperCollins: New York 2003. A number of the documents they cite are reproduced in *Politburo TsK VKP (b) i Sovet Ministrov SSSR*.

72. *Politburo TsK VKP (b) i Sovet Ministrov SSSR* doc. 297.

73. Brent and Naumov, *Stalin's Last Crime* p. 10.

74. Ibid. p. 58.

75. G. Alexopoulos, 'Amnesty 1945: The Revolving Door of Stalin's Gulag', *Slavic Review*, vol. 64, no. 2, Summer 2005.

76. See the table in J. Keep, *Last of the Empires: A History of the Soviet Union, 1945–1991*, Oxford University Press: Oxford 1995 p. 15.

77. Dunmore, *Soviet Politics*.

78. Gorlizki and Khlevniuk, *Cold Peace* pp. 124–32.

79. The section is based on the files on the 19th party congress in Rossiiskii Gosudarstvennyi Arkhiv Sotsial'no-Politicheskoi Istorii (RGASPI) F.592, Op.1. See also: A. Tikhonov and P.R. Gregory, 'Stalin's Last Plan' in P.R. Gregory (ed.), *Behind the Façade of Stalin's Command Economy*, Hoover Institution Press: Stanford 2001.

80. Stalin, *Sochineniya* pp. 227–9.

81. See Y. Gorlizki's, 'Party Revivalism and the Death of Stalin', *Slavic Review*, vol. 54, no. 1, 1995 and 'Stalin's Cabinet: The Politburo and Decision Making in the Post-War Years', *Europe–Asia Studies*, vol. 53, no. 2, 2001.

82. Stalin's speech was published in the newspaper *Glasnost* in 1999 and is widely available on the internet. For further reports on what Stalin said at the plenum see K. Simonov, *Glazami Cheloveka Moego Pokoleniya: Razmyshleniya o I.V. Staline*, Moscow 1989 pp. 240–4; A. Mikoyan, *Tak Bylo*, Moscow 1999 pp. 574–5; A. Resis (ed.), *Molotov Remembers*, Ivan R. Dee: Chicago 1993 pp. 313–16.

83. Cited by Gorlizki and Khlevniuk, *Cold Peace* p. 150.

84. For works which emphasise the role of factional politics in postwar Soviet foreign and domestic policy see: R. Conquest, *Power and Policy in the USSR: The Struggle for Stalin's Succession, 1945–1960*, Harper & Row: New York 1967; W.G. Hahn, *Postwar Soviet Politics: The Fall of Zhdanov and the Defeat of Moderation, 1946–1953*, Cornell University Press: Ithaca, NY 1982; A. Knight, *Beria; Stalin's First Lieutenant*, Princeton University Press: Princeton, NJ 1993; W.O. McCagg, *Stalin Embattled, 1943–1948*, Wayne State University Press: Detroit 1978; and G.D. Ra'anan, *International Policy Formation in the USSR: Factional 'Debates' during the Zhdanovshchina*, Archon Books: Hamden, Conn. 1983.

12 Cold War Confrontation: Stalin Embattled

1. L. Gibianskii, 'The Soviet–Yugoslav Split and the Cominform' in N. Naimark and L.Gibianskii (eds), *The Establishment of Communist Regimes in Eastern Europe, 1944–1949*, Westview Press: Boulder, Col. 1997. Gibianskii has published a number of

articles in English, Russian and other languages on the Stalin–Tito split and has been responsible for the publication of a number of valuable documents from the Soviet archives.

2. 'Na Poroge Pervogo Raskola v "Sotsialisticheskom Lagere"', *Istoricheskii Arkhiv*, no. 4, 1997; *Stalin and the Cold War, 1945–1953: A Cold War International History Project Documentary Reader*, September 1999 pp. 408–19; I. Banac (ed.), *The Diary of Georgi Dimitrov, 1933–1949*, Yale University Press: New Haven 2003 pp. 436–41.

3. 'Sekretnaya Sovetsko–Ugoslavskaya Perepiska 1948 goda', *Voprosy Istorii*, nos 4–5, 1992.

4. G. Procacci (ed.), *The Cominform: Minutes of the Three Conferences, 1947/1948/1949*, Feltrinelli: Milan 2004 pp. 611–21.

5. A.B. Ulam, *Titoism and the Cominform*, Harvard University Press: Cambridge, Mass. 1952 chap. 5.

6. *Vostochnaya Evropa v Dokumentakh Rossiiskikh Arkhivov, 1944–1953*, vol. 1, Moscow 1997 docs 267, 269, 272, 274, 289; *Sovetskii Faktor v Vostochnoi Evrope, 1944–1953*, vol. 1, Moscow 1999 docs 209–12.

7. W. Loth, *Stalin's Unwanted Children: The Soviet Union, the German Question and the Founding of the GDR*, Palgrave: London 1998 chap. 1

8. B. Ruhm von Oppen (ed.), *Documents on Germany under Occupation, 1945–1954*, Oxford University Press: New York 1955 pp. 128–31.

9. G.P. Kynin and J. Laufer (eds), *SSSR i Germanskii Vopros*, vol. 2, Moscow 2000 docs 121–3, 126–8, 137. See also R.B. Levering et al. (eds), *Debating the Origins of the Cold War*, Rowman & Littlefield: Lanham, Maryland 2002 doc. 2 pp. 157–9.

10. 'V.M. Molotov's Statement on the American Draft Treaty for the Disarmament and Demilitarisation of Germany', *Soviet News*, 11/7/46. The exchange between Molotov and Byrnes at the CFM is recorded in Arkhiv Vneshnei Politiki Rossiiskoi Federatsii F.431/II Op.2, D.3, Ll.149–58.

11. G.P. Kynin and J. Laufer (eds), *SSSR i Germanskii Vopros*, vol. 3, Moscow 2003 doc. 35.

12. *Sovetsko–Amerikanskie Otnosheniya, 1945–1948*, Moscow 2004 doc. 185. Stalin made the same argument in his meeting with the East German communists in January 1947.

13. E.S. Mason, 'Reflections on the Moscow Conference', *International Organisation*, vol. 1, no. 3, September 1947 p. 475. Mason also thought, however, that while difficult, it would be possible to arrive at an agreement with the Soviets about the establishment of some kind of liberal democratic regime in a united Germany. For a further analysis of the conference from the western point of view see A. Deighton, *The Impossible Peace: Britain, the Division of Germany and the Origins of the Cold War*, Clarendon Press: Oxford 1990 chap. 6.

14. *Vneshnyaya Politika Sovetskogo Souza 1947 god*, part 1, Moscow 1952 pp. 377–83, 534; 'K Itogam Soveshchaniya Ministrov Inostrannykh Del', *Pravda* 27/4/47. Many Soviet archive documents relating to the Moscow conference may be found in Kynin and Laufer (eds), *SSSR i Germanskii Vopros*, vol. 3. There was very extensive coverage of the conference in the Soviet press; as far as I can see, what the Soviets said in public did not differ much from what they said in private.

15. V.M. Molotov, *Problems of Foreign Policy*, Foreign Languages Publishing House: Moscow 1949 p. 488.

16. Ibid. pp. 503–9.

17. Deighton, *Impossible Peace* chap. 8.

18. Stalin's conversation with the SED leaders on 26 March 1948 in *Istoricheskii Arkhiv*, no. 2, 2002 pp. 9–25.

19. Von Oppen, *Documents* pp. 286–90. On the background to the London communiqué: M. Trachtenberg, *A Constructed Peace: The Making of the European Settlement, 1945–1963*, Princeton University Press: Princeton NJ 1999 pp. 78–91.

20. W. Stivers, 'The Incomplete Blockade: Soviet Zone Supply of West Berlin, 1948–1949', *Diplomatic History*, vol. 21, no. 4, Fall 1997. On Soviet policy in general: M.M.

Narinskii, 'The Soviet Union and the Berlin Crisis' in F. Gori and S. Pons (eds), *The Soviet Union and Europe in the Cold War, 1943–1953*, Macmillan: London 1996.

21. *Sovetsko–Amerikanskie Otnosheniya, 1945–1948* docs 281, 287.
22. Cited by C. Kennedy-Pipe, *Stalin's Cold War*, Manchester University Press: Manchester 1995 pp. 127–8.
23. M.D. Shulman, *Stalin's Foreign Policy Reappraised*, Harvard University Press; Cambridge, Mass. 1963 pp. 73–5. This book remains an essential text on Soviet foreign policy in the late Stalin era. Also of continuing value is W. Taubman, *Stalin's American Policy: From Entente to Détente to Cold War*, W.W. Norton: New York 1982.
24. *Vneshnyaya Politika Sovetskogo Souza 1949 god*, Moscow 1953 pp. 46–71, 88–94, 120–2.
25. Cited by D. Holloway, *Stalin & The Bomb: The Soviet Union and Atomic Energy, 1939–1956*, Yale University Press: New Haven 1994 p. 264.
26. See V. Mastny, *NATO in the Beholder's Eye: Soviet Perceptions and Policies, 1949–1956*, Cold War International History Project Working Paper no. 35, March 2002 and N.I. Egorova, 'Evropeiskaya Bezopastnost'' i "ugroza" NATO v Otsenkakh Stalinskogo Rukovodstva' in V. Gaiduk, N.I. Egorova and A.O. Chubar'yan (eds), *Stalinskoe Desyatiletie Kholodnoi Voiny*, Moscow 1999.
27. *Otnosheniya SSSR s GDR, 1919–1955gg*, Moscow 1974 doc. 114.
28. The historical debate on the so-called 'Stalin Note' may be followed in A. Phillips, *Soviet Policy Reconsidered: The Postwar Decade*, Greenwood Press: New York 1986; R. Steininger, *The German Question and the Stalin Note of 1952*, Columbia University Press: New York 1990; V. Mastny, *The Cold War and Soviet Insecurity*, Oxford University Press: Oxford 1996; J. Zarusky (ed.), *Die Stalin-Note vom 10.Marz 1952*, Munich 2002; R. van Dijk, *The Stalin Note Debate: Myth or Missed Opportunity for German Unification*, Cold War International History Project Working Paper no. 14, May 1996; G. Wettig's, 'The Soviet Union and Germany in the Late Stalin Period, 1950–1953' in Gori and Pons, *Soviet Union* and 'Stalin and German Reunification: Archival Evidence on Soviet Foreign Policy in Spring 1952', *Historical Journal*, vol. 37, no. 2, 1994; W. Loth, 'The Origins of Stalin's Note of 10 March 1952', *Cold War History*, vol. 4, no. 2, January 2004; A.M. Filitov's, 'Stalinskaya Diplomatiya i Germanskii Vopros: poslednii god' in *Stalinskoe Desyatiletie Kholodnoi Voiny* and 'Nota 10 Marta 1952 goda: Prodolzhaushchayasya Diskussiya' in B.M. Tupolev, *Rossiya i Germaniya*, Moscow 2004; J. Laufer, 'Die Stalin-Note vom 10. Marz 1952 im Lichte neuer Quellen', *Vierteljahrshefte für Zeitgeschichte*, January 2004.
29. Stalin, *Sochineniya* p. 224.
30. Report on Stalin's meetings with GDR leaders on 1 April and 7 April 1952, published in *Istochnik*, no. 3, 2003, quotes from pp. 122, 125. Translations of these documents may be found on the Cold War International History Project website.
31. *Otnosheniya SSSR s GDR, 1919–1955gg* doc. 118. This document was drafted by Molotov and Vyshinskii and corrected by Stalin. See *Politburo TsK VKP (b) i Sovet Ministrov SSSR, 1945–1953*, Moscow 2002 doc. 119.
32. *Stalin and the Cold War, 1945–1953* pp. 523–4.
33. Stalin, *Sochineniya*, vol. 16, Moscow 1997 pp. 98–9.
34. *Vneshnyaya Politika Sovetskogo Souza 1949 god* pp. 441ff.
35. B. Ponomaryov et al. (eds), *History of Soviet Foreign Policy, 1945–1970*, Progress Publishers: Moscow 1973.
36. In his original draft Malenkov included a proposal for a 50-year non-aggression pact between Britain, France, the USSR and the USA and the convening of an international conference to make a declaration on peace and related matters, but this whole section was crossed out by Stalin and the quoted words substituted for what was a much longer section presented in list form. Rossiiskii Gosudarstvennyi Arkhiv Sotsial'no-Politicheskoi Istorii (RGASPI) F.592, Op.1, D.6 L.25.
37. Shulman, *Stalin's Foreign Policy*.

38. Stalin, *Sochineniya* pp. 94–5.
39. See F.S. Burin, 'The Communist Doctrine of the Inevitability of War', *American Political Science Review*, vol. 57, no. 2, June 1963.
40. J. Stalin, *Economic Problems of Socialism in the USSR*, Foreign Languages Publishing House: Moscow 1952 pp. 37–41. On the background to the publication of this text see E. Pollack, *Conversations with Stalin on Questions of Political Economy*, Cold War International History Project Working Paper no. 33, July 2001.
41. On Soviet rearmament under Stalin: Holloway, *Stalin & the Bomb* chaps 11–12; Mastny, *NATO*, Y. Gorlizki and O. Khlevniuk, *Cold Peace: Stalin and the Soviet Ruling Circle, 1945–1953*, Oxford University Press: Oxford 2004 pp. 97–101; M. A. Evangelista, 'Stalin's Postwar Army Reappraised' in S.M. Lynn-Jones et al. (eds), *Soviet Military Policy*, MIT Press: Cambridge, Mass. 1989; N. Simonov, *Voenno-Promyshlennyi Kompleks SSSR v 1920–1950-e gody*, Moscow 1996 chap. 5; and *Stalin and the Cold War, 1945–1953* pp. 492–7.
42. *Vneshnyaya Politika Sovetskogo Souza 1949 god* pp. 162–3. The statement is translated in Holloway, *Stalin & the Bomb* pp. 265–6.
43. B. G. Bechhoefer, *Postwar Negotiations for Arms Control*, The Brookings Institution: Washington DC 1961 p. 134. A more sympathetic treatment of Soviet policy on disarmament, arms control and the nuclear question may be found in J.P. Morray, *From Yalta to Disarmament*, Monthly Review Press: New York 1961.
44. Holloway, *Stalin & the Bomb* p. 253.
45. Ibid. p. 242.
46. Ibid. p. 247.
47. Holloway, *Stalin & the Bomb* p. 250. For another analysis of Stalin's attitude to the bomb see V.M. Zubok, 'Stalin and the Nuclear Age' in J.L. Gaddis et al. (eds), *Cold War Statesmen Confront the Bomb: Nuclear Diplomacy since 1945*, Oxford University Press: Oxford 1999.
48. On Soviet policy towards Korea in the early postwar years: E. van Ree, *Socialism in One Zone: Stalin's Policy in Korea 1945–1947*, Berg: Oxford 1989.
49. *Sovetsko–Amerikanskie Otnosheniya, 1945–1948* doc. 68.
50. The texts of the 1945 and 1950 Sino-Soviet treaties may be found in R.L. Garthoff (ed.), *Sino-Soviet Military Relations*, Frederick A. Praeger: New York 1966 Appendices A & B.
51. Ponomaryov et al., *History* chap. 19.
52. The Soviet records of the Mikoyan conversations and of the Stalin–Mao correspondence may be found in *Sovetsko–Kitaiskie Otnosheniya, 1946–1950*, 2 vols, Moscow 2005.
53. *Stalin and the Cold War, 1945–1953* p. 482. The Russian version of this conversation may be found ibid. doc. 544.
54. See further Chen, Jian, *The Sino-Soviet Alliance and China's Entry into the Korean War*, Cold War International History Project Working Paper no. 1, June 1992 pp. 10–12.
55. K. Weathersby, '*Should We Fear This?' Stalin and the Danger of War with America*, Cold War International History Project Working Paper no. 39, July 2002. The quotes from Stalin that follow are from this paper.
56. See K. Weathersby, 'Stalin, Mao, and the End of the Korean War' in O.A. Westad (ed.), *Brothers in Arms: The Rise and Fall of the Sino-Soviet Alliance, 1945–1963*, Stanford University Press: Stanford 1998.
57. *Stalin and the Cold War, 1945–1953* p. 512.
58. See S.N. Goncharov et al., *Uncertain Partners: Stalin, Mao and the Korean War*, Stanford University Press: Stanford 1993.
59. See J. Brent and V.P. Naumov, *Stalin's Last Crime*, HarperCollins: New York 2003 chap. 10. The most authentic-sounding account of Stalin's death is that by his daughter, Svetlana: S. Alliluyeva, *20 Letters to a Friend*, Penguin: London 1968 pp. 13–20.

60. Stalin, *Sochineniya* p. 230.
61. *Stalin and the Cold War, 1945–1953* pp. 529–30.

13 Conclusion: Stalin in the Court of History

1. V. Sokolovskii, 'Velikii Podvig Sovetskogo Naroda', *Pravda* 9/5/54.
2. '75th Anniversary of the Birth of J.V. Stalin', *New Times*, no. 51, 1954; 'Joseph Stalin, 1979–1953', *New Times*, no. 52, 1955.
3. See D. Reynolds, *In Command of History: Churchill Fighting and Writing the Second World War*, Penguin Books: London 2005. Further: D. Reynolds, 'How the Cold War Froze the History of World War Two', Annual Liddell Hart Centre for Military Archives Lecture 2005, www.kcl.ac.uk/lhcma/info/lec05.htm.
4. D.M. Glantz, 'The Failures of Historiography: Forgotten Battles of the German–Soviet War', *Journal of Slavic Military Studies* 8, 1995.
5. Cited by S. Berthon and J. Potts, *Warlords*, Politico's Publishing: London 2005 pp. 166–7.
6. *Churchill and Stalin: Documents from British Archives*, FCO: London 2002 docs 77–78. The Russian version of Churchill's letter may be found in Rossiiskii Gosudarstvennyi Arkhiv Sotsial'no-Politicheskoi Istorii, F.82, Opis.2, D.110, L.820.

Select Bibliography

ARCHIVES

Russian Archives

Arkhiv Vneshnei Politiki Rossiiskoi Federatsii (AVPRF – Foreign Policy Archive of the Russian Federation)

Fond 6	Molotov's Secretariat
Fond 7	Vyshinskii's Secretariat
Fond 12	Dekanozov's Secretariat
Fond 0200	Gusev Papers
Fond 0511	Voroshilov Commission
Fond 0425	European Advisory Commission
Fond 0431	Council of Foreign Ministers
Fond 0432	Paris Peace Conference
Fond 0555	Tehran Conference
Fond 0556	Yalta Conference

Gosudarstvennyi Arkhiv Rossiiskoi Federatsii (GARF – State Archive of the Russian Federation)

Fond 9401	NKVD Reports

Rossiiskii Gosudarstvennyi Arkhiv Noveishei Istorii (RGANI – Russian State Archive of Recent History)

Fond 2	Central Committee Plenums

Rossiiskii Gosudarstvennyi Arkhiv Sotsial'no-Politicheskoi Istorii (RGASPI – Russian State Archive of Social-Political History)

Fond 17	International Department Files, Politburo Protocols, Sovinform Files
Fond 71	Stalin Secretariat
Fond 77	Zhdanov Papers
Fond 82	Molotov Papers
Fond 83	Malenkov Papers
Fond 359	Litvinov Papers
Fond 495	Comintern Files

Fond 558   Stalin Papers
Fond 592   19th Party Congress

American Archives

Averell Harriman Papers, Library of Congress Manuscript Division
Pamela Harriman Papers, Library of Congress Manuscript Division
Volkogonov Papers, Library of Congress Manuscript Division

British Archives

Public Records Office, London

Foreign Office, Cabinet and Prime Minister files on Anglo-Soviet relations

SECONDARY SOURCES

Newspapers and Periodicals

Pravda
Izvestiya
Krasnaya Zvezda
Voina i Rabochii Klass
Novoe Vremya/New Times
Bol'shevik
Mirovoe Khozyaistvo i Mirovaya Politika
World News and Views
The Communist International
Soviet War News/Soviet News
Voprosy Vneshnei Politiki (Central Committee internal bulletin: RGASPI F.17, Op.128)

Reference Works

D. Glantz et al., *Slaughterhouse: The Handbook of the Eastern Front*, Aberjona Press 2004
Kto Byl Kto v Velikoi Otechestvennoi Voine, 1941–1945, Moscow 2000
'Posetiteli Kremlevskogo Kabineta I.V. Stalina', *Istoricheskii Arkhiv*, no. 6, 1994; nos. 2, 3, 4,
    5–6, 1995; nos 2, 3, 4, 5–6, 1996; and no. 1, 1997
'Posetiteli Kremlevskogo Kabineta I.V. Stalina: Alfavitnyi Ukazatel', *Istoricheskii Arkhiv*,
    no. 4, 1998
B. Taylor, *Barbarossa to Berlin: A Chronology of the Campaigns on the Eastern Front, 1941 to
    1945*, 2 vols, Spellmount: Staplehurst, Kent 2004
Vtoraya Mirovaya Voina, 1939–1945: Al'bom Skhem, Moscow 1958

Speeches and Works

B. Franklin, *The Essential Stalin: Major Theoretical Writings, 1905–1952*, Croom Helm:
    London 1973
V.M. Molotov, *Problems of Foreign Policy*, Foreign Languages Publishing House: Moscow
    1949
V.A. Nevezhin, *Zastol'nye Rechi Stalina*, Moscow–St Petersburg 2003
I. Stalin, *O Velikoi Otechestvennoi Voine Sovetskogo Souza*, Moscow 1946
I. Stalin, *Sochineniya*, vol. 16 (1946–1952), Moscow 1997
J. Stalin, *On the Great Patriotic War of the Soviet Union*, Hutchinson: London 1943

N. Voznesenky, *War Economy of the USSR in the Period of the Great Patriotic War*, Foreign Languages Publishing House: Moscow 1948

K.E. Voroshilov, *Stalin i Vooruzhennye Sily SSSR*, Moscow 1951

Published Documents in Russian (listed by title and date of publication)

Vneshnyaya Politika Sovetskogo Souza, vols for 1941–1950, Moscow 1944–1953

Perepiska Predsedatelya Soveta Ministrov SSSR s Prezidentami SShA i Prem'er-Ministrami Velikobritanii vo vremya Velikoi Otechestvennoi Voiny, 1941–1945gg, Moscow 1957

Sovetsko–Frantsuzskie Otnosheniya vo vremya Velikoi Otechestvennoi 1941–1945gg, Moscow 1959

Sovetsko–Kitaiskie Otnosheniya, 1917–1957, Moscow 1959

Dokumenty i Materialy po Istorii Sovetsko–Pol'skikh Otnoshenii, vols 6–7, Moscow, 1969, 1973

Otnosheniya SSSR s GDR, 1919–1955gg, Moscow 1974

Sovetsko–Bolgarskie Otnosheniya i Svyazi, 1917–1944, Moscow 1976

Dokumenty i Materialy po Istorii Sovetsko–Chekhoslovatskikh Otnoshenii, vols 4–5, Moscow 1983, 1984

Sovetsko–Angliiskie Otnosheniya vo vremya Velikoi Otechestvennoi Voiny, 1941–1945, 2 vols, Moscow 1983

Sovetsko–Frantsuzskie Otnosheniya vo vremya Velikoi Otechestvennoi Voiny, 1941–1945, 2 vols, Moscow 1983

Sovetsko–Amerikanskie Otnosheniya vo vremya Velikoi Otechestvennoi Voiny, 1941–1945, 2 vols, Moscow 1984

Sovetskii Souz na Mezhdunarodnykh Konferentsiyakh perioda Velikoi Otechestvennoi Voiny, 1941–1945gg, 6 vols, Moscow 1984

Polpredy Soobshchayut: Sbornik Dokumentov ob Otnosheniyakh SSSR s Latviei, Litvoi i Estoniei, Avgust 1939g–Avgust 1940g, Moscow 1990

Dokumenty Vneshnei Politiki, vols 22–4, Moscow 1992, 1995, 1998, 2000

Sovetsko–Ugoslavskie Otnosheniya, 1917–1941gg, Moscow 1992

Nakanune Voiny: Materialy Soveshchaniya Vysshego Rukovodyashchego Sostava RKKA 23–31 Dekabrya, Moscow 1993 (in the series Russkii Arkhiv)

G.K. Zhukov v Bitve pod Moskvoi: Sbornik Dokumentov, Moscow 1994

Komintern i Vtoraya Mirovaya Voina, 2 vols, Moscow 1994, 1998

NKVD i Pol'skoe Podpol'e, 1944–1945, Moscow 1994

SSSR i Pol'sha, 1941–1945, Moscow 1994

SVAG, 1944–1949, Moscow 1994

Organy Gosudarstvennoi Bezopasnosti SSSR v Velikoi Otechestvennoi Voine, vols 1–3, Moscow 1995, 2000, 2003

Moskva Voennaya, 1941–1945, Moscow 1995

SSSR-Pol'sha: Mekhanizmy Podchineniya, 1944–1949gg, Moscow 1995

Stalingrad, 1942–1943, Moscow 1995

Evreiskii Antifashistskii Komitet v SSSR, 1941–1948, Moscow 1996

Glavnye Politicheskiye Organy Vooruzhennykh Sil SSSR v Velikoi Otechestvennoi Voine 1941–1945gg, Moscow 1996 (series Russkii Arkhiv)

SSSR i Germanskii Vopros, 1941–1949, 3 vols, Moscow 1996, 2000, 2003

Stavka VGK: Dokumenty i Materialy 1941–1945, Moscow 1996–1999

Katyn': Plenniki Neob'yavlennoi Voiny, Moscow 1997

Sovetsko–Yaponskaya Voina 1945 goda: Istoriya Voenno-Politicheskogo Protivoborstva Dvukh Derzhav v 30–40–e gody (series Russkii Arkhiv), Moscow 1997

Voina i Diplomatiya, 1941–1942, Moscow 1997

Vostochnaya Evropa v Dokumentakh Rossiiskikh Arkhivov, 2 vols, Moscow 1997, 1998

1941 God, 2 vols, Moscow 1998

Atomnyi Proekt SSSR: Dokumenty i Materialy, 3 vols, Moscow 1998–2002
Otnosheniya Rossii (SSSR) s Ugoslaviei, 1941–1945gg, Moscow 1998
Soveshchaniya Kominforma, 1947–1949, Moscow 1998
Tri Vizita A.Ya Vyshinskogo v Bukharest, 1944–1946, Moscow 1998
Sovetskii Faktor v Vostochnoi Evrope, 1944–1948, Moscow 1999
Zimnyaya Voina, 1939–1940, Moscow 1999
Moskva Poslevoennaya, 1945–1947, Moscow 2000
Sovetsko–Izrail'skie Otnosheniya, 1941–1949, Moscow 2000
Sovetsko–Rumynskie Otnosheniya, vol. 2, Moscow 2000
Sovetsko–Kitaiskie Otnosheniya, vols 4–5, Moscow 2000, 2005
Stalingradskaya Epopeya, Moscow 2000
Transil'vanskii Vopros: Vengero-Rumynskii Territorial'nyi Spor i SSSR, 1940–1946, Moscow 2000
Georgii Zhukov, Moscow 2001
Iz Varshavy . . . Dokumenty NKVD SSSR o Pol'skom Podpol'e, 1944–1945gg, Moscow 2001
Katyn', 1940–2000, Moscow 2001
Moskva i Vostochnaya Evropa, 1949–1953, Moscow 2002
Neizvestnaya Blokada, 2 vols, Moscow 2002
Politburo Tsk VKP (b) i Sovet Ministrov SSSR, 1945–1953, Moscow 2002
Stalingradskaya Bitva, 2 vols, Moscow 2002
Kurskaya Bitva, 2 vols, Moscow 2003
Sovetskaya Povsednevnost' i Massovoe Soznaniye, 1939–1945, Moscow 2003
Sovetskaya Zhizn', 1945–1953, Moscow 2003
Operatsiya 'Bagration', Moscow 2004
Sovetsko–Amerikanskie Otnosheniya, 1939–1945, Moscow 2004
Sovetsko–Amerikanskie Otnosheniya, 1945–1948, Moscow 2004
Stalin i Cherchill', Moscow 2004
'Zimnyaya Voina': Pabota nad Oshibkami Aprel'-Mai 1940g (Materialy Komissii Glavnogo Voennogo Soveta Krasnoi Armii po Obobshcheniu Opyta Finskoi Kampanii, Moscow 2004
Stalinskiye Deportatsii, 1928–1953, Moscow 2005
Ivan Mikhailovich Maiskii: Izbrannaya Perepiska s Rossiiskimi Korrespondentami, vol. 2, Moscow 2005
Lubyanka: Stalin i NKVD-NKGB-GUKR 'Smersh', 1939–1946, Moscow 2006

Published Documents in English

A.O. Chubaryan and H. Shukman (eds), *Stalin and the Soviet–Finnish War, 1939–1940*, Frank Cass: London 2002
Churchill and Stalin: Documents from British Archives, FCO: London 2002
A. Dallin and F.I. Firsov (eds), *Dimitrov & Stalin, 1934–1943*, Yale University Press: New Haven 2000
J. Degras (ed.), *The Communist International 1919–1943*, vol. 3, Frank Cass: London 1971
J. Degras (ed.), *Soviet Documents on Foreign Policy*, vol. 3 (1933–1941), Oxford University Press: London 1953
The Development of Soviet-Finnish Relations, London 1940
Documents on British Policy Overseas, series 1, vol. 2, HMSO: London 1985
Documents on Israeli–Soviet Relations, 1941–1953, Frank Cass: London 2000
Documents on Polish–Soviet Relations 1939–1945, 2 vols, Heinemann: London 1961
Foreign Relations of the United States: annual volumes, 1941–1946, Government Printing Office: Washington DC 1958–1970
Foreign Relations of the United States: The Conference of Berlin 1945, 2 vols, Government Printing Office: Washington DC 1960

Foreign Relations of the United States: The Conferences of Cairo and Tehran 1943, Government Printing Office: Washington DC 1961

Foreign Relations of the United States: The Conferences of Malta and Yalta, Government Printing Office: Washington DC 1955

K.M. Jensen (ed.), *Origins of the Cold War: The Novikov, Kennan and Roberts 'Long Telegrams' of 1946*, Washington 1991

W. LaFeber (ed.), *The Origins of the Cold War, 1941–1947*, John Wiley: New York 1971

Nazi–Soviet Relations, 1939–1941, Didier: New York 1948

'New Documents about Winston Churchill from Russian Archives', *International Affairs*, vol. 47, no. 5, 2001

A. Polonsky (ed.), *The Great Powers and the Polish Question, 1941–1945*, Orbis Books: London 1976

A. Polonsky and B. Drukier, *The Beginnings of Communist Rule in Poland*, Routledge & Kegan Paul: London 1980

G. Procacci (ed.), *The Cominform: Minutes of the Three Conferences 1947/1948/1949*, Feltrinelli: Milan 1994 (in Russian: *Soveshchaniya Kominforma, 1947, 1948, 1949: Dokumenty i Materialy*, Moscow 1998)

S. Redlich (ed.), *War, Holocaust and Stalinism: A Documentary History of the Jewish Anti-Fascist Committee in the USSR*, Harwood Academic Publishers: Luxembourg 1995

G. Ross (ed.), *The Foreign Office and the Kremlin: British Documents on Anglo-Soviet Relations 1941–1945*, Cambridge University Press: Cambridge 1984

J. Rubenstein and V.P. Naumov (eds), *Stalin's Secret Pogrom: The Postwar Inquisition of the Jewish Anti-Fascist Committee*, Yale University Press: New Haven 2001

B. Ruhm von Oppen (ed.) *Documents on Germany under Occupation, 1945–1954*, Oxford University Press: New York 1955

O.A. Rzheshevsky (ed.), *War and Diplomacy: The Making of the Grand Alliance (Documents from Stalin's Archive)*, Harwood Academic Publishers: Amsterdam 1996

Soviet Foreign Policy during the Patriotic War: Documents and Materials, 2 vols, Hutchinson: London 1944–1945

Stalin and the Cold War, 1945–1953: A Cold War International History Project Documentary Reader, Washington, DC 1999

Stalin's Correspondence with Churchill, Attlee, Roosevelt and Truman, 1941–1945, Lawrence & Wishart: London 1958

'Stalin, Czechoslovakia, and the Marshall Plan: New Documentation from Czechoslovak Archives', *Bohemia Band* no. 32, 1991

G. Takhnenko, 'Anatomy of a Political Decision: Notes on the Marshall Plan', *International Affairs*, July 1992

The Tehran, Yalta and Potsdam Conferences: Documents, Progress Publishers: Moscow 1969

The White House Papers of Harry L. Hopkins, Eyre & Spottiswoode: London 1949

'The Winter War (Documents on Soviet–Finnish Relations in 1939–1940)', *International Affairs*, nos 8 & 9, 1989.

Memoirs and Diaries

S. Alliluyeva, *20 Letters to a Friend*, Penguin: London 1968

I. Kh. Bagramyan, *Tak Shli My k Pobede*, Moscow 1998

I.Banac (ed.), *The Diary of Georgi Dimitrov, 1933–1949*, Yale University Press: New Haven 2003

W. Bedell Smith, *Moscow Mission, 1946–1949*, Heinemann: London 1950

V. Berezhkov, *History in the Making: Memoirs of World War II Diplomacy*, Progress Publishers: Moscow 1983

S. Bialer (ed.), *Stalin and his Generals: Soviet Military Memoirs of World War II*, Souvenir Press: New York 1969

A.H. Birse, *Memoirs of an Interpreter*, Michael Joseph: London 1967

S.S. Biruzov, *Sovetskii Soldat na Balkanakh*, Moscow 1963

C.E. Bohlen, *Witness to History, 1929–1969*, Weidenfeld & Nicolson: London 1973

F.E. Bokov, *Vesna Pobedy*, Moscow 1980

V. Chuikov, *The Beginning of the Road*, MacGibbon & Kee: London 1963

V.I. Chuikov, *Konets Tret'ego Reikha*, Moscow 1973

J.R. Deane, *The Strange Alliance*, Viking Press: New York 1947

M. Djilas, *Wartime*, Secker & Warburg: London 1977

I. Ehrenburg, *Post-War Years, 1945–1954*, MacGibbon & Kee: London 1966

I. Ehrenburg, *The War, 1941–1945*, MacGibbon & Kee: London 1964

F.I. Golikov, *On a Military Mission to Great Britain and the USA*, Progress Publishers: Moscow 1987

W.A. Harriman and E. Abel, *Special Envoy to Churchill and Stalin, 1941–1946*, Random House: New York 1975

L. Kaganovich, *Pamyatnye Zapiski*, Moscow 1996

G. Kennan, *Memoirs*, Hutchinson: London 1968

N. Kharlamov, *Difficult Mission*, Progress Publishers: Moscow 1983

Khrushchev Remembers, Sphere Books: London 1971

I.S. Konev, *Year of Victory*, Progress Publishers: Moscow 1969

I.S. Konev, *Zapiski Komanduyushchego Frontom, 1943–1945*, Moscow 1981

G.A. Kumanev, *Ryadom so Stalinym*, Moscow 1999

I.M. Maiskii, *Vospominaniya Sovetskogo Diplomata*, Moscow 1987

I.M. Maisky, *Memoirs of a Soviet Ambassador*, Hutchinson: London 1967

V.A. Malyshev diary, *Istochnik* no. 5, 1997

The Memoirs of Marshal Zhukov, Jonathan Cape: London 1971

A. Mikoyan, *Tak Bylo*, Moscow 1999

Lord Moran, *Winston Churchill: The Struggle for Survival, 1940–1965*, Sphere Books: London 1968

N.N. Novikov, *Vospominaniya Diplomata*, Moscow 1989

A. Resis (ed.), *Molotov Remembers*, Ivan R. Dee: Chicago 1993 (in Russian: F. Chuev, *Sto Sorok Besed s Molotovym*, Moscow 1991)

K.K. Rokossovskii, *Soldatskii Dolg*, Moscow 2002 (in English: *A Soldier's Duty*, Progress Publishers: Moscow 1970)

H.E. Salisbury (ed.), *Marshal Zhukov's Greatest Battles*, Sphere Books: London 1969

A.M. Samsonov (ed.), *9 Maya 1945 goda*, Moscow 1970

S.M. Shtemenko, *The Soviet General Staff at War, 1941–1945*, 2 vols, Progress Publishers: Moscow 1970, 1973

K. Simonov, *Glazami Cheloveka Moyevo Pokoleniya: Razmyshleniya o I.V. Staline*, Moscow 1990

P. Sudoplatov, *Special Tasks*, Warner Books: London 1995

A.M. Vasilevskii, *A Lifelong Cause*, Progress Publishers: Moscow 1981 (in Russian: *Delo vsei zhizni*, Moscow 1974)

A.I. Yeremenko, *Stalingrad*, Moscow 1961

M.V. Zakharov, *Stalingradskaya Epopeya*, Moscow 1968

G.K. Zhukov, *Vospominaniya i Razmyshleniya*, 10th edn, 3 vols, Moscow 1990

Books and Articles

G.M. Adibekov, E.N. Shakhnazarova and K.K. Shirinya, *Organizatsionnaya Struktura Kominterna, 1919–1943*, Moscow 1997

G. Alexopoulos, 'Amnesty 1945: The Revolving Door of Stalin's Gulag', *Slavic Review*, vol. 64, no. 2, Summer 2005

V.A. Anfilov, *Doroga k Tragedii Sopok Peruogo Goda*, Moscow 1997

A. Axell, *Marshal Zhukov*, Pearson: London 2003

A. Axell, *Stalin's War through the Eyes of his Commanders*, Arms and Armour Press: London 1997

S.J. Axelrod, 'The Soviet Union and Bretton Woods', *Slovo*, April 1995

J. Barber and M. Harrison, 'Patriotic War, 1941–1945' in R.G. Suny (ed.), *The Cambridge History of Russia*, vol. 3, Cambridge University Press: Cambridge 2006

N.I. Baryshnikov, 'Sovetsko–Finlyandskaya Voina 1939–1940gg', *Novaya i Noveishaya Istoriya*, no. 4, 1991

A. Beevor, *Berlin: The Downfall 1945*, Viking: London 2002

A. Beevor, *Stalingrad*, Penguin Books: London 1991

M. Beloff, *Soviet Policy in the Far East, 1944–1951*, Oxford University Press: London 1953

G. Bennett (ed.), *The End of the War in Europe, 1945*, HMSO: London 1996

S. Berthon and J. Potts, *Warlords*, Politico's Publishing: London 2005

L. Bezymenski, *The Death of Adolf Hitler: Unknown Documents from the Soviet Archives*, Michael Joseph: London 1968

N. Bjelakovic, 'Comrades and Adversaries: Yugoslav–Soviet Conflict in 1948', *East European Quarterly*, vol. 33, no. 1, 1999

T.K. Blauvelt, 'Military Mobilisation and National Identity in the Soviet Union', *War & Society*, vol. 21, no. 1, May 2003

H. Boog et al., *Germany and the Second World War*, vols 4 & 6, Clarendon Press: Oxford 1998, 2001

D. Brandenberger, *National Bolshevism: Stalinist Mass Culture and the Formation of Modern Russian National Identity, 1931–1956*, Harvard University Press: Cambridge, Mass. 2002

D. Brandenberger, 'Stalin, the Leningrad Affair and the Limits of Postwar Russocentrism', *Russian Review*, no. 63, April 2004

J. Brent and V.P. Naumov, *Stalin's Last Crime: The Plot against the Jewish Doctors, 1948–1953*, HarperCollins: New York 2003

R.J. Brody, *Ideology and Political Mobilisation: The Soviet Home Front during World War II*, The Carl Beck Papers in Russian and East European Studies no. 1104, University of Pittsburgh, Pittsburgh, Penn. 1994

J. Brooks, *Thank You, Comrade Stalin! Soviet Public Culture from Revolution to Cold War*, Princeton University Press: Princeton NJ 2000

A. Bullock, *Stalin and Hitler*, HarperCollins: London 1991

J. Burds, *The Early Cold War in Soviet West Ukraine*, Carl Beck Papers in Russian and East European Studies, no. 1505, January 2001

F.S. Burin, 'The Communist Doctrine of the Inevitability of War', *American Political Science Review*, vol. 57, no. 2, June 1963.

M.J. Carley, *1939: The Alliance That Never Was and the Coming of World War II*, Ivan R. Dee: Chicago 1999

M.J. Carley, '"A Situation of Delicacy and Danger": Anglo-Soviet Relations, August 1939–March 1940', *Contemporary European History*, vol. 8, no. 2, 1999

D. Carlton, *Churchill and the Soviet Union*, Manchester University Press: Manchester 2000

O.P. Chaney, *Zhukov*, University of Oklahoma Press: London 1996

J. Channon (ed.), *Politics, Society and Stalinism in the USSR*, Macmillan: London 1998

A. Chmielarz, 'Warsaw Fought Alone: Reflections on Aid to and the Fall of the 1944 Uprising', *Polish Review*, vol. 39, no. 4, 1994

A.O. Chubar'yan (ed.), *Voina i Politika, 1939–1941*, Moscow 1999

A.O. Chubar'yan and V.O. Pechatnov (eds), 'Molotov "the Liberal": Stalin's 1945 Criticism of his Deputy', *Cold War History*, vol. 1, no. 1, August 2000

J.M. Ciechanowski, *The Warsaw Rising of 1944*, Cambridge University Press: Cambridge 1974

A.M. Cienciala, 'General Sikorski and the Conclusion of the Polish–Soviet Agreement of July 30, 1941', *Polish Review*, vol. 41, no. 4, 1996

A.M. Cienciala, 'New Light on Oskar Lange as an Intermediary between Roosevelt and Stalin in Attempts to Create a New Polish Government', *Acta Poloniae Historica*, no. 73, 1996

D.S. Clemens, *Yalta*, Oxford University Press: Oxford 1970

M. Cox and C. Kennedy-Pipe, 'The Tragedy of American Diplomacy: Rethinking the Marshall Plan', *Journal of Cold War Studies*, Spring 2005

I.A. Damaskii, *Stalin i Razvedka*, Moscow 2004

N. Davies, *Rising '44: The Battle for Warsaw*, Pan Books: London 2004

S. Davies and J. Harris (eds), *Stalin*, Cambridge University Press: Cambridge 2003

L. E. Davis, *The Cold War Begins: Soviet–American Conflict over Eastern Europe*, Princeton University Press: Princeton NJ 1974

R.B. Day, *Cold War Capitalism: The View from Moscow, 1945–1975*, M.E. Sharpe: London 1995

D. De Santis, *The Diplomacy of Silence: The American Foreign Service, the Soviet Union and the Cold War, 1933–1947*, University of Chicago Press: Chicago 1979

I. Deutscher, *Stalin: A Political Biography*, Pelican: London 1966

L. Dobroszycki and J.S. Gurock (eds), *The Holocaust in the Soviet Union*, M.E. Sharpe: New York 1993

T. Dunmore, *Soviet Politics, 1945–53*, Macmillan: London 1984

D.J. Dunn, *Caught between Roosevelt and Stalin: America's Ambassadors to Moscow*, University Press of Kentucky: Lexington 1998

E. Duraczynski, 'The Warsaw Rising: Research and Disputes Continue', *Acta Poloniae Historica*, no. 75, 1997

Eric Duskin, *Stalinist Reconstruction and the Confirmation of a New Elite, 1945–1953*, Palgrave: London 2001

M. Dyczok, *The Grand Alliance and the Ukrainian Refugees*, Macmillan: London 2000

M. Edele, 'Soviet Veterans as an Entitlement Group, 1945–1955', *Slavic Review*, vol. 65, no. 1 2006

R. Edmonds, *The Big Three*, Penguin Books: London 1991

N.I. Egorova and A.O. Chubar'yan, *Kholodnaya Voina, 1945–1965*, Moscow 2003

N.I. Egorova and A.O. Chubar'yan, *Kholodnaya Voina i Politika Razryadki*, Moscow 2003

J. Erickson, 'Barbarossa: June 1941: Who Attacked Whom', *History Today*, July 2001

J. Erickson, *The Road to Berlin*, Weidenfeld & Nicolson: London 1983

J. Erickson, *The Road to Stalingrad*, Harper & Row: New York 1975

J. Erickson, 'Threat Identification and Strategic Appraisal by the Soviet Union, 1930–1941' in E.R. May (ed.), *Knowing One's Enemies*, Princeton University Press: Princeton NJ 1984

J. Erickson and D. Dilks (eds), *Barbarossa: The Axis and the Allies*, Edinburgh University Press: Edinburgh 1994

F. Falin, *Vtoroi Front*, Moscow 2000

H. Feis, *Churchill–Roosevelt–Stalin*, Princeton University Press: Princeton NJ 1957

A.M. Filitov, 'Nota 10 Marta 1952 goda: Prodolzhaushchayasya Diskussiya' in B.M. Tupolev, *Rossiya i Germaniya*, Moscow 2004

D. Filtzer, *Soviet Workers and Late Stalinism*, Cambridge University Press: Cambridge 2002

I. Fleischhauer, 'The Molotov–Ribbentrop Pact: The German Version', *International Affairs*, August 1991

M. H. Folly, *Churchill, Whitehall and the Soviet Union, 1940–1945*, Macmillan 2000

J.L. Gaddis, *We Now Know: Rethinking Cold War History*, Clarendon Press: Oxford 1997

V. Gaiduk and N.I. Egorova (eds), *Stalin i Kholodnaya Voina*, Moscow 1997

V. Gaiduk, N.I. Egorova and A.O. Chubar'yan (eds), *Stalinskoe Desyatiletie Kholodnoi Voiny*, Moscow 1999

M.P. Gallagher, *The Soviet History of World War II*, Frederick A. Praeger: New York 1963

M.A. Gareev, *Polkovodtsy Pobedy i ikh Voennoe Naslediye*, Moscow 2004

J. and C. Garrard (eds), *World War 2 and the Soviet People*, St. Martin's Press: New York 1993

R.L. Garthoff (ed.), *Sino-Soviet Military Relations*, Praeger: New York 1966

V. Gavrilov and E. Gorbunov, *Operatsiya 'Ramzai'*, Moscow 2004

L. Ya. Gibianskii, 'Doneseniya Ugoslavskogo Posla v Moskve o Otsenkakh Rukovodstvom SSSR Potsdamskoi Konferentsii i Polozheniya v Vostochnoi Evrope', *Slavyanovedeniye*, no. 1, 1994

L. Ya. Gibianskii, *Sovetskii Souz i Novaya Ugoslaviya, 1941–1947*, Moscow 1987

U.S. Girenko, *Stalin–Tito*, Moscow 1991

D.M. Glantz, *Barbarossa: Hitler's Invasion of Russia 1941*, Tempus Publishing: Stroud 2001

D.M. Glantz, *The Battle for Leningrad, 1941–1944*, University Press of Kansas: Lawrence, Kansas 2002

D.M. Glantz, *Colossus Reborn: The Red Army at War, 1941–1943*, University Press of Kansas: Lawrence, Kansas 2005

D.M. Glantz, *Kharkov 1942: Anatomy of a Military Disaster through Soviet Eyes*, Ian Allan Publishing: Shepperton, Surrey 1998

D.M. Glantz, *Zhukov's Greatest Defeat: The Red Army's Epic Disaster in Operation Mars, 1942*, University Press of Kansas: Lawrence, Kansas 1999

D.M. Glantz and J. House, *When Titans Clashed: How the Red Army Stopped Hitler*, University Press of Kansas: Lawrence, Kansas 1995

M.E. Glantz, *FDR and the Soviet Union: The President's Battles over Foreign Policy*, University Press of Kansas: Lawrence, Kansas 2005

S.N. Goncharov et al., *Uncertain Partners: Stalin, Mao and the Korean War*, Stanford University Press: Stanford 1993

F. Gori and S. Pons (eds), *The Soviet Union and Europe in the Cold War, 1943–1953* Macmillan: London 1996

Yu. Gor'kov, *Gosudarstvennyi Komitet Oborony Postanovlyaet (1941–1945)*, Moscow 2002

Y. Gorlizki, 'Ordinary Stalinism: The Council of Ministers and the Soviet Neopatrimonial State, 1945–1953', *Journal of Modern History*, vol. 74, no. 4, 2002

Y. Gorlizki, 'Party Revivalism and the Death of Stalin', *Slavic Review*, vol. 54, no. 1, 1995

Y. Gorlizki, 'Stalin's Cabinet: The Politburo and Decision Making in the Post-war Years, *Europe–Asia Studies*, vol. 53, no. 2, 2001

Y. Gorlizki and O. Khlevniuk, *Cold Peace: Stalin and the Soviet Ruling Circle, 1945–1953*, Oxford University Press: Oxford 2004

G. Gorodetsky, *Grand Delusion: Stalin and the German Invasion of Russia*, Yale University Press: New Haven 1999

G. Gorodetsky (ed.), *Soviet Foreign Policy, 1917–1991*, Frank Cass: London 1994

G. Gorodetsky, 'The Soviet Union and the Creation of the State of Israel', *The Journal of Israeli History*, vol. 22, no. 1, 2003

P.R. Gregory (ed.), *Behind the Façade of Stalin's Command Economy*, Hoover Institution Press: Stanford 2001

A.A. Gromyko et al., *Bor'ba SSSR v OON za Mir, Bezopasnost' i Sotrudnichestvo*, Moscow 1986

J.T. Gross, *Revolution from Abroad: The Soviet Conquest of Poland's Western Ukraine and Western Belorussia*, Princeton University Press: Princeton NJ 1988

W.G. Hahn, *Postwar Soviet Politics: The Fall of Zhdanov and the Defeat of Moderation, 1946–53*, Cornell University Press: Ithaca, NY 1982

T.T. Hammond (ed.), *The Anatomy of Communist Takeovers*, Yale University Press: New Haven 1975

M. Harrison, *Accounting for War: Soviet Production, Employment, and the Defence Burden, 1940–1945*, Cambridge University Press: Cambridge 1996

M. Harrison, *The Economics of World War II: Six Great Powers in International Comparison*, Cambridge University Press: Cambridge 1998

M. Harrison, *Soviet Planning in Peace and War 1938–1945*, Cambridge University Press: Cambridge 1985

M. Harrison, 'The USSR and the Total War: Why Didn't the Soviet Economy Collapse in 1942?' in R. Chickering et al. (eds), *A World at Total War: Global Conflict and the Politics of Destruction, 1939–1945*, Cambridge University Press: Cambridge 2005

T. Hasegawa, *Racing the Enemy: Stalin, Truman, and the Surrender of Japan*, Harvard University Press: Cambridge, Mass. 2005

J. Haslam, 'Stalin's Fears of a Separate Peace, 1942', *Intelligence and National Security*, vol. 8, no. 4, October 1993

J.S.A. Hayward, *Stopped at Stalingrad: The Luftwaffe and Hitler's Defeat in the East, 1942–1943*, University Press of Kansas: Lawrence, Kansas 1998

P.G.H. Holdich, 'A Policy of Percentages? British Policy and the Balkans after the Moscow Conference of October 1944', *International History Review*, February 1987

D. Holloway, 'Jockeying for Position in the Postwar World: Soviet Entry into the War with Japan in August 1945' in T. Hasegawa (ed.), *Reinterpreting the End of the Pacific War: Atomic Bombs and the Soviet Entry into the War*, Stanford University Press: Stanford forthcoming

D. Holloway, *Stalin & the Bomb*, Yale University Press: New Haven 1994

G. Hosking, 'The Second World War and Russian National Consciousness', *Past & Present*, no. 175, 2002

J.M. House and D.M. Glantz, *The Battle of Kursk*, University Press of Kansas: Lawrence, Kansas 1999

Istoriya Velikoi Otechestvennoi Voiny Sovetskogo Souza 1941–1945, 6 vols, Moscow 1960–1964

Istoriya Vtoroi Mirovoi Voiny, 1939–1945, 12 vols, Moscow 1973–1982

R. Ivanov, *Stalin i Souzniki, 1941–1945 gg*, Smolensk 2000

R.F. Ivanov and N.K. Petrova, *Obshchestvenno-Politicheskie Sily SSSR i SShA v Gody Voiny, 1941–1945*, Voronezh 1995

H. and M. James, 'The Origins of the Cold War: Some New Documents', *Historical Journal*, vol. 37, no. 3, 1994

G. Jukes, *Hitler's Stalingrad Decisions*, University of California Press: Berkeley 1985

G. Jukes, *Stalingrad: The Turning Point*, Ballantine Books: New York 1968

V. Karpov, *Generalissimus*, 2 vols, Moscow 2003

C. Kennedy-Pipe, *Stalin's Cold War: Soviet Strategies in Europe, 1943–1956*, Manchester University Press: Manchester 1995

I. Kershaw and M. Lewin, *Stalinism and Nazism*, Cambridge University Press: Cambridge 1997

L. Kettenacker, 'The Anglo-Soviet Alliance and the Problem of Germany, 1941–1945', *Journal of Contemporary History*, vol. 17, 1982

A. Knight, *Beria: Stalin's First Lieutenant*, Princeton University Press: Princeton NJ 1993

J. Knight, 'Russia's Search for Peace: The London Council of Foreign Ministers, 1945', *Journal of Contemporary History*, vol. 13, 1978

A.J. Kochavi, 'Anglo-Soviet Differences over a Policy towards War Criminals', *SEER*, vol. 69, no. 3, July 1991

T.U. Kochetkova, 'Voprosy Sozdaniya OON i Sovetskaya Diplomatiya', *Otechestvennaya Istoriya*, no. 1, 1995

N.V. Kochkin, 'Anglo-Sovetskii Souznyi Dogovor 1942 goda i Nachalo "Kholodnoi Voiny"', *Voprosy Istorii*, no. 1, 2006

N.V. Kochkin, 'SSSR, Angliya, SShA i "Turetskii Krizis" 1945–1947gg', *Novaya i Noveishaya Istoriya*, no. 3, 2002

H. Kohn, 'Pan-Slavism and World War II', *American Political Science Review*, vol. 46, no. 3 1952

N. Ya Komarov and G.A. Kumanev, *Blokada Leningrada: 900 Geroicheskikh Dnei, 1941–1944*, Moscow 2004

M. Korobochin, 'Soviet Policy toward Finland and Norway, 1947–1949', *Scandinavian Journal of History*, vol. 20, no. 3, 1995

V.V. Korovin, *Sovetskaya Razvedka i Kontrrazvedka v gody Velikoi Otechestvennoi Voiny*, Moscow 2003

A. Koshkin, *Yaponskii Front Marshala Stalina*, Moscow 2004

G.V. Kostyrchenko, *Out of the Shadows: Anti-Semitism in Stalin's Russia*, Prometheus Books: New York 1995

G.V. Kostyrchenko, *Tainaya Politika Stalina*, Moscow 2001

E. Kul'kov et al., *Voina, 1941–1945*, Moscow 2004

Y. Lahav, *Soviet Policy and the Transylvanian Question (1940–1946)*, Research Paper no. 27, Soviet and East European Research Centre, Hebrew University of Jerusalem, July 1977

J. Laloy, 'Le General de Gaulle et L'URSS, 1943–1945', *Revue d'istoire diplomatique*, no. 4, 1994

A. Lane and H. Temperley (eds), *The Rise and Fall of the Grand Alliance, 1941–1945*, Macmillan: London 1995

J. Laufer, 'Die Stalin-Note vom 10. Marz 1952 im Lichte neuer Quellen', *Vierteljahrshefte für Zeitgeschichte*, January 2004

N. Lebedeva, *Katyn'*, Moscow 1994

A.M. Ledovskii, *SSSR i Stalin v Sud'bakh Kitaya*, Moscow 1999

M.P. Leffler and D.S. Painter (eds), *Origins of the Cold War*, Routledge: London 2005

C. Leitz (ed.), *Spain in an International Context*, Berghahn Books: Oxford 1999

R.B. Levering, V.O. Pechatnov et al., *Debating the Origins of the Cold War: American and Russian Perspectives*, Rowman & Littlefield: Lanham, Maryland 2002

S.J. Linz (ed.), *The Impact of World War II on the Soviet Union*, Rowman & Allanheld 1985

W. Loth, 'The Origins of Stalin's Note of 10 March 1952', *Cold War History*, vol. 4, no. 2, January 2004

W. Loth, *Stalin's Unwanted Children: The Soviet Union, the German Question and the Founding of the GDR*, Palgrave: London 1998

R.C. Lukas, 'The Big Three and the Warsaw Uprising', *Military Affairs*, vol. 39, no. 3, 1975

D.J. Macdonald, 'Communist Bloc Expansion in the Early Cold War', *International Security*, vol. 20, no. 3, 1995/6

R.H. McNeal, 'Roosevelt Through Stalin's Spectacles', *The International Journal*, vol. 2, no. 18, 1963

R.H. McNeal, *Stalin: Man and Ruler*, Macmillan Press: London 1998

W.H. McNeill, *America, Britain and Russia: Their Co-operation and Conflict, 1941–1946*, Oxford University Press: London 1953

V.L. Mal'kov, 'Domestic Factors in Stalin's Atomic Diplomacy' in P.M. Morgan and K.L. Nelson (eds), *Re-Viewing the Cold War, Domestic Factors and Foreign Policy in the East–West Confrontation*, Praeger: Westport, Conn. 2000

V.V. Mar'ina, 'Sovetskii Souz i Chekhoslovakiya, 1945 god', *Novaya i Noveishaya Istoriya* no. 3, 2001

V. Mar'ina, *Zakarpatskaya Ukraina (Podkarpatskaya Rus') v Politike Benesha i Stalina*, Moscow 2003

E. Mark, *Revolution by Degrees: Stalin's National-Front Strategy for Europe, 1941–1947*, Cold War International History Project Working Paper no. 31, 2001

T. Martin, *The Affirmative Action Empire: Nations and Nationalism in the Soviet Union, 1929–1939*, Cornell University Press: Ithaca NY 2001

A.A. Maslov, 'Forgiven by Stalin – Soviet Generals Who Returned from German Prisons in 1941–45 and Who Were Rehabilitated', *Journal of Slavic Military Studies*, vol. 12, no. 2, June 1999

V. Mastny, *The Cold War and Soviet Insecurity: The Stalin Years*, Oxford University Press: Oxford 1996

V. Mastny, *NATO in the Beholder's Eye: Soviet Perceptions and Policies, 1949–1956*, Cold War International History Project Working Paper no. 35, March 2002

V. Mastny, *Russia's Road to the Cold War*, Columbia University Press: New York 1979

J. Matthaus, 'Operation Barbarossa and the Onset of the Holocaust' in C. Browning, *The Origins of the Final Solution*, University of Nebraska Press: Lincoln NB 2004

E. Mawdsley, 'Crossing the Rubicon: Soviet Plans for Offensive War in 1940–1941', *International History Review*, December 2003

E. Mawdsley, *Thunder in the East: The Nazi-Soviet War, 1941–1945*, Hodder Arnold: London 2005

S. Mazov, 'The USSR and the Former Italian Colonies, 1945–1950', *Cold War History*, vol. 3, no. 3, April 2003.

R. and Z. Medvedev, *The Unknown Stalin*, Overlook Press: Woodstock and New York 2004

Z. Medvedev, *Stalin i Evreiskaya Problema*, Moscow 2003

M.I. Mel'tukhov, ' "Narodny Front" dlya Finlyandii? (K Voprosu o Tselyakh Sovetskogo Rukovodstva v Voine s Finlyandiei 1939–1940gg', *Otechestvennaya Istoriya*, no. 3, 1993

M.I. Mel'tukhov, 'Operatsiya "Bagration" i Varshavskoe Vosstaniye 1944 goda', *Voprosy Istorii*, no. 11, 2004

M.I. Mel'tukhov, *Upushchennyi Shans Stalina*, Moscow 2000

C. Merridale, *Ivan's War: The Red Army 1939–45*, Faber: London 2005

S. Merritt Miner, *Between Churchill and Stalin: The Soviet Union, Great Britain, and the Origins of the Grand Alliance*, University of North Carolina Press: Chapel Hill NC 1988

S. Merritt Miner, *Stalin's Holy War: Religion, Nationalism and Alliance Politics, 1941–1945*, University of North Carolina Press: Chapel Hill NC 2003

J.P. Morray, *From Yalta to Disarmament*, Monthly Review Press: New York 1961

G.P. Murashko, 'Fevral'skii Krizis 1948g v Chekhoslovakii i Sovetskoe Rukovodstvo', *Novaya i Noveishaya Istoriya*, no. 3, 1998

G.P. Murashko and A.F. Noskova, 'Stalin and the National-Territorial Controversies in Eastern Europe, 1945–1947 (Parts 1 & 2)', *Cold War History*, vol. 1, no. 3, 2001, vol. 2, no. 1 2001

D. Murphy, *What Stalin Knew: The Enigma of Barbarossa*, Yale University Press: New Haven 2005

B. Murray, *Stalin, the Cold War and the Division of China*, Cold War International History Project Working Paper, 12 June 1995

M.Yu. Myagkov (ed.), *Mirovye Voiny XX Veka: Vtoraya Mirovaya Voina (Dokumenty i Materialy)*, vols 3–4, Moscow 2002

M.Yu. Myagkov, 'SSSR, SShA i Problema Pribaltiki v 1941–1945godakh', *Novaya i Noveishaya Istoriya*, no. 1, 2005

N.M. Naimark, 'Cold War Studies and New Archival Materials on Stalin', *Russian Review*, no. 61 (January 2002)

N.M. Naimark, 'Post-Soviet Russian History on the Emergence of the Soviet Bloc', *Kritika*, vol. 5, no. 3, Summer 2004

N.M. Naimark, *The Russians in Germany: A History of the Soviet Zone of Occupation, 1945–1949*, Harvard University Press: Cambridge, Mass. 1995

N.M. Naimark, 'Stalin and Europe in the Postwar Period, 1945–53', *Journal of Modern European History*, vol. 2, no. 1, 2004

N. Naimark and L.Gibianskii (eds), *The Establishment of Communist Regimes in Eastern Europe, 1944–1949*, Westview Press: Boulder, Col. 1997

M.M. Narinskii, 'Moscou et le Gouvernement provisoire du général de Gaulle', *Relations internationales*, no. 108, 2001

M.M. Narinskii et al. (eds), *Kholodnaya Voina*, Moscow 1995

J. Nevakivi, 'A Decisive Armistice 1944–1947: Why Was Finland Not Sovietized?' *Scandinavian Journal of History*, vol. 19, no. 2, 1994

V.A. Nevezhin, 'The Pact with Germany and the Idea of an "Offensive War (1939–1941)"', *Journal of Slavic Military Studies*, vol. 8, no. 4, 1995

L.N. Nezhinskii (ed.), *Sovetskaya Vneshnyaya Politika v Gody 'Kholodnoi Voiny'*, Moscow 1995

R. Nisbet, *Roosevelt and Stalin*, Regnery Gateway: Washington DC 1988

R. Overy, *The Dictators: Hitler's Germany and Stalin's Russia*, Allen Lane: London 2004

R. Overy, *Russia's War*, Penguin Books: London 1998

R. Overy, *Why the Allies Won*, Jonathan Cape: London 1995

S.D. Parrish and M.M. Narinsky, *New Evidence on the Soviet Rejection of the Marshall Plan, 1947*, Cold War International History Project Working Paper no. 9, March 1994

T.G. Paterson, *Soviet–American Confrontation: Postwar Reconstruction and the Origins of the Cold War*, Johns Hopkins University Press: Baltimore 1973

V.O. Pechatnov, 'The Allies are Pressing on You to Break Your Will': Foreign Policy Correspondence between Stalin and Molotov and other Politburo Members, September 1945–December 1946, Cold War International History Project, Working Paper No. 26, September 1999

V.O. Pechatnov, *The Big Three after World War II: New Documents on Soviet Thinking about Postwar Relations with the United States and Great Britain*, Cold War International History Project Working Paper no. 13, 1995

V. Pechatnov, 'Exercise in Frustration: Soviet Foreign Propaganda in the Early Cold War, 1945–47', *Cold War History*, vol. 1, no. 2, January 2001

V.O. Pechatnov, 'Moskovskoe Posol'stvo Averella Garrimana', *Novaya i Noveishaya Istoriya*, nos 3–4, 2002

V.O. Pechatnov, 'The Rise and Fall of *Britansky Soyuznik*', *Historical Journal*, vol. 41, no. 1, 1998

A. Perlmutter, *FDR & Stalin*, University of Missouri Press: Columbia 1993

P.V. Petrov and V.N. Stepakov, *Sovetsko–Finlyanskaya Voina, 1939–1940*, 2 vols, St Petersburg 2003

N.K. Petrovka, *Antifashistskie Komitety v SSSR: 1941–1945gg*, Moscow 1999

A. Phillips, *Soviet Policy Reconsidered: The Postwar Decade*, Greenwood Press: New York 1986

H. Piortrowski, 'The Soviet Union and the Renner Government of Austria, April–November 1945', *Central European History*, vol. 20 nos 3/4, 1987

C. Pleshakov, *Stalin's Folly*, Houghton Mifflin: Boston 2005

E. Pollack, *Conversations with Stalin on Questions of Political Economy*, Cold War International History Project Working Paper no. 33, July 2001

B. Ponomaryov et al. (eds), *History of Soviet Foreign Policy, 1945–1970*, Progress Publishers: Moscow 1973

S. Pons, *Stalin and the Inevitable War, 1936–1941*, Frank Cass: London 2002

S. Pons, 'Stalin, Togliatti, and the Origins of the Cold War in Europe', *Journal of Cold War Studies*, vol. 3, no. 2, Spring 2001.

S. Pons and A. Romano, *Russia in the Age of Wars, 1914–1945*, Feltrinelli: Milan 2000

L.V. Pozdeeva, *London–Moskva: Britanskoe Obshchestvennoe Mhenie i SSSR*, Moscow 2000

L.V. Pozdeeva, 'Sovetskaya Propaganda na Angliu v 1941–1945 godax', *Voprosy Istorii*, no. 7, 1998

R.C. Raack, *Stalin's Drive to the West, 1938–1945*, Stanford University Press: Stanford, CA 1995

G. D. Ra'anan, *International Policy Formation in the USSR: Factional 'Debates' during the Zhdanovshchina*, Archon Books: Hamden, Conn. 1983

E. Radzinsky, *Stalin*, Hodder & Stoughton: London 1997

F.S. Raine, 'Stalin and the Creation of the Azerbaijan Democratic Party in Iran, 1945', *Cold War History*, vol. 2, no. 2, October 2001

D. Rayfield, *Stalin and his Hangmen*, Viking: London 2004

C. Read (ed.), *The Stalin Years*, Palgrave: London 2003

E. van Ree, *The Political Thought of Joseph Stalin: A Study in Twentieth Century Revolutionary Patriotism*, Routledge: London 2002

E. van Ree, *Socialism in One Zone: Stalin's Policy in Korea, 1945–1947*, Berg: Oxford 1989

R. Reese, *Stalin's Reluctant Soldiers*, University Press of Kansas: Lawrence, Kansas 1996

A. Resis, 'The Churchill–Stalin Secret "Percentages" Agreement on the Balkans, Moscow, October 1944', *American Historical Review*, April 1978

A. Resis, 'The Fall of Litvinov: Harbinger of the German–Soviet Non-Aggression Pact', *Europe–Asia Studies*, vol. 52, no. 1, 2000

A. Resis, *Stalin, the Politburo, and the Onset of the Cold War, 1945–1946*, The Carl Beck Papers in Russian and East European Studies no. 701, April 1988

D. Reynolds et al., *Allies at War: The Soviet, American and British Experience, 1939–1945*, Macmillan: London 1994

D. Reynolds, 'The "Big Three" and the Division of Europe, 1945–1948', *Diplomacy & Statecraft*, vol. 1, no. 2, 1990

D. Reynolds, *In Command of History: Churchill Fighting and Writing the Second World War*, Penguin Books: London 2005

D. Reynolds (ed.), *The Origins of the Cold War in Europe*, Yale University Press: New Haven 1994

A.J. Rieber, 'Civil Wars in the Soviet Union', *Kritika*, vol. 4, no. 1, Winter 2003

A.J. Rieber, 'The Crack in the Plaster: Crisis in Romania and the Origins of the Cold War', *Journal of Modern History*, no. 76, March 2004

A.J. Rieber, 'Stalin: Man of the Borderlands', *American Historical Review*, no. 5, 2001

A.J. Rieber, *Zhdanov in Finland*, Carl Beck Papers in Russian and East European Studies, no. 1107, University of Pittsburgh, February 1995

C.A. Roberts, 'Planning for War: The Red Army and the Catastrophe of 1941', *Europe–Asia Studies*, vol. 47, no. 8, 1995

Dzh. Roberts, 'Cherchil' i Stalin: Epizody Anglo-Sovetskikh Otnoshenii (Sentyabr' 1939–Iun' 1941 goda)' in A.O. Chubar'yan (ed.), *Voina i Politika, 1939–1941*, Moscow 1999

G. Roberts, 'The Alliance that Failed: Moscow and the Triple Alliance Negotiations, 1939', *European History Quarterly*, vol. 26, no. 3, 1996

G. Roberts, 'Beware Greek Gifts: The Churchill–Stalin "Percentages Agreement" of October 1944', *Mir Istorii*, www/historia.ru/2003/01/roberts.htm

G. Roberts, 'Ideology, Calculation and Improvisation: Spheres of Influence in Soviet Foreign Policy, 1939–1945', *Review of International Studies*, vol. 25, October 1999

G. Roberts, 'From Non-Aggression Treaty to War: Documenting Nazi–Soviet Relations, 1939–1941', *History Review*, December 2001

G. Roberts, 'Litvinov's Lost Peace, 1941–1946', *Journal of Cold War Studies*, vol. 4, no. 2, 2002

G. Roberts, 'Moscow and the Marshall Plan: Politics, Ideology and the Onset of Cold War, 1947', *Europe–Asia Studies*, vol. 46, no. 8, 1994

G. Roberts, 'Sexing up the Cold War: New Evidence on the Molotov–Truman Talks of April 1945', *Cold War History*, vol. 4, no. 3, April 2004

G. Roberts, 'Soviet Policy and the Baltic States, 1939–1940: A Reappraisal', *Diplomacy & Statecraft*, vol. 6, no. 3, 1995

G. Roberts, *The Soviet Union and the Origins of the Second World War*, Macmillan: London 1995

G. Roberts, *The Soviet Union in World Politics: Revolution, Coexistence and the Cold War, 1945–1991*, Routledge: London 1998

G. Roberts (ed.), *Stalin – His Times and Ours*, Irish Association for Russian and East European Studies: Dublin 2005

G. Roberts, 'Stalin and Foreign Intelligence during the Second World War' in E. O'Halpin et al., *Intelligence, Statecraft and International Power*, Irish Academic Press: Dublin 2006

G. Roberts, 'Stalin, the Pact with Nazi Germany and the Origins of Postwar Soviet Diplomatic Historiography', *Journal of Cold War Studies*, vol. 4, no. 3, Summer 2002

G. Roberts, *The Unholy Alliance: Stalin's Pact with Hitler*, I.B. Tauris: London 1989

G. Roberts, *Victory at Stalingrad: The Battle That Changed History*, Pearson/Longman: London 2002

W.R. Roberts, *Tito, Mihailovic and the Allies, 1941–1945*, Rutgers University Press: New Brunswick NJ 1973

N.E. Rosenfeldt et al. (eds), *Mechanisms of Power in the Soviet Union*, Macmillan: London 2000

L. Rotundo, 'Stalin and the Outbreak of War in 1941', *Journal of Contemporary History*, vol. 24, 1989

L. Rotundo (ed.), *Battle for Stalingrad: The 1943 Soviet General Staff Study*, Pergamon-Brassey's: London 1989

I.V. Rubtsov, *Marshaly Stalina*, Moscow 2006

L. Rucker, *Moscow's Surprise: The Soviet–Israeli Alliance of 1947–1949*, Cold War International History Project Working Paper no. 46

E.V. Rusakova, *Polkovodtsy*, Moscow 1995

O.A. Rzheshevskii, 'Poslednii Shturm: Zhukov ili Konev', *Mir Istorii* http://gpw.tellur.ru.

O.A. Rzheshevskii (ed.), *Vtoraya Mirovaya Voina*, Moscow 1995

O.A. Rzheshevskii and O. Vekhvilyainen (eds), *Zimnyaya Voina 1939–1940*, vol.1, Moscow 1999

V.P. Safronov, *SSSR-SShA-Yaponiya v Gody 'Kholodnoi Voiny' 1945–1960gg*, Moscow 2003

K. Sainsbury, *The Turning Point*, Oxford University Press: Oxford 1986

H.E. Salisbury, *The 900 Days: The Siege of Leningrad*, Avon Books: New York 1970

A.M. Samsonov, *Stalingradskaya Bitva*, 4th edn, Moscow 1989

G. Sanford, 'The Katyn Massacre and Polish–Soviet Relations, 1941–1943', *Journal of Contemporary History*, vol. 21, no. 1, 2006

D. Sassoon, 'The Rise and Fall of West European Communism, 1939–1948', *Contemporary European History*, vol. 1, no. 2, 1992

A. Seaton, *Stalin as a Military Commander*, Combined Publishing: Conshohocken, PA 1998

S. Sebag Montefiore, *Stalin: The Court of the Red Tsar*, Weidenfeld & Nicolson: London 2003

A. Sella, '"Barbarossa": Surprise Attack and Communication', *Journal of Contemporary History*, vol. 13, 1978

E.S. Senyavskaya, *1941–1945: Frontovoe Pokolenie*, Moscow 1995

O.V. Serova, *Italiya i Antigitlerovskaya Koalitsiya, 1943–1945*, Moscow 1973

R. Service, *Stalin: A Biography*, Macmillan: London 2004

G.N. Sevost'yanov (ed.), *Voina i Obshchestvo, 1941–1945*, 2 vols, Moscow 2004

S.L. Sharp, 'People's Democracy: Evolution of a Concept', *Foreign Policy Reports*, vol. 26, January 1951

H. Shukman (ed.), *Redefining Stalinism*, Frank Cass: London 2003

H. Shukman (ed.), *Stalin's Generals*, Phoenix Press: London 1997

M.D. Shulman, *Stalin's Foreign Policy Reappraised*, Harvard University Press: Cambridge, Mass. 1963

N. Simonov, *Voenno-Promyshlennyi Kompleks SSSR v 1920–1950–e gody*, Moscow 1996

V. Sipols, *The Road to Great Victory*, Progress Publishers: Moscow 1984

B.N. Slavinskii, *Yaltinskaya Konferentsiya i Problemy 'Severnykh Territorii'*, Moscow 1996

S.Z. Sluch, 'Rech' Stalina, Kotoroi ne Bylo', *Otechestvennaya Istoriya*, no. 1, 2004

N.D. Smirnova, 'Gretsiya v Politke SShA i SSSR, 1945–1947', *Novaya i Noveishaya Istoriya*, no. 5, 1997

B.F. Smith, *Sharing Secrets with Stalin: How the Allies Traded Intelligence, 1941–1945*, University Press of Kansas: Lawrence, Kansas 1996

T. Snyder, '"To Resolve the Ukrainian Problem Once and for All": The Ethnic Cleansing of Ukrainians in Poland, 1943–1947', *Journal of Cold War Studies*, vol. 1, no. 2, Spring 1999

B.V. Sokolov, *Georgii Zhukov*, Moscow 2004

B.V. Sokolov, *Molotov*, Moscow 2005

B.V. Sokolov, 'The Role of Lend-Lease in Soviet Military Efforts, 1941–1945', *Journal of Slavic Military Studies*, vol. 7, no. 3 1994

V.V. Sokolov, 'I.M. Maiskii Mezhdu I.V. Stalinym i U. Cherchillem v Pervye Mesyatsy Voiny', *Novaya i Noveishaya Istoriya*, no. 6, 2001

W.J. Spahr, *Stalin's Lieutenants: A Study of Command under Stress*, Presidio Press: Novato, Calif. 1997

L.M. Spirin, 'Stalin i Voina', *Voprosy Istorii KPSS*, May 1990

P. Spriano, *Stalin and the European Communists*, Verso: London 1985

P.J. Stavrakis, *Moscow and Greek Communism, 1944–1949*, Cornell University Press: New York 1989

R. Steininger, *The German Question and the Stalin Note of 1952*, Columbia University Press: New York 1990

R.W. Stephan, *Stalin's Secret War: Soviet Counterintelligence against the Nazis, 1941–1945*, University Press of Kansas: Lawrence, Kansas 2004

W. Stivers, 'The Incomplete Blockade: Soviet Zone Supply of West Berlin, 1948–1949', *Diplomatic History*, vol. 21, no. 4, Fall 1997

O.F. Suvenirov, *Tragediya RKKA, 1937–1939*, Moscow 1998

Victor Suvorov, *Icebreaker: Who Started the Second World War*, Hamish Hamilton: London 1990

G. Swain, 'The Cominform: Tito's International?', *Historical Journal*, vol. 35, no. 3, 1992

G. Swain, 'Stalin's Wartime Vision of the Postwar World', *Diplomacy & Statecraft*, vol. 7, no. 1, 1996

W. Taubman, *Stalin's American Policy: From Entente to Détente to Cold War*, W.W. Norton: New York 1982

R.W. Thurston and B. Bonwetsch (eds), *The People's War: Responses to World War II in the Soviet Union*, University of Illinois Press: Urbana and Chicago 2000

J. Tomaszewski, *The Socialist Regimes of Eastern Europe: Their Establishment and Consolidation, 1944–1967*, Routledge: London 1989

P. Tsakaloyannis, 'The Moscow Puzzle', *Journal of Contemporary History*, vol. 21 (1986)

A.B. Ulam, *Titoism and the Cominform*, Harvard University Press: Cambridge, Mass. 1952

T.J. Uldricks, 'The Icebreaker Controversy: Did Stalin Plan to Attack Hitler?' *Slavic Review*, vol. 58, no. 3, Fall 1999

A.A. Ulunian, 'Soviet Cold War Perceptions of Turkey and Greece, 1945–58', *Cold War History*, vol. 3, no. 2, January 2003

R. van Dijk, *The Stalin Note Debate: Myth or Missed Opportunity for German Unification*, Cold War International History Project Working Paper no.14, May 1996

C. van Dyke, *The Soviet Invasion of Finland, 1939–1940*, Frank Cass: London 1997

A. Varsori and E. Calandri (eds), *The Failure of Peace in Europe, 1943–48*, Palgrave: London 2002

A.I. Vdovin, 'Natsional'nyi Vopros i Natsional'naya Politika v SSSR v gody Velikoi Otechestvennoi Voiny', *Vestnik Moskovskogo Universiteta: Seriya 8: Istoriya*, no. 5, 2003

V.V. Veshanov, *God 1942– 'Uchebnyi'*, Minsk 2002

D. Volkogonov, *Stalin: Triumph and Tragedy*, Phoenix Press: London 2000

T.V. Volokitina et al. (eds), *Moskva i Vostochnaya Evropa: Stanovlenie Politicheskikh Rezhimov Sovetskogo Tipa, 1949–1953*, Moscow 2002

S. Walsh, *Stalingrad, 1942–1943*, St. Martin's Press: New York 2000

W. Wanger, *The Genesis of the Oder–Neisse Line*, Brentano-Verlag: Stuttgart 1957

D. Watson, *Molotov: A Biography*, Palgrave Macmillan: London 2005

D. Watson, 'Molotov's Apprenticeship in Foreign Policy: The Triple Alliance Negotiations in 1939', *Europe–Asia Studies*, vol. 52, no. 4, 2000

K. Weathersby, '*Should We Fear This?*' *Stalin and the Danger of War with America*, Cold War International History Project Working Paper no. 39, July 2002

A.L. Weeks, *Stalin's Other War: Soviet Grand Strategy, 1939–1941*, Rowman & Littlefield: Oxford 2002

A. Weiner, *Making Sense of War: The Second World War and the Fate of the Bolshevik Revolution*, Princeton University Press: Princeton NJ 2001

A. Werth, *Russia at War, 1941–1945*, Pan Books: London 1964

A. Werth, *Russia: The Postwar Years*, Robert Hale: London 1971

A. Werth, *The Year of Stalingrad*, Hamish Hamilton: London 1946

O.A. Westad, *Brothers in Arms: The Rise and Fall of the Sino-Soviet Alliance, 1945–1963*, Stanford University Press: Stanford 1998

G. Wettig, 'Stalin and German Reunification', *Historical Journal*, vol. 37, no. 2, 1994

B. Whaley, *Codeword Barbarossa*, MIT Press: Cambridge, Mass. 1973

J.L. Wieczynski (ed.), *Operation Barbarossa*, Charles, Schlacks: Salt Lake City 1993

W.C. Wohlforth, *The Elusive Balance: Power and Perceptions during the Cold War*, Cornell University Press: Ithaca NY 1993

N.I. Yegorova, *The 'Iran Crisis' of 1945–1946: A View from the Russian Archives*, Cold War International History Project Working Paper no.15, May 1996

M. Zakharov, *Final: Istoriko-Memuarnyi Ocherk o Razgrome Imperialisticheskoi Yaponii v 1945 gody*, Moscow 1969

M.V. Zakharov, *General'nyi Shtab v Predvoennye Gody*, Moscow 1989 (new edition 2005)

J. Zarusky (ed.), *Die Stalin-Note vom 10.Marz 1952*, Munich 2002

I. N. Zemskov, *Diplomaticheskaya Istoriya Vtorogo Fronta v Evrope*, Moscow 1982

E.F. Ziemke and M.E. Bauer, *Moscow to Stalingrad: Decision in the East*, Center of Military History, US Army: Washington DC 1987

V.A. Zolotarev, *Velikaya Otechestvennaya Istoriya Velikoi Pobedy*, Moscow 2005

V.A. Zolotarev et al. (eds), *Velikaya Otechestvennaya Voina 1941–1945*, 4 vols, Moscow 1998–1999

E. Zubkova, *Poslevoennoe Sovetskoe Obshchestvo*, Moscow 2000

E. Zubkova, *Russia after the War*, M.E. Sharpe: New York 1998

E. Zubkova, 'The Soviet Regime and Soviet Society in the Postwar Years: Innovations and Conservatism, 1945–1953', *Journal of Modern European History*, vol. 2, no. 1, 2004

V.M. Zubok, 'Stalin and the Nuclear Age' in J.L. Gaddis et al. (eds), *Cold War Statesmen Confront the Bomb: Nuclear Diplomacy since 1945*, Oxford University Press: Oxford 1999

V. Zubok and C. Pleshakov, *Inside the Kremlin's Cold War*, Harvard University Press: Cambridge, Mass. 1996

Index

Note: page references in italics indicate maps.

Abakumov, V.S. 338–9, 342
Acheson, Dean (US Secretary of State) 367
agriculture, collectivisation 3, 4, 45, 319
AK *see* Polish Home Army
Akhmatova, Anna 333, 344
Albania, and Yugoslavia 348
Aleksandrov, Georgii F. (propaganda chief)
    264–5, 321, 334
Allied Control Commissions
    for Bulgaria 219, 417 n.4
    for Germany 229, 239, 350
    for Italy 175
    for Japan 300, 303, 366–7
Anders, Gen. W. 170
Anglo-Soviet Treaty of Alliance (1942) 91,
    94, 114, 134, 301–2, 307, 314, 355–6
Anti-Comintern Pact 281
Antonov, A.I. (Deputy Chief, General
    Staff) 123, 159, 180
    and Far Eastern war 283, 289, 291
    and Vistula–Oder operation 256–7,
        259–61
    and Yalta conference 237, 256, 259–60
appeasement, Soviet 63–4
Armistice Commission 174, 228–9
Army Group A 128, 151, 153
Army Group B 128
Army Group Centre 82, 93, 103, 124,
        125–6, 154
    and Kursk 157
    and Moscow 88, 107, 112, 126–7
    and Operation Bagration 199–203
    and Stalingrad 151, 153
    and Warsaw 204
    and Western Direction 99, 100, 103
Army Group Don 153
Army Group North 82, 93

and Leningrad 103–4, 112
and Operation Bagration 199
Army Group South 93
    and Kiev 82, 100, 112
    and Kursk 157
    and Stalingrad 121, 128
Astakhov, Georgii 32
atomic weapons
    American 289, 291–3, 311–12, 363–4,
        369–70
    Soviet 26, 292, 347, 362–4, 368
Attlee, Clement
    and Council of Foreign Ministers 299
    and Potsdam conference 272
Austria
    peace treaty 313–14
    postwar independence 178, 188
Aviators Affair 322
Axis states
    and Balkan states 61
    and battle for Stalingrad 121, 137, 149,
        154
    peace treaties 296, 298, 303, 304, 312,
        314
    troops in Soviet Union 67, 82, 87
    UN membership 296
    and unconditional surrender 166,
        182–3
    and Yugoslavia 59, 61, 62
    see also Bulgaria; Finland; Germany;
        Hungary; Italy; Japan; Romania

Babi Yar massacre 87
Badoglio, Marshal Pietro 175–6
Bagramyan, Marshal I. Kh. 102, 123, 390
    n.43
Bailey, Hugh 312

Baku oilfields 13, 51, 74, 88, 118–19, 126, 128–9
Balkans
  communist federation 348–9
  German allies in 74
  and Soviet sphere of influence 45–6, 55–6, 58, 61–2, 348
  see also Bulgaria; Greece; Romania; Yugoslavia
Baltic Fronts 199, 256
Baltic Sea, Soviet access to 275
Baltic states
  and anti-Soviet resistance 338
  and communist revolutions 72
  and elections to Supreme Soviet 328
  German invasion 104
  Soviet mutual assistance pacts 5, 43–4
  Soviet occupation 5–6, 19, 33–4, 43–5, 55–6
  sovietisation 44–5, 56, 325
Beaverbrook, Max Aitken, Baron 92, 114
Belgrade, Soviet liberation 192, 217
Belorussia
  German occupation 94
  Soviet liberation 192, 199, 200–3
  see also Western Belorussia
Belorussian Fronts
  1st 199, 203–4, 216, 254–8, 261
  2nd 199, 203, 254, 256–7, 261
  3rd 199, 203, 254, 256–7
Beneš, Eduard 210
Berezhkov, Valentin 181
Beria, Lavrentii (Internal Affairs Commissar) 97, 378 n.35
  and atomic weapons programme 292, 362
  and defence of Moscow 108
  and Doctors affair 342
  and Gulag 344
  and Katyn massacre 170
  and Stalin 89, 160
  and State Defence Committee 95
Berlin
  battle for (1945) 4, 11, 14, 254–63, 262, 272
  blockade and airlift (1948–1949) 26, 350, 351, 354–5, 364
  British bombing 142
  and Red Army atrocities 263–5
  as secondary target 260–3
  zones of occupation 229, 263, 350
Bessarabia 114
  revolution 72

and Romania 33, 55–6
Bevin, Ernest (British Foreign Secretary) 23
  and Anglo-Soviet Treaty 307, 314
  and CMF 299, 301, 303
  and Potsdam conference 272
Bialer, Seweryn 10
Bidault, Georges 226–7
Bierut, Boleslaw 222
biographies of Stalin 3, 12
Birse, A.H. 273, 381 n.3
Biruzov, General S.S. 417 n.4
Black Sea, Soviet naval bases 55, 59, 276
Black Sea Straits
  Soviet access to 22–3, 185, 188, 189, 222–3, 272, 275–6, 279
  Soviet–Turkish confrontation 308, 310–11, 364
Bock, Field Marshal Fedor von 112, 128
Bohlen, Charles 179, 182, 190, 273, 401 n.68
Brandenberger, David 346
Brent, Jonathan and Naumov, Vladimir 343
Brest-Litovsk treaty (1918) 378 n.46
Briansk Front 100–1, 107, 129, 159
Britain
  Anglo-Soviet alliance 91–2, 94, 114, 134, 301–2, 307, 314
  and anti-communism 24, 165, 252–3, 308, 330
  and battle for Stalingrad 155
  communist party 360
  declaration of war on Germany 36, 41
  and Far Eastern war 274
  and German peace offers 57, 91
  intention to fight on 91–2
  and Moscow conference of 1943 177–80
  and Poland 209, 213–14, 216, 222
  possibility of separate peace with Germany 141, 165
  and postwar co-operation 114–15
  and postwar peace 168, 174–5, 232, 244
  and second front 102, 134–43, 154, 157, 165, 177, 178–9, 182, 185, 199–200, 281
  and Soviet expansion 22–3, 25, 58
  and Soviet–Finnish War 51–2, 54
  and spheres of interest 23, 190, 196, 217–22, 230–2, 253, 301–4
  and triple alliance 5–6, 30–2, 33–4, 37, 51, 56
  and Turkey 45–6
  see also Grand Alliance

Brooke, Field Marshal Alan 68–9, 188
Browder, Earl 173
Budennyi, Marshal Semyon M., and
    South-Western Direction 97, 101
Bulganin, Gen. Nikolai 324, 360
Bulgaria
    Comintern campaign 61
    and communism 248–9, 251–2, 296,
        303, 319
    mutual defence pact with USSR 231,
        356
    peace treaty 296, 298–9, 304
    and percentages agreement 218–19
    Soviet occupation 192, 217–18, 263
    and Soviet sphere of influence 45, 58,
        59, 274, 278, 296–8, 304
    and tripartite pact 61
    and Turkey 185
    and Yugoslavia 235–7, 245, 348–9
Byrnes, James F. (US Secretary of State)
    273, 290
    and Council of Foreign Ministers
        299–300, 302, 303, 305–6, 352
    and war scares of 1946 312

capitalism
    fascist and democratic 36–7, 42, 236–7
    and new democracy 246–53, 318–19,
        334
    and peaceful coexistence 24, 188,
        311–12, 332, 347, 360, 364
    in Soviet ideology 18, 38, 70, 312, 332,
        333–4, 360–1
Cassidy, Henry C. 140
casualties 10–11, 16
    civilian 5, 16, 106, 143, 199, 216, 325
    Finnish 52
    German 11, 88, 103, 118, 122, 126, 154,
        200, 263
    Japanese 293
    Korean War 370
    Polish 216
    Red Army 11, 80–1, 85, 88, 95, 99–100,
        102, 107, 117, 126, 199
        in Far Eastern war 293
        at Kharkov 122
        at Leningrad 106
        in Moscow 108
        in Operation Bagration 200
        at Sebastopol 122
        at Stalingrad 147, 151, 155
        in Vistula–Oder operation 215, 263
        in Winter War 52

Caucasus
    access to resources in 74, 88–9, 118–19
    German advances in 126, 127, 128–30,
        139, 143
    and Operation Saturn 151, 153
censorship, Soviet 111, 173, 337
Central Front 156, 159
CFM see Council of Foreign Ministers
Chadaev, Yakov 59, 89–90
Chaldei, Yevgeni 263
Chamberlain, Neville 31, 139, 382 n.18
Cheptsov, Alexander 340
Chernyakhovskii, Gen. Ivan 256–7
Chiang Kai-shek 181, 281, 288–9, 292, 367
China 181
    communists in 288–9, 367–8
    and Council of Foreign Ministers 299,
        302, 303
    and Korean War 26, 364–9
    and Manchuria 242, 256, 271, 284
    and Outer Mongolia 271, 283, 287
    and Sino-Soviet alliance 287–8, 291–2
    Soviet relations with 26, 287
    and UN Security Council 197
    war with Japan 197, 281, 287–92
Chou En-lai 358, 369
Chuikov, Gen. Vasilii 144, 147, 258
Churchill, Winston S.
    and cold war 307–8, 347
    and election of 1945 272, 274
    and fall of France 55
    and Far Eastern war 291
    Iron Curtain speech 24, 250, 305–6,
        307–8, 311–12, 330
    and Molotov 331
    in Moscow (1942) 134–43
    in Moscow (1944) 217–24, 282
    and Moscow conference 176–7
    and Nazi–Soviet pact 30–5
    and Operation Overlord 184–5, 200
    percentages agreement 217–25, 274
    and planning for peace 167, 174–5, 191
    and Poland 209, 213–15, 222, 256
    and Potsdam conference 272–4, 278, 321
    relationship with Stalin 188–90, 224
    and second front 102, 134–40, 142, 157,
        180, 184–5, 199–200
    seen as warmonger 312, 330, 347, 359
    and Soviet–Finnish War 51
    and Soviet–German war 92, 102, 125
    and Stalin 8, 31, 38, 56, 114–15, 125,
        136–43, 250, 274, 292, 307, 312,
        330, 347, 371, 373

Churchill, Winston S. (*cont.*)
  and Tehran conference 180–8, 189,
    207–8
  and war criminals 141–2
  and Yalta conference 221, 238–41, 244
Ciano, Galeazzo, conte di Cortellazzo 30
Cienchanowski, Jan M. 206–7
civil war, Russian
  anti-Bolshevik coalition 308
  and defence of Stalingrad 12–13
  and Red Army 53, 134
civilians
  and allied bombing of Germany 137, 142
  casualties 5, 16, 106, 143, 199, 216, 325
  and defence of Moscow 108
  Polish 216
  repatriation 332
class struggle 18, 332
Clausewitz, Carl von 257, 321
cold war 23–9, 296–320
  and anti-communism 23–4, 306, 307,
    311, 330, 337, 360
  beginning 25–6, 253
  and collapse of Grand Alliance 347
  and Cominform 317–20
  effects of Warsaw uprising 216–17
  and Germany 350–9
  and Iron Curtain speech 24, 250, 305–6,
    307–8, 311, 330
  and new democracy 24, 252–3, 318–19,
    334, 350
  and postwar terror 337–8
  and reunification of Germany 358
  and revisionist views of Stalin 372–3
  and Soviet patriotism 337
  and Stalin 24–5, 314, 317–20, 361–4,
    370, 374
  and Truman 25, 268
  and Truman Doctrine 312, 313–14, 317,
    354
  and two-camps doctrine 25–6, 318–20,
    354
  and war scares of 1946 307–12
  see also Berlin, blockade; Korean War
collectivisation, forced 3, 4, 45, 319
colonies, as Trusteeship Territories 272,
    276, 297–8, 303, 305
Cominform (Communist Information
    Bureau)
  and cold war 317–20, 354
  Yugoslav exclusion from 349
Comintern (Communist International)
  abolition 168–74

formation 249
  and Nazi–Soviet pact 36–7, 61
  and Soviet–German war 91, 134
Commission on Armistice Terms 174,
    228–9
Commission on Dismemberment 244
Commission on Peace Treaties and the
    Postwar Order 174, 196, 229
Commission for the Preparation of
    Diplomatic Documents 167, 174
Commission on Reparations 174, 229
communism
  differing forms 236–7
  ideology 18, 38, 48, 72–3, 326, 328–9,
    334, 367
  and new democracy 246–53, 288,
    318–19, 334, 350
  and patriotism 19–23, 25, 28, 111, 172,
    192–5, 246, 331
  and peaceful coexistence 24, 188,
    311–12, 332, 347, 360, 364
  spread 4, 72, 251–3
  western anti-communism 24, 252–3,
    307, 311, 330, 337
Communist Information Bureau *see*
    Cominform
communist parties
  and abolition of Comintern 168–73
  Chinese 288–9
  Eastern Europe 245–51, 317
  French 176, 226, 317–18, 320, 360
  Italian 176, 317–18, 360
Communist Party, Soviet
  Central Committee 1, 327, 333, 335,
    337, 341–2, 345
  and Eastern European parties 349–50
  18th congress 34–5
  elections to Supreme Soviet 327, 328–9
  19th congress 28, 344–6, 359
  postwar membership 326
  and Red Army 19
  rule changes 345
  and Stalin 111
  20th congress 1, 3, 89, 372
  22nd congress 1–2
cosmopolitanism 340–1
Council of Evacuation, Soviet 90, 163
Council of Foreign Ministers (CFM) 279,
    296–306, 354–6
  London meeting (1945) 276, 297–302,
    310, 352
  London meeting (1947) 354
  Moscow meeting (1947) 313–14, 352–4

New York meeting 304
Paris meeting (1946) 304–6, 352
Paris meeting (1949) 355
Council of Ministers 345, 360
Council of People's Commissars 63–4, 95, 327
Crimea
   German conquest 103, 121–4, 128, 135
   German defeat in 192
Crimean conference see Yalta conference
Cripps, Sir Stafford (British ambassador to Moscow) 56–7
Croatia, troops in Soviet Union 82
culture, Soviet
   and patriotism 341, 344
   postwar thaw 328, 344
   and Western influence 23, 332, 333–7
Czechoslovakia
   communist party 248, 251–2, 319, 341, 349
   German occupation 30
   government in exile 210
   as key Soviet ally 231
   and Marshall Plan 316–17
   Soviet occupation 192, 263–4

D Day 199–200, 282
Darien 185, 242, 283, 284, 287, 289, 292, 297
Davies, Joseph E. (US ambassador in Moscow) 176, 371
de Gaulle, Gen. Charles 176, 181, 225–7
   and Stalin 225–7, 238, 241, 320
Deane, Gen. John 261, 282–3
Declaration on Liberated Europe 242, 245
defence expenditure, increase 16, 360
Dekanozov, Vladimir G. (Soviet ambassador to Berlin) 59, 65–6, 68
democracy, new 24, 246–53, 288, 318–19, 334, 350
deportations 3, 19, 45, 326
Deutscher, Isaac xiv, 3, 8
dictatorship of the proletariat, and Eastern Europe 246–9
Dimitrov, Georgi (Comintern leader)
   and Baltic states 44
   and Bulgaria 61, 348–9
   and Cominitern 168–9, 173
   diary 36–7, 38–9, 297, 377 n.31
   and Greek communists 221
   and Potsdam conference 279
   and Soviet–German war 61, 78, 91

and Winter War 48
and Yugoslavia 235–6
Djilas, M. 405 n.62
Doctors affair 341–3
Don Front 148–9
Dumbarton Oaks conference (1944) 195–9, 225, 233
Dunmore, Timothy 344
Duraczynski, Eugeniusz 207
Dyczok, M. 423 n.40

EAC see European Advisory Commission
East Germany
   armed forces 360
   and German reunification 354, 355, 357
   sovietisation 319, 348, 350
East Prussia, Soviet occupation 73–4, 76, 93, 203, 255–8, 260
Eastern Europe
   Anglo-American fears of communism in 233, 274, 307
   communist parties 4, 349–50
   and federation of states 223–4
   and German expansionism 30
   liberation and conquest 228–53
   and Marshall Plan 316–17
   and new democracy 24, 246–53, 319
   and percentages agreement 217–25
   popular front governments 72
   Red Army invasion 175
   as Soviet sphere of influence 5, 23–6, 39, 114–15, 252–3, 274, 278–9, 299, 308, 311, 317, 331, 347
   sovietisation 35, 44–5, 319
   Stalin's aims 245–53, 324
   and western powers 252–3
   and Yalta conference 237–45
Eastern Front
   battle for Stalingrad 118–64
   casualties 10–11, 102–3, 117, 118
   Soviet offensives 11, 112–17, 118, 122–5, 151–3, 157
   and war of attrition 88, 99–100, 102, 119
   see also second front; Vistula–Oder operation
economy, Soviet 162–4, 324, 326–7, 345
   five-year plans 327, 329, 344
   and Germany 350–2
Eden, Anthony 91–2, 114–15, 167
   and Moscow conference 178, 179
   and percentages agreement 219–20
   and Poland 269
   and Potsdam conference 272–3

Eden, Anthony (*cont.*)
  and Tehran conference 186
  and Yalta conference 241
Ehrenburg, Ilya 264–5
Einsatzgruppen (action teams) 84, 87
Eisenhower, Gen. Dwight D. 259, 260–1,
  370
Eisenstein, Sergei, *Ivan the Terrible* 23, 333
ELAS-EAM (Greece) 220–1, 233
Erickson, John xiv, 59, 112, 202
Ericson, Edward E. 42–3
Estonia
  mutual assistance pact 5, 43–4
  Soviet liberation 192
  Soviet occupation 5, 45, 55
  and Soviet sphere of influence 33
ethnic cleansing 3, 18
ethnic minorities
  and nationalism 27, 246, 309–10
  purges 3, 28, 45, 325–6
ethnicity, and postwar borders 223–4, 234,
  309
Etinger, Dr Yakov 342
Europe
  postwar frontiers 167, 190
  Soviet sphere of influence 167
  transition to socialism 190–1, 252–3
  and US aid 314–17
European Advisory Commission (EAC)
  178, 186, 228–9, 234, 239
evacuation, plans for 90, 105–6, 108, 163
extermination camps, German 265

Far East
  and anti-communism 367
  and Soviet sphere of influence 196, 280
  see also China; Japan; Korean War
Far Eastern Advisory Commission (FEAC)
  300, 303
Far Eastern Commission 303
1st and 2nd Far Eastern Fronts 285
Far Eastern war 197, 232, 256, 274, 279–95,
  301
  and peace settlement 299–300
  and Yalta agreement 241–2, 269, 271,
    274, 284, 287, 289, 291
  see also China; Japan
Federal Republic of Germany 354–5
Filtzer, Donald 328
Finland
  and communism 47, 252
  defeat 192, 202
  defeat of German forces in 192

German troops in 58, 59
mutual defence pact with USSR (1949)
  356
peace treaty with Allies 296, 298, 304
peace treaty with Soviet Union (1940) 6,
  50, 52
and postwar settlement 114, 185, 231,
  278
and Soviet sphere of influence 33
troops in Soviet Union 82, 104
war with Soviet Union 170
and Winter War 5–6, 46–55, 49, 72–3, 85
France
  Anglo-American invasion 118
  colonies 181, 190
  communist party 176, 226, 317–18, 320,
    360
  and Council of Foreign Ministers 299,
    302, 303
  declaration of war on Germany 36, 41
  German conquest 54, 55, 56, 70, 272
  and German reparations 270
  and Operation Overlord 182, 184–5,
    200
  and Poland 226–7
  and postwar settlement 181, 190, 225,
    229–31
  and Soviet–Finnish War 51–2, 54
  and triple alliance 5–6, 30–2, 33–4, 37,
    51, 56
  and Turkey 45–6
  and UN Security Council 197
  and zones of occupations in Germany
    239
  see also de Gaulle, Gen. Charles; second
    front
Franco, Francisco 46, 275, 279
Franco-Soviet mutual aid treaty 226–7,
  356

Gat, M. 400 n.42
George VI 184, 274
German Army *see* Wehrmacht
German Democratic Republic 355
Germany
  Allied invasion 260–1
  Ardennes counter-offensive 256, 258–9
  armistice terms 178–9, 228–9
  attempts to divide Grand Alliance 165
  and cold war 350–9
  communist party 353
  demilitarisation 114, 139, 300, 303,
    347–8, 352, 356

dismemberment 114, 179, 183–4, 186, 189, 190, 223, 229–30, 238–9, 244, 350
and European resistance movements 154
expansionism 31, 32, 38–9
invasion of Poland 5, 36, 41, 43, 47, 70
invasion of Soviet Union *see* Soviet–German war
navy and merchant fleet 275, 279
and new democracy 350
peace treaty 313–14, 354, 356–7
planned Soviet invasion 6–7, 76–7, 79, 82–4
possibility of Soviet peace with 165–7
postwar central administration 353–4
postwar recovery 26, 183, 195, 210–11, 213, 223, 236, 277, 288, 347, 367
postwar settlement 139, 177–9, 182–4, 186–8, 189, 231
as postwar Western ally 253
and Potsdam conference 276–8, 279, 352–5
preparations for war 84–5
rearmament 360–1
and reparations 239–40, 243, 264, 270, 275, 277, 279, 327, 352–4
Soviet invasion 4, 254
Soviet–Western demarcation line 261, 412 n.25
and split theory 66, 68
troops on Soviet border 66–9, 74–7, 94
and unconditional surrender 11, 182–3, 229, 239, 265, 288
unity 352–5, 357–8
and Vistula–Oder operation 254–65, *255*
and Yalta conference 238–40, 243, 259, 277, 352–5
zones of occupation 26, 229, 239, 263, 277–8, 350–4
see also Berlin; Nazi–Soviet pact
Gilmore, Eddie 311
GKO *see* State Defence Committee
Glantz, David M. 100, 107, 151, 161, 384 n.75
Goebbels, P. Joseph 270, 308
Golikov, Gen. Filip 67
Gomulka, Wladyslaw 25, 270, 293, 302, 349, 362
Gorbachev, Mikhail, and critique of Soviet past 2
Gordov, Gen. V.N., command of Stalingrad Front 130, 134, 323
Gorodetsky, Gabriel 66, 67, 74

Gottwald, Clement 248
GPU *see* Main Political Administration of the Red Army
Grand Alliance 89, 108–9, 139, 164
and abolition of Comintern 169, 172
collapse 25, 347
and division of Germany 350
and Dumbarton Oaks conference 195–9
and planning for peace 167–8, 174, 180–8, 189–91
as political coalition 165
political problems 23–4, 203, 243–4, 252–3, 258, 271, 296–7, 307–20, 337
and possibility of separate Soviet peace with Germany 167
postwar continuation 24–5, 190–1, 195, 234, 237, 253, 294, 296–307, 317, 331, 359
and second front 134–42, 154, 157
and Warsaw uprising 216–17
see also Britain; Moscow conference; Potsdam conference; Tehran conference; United States
Great Patriotic War *see* Soviet–German war
Greece
German invasion 62–3, 64
Italian invasion 58, 61, 62
partisan movement 23, 220, 233, 298, 348
and percentages agreement 218–22, 235, 274, 299
US aid to 313
Gromyko, Andrei
and Dumbarton Oaks conference 197–8, 233–4
and former colonies 276
and Soviet–American relations 232–3
and Stalin 234
and Truman 268
and United Nations 309, 339
and Yalta conference 221, 237
Groza, Petru 296
Guards Divisions 147, 148, 161
Guderian, Gen. Heinz 100–1, 103
Gulag 344
Gusev, Fedor (Soviet ambassador in London) 229, 237, 244, 409 n.12

Halder, Gen. Franz 85, 88, 126
Harriman, Kathleen 171–2, 224, 237–8

Harriman, W. Averell
  and atomic weapons programme 292
  and Far Eastern war 281–4, 287, 289,
    301
  and Katyn massacre 399 n.29
  and Molotov 267
  and Moscow conference (1943) 166,
    179, 182, 281
  and Poland 208–9, 213–16, 244
  and postwar relations with USSR 114,
    303
  and second front 136–40
  and Stalin 8–9, 22
  and US aid 92
  and Vistula–Oder operation 258, 261,
    265
Harrison, Mark xii, 164, 325
Hebrang, Andrija 234–5
Hess, Rudolf, flight to Britain 66, 91, 141–2
High Command, German, and German
    successes 57, 126, 128–9
High Command, Soviet 10–11, 16, 17
  and defensive strategy 80, 126, 156–7
  and offensive strategy 70, 71–2, 77, 80,
    93, 124
  and Soviet–Finnish War 52
  Stalin and his generals 10, 12, 71, 103,
    159–62, 203, 256, 266–7, 322–3,
    372
  Stavka (Headquarters) 95
  and victory at Stalingrad 155
Himmler, Heinrich 87
Hiroshima, bombing 291–2
Hitler, Adolf
  and access to Soviet resources 42–3, 89,
    118–19, 125–6
  and anti-communism 32
  attempts to divide Grand Alliance 165
  and defeat at Stalingrad 154
  and Leningrad 104
  mistakes 128–9, 373
  and Moscow 104, 109–10, 125–6, 153
  and Nazi–Soviet pact 5–6, 30–60
  possibility of Soviet peace with 165–7
  and racism 84
  and second front in Europe 178
  and Stalin 373
  suicide 263, 270
  and two-front war 115, 118
  and war on Soviet Union 59–60, 65–7,
    70, 82, 117, 118
Hokkaido, Soviet claim to occupation
    rights 293–4, 300

Holloway, David 285–8, 291, 362, 363
Holocaust, and mass murder of Soviet
    Jews 87
honour court 334–5
Hopkins, Harry 92, 102, 188, 270–1
Hoth, Herman 143
House, Jonathan M. 151
Howard, Roy 387 n.44
Hull, Cordell 399 n.10
  and Moscow conference 178, 179, 182,
    281
Hungary
  communist party 251–2, 319
  and invasion of Soviet Union 67, 82,
    121, 137, 149
  mutual defence pact 356
  and new democracy 249, 319
  peace treaty 296, 298, 304
  and percentages agreement 219
  postwar settlement 188, 278
  Red Army occupation 192, 217, 263
  and Romania 58, 59
  and tripartite pact 61

ideology
  Nazi 84–5, 109
  Soviet 18, 38, 48, 70, 72–3, 309, 326,
    328–9, 334, 360, 367
India, and postwar settlement 181–2
industrialisation 2, 3, 4, 20, 22
  and evacuation to the east 163
Institution of Military Commissars 97,
    133
intelligentsia
  and cultural thaw 328
  and honour court 334–5
  and patriotism 333–6
  and postwar terror 337
Iran
  Allied occupation 180
  Soviet troops in 308–9, 364
Israel, and Soviet Union 339–41
Italy
  Allied defeat of 175–6, 185, 202, 219
  and the Balkans 55, 56, 58, 61.62
  communist party 176, 317–18, 360
  former colonies 23, 272, 276, 297–8
  and invasion of Soviet Union 82, 121,
    137, 149
  and NATO 356
  peace treaty 296, 298–9, 304–5, 356
  and postwar settlement 190, 275, 278,
    305

and reparations 305
and tripartite pact 57–8
and Yugoslavia 297, 305

JAFC *see* Jewish Anti-Fascist Committee
Japan
    Anti-Comintern Pact 281
    attack on United States 88
    and bombing of Hiroshima 291–2
    disarmament 303, 366
    and Korea 280, 364, 370
    occupation zones 293–4, 300, 331
    peace treaty 366–7
    postwar settlement 184, 231–2, 304
    recovery 366–7, 369
    Soviet neutrality pact 63, 64–5, 280, 285
    Soviets in war against 182, 242, 256, 267,
        271, 273–4, 279–95
    and tripartite pact 57–8, 63
    and unconditional surrender 271,
        287–90, 292–4, 364
    and war with China 197, 281, 287–90
Jewish Anti-Fascist Committee (JAFC)
    338–41, 343
Jews, Soviet
    and Doctors affair 341–3
    and nationalism 338–43
    and Nazi ideology 84, 87
Jodl, Alfred 128

Kaganovich, Lazar (transport minister),
    and Stalin 90, 97, 160, 378 n.35
Kalinin Front 129, 151
Kardelj, Edvard 318, 348–9
Karpov, Vladimir 166
Katyn massacre 19, 45, 169–72
Kennan, George 306
Kerr, Clark 208–9, 214, 244, 261, 282, 406
    n.87
Kharkov
    disaster 122–6, 129, 135
    Soviet recapture 154, 157
Khlevnuk, O.V. 379 n.60
Khrushchev, Nikita
    and battle of Stalingrad 376 n.15
    as First Secretary of Communist Party
        345
    and 19th party congress 344
    personality cult 4
    secret speech 1, 2, 3–4, 5, 89, 372
    and Stalin as war leader 5, 89, 90, 122–3,
        160
    and Winter War 48

Kiev
    German capture 85, 99, 102–3, 390
        n.68
    Soviet defence 75, 88, 100–1
    Soviet recapture 159
Kim Il Sung 26, 347, 366, 367–9
King, Adm. Ernest 188
King, Harold 169
Kirov, Sergei 16
Kirponos, Gen. Mikhail P. 101–2
Kisilev, V.N. 411 n.6
Kliueva, Nina 334–5
Kolarev, V. 235–6
Kollantai, Alexandra (Soviet ambassador in
    Sweden) 243
Konev, Marshal I.S. 200, 254–7, 261–3, 398
    n.5
Königsberg, Soviet claim to 187–8, 212,
    256, 275, 279, 284
Korea
    division 364–6
    Japanese attacks 280
Korean War (1950–1953) 26, 347, 364–70,
    365
'Korsikanets' (Soviet spy) 67
Kozlov, Gen. Dmitri T. 121–2
Krebs, Col. Hans 63
Kulik, Grigorii (Chief of Soviet artillery)
    93
Kuril Islands 232, 242, 283–4, 291, 293–4
Kursk, battle for (1943) 14, 80, 154, 156–9,
    158, 159
Kuusinen, Otto 48
Kuznetsov, Adm. N. G., and Yalta
    conference 237
Kwantung Army (Japan) 285, 293

Lange, Oscar 210–11
Latvia
    mutual assistance treaty 5, 44
    Soviet liberation 192
    Soviet occupation 5, 45, 55
    and Soviet sphere of influence 33
League of Nations 178, 195–6, 280
    and expulsion of USSR 50
Lenin, V.I. 235, 247–8, 321
    and Soviet nationalities 21
    and Stalin 110–11, 312, 372
Leningrad
    and Finland 33, 47, 48, 52–3, 185
    lifting of blockade 192
    Military Council for Defence 104–5
Leningrad Affair (1949) 337, 343, 344

Leningrad, battle (1941) 85, 99, 103–7
  defence 104–6
  Soviet counterattacks 88, 106–7, 112, 154
Leningrad Front 106, 124, 199
Lippmann, Walter 230–1, 306–7
List, Field Marshal Wilhelm 128
Lithuania
  anti-communist partisans 325
  and elections to Supreme Soviet 328
  German invasion 103
  mutual assistance treaty 5, 44
  Soviet occupation 5, 39, 45, 55
Litvinov, Maksim (Soviet ambassador to
    USA)
  and Anglo-Soviet spheres of interest
    221, 230–2
  and Commission on Peace Treaties 174,
    196, 229
  and Dumbarton Oaks conference 196–7
  and Molotov 174, 196, 234
  and Moscow conference 177–8
  and Roosevelt 267
  and second front 136
  and Stalin 234
London
  CFM meeting (1945) 276, 297–302, 310,
    352
  CFM meeting (1947) 354
Lopatin, Gen. A.I. 396–7 n.107
Lozovskii, S.A. 284, 340
Luftwaffe
  attacks on Sebastopol 122
  attacks on Soviet airfields 85, 98
  attacks on Stalingrad 143, 153
Lvov
  Polish claims to 212, 222
  Soviet recapture 200
Lysenko affair 335
Lysenko, Trofim 335

MacArthur, Gen. Douglas 300, 301, 364,
    369
McCagg, William xiv
Mackintosh, Malcolm 417 n.4
McNeal, Robert H. xiii
Main Command, Soviet, Stavka
    (Headquarters) 90, 95
Main Political Administration of the Red
    Army (GPU) 97, 121
Maiskii, Ivan M. (Soviet ambassador in
    London)
  and Anglo-Soviet relations 51–2, 66,
    91–2

and Churchill 136, 139–40, 141–2
and German troop movements 66
and Hess 91, 165
imprisonment 343
and Kuril Islands 415 n.94
and percentages agreement 220
and postwar settlement 231–2
and Reparations Commission 174, 229,
    240
and Stalin 234
and Winter War 50, 51–2
and Yalta conference 237, 239–40, 242–3
Malenkov, Georgi M.
  and battle for Stalingrad 144
  and cold war 320, 329–30
  and Doctors affair 342
  and 19th party congress 28, 344–5, 359
  and Stalin 160, 378 n.35
  and State Defence Committee 94
Malik, Yakov (Soviet ambassador in Japan)
    196, 284
Malinovskii, R.Y. 284–5, 293
Malyshev, V.A., diary 377 n.31
Manchuria
  and China 242, 271, 284
  Japanese assault on 256, 279–81, 283, 285
  and Soviet Union 185, 285–7, 286, 291,
    292, 293
Mannerheim Line, and defence of Finland
    48–50, 52, 71
Manstein, Field Marshal Eric von 153
Mao Tse-tung 26, 288–9, 367–9
Mark, Eduard 250
Marshall, George (US Secretary of State)
    314, 353
Marshall Plan 25, 314–17, 354
Marzani, Carl 268
Mason, E.S. 426 n.13
Mastny, Vojtech 166
Matsuoka, Yosuke 63, 65
Mawdsley, Evan 70, 72, 102, 106, 397 n.127
Mediterranean
  Allied operations 138, 182
  Soviet access to 22, 276, 297–8
Medvedev, Roy 89
Medvedev, Zhores 89, 341
Meiklejohn, R.P. 215
Meir, Golda 339–40
Mekhlis, Gen. Lev 97, 121
memoirs
  military 4, 8, 10, 13–15, 74, 79–80, 93,
    102, 124, 160, 372
  political 3, 50, 89–90

Mennon, K.P.S. (Indian ambassador to Moscow) 370–1
Meretskov, Gen. K.A. (Chief of General Staff) 48, 53, 73–6, 93, 285
  and purge of officers 98
Merkulov, V.N. (intelligence chief) 67
Meyerson, Golda (Golda Meir) 339–40
Michael, king of Romania 296
Mikhoels, Solomon 338, 342
Mikolajczyk, Stanislaw
  meetings with Stalin 212–14, 222
  and Poland's postwar borders 207
  and provisional government 209, 211, 227, 241, 244, 270
Mikoyan, Anastas (trade minister)
  and China 367
  and Stalin 89–90, 97, 160, 345, 377 n.35, 386 n.19
Military Council for the Defence of Leningrad 104–5
minorities, ethnic
  and nativisation 21, 346
  purges 3, 18, 45, 325–6
Minsk
  German attack 85, 94, 98
  Soviet recapture 200
Mlynar, Zdenek 331
Molotov, Vyacheslav (Soviet foreign minister)
  and Balkans 55, 61–2, 245
  and Baltic states 43–4
  correspondence with Stalin 377 n.31
  and Council of Foreign Ministers 297–302, 305, 310, 352–4
  and Dumbarton Oaks conference 196, 197
  and Far Eastern war 300
  and Great Terror 18
  and individuals
    Churchill 331
    Litvinov 174, 196, 234
    Stalin 1, 63–4, 97, 160, 234, 331, 345, 377 n.35
    Truman 267–9
  and Leningrad 105
  and Marshall Plan 315–16
  and Moscow conference (1943) 178–9
  and Moscow conference (1945) 304
  and Nazi–Soviet pact 30, 34, 36–7, 39, 57, 65
  negotiations with allies 23, 115
  and 19th party congress 344
  and Paris Peace Conference 304–6
  and percentages agreement 219–21
  and Poland 37, 39, 208–9, 214–15, 226–7, 244
  and postwar planning 167, 183, 297–8
  and Potsdam conference 279, 290
  and reconstruction 325
  and second front in Europe 134–5, 140
  and separate peace with Germany 166–7
  Soviet–German war 89–91, 97
  and spheres of interest 231
  and Stalin Note 356–8
  and State Defence Committee 95
  and Tehran conference 186
  and tripartite pact 58–9, 61
  and Turkey 275, 310
  and war criminals 141
  wife 340
  and Winter War 47–8, 52
  and Yalta conference 237, 239, 241, 244
Montefiore, Simon Sebag 160
Montgomery, Field Marshal Bernard 314, 373
Montreux Convention 222–3, 272, 275–6, 310–11
Moscow
  CFM meeting (1947) 313–14, 352–4
  Churchill in (1942) 134–43
  Churchill in (1944) 217–24, 282
  and defence of Leningrad 104, 107
  foreign ministers' conference (Dec. 1945) 303–4
  and VE Day 265–6, 267
  victory parades 14, 266–7, 294, 321
  and Victory Salutes 157, 199
Moscow, battle for (1941) 14, 85, 103, 107–11, 125–6, 160, 166
  defence 14, 88, 107–8
  German deception campaign 126
  and Soviet counter-offensive 111, 112–17, *113*
  and Stalin's Red Square speech 110–11
  as vital to German success 88, 129, 153, 156
Moscow conference (Oct. 1943) 166, 177–80, 187, 196, 228, 281
Moskalenko, Marshal K.S. 122
Mowrer, Edgar A. 268
Mussolini, Benito 175
  and Nazi–Soviet pact 33
Myagkov, Mikhail 153

nationalism, and Jews 338–43
nationalities, Soviet 21, 27, 38, 266

NATO *see* North Atlantic Treaty
      Organisation
navy, German 275, 279
navy, Soviet 55, 59, 275, 285, 360
Nazi–Soviet Pact 5–7, 30–60, *40*, 91
   and anti-Hitler alliance 5–6, 30–1
   and appeasement of Germany 34,
      63–4
   and fall of France 55–6
   as means of gaining time 6, 64, 70, 94
   and misleading Soviet signals 64–70
   and partition of Poland 33–4, 36–9
   and peace offensive 39
   and Polish borders 189
   and preparations for war 19, 66–81
   and Rapallo relationship 41–3, 55, 65–6
   and Soviet territorial gains 115
   and spheres of influence 33–4, 39, 43–6,
      58, 61–2, 68
   strains in 55–60
Nenni, Pietro 362
New York, CFM meeting 304
Ni shagu nazad! (Not a step back!) 131–3
NKVD (People's Commissariat of Internal
      Affairs) 97–8, 108, 111, 132, 141,
      148
   and ethnic group deportations 326
   and Katyn massacre 170–1
   and returnees 332
North Africa
   Allied campaigns 179
   Anglo-American campaign 136, 138,
      142, 153
North Atlantic Treaty Organisation
      (NATO) 26, 355–6, 357–8
North Bukovina, Soviet occupation 55–6,
      72, 114
North Korea, invasion of South Korea
      364–6, 368–70
North Sakhalin, Japanese concessions in
      59, 64–5, 281, 415 n.86
North-Western Direction 97, 106
North-Western Front 93, 97, 106, 123,
      124
Northern Front 93, 97
Norway
   Anglo-Soviet operation 139
   defeat of German forces in 192
   German invasion 43, 64
Nover, Barnet 154
Novikov, Nikolai V. (Soviet ambassador to
      USA) 62, 305–6, 315, 322
nuclear weapons, limitation 359, 364

Odessa
   German capture 87
   liberation 192
officer corps, importance 133
Operation Bagration 199–203, *201*
Operation Barbarossa *see* Soviet–German
      war
Operation Blau *120*, 121, 122, 126–30, 137,
      154
Operation Bodyguard 200
Operation Jupiter 151, *152*
Operation Kreml 126
Operation Little Saturn 153
Operation Mars *152*, 1513
Operation Overlord 182, 184–5, 189, 200
Operation Polar Star 154
Operation Saturn 151, *152*
Operation Torch 138, 139, 142, 153
Operation Uranus *148*, 149–50, *152*, 153,
      163
Operation Wintergewitter 153
Order 227 131–3
Orlemanski, Stanislaw 210
orthodoxy, communist 27
Osobka-Morawski, Edward 270–1
Outer Mongolia, and China 271, 283, 284,
      287
Overy, Richard 10

Paris
   CFM meeting (1946) 304–6, 352
   CFM meeting (1949) 355
Paris Peace Conference (1946) 304–6,
      318
partisans
   in Belorussia 200, 325
   in Greece 23, 220, 233, 298, 348
   Polish 206, 213
   Soviet 87, 90–1
   in Ukraine 325, 338
   in Yugoslavia 177, 211, 217, 297
Paterson, T.G. 420 n.78
patriotism, and communism 172, 192–5,
      246
patriotism, Soviet 19–23, 25, 28, 37, 331,
      337, 341, 346
   and intelligentsia 333–6
   and Jews 339–40
   and Soviet–German war 91, 94–5,
      110–11, 132–4
Paulus, Gen. Fredrich 143, 144–7, 149,
      153–4, 202
Pavlov, Gen. Dmitrii 98, 160–1, 379 n.56

PCNL *see* Polish Committee of National Liberation
peace movement, postwar 347, 359–61, 366
Pearl Harbor attack 88, 182, 280
Pechatnov, Vladimir 305
People's Commissariat of Defence (NKO) 95, 97, 108
People's Commissariat of Foreign Affairs 174, 179
  and CFM conference 301
  and Moscow conference 177
  and postwar planning 184, 197, 228–9
  and Warsaw uprising 215–16
percentages agreement 217–25, 231, 274
personality cult
  attacks on 1–2, 3–4, 372
  development 9, 26, 161, 321, 328
  and infallibility 54
  of Khrushchev 4
  as military strategist 321–3, 374
  of party leaders 319
  and rehabilitation 2
  and succession 346
  in west 24
Pilsudski, Gen. Józéf Klemens 13
Pleshakov, Constantine 389 n.21
Poland
  armed forces 361
  borders 186–8, 326; Curzon Line 37, 186, 207–9, 212, 222, 226, 241, 244; western 114, 183, 187, 189, 207–8, 212, 277–9
  and communism 247–8, 251–2, 319
  and extermination camps 265
  and German expansionism 31, 32, 34
  German invasion 5, 36, 41, 43, 47, 70
  government in exile 169–72, 186, 207–10, 212–13, 216, 222, 227, 241
  and Katyn crisis 169–72
  partition 33–4, 36–9
  and planned Soviet counterattack 76–7
  and postwar settlement 114, 185–8, 190, 207–13, 231, 233, 268–70
  and Potsdam conference 277–8, 279
  provisional government 209–10, 213, 222, 233, 241, 244, 270–1
  Red Army in 5, 37–8, 43, 47, 170, 192, 203–17, 222, 256–7, 263
  and Soviet sphere of influence 5, 33–4, 36, 207
  and Tehran conference 183, 185–6, 188, 207–8

  and Warsaw uprising 206, 212, 213–17
  and Yalta conference 241, 243, 244, 268–70, 277
1st Polish Army 203–4
Polish Committee of National Liberation (PCNL) 209, 212–13, 222, 226–7, 241
Polish Home Army (AK) 172
  and Warsaw uprising 206–7, 212–14, 216–17
Polish Workers' Party 172
Politburo
  and abolition of Comintern 169, 173
  during Soviet–German war 95
  and JAFC 340
  and Katyn massacre 170–1
  and Marshall Plan 314
  and 19th party congress 344
  and Presidium 345
  and Stalin 325, 331–2
political commissars, in Red Army 16, 53, 85, 97, 122, 131, 133–4
politics, and Soviet–German war 165–91, 231
Pollitt, Harry 173
Popov, Gen. M.M. 105–6
Port Arthur 185, 242, 283, 287, 289, 297
Poskrebyshev, A.N. 343
Potsdam conference (July 1945) 219, 271, 272–9, 296, 321
  and Far Eastern war 289
  and former colonies 276
  and Germany 276–7, 279, 352–5
  and Poland 277–9
  and Turkey 275–6
  see also Council of Foreign Ministers
Potsdam Proclamation 289–91
Prague, Red Army occupation 217
Presidium 345
Primorye (1st Far Eastern) Front 285
prisoners of war
  German 202
  Polish 19, 45
  returning 3, 332
  Soviet 84–7, 126–8
  see also Katyn massacre
propaganda, German 38, 82–4, 264–5
propaganda, Soviet 8, 90, 97, 111, 132–4, 161
  and communism 192–5
  and patriotism 193, 210, 266
  postwar 24, 317, 330, 357, 360
Proskurov, Gen. Ivan 98
Ptukhin, Gen. E.S. 98

purges *see* terror
Putin, Vladimir 2

racism
  and anti-Semitism 341, 346
  Nazi 2, 84, 116
Rakosi, Matyas 249
Rapallo Treaty (1922) 41–2, 55, 65–6
rapes, by Red Army personnel 263–5
Rasputitsa (spring muds) 116, 154, 259–60
Razin, Col. 321–2
Red Air Force 204
  and battle for Stalingrad 143–4, 147, 153
  postwar 360, 363
  purge 98, 160
Red Army
  achievements 4
  atrocities and looting 263–5
  in Baltic states 55, 56, 72–3
  and battle for Warsaw 204–8, *205*,
      213–17, 226–7, 256–7
  blocking detachments 98, 132, 148
  cavalry units 97
  and Commissar order 85
  and Communist Party 19
  counter-offensive actions 73, 93, 111,
      112–17, *113*, 143, 148–54, 322, 376
      n.15
  criticism of 131
  defence of Moscow 88, 107–8
  and demobilisation 328, 360
  and democratisation in Eastern Europe
      246
  discipline 97–8, 131–2, 133, 148
  encirclement 11, 85–8, *86*, 94, 98, 104,
      107, 119; at Kharkov 122–3; at Kiev
      100, 102; at Stalingrad 126–8
  encirclement of German forces 149,
      151–4, 192, 200, 203
  and Far Eastern war 271, 273, 280, 283,
      285–7, 289, 293
  and German invasion 4–6, 70, 71, 83,
      92–3
  German views 84–5, 119
  invasion of Eastern Europe 175
  invasion of Finland 47–50, 52–3, 72–3, 85
  invasion of Germany 254–63
  invasion of Poland 37–8, 43, 47, 256–7
  modernisation 15
  occupation of Romania 192, 217–19
  offensive strategy 6–7, 11, 70–81, 93,
      99–100, 107, 112, 116, 122–6, 129,
      157–8, 202–4

  officer corps 133
  peacetime task 323
  penal battalions 132, 148
  planned invasion of Germany 5–7, 76–7
  and political commissars 16, 53, 85, 97,
      122, 131, 133–4
  political loyalty 18–19, 133, 160–1
  and preparations for war 19, 69–74
  purges 15–16, 18, 53, 54, 85, 98, 160–1
  reforms and reorganisations 53, 78,
      97–8, 161–2
  reserves 78, 108, 111, 143, 155, 162–3,
      204
  and siege of Sebastopol 122
  size 16, 69, 88, 163, 199, 360
  and spread of communism 72
  and Stalingrad 126, 143–54, 168
  and strategic defence 71, 77, 80, 125,
      154–7
  tank corps 54, 97, 161
  training 53, 54, 163
  and year of victories 192
  see also casualties; Eastern Front; North-
      Western Direction; North-Western
      Front; Northern Front; South-
      Western Direction; South-Western
      Front; Southern Front; Western
      Direction; Western Front
Reese, R. 379 n.53
reparations
  German 239–40, 243, 264, 270, 275, 277,
      279, 327, 352–4
  Italian 305
Reparations Commission 174, 229, 240
repression, postwar 336–44
Reserve Front 107
Resis, Albert 24, 387 n.45
resistance movements 154
revolution, international
  and abolition of Comintern 72, 168,
      172
  and new democracy 246–53, 289,
      318–19
  and war aims 245
Rhee, Syngman 366, 369
Ribbentrop, Joachim von
  and Nazi–Soviet pact 30, 32–3, 36, 39,
      41, 60
  and separate peace with USSR 167
  and tripartite pact 57–9
Richthogen, Gen. Wolfram von 143
Roberts, Cynthia A. 76, 80
Rodimtsev, A.I. 147

Rokossovskii, Marshal K.K.
  and 1st Polish Army 204, 206, 213, 360
  and preparation for war 80
  rehabilitation 53
  and Stalingrad Front 149, 154, 160
  and Vistula–Oder operation 256–7,
    261–3
Romania
  and Bessarabia 33, 55–6
  communist party 251–2, 296, 319
  and Hungary 58, 59
  and invasion of Soviet Union 67, 82, 87,
    121, 137, 149
  mutual defence pact 356
  peace treaty 296, 298–9, 304
  and percentages agreement 218–19
  Ploesti oil fields 56, 118
  and postwar settlement 231, 245, 278,
    296–7, 303–4
  Soviet occupation 192, 217–19, 263
  Soviet sphere of influence 31, 58, 274,
    297–8, 356
  and Transylvania 58, 223–4
  and tripartite pact 61
Roosevelt, Eleanor 268
Roosevelt, Elliott 312
Roosevelt, Franklin D.
  aid to Soviet Union 92
  death 267–8, 373
  and dismemberment of Germany 189
  and Far Eastern war 280, 282, 291
  and Molotov 306
  and Moscow conference 176–7
  and Operation Overlord 185, 200
  and planning for peace 167, 174–5, 191,
    232–3
  and Poland 40, 209, 215–16, 233, 244
  relationship with Stalin 188–90, 225,
    306
  and second front 136, 140, 157, 179,
    185, 199–200, 281
  and Stalin 8, 102, 267, 274, 373
  and Tehran conference 180–8, 207–8,
    282
  and UN Security Council 198
  and Yalta conference 228, 238, 240–2,
    244
Roskin, Grigorii 334–5
Rostov
  German capture 103, 128, 130–1
  and Operation Saturn 88, 151, 153–4
Russia, and patriotism 21–2, 27, 37, 110,
  266, 336, 337, 341, 346

Russian Orthodox Church 399 n.23
Rybalchenko, Gen. 323
Rychagov, Gen. Pavel 98
Ryumin, Lt Col. M.D. 342

Saburov, M.Z. 344
San Francisco conference (June 1945) 240,
  267, 276, 298
Schulenburg, Friedrich von der 57, 59, 62,
  63–4, 65–6, 91
science
  and honour court 334–5
  postwar advances 335–6
scorched earth policy 91
Sebastopol
  German attack 103, 112, 121–2
  Soviet defence 131
second front 109, 118–19, 155
  and battle for Stalingrad 140–1, 154
  and Britain 102, 134–43, 154, 157, 165,
    177, 178–9, 199–200, 281
  and Hitler 178
  and Molotov 134–5, 140
  and Operation Bagration 199–202
  and Tehran conference 180, 182, 184–5,
    189
  and United States 134–42, 157, 177, 179,
    199–200, 281
Second World War
  declaration 36
  effects of Soviet population 4–5
  Nazi–Soviet pact 5–7, 30–60
  North African campaign 136, 138, 142
  and spread of communism 4
  see also casualties; second front;
    Soviet–German war
security
  Anglo-Soviet zones 230–1
  and Dumbarton Oaks conference 195–9
  international organisation 178, 179,
    183–4, 188, 195, 280
  postwar 167, 347–8
  separate zones 177–8
Shaposhnikov, Marshal Boris (Chief of
  General Staff) 73, 93, 98–9, 101–2
Shcherbakov, A.A. (propaganda chief) 108,
  342, 385 n.13
Shirer, William L. 30
Shostakovich, Dmitrii 333
show trials 17, 349
Shtemenko, S.M. (Chief of Operations)
  and Far Eastern war 285
  and German invasion 93

Shtemenko, S.M. (Chief of Operations)
(*cont.*)
    and Kursk 156, 159
    and Stalin 160, 372, 376 n.17
    and Tehran conference 180
    and Vistula–Oder operation 256, 259,
        261, 412 n.25
Shulman, Marshall 360
Sikorski, Wladyslaw 112, 170
Simonov, Konstantin 333–4
Sino-Soviet alliance 287–8, 291–2, 366–8
Slansky, Rudolph 341
Slavic states, alliances with 22, 210–12,
    217, 236–7, 243, 288
Slavs, and Nazi racism 12, 84
Slovakia
    national uprising 217
    and tripartite pact 61
    troops in Soviet Union 82
Sluch, Sergei Z. 35
Smith, Walter Bedell (US ambassador in
    Moscow) 261–3, 310, 334
Smolensk
    German attack 85, 88, 99
    Red Army recapture 171
    Soviet offensive 112, 157–9
Smushkevich, Gen. Yakov 98
Sokolov, Boris V. 390 n.43
Sokolovskii, Marshal V.D. 372
soldiers, demobilisation 328, 360
Soong, T.V. 287–8, 291, 293
Sorge, Richard (Soviet spy) 67–8
South Korea, invasion by North Korea
    364–6, 368–70
South Sakhalin 232, 242, 281, 283, 291, 294
South-Eastern Front 134, 148
South-Western Direction 6, 97, 101, 122–4
South-Western Front 97, 156, 159
    defence of Kiev 100–2
    defence of Stalingrad 129, 148–9
    initial counter-offensive 77, 93–4
Southern Front 94, 97, 130
Soviet Information Bureau (Sovinform)
    90, 133
Soviet Union
    access to warm-water ports 22, 185, 187,
        189, 222–3
    and atomic bomb 26, 292, 311–12, 347,
        362–4, 368
    borders 114–15, 167, 199, 231
    buffer zone in Eastern Europe 245–6,
        253
    expansionism 22–3, 25, 56, 58, 309, 366

fears of Anglo-German alliance 66
food crisis 1946–1947 327
German invasion *see* Soviet–German war
and German reparations 229, 275, 277,
    279, 327, 352–3
as great power 196–8, 300–1, 305, 307,
    331
as multinational state 2, 20–2, 266, 329
national anthem 266
nationalities 21, 27, 38, 266, 329, 338
and peace-loving state 360–1
possibility of separate peace with 165–7
postwar reconstruction 25, 324, 325–8
postwar society 321–46
reports of imminent German invasion
    65–8
russification 21–2
spheres of influence 22–3, 43–6, 68
    Balkans 45–6, 55–6, 58, 61–2, 348
    Baltic 33–4
    Eastern Europe 5, 23–6, 39, 114–15,
        252–3, 274, 278–9, 299, 308, 311,
        317, 331, 347
    Poland 5, 33–4, 36, 207
    postwar 167, 196, 218–22, 230–2,
        252–3, 278–9, 296–7, 303–4, 307
and tripartite pact 57–9, 63
and United States 92, 94, 115, 270–1
western aid 92, 134, 164, 179, 202, 270,
    315, 327
and year of victories 192–227, *193–4*
see also Baltic States; patriotism; Red
    Army
Soviet–Czechoslovak Treaty of Friendship,
    Mutual Aid and Postwar Co-
    operation 210
Soviet–Estonian Pact of Mutual Assistance
    5, 43–4
Soviet–Finnish War (1939–40) 5–6, 46–55,
    49
Soviet–German war 6–7, 59–60, *83*, *86*, 91,
    94–5
    and appeasement 63–4
    battle for Leningrad 85, 88, 103–7
    costs 10–11
    decision-making structures 95–7, *96*,
        161–2
    and defence of Moscow 88, 107–11
    fears of 61–3
    German invasion (1941) 4–6, 67, 70,
        80–1, 82–95, 163
    German troop concentrations 66–9,
        74–7, 93–4, 119

and misleading signals 64–70
as pan-Slavic struggle 210–11
partisan actions 87, 90–1
and patriotism 91, 94–5, 110–11, 132–4, 246
and planned pre-emptive strike 6–7, 70, 76–7, 79, 82–4
as political 165–91
propaganda war 90, 97, 111, 132–4, 161
scorched earth policy 91
Soviet counter-offensives 93, 103–4, 112–17, 113, 122–6, 157–8
and Soviet nationalities 21–2, 27
Soviet preparations 19, 69–70
Soviet strategy 61–81, 75, 95–103, 374
Soviet troop concentration 74–7, 108
Stalin's personal control 4, 7–15, 95–7, 161–2
Stalin's response 89–95
as war of destruction 82–117
see also second front; South-Western Front; Western Front
Soviet–Japanese Neutrality Pact (1941) 63, 64–5, 280, 285
Sovinform (Soviet Information Buro)
  and political alliances 165, 202
  and Soviet propaganda 330
Spain
  'Blue Division' 82, 106
  and Potsdam conference 275, 279
Spanish civil war
  and communists 246–7
  and Soviet assistance 46
Spriano, Paolo xiv, 173, 189
SS
  Einsatzgruppen (action teams) 84, 87
  extermination camps 265
Stalin, Joseph
  biographies 3, 12
  character: bluntness 9; as bully 325; charm 9, 160, 226, 273, 371; depression 89–90; emotions 11–12; as ideologue 17–18, 26, 32, 48, 190, 231, 309, 328–9; leadership qualities 9, 12–15, 160; memory 10; modesty 371; paranoia 9, 17, 19, 270, 343; rages 101; realism 25, 69, 219; sadism 17; sense of humour 188, 371; shrewdness 371; simplicity 371; toughness 3, 188, 325, 371; vengefulness 17; will to power 17; wit 188, 224
  foreign policies see cold war; Council of Foreign Ministers; Eastern Europe; Grand Alliance; Korean War
  political career: as Chairman of the Council of People's Commissars 63–4; as First Secretary of Communist Party 345; as Generalissimo 8, 303, 321–46; loyalty to 10, 160–1, 323, 332; as Marshal of the Soviet Union 162; as Party General Secretary 63; as People's Commissar for Defence 7, 95, 323–4; as People's Commissar for the Nationalities 21; and postwar policies 23–7; as public speaker 94; as Supreme Commander of Armed Forces 7, 10, 14–15, 95, 100, 124
  as war leader 3, 4, 28–9; abolition of Communist International 168–74; achievements 7–15, 321–2, 332; and appeasement of Germany 34, 63–4; appointments diary 8, 79, 90, 149, 370, 378 n.35, 391 n.68, 406 n.84, 425 n.82; and battle for Leningrad 103–7; and battle for Moscow 107–11, 166, 398 n.5; and battle for Stalingrad 129–34, 143–8; and Churchill 8, 31, 38, 56, 114–15, 125, 136–43, 250, 292, 307, 312, 330, 371, 373; and concentration of troops in south 74–7; coping with emergency 95–103, 374; correspondence 8, 340; and counter-offensive strategy 77, 93, 112–17, 322, 364; and Far Eastern war 279–95, 300, 302; and generals 10, 12, 71, 103, 159–62, 203, 256, 266–7, 322–3, 372; and German invasion (1941) 61–81; and German surrender 265–7; and mechanisation 54–5; and misleading signals 64–70; mistakes 10–14, 26, 122–3, 266, 374; and nationalism 110; Nazi–Soviet pact 5–7, 30–60, 91, 94; and offensive strategy 11, 72–80, 99–102, 103–4, 123–6, 144, 157, 202–4, 256–62, 322; and partition of Poland 33–4, 36–9; and patriotism 110–11, 132–3; personal control of war 95–7; planned invasion of Germany 6; planning for peace

Stalin, Joseph (*cont.*)
  as war leader (cont.)
        167–8, 174–80; and politics of war
        165–91, 231; re-evaluation 372–4;
        relationships with Allied leaders
        188–91, 224, 225–7; response to
        German invasion 89–95; and
        Roosevelt 8, 102, 267, 274, 373;
        sources 8–9, 12; and strategic
        defence 71, 77, 124, 154–7; strategy
        for victory 10, 15, 202–3, 257–8,
        322; war aims 190, 281; and Winter
        War 46–55; year of victories
        192–227, *193–4; see also*
        Dumbarton Oaks conference; High
        Command; Moscow conference;
        Potsdam conference; Tehran
        conference; Yalta conference
  as postwar leader 23–8, 114; campaign
      against the West 329–32; and
      control of culture 333–4, 344; and
      cultural thaw 328, 343–4; as
      dictator 1–3, 9–10, 16–17, 27–9,
      321, 331, 372, 374; and Eastern
      Europe 228–53, 318–19; and
      economic affairs 324, 326–7; and
      Grand Alliance 164, 296–320; as
      international statesman 324; and
      nationalism 309–10, 331;
      neopatrimonialism 27–8; and new
      democracy 246–53, 288, 318–19,
      334, 350; and 19th party congress
      344–5, 359; and patriotism 336–7,
      339–41; and peace campaign 347,
      359–61, 366; and peaceful
      coexistence 24, 188, 311–12, 332,
      347, 360, 364; and percentages
      agreement 217–25; and Poland 183,
      185–8, 189, 190, 207–17, 222, 244,
      260, 270; popular support 328; and
      return of repression 27, 336–44;
      and Soviet society 321–46; and split
      with Tito 347, 348–50; and war
      machine 360–4; xenophobia 25;
      and Zionism 339–41
  private life: declining health 344; death
      1, 3, 370; and Lenin's mausoleum 1,
      2, 372; postwar vacations 27, 325;
  see also personality cult
'Stalin Note' 356–8
Stalin, Vasilii 321
Stalin, Yakov 11
Stalingrad, in Russian civil war 12–13

Stalingrad, battle for 14, 118–64, *146,* 168,
    323
  and access to Soviet resources 119, 125–6
  defence 130, 134, 143–8
  forces deployed 143–7
  German defeat 153–9
  material bases of victory 162–4
  and need for a second front in Europe
      140–1, 154
  and Operation Blau 119–21, *120,*
      126–30, 137, 139, 154
  and Operation Mars 151
  and Operation Uranus *148,* 149–50, 153,
      163
  and patriotic loyalty 131–4
  Red Army counter-offensive 143–4,
      148–54, 376 n.15
  siege 126, 143–8
  significance of Soviet victory 154–5
  stages 394 n.49
  and Timoshenko 129–30
Stalingrad Front 129–30, 134, 148–9, 323
Stamenov, Ivan (Bulgarian ambassador in
    Moscow) 166
'Starshina' (Soviet spy) 67
Stassen, Harold 24, 312, 314, 414 n.71
State Defence Committee (GKO)
  abolition 327
  and Stalin 5, 7, 89, 94, 97–8, 104–5, 108
Stavka (Headquarters) 90, 95–102
  and battle for Leningrad 103–4, 106
  and battle for Moscow 108, 111, 112,
      116, 125–6
  and battle for Stalingrad 130, 134,
      143–4, 148–9, 151–4
  defensive operations 154–7, 159
  and Far Eastern war 280, 285
  and Front commanders 203
  offensive operations 99–102, 103, 112,
      121–6, 129, 157
  troops 154–5
  and Vistula–Oder operation 256–7
  and war strategy 202, 257–8
Stettinius, Edward (US Secretary of State)
    241, 269, 275
Stockholm Appeal (1950) 359
Strachey, Lytton xiii
Sudoplatov, Pavel 166
Supreme Command, Soviet *see* Stavka
    (Headquarters)
Supreme Soviet, elections to 327, 328–9
Suritz, Ya. Z. (Soviet ambassador in Paris)
    50, 383 n.13

Suvenirov, O.F. 379 n.55
Suvorov, Victor (V.B. Rezun) 377 n.24

tanks
  German 157
  Soviet 54, 97, 109, 161
Tarle, Evgenii 308
Tass, and appeasement of Germany 64
Taylor, A.J.P. 51, 100
Tedder, Air Chief Marshal Sir Arthur
  258–9
Tehran conference 180–8, 210, 228, 259
  and Far Eastern war 182, 281, 282
  and Germany 182–3, 184, 186–7, 190
  and international security organisation
    183–4, 188
  and Operation Overlord 182, 184–5, 189
  and Poland 183, 185–6, 188, 207–8
  preparations for 177, 178
  and second front 180
terror, Stalinist 15–19, 27, 319, 343
  and ethnic cleansing 3, 18
  and intelligentsia 333–5, 336–7, 344
  purges of military 15–16, 18, 53, 54, 85,
    98, 160–1
  purges of party officials 3, 16–17, 90,
    337, 342
Thorez, Maurice 173, 176, 319–20
Timoshenko, S.K. (Defence Commissar)
  and battle for Stalingrad 129–30
  and Finnish war 50
  and German invasion 80, 92–3
  and North-Western Front 123
  and preparations for war 53, 71, 73–6,
    79
  and South-Western Direction 101,
    123–4, 129–30
  and wartime planning 90
  and Western Direction 97, 98
Tito, Marshal (Josip Brod) 211, 217, 233,
  235, 245, 247, 264, 274
  and Italian–Yugoslav conflict over
    Trieste 297
  split from communist movement 26,
    347, 348–50
Togliatti, Palmiro 173, 176
totalitarianism 312, 313, 319, 373
trade
  postwar 181, 233, 297–8, 359
  Soviet–German 41–3
Transbaikal Front 285, 293
Transylvania, and Romania 58, 223–4
Trieste dispute 297, 305

triple alliance, proposed 5–6, 30–2, 33–4,
  37, 51
Tripolitania 276, 297–8, 303, 305
Trotsky, Leon 3, 349
Truman Doctrine 313–14, 317, 354
Truman, Harry S. 25, 233
  and Churchill 308
  and cold war 25, 268, 312, 313–14
  and Council of Foreign Ministers 299,
    301
  and Far Eastern war 289, 291, 293–4
  and Molotov 267–9, 306
  and Poland 269–70
  and Potsdam conference 272–5, 277–9,
    289
  and Soviet atomic weapons 362
  and Stalin 267–8, 273–5, 304, 313, 359
Tsaritsyn see Stalingrad
Tukhachevskii, Marshal M.N., and purge
  of military 15–16, 18–19, 98
Tupikov, Gen. V.I. 102
Turkey
  and Allies 178, 185, 188
  and Black Sea Straits 59, 185, 188, 189,
    222–3, 275–6, 308, 310–11, 364
  and Kars and Ardahan districts 275, 310
  mutual assistance pact 45–6, 59
  and United Nations 240–1
  US aid to 313

Ukraine 37–8, 72
  German invasion 82, 83, 93, 103
  and Kharkov disaster 122–6, 129, 154
  natural resources 74, 89, 119
  see also Western Ukraine
1st Ukrainian Front 199, 200, 254–7, 261–3
4th Ukrainian Front 257
United Nations
  Charter 291
  and five-power peace pact 359
  formation 195–9, 267
  and Korean War 26, 366, 370
  membership 240–1, 270, 278–9, 296,
    366
  Relief and Rehabilitation
    Administration 327–8
  voting rights 240–1
United Nations Security Council
  membership 197
  right of veto 198, 234, 240
United States
  and anti-communism 24, 167, 252–3,
    305–6, 330, 360

United States (*cont.*)
  and atomic weapons 291–2, 302,
    311–12, 363–4, 369–70
  and battle for Stalingrad 155
  and cold war 306, 311–12, 360, 370
  entry into Second World War 88–9, 118
  and Far Eastern war 88, 274, 280–1, 301
  and Japan 267
  and Korean War 347, 364, 368–70
  and Moscow conference (1943) 177–80
  and Poland 214–16, 233, 241, 268–70
  and postwar expansionism 232, 305–6,
    313
  and postwar peace 168, 174–5, 232–3,
    301–2, 359
  and second front in Europe 134–42, 157,
    177, 179, 182, 185, 199–200, 281
  and Soviet expansion 22–3, 25
  Soviet Union as ally 92, 94, 115, 270–1,
    301–2
  and spheres of interest 23, 190, 196, 219,
    231, 253, 303–4
  see also Grand Alliance; Marshall Plan;
    Roosevelt, Franklin D.; Truman,
    Harry S.; Truman Doctrine

Varga, Eugene 315, 334
Vasilevskii, Gen. Alexander M. 101,
  102–3
  and battle for Stalingrad 130, 144,
    149–51
  as Defence Minister 324
  and Far Eastern war 284–5, 291
  and Kharkov disaster 123–5
  and Kursk 157, 159
  and Operation Bagration 202, 203
  and Stalin 14, 160, 372
  and Vistula–Oder operation 256
  and war plan 76–9
Vatutin, Gen. Nikolai 129, 149, 157
VE Day 265–6, 267
Veshanov, V.V. 149
Vienna, Allied advance on 258, 261, 263
Vilnius, Soviet recapture 200
Vistula–Oder operation 254–65, *255, 262*
Vladivostok 280, 281, 283–4
Voina i Rabochii Klass 173–4
Volkogonov, Gen. Dmitrii 12, 13, 387
  n.57
Volokitina, T.V. 410 n.54
Voronezh
  German attack 129, 131, 137, 139
  Red Army recapture 154

Voronezh Front 129, 156–7, 159
Voroshilov, Kliment E. (Defence
  Commissar)
  and Leningrad 104–5
  and Leningrad Front 106
  and 19th party congress 344
  and North-Western Direction 97,
    104–5
  and planning for peace 174, 184, 228
  and Stalin 19, 22, 160, 322, 389 n.21
  and State Defence Committee 95
  and Winter War 47, 52, 54
Voznesenski, Nikolai (war economy
  minister)
  and Leningrad Affair 337–8
  and Stalin 97, 378 n.35
Vyshinskii, Andrei (Deputy Commissar for
  Foreign Affairs)
  and Balkans 62
  and five-power peace pact 359
  as Foreign Minister 340, 353, 355
  and Italy 175
  and Marshall Plan 317
  and outbreak of war 91–2
  and Poland 214–15
  and Potsdam conference 279
  and Romania 245
  and Soviet atomic weapons 362
  and Stalin Note 356–8
  and Yalta conference 237
Vyshnevskii, Vsevolod 332

Wallace, Henry 233, 360
Walsh, Stephen 151
war criminals 141, 179
war–revolution nexus 6–7, 35, 36
Warsaw
  battle for 203–6, 212–14, 216, 226–7,
    256–7
  uprising 206, 212, 213–17, 226
Wasilewska, Wanda 172
Weathersby, Kathryn 368
Wehrmacht
  advance through Soviet Union 82, 93–5,
    99, 103, 133
  and battle for Warsaw 206
  Commissar Order 85
  and conduct of war 84–5, 87
  and *Einsatzgruppen* 84, 87
  encirclement by Red Army 149, 151–4,
    192, 200, 203
  and Kursk 157
  and Leningrad 107, 143–8

and Moscow 88, 108–9, 111, 112, 129
and Operation Blau 119–21, 122,
   126–30, 154
panzer divisions 82, 84, 100, 121, 128,
   143, 157, 214
retreat 154, 1579
size 82, 107
and Soviet counter-offensive 112–14,
   117, 118
Soviet underestimation 93–4, 100, 102,
   123, 124, 133
and Stalingrad 126–30, 137, 139
and supplies 111
tactics 85
and Vistula–Oder operation 257
see also Army Group A; Army Group B;
   Army Group Centre; Army Group
   North; Army Group South
Weichs, Field Marshal Baron von 128
Werth, Alexander xiv, 294
   and battle for Warsaw 206
   and cold war 308, 311–12
   and German surrender 265
   and patriotism 110, 132, 134
   and Stalin 325
   and victories of 1944 199
   and Victory Salutes 157
West Germany
   creation 26, 354–5
   and NATO 357–8
   rearmament 356–7
Western Belorussia
   and Poland 13, 37, 186, 207, 222, 326
   Red Army occupation 44–5, 72, 114
Western Direction 97, 98–9
Western Front
   and German successes 93–4, 97, 107–8
   and military purges 98, 160
   and Soviet offensives 76–7, 129, 151,
      159
Western Ukraine
   anti-communist partisans 325, 338
   and Poland 13, 37, 186, 207, 222, 326
   Red Army occupation 44–5, 72, 114
   Soviet recapture 192, 202
Winter War (1939–1940) 5–6, 46–55, 49,
   72–3, 170
women
   rape by Red Army personnel 263–5
   in Red Army 163
world peace congresses 359

xenophobia, postwar 23, 25, 337, 346

Yalta conference (Feb. 1945) 219, 221, 228,
   237–45, 258
   bilateral meetings 238, 242
   Declaration on Liberated Europe 242,
      245
   diplomatic preparations 228–37
   and Far Eastern war 241–2, 269, 271,
      274, 284, 287, 289, 291
   and France 225
   and Germany 238–40, 243, 244, 259,
      277, 352–5
   and Poland 241, 243, 244, 268–70, 277
   and United Nations 240–1
   and Yugoslavia 233, 241, 243
Yel'nya, Soviet recapture 99
Yeltsin, Boris 2
Yeremenko, Gen. A.I. 376 n.15
   and South-Eastern Front 134, 143–5,
      148
   and Western Front 98, 101–2
Yezhov, Nikolai (security chief) 17
Yezhovshchina 17, 19, 337
Yugoslav Committee of National
   Liberation 234–5
Yugoslavia
   and Axis powers 59, 61, 62
   and Bulgaria 235–7, 245, 348–9
   and communism 61, 247, 251–2, 303,
      318–19
   German invasion 62–3, 67
   government in exile 64, 211
   and Italy 297
   and mutual assistance pact 61–3, 65
   partisan movement 177, 211, 217, 297
   and percentages agreement 218–20, 274
   and postwar Slavic alliance 211, 231
   Soviet occupation 192, 217, 263–4
   split from communist movement 26,
      347, 348–50
   and Trieste dispute 297, 305
   and Yalta conference 233, 241, 243

Zakharov, Marshal Matvei V. 74
Zhdanov, A.A.
   and campaign against the West 330
   death 342, 344
   and Jews 339
   and Leningrad 104–7, 333
   and Stalin 23, 160, 318, 334, 385 n.13
   and two-camps doctrine 25–6, 318–19,
      354
Zhdanov, Yuri 335
Zhdanovshchina 23, 333–6, 343, 346

Zhemchuzhina, Polina 340
Zhukov, Georgii K. (Deputy Supreme
      Commander) 11, 266, 321, 376 n.17
   and battle for Berlin 14
   and battle for Kursk 14, 155, 157, 159
   and battle for Leningrad 106
   and battle for Stalingrad 14, 144
   and battle for Warsaw 204, 256–7
   and concentration of forces 74–6
   defence of Moscow 14, 108–9, 111, 112
   demotion 14, 90, 322–3
   and German invasion 92–4
   memoirs 14–15, 64, 79–80, 90, 93–4, 99,
      159, 392 n.128
   and offensive strategy 71–2, 79–80
   and Operation Bagration 203
   and Operation Mars 152
   and South-Western Direction 123,
      124–5, 144, 149–51
   and Stalin 14–15, 90, 372
   and strategic defence 80, 155, 157
   and Vistula–Oder operation 256–8,
      261–3, 265, 272
   and Western Direction 99
   and Western Front 93, 108, 129
Zionism, and Stalin 339–41
Zoshchenko, Mikhail 333
Zubkova, Elena 328